D0163826

ELEMENTS OF SAMPLING THEORY AND METHODS

ZAKKULA GOVINDARAJULU

University of Kentucky

PRENTICE HALL, Upper Saddle River, NJ 07458

Library of Congress Cataloging-in-Publication Data

Govindarajulu, Zakkula
  Elements of Sampling Theory and Methods
      p.   cm.
  Includes bibliographical references and index.
  ISBN: 0-13-743576-2
  1. Statistics. 2. Transformations
  (Mathematics) 3. Sampling analysis. I. Title.
  CIP data available

Executive editor: **Ann Heath**
Editorial/production supervision: **Bayani Mendoza DeLeon**
Managing editor: **Linda Mihatov Behrens**
Executive managing editor: **Kathleen Schiaparelli**
Editor-in-chief: **Jerome Grant**
Vice-president and director of manufacturing and production: **David W. Riccardi**
Manufacturing buyer: **Alan Fischer**
Manufacturing manager: **Trudy Pisciotti**
Marketing manager: **Melody Marcus**
Marketing assistant: **Amy Lysik**
Cover director: **Jayne Conte**
Cover designer: **Bruce Kenselaar**
Editorial assistant: **Joanne Wendelken**
Composition: **PreTEX**

© 1999 by Prentice-Hall, Inc.
Upper Saddle River, NJ 07458

All rights reserved. No part of this book may be reproduced, in any form or by any means, without permission in writing from the publisher.

The author and publisher of this book have used their best efforts in preparing this book. These efforts include the development, research, and testing of the theories and programs to determine their effectiveness. The author and publisher make no warranty of any kind, expressed or implied, with regard to these programs or the documentation contained in this book. The author and publisher shall not be liable in any event for incidental or consequential damages in connection with, or arising out of, the furnishing, performance, or use of these programs.

Printed in the United States of America
10 9 8 7 6 5 4 3 2

ISBN 0-13-743576-2

Prentice-Hall International (UK) Limited,London
Prentice-Hall of Australia Pty. Limited, Sydney
Prentice-Hall Canada Inc., Toronto
Prentice-Hall Hispanoamericana, S.A., Mexico
Prentice-Hall of India Private Limited, New Delhi
Prentice-Hall of Japan, Inc., Tokyo
Pearson Education Asia Pte. Ltd., Singapore
Editora Prentice-Hall do Brasil, Ltda., Rio de Janeiro

MAY 2 5 2004

This book is dedicated to all the research workers who have enriched the theory and methods of sampling.

He hides his faults, the pseudo-wise,
and highlights the faults in others galore.
He knows naught of himself or his self
and the rest that he knows is best unknown.

—Sri Sathya Sai Baba

CONTENTS

▶ **3 SIMPLE RANDOM SAMPLING**   **28**

▶ **4 ESTIMATION OF THE SAMPLE SIZE**   **64**

FOREWORD

Elements of Sampling Theory and Methods by Z. Govindarajulu is the result of his experiments in teaching sample surveys to the graduate students at the University of Kentucky over several years. He evolved a method by which all the basic concepts of sample surveys—designing a survey, collecting data, and analyzing of data through modern statistical methodology—could be covered in one-semester course. This is achieved without sacrificing rigor in the discussion of survey methodology or omitting essential proofs of key results in statistical inference based on survey data.

I have read many books on sample survey theory and methods and participated in the actual planning, collection, and analysis of survey data over a number of years while working at the Indian Statistical Institute. Govindarajulu's book is exceptional in that it provides the theoretical knowledge as well as the practical guidance needed to be a sample survey consultant.

A sample survey properly conducted, with an optimal survey design, can supply information of sufficient accuracy with minimum cost. It can also be claimed that estimates based on sample data collected by well-trained investigators under proper supervision, though subject to sampling errors, are more accurate than those based on complete enumeration which would be subject to nonsampling errors usually of a larger magnitude than the sampling errors. Govindarajulu's book carries this message by emphasizing the designing aspects of sample surveys and analysis of data using modern statistical methodology.

The book covers a vast field beginning with simple sampling designs and the associated estimation procedures and ending with more complex designs and the use of modern statistical methods like jackknife, bootstrap, and imputation of missing values. It is nice to see that all relevant literature on sample surveys is discussed on one volume.

Govindarajulu's book will be useful both as a text book in a graduate course as well as a reference book to practitioners of sample surveys.

C. R. Rao
Eberly Professor of Statistics
Department of Statistics
Penn State University

PREFACE

In sampling one of our interests is estimation of the population total or mean. Thus sampling is central to statistical inference. Sampling is taught in several programs in statistics in a one-semester course. One cannot do justice to sampling theory and methods in one semester, however, by using books like Hansen, Hurwitz, and Madow (1953), Sukhatme et al. (1984), and Cochran (1977), which are designed for a two-semester course. Hence I developed this book, which evolved after teaching a course to the graduate students at the University of Kentucky over several years. It contains as many sampling ideas at an elementary level as can be imparted during a semester's course. This book could serve as a reference as well as a text in a semester's course. The book is self contained, in the sense that all elementary proofs are provided.

Probability varying sampling with replacement is introduced fairly early, namely in Chapter 2. Some may prefer to skip Chapter 2 and come back to it before they do Chapter 10. A semester's course can be based on Chapters 1–9, 11–13, 15, 16, and 18. One can teach a methods course out of this book by omitting most of the proofs.

Unlike existing books on sampling, this book contains new material on topics such as the Bayesian approach, the jackknife method, the bootstrap method, small-area estimation, and imputation methods. Further, most of the concepts are illustrated by numerical examples. Several problems involving real or artificial data are provided at the end of each chapter. Also, relevant references are listed at the end of each chapter and a cumulative list is provided at the end of the book. College algebra and basic statistical inference are prerequisites for a course based on this book.

Owing to the limited scope of this book, it is difficult to do justice to the numerous contributors to this field. The selection of topics is bound to be subjective and is dictated by the level of the course. Thus the bibliography is also highly selective. Hence, my apologies to those whose papers are not cited in the bibliography. I shall appreciate readers drawing my attention to any possible errors.

ACKNOWLEDGMENTS

I learned sampling theory and methodology respectively from Hansen, Hurvitz, and Madow (1953) and P. V. Sukhatme (1954) when taught by Professors Richard B. McHugh and I. Richard Savage at the University of Minnesota. I was influenced greatly by Cochran (1977) when I used it as a text in the course at the University of Kentucky. I am indebted to Professors J. N. K. Rao and D. Raghavarao for reading an earlier draft of this book and making numerous suggestions regarding inclusion and exclusion of topics and for drawing my attention to some important published papers. My gratitude goes to Professors Xiao-Li Meng, C. R. Rao, and John L. Wasik for reading earlier drafts of the book and making very constructive and helpful suggestions for inclusion of examples, problems, and new topics. My sincere thanks go to Ann Heath, the statistics editor of Prentice Hall, and Mindy McClard, Linda Behrens, Bayani DeLeon, Robert Lenz, and Jennifer Pan of Prentice Hall for their generous help and support. I am grateful to Beverly A. Clayborne and Julie Smith for typing earlier drafts, and to Brian Moses for an excellent typing of the later chapters and the final version. Also, I gratefully acknowledge the support I have received from the Department of Statistics at the University of Kentucky. Finally my thanks go to all the graduate students at the University of Kentucky who served as guinea pigs for the earlier versions of the book.

Z. Govindarajulu
Lexington, Kentucky

CHAPTER 1

PRELIMINARIES

1.1 INTRODUCTION

Our behavior, attitudes, and sometimes actions are based on samples. We may generalize on the basis of a sample of size one—for instance, our likes or dislikes of foreign dishes, nationals, or countries. Such a sample is not likely to be representative of the whole population. What size sample should we draw, then? The size of the sample depends on the accuracy we need.

Sampling is widely used in the modern world. The statistical office of the United Nations has sample surveys conducted by member nations on topics of interest such as unemployment, size of labor force, and water consumptions. Sampling is useful in inventories and marketing of products. Airlines and Federal Reserve boards apportion money on the basis of samples of records. Public polls brought sampling techniques to the attention of the public, but surveys have proved to be a useful and important technique for the past several hundred years.

1.2 A BRIEF HISTORY OF SURVEY SAMPLING

An early contribution to sampling theory was made by the French mathematician P. S. Laplace, who tried to estimate the population of France using the theory of *ratio estimation* and the reported births for all areas and counts of inhabitants in a purposive sample of parishes. He also gave a measure of the sampling error under simplified assumptions (see Cochran (1978)). Early in the twentieth century A. A. Tschuprow, a Russian statistician, was active in the International Statistical Institute's (ISI) discussions of the *representative method*. He also developed early theory of sampling and obtained a solution to the problem of *optimum allocation* of a sample to the various strata (see Tschuprow (1923)). In 1924 the ISI set up a commission which presented its report on the representative method in statistics in 1926. In its memoranda, the commission defined the method of *random selection* and *'purposive selection'* (the latter is named for using groups of elements as sampling units). The statistician who brought the concept of *randomization* to the fore was A. L. Bowley (1926), who developed (1) the notion of a *'frame'* (i.e., a complete list of the units in the population serving as sampling units); (2) a theory for *proportionate stratified sampling*, and (3) a theory for *purposive selection*.

R. A. Fisher developed the theory of *experimental design and analysis* for analyzing data from field trials. Fisher's theory consists of six principles, which include replication, local control, and randomization. Randomization was used to minimize the bias of the selection procedure. F. Yates (1946) and others at the Rothamsted Experimental Station developed the theory of *sampling clusters of elements* and of *multistage sampling*. J. Neyman's presentation of a paper in 1934 at a meeting of the Royal Statistical Society provided a catalyst for promoting theoretical research, methodological developments, and applications of *probability sampling*. He presented new sampling designs. He developed the optimum allocation of sampling units to strata quite independently of Tschuprow. At the invitation of W. E. Deming, Neyman gave a series of lectures in Washington, D.C., in 1937. During one of the lectures M. Friedman and S. Wilcox posed a problem which fell in the domain of *double-sampling* or *two-phase sampling* considered by Neyman (1938).

The above developments had a tremendous impact in the United States. The poor predictions made by the *Literary Digest* and the success of the Gallup Poll in forecasting the 1936 presidential election have focused attention on the value of *survey sampling*. In 1942 the sample survey of unemployment was transferred to the Bureau of Census, which made some far-reaching changes in survey design, introducing the use of *probability sampling* at all stages of sampling and ratio estimation. Also the Department of Agriculture launched a program of research and, as a part of it, a research group was established at the Statistical Laboratory of the Iowa State University. W. G. Cochran, who worked with F. Yates at the Rothamsted Experimental Station, joined that group in 1939 and made significant contributions to sampling theory and design. The new developments influenced the efforts of P. C. Mahalanobis at the Indian Statistical Institute and P. V. Sukhatme and V. G. Panse at the Indian Council of Agricultural Research. The Indian school made significant contributions to the survey sampling theory and methodology and, in particular, the control of nonsampling errors in sample surveys. The impact was also felt in Europe with contributions by P. Thionet in France, O. Anderson and H. Kellerer in Germany, and T. Dalenius in Sweden. For further details on the history and early developments of sample surveys the reader is referred to Hansen, Dalenius, and Tepping (1985) or Bellhouse (1988).

1.3   SAMPLING DESIGNS AND AN OVERVIEW OF SAMPLING

Sample design determines the precision of the estimates.   Thus, the way a sample is drawn is as important as the mathematical form of the estimator. Sample design consists of both a sample selection plan and an estimation procedure. Each of these has several features: first we have to define sampling units (*primary*, *secondary*, etc.); sample schemes, such as *simple random sampling* (with or without replacement), *stratified sampling*, *double sampling*, *multistage sampling*, *cluster sampling*, and *systematic sampling*; optimum allocation of sampling units to various strata; and *sampling with varying probabilities*.

We try to estimate the population parameters by linear estimates. We can incorporate auxiliary information into the *ratio estimates* and *regression estimates*.   We try to linearize nonlinear estimators (for example, ratio estimators) before we compute their variances. Also, an important effort in sample surveys is to control and minimize nonresponse errors.   For a list of existing procedures, recommended alternatives, and a proposal for additional research the reader is referred to the panel on Incomplete Data of the Committee on National Statistics (1983).   Also for further references on nonsampling errors see Neter and Waksburg (1964) and Mosteller (1978).

Regarding the foundations, Godambe (1955) formulated a general mathematical theory for survey sampling from finite populations. He showed that no uniformly best linear unbiased estimator exists. However, this does not invalidate the theory of Neyman allocation, because Godambe (1955) defines "linear" in a different fashion. The concept of a super population was devised in order to assert certain properties (such as unbiasedness) of estimators. Such a model can provide an effective guide to sample design within the premise of probability sampling.   If the model is not correct, the estimates may be seriously biased and the confidence coefficient associated with the confidence interval may be less than the nominal coefficient. For an illustration see Hansen, Madow, and Tepping (1983). Some of the open problems are how to further control nonsampling errors, find the rate of convergence in asymptotic properties, and ensure privacy of response in sample surveys.

1.4   INGREDIENTS OF A SURVEY

Sample surveys can be classified as (1) *descriptive*, and (2) *analytical*. In a descriptive survey, for example, we study the proportion of the population watching a certain television program, or the proportion of people afflicted by a certain disease. In analytical surveys we compare groups and employ statistical techniques in order to estimate population parameters (pointwise or by intervals). Most of the surveys available at the United Nations fall in the descriptive category. Carrying out a survey may be easy if the people or subjects are well defined and well organized. For instance, taking a survey of inhabitants in a city is much easier than taking a survey of inhabitants who can be reached only by water or who are suspicious of strangers or who are homeless.

The main ingredients of a survey are:

1. A clear statement of objectives.
2. The population to be sampled.
3. The relevant data to be collected.
4. Required precision of estimates (it is the user's duty to specify this).
5. Well-defined sampling units (a sampling unit could be a field, a person, a family, a block, etc.); the list of sampling units is called a frame.
6. Method of selecting the sample.
7. Plans for handling nonresponse.
8. Summarizing the data; take into consideration large nonresponse.
9. Sample estimation procedures.
10. Identifying mistakes in the present survey to avoid in future surveys.

Sampling theory plays an important role in making sampling more efficient (precise or optimal in the sense of minimizing cost).

If the sample size is large, one can reasonably assume that the sampling distributions of the estimates of parameters of interest are approximately normally distributed. Then the problem is reduced to finding their means and variances. Another approach is distribution-free, in which no normality is assumed. This approach is germane for large surveys in which different measurements with differing frequency distributions are made on the units.

Most of the statistical theory is based on the assumption that the populations are infinite. However, in sample surveys, the populations are finite. Hence, the theory of estimates from samples based on finite populations will be more complicated.

1.5   PROBABILITY SAMPLING

Certain units in the finite population may be more important, hence we wish to assign more probability to their being selected in the sample. This leads us to sampling with varying probabilities.

Let $S_1, S_2, S_3, \ldots$ be groups of sampling units such that $\cup S_i$ constitutes the total population and $S_i \cap S_j = \emptyset$ (the empty set) for $i \neq j$ (that is, the groups are disjoint). We denote the probabilities of selecting the groups $S_1, S_2, \ldots$ by $\pi_1, \pi_2, \ldots$, such that $\pi_1 + \pi_2 + \cdots = 1$. Suppose we draw the ith group S_i. Then we may take the average of all the units in S_i and give that as an estimate of the population mean. Since sampling is done by probability, we can obtain the sampling distribution of the mean of the units in S_i. From a practical convenience point of view we may resort to nonprobabilistic sampling —for instance, picking the first few apples from the top of a truckload of apples. However, these nonprobabilistic sampling methods may not lead to a meaningful sampling theory. Probability sampling will be considered in some detail in Chapter 2.

1.6   PRECISION AND CONFIDENCE INTERVALS

We say that $\hat{\mu}$, an estimate of μ, is unbiased for μ if

$$E(\hat{\mu}) = \sum_{i=1}^{M} \pi_i \hat{\mu}_i = \mu$$

where $\hat{\mu}_i$ is the estimate based on the ith sample and M denotes the number of all possible samples.

$$P\left[|\hat{\mu} - \mu| \le k\sigma_{\hat{\mu}} \right] \doteq 2\Phi(k) - 1$$

where $\sigma_{\hat{\mu}}$ denotes the standard deviation of $\hat{\mu}$ and Φ denotes the standard normal distribution function. For instance, if $k = 1.96$, then the confidence coefficient is 0.95 and the confidence interval for μ is $\hat{\mu} \pm 1.96\sigma_{\hat{\mu}}$. Towards the accuracy of the estimate, we say that there is a 5% chance that the estimate $\hat{\mu}$ is in error by more than 1.96σ ($\sigma = \sigma_{\hat{\mu}}$). If $\sigma_{\hat{\mu}}$ is unknown, we can replace it by the standard error, $s_{\hat{\mu}}$, and use the t distribution in order to set up confidence intervals for μ.

1.7   BIASED ESTIMATORS

Let $\hat{\mu}$ be an estimator of μ such that $E(\hat{\mu}) = m$. Then the bias of $\hat{\mu}$ is defined to be

$$B = m - \mu.$$

Thus, $\hat{\mu}$ is said to be positively (negatively) biased for μ if $B > 0$ ($B < 0$). Consider the error probability

$$P\left(|\hat{\mu} - \mu| > k\sigma \right) = P\left(\frac{\hat{\mu} - m}{\sigma} > \frac{\mu - m}{\sigma} + k \right)$$

$$+ P\left(\frac{\hat{\mu} - m}{\sigma} < \frac{\mu - m}{\sigma} - k \right)$$

$$= 1 - \Phi\left(\frac{\mu - m}{\sigma} + k \right) + \Phi\left(\frac{\mu - m}{\sigma} - k \right)$$

$$= 1 - \Phi\left((-(B/\sigma) + k) \right) + \Phi\left((-(B/\sigma) - k) \right)$$

$$= \Phi\left((B/\sigma) - k \right) + \Phi\left((-B/\sigma) - k \right).$$

From Table 1.1 it is clear that the nominal error probability (namely, 0.1) is unaffected by the bias provided it is less than one-tenth of the standard deviation. Typically B/σ is not known. In some instances such as ratio estimators, however, it is possible to find an upper bound for B/σ. Using this bound, we can assess the error probability of the estimate.

TABLE 1.1   Error Probabilities for Selected Values B/σ

B/σ	Lower tail with $k = 1.645$	Upper tail with $k = 1.645$	Total = sum of the tails
0.02	0.048	0.052	0.10
0.10	0.040	0.061	0.101
0.50	0.016	0.126	0.142
1.00	0.004	0.260	0.264
1.50	0.000	0.442	0.442

1.8   THE MEAN-SQUARED ERROR

In order to compare two estimates that are designed to estimate the same unknown parameter, a useful criterion is the mean-squared error, which takes into account the bias of the estimator. Notice that

$$\text{MSE}(\hat{\mu}) = E\left[(\hat{\mu} - \mu)^2\right] = E\left[(\hat{\mu} - m) + (m - \mu)\right]^2$$

$$= E(\hat{\mu} - m)^2 + (m - \mu)^2 = \text{var}\,\hat{\mu} + (\text{bias of } \hat{\mu})^2$$

since the expectation of the cross-product term is zero. It should be noted that two estimators having the same MSE need not be equivalent, since they may have different biases.

Then the error probability is

$$P\left[|\hat{\mu} - \mu| \geq k\sqrt{\text{MSE}}\right] = P\left[|\hat{\mu} - \mu| \geq k(\sigma^2 + B^2)^{1/2}\right]$$

$$= \Phi\left(-(B/\sigma) - k\left\{1 + (B/\sigma)^2\right\}^{1/2}\right)$$

$$+ \Phi\left((B/\sigma) - k\left\{1 + (B/\sigma)^2\right\}^{1/2}\right)$$

if you proceed as earlier. If B/σ tends to infinity, then the error probability will go to zero, provided $k > 1$, and tends to 0.5 if $k = 1$.

From Table 1.2, it is clear that the error probability is negligibly affected provided $B/\sigma \leq 0.30$.

TABLE 1.2 $P\left(|\hat{\mu} - \mu| \geq k\sqrt{\text{MSE}}\right)$

B/σ	$k = 1$	$k = 1.645$	$k = 1.96$
0	0.317	0.10	0.05
0.1	0.317	0.101	0.05
0.25	0.318	0.100	0.05
0.3	0.320	0.100	0.05
0.5	0.320	0.100	0.049
0.6	0.321	0.099	0.048

1.9 UNBIASED ESTIMATION

Since unbiasedness is a criterion of impartiality, wherever possible we should strive for unbiased estimates. Then among unbiased estimates we choose the one that has the smallest variance. Toward this we have the following results.

Result 1.1. Let $X_i (i = 1, \ldots, n)$ be a set of random variables having common mean μ and $\text{cov}(X_i, X_j) = \sigma_{ij} (1 \le i, j \le n)$. Let $T = W_1 X_1 + \cdots + W_n X_n$ such that $ET = \mu$ and $W_1 + \cdots + W_n = 1$. Then the best weights for which $\text{var } T$ is minimum are given by

$$\mathbf{W} = \Omega^{-1} \mathbf{1}/\mathbf{1}'\Omega^{-1}\mathbf{1}$$

where $\Omega = ((\sigma_{ij}))$, $\mathbf{1} = (1, \ldots, 1)'$ and $\mathbf{W} = (W_1, \ldots, W_n)'$.

Proof: T is unbiased for μ implies that $\mathbf{W}'\mathbf{1} = 1$. Next consider

$$\text{Var } T = \text{var}(\mathbf{W}'\mathbf{X}) = E\left[(\mathbf{W}'\mathbf{X} - \mu)(\mathbf{X}'\mathbf{W} - \mu)\right]$$

$$= E\left[\mathbf{W}'(\mathbf{X} - \mu\mathbf{1})(\mathbf{X} - \mu\mathbf{1})'\mathbf{W}\right] = \mathbf{W}'\Omega\mathbf{W}.$$

Since Ω is symmetric positive definite, we can apply the Cauchy-Schwarz inequality after writing $\mathbf{1}'\mathbf{W} = \mathbf{1}'\Omega^{-1/2}\Omega^{1/2}\mathbf{W}$ and obtain

$$(\mathbf{1}'\mathbf{W})^2 \le (\mathbf{W}'\Omega\mathbf{W})(\mathbf{1}'\Omega^{-1}\mathbf{1}).$$

Also, since $\mathbf{1}'\mathbf{W} = 1$, we have

$$\mathbf{W}'\Omega\mathbf{W} \ge 1/(\mathbf{1}'\Omega^{-1}\mathbf{1})$$

with equality when $\Omega^{1/2}\mathbf{W} = \lambda\Omega^{-1/2}\mathbf{1}$ for some λ—that is, when

$$\mathbf{W} = \lambda\Omega^{-1}\mathbf{1} \text{ or } \mathbf{1}'\mathbf{W} = \lambda\mathbf{1}'\Omega^{-1}\mathbf{1}$$

which implies that $\lambda = 1/\mathbf{1}'\Omega^{-1}\mathbf{1}$. Thus

$$\mathbf{W} = \Omega^{-1}\mathbf{1}/\mathbf{1}'\Omega^{-1}\mathbf{1}$$

and the minimum variance is $1/\mathbf{1}'\Omega^{-1}\mathbf{1}$.

Note that $\Omega^{-1}\mathbf{1}$ is the column made up of sum of the elements in the rows of Ω^{-1} and $\mathbf{1}'\Omega^{-1}\mathbf{1}$ is the sum of all the elements of Ω^{-1}. ∎

Special Case. If

$$\Omega = \text{diag}(\sigma_1^2, \ldots, \sigma_n^2)$$

then

$$W_i = \sigma_i^{-2}/\sum_{j=1}^n \sigma_j^{-2}.$$

Next, let us define minimum-variance unbiased estimators of unknown parameters.

> **Definition 1.1.** An estimator T is said to be minimum variance unbiased (MVU) for θ if $ET = \theta$ and for any other unbiased estimator T', $\operatorname{var} T \leq \operatorname{var} T'$.

The following result pertaining to minimum-variance unbiased estimates is due to C. R. Rao (1952).

Result 1.2. A necessary and sufficient condition for T_0 to be a MVU estimator of a certain unknown parameter is that $\operatorname{cov}(T_0, Z) = 0$ for any Z which is an unbiased estimator of zero.

Proof: Let T_0 be MVU for a certain parameter. Then for all ϵ (since T_0 is MVU),

$$\operatorname{var}(T_0) \leq \operatorname{var}(T_0 + \epsilon Z) = \operatorname{var} T_0 + \epsilon^2 \operatorname{var} Z + 2\epsilon \operatorname{cov}(T_0, Z).$$

That is

$$\epsilon \left[2 \operatorname{cov}(T_0, Z) + \epsilon \operatorname{var} Z \right] \geq 0 \qquad \blacksquare$$

Case 1. Let $\epsilon > 0$ and let $\epsilon \to 0$. Then $\operatorname{cov}(T_0, Z) \geq 0$.

Case 2. Let $\epsilon < 0$ and $\epsilon \to 0$. Then $\operatorname{cov}(T_0, Z) \leq 0$.

Thus $\operatorname{cov}(T_0, Z) = 0$.

Proof: To prove the sufficiency, let T_1 be any other unbiased estimator of the parameter. Writing $T_1 = T_0 + (T_1 - T_0)$, letting $Z = T_1 - T_0$, and using the fact that

$$\operatorname{cov}(T_0, T_1 - T_0) = 0$$

in

$$\operatorname{var} T_1 = \operatorname{var} T_0 + \operatorname{var}(T_1 - T_0) + 2 \operatorname{cov}(T_0, T_1 - T_0)$$

we have

$$\operatorname{var} T_1 \geq \operatorname{var} T_0. \qquad \blacksquare$$

Corollary 1.1. If T_1 is any unbiased estimator and T_0 is MVU for the same parameter, then

$$\operatorname{cov}(T_1, T_0) = \operatorname{cov}(T_0, T_0) = \operatorname{var} T_0.$$

That is, the variance of an MVU T_0 can be obtained by evaluating the covariance of T_0 with any other unbiased estimator of the parameter.

■ PROBLEMS

1.1 Prove the assertion made in Section 1.8 on the mean-square error.

1.2 Solve for the optimal **W** for the following covariance matrices.

(a) $\Omega = \text{diag}(1, 2, \ldots, n)$

(b) $\Omega = \begin{pmatrix} 10 & 6 & -1 \\ 6 & 5 & 4 \\ -1 & 4 & 17 \end{pmatrix}$

Hint: $\Omega^{-1} = \begin{pmatrix} 2.76 & -4.24 & 1.16 \\ & 6.76 & -1.84 \\ & & 0.56 \end{pmatrix}$

(c) $\Omega = ((\sigma_{ij}))$ where $\sigma_{ij} = \dfrac{i(n+1-j)}{(n+1)^2(n+2)}$ for $i \le j$.

Hint: Use $\Omega^{-1} = \begin{pmatrix} 2 & -1 & 0 & \cdots & & 0 \\ -1 & 2 & -1 & & & 0 \\ \vdots & & & & & \vdots \\ \vdots & & & & & 0 \\ \vdots & & & & & -1 \\ 0 & \cdots & & & 0-1 & 2 \end{pmatrix}$.

(d) $\Omega = \begin{pmatrix} 4 & -2 \\ -2 & 3 \end{pmatrix}$

1.3 Let X_i be distributed with mean μ and variance $i\sigma^2$ ($i = 1, \ldots, n$). Assume that the X_i's are uncorrelated. Find the best unbiased estimate of μ.

1.4 Let $X_1, \ldots, X_n$ be a random sample from a population with unknown mean μ and variance σ^2. Let $T = \bar{x}$ and $z = X_1 - X_2$. Verify Result 2.

1.5 Verify Corollary 1.1 for the case considered in Problem 4 with $T_0 = \bar{x}$ and $T_1 = X_1$.

■ REFERENCES

1.1 Bellhouse, D. R. (1988). A brief history of random sampling methods. Chapter 1 of *Handbook of Statistics* #6 (ed. P. R. Krishnaiah and C. R. Rao), New York: North Holland, pp. 1–4.

1.2 Bowley, A. L. (1926). Measurement of the precision attained in sampling. *Bull. Intern. Statist. Inst.* **22**, Supplement to liv. I, 6–62.

1.3 Cochran, W. G. (1978). "Laplace's ratio estimator," in *Contributions to Survey Sampling and Applied Statistics* (ed. H. A. David), New York: Academic Press.

1.4 Godambe, V. P. (1955). A unified theory of sampling from finite populations. *J. Roy. Statist. Soc.* **B17**, 269–278.

1.5 Hansen, M. H., Dalenius, T., and Tepping, B. J. (1985). "The development of sample surveys of finite populations," in *A Celebration of Statistics* (ed. A. C. Atkinson, and S. E. Fienberg). New York: Springer-Verlag, pp. 327–354.

1.6 Hansen, M. H., Madow, W. G., and Tepping, B. J. (1983). An evaluation of model-dependent and probability-sampling inferences in sample surveys. *J. Amer. Statist. Assoc.* **78**, 776–793. Comments and rejoinder, 794–807.

1.7   Mosteller, F. (1978). "Nonsampling errors," in W. M. H. Kruskal and J. M. Tanur (eds.), *The International Encyclopedia of Statistics*. New York: Free Press, 208–229.

1.8   Neter, J., and Waksburg, J. (1964). A study of response errors in expenditure data from households interviews. *J. Amer. Statist. Assoc.* **59**, 18–55.

1.9   Neyman, J. (1934). On the two different aspects of the representative method: The method of stratified sampling and the method of purposive selection. *J. Roy. Statist. Soc.* **97**, 558–606.

1.10   Neyman, J. (1938). Contributions to the theory of sampling human populations. *J. Amer. Statist. Assoc.* **33**, 101–116.

1.11   Panel on Incomplete Data, Committee on National Statistics (1983). *Incomplete Data in Sample Surveys*. Vol 1. *Report and Case Studies* (Madow, Nisselson, Olkin, eds.). Vol 2. *Theory and Bibliographies* (Madow, Olkin, Rubin, eds.). Vol 3. *Proceedings of the Symposium* (Madow and Olkin, eds.). New York: Academic Press.

1.12   Tschuprow, A. A. (1923). On the mathematical expectation of the moments of frequency distributions in the case of correlated observations. *Metron* **2**, 461–493, 646–680.

2

VARYING-PROBABILITY SAMPLING

2.1 INTRODUCTION

You may have heard the saying that all things are created equal, but some are more equal than others. In a population certain units may be more important than others. Thus, selecting units with unequal probabilities yields more efficient estimators than with equal probabilities. This method of sampling is called *varying-probability sampling*. For example, we can select units according to their size, where size denotes the value assigned to a unit or the number of subunits in it. This method is called *probability-proportional-to-size sampling* (pps). In industrial sampling the number of workers in an industrial establishment serves as an example of the size of a unit. Since a large-sized unit is expected to contribute more to the population total than a small unit, it is natural to assign more probability to large units of being included in the sample. In order to overcome the bias in estimators, we weigh the sample observations at the estimation stage.

2.2 OBTAINING VARYING-PROBABILITY SAMPLES

Let N be the number of units and let (x_i, y_i) be the values of x and y (some variables of interest) for the ith unit ($i = 1, \ldots, N$). Then, using x, we set the probability of

---

N. B. Sukhame et al. (1984, Chapters 1 and 3) served as a source for part of this chapter

selecting the ith unit to be $z_i = x_i/X$, $X = \sum_1^N x_i$, and $\bar{Y} = \frac{1}{N}\sum_{i=1}^N y_i$. If we select only one unit, namely i_1th then

$$\hat{\bar{Y}} = \frac{y_{i_1}}{Nz_{i_1}} \left(z_{i_1} = \frac{x_{i_1}}{X}\right).$$

Hence

$$E(\hat{\bar{Y}}) = \sum_{i=1}^N \frac{y_i}{Nz_i} z_i = \bar{Y}$$

and

$$\text{var}\,(\hat{\bar{Y}}) = \sum_{i=1}^N z_i \left(\frac{y_i}{Nz_i} - \bar{Y}\right)^2 = \sum_{i=1}^N \frac{y_i^2}{N^2 z_i} - \bar{Y}^2.$$

If z_i is directly proportional to y_i, then $\text{var}\,(\hat{\bar{Y}}) = 0$ (for example, $z_i = ky_i$, then $k = 1/Y$ and $\text{var}\left(\hat{\bar{Y}}\right) = 0$).

Suppose we wish to obtain a sample of size n from a population of size N with probability proportional to size and with replacement. If X_i is an integer proportional to the size of the ith unit ($i = 1, \ldots, N$), we can form successive cumulative sums $X_1, X_1 + X_2, \ldots$. Draw a random number K ($K \le X_1 + \cdots + X_N$). If it falls in the interval $(X_1 + \cdots + X_{i-1}, X_1 + X_2 + \cdots X_i)$, then the ith unit is selected. Repeat this procedure n times.

EXAMPLE 2.1

Suppose a certain school has 8 classes of sizes 30, 20, 25, 45, 35, 40, 50, and 55. Suppose we wish to select a sample of 3 classes with replacement and with probability proportional to the number of students in the class.

Number of the class	Size X_i	Cumulative total	Range
1	30	30	(1, 30]
2	20	50	(30, 50]
3	25	75	(50, 75]
4	45	120	(75, 120]
5	35	155	(120, 155]
6	40	195	(155, 195]
7	50	245	(195, 245]
8	55	300	(245, 300]

Suppose we choose three random numbers, 104, 223, 71, that are less than or equal to 300. Then we choose the classes numbered 4, 7, 3. ◆

It may be cumbersome and time consuming to write down all the cumulative totals, especially when N is large. Then we can follow Lahiri's (1951) simplified procedure and select a pair of random numbers (i, j) in such a way that $1 \leq i \leq N$ and $1 \leq j \leq M$ where $M = \max_i \ X_i$, X_i being the size of the ith unit in the population. If $j \leq X_i$, select the ith unit; otherwise reject it and draw another pair of random numbers. Repeat this procedure until n units are selected.

Example 2.2

For the data in Example 1, let us choose three classes with replacement and proportionate to size. Suppose the pairs of random numbers as follows:

$$(1, 50), (7, 29), (1, 43), (4, 09), (6, 11)$$

Since $43 > X_1$ and $50 > X_1$, we do not select unit 1. However, we select the seventh unit, fourth unit, and sixth unit.   ◆

As before, let y be the response of interest, y_i be the response associated with the ith unit, and z_i be the probability of selecting the ith unit. Clearly $\sum_1^N z_i = 1$.

Consider the problem of estimating $\bar{Y}$ (the population mean) based on a sample of size n units selected with probabilities z_i and with replacement. Let

$$V_i = \frac{y_i}{N z_i}, \ i = 1, \ldots, N.$$

For an estimator of $\bar{Y}$, consider

$$\bar{v} = n^{-1} \sum_{k=1}^{n} v_k = n^{-1} \sum_{k=1}^{n} \frac{y_{i_k}}{N z_{i_k}}.$$

Then

$$E(\bar{v}) = E(v_k) = \sum_{j=1}^{N} z_j \frac{y_j}{N z_j} = \bar{Y},$$

(since v_k can take on the value V_j with probability z_j).

$$\text{var}(\bar{v}) = n^{-1} \ \text{var} \ v_k = n^{-1} \sum_{j=1}^{N} z_j (V_j - \bar{Y})^2$$

$$= n^{-1} \sum_{j=1}^{N} z_j \left(\frac{y_j}{N z_j} - \bar{Y} \right)^2 = n^{-1} \left[\sum \frac{y_j^2}{N^2 z_j} - \bar{Y}^2 \right].$$

Setting $z_j = 1/N$, we obtain the results that correspond to simple random sampling with replacement.

An unbiased estimate of $\text{var}(\bar{v})$ is given by

$$\hat{\text{var}}(\bar{v}) = s_v^2/n$$

where

$$s_v^2 = (n-1)^{-1} \sum_1^n (v_k - \bar{v})^2$$

$$= (n-1)^{-1} \left[\sum_1^n (v_k - \bar{Y})^2 - n(\bar{v} - \bar{Y})^2 \right]$$

$$E(s_v^2) = n(n-1)^{-1} \left[E(v_1 - \bar{Y})^2 - E(\bar{v} - \bar{Y})^2 \right]$$

$$= n(n-1)^{-1} \left(\sigma_v^2 - \frac{\sigma_v^2}{n} \right)$$

$$= \sigma_v^2$$

where

$$\sigma_v^2 = \sum_{j=1}^N z_j \left(\frac{y_j}{Nz_j} - \bar{Y} \right)^2 .$$

Sometimes, although the correlation between y and the auxiliary variable x is very high, the *pps* (probability proportional to size) sampling estimate may have variance larger than that of the estimate based on simple random sampling with replacement. Consider the following artificial data with $N = 5$ and $n = 2$.

EXAMPLE 2.3

i	x_i	y_i	z_i	$5z_i$
1	2	5	1/15	1/3
2	4	6	2/15	2/3
3	6	7	3/15	1
4	8	8	4/15	4/3
5	10	9	5/15	5/3
Total		30	35	1	5

Then

$$\bar{Y} = 35/5 = 7$$

and

$$\sigma_v^2 = \sum_{i=1}^{5} z_i \left(\frac{y_i}{5z_i} - \bar{Y} \right)^2$$

$$= \frac{1}{15}(15 - 7)^2 + \frac{2}{15}(9 - 7)^2 + \frac{3}{15}(7 - 7)^2 + \frac{4}{15}(6 - 7)^2 + \frac{5}{15}\left(\frac{27}{5} - 7 \right)^2$$

$$= \frac{1}{15}\left(64 + 4 + 0 + 1 + \frac{64}{5} \right) = \frac{88.8}{15} = 5.92 .$$

Also,

$$\sigma^2 = \frac{1}{5} \sum_{1}^{5} (y_j - \bar{Y})^2$$

$$= \frac{1}{5} \left\{ (5 - 7)^2 + (6 - 7)^2 + (7 - 7)^2 + (8 - 7)^2 + (9 - 7)^2 \right\}$$

$$= \frac{1}{5}(4 + 1 + 0 + 1 + 4) = 2 .$$

Thus

$$\text{var}\,(\bar{v}) = \frac{\sigma_v^2}{2} = \frac{5.92}{2} = 2.96$$

whereas

$$\text{var}\,(\bar{y}) = \frac{\sigma^2}{2} = 1 . \qquad \blacklozenge$$

As one can see, the pps sampling estimate is much less efficient than the simple random sampling estimate with replacement, although the correlation between variables x and y is one, since $y = 4 + (x/2)$.

2.3 SAMPLING DESIGNS (ORDERED AND UNORDERED)

D. Basu (1958) extended the sufficiency considerations to sampling from finite populations. Let the finite population consist of N distinct units labeled $(U_1, \ldots, U_N)$. A sample s^* of size $n(s^*)$ is an ordered sequence of labels from the population and is denoted by

$$s^* = (U_{i_1}, U_{i_2}, \ldots, U_{i_{n(s*)}})$$

where U_{i_r} denotes the unit having the label i_r at the rth draw $(r = 1, \ldots, n)$. Notice that the labels need not be distinct, since sampling could be with or without replacement in $n(s^*)$ consecutive draws. Let $W(s^*)$ denote the number of distinct labels in s^*, which is called the effective sample size. Also, let $S^* = \{s^*\}$ denote the totality of all possible samples s^*. For each s^* let $p(s^*) \geq 0$ denote the probability of drawing the sample s^* from the population such that

$$\sum_{s^* \in S^*} p(s^*) = 1.$$

Furthermore, if π_i denotes the probability of U_i being included in s^*

$$\pi_i = P(U_i \in s^*) = \sum_{i \in s^*} p(s^*)$$

where the summation is taken over all possible samples s^* containing U_i. We assume that the $p(s^*)$ are such that $\pi_i > 0$ for $i = 1, \ldots, N$. Then we have the following definition of *ordered sampling design*.

Definition 2.1. The collection $S^* = \{s^*\}$ together with a probability measure $P^* = \{p(s^*)\}$ defined on S^* such that $p(s^*) \geq 0$ and $\sum_{s^* \in S^*} p(s^*) = 1$ is called an ordered sampling design, which is denoted by $D(S^*, P^*)$.

If we ignore the information concerning the order in which the labels occur and the frequencies with which the distinct labels occur in s^*, then we obtain an unordered sample s, which can be written as

$$s = \{U_i : i \in s^*\}$$

Let $W(s)$ denote the number of (distinct) labels in s. Then $W(s) = W(s^*)$. Let S denote the totality of all possible unordered samples s and $p(s) \geq 0$ denote the probability of drawing a sample s from the population such that

$$\sum_{s \in S} p(s) = 1.$$

Then $p(s) = \sum_1 p(s^*)$, where $\sum_1$ denotes the summation taken over all those s^* which yield s. Then $D(S, P)$, the unordered sampling design, can be defined analogous to $D(S^*, P^*)$. Let us illustrate the preceding concepts by the following example.

EXAMPLE 2.4

Let $N = 3, n = 2$. Then there are nine possible samples of size 2 (with replacement).

$$s_1^* = (1, 1), \quad s_4^* = (1, 2), \quad s_7^* = (3, 1)$$

$$s_2^* = (2, 2), \quad s_5^* = (2, 1), \quad s_8^* = (2, 3)$$

$$s_3^* = (3, 3), \quad s_6^* = (1, 3), \quad s_9^* = (3, 2)$$

1. If we are drawing a simple random sample with replacement

$$p(s_i^*) = \frac{1}{9}, \quad i = 1, \ldots, 9.$$

2. If we have simple random sampling without replacement

$$p(s_i^*) = \frac{1}{6}, \quad i = 4, 5, \ldots, 9$$

$$= 0, \quad i = 1, 2, 3.$$

3. If we are doing sampling with probabilities z_i and with replacement,

$$p(s_1^*) = z_1^2, \quad p(s_4^*) = z_1 z_2, \quad p(s_7^*) = z_1 z_3$$

$$p(s_2^*) = z_2^2, \quad p(s_5^*) = z_1 z_2, \quad p(s_8^*) = z_2 z_3$$

$$p(s_3^*) = z_3^2, \quad p(s_6^*) = z_1 z_3, \quad p(s_9^*) = z_2 z_3$$

where $z_1 + z_2 + z_3 = 1$. One can easily verify that

$$\sum_{s^* \in S^*} p(s^*) = (z_1 + z_2 + z_3)^2 = 1.$$

The ordered samples s^* map into the following unordered samples.

$$s_1^* \rightarrow s_1 = (1), \quad s_6^* \text{ and } s_7^* \rightarrow s_5 = (1, 3)$$

$$s_2^* \rightarrow s_2 = (2), \quad s_8^* \text{ and } s_9^* \rightarrow s_6 = (2, 3)$$

$$s_3^* \rightarrow s_3 = (3), \quad s_4^* \text{ and } s_5^* \rightarrow s_4 = (1, 2)$$

If sampling is simple random and without replacement,

$$p(s_i) = 0 \text{ for } i = 1, 2, 3$$

$$= \frac{1}{3} \text{ for } i = 4, 5, 6.$$

Any procedure of selecting a sample s with probability $p(s)$ for $s \in S$ is called a *probability sampling procedure* and the resulting sample is a *probability sample*. ◆

In order to obtain a probability sample we need to provide

$$P(U_{i_r} | U_{i_1}, \ldots, U_{i_{r-1}})$$

which is the conditional probability of drawing U_{i_r} at the rth draw given that $U_{i_1}, \ldots,$ $U_{i_{r-1}}$ have been drawn at the first, second, $\ldots$, $(r-1)$th draws, respectively. We define $P(U_{i_1} | U_{i_0}) = z_{i_1}$. We also assume that

$$\sum_{i_r} P(U_{i_r} | U_{i_1}, \ldots, U_{i_{r-1}}) = 1.$$

For example, we have

Method of Sampling	$P(U_{i_r}|U_{i_1}, \ldots, U_{i_{r-1}})$
Simple random sampling with replacement	$1/N$
Simple random sampling without replacement	$1/(N-r+1)$
Sampling with probabilities z_i and with replacement	z_{i_r}
Sampling with probabilities z_i and without replacement	$z_{i_r}/(1-z_{i_1}-z_{i_2}-\ldots-z_{i_{r-1}})$

Given the ordered sampling design $D(S^*, P^*)$, the data d^* obtained from a sample s^* of size $n(s^*)$ is

$$d^* = \{(U_{i_r}, y_{i_r}) : i_r \in s^*, \quad r = 1, \ldots, n(s^*)\}$$

where y_{i_r} denotes the Y value associated with U_{i_r} $(r = 1, \ldots, n(s^*))$. The totality of values $\{d^*\}$ is the sample space denoted by $\mathcal{X}^*$. A statistic is a function of d^* defined on the sample space $\mathcal{X}^*$, which depends on the population vector $\underline{Y}$ through the values of Y_k, where $k \in s^*$. Similarly for an unordered sampling design $D(S, P)$, data d in a sample s of size $n(s)$ is given by

$$d = \{(U_{i_r}, y_{i_r}) : i_r \in s, \quad r = 1, \ldots, n(s)\}$$

and the corresponding sample space is denoted by $\mathcal{X}$. The linear classes of statistics considered in the literature are

1. $T_1 = \sum_{j=1}^{n} \alpha_j y_{i_j}$, where α_j is the coefficient attached to the Y value associated with U_{i_j} which is in the sample $(j = 1, \ldots, n)$. For example, in random sampling with replacement, $\alpha_j = \frac{N}{n}$ belongs to this class.

2.
$$T_2 = \sum_{i \in s} \beta_i y_i$$

where β_i is the coefficient of y_i associated with U_i when it is included in the sample $(i = 1, \ldots, N)$. In simple random sampling without replacement, $\beta_i = \frac{N}{n}$ belongs to this class.

3.
$$T_3 = \gamma_s \sum_{i \in s} y_i$$

where γ_s is the coefficient associated with each of the units in the sample, and it is defined in advance for all s. Ratio estimates are included in this class.

4. The generalized linear estimator proposed by Godambe (1955) is
$$T_4 = \sum_{i \in s} \beta_{s,i} y_i$$

where $\beta_{s,i}$ is the coefficient associated with the Y value of U_i whenever it is included in the sample and is defined in advance for all s and all i in s.

$T = n^{-1} \sum_{i \in s} y_i / z_i$ does belong to class (4). Koop (1963) points out that the above classification is not exhaustive.

Next we consider a result pertaining to minimum-variance unbiased estimation.

> **Definition 2.2.**   A sampling design is said to be a unicluster design if for any two possible samples s_1 and s_2 such that $p(s_1) > 0$, $p(s_2) > 0$, $s_1 \neq s_2$ implies that $s_1 \cap s_2$ is empty (that is, when two possible samples are either identical or disjoint).

Hence, the sample is obtained by choosing one subset in a given nonrandom partition of the label space $\mathcal{U} = (U_1, \ldots, U_N)$. For example, the systematic sampling is a unicluster design.

According to Lanke (1975, p. 13) Godambe's (1955) proof that no sampling design admits a uniformly minimum-variance linear unbiased estimate (UMVUE) of population total Y contains a slip. This makes Godambe overlook the fact that the unicluster designs form an exception. Lanke (1975) provides the correct version of the theorem which is stated below without proof.

Theorem 2.1.   A sampling design admits a UMV estimator in the class of linear unbiased estimators of the population total if and only if it is a unicluster design with $\pi_i > 0$ for all i, where π_i denotes the probability of including the ith unit in the sample.

2.4   SUFFICIENCY IN SAMPLING FROM FINITE POPULATIONS

D. Basu (1958) and M. N. Murthy (1957) extended the sufficiency considerations to sampling from finite populations. Let the finite population consist of N distinct units labeled $(U_1, \ldots, U_N)$. Let s^* and s denote an ordered and unordered sample of size n, respectively drawn from this population. Let d^* and d be the corresponding data. Then

$$P(d^* | d) = P(d^*) / P(d) = \frac{p(s^*)}{\Sigma_1 p(s^*)}$$

where the summation Σ_1 is over all those samples s^* which yield s. Hence $P(d^* | d)$ is independent of the population parameter $\underline{Y} = (y_1, \ldots, y_N)'$. Thus d is a sufficient statistic, and it is reasonable to confine ourselves to estimators that are functions of d. Then we have the following analogue of Rao-Blackwell theorem.

Result 2.1.   Let $t^* = t^*(d^*)$ be a statistic designed to estimate a certain unknown parameter θ of the population. Let $t = E(t^* | d)$. Then

1. $E(t) = E(t^*)$
2. MSE $(t^*) =$ MSE $(t) + E(t - t^*)^2$.

Proof:

$$E(t) = E\{E(t^*|d)\} = E\left\{\Sigma_1 t^*(d^*)\frac{p(s^*)}{p(s)}\right\}$$

$$= \sum_s \left\{\Sigma_1 t^*(d^*)\frac{p(s^*)}{p(s)}\right\} p(s)$$

$$= \sum_{s^*} t^*(d^*)p(s^*) = E(t^*).$$

Next consider

$$\text{MSE}(t^*) = E(t^* - \theta)^2 = E(t^* - t + t - \theta)^2$$

$$= E(t^* - t)^2 + E(t - \theta)^2 + 2E(t - \theta)(t^* - t).$$

However,

$$E(t - \theta)(t^* - t) = E\left\{E(t - \theta)(t^* - t)|d\right\}$$

$$= E(t - \theta)E\left\{(t^*|d) - t\right\} = 0.$$

That is, for any estimator t^* there exists an estimator t which is more efficient than t^* unless t^* coincides with t.   ∎

EXAMPLE 2.5

Suppose we are interested in estimating the population mean $\bar{Y}$ on the basis of data d^* obtained from an ordered sample s^* of size n drawn by simple random sampling with replacement. Then

$$d^* = \{U_i, y_i : i \in s^*\}$$

where s^* has W distinct units, namely $U_{i_1}, \ldots, U_{i_w}$, with U_{i_r} occurring n_r times such that $\sum_{r=1}^{W} n_r = n$.

Then $\bar{y}$, the sample mean based on d^*, is an unbiased estimator of $\bar{Y}$ with var $(\bar{y}) = \sigma^2/n$. Also $d = (U_{i_r}, y_{i_r} : i_r \in s)$ is a sufficient statistic for $\underline{Y} = (y_1, \ldots, y_N)'$.

From Result 2.1,

$$t = E(\bar{y}|d) = E(\frac{1}{n}\sum_{r=1}^{W} n_r y_{i_r}|d)$$

$$= \sum_{r=1}^{W} y_{i_r} E(\frac{n_r}{n}|d)$$

$$= \sum_{r=1}^{W} \frac{1}{W} y_{i_r}, \quad \text{since } E(n_r|d) = n \cdot \frac{1}{W}$$

$$= \bar{y}_W \text{ (the mean of the distinct units in the sample)}$$

is uniformly better than $\bar{y}$.

Also

$$\text{var}\,(\bar{y}_W) = E\,(\,\text{var}\,(\bar{y}_W|W) + \text{var}\,(E\bar{y}_W|W))$$

$$= E\left\{\left(\frac{1}{W} - \frac{1}{N}\right)S^2\right\} + \text{var}\,(\bar{Y})$$

$$= \left\{E\left(\frac{1}{W}\right) - \frac{1}{N}\right\}S^2 + 0$$

where
$$S^2 = \frac{N}{N-1}\sigma^2 = (N-1)^{-1}\sum_{i=1}^{N}(y_i - \bar{Y})^2.$$

$E\left(\frac{1}{W}\right)$ and the optimal properties of $\bar{y}_W$ will be dealt with more detail in Chapter 3.   ◆

EXAMPLE 2.6

Consider estimating the population mean $\bar{Y}$ based on data d^* obtained from an ordered sample of size $n = 4$ drawn with probability z_i and with replacement. Let

$$d^* = (U_{i_1},\ y_{i_1};\ U_{i_2},\ y_{i_2};\ U_{i_3},\ y_{i_3};\ U_{i_2},\ y_{i_2})$$

So, we have $W = 3$ and $d = (U_{i_1},\ y_{i_1},\ U_{i_2},\ y_{i_2},\ U_{i_3},\ y_{i_3})$. Then $\bar{v} = \frac{1}{4}\Sigma_1^4 \frac{y_{i_j}}{Nz_{i_j}}$ based on d^* is an unbiased estimator for $\bar{Y}$. Also from Result 2.1, $t = E(\bar{v}|d)$ will be uniformly better than $\bar{v}$. Here $W = 3$.

$$t = E(\bar{v}|d)$$

$$= \frac{1}{4}\left(\frac{2y_{i_1}}{Nz_{i_1}} + \frac{y_{i_2}}{Nz_{i_2}} + \frac{y_{i_3}}{Nz_{i_3}}\right)q_1$$

$$+ \frac{1}{4}\left(\frac{y_{i_1}}{Nz_{i_1}} + \frac{2y_{i_2}}{Nz_{i_2}} + \frac{y_{i_3}}{Nz_{i_3}}\right)q_2$$

$$+ \frac{1}{4}\left(\frac{y_{i_1}}{Nz_{i_1}} + \frac{y_{i_2}}{Nz_{i_2}} + \frac{2y_{i_3}}{Nz_{i_3}}\right)q_3$$

where

$$q_1 = P(n_{i_1} = 2, n_{i_2} = 1, n_{i_3} = 1) = \frac{z_{i_1}^2 z_{i_2} z_{i_3}}{D} = \frac{z_{i_1}}{z_{i_1} + z_{i_2} + z_{i_3}}$$

$$q_2 = P(n_{i_1} = 1, n_{i_2} = 2, n_{i_3} = 1) = \frac{z_{i_2}}{z_{i_1} + z_{i_2} + z_{i_3}}$$

$$q_3 = \frac{z_{i_3}}{z_{i_1} + z_{i_2} + z_{i_3}}$$

where $D = z_{i_1}^2 z_{i_2} z_{i_3} + z_{i_1} z_{i_2}^2 z_{i_3} + z_{i_1} z_{i_2} z_{i_3}^2 = z_{i_1} z_{i_2} z_{i_3}(z_{i_1} + z_{i_2} + z_{i_3})$.

Then

$$t = \frac{1}{4N(z_{i_1} + z_{i_2} + z_{i_3})}$$

$$\left\{ \frac{y_{i_1}}{z_{i_1}}(2z_{i_1} + z_{i_2} + z_{i_3}) + \frac{y_{i_2}}{z_{i_2}}(z_{i_1} + 2z_{i_2} + z_{i_3}) + \frac{y_{i_3}}{z_{i_3}}(z_{i_1} + z_{i_2} + 2z_{i_3}) \right\}$$

Thus

$$t = \frac{1}{4N} \left\{ \sum_{j=1}^{3} \frac{y_{ij}}{z_{ij}} + \frac{\sum_{j=1}^{3} y_{ij}}{\sum_{j=1}^{3} z_{ij}} \right\}.$$

Proceeding in an analogous fashion, one can show that if a sample of n units is drawn with probability sampling with replacement having $(n-1)$ distinct units, then the more efficient estimator based on the sufficient statistic d is

$$t = \frac{1}{nN} \left[\sum_{j=1}^{n-1} \frac{y_{ij}}{z_{ij}} + \frac{\sum_{j=1}^{n-1} y_{ij}}{\sum_{j=1}^{n-1} z_{ij}} \right]. \qquad \blacklozenge$$

Pathak (1962) has given the general form of the estimator for any value of W, and it is too complicated to be of practical use.

> **Definition 2.3.** A statistic t is said to be complete if and only if for any $h(t)$, $Eh(t) = 0$ for all $\underline{Y} = (y_1, \ldots, y_N)'$ implies that $h(t) = 0$ with probability one for all $\underline{Y}$.

If the data d is complete, then there will be a unique unbiased estimator of θ which is a function of the sufficient statistic d. However, Cassel, Sarndal, and Wretman (1977, p. 44) have shown that d is not complete. Hence, the best unbiased estimator is not unique.

Cassel et al. (1977) have produced a nontrivial estimator based on the sufficient statistic, the expectation of which is zero. This will be given below.

EXAMPLE 2.7

In order to show that d is not complete, it suffices to find one function $g(d)$ such that $Eg(d) = 0$ for all $\underline{Y}$ and $P(g(d) \neq 0 | \underline{Y}) > 0$ for at least one $\underline{Y}$. Choose some fixed $k_0 (1 \leq k_0 \leq N)$ such that $0 < z_{k_0} < 1$ and let $g_c(d)$ be defined for some real constant $c \neq 0$ by

$$g_c(d) = \begin{cases} c/z_{k_0}, & \text{if } s \in C_{k_0} \\ -c/(1 - z_{k_0}), & \text{if } s \notin C_{k_0} \end{cases}$$

where

$$C_{k_0} = \{s: k_0 \in s\}.$$

Then

$$E\{g_c(d)\} = z_{k_0} \cdot \frac{c}{z_{k_0}} + (1 - z_{k_0})\frac{-c}{(1 - z_{k_0})} = 0$$

for all $\underline{Y}$. However when $c \neq 0$, $P(g_c(d) \neq 0|\underline{Y}) = 1$ for all $\underline{Y}$. Thus d is not complete. ◆

2.5   SAMPLING WITH VARYING PROBABILITIES AND WITHOUT REPLACEMENT

Here we just introduce the reader to the probability sampling without replacement and show how quickly analysis can become complicated. Let $p_{i,r}$ denote the probability of selecting U_i at the rth draw $r = 1, \ldots, n$ and $i = 1, 2, \ldots, N$. To be consistent

$$p_{i,1} = z_i (i = 1, \ldots, N)$$

where z_i denotes the probability of selecting U_i at the first draw, $p_{i,2} = \sum_{j \neq i}^{N} P(U_j$ is selected at the first draw) P (selecting U_i at second draw given U_j at first draw)

$$= \sum_{j \neq i}^{N} z_j \cdot \frac{z_i}{1 - z_j} = z_i \left\{ \sum_{j=1}^{N} \frac{z_j}{1 - z_j} - \frac{z_i}{1 - z_i} \right\}.$$

Clearly $p_{i,2} \neq z_i$ for $i = 1, \ldots, N$ unless $z_i = \frac{1}{N}$.

Hence, we need to develop new theory for sampling with varying probabilities and without replacement which will be more complicated than that with replacement. Also $E(\frac{y_i}{z_i})$ will change with successive draws. In order to overcome this difficulty, we may associate a new variable at each draw, so that its expected value equals the population value of the original variable. Estimates based on such schemes, which take into consideration the order of the draw, are called *ordered estimates* and have been studied by Das (1951) and DesRaj (1956). M. N. Murthy (1957) has obtained the corresponding unordered estimates via the Rao-Blackwell theorem (see Result 2.1).

Let us consider the ordered estimator proposed by DesRaj (1956). Let $(y_1, \ldots, y_n)$ and $(z_1, \ldots, z_n)$ be, respectively, the values of the sample units and their initial probabilities in the order of their selection. Then the proposed estimator is

$$\hat{\bar{Y}}_D = \frac{1}{n} \sum_{i=1}^{n} t_i = \bar{t} \quad \text{(say)}$$

where

$$t_i = N^{-1} \left\{ y_1 + \cdots + y_{i-1} + \frac{y_i}{z_i}(1 - z_1 - z_2 - \cdots - z_{i-1}) \right\}$$

and

$$E(t_i|y_i \ \ldots \ y_{i-1}) = N^{-1}\left\{(y_1 + \cdots + y_{i-1}) + \sum_{j=i}^{N} \frac{y_j}{z_j} \frac{z_j(1 - z_1 \cdots - z_{j-1})}{(1 - z_1 - \cdots - z_{j-1})}\right\}$$

$$= N^{-1}\{y_1 + \cdots + y_{i-1} + Y - y_1, \ \ldots \ - y_{i-1}\}$$

$$= \bar{Y}.$$

Thus t_i is an unbiased estimator of $\bar{Y}$ and hence $\hat{\bar{Y}}_D$ is unbiased for $\bar{Y}$.

Now, for $i < j$,

$$E(t_i t_j) = Et_i(Et_j|y_i, \ \ldots, \ y_{i-1})$$

$$= Et_i \bar{Y} = \bar{Y}^2.$$

Same result holds for $i > j$.

Hence t_i and $t_j (i \neq j)$ are uncorrelated. Thus one can easily show that

$$\{n(n-1)\}^{-1} E(\sum\sum_{i\neq j} t_i t_j) = \{n(n-1)\}^{-1} E\left(\sum\sum_{i<j} + \sum\sum_{i>j}\right) t_i t_j$$

$$= \bar{Y}^2.$$

Although it is too complicated to obtain an expression for the variance of $\hat{\bar{Y}}_D$, one can obtain an unbiased estimate given by

$$\hat{\text{var}}(\hat{\bar{Y}}_D) = \bar{t}^2 - (\hat{\bar{Y}})^2$$

$$= \bar{t}^2 - \{n(n-1)\}^{-1} \sum\sum_{i\neq j} t_i t_j$$

$$= \bar{t}^2 + \{n(n-1)\}^{-1} \left[\sum t_i^2 - n^2\bar{t}^2\right]$$

$$= \{n(n-1)\}^{-1} \sum_{1}^{n}(t_i - \bar{t})^2.$$

Roy Choudury (1956) has shown that $\text{var}(\hat{\bar{Y}}_D)$ is less than the variance of the usual unbiased estimator obtained with probability sampling with replacement. In the case of $n = 2$, we can get an explicit expression for $\text{var}(\hat{\bar{Y}}_D)$. Then

$$t_1 = \frac{y_1}{Nz_1}, \qquad t_2 = N^{-1}\left\{y_1 + y_2\frac{(1 - z_1)}{z_2}\right\}$$

$$\bar{t} = (t_1 + t_2)/2 = \frac{1}{2}\left\{(1 + z_1)\frac{y_1}{Nz_1} + (1 - z_1)\frac{y_2}{Nz_2}\right\}.$$

Let

$$r_i = \frac{y_i}{N z_i} - \bar{Y}, \qquad i = 1, 2 .$$

Since $E\bar{t} = \bar{Y}$, one can write

$$2(\bar{t} - \bar{Y}) = (1 + z_1)r_1 + (1 - z_1)r_2 .$$

Hence

$$4 \text{ var } \bar{t} = E\left[(1 + z_1)r_1 + (1 - z_1)r_2\right]^2$$

$$= \sum_{i \neq j}^{N} \sum^{N} \left\{(1 + z_i)r_i + (1 - z_i)r_j\right\}^2 \cdot \frac{z_i z_j}{1 - z_i}$$

$$= \sum_{i=1}^{N} \sum_{j=1}^{N} \{\quad\}^2 \cdot \frac{z_i z_j}{1 - z_i} - 4 \sum_{i=1}^{N} r_i^2 \frac{z_i^2}{1 - z_i} .$$

After squaring the quantity in braces and summing, we obtain

$$4 \text{ var } \bar{t} = \sum_{i=1}^{N} \frac{(1 + z_i)^2 z_i}{1 - z_i} r_i^2 + \left(\sum_{1}^{N} z_i(1 - z_i)\right)\left(\sum_{j} z_j r_j^2\right) - 4 \sum \frac{z_i^2}{1 - z_i} r_i^2 .$$

(The cross-product term vanishes because $\sum_1^N z_j r_j = 0$.) Thus

$$4 \text{ var } \bar{t} = \sum_{i} \left\{\frac{(1 + z_i)^2 z_i - 4 z_i^2}{1 - z_i}\right\} r_i^2 + \left(1 - \sum z_i^2\right)\left(\sum z_j r_j^2\right)$$

$$= \sum (1 - z_i) z_i r_i^2 + \left(1 - \sum z_i^2\right)\left(\sum z_j r_j^2\right)$$

$$= \left(2 - \sum z_i^2\right)\left(\sum_{1}^{N} z_j r_j^2\right) - \sum_{1}^{N} z_j^2 r_j^2 .$$

$$2 \text{ var } \bar{t} = \left(1 - \frac{1}{2}\sum z_i^2\right)\left(\sum_{1}^{N} z_j r_j^2\right) - \frac{1}{2}\sum_{1}^{N} z_j^2 r_j^2$$

$$< \sum z_j r_j^2$$

= twice the variance of the unbiased estimate with probability sampling and with replacement.

This establishes Roy Choudury's (1956) result for $n = 2$.

Murthy (1957) obtained unordered estimates from the ordered estimate of DesRaj (1956). Sampling procedures with unequal probabilities and without replacement may be classified into two categories. The first category is IPPS (inclusive probability proportional to size) sampling procedures in which the probability of including U_i in the sample of size n is nz_i. A commonly used procedure for estimating the population mean or total with such procedures is the celebrated Horvitz-Thompson procedure. The second category consists of non-IPPS sampling procedures, in which some other estimator is used for estimating the population mean or total. In Chapter 10 we will consider in great detail Murthy's method and the Horvitz-Thompson estimator.

■ PROBLEMS

2.1   Suppose a certain district has 10 counties of population sizes (in thousands)

$$15, 18, 21, 12, 16, 10, 8, 5, 3, 9$$

Suppose we wish to select a sample of 3 counties with replacement and with probability proportional to the size of the county. Use the method presented in Example 2.1.

2.2   For the same data, use Lahiri's (1951) method discussed in Section 2.2 in selecting 3 counties with replacement and with probability proportional to the size of the county.

2.3   Consider the following population configuration:

Unit	x_i	y_i	z_i
1	2	4	1/10
2	3	5	1/5
3	4	6	1/5
4	5	10	2/5
5	6	15	1/10
Total	20	40	1

Suppose we draw a sample of size $n = 2$ with replacement. Compute the variance of the estimate of $\bar{Y}$ when sampling is proportional to size and compare it with the variance of the estimate based on simple random sampling with replacement.

2.4   Consider the following population configuration:

Unit	y_i	z_i	y_i/z_i
1	0.5	0.1	5
2	1.2	0.2	6
3	2.1	0.3	7
4	3.2	0.4	8

For probability sampling of size 2 without replacement, find the variances of the Horvitz-Thompson estimator (H-T) and the DesRaj estimator D.

Hint: Note that the H-T estimator of $\bar{Y}$ is $\hat{\bar{Y}}_{HT} = \sum_{i \in s} y_i/N\pi_i$ where $\pi_i = P$ (ith unit is included in the sample). When $n = 2$,

$$\pi_i = z_i + \sum_{j=1, j \neq i}^{N} z_j z_i/(1 - z_j).$$

Also, probability of selecting both ith and jth units in a sample of size $2 = z_i z_j \{(1 - z_i)^{-1} + (1 - z_j)^{-1}\}$.)

2.5   Let $N = 10$ and the values of the units in the population be

$$1, 2, 3, \ldots, 10.$$

Let the probability of their selection be given by

$$P(i\text{th unit is selected}) = z_i = \frac{i}{55}, \quad i = 1, \ldots, 10.$$

Draw a sample of size 3 without replacement and with the above probabilities of sampling. Obtain DesRaj's estimate $\bar{Y}_D$.

2.6   Suppose a club consists of $N = 15$ members and their annual incomes are 4, 7, 9, 10.8, 13, 17, 22, 26, 28, 32, 45, 60, 78, 100, and 125 (in thousands of dollars). We wish to draw a random sample $n = 4$ without replacement and with probabilities proportional to their annual incomes. Carry out the sampling procedure of Lahiri with the help of a table of random numbers.

■ REFERENCES

2.1   Basu, D. (1958). On sampling with and without replacement. *Sankhyā* **20**, 287–294.

2.2   Cassel, C. M., Sarndal, C. E., and Wretman, J. H. (1977). *Foundations of Inference in Survey Sampling*. New York: John Wiley & Sons, p. 44.

2.3   Das, A. C. (1951). On two phase sampling and sampling with varying probabilities without replacement. *Bull. Internat. Statist. Inst.* **33**, 105–112.

2.4   Des Raj (1956). Some estimates in sampling with varying probabilities without replacement. *J. Amer. Statist. Assoc.* **51**, 269–284.

2.5   Godambe, V. P. (1955). A unified theory of sampling from finite populations. *J. Roy. Statist. Soc.* B**17**, 269–278.

2.6   Koop, J. C. (1963). On the axioms of sample formation and their bearing on the construction of linear estimators in sampling theory for finite universes. *Metrika* **17**, 81–114, 165–204.

2.7   Lahiri, D. B. (1951). A method for sample selection providing unbiased ratio estimates. *Bull. Intern. Statist. Inst.* **31**, 24–57.

2.8   Lanke, J. (1975). *Some Contributions to the Theory of Survey Sampling*. Lund: A B Svenska Siffror, pp. 41–42.

2.9   Murthy, M. N. (1957). Ordered and unordered estimators in sampling without replacement. *Sankhyā* **18**, 379–390.

2.10   Roy Choudhury, D. K. (1956). Integration of several pps. surveys. *Science and Culture* **22**, 119–120.

CHAPTER 3

SIMPLE RANDOM SAMPLING

3.1 INTRODUCTION

Simple random sampling is a scheme for selecting n units out of N sampling units such that all possible distinct samples, namely $\binom{N}{n}$, are equally likely to be chosen. The sampling units in the population are labeled $1, 2, \ldots, N$. A set of n random distinct numbers lying between 1 and N are selected, and the units having these numbers are selected for the sample. If you are randomly selecting the sample, we can show by the following argument that all $\binom{N}{n}$ samples are equally likely. Several other schemes of drawing simple random samples are also available and designed for particular situations—for example, drawing from a large file sequentially.

At the first draw, the probability that one of the n specified units will be selected is n/N. At the second draw, the probability that some one of the remaining $n-1$ units will be selected is $(n-1)(N-1)$, etc. Hence the probability of selecting the n specified units is

$$\frac{n}{N} \cdot \frac{n-1}{N-1} \cdots \frac{1}{N-n+1} = \frac{n!(N-n)!}{N!} = 1/\binom{N}{n}.$$

In the above scheme we have been sampling *without replacement*. Sampling with replacement is also possible. Then all members of the population are equally likely to be chosen at each stage. There are certain mathematical niceties that follow in the case of sampling *with replacement*. For instance, the expressions for the variances of estimates are simple and easy to evaluate. However, since the duplicates are avoided, sampling without replacement is more informative. Study of simple random sampling is important, because it serves as a stepping stone for other sampling schemes.

3.2   NOTATION

Let the values in the population be denoted by $y_1, y_2, \ldots, y_N$ and the values in the sample by $y_{i_1}, \ldots, y_{i_n}$. (For the sake of simplicity, sometimes we denote it by $(y_1, \ldots, y_n)$.)

$$\text{population total} = Y = \sum_{i=1}^{N} y_i \,,$$

$$\text{population mean} = \bar{Y} = N^{-1} \sum_{1}^{N} y_i \,,$$

$$\text{sample total} = \sum_{j=1}^{n} y_{i_j} \,,$$

$$\text{sample mean } \bar{y} = n^{-1} \sum_{j=1}^{n} y_{i_j} \,.$$

Parameters of interest to be estimated are:

1. Mean $= \bar{Y}$ (e.g., the average number of children per school).
2. Total $= Y$ (e.g., the total number of acres of corn in a region).
3. Ratio of two totals or means $= R = Y/X = \bar{Y}/\bar{X}$ (e.g., the ratio of girls to boys in a certain school district).
4. Proportion of units that fall in a certain category (e.g., the proportion of people having hearing aids).

The circumflex on a letter denotes its estimate. For example,

$$\hat{\bar{Y}} = \bar{y} = \text{ sample mean}$$

$$\hat{Y} = N\bar{y} = N \sum_{1}^{n} y_{i_j}/n$$

$$\hat{R} = \bar{y}/\bar{x} = \sum y_{i_j} / \sum x_{i_j} \,.$$

The factor N/n is called the *expansion or inflation* factor, and n/N is called the *sampling fraction* and is denoted by the letter f.

3.3   PROPERTIES OF ESTIMATES

In this section we define some of the important properties of estimators.

Definition 3.1. An estimate is said to be *consistent* if the estimate tends to the unknown parameter as n tends to ∞ and N tends to ∞ such that n/N is bounded away from 0 and 1.

For example, $\bar{y}$ and $N\bar{y}$ are consistent estimators of the population mean and total. Although consistency is a desirable property to have, inconsistent estimators are not always useless.

Definition 3.2. An alternate definition of consistency: An estimator $\hat{\mu}$ is said to be consistent for μ if the MSE $(\hat{\mu})$ tends to zero as n and $N \to \infty$ such that n/N is bounded away from 0 and 1.

Note that Definition 3.2 implies Definition 3.1. We have already defined unbiasedness of an estimator.

Lemma 3.1. $P[y_{i_j} = y_l] = \frac{1}{N}$.

Proof: There are $\binom{N}{n}$ possible ways of choosing n numbers out of N and n possibilities for the jth draw. However, if $y_{i_j} = y_l$, then there are $\binom{N-1}{n-1}$ ways of drawing the remaining $n-1$ numbers out of $N-1$. Hence $P(y_{i_j} = y_l) = \binom{N-1}{n-1} / n \binom{N}{n} = 1/N$. ∎

Result 3.1. $\bar{y}$ is an unbiased estimator of $\bar{Y}$.

Proof:

$$E\bar{y} = \frac{1}{n} \sum_{j=1}^{n} E(y_{i_j})$$

Now

$$E(y_{i_j}) = \sum_{l=1}^{N} y_l P(y_{i_j} = y_l) = \binom{N-1}{n-1} \sum y_l / n \binom{N}{n} = \frac{1}{N} \sum_{1}^{N} y_l = \bar{Y}. \quad ∎$$

Corollary 3.1. $\hat{Y} = N\hat{y}$ is an unbiased estimate of Y.

3.4   VARIANCES OF ESTIMATORS

In this section we derive explicit expressions for the variances of estimators.

Lemma 3.2. $P[y_{i_j} = y_r \text{ and } y_{i_k} = y_s] = \frac{1}{N} \cdot \frac{1}{N-1}$, for all $j \neq k$, $r \neq s$.

Proof: Required probability $= \binom{N-2}{n-2} / n(n-1) \binom{N}{n}$.

The variance of the population $= \sigma^2 = N^{-1} \sum_{i=1}^{N} (y_i - \bar{Y})^2$. Let us denote the population MSE by $S^2 = (N-1)^{-1} \sum_{i=1}^{N} (y_i - \bar{Y})^2$. ∎

Result 3.2. $\text{var } \bar{y} = E(\bar{y} - \bar{Y})^2 = \frac{S^2}{n} \left(\frac{N-n}{N} \right) = \frac{S^2}{n}(1-f), f = n/N$.

Proof: One can write

$$n(\bar{y} - \bar{Y}) = (y_{i_1} - \bar{Y}) + \cdots + (y_{i_n} - \bar{Y}),$$

$$n^2(\bar{y} - \bar{Y})^2 = \sum_{j=1}^{n}(y_{i_j} - \bar{Y})^2 + \sum\sum_{j \neq k}(y_{i_j} - \bar{Y})(y_{i_k} - \bar{Y})$$

So, $n^2 \text{ var } \bar{y} = \sum_{j=1}^{n} E(y_{i_j} - \bar{Y})^2 + \sum\sum_{j \neq k} E(y_{i_j} - \bar{Y})(y_{i_k} - \bar{Y})$.

Since the $y_{i_1}, \ldots, y_{i_n}$ are identically distributed,

$$n^2 \text{ var } \bar{y} = n E\left\{ (y_{i_1} - \bar{Y})^2 \right\} + n(n-1)E\left\{ (y_{i_1} - \bar{Y})(y_{i_2} - \bar{Y}) \right\}.$$

Now

$$E\left\{ (y_{i_1} - \bar{Y}) \right\}^2 = \sum_{l=1}^{N} \frac{1}{N}(y_l - \bar{Y})^2 = \frac{N-1}{N} S^2$$

and

$$E\left\{ (y_{i_1} - \bar{Y})(y_{i_2} - \bar{Y}) \right\} = \frac{1}{N(N-1)} \sum\sum_{j \neq k}^{N} (y_j - \bar{Y})(y_k - \bar{Y})$$

$$= \frac{1}{N(N-1)} \left[\left\{ \sum_{1}^{N}(y_l - \bar{Y}) \right\}^2 - \sum_{1}^{N}(y_l - \bar{Y})^2 \right]$$

$$= \frac{1}{N(N-1)} \left[0 - (N-1)S^2 \right]$$

$$= -\frac{S^2}{N}.$$

Hence,

$$n \text{ var } \bar{y} = \frac{N-1}{N} S^2 - \frac{n-1}{N} S^2 = \left(\frac{N-n}{N} \right) S^2. \qquad \blacksquare$$

Corollary 3.2.   var $\hat{Y} = E(\hat{Y} - Y)^2 = N^2 S^2 (1 - f)/n$.

Proof: Note that $\hat{Y} = N\bar{y}$ and var $\hat{Y} = N^2$ var $\bar{y}$. The formula for the var $\bar{y}$ involves S^2 which will be unknown. Hence it is of interest to derive an unbiased estimate for S^2.   ∎

Result 3.3.   Let $s^2 = (n - 1)^{-1} \sum_{j=1}^{n} (y_{i_j} - \bar{y})^2$. Then s^2 is an unbiased estimator for S^2.

Proof: One can easily show that

$$S^2 = \frac{1}{N(N - 1)} \sum_{i<j}^{N} \sum^{N} (y_i - y_j)^2 .$$

Let

$$s^2 = \frac{1}{n(n - 1)} \sum_{j<k}^{n} \sum^{n} (y_{i_j} - y_{i_k})^2 .$$

We can write s^2 as

$$s^2 = \frac{1}{2n(n - 1)} \sum_{i \neq j}^{N} \sum^{N} (y_i - y_j)^2 a_i a_j$$

where

$$a_i = 1 \qquad \text{if the } i\text{th unit is included in the sample}$$
$$= 0, \qquad \text{otherwise} .$$

Then

$$E(a_i a_j) = n(n - 1)/N(N - 1) .$$

Hence

$$E s^2 = \frac{1}{2n(n - 1)} \sum_{i \neq j}^{N} \sum^{N} (y_i - y_j)^2 \frac{n(n - 1)}{N(N - 1)}$$

$$= \frac{1}{2N(N - 1)} \sum_{i \neq j}^{N} \sum^{N} (y_i - y_j)^2 = S^2 .$$

Now we can write

$$s^2 = \frac{1}{2n(n - 1)} \sum_{j}^{n} \sum_{k}^{n} \{(y_{i_j} - \bar{y}) - (y_{i_k} - \bar{y})\}^2$$

$$= \frac{1}{n - 1} \sum_{j=1}^{n} (y_{i_j} - \bar{y})^2 .$$ ∎

Corollary 3.3. Standard errors of $\bar{y}$ and $\hat{Y}$ are given by

$$s_{\bar{y}} = s\,\{(1 - f)/n\}^{\frac{1}{2}} \quad\text{and}\quad s_{\hat{Y}} = Ns\,\{(1 - f)/n\}^{\frac{1}{2}}\,.$$

3.5 CONFIDENCE INTERVALS

One can set up confidence intervals for $\bar{Y}$ or Y, provided we can reasonably assume that $\bar{y}$ is asymptotically normally distributed. Then we obtain

$$P\left[\bar{y} - zs\sqrt{\frac{1 - f}{n}} \le \bar{Y} \le \bar{y} + zs\sqrt{\frac{1 - f}{n}}\right] = 1 - \alpha$$

or

$$P\left[N\bar{y} - zNs\sqrt{\frac{1 - f}{n}} \le Y \le N\bar{y} + zNs\sqrt{\frac{1 - f}{n}}\right] = 1 - \alpha$$

where z is the upper $\alpha/2$ point on the standard normal distribution. If $n < 50$, we can replace z by t, where t denotes the upper $\alpha/2$ point on the Student's t distribution with $n - 1$ degrees of freedom. Since t is robust with respect to moderate departures from normality, the confidence intervals for $\bar{Y}$ or Y should be reasonable.

EXAMPLE 3.1

A typed manuscript consists of 500 pages, and a sample of 10 pages are taken and the number of typographical errors counted. The data are as follows:

$$2, 4, 2, 3, 6, 5, 4, 1, 0, 1$$

$$\bar{y} = 28/10 = 2.8$$

$$\sum y_i^2 = 112, \; s^2 = (112 - 78.4)/9 = 33.6/9 = 3.73\,.$$

Hence

$$s = 1.93\,.$$

A 95% confidence interval for Y, the total number of errors, is

$$\hat{Y} \pm tNs\left(\frac{1 - f}{n}\right)^{\frac{1}{2}}\,.$$

That is,

$$1400 \pm (2.26)500(1.93)\left(\frac{1 - .02)}{10}\right)^{\frac{1}{2}}$$

or

$$1400 \pm 682.7 = (717.3, 2082.7)\,.$$

◆

3.6   ALTERNATE METHOD FOR EVALUATING $\text{var}(\bar{y})$

Cornfield (1944) suggested an elegant method which enables one to use results that are relevant for infinite populations. Recall that $a_i = 1$ if y_i is included in the sample, $= 0$ otherwise, for $i = 1, \ldots, n$. Then, one can write

$$n\bar{y} = \sum_{i=1}^{N} a_i y_i, \qquad \sum_{1}^{N} a_i = n.$$

Notice that $P(a_i = 1) = (n/N)$, $P(a_i = 0) = 1 - (n/N)$, and hence $E(a_i) = n/N$ and $\text{var } a_i = f(1 - f)$, where $f = n/N$. Also,

$$
\begin{aligned}
\text{cov}(a_i, a_j) &= E(a_i a_j) - E(a_i)E(a_j) \\
&= \frac{n(n-1)}{N(N-1)} - \left(\frac{n}{N}\right)^2 = -(N-1)^{-1} f(1-f).
\end{aligned}
$$

The random variables $(a_1, \ldots, a_N)$ are exchangeable . That is, the joint probability function of $(a_1, \ldots, a_N)$ does not change if the subscripts of the random variables, namely $(1, 2, \ldots, N)$ are replaced by a random permutation $(i_1, \ldots, i_N)$. This implies that the joint probability function of $(a_1, \ldots, a_k)$ depends only on k and not on the specific subscripts of the a's $(k = 1, \ldots, N)$. In particular, the a_i are identically distributed, and the pairs (a_{i_1}, a_{i_2}) are identically distributed.

$$P(a_1 = 1, a_2 = 1) = \frac{n}{N} \cdot \frac{n-1}{N-1}$$

$$P(a_1 = 1, a_2 = 0) = \frac{n}{N} \cdot \left[1 - \frac{n-1}{N-1}\right]$$

$$P(a_1 = 0, a_2 = 1) = \left[1 - \frac{n}{N}\right]\frac{n}{N-1}$$

$$P(a_1 = 0, a_2 = 0) = \left[1 - \frac{n}{N}\right]\left[1 - \frac{n}{N-1}\right].$$

Since right-hand quantities are free of the subscripts of the two a's, we infer that the bivariate distributions are the same. Thus,

$$
\begin{aligned}
P(a_2 = 1) &= P(a_2 = 1, a_1 = 1) + P(a_2 = 1, a_1 = 0) \\
&= \frac{n}{N} \cdot \frac{n-1}{N-1} + \left[1 - \frac{n}{N}\right]\frac{n}{N-1} \\
&= \frac{n}{N-1}\left[\frac{n-1}{N} + 1 - \frac{n}{N}\right] \\
&= \frac{n}{N}.
\end{aligned}
$$

In general,

$$P(a_i = 1) = P(i\text{th unit is included in the sample})$$

$$= \begin{bmatrix} N-1 \\ n-1 \end{bmatrix} \bigg/ \begin{bmatrix} N \\ n \end{bmatrix} = n/N.$$

Similarly, $P(a_i = 1, a_j = 1) = n(n-1)/N(N-1), i \neq j,$

$$n^2 \text{ var } \bar{y} = \sum_{i=1}^{N} y_i^2 \text{ var}(a_i) + \sum\sum_{i \neq j} y_i y_j \text{ cov}(a_i, a_j)$$

$$= (1-f)f \left\{ \sum y_i^2 - (N-1)^{-1} \sum\sum_{i \neq j} y_i y_j \right\}$$

$$= f(1-f) \left\{ N(N-1)^{-1} \sum y_i^2 - (N-1)^{-1} Y^2 \right\}$$

$$= \frac{Nf(1-f)}{N-1} \sum (y_i - \bar{Y})^2 = Nf(1-f)S^2.$$

That is,

$$\text{var } \bar{y} = (1-f)S^2/n.$$

Remark 3.1. This method of Cornfield (1944) will be very useful in evaluating higher moments of $\bar{y}$. Tukey's (1950) approach will also be helpful in this regard.

3.7   RANDOM SAMPLING WITH REPLACEMENT

If sampling is with replacement, there are N^n possible random samples of size n drawn out of N. Let t_i be the frequency with which y_i is observed in the sample ($i = 1, \ldots, N$). Then we can write

$$\bar{y} = n^{-1} \sum_{i=1}^{N} t_i y_i, \quad \text{where } 0 \leq t_i \leq n, \quad i = 1, \ldots, N, \quad \sum_{1}^{N} t_i = n.$$

Also, t_i is distributed as binomial $(n, 1/N)$ and $(t_1, \ldots, t_N)$ is multinomial $\left(\sum_{1}^{N} t_i = n \right)$ with

$$Et_i = n/N, \quad \text{var } t_i = n(N-1)/N^2$$

and $\text{cov}(t_i, t_j) = -n \cdot \frac{1}{N} \cdot \frac{1}{N}$ for $1 \leq i, j \leq N$. Hence

$$n^2 \text{ var } \bar{y} = \sum_{i=1}^{N} y_i^2 n(N-1)N^{-2} - \sum\sum_{i \neq j} y_i y_j n N^{-2}$$

$$n \text{ var } \bar{y} = N^{-1} \sum y_i^2 - N^{-2} \left(\sum y_i \right)^2 = N^{-1} \sum (y_i - \bar{Y})^2 = \frac{N-1}{N} S^2.$$

Thus, the variance of $\bar{y}$ in sampling without replacement is $(N - n)/(N - 1)$ times its value in sampling with replacement.

Let $\bar{y}_d$ denote the mean of the distinct elements in the sample when sampling is with replacement. If the cost of the sample is proportional to the number of distinct units in the sample, Seth and J. N. K. Rao (1964) have shown that for specified average cost of sampling, the variance of $\bar{y}$ in sampling without replacement is smaller than var $(\bar{y}_d)$ in sampling with replacement.

3.8   ESTIMATES FOR RATIOS

Often we are interested in ratios of two parameters. For example, consider (1) average amount spent on cosmetics by an adult female; (2) average number of hours per week spent by a teenager watching television. In order to estimate the ratio in (1) for the ith household, let x_i denote the number of adult females and y_i denote the amount spent on cosmetics in the ith household ($i = 1, \ldots, N$). Then the population parameter to be estimated is the ratio

$$R = \frac{\text{total amount}}{\text{total number of adult females}} = \frac{\sum_1^N y_i}{\sum_1^N x_i}.$$

The estimate based on sample of size n is

$$\hat{R} = \sum_{j=1}^n y_{i_j} / \sum_{j=1}^n x_{i_j}.$$

Examples of this nature occur frequently when the sampling unit (namely the household) consists of a group of cluster of elements (the number of adult females) and we are interested in estimating the population mean for a member of the group.

The distribution of $\hat{R}$ is more complicated than that of a sample mean, and $\hat{R}$ may not even be unbiased for R.

Result 3.4.   If x_i, y_i are taken on each unit of a simple random sample of size n (assumed to be large), then

$$\text{MSE}\,(\hat{R}) \doteq \text{var}\,(\hat{R}) \doteq \frac{(1 - f)}{(N - 1)n\bar{X}^2} \sum_{i=1}^N (y_i - Rx_i)^2$$

where $R = \bar{Y}/\bar{X}$ and $f = n/N$.

Proof: Let $g(\bar{y}, \bar{x}) = \bar{y}/\bar{x}$. Then for sufficiently large n, we have $g(\bar{y}, \bar{x}) = g(\bar{Y}, \bar{X}) + (\bar{x} - \bar{X})\, \partial g(\bar{Y}, \bar{X})/\partial \bar{X} + (\bar{y} - \bar{Y})\, \partial g(\bar{Y}, \bar{X})/\partial \bar{Y}$. Hence

$$\hat{R} - R \doteq \frac{\bar{y} - \bar{Y} - R(\bar{x} - \bar{X})}{\bar{X}} = \frac{\bar{y} - R\bar{x}}{\bar{X}}$$

provided n is large (then $\bar{x}$ will be close to $\bar{X}$). Thus

$$E(\hat{R} - R) \doteq \frac{E(\bar{y} - R\bar{x})}{\bar{X}} = \frac{\bar{Y} - R\bar{X}}{\bar{X}} = 0.$$

That is, $\hat{R}$ is approximately unbiased for R. Next

$$\text{MSE}\,(\hat{R}) \doteq \frac{E(\bar{y} - R\bar{x})^2}{\bar{X}^2}.$$

Now let $d_j = y_{i_j} - Rx_{i_j} (j = 1, \ldots, n)$ and $\bar{D} = \bar{Y} - R\bar{X} = 0$. Then we can find var $(\bar{R})$ by applying the previous result on the variance of a sample mean, namely $\bar{d}$. Hence

$$\text{var}\,\hat{R} = \frac{1}{\bar{X}^2} \cdot \frac{S_d^2}{n}(1 - f)$$

where $S_d^2 = \sum_{i=1}^{N}(y_i - Rx_i)^2/(N - 1)$ (since $\bar{D} = 0$). A sample estimate of S_d^2 will be

$$s_d^2 = \sum_{j=1}^{n}(y_{i_j} - \hat{R}x_{i_j})^2/(n - 1) = \left[\sum y_{i_j}^2 - 2\hat{R}\sum x_{i_j}y_{i_j} + \hat{R}^2\sum x_{i_j}^2\right]/(n - 1).$$

Thus the standard error of $\hat{R}$ is given by

$$s(\hat{R}) = \left(\frac{1 - f}{n}\right)^{\frac{1}{2}} s_d/\bar{x}$$

where, since $\bar{X}$ will not be available, we replace it by $\bar{x}$.   ∎

EXAMPLE 3.2

From a list of 250 small 2-year colleges, a simple random sample of 50 colleges was drawn. The data for the number of students (y) and the number of teachers (x) are as follows:

n	$\sum y$	$\sum x$	$\sum y^2$	$\sum yx$	$\sum x^2$
50	30.2×10^3	2.02×10^3	30.1×10^6	1.7×10^6	0.11×10^6

Estimate the ratio, number of students per teacher. Compute the standard error of your estimate. Also, find a 95% confidence interval for R. $N = 250$, $n = 50$ yields

$$\hat{R} = \sum y/\sum x$$

$$= 30.2/2.02 = 14.95, \quad \bar{x} = 0.0404 \times 10^3$$

$$s^2(\hat{R}) = \frac{0.8}{50(.0404)^2} \cdot \frac{\{30.1 - 2(14.95)(1.7) + (14.95)^2(0.11)\}}{49}$$

$$= (9.803)(30.1 - 50.83 + 24.58)/49$$

$$= 0.7713.$$

Thus,

$$s(\hat{R}) = 0.878,$$

$$95\% \ \text{CI for } R = \hat{R} \pm zs(\hat{R})$$

$$= 14.95 \pm 1.96(0.878)$$

$$= 14.95 \pm 1.72$$

$$= (13.23, 16.67).$$ ◆

3.9   ESTIMATES OF MEANS OR TOTALS OVER SUBPOPULATIONS

If a population is divided into certain classes (called domains of study) and if a simple random sample of size n is drawn from the overall population, let $n_1, n_2, \ldots, n_c$ denote the subsample sizes from the c classes of subpopulations. Then the estimate of the mean or total of the jth class can be obtained as a ratio estimator, since the n_i's are random, although their sum, namely n, is nonrandom. If the population for the jth class, namely N_j, is unknown, one can replace n_j/N_j by n/N.

3.10   JUSTIFICATION OF THE NORMAL APPROXIMATION

While we are setting up confidence intervals for the population mean, total, or ratio of means, we have implicitly used the normal approximation of the sampling distribution of the relevant statistic, when the sample size is large. The following theorem of Erdös, Rényi, and Hájek gives a justification for the normal approximation. Notice that, since we are sampling from finite populations, the random variables are dependent. However, the dependence is weak. So, when n and N are large, the usual estimators behave like sums of independent random variables, and the criterion for the asymptotic normality is essentially of the Lindberg type. This result will be given below.

3.11   ASYMPTOTIC NORMALITY OF ESTIMATES ARISING FROM SIMPLE RANDOM SAMPLING

Sampling from a finite population may be conceived as a random experiment whose outcomes are subsets s of the set $\mathcal{U} = \{1, 2, \ldots, N\}$. Let s_k denote the subset s consisting of k elements and $P(s_k)$ denote the probability of obtaining s_k. Recall that

$$P(s_k) = \begin{cases} \binom{N}{n}^{-1} & \text{if } k = n \quad \text{(simple random sampling of size } n) \\ 0 & \text{otherwise.} \end{cases}$$

Let $y_1, y_2, \ldots, y_N$ be a sequence of real numbers and let

$$T = \sum_{i_j \in s_n} y_{i_j}/n$$

where s_n is a simple random sample and $\sum_{i_j \in s_n}$ extends over all i_j contained in the sample s_n.

$$ ET = \frac{1}{N} \sum_1^N y_i = \frac{1}{N}Y = \bar{Y} $$

$$ \text{var } T = \left[\frac{n}{N}\right]\left[\frac{N-n}{N-1}\right] \frac{\sum(y_i - \bar{Y})^2}{n^2} = n^{-1}(1-f)S^2 . $$

In the above computations, we use $ET = \sum_{i_j \in s_n} \sum_{k=1}^N P(y_{i_j} = y_k)\frac{y_k}{n} = \sum_{i_j \in s_n} \sum_{k=1}^N \frac{1}{N} \cdot \frac{y_k}{n}$ and $\text{var } T = \sum \text{var } y_{i_j} + \underset{i \neq k}{\sum \sum} \text{cov}(y_{i_j}, y_{i_k})$.

Theorem 3.1.   (Erdös, Rényi, and Hájek). Let $\mathcal{U}_\tau$ be a subset of the elements of $\mathcal{U} = \{1, \dots, N\}$ on which the inequality

$$ (y_i - \bar{Y}) > \tau\sqrt{\text{var } T} $$

holds. Let $n \to \infty$ and $N - n \to \infty$. Then

$$ P\left[\frac{T - ET}{(\text{var } T)^{1/2}} \leq x\right] \to \Phi(x) $$

provided $\displaystyle\lim_{n, N-n \to \infty} \frac{\sum_{i \in \mathcal{U}_\tau}(y_i - \bar{Y})^2}{\sum_{i=1}^N (y_i - \bar{Y})^2} = 0$ for any $\tau > 0$.

Remark 3.2.   Erdös and Rényi (1959) showed the sufficiency of the condition of Theorem 3.1, whereas Hájek (1960) showed its necessity.

Remark 3.3.   The condition of Erdös, Rényi, and Hájek is satisfied provided

1. $\frac{n}{N}$ is bounded away from 0 and 1, i.e.,

$$ 0 < \epsilon < \frac{n}{N} < 1 - \epsilon \qquad \text{for some } \epsilon < \frac{1}{2} $$

and

2. $\displaystyle\lim_{N \to \infty} \frac{\max_{1 \leq i \leq N}(y_i - \bar{Y})^2}{\sum_1^N (y_i - \bar{Y})^2} = 0$ (Noether's condition).

EXAMPLE 3.3

Let $N = 4$, $n = 2$, $(y_1, \dots, y_4) = (3.2, 1.7, 2.6, 4.9)$. Then $\bar{Y} = 3.1$, $S^2 = 1.82$, var $T = 0.455$, $\sigma_T = 0.674$, $\tau = 1$ implies that $\mathcal{U}_\tau = \{4\}$, since $4.9 - 3.1 = 1.8 > 0.674$. ◆

Remark 3.4.   One might ask how large n should be before one can apply the normal approximation. For populations of marked positive skewness, Cochran (1977, p. 42) gives the following rule of thumb:

$$n \geq 25G_1^2$$

where $G_1 = (N\sigma^3)^{-1} \sum_{i=1}^{N}(y_i - \bar{Y})^3$, namely Fisher's measure of skewness, and σ^2 denotes the population variance.

Remark 3.5.   Rosen (1964) obtains weak and strong laws and central limit theorems for sample sums under general regularity assumptions.

3.12   BEST UNBIASED ESTIMATORS

The Gauss-Markov theorem pertaining to best linear unbiased estimation exists for linear models. However, no such analogous result exists for survey designs. Consider the problem of estimating a parameter $T(y_1, \ldots, y_N)$ by an unbiased estimator t obtained from a random sample of size $n(< N)$. Then we have the following result of D. Basu (1971).

Result 3.5.   There is no uniformly minimum-variance unbiased estimator of T.

Proof: Let t be an unbiased estimator of T and let t_0 be the estimator t when $y_i = y_{i0}$ for $i = 1, \ldots, N$, where the y_{i0} are fixed values. Let

$$t^* = t - t_0 + T(y_{10}, \ldots, y_{N0}).$$

Then it is easy to verify that $t^* \equiv T(y_{10}, \ldots, y_{N0})$ for any sample, whenever $y_i = y_{i0}$ and hence $\text{var}(t^*) = 0$. Furthermore, t^* is an unbiased estimator of T. Hence for any given population values, we can construct a suitable estimator with zero variance. That is, there does not exist a uniformly minimum-variance unbiased estimator.   ∎

Suppose we restrict our attention to linear estimators of the form $t = \sum_{i=1}^{n} w_i y_i$, where $\{y_1, \ldots, y_n\}$ is the sample and w_i are some weights which do not depend on the other units drawn in the sample, but depend solely on the specific units drawn. Then the Horvitz-Thompson estimator is the best unbiased estimator. However, if the weights w_i are allowed to depend on the other units drawn in the sample, Godambe (1955) has shown that no minimum-variance unbiased estimator of $\bar{Y}$ exists for all populations.

EXAMPLE 3.4[1]

Consider the case of $N = 3$ and $n = 2$ and let $S = (S_1, S_2, S_3)$ be the support with

$$S_1 = \{U_1, U_2\}, \qquad S_2 = \{U_1, U_3\}, \quad \text{and} \quad S_3 = \{U_2, U_3\},$$

where U_1, U_2, U_3 denote the units in the population. Then the Horwitz-Thompson estimator of $\bar{Y}$ is

$$\hat{\bar{Y}}_{HT} = \sum_{i \in s} \frac{y_i}{N\pi_i}.$$

---

[1] I thank Professor D. Raghavarao for drawing my attention to this example.

When $N = 3$ and $\pi_i = 2/3$,

$$\hat{\bar{Y}}_{HT} = \sum_{i \in s} \frac{y_i}{2} = \bar{y}.$$

Writing

$$\hat{\bar{Y}}_{HT} = \sum_{i=1}^{N} \frac{y_i a_i}{N \pi_i}$$

where

$$a_i = 1 \qquad \text{if the } i\text{th unit is included in the sample}$$

$$= 0 \qquad \text{otherwise}$$

we obtain

$$\text{var}(\hat{\bar{Y}}_{HT}) = \frac{1}{N^2} \left\{ \sum_{i=1}^{N} \frac{y_i^2}{\pi_i^2} \text{ var } a_i + \sum\sum_{i \neq j} y_i y_j \frac{\text{cov}(a_i, a_j)}{\pi_i \pi_j} \right\}.$$

Here

$$\text{var } a_i = \pi_i(1 - \pi_i) = \frac{2}{3} \cdot \frac{1}{3} = \frac{2}{9}$$

$$\text{cov}(a_i, a_j) = E(a_i a_j) - \pi_i \pi_j = \frac{2}{3} \cdot \frac{1}{2} - \left(\frac{2}{3}\right)^2 = \frac{-1}{9}, \qquad \text{since } \pi_i = n/N.$$

Hence,

$$\text{var } \hat{\bar{Y}}_{HT} = \frac{1}{4} \left[\frac{2}{9}(y_1^2 + y_2^2 + y_3^2) - \frac{2}{9}(y_1 y_2 + y_1 y_3 + y_2 y_3) \right]. \qquad \blacklozenge$$

Thus the variance of the Horvitz-Thompson estimator $\bar{y}$ of $\bar{Y}$ is given by

$$\text{var}(\bar{y}) = (y_1^2 + y_2^2 + y_3^2 - y_1 y_2 - y_1 y_3 - y_2 y_3)/18.$$

Consider the estimator t given by

$$t(S_1) = a_{12} y_1 + a_{21} y_2$$

$$t(S_2) = a_{13} y_1 + a_{31} y_3$$

$$t(S_3) = a_{23} y_2 + a_{32} y_3$$

where a_{ij} is the weight given to y_i in the presence of y_j in the sample. Since t is an unbiased estimator of $\bar{Y}$, we obtain

$$Et = \frac{1}{3} \{(a_{12} + a_{13}) y_1 + (a_{21} + a_{23}) y_2 + (a_{31} + a_{32}) y_3\} = \bar{Y}$$

which implies that

$$a_{12} + a_{13} = a_{21} + a_{23} = a_{31} + a_{32} = 1.$$

Further

$$\text{var}(t) = \frac{1}{3}\sum_{i=1}^{3}\{t(S_i)\}^2 - \bar{Y}^2$$

$$= \frac{1}{3}\left[(a_{12}y_1 + a_{21}y_2)^2 + (a_{13}y_1 + a_{31}y_3)^2 \right.$$

$$\left. + (a_{23}y_2 + a_{32}y_3)^2 - 3\bar{Y}^2\right].$$

Taking $a_{1,2} = \frac{1}{2}$, $a_{21} = \frac{1}{2}$, and $a_{31} = \frac{2}{3}$, we see that

$$3\,\text{var}\,t = \frac{1}{4}(y_1 + y_2)^2 + \left(\frac{1}{2}y_1 + \frac{2}{3}y_3\right)^2 + \left(\frac{1}{2}y_2 + \frac{1}{3}y_3\right)^3 - 3\bar{Y}^2$$

$$= \frac{1}{18}\left(3y_1^2 + 3y_2^2 + 4y_3^2 - 3y_1y_2 - 6y_2y_3\right).$$

Hence $\text{var}\,t = \frac{1}{18}\left(y_1^2 + y_2^2 + \frac{4}{3}y_3^2 - y_1y_2 - 2y_2y_3\right).$

So, $\text{var}\,\bar{y} > \text{var}\,t$, provided $y_3(y_2 - \frac{y_3}{3} - y_1) > 0$, which holds in particular when $y_2 = 2$, $y_1 = y_3 = 1$.

Consider the class of linear estimators for $\bar{Y}$ given by

$$\sum_{i \in s} w_i y_i.$$

Suppose we write $\sum w_i y_i = \sum_t w_t n_t y_t$, $\sum_t n_t = n$ where y_t appears n_t times. Then Hartley and J. N. K. Rao (1968) have shown that the ordinary sample mean $\bar{y}$ has minimum variance among unbiased estimators of $\bar{Y}$ that are functions of n_t and y_t only. Much work has been done regarding the role of maximum likelihood, the use of auxiliary information the labels may carry about the y_i, and Bayesian estimators. For survey results see J. N. K. Rao (1975) and Smith (1976).

3.13   DISTINCT UNITS

We need the following lemma on conditional variance and covariance.

Lemma 3.3.   For any random variables U, V, and W defined on the same sample space

$$\text{cov}(U, V) = E\{\text{cov}(U, V)|W\} + \text{cov}(E(U|W), E(V|W)).$$

Proof:

$$\mathrm{cov}\,(U, V) = E(UV) - (EU)(EV)$$

$$= EE(UV|W) - E\tilde{E}U \cdot E\tilde{E}V, \qquad \text{where } \tilde{E}(\cdot) = E(\cdot|W).$$

$$= E\left\{\tilde{E}(UV) - \tilde{E}U \cdot \tilde{E}V\right\}$$

$$+ E\left\{\tilde{E}U \cdot \tilde{E}V - E\tilde{E}U \cdot E\tilde{E}V\right\}$$

$$= E\{\,\mathrm{cov}(U, V|W)\} - \mathrm{cov}\left\{(\tilde{E}U, \tilde{E}V)\right\}. \qquad \blacksquare$$

Corollary 3.4. $\mathrm{var}\,U = \mathrm{cov}\,(U, U) = E\,\mathrm{var}\,(U|W) + \mathrm{var}\,(EU|W).$

Result 3.6.   (DesRaj and Khamis (1958)). Let W denote the number of distinct units in a random sample of size n drawn with replacement. Let b_r be the number of times the rth district unit appears in the sample. Then

$$E\,(\bar{y}_W) = \bar{Y} \quad \text{and} \quad \mathrm{var}\,(\bar{y}_W) \leq \mathrm{var}\,(\bar{y}_n)$$

where

$$\bar{y}_W = W^{-1}\sum_{r=1}^{W} y_r \quad \text{and} \quad \bar{y}_n = n^{-1}\sum_{r=1}^{W} b_r y_r.$$

Proof: For given W, the sample of distinct units is a random sample of W selected without replacement. Thus

$$E(\bar{y}_W|W) = \bar{Y}$$

and hence $E(\bar{y}_W) = EE(\bar{y}_W|W) = \bar{Y}$. Further, for a given sample $A_W = (y_1, y_2, \ldots, y_W)$ of W distinct units, $P(\text{the unit } U_r \text{ will be selected}|A_W) = \frac{1}{W}$ and hence $E(b_r|A_W) = \frac{n}{W}$. Thus $E(\bar{y}_n|A_W) = n^{-1}\sum y_r E(b_r|A_w) = \frac{1}{W}\sum y_r = \bar{y}_W$. Now by the above corollary,

$$\mathrm{var}\,(\bar{y}_n) = E\,\mathrm{var}\,(\bar{y}_n|A_W) + \mathrm{var}\,(E\bar{y}_n|A_W)$$

$$= E\,\mathrm{var}\,(\bar{y}_n|A_W) + \mathrm{var}\,(\bar{y}_W) \geq \mathrm{var}\,(\bar{y}_W). \qquad \blacksquare$$

Basu (1958) obtained Result 3.6 using sufficiency considerations. Also, using Corollary 3.4, we have

$$\mathrm{var}\,(\bar{y}_W) = E\,\mathrm{var}\,(\bar{y}_W|W) = (EW^{-1} - N^{-1})S^2.$$

3.14   THE DISTRIBUTION OF W

The distribution of W is closely related to the occupancy problem when n balls are distributed to N cells. Here W equals the number of cells that are not empty. Feller (1968, p. 102) gives the distribution of W as

$$P(W = s|N, n) = \binom{N}{s} N^{-n} \sum_{v=0}^{s} (-1)^v \binom{s}{v} (s-v)^n, \quad s = 1, 2, \ldots, \min(n, N).$$

D. Basu (1958) was able to obtain explicit expressions for the factorial moment generating function, and from it he obtains

$$EW = N\left[1 - \left(\frac{N-1}{N}\right)^n\right]$$

and

$$\text{var } W = N\left(\frac{N-1}{N}\right)^n - N^2\left(\frac{N-1}{N}\right)^{2n} + N(N-1)\left(\frac{N-2}{N}\right)^n.$$

If N and n become large, such that $\lambda = Ne^{-n/N}$ is bounded, then

$$P(W = s|N, n) \doteq e^{-\lambda}\lambda^{N-s}/(N-s)!$$

Alternatively, one can see that A_W is sufficient for $\bar{Y}$. By the Rao-Blackwell theorem $E(\bar{y}_n|A_W) = \bar{y}_W$ is unbiased for $\bar{Y}$ and $\text{var } \bar{y}_W \le \text{var } \bar{y}_n$.

Using the Cauchy-Schwarz inequality,

$$1 = \left\{E\left(W^{\frac{1}{2}}W^{-\frac{1}{2}}\right)\right\}^2 \le (EW)E(W^{-1}).$$

That is, $E(W^{-1}) \ge (EW)^{-1} = \left\{N\left(1 - \left(\frac{N-1}{N}\right)^n\right)\right\}^{-1}$. Now

$$1 - \left(\frac{N-1}{N}\right)^n = 1 - (1 - \frac{1}{N})^n = 1 - \left\{1 - \frac{n}{N} + \frac{n(n-1)}{2N^2} - \cdots\right\}$$

$$= \frac{n}{N} - \frac{n(n-1)}{2N^2} + \frac{n(n-1)(n-2)}{6N^3} \cdots.$$

Thus

$$E(W^{-1}) \ge \left\{n - \frac{n(n-1)}{2N} + \cdots\right\}^{-1}$$

$$= n^{-1}\left\{1 - \frac{n-1}{2N} + \frac{(n-1)(n-2)}{6N^2} - \cdots\right\}^{-1}$$

$$= n^{-1}\left\{1 + \frac{n-1}{2N} - \frac{(n-1)(n-2)}{6N^2} + \frac{(n-1)^2}{4N^2} - \cdots\right\}$$

$$= n^{-1}\left\{1 + \frac{n-1}{2N} + \frac{(n-1)(n+1)}{12N^2} + \cdots\right\}$$

Hence

$$S^{-2}\{\text{var } \bar{y}_W\} = \left\{E\frac{1}{W} - \frac{1}{N}\right\} \geq \frac{1}{n} + \frac{n-1}{2nN} + \frac{n^2-1}{12nN^2} - \frac{1}{N}$$

$$= \frac{1}{n} - \frac{1}{2N} - \frac{1}{2nN} + \frac{n^2-1}{12nN^2}.$$

Pathak (1961) derives exact expressions for the regular as well as inverse moments of W under any sampling scheme (including sampling with varying probabilities and with or without replacement). In particular, in simple random sampling with replacement,

$$E\left(\frac{1}{W}\right) = \frac{1}{N} + \sum_{m=1}^{N-1} \frac{(N-m)^n}{(N-m)N^n} = \frac{1^{n-1} + 2^{n-1} + \cdots + N^{n-1}}{N^n}$$

or in terms of Bernoulli numbers

$$E\left(\frac{1}{W}\right) = \frac{1}{n} + \frac{1}{2N} + \frac{1}{n} \sum_{s=1}^{\leq (n-1)/2} (-1)^{s-1} \binom{n}{2s} \frac{B_s}{N^{2s}}$$

where B_s is the sth Bernoulli number, given by

$$B_1 = \frac{1}{6}, \quad B_2 = \frac{1}{30}, \quad B_3 = \frac{1}{42}, \quad B_4 = \frac{1}{30}, \quad \text{etc.}$$

Hence

$$E\left(\frac{1}{W}\right) - \frac{1}{N} = \frac{1}{n} - \frac{1}{2N} + \frac{(n-1)}{12N^2} + \cdots.$$

Also, note that

$$E\left(\frac{1}{W}\right) - \frac{1}{N} = N^{-n}\left(1^{n-1} + 2^{n-1} + \cdots + (N-1)^{n-1}\right)$$

$$= N^{-n} \int_1^{N-1} x^{n-1}\, dx = \frac{N^{-n}}{n}\left((N-1)^n - 1\right)$$

$$= \left(\frac{1}{n} - \frac{1}{N} + \frac{n-1}{2N^2}-\right) - \frac{N^{-n}}{n}.$$

Korwar and Serfling (1970) have given a simple proof of the exact expression for $E\left(\frac{1}{W}\right)$ without using the distribution of W. This will be presented below.

Result 3.7.

$$E\left(\frac{1}{W}\right) = N^{-n} \sum_{j=1}^{N} j^{n-1}.$$

Proof: Let $U_1, \ldots, U_N$ denote the population units and let $i_1, \ldots, i_n$ be the subscripts (or labels) of units selected in the sample. Also let $i_{(1)} < i_{(2)} < \cdots < i_{(W)}$ be their ordered distinct values. Then

$$P(i_1 = i_{(W)}) = E P(i_1 = i_{(W)} | i_{(1)}, \ldots, i_{(W)})$$

$$= E\left(\frac{1}{W}\right)$$

since any one of the distinct units is equally likely. On the other hand

$$P(i_1 = i_{(W)}) = P(i_1 \geq i_2, i_1 \geq i_3, \ldots, i_1 \geq i_n)$$

$$= \sum_{j=1}^{N} P(i_1 = j) P(i_2 \leq j, \ldots, i_n \leq j)$$

$$= \sum_{j=1}^{N} \left(\frac{1}{N}\right) \left(\frac{j}{N}\right)^{n-1}.$$

after using symmetry and the independence of $i_1, \ldots, i_n$. This completes the proof of Result 3.7. Lanke (1975, pp. 41–42) also gives an independent proof of Result 3.7.

Korwar and Serfling (1970) also show that

$$Q^* - \frac{1}{720N} \leq E\left(\frac{1}{W}\right) \leq Q^*$$

where

$$Q^* = \frac{1}{n} + \frac{1}{2N} + \frac{n-1}{12N^2}.$$

Since $\frac{n^{-1} - (Nn)^{-1}}{Q^* - N^{-1}} \doteq (1 - \frac{1}{2}f)^{-1}$, where $f = \frac{n}{N}$, the relative benefit due to averaging over distinct units only is an increasing function of f (Note that $\operatorname{var} \bar{y} = \frac{N-1}{Nn} S^2$). ∎

Pathak (1962) has shown the admissibility of $\bar{y}_W$ in the class of all estimators that are functions of $\bar{y}_W$ and W, provided the loss function is squared error.

Result 3.8. If the loss function is squared error, $\bar{y}_W$ is admissible in the class of all functions of $\bar{y}_W$ and W.

Proof: Let $T = \bar{y}_W + f(\bar{y}_W, W)$ be a function of $\bar{y}_W$ and W. Suppose that T is uniformly better than $\bar{y}_W$. Then

$$R(T) = E(\bar{y}_W - \bar{Y})^2 + E\left[f(\bar{y}_W, W)\right]^2 + 2E\left[(\bar{y}_W - \bar{Y}) f(\bar{y}_W, W)\right] \leq E(\bar{y}_W - \bar{Y})^2.$$

That is,

$$E\left[f(\bar{y}_W, W)\right]^2 + 2E\left[(\bar{y}_W - \bar{Y})f(\bar{y}_W, W)\right] \leq 0$$

for all $y_1, y_2, \ldots, y_N$. In particular take

$$y_1 = \ldots = y_N = C.$$

Then the above inequality implies that $f(C, W) = 0$. Since the choice of C is arbitrary, it follows that $f(\bar{y}_W, W) \equiv 0$, which completes the proof.

Let $\bar{y}_{W(2)} = \frac{NW/(N-W)}{E\{NW/(N-W)\}} \bar{y}_W$.

If $\frac{n}{N}$ can be ignored, $y_{W(2)}$ is equivalent to

$$\bar{y}^*_{W(2)} = \frac{W}{E(W)} \bar{y}_W .$$ ∎

Then we have the following result of Pathak (1962, pp. 270–291), which we state without proof.

Result 3.9. We have

$$\begin{aligned}
\mathrm{var}\,(\bar{y}_W) - \mathrm{var}\,(\bar{y}^*_{W(2)}) &< 0 \qquad \text{if } \frac{S^2}{\bar{Y}^2} < \frac{C_2}{C_1} \\[2mm]
&> 0 \qquad \text{if } \frac{S^2}{\bar{Y}^2} > \frac{C_2}{C_1}
\end{aligned}$$

where

$$C_1 = \frac{1}{2nN} + \frac{5(n-1)}{12nN^2} + o(N^{-2})$$

and

$$C_2 = \frac{n-1}{2nN} - \frac{(n-1)(n-2)}{3nN^2} + o(N^{-2}).$$

DesRaj and Khamis (1958) provide an unbiased estimator for $\mathrm{var}\,(\bar{y}_W)$ which is given by

$$G(W) = \left[\left(\frac{1}{W} - \frac{1}{N}\right) + N^{1-n}\left(1 - \frac{1}{W}\right)\right] s^2_W .$$

Let us show that $E(G_W | W \geq 2) = \mathrm{var}\,(\bar{y}_W)$.

Notice that $P(W \geq 2) = 1 - P(W = 1) = 1 - N^{1-n}$. Then

$$E\{G(W)|W \geq 2\}$$

$$= \sum_{u=2}^{n} \{EG(W)|W = u\} \, P(W = u|W \geq 2)$$

$$= \sum_{u=2}^{n} EG(W)|W = u)P(W = u)/P(W \geq 2)$$

$$= (1 - N^{1-n})^{-1} \sum_{u=2}^{n} P(W = u) \{EG(W|W = u)\}$$

$$= (1 - N^{1-n})^{-1} \sum_{u=2}^{n} \left\{ \frac{1}{u} - \frac{1}{N} - N^{1-n}\left(1 - \frac{1}{u}\right) \right\} P(W = u) E(s_W^2|W)$$

$$= (1 - N^{1-n})^{-1} S^2 \sum_{u=2}^{n} \left\{ \frac{1}{u} - \frac{1}{N} - N^{1-n}\left(1 - \frac{1}{u}\right) \right\} P(W = u)$$

$$= (1 - N^{1-n})^{-1} S^2 \left[\sum_{u=1}^{n} \left\{ \frac{1}{u} - \frac{1}{N} - N^{1-n}\left(1 - \frac{1}{u}\right) \right\} P(W = u) \right.$$

$$\left. - \left(1 - \frac{1}{N}\right) N^{1-n} \right]$$

$$= (1 - N^{1-n})^{-1} S^2 \left[\sum_{u=1}^{n} \left\{ \frac{1}{u} - \frac{1}{N} - N^{1-n}\left(1 - \frac{1}{u}\right) \right. \right.$$

$$\left. \left. - (1 - \frac{1}{N})N^{1-n} \right\} P(W = u) \right]$$

$$= (1 - N^{1-n})^{-1} S^2 \left[\sum_{u=1}^{n} (1 - N^{1-n})\left(\frac{1}{u} - \frac{1}{N}\right) P(W = u) \right]$$

$$= S^2 \left[\sum_{u=1}^{n} \left(\frac{1}{u} - \frac{1}{N}\right) P(W = u) \right] = \left(E\frac{1}{W} - \frac{1}{N} \right) S^2 = \text{var } \bar{y}_W .$$

DesRaj and Khamis (1958) provide another unbiased estimator given by

$$G'(u) = \left[\left(\frac{1}{u} - \frac{1}{N} \right) + \frac{N-1}{N^n - N} \right] s^2$$

where

$$s^2 = \begin{cases} s_w^2 & \text{for } w \geq 2 \\ 0 & \text{for } w = 1. \end{cases}$$

Pathak (1962, p. 295) gives some other unbiased estimators for $\text{var}(\bar{y}_w)$.

Consider the sampling scheme where the total sample size is random with the number of distinct units specified. Then also, DesRaj and Khamis (1958) show that the average based on the distinct units has a smaller variance than the average based on all the sampled units. The same is true of ratio estimates.

3.15   COMPARISON OF SIMPLE RANDOM SAMPLING WITH AND WITHOUT REPLACEMENT

If you look at the variances of estimators for the population mean, we obtain

$$\frac{\sigma^2}{n} \quad \text{and} \quad \frac{\sigma^2}{n}\left(\frac{N-n}{N-1}\right)$$

for sampling with and without replacement, respectively. We infer that sampling without replacement is better. However, Basu (1958) and Pathak (1962) point out that the comparison is unfair, because cost in sampling without replacement is greater than the cost in sampling with replacement. It would be appropriate to take into account the cost involved in the selection of the two different samples. For instance, if the cost is proportional to the number of distinct units drawn, the expected cost in sampling with replacement is proportional to

$$E(W) = N\left[1 - \left(\frac{N-1}{N}\right)^n\right]$$

for instance, for $N = 100, n = 25, E(W) = 22.2$.

Basu (1958) has shown that in this situation the sample mean of the sample with replacement is worse than the sample mean of the equivalent sample without replacement (i.e., the one based on a sample of size $E(W)$ without replacement). Pathak (1962) compares the sample means $\bar{y}$ of the equivalent sample without replacement with the estimator $\bar{y}_{W(2)}$ given by

$$\bar{y}_{w(2)} = \frac{NW/(N-W)}{E\{NW/(N-W)\}}\bar{y}_W .$$

Then

$$\text{var}(\bar{y}_{W(2)}) = \frac{S^2}{E[NW/(N-W)]} + \bar{Y}^2 \text{ var}\left[\frac{NW/(N-W)}{ENW/(N-W)}\right]$$

and

$$\text{var}(\bar{y}) = \left(\frac{1}{EW} - \frac{1}{N}\right)S^2 .$$

Now, since $NW/(N-W)$ is a convex function of W, we have by Jensen's inequality [2]

$$E\left[NW/(N-W)\right] \geq NEW/(N-EW) = \left(\frac{1}{EW} - \frac{1}{N}\right)^{-1}.$$

Thus, the first component in the var $(\bar{y}_{W(2)})$ is smaller than var $(\bar{y})$.

Since $E\left(\frac{1}{W}\right) > \frac{1}{E(W)}$ for $n > 1$, it readily follows that $\bar{y}_{EW} = \frac{1}{EW} \sum_1^{EW} y_i$ (where EW is assumed to be an integer) is uniformly more efficient than $\bar{y}_W$.

Let

$$\bar{y}_{g(W)} = \frac{g(W)}{Eg(W)} \bar{y}_W$$

where g is a function of W. In particular we could have

$$g(W) = 1, \qquad g(W) = W \quad \text{or} \quad g(W) = NW/(N-W).$$

Then

$$\text{var } \bar{Y}_{EW} = \left(\frac{1}{EW} - \frac{1}{N}\right) S^2$$

$$= \left[\left(1 - \frac{n}{2N}\right) - \frac{1}{2N} + \frac{n^2-1}{12N^2}\right] S^2 + O(N^{-2}).$$

Also we have the following general theorem of Seth and J. N. K. Rao (1964) (see also J. N. K. Rao (1966, p. 130)).

Result 3.10.   The variance of $\bar{y}_{EW}$ is always smaller than the variance of $\bar{y}_{g(W)}$ if $S^2/\bar{Y}^2$ is less than N. If $g(W)$ is a constant, then var $(\bar{y}_{EW})$ is always smaller than the var $(\bar{y}_{g(W)})$.

Proof:

$$\text{var}\,(\bar{y}_{g(W)}) = E\left\{\text{var}(\bar{y}_{g(W)}|W)\right\} + \text{var}\left\{E(\bar{y}_{g(W)}|W)\right\}$$

$$= \left(\frac{E(g^2(W)/W)}{E^2 g(W)} - \frac{1}{N}\right) S^2 + \frac{\text{var}\,g(W)}{E^2 g(W)}\left(\bar{Y}^2 - \frac{S^2}{N}\right).$$

By the Cauchy-Schwarz inequality we have

$$1 = E^2\left(\frac{g}{\sqrt{W}} \cdot \frac{\sqrt{W}}{Eg}\right) \leq E\left(\frac{g^2}{W}\right) \cdot E\left(\frac{W}{(Eg)^2}\right).$$

Hence

$$\frac{E\{g^2(W)/W\}}{E^2 g(W)} \geq \frac{1}{EW}.$$

---

[2] Jensen's inequality says that if Ψ is convex in an open interval I and W is a random variable such that $P(W \in I) = 1$ and $EW < \infty$, then $E\Psi(W) \geq \Psi(EW)$.

That is, var $(\bar{y}_{EW})$ is always smaller than var $(\bar{y}_{g(W)})$ if $S^2/\bar{Y}^2$ is less than N. If $g(W)$ is a constant, the second term in the expression for var $(\bar{y}_{g(W)})$ is zero, so that

$$\text{var}\,(\bar{y}_{EW}) \;<\; \text{var}\,(\bar{y}_{g(W)}) \;=\; \text{var}\,(\bar{y}_W).$$

It should be pointed out that in practice one seldom comes across populations having coefficient of variation larger than $N^{\frac{1}{2}}$.   ■

3.16   USE OF BALANCED INCOMPLETE BLOCK DESIGNS IN SIMPLE RANDOM SAMPLING

In simple random sampling without replacement the support size $K = \binom{N}{n}$ could be very large. Ideas for reducing the size K are contained in Chakrabarti (1963), who used the well known balanced incomplete block (BIB) designs,   defined as follows.

Definition 3.3.   A BIB design is an arrangement of v symbols into b sets each of size $k^*(k^* < v)$ such that

1. every symbol occurs at most once in a set,
2. every symbol occurs in exactly r sets, and
3. every pair of symbols occur together in λ sets.

v, b, r, k^* and λ are known as the design parameters and they satisfy the relations

$$vr = bk^*, \qquad r(k^* - 1) = \lambda(v - 1), \qquad b \geq v.$$

EXAMPLE **3.5** _____

A design for $v = 13, b = 13, r = 4, k^* = 4, \lambda = 1$ is given below with columns as sets of the design.

1	2	3	4	5	6	7	8	9	10	11	12	13
2	3	4	5	6	7	8	9	10	11	12	13	1
4	5	6	7	8	9	10	11	12	13	1	2	3
10	11	12	13	1	2	3	4	5	6	7	8	9

◆

For further details on these designs, please refer to Raghavarao (1971).   The analogy between simple random sampling and BIB is that the v symbols correspond to N population units and the sets correspond to samples of size $n = k^*$. Then the support has b samples. It should be noted that $b \leq K = \binom{N}{n}$. By selecting a set of the design with probability $1/b$ and using the sample corresponding to the units identified with the symbols in the set, we obtain the selection and inclusion probabilities.

$$p_\alpha = \text{probability of a particular sample} = 1/b$$

$$\pi_i = P(i\text{th unit is included in the sample}) = \frac{r}{b} = \frac{vr}{bv} = \frac{k^*}{v} = \frac{n}{N},$$

$$\pi_{ij} = P(i\text{th and }j\text{th units are included in the sample})$$

$$= \frac{\lambda}{v} = \frac{\lambda(v-1)}{b(v-1)} = \frac{r(k^*-1)}{b(v-1)} = \frac{vr(k^*-1)}{bv(v-1)}$$

$$= \frac{k^*(k^*-1)}{v(v-1)} = \frac{n(n-1)}{N(N-1)}.$$

The above computations indicate that the resulting sampling design is simple random sampling without replacement.

3.17   ESTIMATING PROPORTIONS AND PERCENTAGES

Estimating the proportions or percentages arises naturally in sample surveys. For example, we want to estimate the proportion of the population suffering from a certain ailment. If N is the size of the population and M is the number of people in the population having a certain characteristic, we can define

$$y_i = 1, \quad \text{if the }i\text{th unit in the population has the characteristic}$$

$$= 0, \quad \text{otherwise } (i = 1, \ldots, N).$$

Then

$$Y = \sum_{i=1}^{N} y_i = M, \qquad \bar{Y} = N^{-1}\sum_{1}^{N} y_i = M/N = P$$

the true proportion. If we draw a sample of size n, then

$$\bar{y} = n^{-1}\sum_{j=1}^{n} y_{i_j} = m/n = p$$

m denoting the number in the sample having the characteristic and p denoting the sample proportion. Also note that since

$$\sum_{i=1}^{N} y_i^2 = \sum_{1}^{N} y_i = M = NP$$

and

$$\sum_{j=1}^{n} y_{i_j}^2 = m = np$$

$$S^2 = (N-1)^{-1} \sum_{i=1}^{N} (y_i - \bar{Y})^2 = (N-1)^{-1} \left[\sum y_i^2 - N\bar{Y}^2 \right]$$
$$= (N-1)^{-1}[NP - NP^2]$$
$$= NPQ/(N-1), \quad Q = 1 - P$$

and

$$s^2 = (n-1)^{-1} \sum_{1}^{n} (y_{i_j} - \bar{y})^2 = npq/(n-1), \quad q = 1 - p.$$

We have the following results parallel to those developed earlier in this chapter.

Result 3.11.   The sample proportion p is unbiased for P.

Result 3.12.   The variance of p is

$$\text{var } p = E(p - P)^2 = (1 - f)S^2/n = (1 - f)PQN/n(N-1).$$

Corollary 3.5. $\text{var } \hat{M} = N^2 \text{ var } p = N^3(1 - f)PQ/n(N-1)$ where $\hat{M} = Np$.

Result 3.13.   An unbiased estimate of the variance of p is

$$\widehat{\text{var }} p = s_p^2 = (1 - f)pq/(n-1).$$

Proof: We have shown in Result 3.3 that $(1 - f)s^2/n$ is an unbiased estimator of var $(\bar{y})$. Now, substituting $s^2 = npq/(n-1)$, we obtain the desired result.   ∎

Notice that if N is large $1 - f \doteq 1$ and hence $pq/(n-1)$ is approximately unbiased for var p.

Corollary 3.6.   An unbiased estimate of the variance of $\hat{M} = Np$ is

$$\widehat{\text{var }} M = N^2(1 - f)pq/(n-1).$$

EXAMPLE 3.6

In a small city consisting of 1250 people we are interested in estimating the number that are of blood type AB. A simple random sample of size $n = 100$ is taken and it yields $p = 0.11$. Then

$$\hat{M} = Np = 1250 \times 0.11 = 137.5,$$

$$\text{standard error of } \hat{M} = s_{\hat{M}} = N\{(1 - f)pq/(n-1)\}^{1/2}$$

$$= 1250 \left\{ \left(1 - \frac{1}{12.5}\right)(0.11)(0.89)/99 \right\}^{1/2}$$

$$= 1250\{0.03\} = 37.5.$$ ◆

Remark 3.6. In many surveys, each sampling unit consists of a group of elements. For example, a family consists of its members. If a simple random sample of units is drawn in order to estimate the proportion P of elements that belong to a certain category, the preceding formulae are not applicable.

Remark 3.7. $\sigma_{\hat{M}}/M$ is called the coefficient of variation of the estimate. If f is ignored,

$$\sigma_{\hat{M}}/M = (Q/nP)^{1/2}.$$

Note that $Q/P \doteq (P^{-1} - 1)$ is decreasing in P and goes from ∞ to 0 as P increases from 0 to 1.

If we wish to estimate M such that the coefficient of variation of $\hat{M}$ is 20%, then

$$(Q/nP)^{\frac{1}{2}} = 1/5$$

$$nP/Q = 25$$

$$n = 25(Q/P) \leq 25 \max(Q/P).$$

If we have prior information that P is near 1%, then

$$n = 25 \times 99 = 2475.$$

3.18 BINOMIAL AND HYPERGEOMETRIC DISTRIBUTIONS AND THEIR USE IN SAMPLING

If you sample with replacement, then the number of units in the sample of size n having the characteristic is binomially distributed. In other words,

$$f(m) = \binom{n}{m} P^m (1 - P)^{n-m}, \qquad m = 0, 1, \ldots, n.$$

Extensive tables of the binomial distribution do exist.

On the other hand, if we perform sampling without replacement, then

$$f(m) = f(m|M) = \binom{M}{m} \binom{N - M}{n - m} \binom{N}{n}$$

$$= (M)_m (N - m)_{n-m} / (N)_n$$

where $(K)_r = K(K - 1) \cdots (K - r + 1)$ for $r \leq K$. In this case, it is well known that if $p = m/n$, then

$$E(np) = nP$$

and $$\text{var}(np) = nPQ(1 - f)N/(N - 1).$$

3.19   CONFIDENCE LIMITS FOR M

For specified α_U the upper confidence limit M_U is defined as the smallest integral value of M such that

$$\sum_{j=0}^{m} f(j|M_U) \leq \alpha_U$$

where m denotes the number of units in the sample having the characteristic. Similarly, we define the lower confidence limit M_L (for specified α_L) as the largest integral value of M for which

$$\sum_{j=m}^{n} f(j|M_L) \leq \alpha_L .$$

(M_L, M_U) constitutes a confidence interval with confidence coefficient $\geq 1 - \alpha_U - \alpha_L$. Chung and De Lury (1950) present charts of the 90%, 95%, 99% confidence limits for $P = M/N$ for $N = 500, 2500$, and $10,000$.

Lemma 3.4.   Let X be $b(n, \theta)$ and Y be distributed as beta with parameters $X + 1$ and $n - X$. Then

$$P[X \leq k|\theta] = [Y \geq \theta|X = k].$$

Proof:

$$P[X \leq k|\theta] = \sum_{i=0}^{k} \binom{n}{i} \theta^i (1 - \theta)^{n-i} = \frac{n!}{k!(n-k-1)!} \int_{\theta}^{1} u^k (1 - u)^{n-k-1} \, du$$

$$= P[Y(k+1, n-k) \geq \theta].$$

So,

$$p[X \leq k|\theta] \leq \alpha_1 (=) P[Y(k+1, n-k) \geq \theta|X = k] \leq \alpha_1 . \qquad \blacksquare$$

3.20   CONFIDENCE INTERVALS FOR UNKNOWN DISCRETE POPULATION PARAMETER

Let $(X_1, \ldots, X_n)$ denote a random sample from a population having a discrete distribution function denoted by $F(x; \theta)$, where θ is the unknown parameter and $\theta \in (a, b)$. Let $\hat{\theta}$ be an estimator of θ defined at every mass point in the sample space R_n, namely, the n-dimensional Euclidean space, and $\hat{\theta} \in (a, b)$. Let $V(\hat{\theta}; \theta)$ denote the distribution function of $\hat{\theta}$ evaluated at $\hat{\theta}$ and $V^*(\hat{\theta}, \theta) = 1 - V(\hat{\theta}, \theta)$. Furthermore, let $V(\hat{\theta}; \theta)$ be continuous and decreasing in θ at each mass point of $\hat{\theta}$ so that

$$\lim_{\theta \to a} V(\hat{\theta}, \theta) = 1, \qquad \lim_{\theta \to b} V(\hat{\theta}, \theta) = 0, \qquad \hat{\theta} \in (a, b).$$

N.B. S. S. Wilks (1962, pp. 368–369) served as a source for the material of Section 3.20.

Let $\underline{\theta}$ and $\bar{\theta}$ be the values of θ for which

$$V(\hat{\theta}; \underline{\theta}) = \alpha_1 \quad \text{and} \quad V^*(\hat{\theta}; \bar{\theta}) = \alpha_2, \quad \text{respectively,}$$

where α_1 and α_2 are nonnegative and $0 < \gamma = 1 - \alpha_1 - \alpha_2 < 1$.

Result 3.14.   With the above notation, $(\underline{\theta}, \bar{\theta})$ is a confidence interval for θ with confidence coefficient $\geq \gamma$.

Proof: Let $\theta_1[\theta_2]$ be the largest (smallest) value of $\hat{\theta}$ for which

$$V(\hat{\theta}; \theta) \leq \alpha_1, \quad [V^*(\hat{\theta}; \theta) \leq \alpha_2].$$

Then,

$$P(\theta_1 < \hat{\theta} < \theta_2) \geq \gamma, \quad \gamma = 1 - \alpha_1 - \alpha_2.$$

However, since $V(\hat{\theta}, \theta)$ is monotonically decreasing in θ and nondecreasing in $\hat{\theta}$ and $V^*(\hat{\theta}; \theta)$ is monotonically increasing in θ and nonincreasing in $\hat{\theta}$, it is clear that

$$\theta_1 < \hat{\theta} < \theta_2 \quad \text{if and only if} \quad V(\hat{\theta}; \theta) < \alpha_1 \quad \text{and} \quad V^*(\hat{\theta}; \theta) < \alpha_2$$

that is, if and only if $\underline{\theta} \leq \theta \leq \bar{\theta}$. Hence,

$$P(\underline{\theta} \leq \theta \leq \bar{\theta}|\theta) \geq \gamma. \qquad \blacksquare$$

EXAMPLE 3.7

Let $(X_1, \ldots, X_n)$ be a random sample from the Bernoulli density function given by

$$f(x; P) = P^x (1 - P)^{1-x}, \quad x = 0 \text{ or } 1 \quad \text{and} \quad 0 < P < 1.$$

p has the binomial distribution over the sample space $0, 1/n, \ldots, n/n$ and

$$V(p; P) = \sum_{i=0}^{[np]} \binom{n}{i} P^i (1 - P)^{n-i}$$

$$= \frac{n!}{[np]!(n - [np] - 1)!} \int_P^1 u^{[np]} (1 - u)^{n-[np]-1} \, du$$

and

$$V^*(p; P) = 1 - V(p; P).$$

Now $V(p; P)$ is monotonically decreasing in P and $V^*(p; P)$ is monotonically increasing in P for $0 < p < 1$. Furthermore, $V(p; 0) = 1$ and $V(p; 1) = 0$ for all $p \in (0, 1)$. Hence from the previous result, if $\underline{p}$ and $\bar{p}$ are the solutions of the equations

$$V(p; P) = \alpha_1 \quad \text{and} \quad V^*(p; P) = \alpha_2, \quad \text{respectively}$$

and if $\gamma = 1 - \alpha_1 - \alpha_2$, we have

$$P(\underline{p} \leq P \leq \bar{p}|P) \geq \gamma.$$

That is, $(\underline{p}, \bar{p})$ is a γ-confidence interval for P. $\blacklozenge$

Remark 3.8. Clopper and Pearson (1934) have graphically constructed confidence intervals of this type for the case $\alpha_1 = \alpha_2 = .05, .025$ for various values of $n (10 \leq n \leq 1000)$.

Remark 3.9. A similar procedure can be given for the Poisson parameter and the hypergeometric case. In the latter, the distribution function is $H(M; N, n)$, where N, n are known and M is the unknown parameter.

3.21 USE OF THE FINITE POPULATION CORRECTION FOR BINOMIAL CONFIDENCE LIMITS

Let N be the population size, n the sample size, and m the number of units in the sample that have the characteristic of interest. Also, let P_L and P_U denote the lower and upper confidence limits for the true binomial proportion p having confidence coefficient γ. Then Burnstein (1975) suggests the following confidence limits in order to take the population size into consideration:

$$P_{1L} = m/n - (m/n - P_L)[(N - n)/(N - 1)]^{\frac{1}{2}} = gP_L + (m/n)(1 - g)$$

$$P_{1U} = m/n + (P_U - m/n)[(N - n)/(N - 1)]^{\frac{1}{2}} = gP_U + (m/n)(1 - g)$$

where

$$g = \{(N - n)/(N - 1)\}^{\frac{1}{2}} .$$

More accurate confidence limits (P_{2L}, P_{2U}) for P are obtained replacing m by $m - 0.5$ in P_{1L} and m by $m + 0.5$ in P_{1U}.

Remark 3.10. One will get confidence limits for M as follows:

$$M_L = [P_{2L}N], \qquad M_U = [P_{2U}N]$$

where $[x]$ denotes the largest integer contained in x. If we use $P_L^* = M_L/N$ and $P_U^* = M_U/N$ for P, then the confidence coefficient is affected. Burnstein (1975, Tables 2 and 3) studies the effect of this modification on the nominal confidence coefficient.

3.22 CLUSTER SAMPLING: ESTIMATION OF PROPORTIONS

We take a simple random sample of n units. Let each unit have the same number of elements, namely k. Let m_i denote the number of elements of ith unit having the characteristic of interest. Then define

$$p_i = m_i/k \qquad \text{and} \qquad p = \frac{\sum_1^n m_i}{nk} = n^{-1} \sum_1^n p_i .$$

That is, the estimate of p is the unweighted mean of the p_i. Then by using the formulae developed in this chapter (that is, replacing y_i by p_i), we have

$$\text{var}(p) = (1 - f) \sum_{i=1}^N (p_i - P)^2/n(N - 1), \qquad \text{where } P = N^{-1} \sum_1^N p_i$$

and an unbiased estimate of the variance of p is

$$\widehat{var}(p) = (1 - f) \sum_{j=1}^{n} (p_{i_j} - p)^2 / n(n-1)$$

assuming that units $i_1, \ldots, i_n$ are included in the sample.

EXAMPLE 3.8

A simple random sample of 50 newly married couples (in the month of June) in the U.S. were asked whether they were 21 or older. The following data are obtained. Let y_i = # of persons in ith couple who are 21 years or older.

$y_i = 2p_i$	0	1	2	Total
f_i = freq	10	20	20	50
$f_i y_i$	0	20	40	60

Here we assume that $1 - f = 1$.

$$p = \frac{60}{100} = 0.6 = 60\%$$

$$\sum fy^2 = 0 + 20 + 80 = 100$$

$$s_y^2 = \sum f_i(y_i - \bar{y})^2 / (n-1)$$

$$= \{100 - (60)^2/50\}/49 = 1400/50(49) = 0.5714$$

$$s_y = 0.756, \qquad s_p = \frac{1}{2}(0.756) = 0.378 .$$

That is, s_p is 37.8%.   ◆

If the size of the cluster varies from unit to unit, let k_i be the number of elements in ith cluster. Then

$$p_i = m_i/k_i, \qquad p = \sum_{1}^{n} m_i / \sum_{1}^{n} k_i .$$

Now, p is of the form of a ratio estimator. Hence,

$$var(p) = (1 - f) \sum_{i=1}^{N} (m_i - Pk_i)^2 / n\bar{K}^2(N-1)$$

where P is the proportion of elements in the population having the characteristic and $\bar{K} = \sum_{1}^{N} k_i/N$. One can also write

$$var(p) = (1 - f) \sum_{1}^{N} (k_i/\bar{K})^2 (p_i - P)^2 / (N-1)n .$$

An estimate of var (p) is

$$\widehat{\text{var}}\ (p) = (1 - f)\left[\sum_1^n m_i^2 - 2p \sum_1^n m_i k_i + p^2 \sum_1^n k_i^2\right]/\bar{k}^2(n)(n - 1)$$

where $\bar{k} = \sum_1^n k_i/n = $ the average number of elements per cluster in the sample.

■ PROBLEMS

In the following problems sampling is without replacement unless specified otherwise.

3.1 A random sample of size 2 is taken from a population with $N = 4$ and the values of the y_i being 1, 2, 3, 4. Calculate the sample mean for all possible simple random samples of size 2. Show that $\bar{y}$ is an unbiased estimator of $\bar{Y}$ and its variance agrees with the formula.

3.2 For the population in (1), calculate s^2 for all possible simple random samples of size 2 and show that s^2 is unbiased for S^2.

3.3 A simple random sample of 15 households was drawn from a city containing 15,000 households. The number of people per household is as follows:

$$4,\ 3,\ 5,\ 6,\ 4,\ 7,\ 3,\ 2,\ 1,\ 6,\ 4,\ 3,\ 2,\ 3,\ 5\,.$$

Estimate the population of that city and find a 95% confidence interval for the true population of that city.

3.4 Continuing Example 3.2 worked out to illustrate the ratio estimates, suppose we have the following data:

	N	n	$\sum y$	$\sum x$	$\sum y^2$	$\sum xy$	$\sum x^2$
public	250	50	30.2×10^3	2.02×10^3	30.1×10^6	1.7×10^6	0.11
private	250	50	13.6×10^3	1.05×10^3	6.2×10^6	0.42×10^6	0.03×10^6

Estimate the student/teacher ratio for the private colleges. Compute the standard error of the estimate. Find an estimate of the difference between the student/teacher ratios between the public and private colleges and a 95% confidence interval for the same.

3.5 A village consists of 150 children. Dr. Jones selects a simple random sample of 15 children and counts the number of cavities in each child's mouth yielding the following results.

$$\text{No. of cavities}\ \ 0\ 1\ 2\ 3\ 4\ 5$$
$$\text{No. of children}\ \ 6\ 3\ 2\ 2\ 1\ 1$$

Dr. Smith examines all the 150 children and records that 50 children have no cavities in their mouths. Estimate the total number of cavities in the village children (a) using Dr. Jones' results only; (b) using both Dr. Jones' and Dr. Smith's results. (c) Are the estimates unbiased? (d) Which estimate do you expect to have a smaller variance?

3.6 A simple random sample of size 4 is drawn from a population of size N with replacement. Show that the probabilities that the sample contains 1, 2, and 3 distinct units are

$$P_1 = N^{-3}, \qquad P_2 = 7(N - 1)/N^3, \qquad P_3 = 6(N - 1)(N - 2)/N^3$$

and $P_4 = (N - 1)(N - 2)(N - 3)/N^3$.

Let $\bar{y}'$, the unweighted mean of the distinct units in the sample, be an estimate of $\bar{Y}$ (the population mean). Obtain the variance of $\bar{y}'$. Hence show that $\text{var}\ \bar{y} > \text{var}\ \bar{y}'$.

Hint:

$$\bar{y}' = y_1 \text{ if one distinct unit exists}$$

$$= (y_1 + y_2)/2, \text{ if two distinct units exists}$$

$$= (y_1 + y_2 + y_3)/3, \text{ if three distinct units exists}$$

$$= (y_1 + y_2 + y_3 + y_4)/4, \text{ if four distinct units exist.}$$

So,

$$E\bar{y}' = \bar{Y}$$

and

$$\text{var } \bar{y}' = E(\bar{y}' - E\bar{y}')^2 = \sum_{i=1}^{4} P_i E\left\{(\bar{y}' - E\bar{y}')^2 | i \text{ units are distinct}\right\}.$$

3.7   From a list of 100 households in a certain small town, 10 households are drawn at random. The data for the number of teenagers (x) and the average number of hours per week (y) spent by a teenager watching television are as follows:

x:	2	1	3	2	4	3	2	0	3	1
y:	15	20	16	14	17	12	18	0	15	18

Find a ratio estimate of the average number of hours spent by a teenager watching television in that town. Also, find a 95% confidence interval for R.

3.8   According to Cochran's rule of thumb, how large the sample size should be if $G_1 = 1.2$ (Fisher's measure of skewness)?

3.9   In Example 4, set $a_{12} = \frac{1}{3}$, $a_{21} = \frac{1}{2}$, $a_{31} = \frac{2}{3}$ and $y_2 = 2$, $y_1 = 1$, and $y_3 = 0$. Show that var $\bar{y} >$ var t.

3.10   A more rigorous proof of the assertion that $P(a_i = 1) = n/N$ can be based on the induction argument.

Hint: If $n = 1$, then $P(a_i = 1) = P(y_{i_1} = y_i) = 1/N$.

Next assume that the claim is true for every m such that $1 \leq m < n$. We want to show the claim is true for sample size n. Toward this, notice that

$$\{a_i = 1\} = \bigcup_{m=1}^{n} \{y_{i_m} = y_i, \ y_{i_j} \neq y_i \text{ for } 1 \leq j < m\}$$

is a disjoint union, which implies that

$$P(a_i = 1) = \sum_{m=1}^{n} P(y_{i_m} = y_i, \ y_{i_j} \neq y_i \text{ for } 1 \leq j < m).$$

However,

$$P(y_{i_m} = y_i, \ y_{i_j} \neq y_i \text{ for } 1 \leq j < m) = P(y_{i_m} = y_i | y_{i_j} \neq y_i \text{ for } 1 \leq j < m)\cdot$$

$$P(y_{i_j} \neq y_i \text{ for } 1 \leq j < m) = \frac{1}{N - m + 1} \cdot \left(1 - \frac{m-1}{N}\right) = \frac{1}{N}.$$

Hence,

$$P(a_i = 1) = \sum_{m=1}^{n} \frac{1}{N} = \frac{n}{N}.$$

3.11 Show that for $n = 1$ and 2,

$$E\left(\frac{1}{W}\right) = \frac{1}{n} - \frac{1}{Nn}$$

and for $n = 3$,

$$E\left(\frac{1}{W}\right) = \frac{1}{3} - \frac{1}{2N} + \frac{1}{6N^2}.$$

3.12 Show that $G'(u)$ (see p. 48) is unbiased for (var $(\bar{y}_W)$.

Hint: Start with

$$EG'(W) = E\left\{E\left(G'(W)|W = u\right)\right\}$$

$$= \sum_{u=1}^{n} \left\{\frac{1}{u} - \frac{1}{N} + \frac{N-1}{N^n - n}\right\} E(s^2|W = u)P(W = u).$$

3.13 Let $N = 101, n = 20, m = 5$, and $\gamma = 0.95$. Taking P_L to be $0.25 - 1.96\sqrt{(0.25)(0.75)/20}$ $= 0.25 - 0.19 = 0.06$ and P_U to be $0.25 + 1.96\sqrt{(0.25)(0.75)/20} = 0.25 + 0.19 = 0.44$, compute more accurate confidence intervals (P_{L1}, P_{U1}) and (P_{L2}, P_{U2}).

3.14 In a small town of population $N = 100$, a random sample of size 10 was drawn and found that one of them has AIDS. Estimate the total number in the town that are suffering from AIDS. Also, find a 95% confidence interval for that number.

3.15 In a random sample of size 25, a certain diagnostic machine gave false alarms in one case. Find a 95% confidence interval for the true proportion of cases in which the machine will give a false alarm.

Hint: Assume that N is effectively infinite.

3.16 Compute EW where $N = 10$ and $n = 5$ and sampling is simple random with replacement. Let the population consist of values $1, 2, \ldots, 10$. Evaluate exactly or approximately var $\bar{y}_W$ and var $\bar{y}_{EW}$. Let $\bar{Y}$ and S^2, respectively, denote the population mean and variance.

3.17 [3]In a survey conducted in fall, 1995, by the Survey Research Center at the University of Kentucky, it was found that 268 out of 534 households have no children under age 18 living at home. Find a 95% confidence interval for the true proportion of households in the state of Kentucky that have no children under age 18 living at home.

Hint: Assume that N is effectively infinite.

3.18 In the survey mentioned in Problem 17, 485 out of 663 households responded that the state government should not regulate abortion. Find a 95% confidence interval for the true proportion of households in the state of Kentucky that are not in favor of the state regulating abortion.

---

[3] The data in Problems 17–20 are based on: University of Kentucky Survey Research Center, "Fall 1995 Kentucky Survey."

3.19   In the above survey, only 48 out of 662 respondents have at most an 8th-grade education. Find a 95% confidence interval for the true proportion of adults in Kentucky who have at most an 8th-grade education.

3.20   In the above survey, 291 out of 663 respondents said that they attend religious services every week or almost every week. Find a 95% confidence interval for the true proportion in the state of Kentucky who attend religious services every week or almost every week.

3.21   [4]In a 1995 survey of Kentucky schools' education technology programs, a sample of 107 schools was taken from the 1371 Kentucky schools. It was determined that,

>   37 schools had high implementation of education technology,
>   35 schools had medium implementation of education technology,
>   35 schools had low implementation of education technology.

   (a) Estimate the number of schools in Kentucky with high implementation.

   (b) Obtain a 95% confidence interval for the number of schools that have high implementation of education technology.

3.22   From the same 1995 survey on Kentucky education technology, the sample of 107 schools was comprised of 40 elementary schools, 31 middle schools, and 36 high schools. The enrollment or number of students (y) and the number of teachers (x) per school was as follows:

Level	n	Σx	Σy	Σx^2	Σy^2	Σxy
Elementary	40	803.9	16,624	21,886.47	8,962,370	429,187.5
Middle	31	921.8	19,246	30,244.90	12,978,958	608,517.4
High school	36	1170.0	27,595	50,504.84	28,316,961	1,154,434.9
Total	107	2895.7	63,465	102,636.21	50,258,289	2,192,139.8

   (a) For each level, estimate the student/teacher ratio.

   (b) Find a 90% confidence interval for elementary schools of the student/teacher ratio.

   (c) Kentucky's student/teacher ratio in 1995 was 17:1 (total public school teachers was 38,000 and the total public school enrollment was 660,000). Compare the 90% confidence interval with the population ratio.

3.23   Suppose the total number of Kentucky schools by level are:

>   Elementary 830
>   Middle   224
>   High school 317

   (a) For each level of schools estimate the total number of teachers (refer to Problem 22).

   (b) For each level of schools estimate the total number of students (refer to Problem 22).

---

[4] Problems 21, 22, and 23 are based on the report: Joan M. Mazur, (1995), *The Implementation of the Kentucky Education Technology System* (KETS). The Kentucky Institute for Educational Research, Frankfort, Kentucky.

■ REFERENCES

3.1   Basu, D. (1958). On sampling with and without replacement. *Sankhyā* **20**, 287–294.

3.2   Basu, D. (1971). An essay on the logical foundations of survey sampling I. In *Foundations of Statistical Inference.* (Godambe, V. P. and Sprott, D. S., eds.) Toronto: Holt, Rinehart and Winston, pp. 203–242.

3.3   Burstein, H. (1975). Finite population correction for binomial confidence limits. *J. Amer. Statist. Assoc.* **70**, 67–69.

3.4   Chakrabarti, M. C. (1963). On the use of incidence matrices of designs in sampling from finite populations. *J. Indian Statist Assoc.* **1**, 78–85.

3.5   Chung, J. H. and DeLury, D. B. (1950). *Confidence Limits for the Hypergeometric Distribution.* University of Toronto Press, Toronto, Canada.

3.6   Clopper, C. J. and Pearson, E. S. (1934). The use of confidence or fiducial limits illustrated in the case of the binomial. *Biometrika* **26**, 404–413.

3.7   Cornfield, J. (1944). On samples from finite populations. *J. Amer. Statist. Assoc.* **39**, 236–239.

3.8   Des Raj and Khamis, S. H. (1958). Some remarks on sampling with replacement. *Ann. Math. Statist.* **29**, 550–557.

3.9   Erdös, P. and Rényi, A. (1959). On the central limit theorem for samples from a finite population. *Pub. Math. Inst. Hungarian Acad. Sci.* **4**, 49–57.

3.10   Feller, W. (1968). *An Introduction to Probability Theory and its Applications.* Vol. 1 (Third Edition), New York: John Wiley & Sons.

3.11   Godambe, V. P. (1955). A unified theory of sampling from finite populations. *J. Roy. Statist. Soc.* **B17**, 269–278.

3.12   Hájek, J. (1960). Limiting distribution in simple random sampling from a finite population. *Pub. Math. Inst. Hungarian Acad. Sci.* **5**, 361–374.

3.13   Korwar, R. M. and Serfling, R. J. (1970). On averaging over distinct units in sampling with replacement. *Ann. Math. Statist.* **41**, 2132–2134.

3.14   Pathak, P. K. (1961). On the evaluation of moments of distinct units in the sample. *Sankhyā* **A23**, 415–420.

3.15   Pathak, P. K. (1962). On simple random sampling with replacement. *Sankhyā* **A24**, 287–302.

3.16   Rao, J. N. K. (1966). Alternative estimators in pps sampling for multiple characteristics. *Sankhyā* **A23**, 47–60.

3.17   Rao, J. N. K. (1968). Some small sample results in ratio and regression estimation. *Jour. Ind. Stat. Assoc.* **6**, 160–168.

3.18   Rao, J. N. K. (1975). On the foundations of survey sampling. In A *Survey of Statistical Design and Linear Models*, J. N. Srivastava (ed.), American Elsevier Publishing Co., New York, 489–505.

3.19   Rosen, B. (1964). Limit theorems for sampling from finite populations. *Ark. Mat.* **28**, 383–424.

3.20   Seth, G. R. and Rao, J. N. K. (1964). On the comparison between simple random sampling with and without replacement. *Sankhyā* **A26**, 85–86.

3.21   Smith, T. M. F. (1976). The foundations of survey sampling.: A review. *J. Roy. Statist. Soc.* **A139**, 183–204.

3.22   Tukey, J. W. (1950). Some sampling simplified. *J. Amer. Statist. Assoc.* **45**, 501–519.

3.23   Wilks, S. S. (1962). *Mathematical Statistics.* New York: John Wiley & Sons, p. 369.

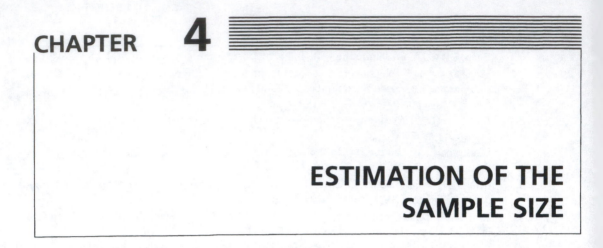

CHAPTER 4

ESTIMATION OF THE SAMPLE SIZE

4.1 INTRODUCTION

In planning a survey, one needs to know how big a sample he should draw. This depends on the precision of the estimate to be specified. The specified precision is usually in terms of the error that can be tolerated.

4.2 SAMPLE SIZE IN ESTIMATING PROPORTIONS

Suppose the units belong either to class C or to class C'. We would like to estimate P, the true proportion belonging to C within d. Also, suppose that we are willing to tolerate $100\alpha\%$ of the samples that yield values of p falling outside of $P \pm d$. That is,

$$P\left[|p - P| \geq d\right] = \alpha.$$

Since $\sigma_p^2 = N(1 - f)PQ/(N - 1)n$, we require

$$d^2 = (1 - f)z^2 PQN/(N - 1)n$$

or

$$n(N - 1)d^2 = (N - n)PQz^2.$$

That is,

$$n\left[(N-1)d^2 + PQz^2\right] = NPQz^2$$

or

$$n = NPQz^2/\left[(N-1)d^2 + PQz^2\right]$$
$$= d^{-2}PQz^2/\left\{1 + N^{-1}(z^2PQd^{-2}-1)\right\},$$

where z is the upper $(\alpha/2)th$ point on the standard normal curve.   For practical purposes one can take

$$n_0 = PQz^2d^{-2} = \frac{PQ}{V} \quad \text{(say)}$$

where $V = PQ/n_0$ is the desired variance of the sample proportion. In practice we first compute $\hat{n}_0 = pq/V$, and, if $\hat{n}_0/N$ is negligible, n_0 is deemed satisfactory. If not, n is obtained as

$$n = \hat{n}_0/\left\{1 + (\hat{n}_0 - 1)/N\right\} \doteq \hat{n}_0/\{1 + \hat{n}_0/N\}.$$

Sometimes in estimating the population total NP of units having the characteristic, we wish to control the relative error r instead of the absolute error in Np. For example, we want

$$P\left(|Np - NP|/NP \geq r\right) = P(|p - P| \geq rP) = \alpha.$$

Substituting rP or rp for d in the earlier formula we get

$$n_0 = z^2PQ/r^2P^2 = z^2Q/r^2P$$
$$\hat{n}_0 = z^2q/r^2p.$$

EXAMPLE 4.1

Let $\alpha = 0.05$ and $r = 0.2$, $p = 0.05$. Then

$$\hat{n}_0 = (1.96)^2(.95)/(.04)(0.05)$$
$$= 3.64952/(.002) = 1824.76.$$

$\blacklozenge$

EXAMPLE 4.2

Let $\alpha = 0.05$ and $r = 0.2$, $p = 0.20$. Then

$$\hat{n}_0 = (1.96)^2(0.8)/(0.04)(0.20)$$
$$= 3.07328/(0.008) = 384.16.$$

$\blacklozenge$

4.3 INVERSE SAMPLING FOR RARE ATTRIBUTES

If the true proportion is small, say less than 0.1, we need a much larger sample in order to estimate p with a specified relative error r. Then we are better off conducting the *inverse sampling* method proposed by Haldane (1945), in which we stop sampling as soon as m of the rare items are found in the sample. If n denotes the required sample to produce m rare items, then

$$P(n|m) = \frac{\binom{M}{m-1}\binom{N-M}{n-m}}{\binom{N}{n-1}} \cdot \frac{M-m+1}{N-n+1}, \qquad n = m, m+1, \ldots, N.$$

One can easily show that $p = (m-1)/(n-1)$ is an unbiased estimate of $P = M/N$. Toward this consider

$$E\left(\frac{m-1}{n-1}\right) = \sum_{n=m}^{N} \frac{m-1}{n-1} \frac{\binom{M}{m-1}\binom{N-M}{n-m}}{\binom{N}{n-1}} \cdot \frac{M-m+1}{N-n+1}$$

$$= \frac{M}{N} \sum_{n-1=m-1}^{N-1} \frac{\binom{M-1}{m-2}\binom{N-M}{n-m}}{\binom{N-1}{n-2}} \cdot \frac{M-1-m+2}{N-n+1}.$$

We also write

$$\left(\frac{m-1}{n-1}\right)^2 = \frac{(m-1)^2}{(n-1)(n-2)\left\{1 + (n-2)^{-1}\right\}}$$

$$\doteq \frac{(m-1)^2}{(n-1)(n-2)}\left\{1 - (n-2)^{-1} + \cdots\right\}$$

$$= \frac{(m-1)^2}{(n-1)(n-2)} - \frac{(m-1)^2}{(n-1)(n-2)^2} + \cdots$$

$$= \frac{(m-1)^2}{(n-1)(n-2)} - \frac{(m-1)^2}{(n-1)(n-2)(n-3)} + \cdots.$$

So,

$$E(p^2) \doteq \frac{m-1}{m-2} \cdot \frac{M}{N} \cdot \frac{(M-1)}{N-1} - \frac{m-1}{(m-2)(m-3)} \cdot \frac{M}{N} \cdot \frac{(M-1)}{N-1} \cdot \frac{(M-2)}{N-2}$$

$$= \frac{(m-1)}{(m-2)(m-3)} P\left(P - \frac{1}{N}\right)\left(1 - \frac{1}{N}\right)^{-1}$$

$$\left[(m-3) - \left(P - \frac{2}{N}\right)\left(1 - \frac{2}{N}\right)^{-1}\right].$$

So,

$$\text{var } p = \frac{(m-1)}{(m-2)(m-3)} P[(m-3)P - P^2 + 0(N^{-1})] - P^2$$

$$= \frac{(m-1)}{(m-2)(m-3)} P^2[(m-3) - \frac{(m-2)(m-3)}{m-1} - P + 0(N^{-1})]$$

$$= \frac{(m-1)}{(m-2)(m-3)} P^2[\frac{(m-3)}{m-1} - P + 0(N^{-1})]$$

$$= \frac{(m-1)}{(m-2)(m-3)} P^2[Q - \frac{2}{m-1} + 0(N^{-1})]$$

$$= \frac{(m-1)}{(m-2)(m-3)} P^2 Q - \frac{2P^2}{(m-2)(m-3)} + 0(N^{-1})$$

$$\doteq \frac{(m-1)}{(m-2)(m-3)} P^2 Q - \frac{2P^2}{(m-2)(m-3)}.$$

$$= \frac{P^2}{m-2} - \frac{P^3(m-1)}{(m-2)(m-3)} < \frac{P^2}{m-2}.$$

Thus, the coefficient of variation of p is

$$CV(p) < (m-2)^{-1/2}.$$

Thus, by fixing m in advance, we can control the coefficient of variation $CV(p)$ without the knowledge of P. For instance, $m = 27$ gives $CV(p) < 20\%$ and $m = 102$ gives $CV(p) < 10\%$. The value of n will be very large if p is small.

Alternatively, since $p = (m-1)/(n-1)$, using the delta method (assuming that n is a continuous variable), we obtain

$$\text{var } p \doteq \frac{(m-1)^2}{(En-1)^4} \cdot \text{var } n.$$

One can easily obtain

$$E(n) = \frac{m(N+1)}{M+1} \doteq \frac{m}{P}, \quad E\{n(n+1)\}$$

$$= \frac{m(m+1)(N+1)(N+2)}{(M+1)(M+2)} \doteq m(m+1)/P^2.$$

Thus

$$\text{var } n \doteq m(m+1)P^{-2} - mP^{-1} - m^2 P^{-2}$$

$$\doteq \frac{mQ}{P^2}.$$

Since $En - 1 = \frac{m-1+Q}{P}$, we have

$$\text{var } p \doteq \frac{m(m-1)^2 P^2 Q}{(m-1+Q)^4}$$

and

$$CV(p) \doteq (mQ)^{1/2}(m-1)/(Q+m-1)^2.$$

Thus, for $m = 27$, $CV(p) < 20\%$ and for $m = 102$, $CV(p) < 10\%$.

4.4   ESTIMATING SAMPLE SIZE WITH CONTINUOUS DATA

Suppose it is specified that the relative error in estimating $\bar{Y}$ by $\bar{y}$ exceeds r with probability α, then

$$P\left[\frac{|\bar{y} - \bar{Y}|}{\bar{Y}} \geq r\right] = P(|\bar{y} - \bar{Y}| \geq r\bar{Y}] = \alpha.$$

If we assume that $\bar{y}$ is approximately normal with mean $\bar{Y}$ and variance $\sigma_{\bar{y}}^2 = (N - n)S^2/nN$, then

$$r\bar{Y} = z\sigma_{\bar{y}} = z\left(\frac{N-n}{N}\right)^{1/2} S/\sqrt{n}, \qquad z = z_{1-\alpha/2}$$

or

$$r^2\bar{Y}^2 = z^2\left(\frac{N-n}{N}\right)\frac{S^2}{n}.$$

Solving for n yields

$$n = (zS/r\bar{Y})^2 / \left[1 + N^{-1}(zS/r\bar{Y})^2\right]$$

which is a function of $S/\bar{Y}$, the population coefficient of variation. As a first approximation we can set

$$n_0 = (zS/r\bar{Y})^2 = (z/r)^2 C$$

where C denotes the specified square of the coefficient of variation (CV) of $\bar{y}$. Then

$$n = n_0/\{1 + N^{-1}n_0\}.$$

Instead of the relative error r, if we wish to control the absolute error d in $\bar{y}$, we set

$$n_0 = z^2 S^2/d^2 = S^2/V$$

where V is the desired variance of $\bar{y}$.

4.5   ESTIMATION OF S^2

Typically we do not know S^2 and we need to obtain estimates or guesstimates of the same, based on either two-stage sampling or pilot surveys. Cox (1952) has given a double-sampling scheme by which we can compute n, and we will give his results below.

4.6   ESTIMATION BY DOUBLE SAMPLING

Suppose we are interested in estimating an unknown parameter θ with specified accuracy, which could be in terms of variance $a(\theta)$, some given function of θ. Another problem of interest is to estimate θ by a confidence interval having a specified width and a specified confidence coefficient γ. In general, it is not possible to construct an estimate meeting the specifications on the basis of a sample of fixed size. Thus, one has to resort to some kind of sequential sampling. It is somewhat difficult to construct a sequential sampling procedure leading to an estimate having the specified properties, although these properties may hold asymptotically. Also, the sequential procedure suffers from the drawback of calculation at each stage. Cox (1952) proposed a double-sampling scheme for the above problem. The basic idea is to draw a preliminary sample of observations which determines how large the total sample size should be. The double-sampling methods of Cox (1952) differ from those used in industrial inspection, because, in the latter case, the second sample size is fixed. In the following, we present an estimate of θ having bias $O(n_1^{-2})$ and variance $a(\theta)\left[1 + O(n_1^{-2})\right]$ where n_1 is the preliminary sample size and $a(\theta)$ the specified variance.

4.7   ESTIMATION WITH GIVEN VARIANCE: SINGLE UNKNOWN PARAMETER

Let θ denote the unknown parameter which we wish to estimate with variance equal to a given function of θ. Let $\{S_\lambda\}$ denote a sequence of problems, where S_λ denotes the problem of estimating θ with variance $a(\theta)/\lambda$ and λ tends to infinity. Assume that from random samples of any fixed size r one can construct an estimate $T^{(r)}$ of θ such that

1. $T^{(r)}$ is unbiased for θ with variance $v(\theta)/r$;
2. The skewness coefficient γ_1 of $T^{(r)}$ is asymptotically $\gamma_1(\theta)/r^{1/2}$, where $\gamma_1(\theta)$ denotes the skewness in the population and γ_2 (kurtosis) of $T^{(r)}$ is $O(r^{-1})$ as $r \to \infty$.
3. Asymptotic means and standard errors can be derived for $a(T^{(r)})$, $v(T^{(r)})$ and combinations of these functions by expansion in series.

If θ were known, a sample of size $\lambda n(\theta) = \lambda v(\theta)/a(\theta)$ would give the required accuracy $\left(\because \frac{v(\theta)}{n} = a(\theta)\right)$.

4.8   SAMPLING PROCEDURE

Take a random sample of size $n_0\lambda$ and let T_1 be the resulting estimate of θ. Let

$$n(T_1) = v(T_1)/a(T_1).$$

Also, let

$$m(T_1) = 1/n(T_1) = a(T_1)/v(T_1)$$

and

$$b(\theta) = n(\theta)v(\theta) \cdot$$

$$\left\{ 2m(\theta)m'(\theta)\gamma_1(\theta)v^{-1/2}(\theta) + m'^2(\theta) + 2m(\theta)m''(\theta) + m''(\theta)/2n_0 \right\}$$

where

$$m' = dm(\theta)/d\theta, \qquad m'' = d^2m(\theta)/d\theta^2 .$$

Now set

$$\tilde{n}(T_1) = n(T_1)\{1 + b(T_1)/\lambda\}$$

and take a second sample of size max $\{0, [\tilde{n}(T_1) - n_0]\lambda\}$ and let $\tilde{T}_2$ be the estimate of θ based on the second sample. Let

$$\tilde{T} = \begin{cases} \left\{ n_0 T_1 + (\tilde{n}(T_1) - n_0)\tilde{T}_2 \right\} /\tilde{n}(T_1), & \text{if } \tilde{n}(T_1) \geq n_0 \\ T_1, & \text{if } \tilde{n}(T_1) \leq n_0 \end{cases}$$

and let

$$T' = \begin{cases} \tilde{T} - m'(\tilde{T})v(\tilde{T})\lambda^{-1}, & \text{if } n_0 \leq \tilde{n}(T_1) \\ T_1 & \text{if } n_0 > \tilde{n}(T_1) \end{cases} .$$

Then Cox (1952) shows that T' has bias $O(\lambda^{-2})$ and variance $a(\theta)\lambda^{-1}\left[1 + O(\lambda^{-2})\right]$.

In any specified application, we must have one variance function small and one particular preliminary sample size which must be large. So, without loss of generality, we can set $\lambda = 1$. Possible applications are estimation of Poisson and binomial means and the normal mean when the population variance is known.

4.9   ESTIMATION OF P WITH SPECIFIED VARIANCE V

Let p_1 be the estimate of P based on the first-stage sample of size of Vn_0. Then set $a(\theta) = V$, $v(\theta) = \theta(1 - \theta)$, $\gamma_1(\theta) = (1 - 2\theta)\{\theta(1 - \theta)\}^{-1/2}$, and hence $m(\theta) = V/\theta(1 - \theta)$. Thus

$$b(\theta)n(\theta) = \frac{3 - 8\theta(1 - \theta)}{\theta(1 - \theta)} + \frac{1 - 3\theta(1 - \theta)}{Vn_0} .$$

Consequently,

$$n = \frac{p_1 q_1}{V} + \frac{3 - 8p_1 q_1}{p_1 q_1} + \frac{1 - 3p_1 q_1}{Vn_0}$$

where the first term is the required sample size if P is known. In order to correct for bias, Cox (1952) suggests to use

$$\hat{P} = p + V(1 - 2p)/pq .$$

EXAMPLE 4.3 _____

Let $n_0 = 20$, $p_1 = 0.1$, and $V = 0.005$. Then $n = 18 + 25.33 + 7.3 = 50.63$.   ◆

4.10   ESTIMATION OF P WITH SPECIFIED $CV = C^{1/2}$

Here we set $a(\theta) = \theta^2 C$, $v(\theta)$ and $\gamma_1(\theta)$ as in the previous case. Then $m(\theta) = C\theta/(1-\theta)$. Straightforward computations yield $b(\theta) = 3C(1-\theta)^{-2} + \{n_0(1-\theta)\}^{-1}$. Thus

$$n = \frac{q_1}{Cp_1} + \frac{3}{p_1 q_1} + \frac{1}{Cp_1 n_0}$$

and estimate P by

$$\hat{P} = p - C(p/q).$$

EXAMPLE 4.4

Let $n_0 = 100$, $p = 0.1$, and $C = 0.04$. Then $n = 225 + 33.3 + 2.5 = 260.8$ and $\hat{P} = 0.0956$.   ◆

Notice that in all the above results the finite population correction factor (fpc) is neglected.

Cox (1952) extended the above considerations to the case where there is an unknown nuisance parameter ψ. The main application is estimation of the normal mean with a specified coefficient of variation when the population variance is unknown. However, we do not present the general two-sample procedure with nuisance parameter here. Instead we will give the following applications to the normal case.

4.11   ESTIMATION OF $\bar{Y}$ WITH SPECIFIED $CV = C^{1/2}$

Assume that the y_i are normally distributed. If $\bar{y}_1$ is the sample mean and s_1^2 is the sample variance based on the first-stage sample of size n_1, then sample additional units so that the combined total sample is n. In Cox's (1952) formula (in the presence of a nuisance parameter) set $\theta = \mu$, $\psi = \sigma^2$, $a(\theta) = \theta^2 C$, $T_{n_1} = \bar{y}_1$, $\psi_{n_1} = s_1^2$ and obtain

$$n = s_1^2 (C\bar{y}_1^2)^{-1} \left\{ 1 + 8C + s_1^2(n_1\bar{y}_1^2)^{-1} + 2n_1^{-1} \right\}.$$

The last term is the additional observations one has to take for not knowing S. Then take

$$\hat{\bar{Y}} = \bar{y}(1 - 2C).$$

EXAMPLE 4.5

$n_1 = 15$, $s_1^2 = 20$, $\bar{y}_1 = 5$, and $C = 0.04$ yield $n = 30.1$.   ◆

4.12   ESTIMATION OF $\bar{Y}$ WITH SPECIFIED VARIANCE V

Then, in Cox's (1952) formula set $\theta = \mu$, $\psi = \sigma^2$, $a(\theta) = V$, $C_1 = s_1^2$, and $\tau = 2$ and obtain

$$n = s_1^2 V^{-1}(1 + 2n_1^{-1})$$

where $2s_1^2/n_1 V$ is the additional number of observations one has to take when S is unknown.

4.13   COMPUTING SAMPLE SIZE: DECISION-THEORETIC APPROACH

Let $l(z)$ denote the loss incurred while making an error of amount z in population parameter. Let $f(z; n)$ denote the probability density of Z which depends on n. Then the expected loss or the risk is given by

$$r(n) = \int l(z) f(z; n) dz = E\{l(Z)|n\}\ .$$

If $C(n)$ denotes the cost of sampling n units, then we wish to choose n which minimizes

$$r(n) + C(n)$$

which denotes the total expected cost. As a special case let

$$C(n) = c_0 + c_1 n \quad \text{and} \quad r(n) = \lambda E Z^2 = \lambda E(\bar{y} - \bar{Y})^2\ ;$$

then $r(n) = \lambda S^2 (n^{-1} - N^{-1})$, where c_0 is the overhead cost. Thus

$$n = (\lambda S^2 / c_1)^{1/2}\ .$$

EXAMPLE 4.6

The selling price of a lot of personal computers (PCs) is $4000 each and the lot contains N of them. The cost of each PC to the seller is $2000. The manufacturer informs the seller that he should expect M of them to be defective. The seller tests n of the PCs and reimburses $\$(\hat{M} - M)^2$ to the buyers, where $\hat{M} = \frac{m}{n}N$ and m denotes the number of defectives in the sample of size n. Let c denote the cost of testing each PC to the seller. Find the optimum value of n so that the expected profit to the seller is maximized.

$$\text{Net profit to the seller} = 4N - 2N - (\hat{M} - M)^2 - cn$$

$$= 2N - N^2 \left(\frac{m}{n} - P\right)^2 - cn$$

where $P = M/N$,

$$E(\text{profit}) = A(n) = 2N - N^2 \cdot \frac{PQ}{n} - cn$$

$$\frac{\partial A}{\partial n} = \frac{N^2 PQ}{n^2} - c = 0$$

implies that

$$n = N(PQ/c)^{1/2}\ .$$

So

$$\hat{n} = N(pq/c)^{1/2}$$

if a preliminary estimate p of P is available. Also, $n \leq N(4c)^{-1/2}$ for all P, which may be too large. Notice that the solution of the equation $\partial A/\partial n = 0$ maximizes the function A because the second derivative of A w.r.t. n is negative. In particular, $N = 1000$, $p = 0.01$, and $c = 0.1$ gives $n \approx 315$.   ◆

■ PROBLEMS

4.1 The population of a certain small town consists of $N = 1000$ people. We wish to estimate the proportion of the population having blood type AB. How large a sample should we choose if we wish to estimate the true proportion with 30% relative error and with confidence 90%? Assume that we have a preliminary estimate of P to be 0.10.

4.2 In a large metropolitan city of $N = 1.5 \times 10^6$ people, we wish to estimate the proportion of people afflicted with AIDS, with relative error 20% and confidence coefficient 0.95. A preliminary estimate of P is 0.10.

4.3 In 1995 there were 77,853 public schools in the United States. We wish to estimate the percentage of schools having Internet access. How large a sample should we draw if we wish to estimate the true percentage within 10 % of the true percentage and with confidence 95%? Assume that a preliminary estimate of the true percentage is 20%.

4.4 Let $N = 77,853$ be the number of public schools in the United States. We wish to estimate $P = \frac{M}{N}$, where M is the number of those that have Internet access. If we do inverse binomial sampling with $m = 10$, what is the expected number of schools we have to sample?

Hint: Assume a preliminary estimate of P to be 10%.

4.5 Let the number of public schools in the United States be 77,850. Suppose we wish to estimate $\bar{Y}$, the average number of computers used in a public school in the United States. Assume that an estimate of the population variance S^2 is given by $s^2 = 96$. How large a sample should one draw in order to estimate $\bar{Y}$ within 4 units and with confidence 95%?

Hint: You are given $P\left(|\bar{y} - \bar{Y}| \leq 4\right) = 0.95$.

4.6 The state of Kentucky has 224 middle schools. In 1990 the Kentucky Education Reform Act (KERA) initiated the creation of School Based Decision Making (SBDM) committees. A study was launched to determine the impact of SBDM over five years. How large a sample of middle schools must be drawn in order to determine the true proportion of schools that have SBDM in place, within 30% of the true proportion and with confidence 95%? (A preliminary estimate of $P = 0.10$.)

4.7 We wish to estimate the percentage of population in the United States who are opposed to governmental regulation of abortion. How large a sample must be drawn in order to determine the true proportion of people opposed to governmental regulation of abortion, with 2% standard error and with confidence 95%?

Hint: Assume that a preliminary estimate of the true proportion is 0.70.

4.8 Suppose we wish to find out the percentage of accounting consultants in the United States who think that "perceived usefulness" and "perceived ease of use" are the two most important factors that influence their usage of the World Wide Web. How large a sample should we draw if we wish to estimate this percentage with 95% confidence? Assume that we are willing to tolerate a relative error of 10% and that a preliminary estimate of P is 0.45.

4.9 The selling price of a CD ROM is $200, and a lot contains N of them. The cost of each CD ROM to the seller is $100. The seller expects M of them in the lot to be defective. The seller tests n of the CD ROMs and reimburses $\$(\hat{M} - M)^2$ to the buyers, where $\hat{M} = \frac{m}{n} N$ and m is the number of defectives in the sample of size n. Let c denote the cost of testing each CD ROM to the seller. Find the optimum value of n that maximizes the expected profit to the seller when $N = 500$, $p = 0.01$, and $c = 0.05$.

4.10   A survey of 9th-grade students in a certain state was to determine the proportion of those students who graduate from high schools. How large a sample is needed to estimate the true proportion P of 9th graders who graduate from high schools, with relative error not exceeding 5%? Use a preliminary estimate of P of 0.45.

■ REFERENCES

4.1   Cox, D. R. (1952). Estimation by double sampling. *Biometrika* **39**, 217–227.

4.2   Haldane, J. B. S. (1945). On a method of estimating frequencies. *Biometrika* **33**, 222–225.

CHAPTER 5

STRATIFIED SAMPLING

5.1 INTRODUCTION

In simple random sampling, the variance of the population mean depends not only on the sample size but also on the variability of the response y in the population. If the population is heterogeneous and cost considerations limit the sample size not to be large, it is not possible to obtain a precise estimate of the population parameter. For example, the populations of manufacturing companies are heterogeneous. Some employ more than 1000 people and some as few as 3 or 4. If we are able to divide the population into homogeneous strata, then we can take random subsamples from these strata, thereby ensuring better estimates of the strata parameters. If the main purpose of stratification is to achieve more precise estimates, then the following questions should be addressed:

1. How should the strata be constructed and how many?
2. How should we allocate the total sample size to the various strata?
3. How should we obtain precise estimates from the stratified sample?
4. What effect would post stratification have on the estimates?

In the following we try to answer these questions.

Let $N_1, N_2, \ldots, N_L$ denote the strata sizes. If a simple random sample is drawn from each stratum, then the sampling scheme is called stratified random sampling. We shall use the following notation:

N_h = size of the hth stratum

n_h = size of the sample from hth stratum

y_{hi} = value of ith unit from hth stratum

$W_h = N_h/N$ = proportion of the population size attributable to hth stratum.

$f_h = n_h/N_h$ = sampling fraction of hth stratum.

$$\bar{Y}_h = \sum_{i=1}^{N_h} y_{hi}/N_h = \text{true mean of } h\text{th stratum.}$$

$$\bar{y}_h = \sum_{i=1}^{n_h} y_{hi}/n_h = \text{sample mean of } h\text{th stratum.}$$

$$S_h^2 = (N_h - 1)^{-1} \sum_{i=1}^{N_h} (y_{hi} - \bar{Y}_h)^2 = h\text{th stratum variance}$$

and $N = N_1 + \cdots + N_L$.

5.2   ESTIMATORS OF MEAN AND TOTAL AND THEIR PROPERTIES

An estimator of the population mean $\bar{Y} = \sum_{h=1}^{L} W_h \bar{Y}_h$ is the stratified mean $\bar{y}_{\text{st}}$ given by

$$\bar{y}_{\text{st}} = \sum_{h=1}^{L} W_h \bar{y}_h.$$

The overall sample mean is denoted by $\bar{y}$, where

$$\bar{y} = \sum_{h=1}^{L} n_h \bar{y}_h/n.$$

Notice that $\bar{y}_{\text{st}} = \bar{y}$ provided

$$\frac{n_h}{n} = \frac{N_h}{N}.$$

That is, we have proportional sampling or allocation; the sample size in each stratum is proportional to its size.

Result 5.1.   If $\bar{y}_h$ is unbiased for $\bar{Y}_h (h = 1, \ldots, L)$, then $\bar{y}_{\text{st}}$ is unbiased for $\bar{Y}$.

Proof: $E\bar{y}_{\text{st}} = \Sigma W_h E\bar{y}_h = \Sigma W_h \bar{Y}_h = \bar{Y}.$ ■

Result 5.2.   If sampling is done independently in various strata, then

$$\text{var}(\bar{y}_{st}) = \Sigma W_h^2 \,\text{var}(\bar{y}_h).$$

Result 5.3.   In stratified random sampling, we have

$$\text{var}(\bar{y}_{st}) = N^{-2}\Sigma N_h(N_h - n_h)S_h^2/n_h$$

$$= \Sigma W_h^2(1 - f_h)S_h^2/n_h.$$

Proof: In Result 5.2, replace var $\bar{y}_h$ by $(1 - f_h)S_h^2/n_h$. ■

Special Case 1.   If the f_h are negligible,

$$\text{var}(\bar{y}_{st}) = \Sigma W_h^2 S_h^2/n_h.$$

Special Case 2.   If sampling is proportional, then

$$\text{var}(\bar{y}_{st}) = (1 - f)n^{-1}\Sigma W_h S_h^2.$$

Proof:

$$\text{var}(\bar{y}_{st}) = \Sigma W_h \left(\frac{N_h}{Nn_h} - \frac{1}{N}\right) S_h^2$$

$$= \Sigma W_h \left(\frac{1}{n} - \frac{1}{N}\right) S_h^2 = (1 - f)n^{-1}\Sigma W_h S_h^2. ■$$

Special Case 3.   If sampling is proportional and the variances in all the strata have the same value, S_W^2, then

$$\text{var}(\bar{y}_{st}) = (1 - f)n^{-1}S_W^2.$$

Result 5.4. $\text{var}(\hat{Y}_{st}) = N^2\,\text{var}(\bar{y}_{st}) = \Sigma N_h(N_h - n_h)S_h^2/n_h$, where $\hat{Y}_{st} = N\bar{y}_{st}$.

Lemma 5.1.   Let

$$T^* = \sum_{h=1}^{L} a_i \chi^2(f_i)$$

where $\chi^2(f_i)$ denotes a chi-square variable with f_i degrees of freedom. Also assume that the chi-square variables are independent and the a_i are some fixed constants. We approximate the distribution of T^* by $\tilde{T} = a\chi^2(f)$ and we estimate a and f by equating the first two moments of T^* and $\tilde{T}$;

$$ET^* = \Sigma a_i f_i = E\tilde{T} = af$$

$$\text{var}\,T^* = 2\Sigma a_i^2 f_i = \text{var}\,\tilde{T} = 2a^2 f.$$

So

$$a = \Sigma a_i^2 f_i/\Sigma a_i f_i$$

and

$$f = (\Sigma a_i f_i)^2/\Sigma a_i^2 f_i.$$

Remark 5.1.   This kind of approximation is used in finding the approximate distribution of estimates of variance components (see, for instance, Satterthwaite (1946)).

5.3   CONFIDENCE LIMITS (CI'S)

In stratified random sampling an unbiased estimate of S_h^2 is

$$s_h^2 = (n_h - 1)^{-1} \sum_{i=1}^{n_h} (y_{hi} - \bar{y}_h)^2 .$$

Result 5.5.   With stratified random sampling, an unbiased estimate of the variance of $\bar{y}_{st}$ is

$$\widehat{var}\,(\bar{y}_{st}) = s^2(\bar{y}_{st}) = N^{-2} \Sigma N_h (N_h - n_h) s_h^2 / n_h$$

$$= \sum_1^L \frac{W_h^2 s_h^2}{n_h} - \sum_1^L \frac{W_h s_h^2}{N} .$$

Notice that the second term on the right gives the correction due to the finiteness of the population. Also note that in order for s_h^2 to be meaningful, one should draw at least two units from each stratum.

If the n_i are fairly large, then the confidence intervals for population mean $\bar{Y}$ is $\bar{y}_{st} \pm z s(\bar{y}_{st})$, $z = z_{1-\alpha/2}$. The confidence interval for the population total Y is $N\bar{y}_{st} \pm N z s(\bar{y}_{st})$. If the n_i are moderate, we would like to approximate the distribution of

$$T = (\bar{y}_{st} - \bar{Y})/s(\bar{y}_{st})$$

by a Student's t distribution. Let V denote $var\,(\bar{y}_{st})$. Then we can rewrite T as

$$T = \frac{(\bar{y}_{st} - \bar{Y})/V^{\frac{1}{2}}}{s(\bar{y}_{st})/V^{\frac{1}{2}}} .$$

$(\bar{y}_{st} - \bar{Y})/V^{\frac{1}{2}}$ is approximately normal with mean 0 and variance 1. Consider the distribution of

$$s^2(\bar{y}_{st})/V = \sum_{h=1}^{L} \frac{N_h (N_h - n_h)}{N^2 n_h (n_h - 1) V} S_h^2 \cdot (n_h - 1) \frac{s_h^2}{S_h^2}$$

$$\doteq \Sigma a_h \cdot \chi^2 (n_h - 1) ,$$

where

$$a_h = \frac{N_h (N_h - n_h) S_h^2}{N^2 n_h (n_h - 1) V}$$

and

$$(n_h - 1) s_h^2 / S_h^2 = \chi^2 (n_h - 1) .$$

Applying Lemma 5.1, we have

$$s^2(\bar{y}_{st})/V \text{ is approximately distributed as } a\chi^2(f)$$

where

$$a = \Sigma a_h^2(n_h - 1)/\Sigma a_h(n_h - 1)$$

and

$$f = [\Sigma a_h(n_h - 1)]^2 / \Sigma a_h^2(n_h - 1).$$

i.e.,

$$T \doteq Z/\sqrt{a\chi^2(f)}, \qquad Z \underset{d}{=} n(0, 1) \qquad (d \text{ stands for distributed as})$$

$$\sqrt{af}\,T \doteq Z\sqrt{f}/\sqrt{\chi^2(f)} = Z/\sqrt{\chi^2(f)/f} = t_f \qquad \text{(approximately)}.$$

That is, $\sqrt{af}\,T$ is approximately distributed as t with f degrees of freedom. However, since $af = \Sigma a_h(n_h - 1) = 1$,

$$T = (\bar{y}_{st} - \bar{Y})/s(\bar{y}_{st}) \underset{d}{=} t_f.$$

So CI for $\bar{Y}$ is $\bar{y}_{st} \pm t_f s(\bar{y}_{st})$, and

$$\Sigma a_h^2(n_h - 1) = \Sigma \frac{N_h^2(N_h - n_h)^2}{N^4 n_h^2(n_h - 1)} \frac{S_h^4}{V^2}.$$

Notice that $\Sigma a_i f_i = 1$ because of the definition of V. So

$$a = \Sigma a_i^2 f_i$$

$$f = (\Sigma a_i^2 f_i)^{-1}$$

$$= \frac{V^2}{\Sigma \frac{N_h^2(N_h - n_h)^2}{N^4 n_h^2(n_h - 1)} S_h^4}$$

$$\doteq \frac{\left\{ \Sigma N_h(N_h - n_h)s_h^2/n_h \right\}^2}{\Sigma \frac{N_h^2(N_h - n_h)^2}{n_h^2(n_h - 1)} S_h^4}.$$

5.4 OPTIMUM ALLOCATION OF A RANDOM SAMPLE

For fixed n, we wish to optimally choose the n_h. The optimality could be in terms of minimizing var $(\bar{y}_{st})$ subject to a specified overall cost or maximizing the overall cost subject to a specified var $(\bar{y}_{st})$. Surprisingly, the result is the same. We assume that the total cost is

$$C = c_0 + \Sigma_1^L c_h n_h$$

where c_0 is the overhead and c_h is the unit cost in the hth stratum.

Result 5.6. If we have stratified random sampling and the cost is linear, var $(\bar{y}_{st})$ is a minimum for specified cost C, and the cost is a minimum for a specified var $(\bar{y}_{st})$ when n_h is proportional to $W_h S_h/\sqrt{c_h}$.

Proof: We follow Cochran's (1977, pp. 97–99) method of proof. Thus,

$$C = c_0 + \Sigma c_h n_h$$

and

$$V = \text{var}(\bar{y}_{st})$$

$$= \Sigma W_h^2 S_h^2 (1 - f_h)/n_h$$

$$= \Sigma W_h^2 S_h^2/n_h - \Sigma W_h^2 S_h^2/N_h .$$

Now minimizing V for fixed C or minimizing C for fixed V is equivalent to minimizing

$$V'C' = (V + \Sigma W_h^2 S_h^2/N_h)(C - c_0)$$

$$= (\Sigma W_h^2 S_h^2/n_h)(\Sigma c_h n_h) .$$

Now because of the identity

$$(\Sigma a_i^2)(\Sigma b_i^2) - (\Sigma a_i b_i)^2 = \sum_i \sum_{j=i+1} (a_i b_j - a_j b_i)^2$$

it follows that (or from the Cauchy-Schwarz inequality)

$$(\Sigma a_i^2)(\Sigma b_i^2) \geq (\Sigma a_i b_i)^2 .$$

Now set $a_h = W_h S_h/\sqrt{n_h}$, $b_h = (c_h n_h)^{\frac{1}{2}}$. Then

$$(\Sigma W_h^2 S_h^2/n_h)(\Sigma c_h n_h) \geq (\Sigma W_h S_h \sqrt{c_h})^2 .$$

Thus the minimum value is achieved when

$$b_h/a_h = n_h \sqrt{c_h}/W_h S_h = \text{constant} = D \quad \text{(say)}$$

i.e.,

$$n_h = DW_h S_h/\sqrt{c_h} ,$$

$$\Sigma n_h = n \text{ implies that } D = n(\Sigma W_h S_h/\sqrt{c_h})^{-1} .$$

Hence

$$\frac{n_h}{n} = \frac{W_h S_h/\sqrt{c_h}}{(\Sigma W_h S_h/\sqrt{c_h})} = \frac{N_h S_h/\sqrt{c_h}}{\Sigma(N_h S_h/\sqrt{c_h})} .$$

Consequently

1. n_h increases with N_h,
2. n_h increases with S_h,
3. n_h decreases with c_h.

The preceding allocation expresses the n_h in terms of n which is unknown. If the cost is fixed, then substituting the optimum n_h in the cost we have

$$C - c_0 = \Sigma n_h c_h = \frac{n \Sigma N_h S_h \sqrt{c_h}}{\Sigma (N_h S_h / \sqrt{c_h})}.$$

That is

$$n = (C - c_0)(\Sigma N_h S_h / \sqrt{c_h}) / \Sigma N_h S_h \sqrt{c_h}.$$

On the other hand, if $V = \text{var}(\bar{y}_{st})$ is fixed, substitute the optimum n_h in the formula for V

$$V + \Sigma W_h^2 S_h^2 / N_h = \sum_{h=1}^{L} W_h^2 S_h^2 \cdot \frac{(\Sigma W_h S_h / \sqrt{c_h})}{n W_h S_h / \sqrt{c_h}}$$

$$n = \frac{(\sum_{h=1}^{L} W_h S_h \sqrt{c_h})(\Sigma W_h S_h / \sqrt{c_h})}{V + N^{-1} \Sigma W_h S_h^2}. \qquad \blacksquare$$

Special Case.   If $c_h = c$, then $C = c_0 + cn$. Hence, fixing C is equivalent to fixing n. Thus optimum allocation for fixed cost reduces to optimum allocation for fixed sample size. For this special case we have the following result.

Result 5.7.   In stratified random sampling, $\text{var}(\bar{y}_{st})$ is minimized for a fixed total sample size n if

$$n_h = n N_h S_h / (\Sigma N_h S_h).$$

This is called Neyman's allocation. (See Neyman (1934) and Tschuprow (1923)). With this allocation

$$\min \text{var}(\bar{y}_{st}) = n^{-1}(\Sigma W_h S_h)^2 - N^{-1} \Sigma W_h S_h^2.$$

EXAMPLE 5.1

Let $L = 3$,

$$N_1 = 500, \qquad N_2 = 1000, \qquad N_3 = 1500;$$
$$S_1^2 = 100, \qquad S_2^2 = 200, \qquad S_3^2 = 225;$$
$$c_1 = c_2 = c_3 = c, \qquad n = 84;$$
$$W_1 = 1/6, \qquad W_2 = 1/3, \qquad W_3 = 1/2;$$
$$S_1 W_1 = 10/6, \qquad S_2 W_2 = 10\sqrt{2}/3, \qquad S_3 W_3 = 15/2.$$

Hence

$$n_1 = n \frac{10/6}{10/6 + 10\sqrt{2}/3 + 15/2} = n \frac{10}{10 + 20\sqrt{2} + 45} = n \frac{10}{83.28} \doteq 10$$

$$n_2 = \qquad n(20\sqrt{2}/83.28) \qquad = 28.52 \doteq 29,$$
$$n_3 = \qquad n(45/83.28) \qquad = 45.4 \doteq 45.$$

Then

$$\min \text{var}(\bar{y}_{st}) = (1/84)(83.28/6)^2 - (1/3000)(100/6 + 200/3 + 225/2)$$

$$= 2.2935 - .065 = 2.23. \qquad \blacklozenge$$

5.5   MERITS OF STRATIFIED SAMPLING (SS) RELATIVE TO SIMPLE RANDOM SAMPLING (SRS)

Here we would like to compare the precisions of the stratified (optimal) sampling, proportionate sampling (PS), and simple random sampling. Of course (optimal) stratified sampling is more efficient than PS or SRS. However, PS may not always be more efficient than SRS. Let the variances of the estimates of the population mean by SRS, PS, and SS be denoted by $V(SRS)$, $V(PS)$, and $V(SS)$, respectively. Then we have the following result.

Result 5.8.   If terms of the order N_h^{-1} and N^{-1} are ignored, then

$$V(SRS) \geq V(PS) \geq V(SS).$$

where the optimal allocation in SS is for fixed n (that is, n_h is proportional to $N_h S_h$).

Proof: Recall that

$$V(SRS) = (1 - f)S^2/n = S^2/n - S^2/N$$

$$V(PS) = (1 - f)n^{-1}\Sigma W_h S_h^2 = n^{-1}\Sigma W_h S_h^2 - N^{-1}\Sigma W_h S_h^2,$$

and

$$V(SS) = n^{-1}(\Sigma W_h S_h)^2 - N^{-1}\Sigma W_h S_h^2.$$

We also have the identity

$$(N - 1)S^2 = \sum_h \sum_i (y_{hi} - \bar{Y})^2 = \sum_h \sum_i (y_{hi} - \bar{Y}_h)^2 + \sum_h N_h(\bar{Y}_h - \bar{Y})^2$$

$$= \sum_h (N_h - 1)S_h^2 + \sum_h N_h(\bar{Y}_h - \bar{Y})^2.$$

So, ignoring terms of order N_h^{-1} and N^{-1}, we have

$$S^2 = \Sigma W_h S_h^2 + \Sigma W_h(\bar{Y}_h - \bar{Y})^2.$$

Thus

$$V(SRS) = n^{-1}(1 - f)\Sigma W_h S_h^2 + n^{-1}(1 - f)\Sigma W_h(\bar{Y}_h - \bar{Y})^2$$

$$= V(PS) + n^{-1}(1 - f)\Sigma W_h(\bar{Y}_h - \bar{Y})^2$$

$$= V(SS) + n^{-1}\Sigma W_h(S_h - \bar{S})^2 + n^{-1}(1 - f)\Sigma W_h(\bar{Y}_h - \bar{Y})^2$$

where $\bar{S} = \Sigma W_h S_h$. This completes the proof of the assertion. Notice that the second term is due to differences in strata variances and the last term is due to differences in strata means.   ∎

Remark 5.2.   If no terms are ignored,

$$V(SRS) - V(PS) = \frac{(1-f)}{n(N-1)}\left[\Sigma(N_h - 1)S_h^2 + \Sigma N_h(\bar{Y}_h - \bar{Y})^2\right]$$

$$- n^{-1}(1-f)\Sigma W_h S_h^2$$

$$= \frac{(1-f)}{n(N-1)}\left[-\Sigma\frac{(N-N_h)}{N}S_h^2 + \Sigma N_h(\bar{Y}_h - \bar{Y})^2\right].$$

So $V(SRS) - V(PS) < 0$ when

$$\Sigma N_h(\bar{Y}_h - \bar{Y})^2 \leq \Sigma\frac{(N-N_h)}{N}S_h^2.$$

This is quite conceivable. For instance, let $S_h^2 \equiv S_W^2$ (i.e., all the strata variances have the same value), so that proportional allocation is optimum in the sense of Neyman. Then the above inequality becomes

$$\Sigma N_h(\bar{Y}_h - \bar{Y})^2 \leq (L-1)S_W^2$$

or

$$\frac{\Sigma N_h(\bar{Y}_h - \bar{Y})^2}{L-1} \leq S_W^2.$$

That is, the ratio of the mean-square error among strata to the mean-square error within the strata is less than unity.

The ideal stratification variable is the response variable y itself. However, in practice, we cannot stratify by the values of y. We stratify the population under the following circumstances:

1. The population consists of heterogeneous institutions which vary in size;

2. The response variable of interest is closely related to the sizes of the institutions;

3. The response variable is highly correlated with the stratification variable;

4. Certain strata are more expensive to sample than others.

For instance, the yield of some crop by a farm is closely related to the size of the farm. So, we can stratify the farms by their sizes. Similarly, we stratify the counties by the population size.

Recall that the optimum allocation assumes that the strata variances S_h^2 are known. Typically they are unknown. We need to estimate them or use the figures from an earlier survey or previous year. Then the question arises how much we gain from optimum allocation relative to proportional allocation. Sometimes because of the gross errors in estimating the S_h^2, and because of the simplicity of the proportional allocation, one may be better off with proportional allocation.

5.6   MODIFICATION OF OPTIMAL ALLOCATION

Sometimes the optimum allocation calls for subsample sizes that exceed the stratum sizes. In that case, we replace the optimal n_h by N_h and recompute the rest of the n_h by the revised optimum allocation. For example, suppose $n_1 \geq N_1$. Then take

$$\tilde{n}_1 = N_1 \quad \text{and} \quad \tilde{n}_h = (n - N_1)(W_h S_h) / \left(\sum_{h=2}^{L} W_h S_h \right) \qquad (h \geq 2)$$

provided $\tilde{n}_h \leq N_h$ for $h \geq 2$. If it were to happen that $\tilde{n}_2 \geq N_2$ the re-revised allocation would be to take

$$\tilde{n}_1 = N_1, \quad \tilde{n}_2 = N_2, \quad \text{and } \tilde{n}_h = (n - N_1 - N_2)(W_h S_h) / \left(\sum_{h=3}^{L} W_h S_h \right), \qquad h \geq 3$$

provided $\tilde{n}_h \leq N_h$ for $h \geq 3$. We continue this process until every $\tilde{n}_h \leq N_h$.

Notice that the formula for min var $(\bar{y}_{st})$ is not valid. It should be modified to

$$\text{min var}(\bar{y}_{st}) = \frac{(\Sigma' W_h S_h)^2}{n'} - \frac{\Sigma' W_h S_h^2}{N}$$

where Σ' denotes summation over the strata in which $\tilde{n}_h \leq N_h$ and n' is the revised total sample size in the strata.

EXAMPLE 5.2

Let $L = 3$,

$$N_1 = 50, \qquad N_2 = 100, \qquad N_3 = 150;$$
$$S_1^2 = 625, \qquad S_2^2 = 100, \qquad S_3^2 = 225;$$
$$c_1 = c_2 = c_3 = c, \qquad n = 200.$$

Then

$$W_1 = 1/6, \qquad W_2 = 1/3, \quad \text{and} \quad W_3 = 1/2$$

and

$$S_1 W_1 = 25/6, \qquad S_2 W_2 = 10/3, \qquad S_3 W_3 = 15/2, \qquad \sum_1^3 S_i W_i = 15$$

$$n_1 = n \cdot \frac{25/6}{15} = n \frac{5}{18}.$$

Since $n_1 = \frac{200 \times 5}{18} \doteq 56 \geq N_1$ we set $\tilde{n}_1 = N_1$ and

$$\tilde{n}_2 = (200 - 50)\frac{(10/3)}{10/3 + 15/2} = 150 \cdot \frac{20}{65} = 46.15 \approx 46$$

$$\tilde{n}_3 = 150(15/2)/\{10/3 + 15/2\} = 150(45)/65 = 103.8 \approx 104$$

$$\text{min var}\,(\bar{y}_{st}) = \frac{(10/3 + 15/2)^2}{150} - \frac{(100/3 + 225/2)}{300}$$

$$= 4.6944 - 0.4861 = 4.21\,. \qquad \blacklozenge$$

5.7   ESTIMATION OF SAMPLE SIZES IN STRATIFIED SAMPLING: CONTINUOUS RESPONSE DATA

Assume that the estimate has a specified variance V, then the sample size can be determined. On the other hand, if d denotes the margin of error in the estimate (i.e., $P(|\bar{y}_{st} - \bar{Y}| \leq d) = 1 - \alpha$), then $V = (d/z)^2$ where z denotes the $1 - d/z^{\text{th}}$ quantile of the standard normal distribution.

5.8   ESTIMATION OF THE POPULATION MEAN $\bar{Y}$

Let s_h denote an estimate of S_h and let $n_h = nw_h$ where the w_h have been chosen according to some criterion. Then the variance of $\bar{y}_{st}$ is

$$\text{var}\,(\bar{y}_{st}) \doteq n^{-1}\Sigma \frac{w_h^2 s_h^2}{w_h} - N^{-1}\Sigma W_h s_h^2$$

where $W_h = N_h/N$. Solving for n we obtain

$$n \doteq \frac{\Sigma W_h^2 s_h^2/w_h}{V + N^{-1}\Sigma W_h s_h^2}\,.$$

If the fpc can be ignored, we get the first approximation to n as

$$n_0 = V^{-1}\Sigma W_h^2 s_h^2/w_h\,.$$

If n_0/N cannot be ignored, we have

$$n = \frac{n_0}{1 + (NV)^{-1}\Sigma W_h s_h^2}\,.$$

Special Cases

   1. Optimal allocation (for fixed n): $w_h \propto W_h s_h$. (Since $\Sigma w_h = 1$ implies that $w_h = W_h s_h/\Sigma W_h s_h$.)

$$n = (\Sigma W_h s_h)^2/\{V + N^{-1}\Sigma W_h s_h^2\}$$

2. Proportional allocation: $w_h = W_h = N_h/N$. Then

$$n_0 = \Sigma W_h s_h^2 / V$$

and

$$n = n_0 / \{1 + n_0/N\}.$$

5.9   ESTIMATION OF THE POPULATION TOTAL

If V is the desired $\mathrm{var}\,(\hat{Y}_{\mathrm{st}})$, then we have the following formulae for the sample sizes. (Note that $V = \mathrm{var}\,(\hat{Y}_{\mathrm{st}}) = \Sigma N_h^2 S_h^2 / n w_h - \Sigma N_h S_h^2.$)

General: $$n = \frac{\Sigma N_h^2 s_h^2 / w_h}{V + \Sigma N_h s_h^2}$$

Optimal (fixed n): $$n = \frac{(\Sigma N_h s_h)^2}{V + \Sigma N_h s_h^2} \qquad \left(\text{set } w_h = \frac{W_h s_h}{\Sigma W_h s_h} = \frac{N_h s_h}{\Sigma N_h s_h} \right)$$

Proportional: $$n_0 = N V^{-1} \Sigma W_h s_h^2$$

$$n = n_0 / \{1 + n_0/N\}$$

where n_0 is the approximate value of n when the fpc are ignored.

5.10   APPLICATION TO STRATIFIED SAMPLING FOR PROPORTIONS

If A_h denotes the number of units in the stratum that fall into a class C, then

$$P_h = A_h/N_h.$$

An estimate of P_h is $p_h = a_h/n_h$, where a_h denotes the number of units in the sample of size n_h from N_h that belong to class C. Suppose we are interested in estimating

$$P = \sum_{h=1}^{L} W_h P_h.$$

Then the stratified sample estimate of P is

$$p_{\mathrm{st}} = \Sigma W_h p_h.$$

Result 5.9.   In stratified random sampling, we have

$$\mathrm{var}\,(p_{\mathrm{st}}) = N^{-2} \Sigma N_h^2 \frac{(N_h - n_h)}{(N_h - 1)} \frac{P_h Q_h}{n_h}.$$

Proof: In the general formula obtained in Result 5.3 replace S_h^2 by $N_h P_h Q_h / (N_h - 1)$.   ∎

Remark 5.3.   In most of the applications, even if the fpc is not negligible, we can reasonably ignore terms of the order N_h^{-1}. Then the above formula simplifies to

$$\mathrm{var}\,(p_{\mathrm{st}}) = N^{-2} \Sigma N_h (N_h - n_h) \frac{P_h Q_h}{n_h} = \Sigma \frac{W_h^2 P_h Q_h}{n_h} (1 - f_h).$$

Corollary 5.1.   If the fpc is ignored,

$$\text{var}\,(p_{\text{st}}) \;=\; \Sigma W_h^2 \frac{P_h Q_h}{n_h}\,.$$

Corollary 5.2.   If proportional allocation is carried out,

$$\text{var}\,(p_{\text{st}}) \;=\; \frac{N-n}{N} \cdot \frac{1}{nN} \cdot \Sigma \frac{N_h^2 P_h Q_h}{N_h - 1}$$

$$\doteq (1-f)n^{-1}\Sigma W_h P_h Q_h\,.$$

Estimates of var (p_{st}) can be obtained by replacing $P_h Q_h / n_h$ by $p_h q_h / (n_h - 1)$ in any one of the above formulae. The best choice of the n_h for minimizing var (p_{st}) follows from the general theory.

5.11   MINIMUM VARIANCE FOR FIXED n (TOTAL SAMPLE SIZE)

$$n_h \propto N_h \cdot \sqrt{N_h/(N_h - 1)}\sqrt{P_h Q_h} \doteq \sqrt{P_h Q_h}\,N_h\,.$$

That is

$$n_h \doteq n\frac{N_h\sqrt{P_h Q_h}}{\Sigma N_h\sqrt{P_h Q_h}}\,.$$

Minimum variance for fixed cost, where cost $= c_0 + \Sigma c_h n_h$,

$$n_h \doteq n\frac{N_h\sqrt{P_h Q_h/c_h}}{\Sigma N_h\sqrt{P_h Q_h/c_h}}\,.$$

The value of n is as given by the general theory (see Section 5.4).

5.12   GAIN BY STRATIFIED SAMPLING FOR PROPORTIONS

If we ignore the fpc, then

$$\min V(SS) = (\Sigma W_h\sqrt{P_h Q_h})^2/n$$

and

$$\min V(PS) = \Sigma W_h P_h Q_h/n\,.$$

Thus the precision of PS relative to SS is

$$\min V(SS)/\min V(PS) = (\Sigma W_h\sqrt{P_h Q_h})^2/(\Sigma W_h P_h Q_h)\,.$$

EXAMPLE **5.3**

Let $L = 3$, $W_1 = 0.6$, $W_2 = 0.3$, $W_3 = 0.1$ and $P_1 = 0.25$, $P_2 = 0.2$, $P_3 = 0.15$. Then

$$\min V(SS)/\min V(PS) = \frac{\left\{0.6\sqrt{(.25)(.75)} + 0.3\sqrt{0.16} + 0.1\sqrt{(.15)(.85)}\right\}^2}{0.6(.25)(.75) + 0.3(0.16) + 0.1(0.15)(.85)}$$

$$= \frac{(0.2598 + 0.12 + 0.0357)^2}{(0.1275 + 0.048 + 0.0128)}$$

$$= \frac{0.17264}{0.1883} = 0.92 .$$

That is, proportional sampling is 92% as efficient as stratified sampling.   ◆

5.13   SAMPLE SIZE FOR PROPORTIONS

Let V be the desired variance of the estimate of P.

Proportional sampling: $n_0 = \Sigma W_h p_h q_h / V$, $n = n_0 / \{1 + n_0/N\}$

Optimal allocation: $n_0 = (\Sigma W_h \sqrt{p_h q_h})^2 / V$, $n = n_0 / \{1 + (NV)^{-1} \Sigma W_h p_h q_h\}$

where n_0 is the approximate value of n when the fpc is ignored.

EXAMPLE **5.4**

In a certain state, we wish to estimate the average amount of money invested in farm machinery. The farms are classified as big and small. (A farm is big if the total acreage is more than 600; otherwise it is small.) The number of big farms is 5000 and the number of small farms 20,000. On the average, a farm in the big category is thought to have invested four times as much money in farm machinery as a farm in the small category. Also it is assumed that S_h is proportional to the square root of the stratum mean. Then (a) how would you allocate a sample of 300 farms between the two categories? (b) If we wish to estimate the difference between the value of machinery in the two categories of farms, how should the sample be allocated?

	Big farms	Small farms
	$N_1 = 5000$	$N_2 = 20,000$
	$W_1 = 1/5$	$W_2 = 4/5$
Stratum mean $=$	$\bar{Y}_1$	$\bar{Y}_2$
Stratum variance $=$	S_1^2	S_2^2
Sample size $=$	n_1	n_2
Sample mean $=$	$\bar{y}_1$	$\bar{y}_2$

(b) We are interested in estimating $\bar{Y}_1 - \bar{Y}_2$. Sample estimate is $\bar{y}_1 - \bar{y}_2$

$$V = \text{var}(\bar{y}_1 - \bar{y}_2) = \text{var}\,\bar{y}_1 + \text{var}\,\bar{y}_2$$

$$= \frac{(1-f_1)S_1^2}{n_1} + \frac{(1-f_2)S_2^2}{n_2}$$

$$n_1 + n_2 = 300$$

It is given that $S_1 \propto \sqrt{\bar{Y}_1}$ and $S_2 \propto \sqrt{\bar{Y}_2}$ and that $\bar{Y}_1 = 4\bar{Y}_2$. So

$$\text{var}(\bar{y}_1 - \bar{y}_2) + \frac{S_1^2}{N_1} + \frac{S_2^2}{N_2} = \frac{S_1^2}{n_1} + \frac{S_2^2}{n_2}$$

That is

$$V' = V + c\left(\frac{\bar{Y}_1}{N_1} + \frac{\bar{Y}_2}{N_2}\right) = c\left(\frac{\bar{Y}_1}{n_1} + \frac{\bar{Y}_2}{n_2}\right).$$

Since $\bar{Y}_1 = 4\bar{Y}_2$, we obtain

$$V' = V + c\bar{Y}_2\left(\frac{4}{N_1} + \frac{1}{N_2}\right) = c\bar{Y}_2\left(\frac{4}{n_1} + \frac{1}{n_2}\right).$$

Hence, we wish to minimize V' subject to $n_1 + n_2 = 300$. Consider

$$\bar{Y}_2\left(\frac{4}{n_1} + \frac{1}{300 - n_1}\right)$$

and set its derivative with respect to n_1 equal to zero. We obtain

$$4/n_1^2 \equiv 1/(300 - n_1)^2$$

Hence

$$2/n_1 = 1/(300 - n_1), \qquad \text{i.e.,} \quad n_1 = 200 \text{ and } n_2 = 100.$$

(a) Here we wish to estimate $\bar{Y} = \sum_1^L W_h \bar{Y}_h$. We choose n_1 and n_2 such that $\text{var}(\bar{y}_{st}) = \text{var}(W_1\bar{y}_1 + W_2\bar{y}_2)$ is minimized subject to $n_1 + n_2 = 300$.

$$\frac{n_1}{n} = \frac{W_1 S_1}{W_1 S_1 + W_2 S_2} = \frac{W_1\sqrt{\bar{Y}_1}}{W_1\sqrt{\bar{Y}_1} + W_2\sqrt{\bar{Y}_2}} = \frac{2W_1}{2W_1 + W_2} = \frac{2/5}{2/5 + 4/5} = \frac{1}{3}$$

$$n_1 = 300(1/3) = 100 \text{ and } n_2 = 200. \qquad \blacklozenge$$

5.14   POSTSTRATIFICATION

Sometimes, it is possible to stratify the data only after the data has been collected. For instance, the stratification variables could be age, sex, race, and educational training. Although the N_h can be obtained from official statistical sources, we assume that the units can be classified into the strata only after the sample is drawn. Let n denote the size of the simple random sample. Instead of the usual $\bar{y}$, we use

$$\bar{y}_w = \sum W_h \bar{y}_h$$

where $\bar{y}_h$ denotes the sample mean of units that fall in stratum h. $(h = 1, \ldots, L)$ and $W_h = N_h/N$. This method is almost as precise as the proportional sampling procedure, provided

1. $E(m_h) \geq 20 (h = 1, \ldots, L)$, where m_h denotes the number of units that fall in stratum h, and
2. the effects of errors in the weights W_h are negligible.

This will be shown in the following.

Let m_h be the subsample size in stratum h. Then for fixed m_h,

$$\text{var}\,(\bar{y}_w | m_1, \ldots, m_L) = \sum \frac{W_h^2 S_h^2}{m_h} - \frac{1}{N} \sum W_h S_h^2.$$

Now we wish to find the unconditional variance or the expectation of the above conditional variance (since $E\bar{y}_w = \bar{Y}$). Toward this we need $E(m_h^{-1})$. Write

$$m_h^{-1} = (m_h - nW_h + nW_h)^{-1} = (nW_h)^{-1} (1 + \frac{m_h - nW_h}{nW_h})^{-1}$$

$$= (nW_h)^{-1} \left[1 - \left(\frac{m_h - nW_h}{nW_h} \right) + \left(\frac{(m_h - nW_h)}{nW_h} \right)^2 - \cdots \right].$$

Hence,

$$E(m_h^{-1}) = (nW_h)^{-1} + (nW_h)^{-1} \left[\frac{nW_h(1 - W_h)}{n^2 W_h^2} \right] - \cdots$$

$$\doteq (nW_h)^{-1} + \frac{1 - W_h}{n^2 W_h^2} - \cdots .$$

Then

$$\text{var}\,(\bar{y}_w) \doteq \frac{(1 - f)}{n} \sum W_h S_h^2 + \frac{1}{n^2} \sum (1 - W_h) S_h^2 \qquad \text{(see also Stephan, 1945)}.$$

Notice that the first term in the above approximation is the variance of a stratified sample of size n with proportional allocation, and the second term represents the increase in variance due to the fact that the m_h, in general, are not proportional to the stratum sizes. However,

$$n^{-2} \sum (1 - W_h) S_h^2 = n^{-1}(L/n) \bar{S}^2 - n^{-2} \sum W_h S_h^2$$

$$= (n\bar{n})^{-1} \bar{S}^2 - n^{-2} \sum W_h S_h^2$$

where $\bar{S}^2$ is the average of the S_h^2 and $\bar{n} = n/L$ is the average number of units per stratum. Thus if the S_h^2 do not differ significantly among themselves, the increase is about $(L - 1)/L\bar{n}$ times the variance for proportional sampling (of course, after ignoring the fpc).

$$\left(\text{var}\,\bar{y}_w \doteq \frac{1}{n} \bar{S}^2 \left(1 + \frac{L - 1}{L\bar{n}} \right) \right).$$

The increase is small if $\bar{n}$ is fairly large.

Also, for any positive random variable X, using the Cauchy-Schwarz inequality, we have

$$1 = \left\{ E\left(\frac{1}{\sqrt{X}} \cdot \sqrt{X} \right) \right\}^2 \leq E(X) \cdot E(X^{-1})$$

and setting $X = m_h^{-1}$, we have

$$E(m_h^{-1}) \geq 1/E(m_h) = \frac{1}{nW_h} \qquad (\text{i.e., } \operatorname{var}(\bar{y}_w) \geq \operatorname{var}(\bar{y}_{\text{PS}})).$$

Replacing S_h^2 by the sample estimates, we have

$$\widehat{\operatorname{var}}(\bar{y}_w) \doteq \frac{(1-f)}{n} \sum W_h s_h^2 + \frac{1}{n^2} \sum (1 - W_h) s_h^2.$$

The real advantage of post stratification is that it gives conditionally unbiased estimates given $(m_1, \ldots, m_L)$, which is an ancillary statistic,[1] whereas $\bar{y}$ (see p. 76 for the definition) is conditionally biased. For more on conditional inference on survey sampling, see J. N. K. Rao (1985) or Holt and Smith (1979).

EXAMPLE 5.5

Suppose $L = 2$ with men in stratum one and women in the other stratum. Let $n = 100$, $n_1 = 45$, $n_2 = 55$. Suppose that 40% of men and 60% of women are in favor of a curfew hour for teenagers. Let us assume that $W_1 = W_2 = 0.5$. Then the poststratified estimate of the true proportion is

$$p_W = 0.5(0.4) + (0.5(0.60) = 0.50.$$

Also,

$$s_1^2 = (0.4)(0.6) = 0.24, \qquad s_2^2 = (0.6)(0.4) = 0.24.$$

Ignoring the finite population correction f, we obtain

$$\widehat{\operatorname{var}}(p_W) = \frac{1}{100}\{(0.5)(0.24) + (0.5)(0.24)\} + \frac{1}{10^4}\{(0.5)(0.24) + (0.5)(0.24)\}$$

$$= \frac{0.24}{100} + \frac{0.24}{10^4} = (24.24)10^{-4}.$$

95% confidence interval for the true proportion is

$$p_W \pm 2\{\widehat{\operatorname{var}}(p_W)\}^{1/2} = 0.50 \pm 2\{4.9\}10^{-2} = 0.50 \pm 0.098. \qquad \blacklozenge$$

---

[1] An ancillary statistic is a statistic the distribution of which is free of the population parameters and hence contains no information about these parameters.

5.15   HOW SHOULD THE STRATA BE FORMED?[2]

We impose one criterion—namely, the strata should be internally as homogeneous as possible, because the smaller the strata variances, the smaller is the variance of the sample estimate. If the distribution of the response variable y is approximately known, we can create various strata by suitably partitioning the support of this distribution into disjoint intervals. Let $y_1 < y_2 < \cdots < y_{L-1}$ denote such a partition and let $\bar{Y}_h$ and σ_h^2 denote the mean and variance of the hth stratum. Then

$$W_h = \int_{y_{h-1}}^{y_h} f(u)\,du$$

$$W_h \bar{Y}_h = \int_{y_{h-1}}^{y_h} u f(u)\,du$$

$$W_h \sigma_h^2 = \int_{y_{h-1}}^{y_h} u^2 f(u)\,du - W_h \bar{Y}_h^2$$

where $f(u)$ denotes the density of y. Then the population mean is

$$\bar{Y} = \sum W_h \bar{Y}_h\,; \qquad \text{its estimate is } \bar{y}_{st} = \sum W_h \bar{y}_h$$

and

$$\mathrm{var}\,(\bar{y}_{st}) = \sum W_h^2 \frac{\sigma_h^2}{n_h}\,.$$

Thus, $\mathrm{var}\,(\bar{y}_{st})$ depends on $(y_1 \ldots y_{L-1})$, and the problem is to determine the best values of $y_1 \ldots y_{L-1}$ which minimize $\mathrm{var}\,(\bar{y}_{st})$ for a specified allocation of the n_h. Dalenius (1950) has considered this problem, and we present some of his results in the following:

Let us use the following notation:

$$\text{Let } \mu = \int_a^b u f(u)\,du \quad \text{and} \quad \mu_2' = \int_a^b u^2 f(u)\,du\,.$$

Let us consider the three important types of allocations

(a) Proportional Allocation

Under this scheme $n_h = n W_h$. Then

---

[2]**N.B.** DesRaj (1968, sec. 4.6) served as a source for part of this section

$$\text{var}(\bar{y}_{st}) = n^{-1} \sum W_h \sigma_h^2 = n^{-1} \left[\sum \int_{y_{h-1}}^{y_h} u^2 f(u)\, du - \sum W_h \bar{Y}_h^2 \right]$$

$$= n^{-1} \mu_2' - n^{-1} \sum W_h \bar{Y}_h^2$$

$$= n^{-1} \mu_2' - n^{-1} \sum \frac{(W_h \bar{Y}_h)^2}{W_h}$$

$$= n^{-1} \mu_2' - n^{-1} \sum_{h=1}^{L} \left\{ \int_{y_{h-1}}^{y_h} u f(u)\, du \right\}^2 / W_h$$

So minimization of $\text{var}(\bar{y}_{st})$ with respect to the y_i is equivalent to maximizing

$$A = \sum_{j=1}^{L} W_j^{-1} \left\{ \int_{y_{j-1}}^{y_j} u f(u)\, du \right\}^2 .$$

Noting that the only terms that involve y_h will be those corresponding to $j = h$ and $j = h + 1$ in the summation, we find that

$$\frac{\partial A}{\partial y_h} = - W_h^{-2} \frac{\partial W_h}{\partial y_h} \left(W_h \bar{Y}_h \right)^2 + W_h^{-1} \cdot 2 W_h \bar{Y}_h \, y_h f(y_h)$$

$$- W_{h+1}^{-2} \frac{\partial W_{h+1}}{\partial y_h} \left(W_{h+1} \bar{Y}_{h+1} \right)^2 - W_{h+1}^{-1} \cdot 2 W_{h+1} \bar{Y}_{h+1} \cdot y_h f(y_h) = 0 .$$

That is

$$-f(y_h) \bar{Y}_h^2 + 2 \bar{Y}_h y_h f(y_h) + f(y_h) \bar{Y}_{h+1}^2 - 2 \bar{Y}_{h+1} y_h f(y_h) = 0$$

or

$$\bar{Y}_{h+1}^2 - \bar{Y}_h^2 = 2 y_h \left(\bar{Y}_{h+1} - \bar{Y}_h \right)$$

or

$$y_h = \frac{1}{2} \left(\bar{Y}_{h+1} + \bar{Y}_h \right), \qquad h = 1, \ldots, L .$$

For an arbitrary $f(u)$, one can solve for y_h by iterative methods.

Particular forms of $f(u)$

$$(1) \text{ Let } f(u) = (b - a)^{-1}, \qquad \text{if } a < u < b$$

$$= 0, \qquad\qquad\qquad \text{otherwise} .$$

Then

$$W_h = (y_h - y_{h-1})/(b - a),$$

$$W_h \bar{Y}_h = (y_h^2 - y_{h-1}^2)/2(b - a)$$

$$\bar{Y}_h = (y_h + y_{h-1})/2, \qquad h = 1, \ldots, L.$$

So

$$y_h = \frac{1}{2}(\bar{Y}_{h+1} + \bar{Y}_h)$$

implies that

$$y_h - y_{h-1} = y_{h+1} - y_h = c, h = 1, \ldots.$$

Then

$$\sum_{h=1}^{L}(y_h - y_{h-1}) = b - a = Lc$$

or

$$c = (b - a)/L.$$

Thus

$$y_h = a + h(b - a)/L, \qquad h = 1, \ldots, L.$$

EXAMPLE 5.6

Suppose that $L = 3$ and y the response variable is the score of students on a certain test. Let $a = 40$, and $b = 100$. Then

$$y_h = 40 + h(100 - 40)/3 = 40 + 20h, \qquad h = 1, 2, 3. \qquad \blacklozenge$$

Remark 5.4. The above approximation has been proposed by Aoyama (1954) for an arbitrary $f(u)$.

$$(2) \text{ Similarly if } f(u) = e^{-u}, \qquad 0 < u < \infty$$

$$= 0, \qquad \text{elsewhere}$$

we obtain

$$W_h = e^{-y_{h-1}} - e^{-y_h}$$

and

$$\bar{Y}_h = 1 + (y_{h-1}e^{-y_{h-1}} - y_h e^{-y_h})/W_h$$

$$y_h = (\bar{Y}_{h+1} + \bar{Y}_h)/2$$

implies that $y_h = 1 + \dfrac{y_h e^{-y_h} - y_{h+1}e^{-y_{h+1}}}{2(e^{-y_h} - e^{-y_{h+1}})} + \dfrac{y_{h-1}e^{-y_{h-1}} - y_h e^{-y_h}}{2(e^{-y_{h-1}} - e^{-y_h})},$

$$h = 1, 2, \ldots, L.$$

Other candidates for $f(u)$ are

$$f(u) = (2/\pi)^{\frac{1}{2}}e^{-u^2/2} \qquad 0 < u < \infty \qquad \text{(folded normal density)}$$

$$f(u) = ue^{-u}, \ldots, u > 0$$

$$f(u) = 2(1 - u), \qquad 0 \le u \le 1 \qquad \text{(triangular density)}.$$

(b) Equal Allocation.

Here

$$n_h = n/L$$

and consequently

$$\text{var}(\bar{y}_{st}) = \frac{L}{n}\sum W_h^2\sigma_h^2$$

$$= \frac{L}{n}\sum W_h(W_h\sigma_h^2)$$

$$= \frac{L}{n}\sum W_h\left\{W_h(\sigma_h^2 + \bar{Y}_h^2) - W_h\bar{Y}_h^2\right\}$$

$$= \frac{L}{n}\sum_h W_h\int_{y_{h-1}}^{y_h} u^2 f(u)\,du - \frac{L}{n}\sum\left(\int_{y_{h-1}}^{y_h} uf(u)\,du\right)^2.$$

Now differentiating w.r.t. y_h and proceeding as before, one can obtain a set of equations for minimizing $\text{var}(\bar{y}_{st})$ with respect to the y_i's.

(c) Optimum Stratification

Here we have $\frac{n_h}{n} = \frac{W_h\sigma_h}{\sum W_j\sigma_j}$ and $\text{var}(\bar{y}_{st}) = n^{-1}(\sum W_j\sigma_j)^2$. We choose the y_h such that $\sum W_j\sigma_j$ is minimum. Note that

$$\frac{\partial}{\partial y_h}\left(\sum W_j\sigma_j\right) = \frac{\partial}{\partial y_h}(W_h\sigma_h + W_{h+1}\sigma_{h+1}).$$

Considering

$$\frac{\partial}{\partial y_h}(W_h\sigma_h) = \sigma_h\frac{\partial W_h}{\partial y_h} + W_h\frac{\partial\sigma_h}{\partial y_h} = \sigma_h f(y_h) + W_h\frac{\partial\sigma_h}{\partial y_h}$$

and

$$f(y_h)(y_h - \bar{Y}_h)^2 = \frac{\partial}{\partial y_h}(W_h\sigma_h^2) = \sigma_h^2 f(y_h) + 2W_h\sigma_h\frac{\partial\sigma_h}{\partial y_h}$$

we have

$$\frac{\partial}{\partial y_h}(W_h\sigma_h) = (2\sigma_h)^{-1}f(y_h)\left[(y_h - \bar{Y}_h)^2 + \sigma_h^2\right].$$

Analogously

$$\frac{\partial}{\partial y_h}(W_{h+1}\sigma_{h+1}) = -(2\sigma_{h+1})^{-1}f(y_h)\left[(y_h - \bar{Y}_{h+1})^2 + \sigma_{h+1}^2\right].$$

Thus the set of equation yielding the optimal $y_1, \ldots, y_L$ are

$$\sigma_h^{-1}\left\{(y_h - \bar{Y}_h)^2 + \sigma_h^2\right\} - \sigma_{h+1}^{-1}\left\{(y_h - \bar{Y}_{h+1})^2 + \sigma_{h+1}^2\right\} = 0, h = 1, \ldots, L.$$

However these equations are nonlinear and can be solved only numerically by iterative methods. Some approximations has been suggested by Dalenius and Hodges (1959), who propose that we assume the distribution within strata be uniform when the number of strata is large. Then

$$W_h = (y_h - y_{h-1}) f_h$$

$$\bar{Y}_h = (y_h + y_{h-1})/2 \quad \text{and} \quad \sigma_h = \frac{y_h - y_{h-1}}{\sqrt{12}} \text{ with } f_h = f(y_h).$$

Hence

$$\Sigma\sqrt{12}W_h\sigma_h = \sum f_h(y_h - y_{h-1})^2 = \sum \left[\sqrt{f_h}(y_h - y_{h-1})\right]^2.$$

Now let $G(h) = \int_a^{y_h} \sqrt{f(u)} \, du$. Then we have

$$G(h) - G(h - 1) = \int_{y_{h-1}}^{y_h} \sqrt{f(u)} du \doteq \sqrt{f_h}(y_h - y_{h-1})$$

and consequently

$$\Sigma\sqrt{12}W_h\sigma_h \doteq \sum_h [G(h) - G(h - 1)]^2$$

$$0 = \frac{\partial}{\partial y_h} \Sigma W_j\sigma_j = 2[G(h) - G(h - 1)]\sqrt{f(y_h)} - 2[G(h + 1) - G(h)]\sqrt{f(y_h)}.$$

That is, $G(h) - G(h - 1) = c$, where c may depend on L. Thus we should take equal intervals on the cumulative values of $\sqrt{f(u)}$. That is,

$$y_h = \frac{h}{L} \int_a^b \sqrt{f(u)} \, du, \qquad h = 1, 2, \ldots, L - 1, \qquad \text{with } y_L = b.$$

If the density is over a finite interval (y_0, y_L) and if $f'(u)$, $f''(u)$ exist and are continuous over the whole range, then Ekman (1959) obtains

$$\left\{ \frac{\sigma_h^2 + (y_h - \bar{Y}_h)^2}{\sigma_h} \right\}^2 \sim \frac{4(y_h - y_{h-1})W_h}{3f(y_h)}$$

and

$$\left\{ \frac{\sigma_{h+1}^2 + (y_h - \bar{Y}_{h+1})^2}{\sigma_{h+1}} \right\}^2 \sim \frac{4(y_{h+1} - y_h)W_{h+1}}{3f(y_h)}.$$

So, equality of the left sides of the above two equations (in the optimal allocation case) implies that

$$(y_h - y_{h-1})W_h = (y_{h+1} - y_h)W_{h+1} = c, h = 1, \ldots, L.$$

If we have infinite range (i.e., $y_0 = -\infty$ and $y_L = \infty$), Ekman (1959) suggests to replace the above system by the following system of equations:

$$(y_h - y_{h-1})W_h = c, h = 2, \ldots L - 1$$

$$\frac{3f(y_1)}{4} \left[\frac{\sigma_1^2 + (y_1 - \bar{Y}_1)^2}{\sigma_1} \right]^2 = \frac{3f(y_{L-1})}{4} \left[\frac{\sigma_L^2 + (y_{L-1} - \bar{Y}_L)^2}{\sigma_L} \right]^2 = c$$

Dalenius and Gurney (1951) conjecture and Dalenius and Hodges (1957) support their conjecture to use

$$W_h \sigma_h = c, \qquad h = 1, \ldots, L.$$

Cochran (1961) based on numerical study suggests that the rules given by Dalenius and Hodges (1959) and Ekman (1959) are better than the other rules. Hess, Sethi, and Balakrishnan (1966) have conducted an empirical study comparing the various approximate methods of optimal stratification. Mahalanobis (1952) and Hansen, Hurwitz, and Madow (1953) suggested that strata be formed by using

$$W_h \bar{Y}_h = c, \qquad h = 1, \ldots, L.$$

However, it has been found not to lead to satisfactory results (see Sethi (1963) and DesRaj (1968, p. 73)).

cum $\sqrt{f}$ formulas for var $(\bar{y}_{st})$. Let $K = \int_{-\infty}^{\infty}[f(u)]^{\frac{1}{2}} du$, $K^* = \int_{-\infty}^{\infty}[f(u)]^{\frac{3}{2}} du$. We assume that the density of y, namely $f(y)$, has finite variance $\sigma^2 > 0$, finite cum $\sqrt{f}$, and mean $\sqrt{f}$. Also let

$$k = K^4/12\sigma^2, \qquad k^* = KK^*.$$

We will confine to the interval $[a, b]$ outside of which $f(u)$ is either zero or approximately zero. Let

$$A_h = \int_{y_{h-1}}^{y_h} [f(y)]^{\frac{1}{2}} dy, \qquad h = 1, \ldots, L - 1.$$

Then

$$\sum_{h=1}^{L} A_h = K.$$

Let θ_h be the mean value of $f(u)$ within the hth stratum. Then we have (approximately) for the weight, variance, and $\text{cum}\sqrt{f}$ of the hth stratum

$$W_h \doteq \theta_h(y_h - y_{h-1})$$

$$\sigma_h^2 \doteq (y_h - y_{h-1})^2/12$$

$$A_h \doteq \theta_h^{\frac{1}{2}}(y_h - y_{h-1})$$

which imply that

$$W_h\sigma_h \doteq A_h^2/\sqrt{12}.$$

So, by minimizing $\sum W_h\sigma_h$ (or equivalently by minimizing $\sum A_h^2$ subject to $\sum A_h = K$), we find that

$$A_h = K/L \quad (h = 1, \dots, L.)$$

i.e., by equal partition of the $\text{cum}\sqrt{f}$ scale. Then the "$\text{cum}\sqrt{f}$" approximation to Neyman-Tschuprow allocation (under constant cost per sample unit in all strata) becomes

$$n_h \doteq n.\frac{W_h\sigma_h}{\sum W_h\sigma_h} \doteq \frac{n \cdot K^2/\sqrt{12}L^2}{L \cdot (K^2/\sqrt{12}L^2)} = \frac{n}{L} \quad (h = 1, \dots, L)$$

which is nothing but equal allocation.

Next let us approximate $\text{var}(\bar{y}_{st})$ under $\text{cum}\sqrt{f}$ rule.

$$\text{min var}(\bar{y}_{st}) = \frac{1}{n}\left(\sum W_h\sigma_h\right)^2 \doteq \left(\sum A_h^2\right)^2/12 = K^4/12nL^2$$

$$= k\sigma^2/nL^2.$$

As L increases, the approximation becomes more precise, since the strata become narrower.

EXAMPLE 5.7

Suppose the distribution of scores of students in a large statistics class is given as follows (the intervals being closed at the left and open at the right boundaries):

Score	Frequency	$\sqrt{\text{Frequency}}$	Cumulative $\sqrt{\text{Frequency}}$
30 – 40	4	2	2
40 – 50	4	2	4
50 – 60	9	3	7
60 – 70	25	5	12
70 – 80	16	4	16
80 – 90	9	3	19
90 – 100	9	3	22
Total	76		

If we follow the cumulative square-root frequency method for determining the strata with $L = 3$, then $22/3 = 7.3$ and $2(22/3) = 14.7$. In the scale of the above example, 7 is close to 7.3 and 16 is close to 14.7. thus the resulting strata are:

> Stratum 1: students with scores in $[30–60)$
> Stratum 2: students with scores in $[60–80)$
> Stratum 3: students with scores in $[80–100)$.

Then the "cum$\sqrt{f}$" approximation to Neyman-Tschuprow allocation (under constant cost per sample unit in all strata) becomes

$$n_h = \frac{n}{3} \quad (h = 1, 2, 3).$$

In particular, if $n = 15$, we sample 5 students from each of the newly chosen strata. We assume that the students in each stratum can be identified before samples are drawn.   ◆

Number of Strata.   It was pointed out that by stratifying we can increase the precision of the estimate. One can carry this logic to the maximum and try to have as many strata as the number of units in the sample. However, the reduction in the variance is not proportional to the increase in the number of strata. DesRaj (1968, p. 73) illustrates this with an example which will be given below.

Let x be a random variable distributed uniformly in $(0, a)$. Let

$$y = x + \epsilon$$

where x and ϵ are uncorrelated. Let g strata of equal width, namely a/L be formed. Then

$$\sigma_y^2 = \sigma_x^2 + \sigma_\epsilon^2$$

and the variance in hth stratum is

$$\sigma_{x,h}^2 \doteq \frac{1}{12}\left(\frac{a}{L}\right)^2 .$$

Also $W_h = \frac{N_h}{N} = \frac{1}{L}, h = 1, \ldots, L.$

If the sample is allocated equally to the strata (i.e., $n_h = n/L$), the variance of the estimate of the population mean is given by

$$\frac{L}{n}\sum W_h^2 \sigma_{y,h}^2 = \frac{L}{n}\sum L^{-2}\left(\frac{a^2}{12L^2} + \sigma_\epsilon^2\right)$$

$$= \frac{a^2}{12nL^2} + \frac{\sigma_\epsilon^2}{n} .$$

Now, if the number of strata is increased by a factor of m, the variance based on mL strata is

$$\frac{a^2}{12nm^2L^2} + \frac{\sigma_\epsilon^2}{n}$$

where the first component has decreased by increasing the number of strata, whereas the second component remains the same. If m is large, the second component will be significant and the first component will be insignificant. Hence, the precision of the estimate will not be effected.

5.16   OPTIMAL CHOICE OF L AND N

It remains to optimize with respect to n and L, given that allocation of sample sizes is optimal in the Neyman sense and that the strata have been constructed optimally. A heuristic discussion of the best choice of L is available in Dalenius (1957) and Cochran (1977). Taga (1953, 1967) considers optimization with respect to L and n for some specific populations; however, neither the construction of strata nor the allocation of sample sizes is optimal. Serfling (1968) considers the optimal choice of L and n for fixed cost. This will be discussed below.

Let the cost function be of the form

$$C = c_0 + c_1 n + \psi(L)$$

where c_0 denotes the overhead cost, c_1 is the cost per sample unit and $\psi(L)$ denotes the cost of forming L strata. We further assume that $\psi(t) \geq 0$, increasing in t and differentiable. Linear ψ will be of interest. So, we wish to

$$\text{minimize } ka^2/nL^2 \quad (\text{or } (nL^2)^{-1})$$

subject to fixed cost C. Then consider

$$H(L) = (nL^2)^{-1} + \lambda (c_0 + c_1 n + \psi(L) - C)$$

$$\frac{\partial H}{\partial L} = 0 \text{ gives } n^{-1}(-2)L^{-3} + \lambda\psi'(L) = 0$$

$$\text{i.e.,} \lambda n L^3 \psi'(L) = 2$$

$$\frac{\partial H}{\partial n} = 0 \text{ gives } - n^{-2}L^{-2} + c_1\lambda = 0$$

$$\text{i.e.,} c_1 \lambda n^2 L^2 = 1.$$

Hence
$$n = L\psi'(L)/2c_1 .$$

Substituting this in the expression for C, we obtain the differential equation

$$C = c_0 + \frac{1}{2}L\psi'(L) + \psi(L) .$$

After solving for L, we can solve for n.

If

$$\psi(L) = c_0' + c_2 L^m \quad (m > 0)$$

and

$$d_i = (C - c_0 - c_0')/c_i \qquad (i = 1, 2).$$

Then

$$C = c_0 + \frac{1}{2}L(c_2 m L^{m-1}) + c_2 L^m + c_0'.$$

That is

$$L = \left(\frac{2}{m+2}d_2\right)^{1/m}$$

and

$$n = \frac{m}{m+2}d_1.$$

Hence

$$\frac{n}{L} \doteq \left(\frac{m}{m+2}d_1\right) \bigg/ \left(\frac{2}{m+2}d_2\right)^{1/m}.$$

Special Case. $m = 1$ (i.e., ψ is linear)

$$L = 2d_2/3, \qquad n = d_1/3, \qquad n/L = c_2/2c_1.$$

EXAMPLE 5.8

If $C^* = 10n + 200L$ (i.e., $C^* = C - c_0 - c_0'$, $c_1 = 10$, $c_2 = 200$),

$$L = C^*/300, \qquad n = C^*/30, \qquad n/L = 10,$$

where C^* is the total budget above overhead costs.   ◆

5.17   OPTIMAL CHOICE OF L AND N VIA A REGRESSION VARIABLE

Suppose there exists another variable x whose density $g(x)$ is known, x is highly correlated with y, and the regression of y on x is linear and is given by

$$y = \alpha + \beta x + e$$

such that $E(e|x) = 0$, $E(xe) = 0$, and $\text{var}(e|x) = \sigma_e^2$. Since $\sigma_y^2 = \beta^2\sigma_x^2 + \sigma_e^2$, the optimal points $x_i (i = 1, \ldots, L-1)$ based on x are obtained by minimizing

$$n^{-1}\left[\sum_{h=1}^{L} W_h\left(\beta^2\sigma_{x,h}^2 + \sigma_{e,h}^2\right)\right]^2.$$

The resulting minimizing equations will be too complicated to solve for $x_1, \ldots, x_{L-1}$. However, we can proceed approximately as before by the cum$\sqrt{g(x)}$ rule. We define K_x, K_x^* corresponding to $g(x)$ and $k_x^* = K_x K_x^*$.

Now assume that $\sigma_{eh}^2 = \sigma_e^2$ for all h. Then

$$\text{var}(\bar{y}_{st}) = \text{var}(\alpha + \beta \bar{x}_{st} + \bar{e}_{st})$$

$$= \beta^2 \text{var}(\bar{x}_{st}) + \frac{L}{n}\sigma_e^2 \sum_{h=1}^{L} W_h^2$$

because $n_h = n/L$. Now $\text{var}(\bar{x}_{st})$ can be approximated by $\text{var}(\bar{x}_{st}) = k_x\sigma_x^2/nL^2$. Thus

$$\text{var}(\bar{y}_{st}) = \beta^2\frac{k_x\sigma_x^2}{nL^2} + \frac{L}{n}(1 - \rho^2)\sigma_y^2 \sum_{h=1}^{L} W_h^2 .$$

where ρ denotes the correlation between x and y. Now $L\sum_{h=1}^{L} W_h^2 \doteq L\sum_{h=1}^{L} \eta_h^2 \times (x_h - x_{h-1})^2$, where η_h is the mean value of $g(x)$ in the hth stratum. So

$$L\sum_{h=1}^{L} W_h^2 \doteq L\sum A_h\eta_h^{\frac{3}{2}}(x_h - x_{h-1}) \qquad \text{(where } A_h \text{ is specified on p. 97)}$$

$$\doteq K_x \sum_{1}^{L} \eta_h^{\frac{3}{2}}(x_h - x_{h-1})$$

$$= K_x \int_a^b [g(x)]^{\frac{3}{2}}dx$$

$$= K_x K_x^* = k_x^* .$$

Noting that $\beta^2\sigma_x^2 = \rho^2\sigma_y^2$ and $\sigma_e^2 = (1 - \rho^2)\sigma_y^2$, we have

$$\text{var}(\bar{y}_{st}) = \frac{\sigma_y^2}{n}\left[\frac{\rho^2 k_x}{L^2} + k_x^*(1 - \rho^2)\right] = \frac{\sigma_y^2 k_x^*(1 - \rho^2)}{n}\left(\frac{\gamma}{L^2} + 1\right)$$

where $\gamma = k_x\rho^2/k_x^*(1 - \rho^2)$. Now minimize $(\gamma L^{-2} + 1)/n$ subject to the total cost $C \leq C_0$ and obtain $n = (\gamma L + L^3)\psi'(L)/2c_1\gamma$, where L is the root of the equation

$$2\gamma[C_0 - c_0 - \psi(L)] - (\gamma L + L^3)\psi'(L) = 0.$$

It should be noted that in the case of stratification on the y variable the optimal values of n and L do not depend on the distribution of y. However, if the stratification is on the x variable, they do depend on k_x, k_x^*, and ρ. However, k_x and k_x^* can be obtained from the density of x. So, we must specify only ρ in order to obtain the optimal values of L and n.

Special Case.   Let $\psi(L) = c_0' + c_2 L^m$. Then

$$n = (\gamma L + L^3) m c_2 L^{m-1} / 2 c_1 \gamma .$$

and L is the root of the equation

$$m L^{m+2} + (m + 2)\gamma L^m - 2\gamma d_2 = 0$$

where $d_i = (C - c_0 - c_0')/c_i \, (i = 1, 2)$.

By Descartes' rule of signs the equation in L has exactly one positive real root. If $\psi(L)$ is linear (i.e., $m = 1$) the equations simplify to

$$L^3 + 3\gamma L - 2\gamma d_2 = 0$$

$$n = (\gamma L + L^3) c_2 / 2 c_1 \gamma .$$

Note that we could determine n from the equation

$$n = d_1 - (c_2 / c_1) L .$$

For a variety of densities $g(x)$ (including the rectangular, exponential, and normal) we can reasonably assume that $1 \le k_x / k_x' \le 1.75$ (see Serfling (1968, p. 1307)), and we can assume that $0.8 \le \rho \le 0.95$.

Thus for several situations, γ will satisfy

$$1.8 \le \gamma \le 16 .$$

When $c_1 = 10$, $c_2 = 200$, i.e., $C^* = 10n + 200L$ (values considered by Dalenius (1957, p. 191)), Serfling (1968, p. 1307) finds that the values of L and n are essentially the same for $\gamma = 5$ and 10. For instance, $C^* = 2000$ yields $L = 4$, $n = 120$ when $r = 5$ or 10.

That is, the optimal values of L and n are robust $w \cdot r \cdot t \cdot$ small errors in the value of ρ.

The optimal number of strata is considerably lower for the covariate case than for the no-covariable case.

Serfling (1968) compares stratified and simple random sampling and, on the basis of numerical study, finds that the gain due to stratification is far less in the covariate case than in the no-covariate case.

5.18   CONTROLLED SAMPLING

Let N denote the size of the population of fields. Suppose we draw a simple random sample of size 2 without replacement. The fields are of two types, those that are irrigated and the rest that are not. Also suppose we are interested in estimating the average yield per field. If the random sample consists of both irrigated or both unirrigated fields, the resultant estimate will not be very precise. Hence, we may wish to stratify the population into irrigated and unirrigated fields and draw a random sample of size one from each of the strata. Such sampling is called *preferred* or *controlled sampling*.   By this sampling we minimize the selection probabilities of nonpreferred samples. Similarly if a mayor appoints a citizens' committee which is supposed to articulate the concern in his or her town, he or she makes sure that all the minorities are represented in the committee. This calls for controlled selection. Even within each stratum, we may have to further control the selection of the subsample. Goodman and Kish (1950) were the first to propose the technique of controlled selection. Avadhani and B. V. Sukhatme (1965, 1967) have given a technique of controlled sampling with equal probabilities and without replacement which minimizes the risk of drawing nonpreferred samples. They (1973) also provide some simplified procedures of controlled selection that are useful in practical situations.

5.19   MULTIPLE STRATIFICATION

If the response variables are related to one single auxiliary variable x for which information is available for all population units, then stratification and optimum allocation can be made using the data on x. However, all the responses of interest may not be related to a single supplementary variable. For example, acreage under corn is likely to be related to geographical or cultivated area. In such cases, the units are first grouped into primary strata with respect to the most important stratification variable; then, within each of the primary strata, secondary or substrata are constructed according to another supplementary variable, etc. This method is called *multiple stratification* or *deep stratification*.

When once the multiple strata are formed, allocation of the sample sizes may be made on the basis of each of the stratification variables according to the Neyman allocation. However, the sample size n may not warrant sampling from each substratum. Then the problem is how to design the sample and come up with proper estimates. To fix ideas, let us consider two stratification variables A and B. For simplicity let there be L substrata in each of the variables A and B, and let each substratum or cell in the population contain M units. Suppose we wish to take one observation in L of the substrata. In order that each substratum of variable A and each substratum of variable B be represented, we use the Latin-square design, which is as follows. Select one cell at random from the first row and delete

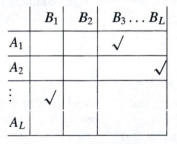

from the population the $L-1$ cells occurring in the column to which the selected cell belongs. From the second row select one cell at random from the $L-1$ remaining cells and exclude from the population the $L-1$ cells that occur in the column to which the second selection belongs, and so on. Thus we end up with L cells and within each cell select one unit at random.

Let y_{rc} be the response on the unit in the sample (r, c)th cell occurring in the rth row and cth column. Then an unbiased estimate of the population total is

$$\hat{Y} = LM \sum_r y_{rc}.$$

One can obtain an explicit expression for the variance of $\hat{Y}$. For details see, for instance, DesRaj (1968, pp. 81–83).

If the variables A and B are not amenable to the same number of strata and if the sample size n is smaller than $L_1 L_2$ (where L_1 is the number of strata on A and L_2 is the number of strata on B), one can come up with a sampling design using the Latin-square ideas. For details see DesRaj (1968, section 9.6) or Sukhatme et al. (1984, section 4.11). This design was originally proposed by Bryant, Hartley, and Jessen (1960).

5.20 INTERPENETRATING SUBSAMPLING

If a sample consists of two or more subsamples drawn according to the same sampling scheme, such that each subsample yields an estimate of the parameter of interest, the subsamples are called interpenetrating subsamples. The subsamples may or may not be independent. However, it is desirable for them to be independent, because one can easily obtain an unbiased estimate of the variance of the composite estimator, even if the sample design is complicated and the expression for the variance of the composite estimator is not simple. Let $t_1, \ldots, t_k$ be k unbiased estimates of the parameter θ based on k independent interpenetrating subsamples. Then an unbiased estimator of θ is given by

$$\hat{\theta} = \frac{1}{k} \sum_{i=1}^{k} t_i = \bar{t} \quad \text{(say)}.$$

Then

$$E(\hat{\theta}) = \theta$$

and

$$\widehat{\text{var}}\,(\bar{t}) = \frac{1}{k(k-1)} \sum_{i=1}^{k} (t_i - \bar{t})^2$$

because

$$E\left\{\widehat{\text{var}}\,(\bar{t})\right\} = \frac{1}{k(k-1)} E\left\{\sum_{i=1}^{k} (t_i - \theta)^2 - k(\bar{t} - \theta)^2\right\}$$

$$= \frac{1}{k(k-1)} \left[\sum_{i=1}^{k} \text{var}\,(t_i) - k\,\text{var}\,\bar{t}\right]$$

$$= \frac{1}{k(k-1)} (k^2 - k)\,\text{var}\,(\bar{t}) = \text{var}\,\bar{t}.$$

Furthermore, if each of the estimators is symmetrically distributed about θ, then

$$P(t_{(1)} < \theta < t_{(k)}) = 1 - \left(\frac{1}{2}\right)^{k-1}$$

where $t_{(1)} = \min(t_1, \ldots, t_k)$ and $t_{(k)} = \max(t_1, \ldots, t_k)$, thus yielding a confidence interval.

The method of interpenetrating subsampling was developed by Mahalanobis (1946), and it has been extensively used in surveys for assessing sampling and nonsampling errors. The subsamples could arise due to different teams of workers. Deming (1960) has used this method for obtaining quick estimates of sampling variance when we have several sampling schemes.

In stratified sampling, suppose that we have k independent interpenetrating subsamples of the same size from each stratum, drawn according to the same sampling design, such as simple random sampling, systematic sampling, or probability proportional to size. Let $\hat{Y}_{s,i}$ be the unbiased estimator of the total of the sth stratum based on the ith subsample ($i = 1, \ldots, k$ and $s = 1, \ldots, L$). Then an unbiased estimator of the sth stratum total is given by

$$\hat{Y}_s = k^{-1} \sum_{i=1}^{k} \hat{Y}_{s,i}.$$

Also an unbiased estimator of the variance of $\hat{Y}_s$ is

$$\widehat{\text{var}}(\hat{Y}_s) = \frac{1}{k(k-1)} \sum_{i=1}^{k} (\hat{Y}_{si} - \hat{Y}_s)^2.$$

Hence, an unbiased estimator of the population total Y and its variance estimator are given by

$$\hat{Y} = \sum_{s=1}^{L} \hat{Y}_s = \frac{1}{k} \sum_{s=1}^{L} \sum_{i=1}^{k} \hat{Y}_{si}$$

and

$$\widehat{\text{var}}_1(\hat{Y}) = \sum_{s=1}^{L} \widehat{\text{var}}(\hat{Y}_s) = \frac{1}{k(k-1)} \sum_{s=1}^{L} \sum_{i=1}^{k} (\hat{Y}_{si} - \hat{Y}_s)^2.$$

One can obtain another unbiased estimator of $\text{var}(\hat{Y})$ which is easier to compute and is based on the k estimates of the population total derived by adding the estimates of $\hat{Y}_s$ separately for the k subsamples. The k subsample estimates of Y_s that are independent and unbiased estimates having the same sampling variance, are defined by

$$\tilde{Y}_i = \sum_{s=1}^{L} \hat{Y}_{si}, \qquad i = 1, \ldots, k$$

are k unbiased estimates of Y having the same variance.

Then

$$\hat{Y} = \frac{1}{k}\sum_{i=1}^{k}\tilde{Y}_i$$

is also unbiased for Y and $\mathrm{var}\,(\hat{Y}) = \frac{1}{k}\,\mathrm{var}\,(\tilde{Y}_i)$. Hence

$$\widehat{\mathrm{var}}_2\,(\hat{Y}) = \frac{1}{k(k-1)}\sum_{i=1}^{k}(\tilde{Y}_i - \hat{Y})^2 .$$

Murthy (1962) has shown that $\widehat{\mathrm{var}}_1\,(\hat{Y})$ is more efficient than $\widehat{\mathrm{var}}_2\,(\hat{Y})$, obtaining

$$\mathrm{var}\left\{\widehat{\mathrm{var}}_1\,(\hat{Y})\right\} = \frac{1}{k^3(k-1)}\sum_{s=1}^{L}\{(k-1)\mu_{4s} + (3-k)\mu_{2s}^2\}$$

and

$$\mathrm{var}\left\{\widehat{\mathrm{var}}_2\,(\hat{Y})\right\} = \mathrm{var}\left\{\widehat{\mathrm{var}}_1\,(\hat{Y})\right\} + \frac{4}{k^2(k-1)}\sum\sum_{r<s}\mu_{2r}\mu_{2s}$$

where μ_{2s} and μ_{4s} are the second and fourth moments of the estimate $\hat{Y}_{si}$. Thus the loss of efficiency in using $\widehat{\mathrm{var}}_2\,(\hat{Y})$ instead of $\widehat{\mathrm{var}}_1\,(\hat{Y})$ is given by

$$\frac{\mathrm{var}\{\widehat{\mathrm{var}}_2\,(\hat{Y})\} - \mathrm{var}\{\widehat{\mathrm{var}}_1\,(\hat{Y})\}}{\mathrm{var}\{\widehat{\mathrm{var}}_1\,(\hat{Y})\}} = \frac{k}{k-1}\frac{4\sum\sum_{r<s}^{L}\mu_{2r}\mu_{2s}}{\sum_{s=1}^{L}(\beta_s - \frac{k-3}{k-1})\mu_{2s}^2}$$

where $\beta_s = \mu_{4s}/\mu_{2s}^2$.

If the distribution of the estimate within each stratum is approximately normal, then one can set $\beta_s \doteq 3$ for all s. Then the loss of efficiency becomes

$$\left(\sum_{1}^{L}\mu_{2s}\right)^2\left(\sum_{s=1}^{L}\mu_{2s}^2\right)^{-1} - 1 .$$

Furthermore, if we can assume that the variance of the estimate in each stratum is the same, then the loss in efficiency is equal to $L - 1$, which can be substantial if L is large.

■ PROBLEMS

5.1   In 1987 the Survey Research Center (SRC)*at the University of Kentucky conducted a telephone survey consisting of 745 people and obtained the following data (post-stratified) as response to the question:

"Should children with AIDS virus be allowed to go to school?"

Level of Education	Sample Size	# of Yeses
High school drop-out	181	86
High school diploma	450	259
College diploma	114	84
Total	745	429

Religious Affiliation	Sample Size	# of Yeses
Protestant	582	313
Catholic	105	75
Other	58	41
Total	745	429

Political Affiliation	Sample Size	# of Yeses
Republican	153	83
Democrat	408	233
Not registered	150	90
Others	34	23
Total	745	429

Obtain the stratified estimate of the true proportion of yeses using the three different stratification variables. (According to 1990 census, in Kentucky, 49.6% are Democrats, 21.7% are Republicans, 26.2% are not registered, and 2.5% are others. For level of education, use $W_1 = 0.3$, $W_2 = 0.5$, $W_3 = 0.2$ and for religious affiliation use $W_1 = 0.6$, $W_2 = 0.3$, $W_3 = 0.1$.)

5.2   In 1987 the SRC at the University of Kentucky conducted a survey consisting of 745 people and obtained the following data (poststratified) in response to the statement:

"I am well informed about AIDS."

*University of Kentucky Survey Research Center, Spring 1987 Kentucky Survey.

LEVEL OF EDUCATION

	High School Drop-out	High School Diploma	College Diploma	TOTAL
1. Strongly Agree	9	42	23	74
2. Agree	76	240	70	386
3. Disagree	71	137	18	226
4. Strongly Disagree	7	11	1	19
5. Don't Know	18	17	1	36
6. Refuse to Answer	0	3	1	4
Total	181	450	114	745

RELIGIOUS AFFILIATION

	Protestant	Catholic	Other	Total
1	54	10	10	74
2	296	64	26	386
3	182	27	17	226
4	16	2	1	19
5	33	0	3	36
6	1	2	1	4
Totals	582	105	58	745

By computing the standard errors of the estimates of proportion who agree (categories 1 and 2), determine which method of poststratification is better.

5.3   In 1987 the SRC at the University of Kentucky conducted a telephone survey of 745 individuals in the state of Kentucky and obtained the following data in response to the statement:

"There is no chance of getting AIDS from public toilets."

LEVEL OF EDUCATION

	High School Drop-out	High School Diploma	College Diploma	TOTAL
1. Strongly Agree	6	33	24	63
2. Agree	35	176	58	269
3. Disagree	60	126	16	202
4. Strongly Disagree	5	18	2	25
5. Don't Know	74	93	13	180
6. Refuse to Answer	1	4	1	6
Total	181	450	114	745

RELIGIOUS AFFILIATION

	Protestant	Catholic	Other	Total
1	39	14	10	63
2	206	45	18	269
3	163	25	15	202
4	19	2	4	25
5	152	18	10	180
6	4	1	1	6
Totals	582	105	58	745

By computing the standard errors of the estimates of proportion who agree (categories 1 and 2), determine which method of poststratification is better.

5.4   For the following data:

$df = f_i$	60	60	60	60	60	60	60	60
mean	3.88	4.02	3.63	3.97	4.15	3.50	4.10	4.45
s_h: sample standard deviation	0.78	0.89	0.84	0.55	0.76	0.85	0.77	0.67

obtain the approximate distribution of $(\bar{y}_{st} - \bar{Y})/s(\bar{y}_{st})$ and hence obtain a 95% confidence interval for $\bar{Y}$. (Assume that $W_1 = \cdots = W_8 = 1/8$.)

5.5   In a certain community, 60% are white, 15% are black, and 25% are other minorities. We wish to obtain the proportion of people having a rare blood type. We wish to take a sample of 50 residents. Obtain a Neyman allocation of this sample to the three groups assuming that $P_1 = 0.05$, $P_2 = 0.03$, and $P_3 = 0.02$. Also evaluate min var (p_{st}).

5.6   A certain city has $N = 500,000$ people, of whom 60% are white, 20% black, and 20% others. We wish to estimate the average income for that city. Assume that the variances within the three strata are $S_1 = 5000$, $S_2 = 500$, $S_3 = 100$. We wish to draw a total sample of $n = 100$ people from this city. Via Neyman allocation obtain the subsample sizes.

5.7   A survey conducted in fall 1995 by the Survey Research Center* at the University of Kentucky obtained the following data on the amount of money (in dollars) earned in the last 12 months from odd jobs and extra work.

Strata:	[0 – 100) (dollars)	(100 – 1000]	(1000 – 10,000]	> 10,000
	0	150	1200	10,400
	20	200	1500	12,000
	25	250	1700	14,000
	30	300	2000	15,000
	40	350	2500	40,000
	50	400	3000	
	60	500	3500	
	75	700	4000	
	98	800	4300	
	100	998	5000	
		998	6000	
		999	7000	
		1,000	8000	
			9998	
			10,000	
n_i	10	12	15	5

Find the stratified mean and its standard error.
Hint: Use $W_1 = 0.17$, $W_2 = W_3 = 0.39$, and $W_4 = 0.05$.

5.8   Let $L = 3$, $N_1 = 50$, $N_2 = 80$, $N_3 = 120$, $S_1 = 20$, $S_2 = 10$, $S_3 = 15$. Assume that $c_1 = c_2 = c_3 = c$. Obtain a Neyman (or modified Neyman) allocation of $n = 150$ to the three strata. Also compute min var $(\bar{y}_{st})$.

5.9   Evaluate the gain in precision by stratified sampling relative to proportional sampling for the following case:

$$L = 3, \quad W_1 = 0.6, \quad W_2 = 0.2, \quad W_3 = 0.3$$

and

$$P_1 = 0.2, \quad P_2 = 0.25 \quad \text{and} \quad P_3 = 0.1.$$

Compute the variance of the poststratified mean for the configuration given in Problem 5.7.

5.10   In a large city we are interested in estimating the proportion of people who are in favor of capital punishment. We draw a simple random sample of size $n = 100$ and find $n_1 = $ number of white are 60, $n_2 = $ number of black are 20, and $n_3 = $ others $= 20$. We also find 70% of the white, 40% of the black, and 50% of the rest in the sample are in favor of

---

*University of Kentucky Servey Research Center, Fall 1995 Kentucky Survey

capital punishment. Assuming that $W_1 = 0.70$, $W_2 = 0.15$, and $W_3 = 0.15$, and ignoring the finite population correction, obtain a 95% confidence interval for the poststratified estimate of the mean of the true proportion of people in that city who are in favor of capital punishment.

5.11 Assume that 36 tests were carried out on the tensile strengths of screwdrivers of 34 valve caps produced by a certain manufacturing company and are classified as follows:

Tensile Strength	Frequency
[130 – 140)	6
140 – 150	7
150 – 160	13
160 – 170	5
170 – 180	3
	34

Following the cum $\sqrt{f}$ method, determine the strata with $L = 2$.

5.12 We wish to estimate the amount of money spent by a household on grocers per week in a certain city. The city has three groups of people: urban, suburban, and rural. It costs $9, $16, and $25, respectively, to sample a household in the urban, suburban, and rural locations. Assume that $W_1 = 0.6$, $W_2 = 0.30$, and $W_3 = 0.1$ and $S_1 = \$10$, $S_2 = \$12$, $S_3 = \$15$. If we wish to take a total sample of $n = 100$, how do you allocate them optimally to the three groups?

5.13 One hundred residents of a certain suburb were asked whether they are in favor of increasing property taxes for the betterment of schools. We have the following responses:

	Male	Female
n_i	55	45
yes	30	25

Estimate the proportion of residents who are in favor of the tax increase and find a 95% confidence interval for the true proportion.

5.14 A certain electronic store buys 9-volt batteries from two different manufacturers: A and B. A produces 5% defectives and B produces 1% defectives. In a random sample of size $n = 100$, we found the following results:

	A	B
n_i	60	40
defectives	5	1

(a) Estimate the true proportion of defectives in the stock of 9-volt batteries in the electronic store, and obtain a 95% confidence interval for the same, using the simple random sample approach. (Assume that $W_1 = W_2 = 1/2$.)

(b) Answer the same questions as in (a) using a stratified sampling approach.
Hint: Ignore the finite population correction.

(c) Which procedure is more precise?

5.15 Mars University wants to estimate, for this year, the total number of days used for sick leave among its 3000 staff and 2000 faculty members. From past data, it is surmised that the staff members use 20–200 days of sick leave and the faculty members use 0–120 days. A random sample of 100 employees is to be selected. Find the appropriate allocation of the sample of the two strata.

Hint: Use range $\doteq$ six times the standard deviation.

5.16 We wish to know how much money a company spends annually on its Web site building (including maintenance and update). The companies are stratified into three strata according to their annual sales. There are 50 large companies, 80 medium-size companies, and 300 small companies. According to historical data, the standard deviation in the strata are 20, 10, and 15, respectively (in thousands of dollars). We further assume that the sampling costs in each stratum are the same. Obtain a Neyman allocation of $n = 100$ to the three strata and also evaluate min var $(\bar{y}_{st})$.

5.17 Assume that tests were carried out on the deflation time of 40 airbags produced by GM. They are classified as follows:

Time (seconds)	frequency
(0.8 – 0.85]	4
0.85 – 0.9	7
0.9 – 0.95	9
0.95 – 1.0	11
1.0 – 1.05	5
1.05 – 1.10	4
	40

Following the cum$\sqrt{f}$ method, determine the strata with $L = 3$.

5.18 There are 77,853 public schools, of which 23% are in the city, 24% are in urban areas, 25% are in towns, and 28% are in rural areas. We wish to estimate the average income earned by teachers. Assume the variances within the strata are $S_1 = \$4000$, $S_2 = \$2500$, $S_3 = \$1850$, and $S_4 = \$2000$. We wish to draw a total SRS of $n = 1500$ schools. Use a Neyman allocation to obtain the subsample sizes.

5.19 We are interested in estimating the proportion of schools having access to the Internet. We draw an SRS of size $n = 876$ and find $n_1 = $ # of elementary schools $= 455$, $n_2 = $ # of secondary schools $= 421$. We also find that 30% of elementary schools and 49% of secondary schools have access. Assume $W_1 = .74$ and $W_2 = .26$ and, ignoring finite population correction, obtain a 95% confidence interval for the poststratified estimate of the true proportion of schools that have access to the Internet.

5.20 In 1995 the U.S. Department of Education commissioned a survey of 917 schools and obtained the following data (poststratified) in response to this question:

"Do you have access to the Internet?"

Size of Enrollment	Sample Size	# of Yeses
< 300	181	71
300 – 999	537	279
≥ 1000	199	137
TOTAL	917	487

Metropolitan Status	Sample Size	# of Yeses
City	208	98
Urban	230	136
Town	237	111
Rural	242	116
TOTAL	917	461

Geographic Region	Sample Size	# of Yeses
NE	162	96
SE	206	91
Central	269	140
West	280	134
TOTAL	917	461

(For Enrollment Size, $W_1 = .27$, $W_2 = .64$, $W_3 = .09$; for Metropolitan Status, $W_1 = .23$, $W_2 = .24$, $W_3 = .25$, $W_4 = .28$; and for Geographic Region, $W_1 = .18$, $W_2 = .21$, $W_3 = .31$, $W_4 = .30$.) Which method of poststratification is better?

■ REFERENCES

5.1 Aoyama, H. (1954). A study of the stratified random sampling. *Ann. Inst. Statist. Math.* **6**, 1–36.

5.2 Avadhani, M. S. and Sukhatme, B. V. (1965). Controlled simple random sampling. *J. Ind. Soc. Agri. Statist.* **17**, 34–42.

5.3 Avadhani, M. S. and Sukhatme, B. V. (1967). Controlled sampling with varying probabilities with and without replacement. *Aust. J. Statist.* **9**, 8–15.

5.4 Avadhani, M. S. and Sukhatme, B. V. (1973). Controlled sampling with equal probabilities and without replacement. *Internat. Statist. Rev.* **41**, 175–182.

5.5 Bryant, E. C., Hartley, H. O., and Jessen, R. J. (1960). Design and estimation in two-way stratification. *J. Amer. Statist. Assoc.* **55**, 105–124.

5.6 Cochran, W. G. (1961). Comparison of methods for determining strata boundaries. *Bull. Internat. Statist. Inst.* **38** (Part II), 345–358.

5.7 Cochran, W. (1977). *Sampling Techniques,* 3d ed. New York: John Wiley & Sons.

5.8 Dalenius, T. (1950). The problem of optimum stratification. *Skand. Aktuartidskr* **33**, 203–213.

5.9 Dalenius, T. (1957). *Sampling in Sweden.* Stockholm: Almquist and Wiksell.

5.10 Dalenius, T. and Gurney, M. (1951). The problem of optimum stratification II. *Skand. Aktuartidskr.* **34**, 133–148.

5.11 Dalenius, T. and Hodges, J. L. (1957). The choice of stratification points. *Skand. Aktuartidskr.* **3–4**, 198–203.

5.12 Dalenius, T. and Hodges, J. L. (1959). Minimum variance stratification. *J. Amer. Statist. Assoc.* **54**, 88–101, correction *JASA*, **58** (1963), p. 1161.

5.13 Deming, W. E. (1960). *Sampling Design in Business Research*. New York: John Wiley & Sons.

5.14 DesRaj (1968). *Sampling Theory*. New York: McGraw Hill Book Company.

5.15 Ekman, G. (1959). An approximation useful in univariate stratification. *Ann. Math. Statist.* **30**, 219–229.

5.16 Goodman, R. and Kish, L. (1950). Controlled selection—a technique in probability sampling. *J. Amer. Statist. Assoc.,* **45**, 350–372.

5.17 Hansen, M.H., and Hurwitz, W. N. (1943). On the theory of sampling from finite populations. *Ann. Math. Statist.* **14**, 333–362.

5.18 Hess, I., Sethi, V. K., and Balakrishnan, T. R. (1966). Stratification: A practical investigation. *J. Amer. Statist. Assoc.* **61**, 74–90.

5.19 Holt, D. and Smith, T. M. F. (1979) Post-stratification *J. Roy. Statist. Soc.* **A142**, 33–46.

5.20 Mahalanobis, P. C. (1946). Recent experiments in statistical sampling in the Indian Statistical Institute. *J. Roy. Statist. Soc.* **A109**, 325–378, reprinted in *Sankhyā* **20** (1958), 1–68.

5.21 Mahalanobis, P. C. (1952). Some aspects of the design of sample surveys. *Sankhyā* **12**, 1–7.

5.22 Murthy, M. N. (1962). Variance and confidence interval estimation *Sankhyā* **24**(B), 1–12.

5.23 Neyman, J. (1934). On the two different aspects of the representative method: The method of stratified sampling and the method of purposive selection. *J. Roy. Statist. Soc.* **97**, 558–606.

5.24 Rao, J. N. K. (1985). Conditional inference in survey sampling. *Survey Methodology*, **II**, No. 1, 15–31.

5.25 Satterthwaite, F. E. (1946). An approximate distribution of estimates of variance components. *Biometrics* **2**, 110–114.

5.26 Serfling, R. J. (1968). Approximately optimal stratification. *J. Amer. Statist. Assoc.* **63**, 1298–1309.

5.27 Sethi, V. K. (1963). A note on optimum stratification of populations for estimating the population means. *Aust. J. Statist.* **5**, 20–33.

5.28 Stephan, F. F. (1945). The expected value and variance of the reciprocal and other negative powers of a positive Bernoulli variate. *Ann. Math. Statist.* **16**, 50–61.

5.29 Sukhatme, P. V., Sukhatme, B. V., Sukhatme, S., and Ashok, C. (1984). *Sampling Theory of Surveys with Applications*, 3d ed., Ames (Iowa): Iowa State University Press.

5.30 Taga, Y. (1953). On optimum balancing between sample size and number of strata in subsampling. *Ann. Inst. Statist. Math.* (Tokyo) **4**, 95–102.

5.31 Taga, Y. (1967). On optimum stratification for the objective variable based on concomitant variables using prior information. *Ann. Inst. Statist. Math.* (Tokyo) **19**, 101–129.

5.32 Tschuprow, A. A. (1923). On the mathematical expectation of the moments of frequency distributions in the case of correlated observations. *Metron* **2**, 461–493, 646–680.

CHAPTER  6

RATIO ESTIMATORS

6.1 INTRODUCTION

Although a large amount of theory is available for statistical estimation, it is not amenable to sample survey purposes. In sample surveys we do not assume a parametric form for the response. So, we need to develop simple techniques that are applicable under a variety of distributions. For the response variable, the ratio estimates arise naturally in sample survey problems. Let x be an auxiliary variable. Then x could be the number of acres in the sample on which corn is grown and y could be the total produce of corn by the number of farms in the sample. Then y/x gives an estimate of the average production of corn per acre. An estimate of the population mean $\bar{Y}$ is given by

$$\hat{\bar{Y}}_R = \frac{y}{x}\,\bar{X}$$

where $\bar{X}$ denotes the population mean of the x's. Often we wish to estimate a ratio instead of a mean or total—for example, the ratio of corn acres to wheat acres.

EXAMPLE 6.1

The total population of greater Lexington (in the state of Kentucky) was 200,000 in 1980. In 1987 we took a census of two suburbs and the total was 76,000. In these two

116

suburbs the total population in 1980 was 72,000. What is the ratio estimate of the total population of greater Lexington in 1987?

$$\hat{Y}_R = \frac{76,000}{72,000} \times 200,000 = 211,111.$$

◆

6.2 VARIANCE OF THE RATIO ESTIMATE

It is almost impossible to find the distribution of a ratio estimator since the numerator and the denominator are both random. It is also clear that the ratio estimates are consistent. Invariably, ratio estimates are biased, although the bias goes to zero as the sample size increases. Furthermore, in large samples, the ratio estimates are normally distributed.

Result 6.1. Let $\hat{\bar{Y}}_R = \frac{\bar{y}}{\bar{x}}\bar{X}$, and $\hat{R} = \frac{\bar{y}}{\bar{x}}$. Then in a random sample of size (sufficiently large) n, we have

$$\text{var}(\hat{\bar{Y}}_R) \doteq \frac{(1-f)}{n}\left[\sum_{i=1}^{N}(y_i - Rx_i)^2/(N-1)\right]$$

and

$$\text{var}(\hat{R}) \doteq \frac{(1-f)}{n\bar{X}^2}\left[\sum_{i=1}^{N}(y_i - Rx_i)^2/(N-1)\right]$$

where $f = n/N$.

Proof: See Result 3.4. ∎

Let

$$\rho = \sum_{1}^{N}(y_i - \bar{Y})(x_i - \bar{X})/(N-1)S_x S_y$$

and

$$S_{xy} = \sum_{1}^{N}(y_i - \bar{Y})(x_i - \bar{X})/(N-1)$$

and $S_x^2 = S_{xx}$ and $S_y^2 = S_{yy}$. Then one can write

$$\text{var}(\hat{\bar{Y}}_R) \doteq \frac{(1-f)}{n}\left[S_y^2 + R^2 S_x^2 - 2RS_{yx}\right]$$

$$(\text{C.V. }\hat{\bar{Y}}_R)^2 = \frac{(1-f)}{n}\left[\frac{S_y^2}{\bar{Y}^2} + \frac{S_x^2}{\bar{X}^2} - \frac{2S_{yx}}{\bar{Y}}\bar{X}\right].$$

6.3   ESTIMATES FOR $\text{var}(\hat{\bar{Y}}_R)$

Replacing $\sum_1^N (y_i - Rx_i)^2 / (N-1)$ by $\sum_1^n (y_i - \hat{R}x_i)^2 / (n-1)$, we have

$$\widehat{\text{var}}(\hat{\bar{Y}}_R) = s_{\hat{\bar{Y}}_R}^2 = \frac{(1-f)}{n(n-1)} \sum_1^n (y_i - \hat{R}x_i)^2.$$

Similarly,

$$\widehat{\text{var}}(\hat{R}) = \frac{(1-f)}{n\bar{X}^2} \sum_1^n (y_i - \hat{R}x_i)^2 = \frac{(1-f)}{n\bar{X}^2} \left[s_y^2 + \hat{R}^2 s_x^2 - 2\hat{R} s_{yx} \right].$$

If $\bar{X}$ is unknown, we can have

$$\widehat{\text{var}}(\hat{R}) = \frac{(1-f)}{n\bar{x}^2} \left(s_y^2 + \hat{R}^2 s_x^2 - 2\hat{R} s_{yx} \right).$$

Next assume that the joint distribution of $\bar{x}$ and $\bar{y}$ is approximately bivariate normal. As a consequence

$$P \left\{ \frac{|\bar{y} - R\bar{x}|}{\left(\frac{N-n}{Nn}\right)^{1/2} \left\{ s_y^2 + R^2 s_x^2 - 2R s_{yx} \right\}^{1/2}} \leq z_{1-\alpha/2} \right\} \doteq 1 - \alpha$$

or

$$P \left\{ (\bar{y} - R\bar{x})^2 \leq z_{1-\alpha/2}^2 \left(\frac{N-n}{Nn} \right) \left(s_y^2 + R^2 s_x^2 - 2R s_{yx} \right) \right\} \doteq 1 - \alpha.$$

Alternatively, one can use Fieller's theorem.*

6.4   CONFIDENCE INTERVALS FOR R

Inverting the previous probability statement for R, one can easily obtain the confidence interval for R. Note that the limits could be imaginary.

Result 6.2.   The confidence interval for R is given by

$$\frac{\hat{R}}{(1 - z^2 C_{\bar{x}\bar{x}})} \left[(1 - z^2 C_{\bar{y}\bar{x}}) \pm z \left\{ C_{\bar{y}\bar{y}} + C_{\bar{x}\bar{x}} - 2C_{\bar{y}\bar{x}} - z^2 \left(C_{\bar{y}\bar{y}} C_{\bar{x}\bar{x}} - C_{\bar{y}\bar{x}}^2 \right) \right\}^{1/2} \right].$$

Ignoring z^2 terms (assuming the coefficients of z^2 are small), the confidence interval for R simplifies to

$$\hat{R} \left[1 \pm z \left\{ C_{\bar{y}\bar{y}} + C_{\bar{x}\bar{x}} - 2C_{\bar{y}\bar{x}} \right\}^{1/2} \right]$$

where $z = z_{1-\alpha/2}$, $C_{\bar{x}\bar{x}} = \frac{s_x^2}{n\bar{x}^2}$, $C_{\bar{y}\bar{x}} = \frac{s_{y,x}}{n\bar{x}\bar{y}}$, and $C_{\bar{y}\bar{y}} = \frac{s_y^2}{n\bar{y}^2}$.

---

*See *Biometrika* **24** (1932), 422–440

6.5   EFFICIENCY COMPARISONS

One can ask the following question. When does

$$\text{var}\left(\hat{\bar{Y}}_R\right) < \text{var}\left(\hat{\bar{Y}}\right)?$$

Recall that

$$\text{var}\left(\hat{\bar{Y}}_R\right) = \frac{(1-f)}{n}(S_y^2 + R^2 S_x^2 - 2R\rho S_x S_y)$$

and

$$\text{var}\left(\hat{\bar{Y}}\right) = \frac{(1-f)}{n}S_y^2$$

where

$$\rho = \sum_1^N (y_i - \bar{Y})(x_i - \bar{X})/(N-1)S_x S_y.$$

So,

$$\text{var}\left(\hat{\bar{Y}}_R\right) < \text{var}\left(\hat{\bar{Y}}\right) \qquad \text{if } R^2 S_x^2 - 2R\rho S_x S_y < 0.$$

That is when

$$\rho > \frac{RS_x}{2S_y} = \frac{S_x/\bar{X}}{2S_y/\bar{Y}} = \frac{C.V.(x)}{2C.V.(y)}.$$

P. S. R. S. Rao and J. N. K. Rao (1971) have studied the biases and the stability of the two estimators for a certain regression model.

EXAMPLE 6.2

McDonald Corporation wishes to estimate the average annual sales at its various Mc-Donald Restaurants for the current year. It takes a random sample of $n = 9$ and obtains the following data. Let x denote the receipts (in millions of dollars) for the previous year and y^* be the sales for the first quarter of the current year. Assume that $N = 10,000$ and $\bar{X} = 2.43$ million dollars.

Restaurant	x	y^*	$y = 4y^*$	$\hat{R}x$	$y - \hat{R}x$
1	2.1	0.6	2.4	2.33	0.07
2	3.2	0.9	3.6	3.56	0.04
3	5.1	1.4	5.6	5.67	-0.07
4	1.7	0.5	2.0	1.89	0.11
5	4.3	1.1	4.4	4.78	-0.38
6	1.9	0.5	2.0	2.11	-0.11
7	4.8	1.3	5.2	5.33	-0.13
8	2.3	0.7	2.8	2.56	0.24
9	1.6	0.5	2.0	1.78	0.12
Total	27.0	7.5	30.0		

Obtain a ratio estimate of the average annual sales for the current year at a McDonald Restaurant and also a 95% confidence interval for the same.

$$\sum_{1}^{9} x_i^2 = 96.54, \qquad \sum_{1}^{9} y_i^{*2} = 9.27, \qquad \sum_{1}^{9} x_i y_i^* = 26.46;$$

$$s_x^2 = \frac{9\Sigma x_i^2 - (\Sigma x_i)^2}{72} = \frac{139.86}{72} = 1.9425;$$

$$s_{y^*}^2 = \frac{9\Sigma y_i^{*2} - (\Sigma y_i^*)^2}{72} = \frac{9.18}{72} = 0.1275;$$

$$s_{y^*x} = \frac{9\Sigma y_i^* x_i - (\Sigma x_i)(\Sigma y_i^*)}{72} = \frac{35.64}{72} = 0.495;$$

$$\hat{R} = \bar{y}/\bar{x} = 30/27 = 1.1111$$

$$\hat{\bar{Y}}_R = \hat{R}\bar{X} = 2.7 \quad \text{(millions)}.$$

Ignoring the finite population correction,

$$\widehat{\text{var}}\,\hat{\bar{Y}}_R = \frac{1}{72}\Sigma(y_i - \hat{R}x_i)^2 = 0.2689/72 = 0.00373.$$

So,

$$s_{\hat{\bar{Y}}_R} = 0.061.$$

Hence, a 95% confidence interval for $\bar{Y}$ is $\hat{\bar{Y}}_R \pm (1.96)(0.061)$,

$$\text{i.e.,} 2.7 \pm 0.12$$

$$\text{i.e.,} (2.58, 2.82). \qquad \blacklozenge$$

Remark 6.1. We have made use of the definitional form for $\text{var}\,(\hat{\bar{Y}}_R)$. It is recommended to use the computational form.

6.6   AN OPTIMUM PROPERTY OF THE RATIO ESTIMATORS

A well-known result in regression analysis establishes the optimum property of the ratio estimator arising from infinite populations. Brewer (1963b) and Royall (1970) have shown that this result holds even in finite populations, provided the following assumptions are satisfied.

Assumptions:

1. The relation between y_i and x_i is a straight line passing through the origin.

2. The variance of y_i for given x_i is proportional to x_i.

A linear estimator for Y is of the form $\sum_1^n l_i y_i$ where the l_i do not depend on y_i but may depend on x_i. Furthermore, the l_i's are subject to the constraint

$$E \left(\sum_{i=1}^n l_i y_i \right) = Y$$

Brewer (1963b) and Royall (1970a) assume that there exists a super population from which a random sample (y_i, x_i), $i = 1, \ldots, N$ is drawn and y_i are related by

$$y_i = \beta x_i + \epsilon_i$$

where $E(\epsilon_i | x_i) = 0$, $\text{var}(\epsilon_i | x_i) = \lambda x_i$, $\text{cov}(\epsilon_i, \epsilon_j | x_i, x_j) = 0$, $i \neq j$, and ϵ_i is independent of $x_j (j \neq i)$. Throughout we assume that the x's are known.

So far (in the earlier chapters) we assumed that Y is a fixed quantity. However, under the super population model, we have

$$Y = \sum_{i=1}^N y_i = \beta X + \sum_{i=1}^N \epsilon_i, \qquad \text{where } X = \sum_1^N x_i,$$

and hence Y is a random variable.

Brewer and Royall define an estimate $\hat{Y}$ to be unbiased if $E(\hat{Y}) = E(Y)$ in repeated selections of the finite population of size N from the super population and a random sample of size n from this finite population. Such an estimator $\hat{Y}$ so that $E(\hat{Y}) = E(Y)$ is called *model unbiased*. Also note that $E(\hat{Y} - Y)^2 = \text{var}(\hat{Y} - Y)$ if $\hat{Y}$ is model unbiased, where the expectation is with respect to the model distribution. Then we have the following result.

Result 6.3.   Under the preceeding model, the ratio estimator $\hat{Y}_R = X\bar{y}/\bar{x}$ is the best linear unbiased estimator of the total for any sample (random or nonrandom), selected only according to the values of the x_i's.

Proof: From the assumed model, it follows that

$$Y = \beta X + \sum_1^N \epsilon_i, \qquad E(Y) = \beta X.$$

A linear estimator[1]

$$\hat{Y} = \Sigma l_i y_i = \beta \Sigma l_i x_i + \Sigma l_i \epsilon_i.$$

---

[1] It should be of the form $\sum_{j=1}^n l_j x_{i_j}$. Here without loss of generality we take $i_j = j$.

Then

$$E(\hat{Y}|x_1, \ldots, x_n) = \beta \Sigma_1^n l_i x_i$$

and

$$\text{var}\,(\hat{Y}|x_1, \ldots, x_n) = \lambda \Sigma l_i^2 x_i\,.$$

Thus $\hat{Y}$ is model unbiased if $\sum_1^n l_i x_i = X$ and we wish to minimize $\lambda \Sigma l_i^2 x_i$ subject to $\Sigma l_i x_i = X$. So consider

$$h(l_1, \ldots, l_n) = \lambda \Sigma l_i^2 x_i - 2\lambda c(\Sigma l_i x_i - X)\,.$$

$\partial h/\partial l_i = 0$ implies that $l_i x_i = cx_i$ or $l_i = c = X/n\bar{x}$, $(i = 1, \ldots, n)$ because $\Sigma l_i x_i = X$. Hence the BLUE (best linear unbiased estimator) of Y is $\hat{Y} = n\bar{y}X/n\bar{x} = X\bar{y}/\bar{x} = \hat{Y}_R$, the usual ratio estimator. The proof is complete. ∎

Next, if $l_i = X/n\bar{x}$, then

$$\hat{Y}_R - Y = \sum_1^n l_i \epsilon_i - \sum_1^N \epsilon_i = (X/n\bar{x}) \left(\sum_1^n \epsilon_i \right) - \sum_1^N \epsilon_i$$

$$= \frac{(X - n\bar{x})}{n\bar{x}} \sum_1^n \epsilon_i - \sum_{n+1}^N \epsilon_i\,.$$

Now

$$\text{var}\,(\hat{Y}_R|x_1, \ldots, x_n) = E\left\{ (\hat{Y}_R - \beta X)^2|x_1, \ldots, x_n \right\}$$

$$= E^*(\hat{Y}_R - Y)^2 + E^*(Y - \beta X)^2 + 2E^*(Y - \beta X)(\hat{Y}_R - Y)$$

where E^* denotes the conditional expectation given $x_1, \ldots, x_n$. Hence

$$E^*(Y - \beta X)^2 = E^* \left(\sum_1^N \epsilon_i \right)^2 = \sum_{i=1}^N \lambda x_i = \lambda X,$$

$$E^*(\hat{Y}_R - Y)^2 = \frac{(X - n\bar{x})^2}{(n\bar{x})^2} \lambda \sum_1^n x_i + \lambda(X - n\bar{x}) = \lambda(X - n\bar{x})X/n\bar{x}\,.$$

Next,

$$E^*(Y - \beta X)(\hat{Y}_R - Y) = E^* \left(\sum_{i=1}^N \epsilon_i \right) \left(\frac{(X - n\bar{x})}{n\bar{x}} \sum_1^n \epsilon_i - \sum_{i=n+1}^N \epsilon_i \right)$$

$$= \frac{(X - n\bar{x})}{n\bar{x}} \sum_1^n \lambda x_i - \sum_{i=n+1}^N \lambda x_i$$

$$= X - n\bar{x} - (X - n\bar{x}) = 0\,.$$

Thus

$$\text{var}\left(\hat{Y}_R | x_1, \ldots, x_n\right) = \lambda X + \lambda(X - n\bar{x})X/n\bar{x} = \lambda X^2/n\bar{x}.$$

Remark 6.2. So, if we are sampling nonrandomly (i.e., purposively) the $\text{var}(\hat{Y}_R | \cdots)$ can be minimized by selecting the n items in the population having the n largest x_i values.

Remark 6.3. Sometimes the variance of y_i for given x_i may be a function of x_i, say $v(x_i)$. Then the best linear unbiased estimator for Y is (see, for instance Royall, 1970a),

$$\hat{Y} = \frac{\Sigma^n w_i y_i x_i}{\Sigma^n w_i x_i^2} \cdot X, \qquad \text{where } w_i = 1/v(x_i).$$

In particular, if $v(x_i) = x_i^2$, we get the special case of Horwitz-Thompson estimator given by

$$\hat{Y} = \frac{X}{n} \sum_1^n (y_i/x_i).$$

$v(x_i) \equiv 1$ gives

$$\hat{Y} = \frac{\Sigma y_i x_i}{\Sigma x_i^2} X.$$

Properties of these latter estimators have been studied in great detail by Royall (1970).

A model-unbiased estimator of λ from the sample of size n can easily be shown to be

$$\hat{\lambda} = \sum_{i=1}^n (y_i - \hat{R} x_i)^2 / x_i (n - 1)$$

where $\hat{R} = \bar{y}/\bar{x}$. Substituting this value of $\hat{\lambda}$ into the $\text{var}(\hat{Y}_R | x_1, \ldots, x_n)$, we obtain a model-unbiased sample estimate of $\text{var}(\hat{Y}_R | x_1, \ldots, x_n)$.

6.7   BIAS IN THE RATIO ESTIMATE

In the following we will establish that the bias of a ratio estimate is of the order $O(n^{-1})$, whereas its standard error is of the order $O(n^{-1/2})$, and consequently the ratio of bias to standard error is of the order $O(n^{-1/2})$ and goes to zero if n becomes large. We can write

$$\hat{R} - R = (\bar{y}/\bar{x}) - R = (\bar{y} - R\bar{x})/\bar{x}.$$

Now we can expand

$$\bar{x}^{-1} = \left[\bar{X} + (\bar{x} - \bar{X})\right]^{-1} = (1/\bar{X})\left\{1 + \left(\frac{\bar{x} - \bar{X}}{\bar{X}}\right)\right\}^{-1} \doteq \frac{1}{\bar{X}}\left(1 - \frac{\bar{x} - \bar{X}}{\bar{X}}\right)$$

and consequently

$$\hat{R} - R \doteq \frac{(\bar{y} - R\bar{x})}{\bar{X}} \left(1 - \frac{\bar{x} - \bar{X}}{\bar{X}} \right) .$$

$$E(\bar{y} - R\bar{x}) = \bar{Y} - R\bar{X} = 0; \text{ hence}$$

$$E(\hat{R} - R) \doteq (\bar{X})^{-2} E \left\{ -\bar{y} (\bar{x} - \bar{X}) + R\bar{x} (\bar{x} - \bar{X}) \right\}$$

$$= (\bar{X})^{-2} E \left\{ -(\bar{y} - \bar{Y}) (\bar{x} - \bar{X}) + R (\bar{x} - \bar{X})^2 \right\}$$

$$= (\bar{X})^{-2} \frac{(1 - f)}{n} \left\{ -\rho S_x S_y + R S_x^2 \right\}$$

$$= \frac{(1 - f)}{n} R \{ C_{xx} - \rho C_{yx} \} .$$

We also have

$$\text{var} (\hat{R}) = \frac{(1 - f)}{n\bar{X}^2} \left(S_y^2 + R^2 S_x^2 - 2R\rho S_y S_x \right) .$$

Thus, we have

$$\frac{E(\hat{R} - R)}{\sigma_{\hat{R}}} = cv(\bar{x}) \frac{\left(R S_x - \rho S_y \right)}{\left(S_y^2 + R^2 S_x^2 - 2R\rho S_y S_x \right)^{1/2}} \leq cv(\bar{x})$$

since $S_y^2 \geq \rho^2 S_y^2$, where $cv(\bar{x}) = (1 - f)^{1/2} S_x / \sqrt{n} \bar{X}$. At this point we can substitute $\hat{R} = \hat{Y}_R / N\bar{X}$ and other sample estimates for the unknown quantities.

6.8 AN EXACT EXPRESSION FOR THE BIAS OF THE RATIO ESTIMATE

Hartley and Ross (1954) obtained an exact expression for the bias in $\hat{R}$. Consider

$$\text{cov} (\hat{R}, \bar{x}) = E \left(\frac{\bar{y}}{\bar{x}} \cdot \bar{x} \right) - E(\hat{R}) E(\bar{x})$$

$$= \bar{Y} - E(\hat{R}) \bar{X} .$$

Hence

$$E(\hat{R}) = \frac{\bar{Y}}{\bar{X}} - \frac{1}{\bar{X}} \text{cov} (\hat{R}, \bar{x}) ,$$

or

$$E(\hat{R}) - R = - \text{cov} (\hat{R}, \bar{x}) / \bar{X} .$$

Thus

$$\frac{\left| E(\hat{R}) - R \right|}{\sigma_{\hat{R}}} \leq \frac{\sigma_{\bar{x}}}{\bar{X}} = cv(\bar{x}) .$$

Since $\operatorname{cov}(\hat{\bar{Y}}_R, \bar{x}) = \bar{Y}\bar{X} - E(\hat{\bar{Y}}_R)E(\bar{x}) = -\bar{X}(E\hat{\bar{Y}}_R - \bar{Y})$, the same bound applies to the bias in $\hat{Y}_R$ and $\hat{\bar{Y}}_R$. As a rule of thumb, if $\operatorname{cv}(\bar{x})$ is less than 0.1, then the bias in $\hat{R}$ relative to its standard error is negligible.

6.9   RATIO ESTIMATES IN STRATIFIED RANDOM SAMPLING

The population total can be estimated in two ways. One is to estimate each stratum total by a ratio estimator and sum over the strata. That is, the separate ratio estimator is given by

$$\hat{Y}_{Rs} = \sum_h \frac{y_h}{x_h} X_h = \sum_h \frac{\bar{y}_h}{\bar{x}_h} X_h .$$

Result 6.4.   If the sampling is independent in each stratum, and each n_h is large,

$$\operatorname{var}(\hat{Y}_{Rs}) = \sum_h \operatorname{var}\left(\frac{\bar{y}_h}{\bar{x}_h} X_h\right) = \sum_h \operatorname{var}(\hat{Y}_{Rh})$$

where

$$\operatorname{var}\left(\frac{\bar{y}_h}{\bar{x}_h} X_h\right) = N_h^2 \frac{(1 - f_h)}{n_h}(S_{yh}^2 + R_h^2 S_{xh}^2 - 2R_h\rho_h S_{yh}S_{xh}) \qquad \text{(see p. 117)}$$

and $R_h = Y_h/X_h$ and ρ_h is the correlation in the hth stratum.

Remark 6.4.   If the number of strata is large and the n_h are small, then the bias in $\hat{Y}_{RS}$ relative to its standard error may not be negligible, because the bias will be of the order L and the standard error is of the order $L^{1/2}$. (As a special case one can assume that the bias and the variance in each stratum are independent of the stratum.)

An alternative estimate for Y would be the combined estimate. We have

$$\hat{Y}_{st} = \sum_h N_h \bar{y}_h , \qquad \hat{X}_{st} = \sum_h N_h \bar{x}_h .$$

So

$$\hat{Y}_{Rc} = \frac{\hat{Y}_{st}}{\hat{X}_{st}} X = \frac{\bar{y}_{st}}{\bar{x}_{st}} X$$

where

$$\bar{y}_{st} = \hat{Y}_{st}/N , \qquad \bar{x}_{st} = \hat{X}_{st}/N .$$

Notice that the combined estimate $\hat{Y}_{Rc}$ does not require the knowledge of X_h but only of their sum, namely X.

Following the method of Hartley and Ross (1954), one can readily obtain

$$E(\hat{R}_c) = R - \frac{1}{X} \operatorname{cov}(\hat{R}_c, \bar{x}_{st})$$

and hence

$$\frac{|\text{bias in } \hat{R}_c|}{\sigma_{\hat{R}_c}} = \frac{|\rho_{\hat{R}_c, \bar{x}_{st}} \sigma_{\bar{x}_{st}}|}{\bar{X}} \le \text{cv}(\bar{x}_{st}) .$$

So, the bias in $\hat{R}_c$ or $\hat{Y}_{RC}$ relative to their standard errors is negligible, provided $\text{cv}(\bar{x}_{st}) \le 0.1$.

Result 6.5.   If the total sample size n is large,

$$\text{var}(\hat{Y}_{RC}) = \sum_h N_h^2 \frac{(1 - f_h)}{n_h} (S_{yh}^2 + R^2 S_{xh}^2 - 2R\rho_h S_{yh} S_{xh}) .$$

Proof: Write

$$\hat{Y}_{R_c} - Y = \frac{N\bar{X}}{\bar{x}_{st}} (\bar{y}_{st} - R\bar{x}_{st}) \doteq N(\bar{y}_{st} - R\bar{x}_{st}) .$$

Now let $u_{hi} = y_{hi} - Rx_{hi}$. Then $\bar{y}_{st} - R\bar{x}_{st} = \bar{u}_{st}$, where $\bar{u}_{st}$ is the weighted mean of the variate u_{hi} in stratified sampling. Furthermore, the population mean $\bar{U}$ of u_{hi} is zero, since $R = \bar{Y}/\bar{X}$. Thus, using Result 5.3, we have

$$\text{var}(\hat{Y}_{R_c}) \doteq N^2 \text{var}(\bar{u}_{st}) = \sum_h \frac{N_h(N_h - n_h)}{n_h} S_{uh}^2$$

where

$$S_{uh}^2 = (N_h - 1)^{-1} \sum_{i=1}^{N_h} (u_{hi} - \bar{U}_h)^2$$

$$= (N_h - 1)^{-1} \sum_{i=1}^{N_h} \left[(y_{hi} - \bar{Y}_h) - R(x_{hi} - \bar{X}_h) \right]^2 .$$

After expanding the quadratic, we obtain the desired result. Notice that the difference between the $\text{var}(\bar{Y}_{RS})$ and $\text{var}(\bar{Y}_{RC})$ is that the former has R_h instead of R. ∎

6.10   COMPARISON OF $\hat{Y}_{RS}$ AND $\hat{Y}_{RC}$

$$\text{var}(\hat{Y}_{Rc}) - \text{var}(\hat{Y}_{Rs}) = \sum_h \frac{N_h^2(1 - f_h)}{n_h} \left[(R^2 - R_h^2)S_{xh}^2 - 2(R - R_h)\rho_h S_{yh} S_{xh} \right]$$

$$= \sum_h \frac{N_h^2(1 - f_h)}{n_h} \times$$

$$\left[(R - R_h)^2 S_{xh}^2 + 2(R_h - R)(\rho_h S_{yh} S_{xh} - R_h S_{xh}^2) \right] .$$

The last term on the right side is usually small. It is equal to zero if within each stratum the relation between y_{hi} and x_{hi} is a line passing through the origin (i.e., $y_i = \beta x_i, i = 1, \dots$, where $\beta = \rho S_y/S_x$).

Hence, unless R_h is a constant free of h, the $\hat{Y}_{Rs}$ is more precise than $\hat{Y}_{Rc}$. However, if the strata subsamples are small, the combined estimate is recommended.

In order to get sample estimates of these values, we replace R_h, R by their estimates, the stratum variances and covariances by their sample estimates.

6.11 OPTIMUM ALLOCATION WITH A RATIO ESTIMATOR

Consider

$$\mathrm{var}\,(\hat{Y}_{Rs}) = \sum_h \frac{N_h(N_h - n_h)}{n_h}\,S_{dh}^2$$

where

$$S_{dh}^2 = (N_h - 1)^{-1}\sum_{i=1}^{N_h} d_{hi}^2, \quad d_{hi} = y_{hi} - R_h x_{hi}\,.$$

Proceeding as in Chapter 5, the optimum n_h are

$$n_h \propto N_h S_{dh}/\sqrt{c_h}\,.$$

Typically S_{dh} are unknown. Consider the following special cases.

Special Cases.

1. $S_{dh} \propto \sqrt{\bar{X}_h}$. Then $n_h \propto N_h(\bar{X}_h/c_h)^{1/2}$.
2. If $S_{dh} \propto \bar{X}_h$, then $n_h \propto N_h \bar{X}_h/\sqrt{c_h}$.

If $\hat{Y}_{Rc}$ is used, similar optimum allocation formulae hold.

EXAMPLE 6.3

Let $L = 3$, $N_1 = 100$, $N_2 = 150$, $N_3 = 250$ (i.e., $N = 500$). Let $c_1 = 4$, $c_2 = 9$, and $c_3 = 25$. How do you allocate a sample of $n = 50$ to the three strata if $s_{d_1} = 15$, $s_{d_2} = 20$, and $s_{d_3} = 25$? Then

$$\begin{aligned}
N_1 s_{d_1}/\sqrt{c_1} &= 100\,(15)/2 = 750\\
N_2 s_{d_2}/\sqrt{c_2} &= 150\,(20)/3 = 1000\\
N_3 s_{d_3}/\sqrt{c_3} &= 250\,(25)/5 = 1250
\end{aligned}$$

$$\overline{\phantom{N_3 s_{d_3}/\sqrt{c_3} = 250\,(25)/5 = 1250}}$$

Total   3000

Hence

$$\begin{aligned}
n_1 &= 50(750/3000) = 50(0.25) = 12.5 \approx 12\\
n_2 &= 50(1000/3000) = 50/3 = 16.78 \approx 17\\
n_3 &= 50(1250/3000) = 50(0.417) = 20.8 \approx \underline{21}
\end{aligned}$$

◆

6.12   UNBIASED RATIO ESTIMATES

Ratio-type estimators that are unbiased or have smaller bias than $\hat{R}$ or $\hat{Y}_R$ are useful in sample surveys. In the following we give an unbiased estimate proposed by Hartley and Ross (1954). Let

$$\bar{r} = n^{-1} \sum_1^n r_i = n^{-1} \sum_1^n (y_i/x_i) .$$

Next

$$N^{-1} \sum_{i=1}^N r_i(x_i - \bar{X}) = \bar{Y} - \bar{X}(N^{-1} \sum_{i=1}^N r_i) = \bar{Y} - \bar{X}E(r_i)$$

$$= \bar{X}(R - E(r_i)) .$$

However, in simple random sampling $E(\bar{r}) = E(r_i)$. Hence the bias in

$$\bar{r} = E(\bar{r}) - R = -\sum_{i=1}^N r_i(x_i - \bar{X})/N\bar{X} .$$

Also, an unbiased estimate of

$$(N - 1)^{-1} \sum_{i=1}^N r_i(x_i - \bar{X})$$

is

$$(n - 1)^{-1} \sum_{i=1}^n r_i(x_i - \bar{x}) = n(\bar{y} - \bar{r}\bar{x})/(n - 1) .$$

Hence, the estimate $\bar{r}$ corrected for bias is

$$\hat{R}_{HR} = \bar{r} + \frac{n(N - 1)}{(n - 1)N\bar{X}} (\bar{y} - \bar{r}\bar{x}) .$$

The associated unbiased estimate of the population total $\hat{Y}$ is

$$\hat{Y}_{HR} = X\hat{R}_{HR} = \bar{r}X + \frac{n(N - 1)}{n - 1} (\bar{y} - \bar{r}\bar{x}) .$$

6.13   JACKKNIFE METHOD FOR OBTAINING A RATIO ESTIMATE WITH BIAS $O(N^{-2})$

Quenouille (1956) has proposed a *jackknife* method for getting rid of the term of order $1/n$ from the bias of an estimator. Durbin (1959) has pointed out the use of this method in reducing the bias of ratio estimates. This will be described below.

Ignore the fpc and assume that the expected value of R can be expanded as

$$E(\hat{R}) = R + (b_1/n) + (b_2/n^2) + \cdots .$$

Let $n = mg$ and the sample be divided at random into g groups of size m. Then

$$E(g\hat{R}) = gR + (b_1/m) + (b_2/gm^2) + \cdots .$$

Next, let $\hat{R}_j$ denote the ratio $\sum y / \sum x$, where the summation is on all values of the sample except the jth group. Since $\hat{R}_j$ is based on a simple random sample of size $m(g-1)$, we have

$$E(\hat{R}_j) = R + \frac{b_1}{m(g-1)} + \frac{b_2}{m^2(g-1)^2} + \cdots .$$

Hence

$$E\left[(g-1)\hat{R}_j\right] = (g-1)R + \frac{b_1}{m} + \frac{b_2}{m^2(g-1)} + \cdots .$$

Thus

$$E((g\hat{R} - (g-1)\hat{R}_j) = R - \frac{b_2}{g(g-1)m^2} + \cdots = R - \frac{b_2}{n^2}\frac{g}{g-1} + \cdots .$$

Hence, the bias is of the order n^{-2}. Now, we have g estimates of the above form, one for each group. Then Quenouille's estimator (the jackknife) is the average of these g estimates and is given by

$$\hat{R}_Q = g\hat{R} - (g-1)\hat{R}_- , \qquad \hat{R}_- = \sum_{i=1}^{g}\hat{R}_j/g .$$

As a special case we can set $g = n$, and $m = 1$, which will be appropriate for small sample sizes. The optimality of the choice $g = n$ was shown by P. S. R. S. Rao and J. N. K. Rao (1971).

EXAMPLE 6.4

A random sample of 5 is taken in a women's dormitory and the following data obtained on annual income of parents and the amount spent on cosmetics per month:

| x income in thousands of dollars: | 50 | 60 | 45 | 70 | 68 |
| y amount in dollars spent on cosmetics: | 25 | 30 | 20 | 36 | 35 |

Let $g = 5 (= n)$ and $m = 1$. Obtain a jackknife estimate of the average amount spent by the women students on cosmetics.

$$\hat{R}_1 = \frac{30 + 20 + 36 + 35}{60 + 45 + 70 + 68} = \frac{121}{243} = 0.498$$

Similarly,

$$\hat{R}_2 = \frac{116}{233} = 0.498$$

$$\hat{R}_3 = \frac{126}{248} = 0.508$$

$$\hat{R}_4 = \frac{110}{223} = 0.493$$

and

$$\hat{R}_5 = \frac{111}{225} = 0.493 \,.$$

Hence,

$$\hat{R}_- = \sum_1^5 \hat{R}_j/5 = 2.49/5 = 0.498$$

and

$$\hat{R} = \frac{146}{293} = 0.498 \,.$$

Thus,

$$R_Q \equiv 5(\hat{R}) - 4\hat{R}_- = 0.498 \,. \qquad \blacklozenge$$

6.14   MULTIVARIATE RATIO ESTIMATORS

Olkin (1958) generalized the case of one auxiliary variable to the case of k variables. It is given by

$$\hat{Y}_{MR} = \sum_{i=1}^k W_i \frac{\bar{y}}{\bar{x}_i} = \sum_{i=1}^k W_i \hat{Y}_{Ri} \,,$$

where the weights W_i are chosen so as to minimize the variance of $\hat{Y}_{MR}$, subject to the constraint $\sum W_i = 1$. We assume that the X_i are known. Let V denote the variance-covariance matrix of the $\hat{Y}_{Ri}$. Then we wish to minimize

$$\mathbf{W}'V\mathbf{W} - 2\lambda(\mathbf{1}'\mathbf{W} - 1)$$

where 2λ denotes the Lagrange multiplier. By differentiating with respect to $\mathbf{W}$ we obtain

$$V\mathbf{W} = \lambda\mathbf{1}, \qquad \mathbf{W} = \lambda V^{-1}\mathbf{1}$$

and λ is determined from the relation $\mathbf{1}'\mathbf{W} = 1 = \lambda\mathbf{1}'V^{-1}\mathbf{1}$. That is, $\lambda = 1/\mathbf{1}'V^{-1}\mathbf{1}$. Hence the optimum $\mathbf{W}$ is

$$\mathbf{W} = V^{-1}\mathbf{1}/\mathbf{1}'V^{-1}\mathbf{1} \,.$$

In practice, we replace the unknown variances V_{ij} by the sample variances

$$v_{ii} = \frac{(1-f)\hat{Y}^2}{n}(c_{yy} + c_{ii} - 2c_{yi}), \qquad v_{ij} = n^{-1}(1-f)\hat{Y}^2(c_{yy} + c_{ii} + c_{jj} - c_{yi} - c_{yj})$$

where $c_{yy} = s_y^2/\bar{y}^2$, $c_{ii} = s_i^2/\bar{x}_i^2$, etc. Note that the optimum $\mathbf{W}$ is free of the factor $(1 - f)\hat{Y}^2/n$. So

$$\hat{\mathbf{W}} = w = v^{-1}\mathbf{1}/\mathbf{1}'v^{-1}\mathbf{1}$$

where

$$v = ((v_{ij})) \,.$$

So, use of several auxiliary variables will increase the precision of the estimate.

6.15   A DUAL RATIO ESTIMATOR

Let Y and X denote the population totals on the y and x variables. We assume that X is known and that all the measurements are nonnegative. Let $\hat{Y}$ and $\hat{X}$ denote unbiased estimators of Y and X, respectively, where we further assume that X and $\hat{X}$ are positive. Let N and n, respectively, denote the population and sample sizes. The ratio estimator of Y is

$$\hat{Y}_R = \hat{Y}X/\hat{X} \,.$$

Srivenkataramana (1980) has proposed a product type of estimator which is given by

$$\hat{Y}_a = \hat{Y}\hat{X}^*/X$$

where

$$\hat{X}^* = (NX - n\hat{X})/(N - n) \,.$$

Notice that $\hat{X}^*$ is also unbiased for X and

$$\text{Corr}\,(\hat{Y}, \hat{X}^*) = -\text{Corr}\,(\hat{Y}, \hat{X}) = -\rho \quad \text{(say)}.$$

Bias and Mean-Squared Error of $\hat{Y}_a$

Let $\hat{Y} = Y(1 + e_1)$ and $\hat{X} = X(1 + e_2)$, where

$$E(e_1) = E(e_2) = 0 \,.$$

Bias in

$$\hat{Y}_a = B(\hat{Y}_a) = E(\hat{Y}\hat{X}^*/X) - Y$$

$$= \frac{1}{X(N - n)}E\left\{\hat{Y}(NX - n\hat{X})\right\} - Y$$

$$= \frac{1}{X(N - n)}\{nYX - nXY - nXYV_{11}\}$$

$$= -\frac{n}{N - n}YV_{11} = -gYV_{11} = -gkYV_{02}$$

where

$$V_{ij} = E(e_1^i e_2^j) = E\left\{(\hat{Y} - Y)^i (\hat{X} - X)^j\right\} / (Y^i X^j),$$

$$g = n/(N - n)$$

and

$$k = V_{11}/V_{02}.$$

Thus, when $k > 0$, that is, $\rho > 0$, the bias in $\hat{Y}_a$ is always negative. Next consider

$$M(\hat{Y}_a) = E(\hat{Y}_a - Y)^2$$

$$= E\left[\frac{Y(1 + e_1)}{X} \frac{\{NX - n(1 + e_2)X\}}{N - n} - Y\right]^2$$

$$= Y^2 E\left[(1 + e_1)\{1 - ge_2\} - 1\right]^2$$

$$= Y^2 E\left[e_1 - ge_2 - ge_1 e_2\right]^2$$

$$= Y^2 E\left[e_1^2 + g^2 e_2^2 + g^2 e_1^2 e_2^2 - 2ge_1 e_2 - 2ge_1^2 e_2 + 2g^2 e_1 e_2^2\right]$$

$$= Y^2 (V_{20} - 2gV_{11} + g^2 V_{02} - 2gV_{21} + 2g^2 V_{12} + g^2 V_{22}).$$

When $k > 0$ (i.e., $\rho > 0$), the bias is always negative.

6.16   COMPARISON OF VARIOUS ESTIMATORS

We have three estimators for the population total, namely $\hat{Y}_a$, $\hat{Y}_R$, and $\hat{Y}$. Their mean-square errors up to second-order moments are given by

$$M_1(\hat{Y}_a) = Y^2 (V_{20} - 2gV_{11} + g^2 V_{02})$$

$$M_1(\hat{Y}_R) = Y^2 (V_{20} - 2V_{11} + V_{02})$$

and

$$\mathrm{var}\,(\hat{Y}) = Y^2 V_{20}.$$

$\hat{Y}_a$ is more efficient than $\hat{Y}_R$ if

$$-2gV_{11} + g^2 V_{02} < -2V_{11} + V_{02}$$

i.e.,

$$-2gk + g^2 < -2k + 1$$

$$g^2 - 1 < 2k(g - 1)$$

$$g + 1 > 2k, \qquad \text{provided } g < 1 \text{ or } N > 2n$$

that is, when $k < (g + 1)/2$. Also, $\hat{Y}_R$ is more efficient than $\hat{Y}$ when

$$-2V_{11} + V_{02} < 0$$

$$-2k + 1 < 0 \quad \text{or} \quad k > 1/2.$$

Thus, $\hat{Y}_a$ is more efficient than $\hat{Y}$ or $\hat{Y}_R$ when

$$\frac{g}{2} < k < \frac{1}{2}(1 + g).$$

Typically g is small, and the above inequalities imply that for most of the time $\hat{Y}_a$ is superior, in terms of m.s.e., to $\hat{Y}$ just when $\hat{Y}_R$ is inferior to $\hat{Y}$. In this sense, $\hat{Y}_a$ and $\hat{Y}_R$ complement each other.

Special Case. Let $V_{20} = V_{02}$ and $n = N/5$. Then k reduces to ρ. Then $\hat{Y}_a$ is more efficient than $\hat{Y}$ or $\hat{Y}_R$ (provided $0.125 < \rho < 0.675$) and $\hat{Y}_R$ is better than $\hat{Y}$ when $\rho > 1/2$.

For simple random or varying probability sampling with replacement or any other plan involving independent subsamples, the bias and mean-square error of $\hat{Y}_a$ are

$$B(\hat{Y}_a) = -g V_{11}'/n$$

and

$$M(\hat{Y}_a) = M_1(\hat{Y}_a) + O(n^{-2})$$

where

$$M_1(\hat{Y}_a) = Y^2 n^{-1}(V_{20}' - 2g V_{11}' + g^2 V_{02}')$$

and V_{ij}' denotes V_{ij} for a sample of one unit or for one subsample and n is the sample size or the number of subsamples. Now, one can easily verify that $M_1(\hat{Y}_a)$ decreases as n increases only until $n/N = k/(1 + k)$ obtains a minimum, increasing with n thereafter. Thus the knowledge of the magnitude of k will help us choose one of the three estimators and also in determining the suitable sample size with respect to the precision when $\hat{Y}_a$ is used.

Srivenkataramana (1980) provides some jackknife type of estimators that are unbiased. Here we will provide one of those.

Let $n = 2m$ where m is a positive integer. Split the sample at random into two subsamples of m units each. Let $\hat{Y}_i$, $\hat{X}_i$ ($i = 1, 2$) be unbiased estimators of Y and X based on the subsamples and $\hat{Y}$, $\hat{X}$ those unbiased estimates based on the entire sample. Take $\hat{X}_i^* = (NX - n\hat{X}_i)/(N - n)$ and $\hat{X}^* = (NX - n\hat{X})/(N - n)$. Consider the product type of estimators

$$\hat{Y}_{ai} = \hat{Y}_i \hat{X}_i^*/X \quad (i = 1, 2).$$

Define

$$\hat{Y}_1 = \frac{(2N - n)}{N}\hat{Y}_a - \frac{(N - n)}{2N}(\hat{Y}_{a1} + \hat{Y}_{a2}).$$

The author (1980) surmises that $\hat{Y}_1$ is unbiased and the variance of $\hat{Y}_1$ and the m.s.e. of $\hat{Y}_a$ are equal up to second-order moments.

6.17 UNBIASED RATIO ESTIMATOR

If we slightly modify the usual selection procedure, we can make the ratio estimator unbiased. Let p_s denote the probability of obtaining sample s. If p_s is proportional to $\hat{X}_s p_s'$, where p_s' denotes the probability of selecting the sample s in the original sample design, then $\hat{R} = \hat{Y}/\hat{X}$ will be unbiased for $R = Y/X$. That is, let

$$p_s = \hat{X}_s p_s' / \sum_s \hat{X}_s p_s' .$$

Then

$$E(\hat{R}) = \sum_s \frac{\hat{Y}_s}{\hat{X}_s} p_s = \frac{\sum \hat{Y}_s p_s'}{\sum \hat{X}_s p_s'} = \frac{Y}{X} = R$$

since $\hat{Y}$ and $\hat{X}$ are unbiased for Y and X, respectively in the original design. In particular, if p_s' is the same for all samples, then p_s should be proportional to $\hat{X}_s$ in order to make the ratio estimator unbiased. This method of changing the selection procedure for obtaining unbiased ratio estimates is given by Nanjamma, Murthy, and Sethi (1959). For the many commonly used sampling schemes, the modification called for is first selecting one unit with probability proportional to its value of the characteristic occurring in the denominator of the ratio and then selecting the remaining units according to the original scheme of sampling.

Special Cases. In simple random sampling without replacement, $\bar{y}/\bar{x}$ (the ratio of the sample means) will be unbiased for R if we make the following modification. Since $p_s' = 1/\binom{N}{n}$ for all s, we set

$$p_s = \frac{\hat{X}_s p_s'}{X} = \frac{1}{\binom{N}{n}} \frac{\bar{X}_s}{\bar{X}} .$$

That is, make the probability of selecting the sample proportional to its mean or its total size. This can be achieved by selecting one unit proportional to x and the rest with simple random sampling without replacement from the remaining units of the population. Murthy (1967, p. 387) gives an unbiased variance estimator of the unbiased ratio estimator based on a sample selected by this method.

■ **PROBLEMS**

6.1 The following artificial data pertains to a small population consisting of $N = 10$ and two strata of equal size.

Stratum 1		Stratum 2	
x_{1i}	y_{1i}	x_{2i}	y_{2i}
2	1	8	1
4	3	16	13
8	7	20	12
10	8	25	15
14	10	30	17

For a stratified random sample with $n_1 = n_2 = 2$, compare the MSE's of $\hat{Y}_{Rs}$ and $\hat{Y}_{Rc}$ by obtaining the results for all possible samples. Can you attribute the differences in MSE's to biases in the estimates?

6.2   A fictitious survey of 10 households in a small village gave the following data for number of members (x), children (y), cars (y_2), and bicycles (y_3).

x	y_1	y_2	y_3
4	2	1	2
5	3	2	3
2	0	1	2
4	2	1	1
6	3	2	2
3	1	1	1
5	2	2	2
3	1	1	1
2	0	2	1
1	0	1	1

Assuming that for the total population of that town, $X = 100$, and $N = 25$, obtain ratio estimates of the total number of children, cars, and bicycles in that town.

6.3   Toyota Manufacturing Company in Georgetown, Kentucky, wants to estimate the ratio of the number of man-hours lost due to sickness of its employees. It has $N = 7000$ employees and it takes a random sample of $n = 10$ employees and obtains the following data. Let x (y) denote the number of man hours lost during the previous (current) year.

Employee	x	y
1	15	14
2	18	20
3	30	34
4	25	18
5	10	15
6	20	25
7	16	20
8	12	15
9	13	10
10	2	5
Total	161	176

Estimate the desired ratio and obtain a 95% confidence interval for it.

6.4 Suppose we wish to estimate the grade-point average of the graduating seniors at Mars University. Let $N = 1000$, the number of graduating seniors. We take a random sample of $n = 9$ students. Let x denote their SAT scores and y denote the grade-point average at the university. Assume that $\bar{X} = 600$.

Student #	x	y
1	550	2.8
2	630	3.1
3	570	2.9
4	650	3.3
5	700	3.5
6	520	3.0
7	720	3.6
8	660	3.5
9	575	3.2
Total	5575	28.9

Obtain a ratio estimate of the average grade-point average of a graduating senior at the University of Mars and also set up a 95% confidence interval for the same.

6.5 Let the population of a small town have the strata: Men, Women, and Children under 18. Let $N_1 = 100$, $N_2 = 150$, and $N_3 = 120$. Assume that $S_{d_1} = 10$, $S_{d_2} = 12$, and $S_{d_3} = 15$, and $c_1 = 5$, $c_2 = 6$, and $c_3 = 4$. Find an optimal allocation of $n = 25$ to the three strata.

6.6 Suppose a random sample of 11 students yield the following amounts of money spent on entertainment per month, and their families' incomes are as follows: $x =$ annual income in thousands of dollars and y is the amount in dollars spent on entertainment per month.

$$y: \quad 20, 15, 22, 30, 40, 35, 25, 32, 42, 45, 24$$
$$x: \quad 50, 45, 60, 70, 80, 75, 62, 75, 85, 80, 58$$

Letting $g = n$ and $m = 1$, obtain the jackknife estimates of the average amount spent by students on entertainment.

6.7 A simple random sample of 10 customers was taken at a local grocery store and the following data were obtained:

Customer	Total Annual Income x (in thousands)	Annual Amount Spent on Food y (in thousands)
1	25	3.7
2	32	4.1
3	40	4.5
4	35	3.9
5	29	3.8
6	42	4.6
7	50	4.8
8	38	4.0
9	41	4.5
10	44	4.4

Assuming that N is effectively infinite, estimate R, the population ratio $(R = Y/X)$, and obtain its standard error.

6.8 A simple random sample of 5 people who completed a Weight Watcher's program was taken and the following data were obtained:

Customer	Wt. before entering program x	Wt. at end of program y
1	120	100
2	140	105
3	160	110
4	130	115
5	180	120

Estimate R and obtain its standard error.

6.9 The American Hotel and Motel Association monitors the profits of the hotel industry and the average occupancy rate and average room rates. For the six-year period 1981–1986 these figures were as follows:

Year	Occupancy Rate	Average Room Rate
1981	70.0%	$39.15
1982	66.0%	43.55
1983	66.1%	46.70
1984	68.0%	52.15
1985	65.5%	53.81
1986	65.0%	54.90

Obtain a ratio estimate of the average room rate and find a 90% confidence interval for the same. Assume $N = 25$ and $\bar{X} = 70$.

6.10   An airline company plans to initiate service in a city of approximately 500,000 people. Suppose we want to determine the staffing requirements. The following data were collected on similar cities as well as competitors already servicing the airport.

Airline	Flights Departing Weekly	Total Employees
1	105	85
2	90	70
3	95	53
4	63	40
5	50	42

Obtain a ratio estimate of the average employees needed and also obtain a 95% confidence interval. Assume $N = 10$ and $\bar{X} = 55$.

6.11   We are interested in the annual percent yield of mutual funds in the United States. Let x denote the yield for 95 and y, the yield for 96. We take a random sample of 5 mutual funds and obtain the following data.

Mutual Fund Co.	x	y
1	12.3	11.9
2	13.1	16.2
3	9.8	14.5
4	18.7	19.1
5	15.5	15.7

Assume that $N = 100$ and $\bar{X} = 17.2\%$. Obtain a ratio estimate of the average annual yield of mutual funds in the United States in 1996 and also obtain a 95% confidence for the same.

6.12   ABC Company wants to estimate the total number of hours of breakdown of its assembly lines. They collect data on a random sample of 8 days. Let x denote the breakdown hours in 95 and y, the breakdown hours in 96.

Day	x	y
1	0.2	0.2
2	0.1	0.2
3	0.1	0.1
4	0.2	0.3
5	0.3	0.3
6	0.4	0.4
7	0.1	0.2
8	0.1	0.2

Assume $N = 250$ (total working days in a year) and $\bar{X} = 0.232$ hours. Obtain a ratio estimate of average hours of breakdown per day in 96.

6.13 A university wishes to estimate the annual income of all of its graduates. Let $N = 100,000$, the number of graduates. We take a random sample of $n = 10$. Let x denote their GPA and y denote their annual income (in thousands of dollars). Assume that $\bar{X} = 3.0$.

Client #	x	y
1	3.5	45
2	3.1	41
3	2.6	32
4	4.0	50
5	2.3	40
6	3.2	37
7	3.1	38
8	2.8	31
9	2.1	28
10	3.5	39

Obtain a ratio estimate of the average annual income of a graduate and set up a 95% confidence interval for the same.

6.14 Suppose we wish to estimate the weight loss of clients at a popular weight-loss clinic. Let $N = 300$, the number of clients who are taking a diet pill daily. We take a random sample of $n = 8$. Let x denote the number of hours per week spent exercising and y denote their weight loss in one month. Assume $\bar{X} = 6$.

Client #	x	y
1	4	20
2	5	22
3	3	17
4	6	25
5	8	30
6	7	23
7	2	15
8	5	20

Obtain a ratio estimate of the average weight loss of a client at the weight-loss clinic and set up a 95% confidence interval for the same.

6.15 The Lexington-Fayette County area is divided into 24 districts. A random sample of 5 districts were chosen and the following data was obtained:

$x =$ total population, $y =$ elderly population;

x:	5212	7247	3907	14,240	16,775
y:	806	551	400	2,352	2,296

Let $g = n$ and $m = 1$. Obtain the Quenouille's estimate (the jackknife) of the average number of elderly.

6.16   The governor of Kentucky wants to know the ratio of population below poverty level (x) to the total population (y) in the Lexington-Fayette County area. The area is divided into 24 districts. A random sample of 5 of these districts provided the following:

District	x	y
1	1879	5212
2	1221	7247
3	1176	3907
4	1781	14,240
5	956	16,775
	7013	47,381

Estimate the desired ratio and obtain a 95% confidence interval for it.

6.17   In 1995, 176 athletes from Kentucky's small colleges had various preseason fitness measurements taken by trainers. There were 104 male athletes and 72 female athletes. The trainers want to determine the average strength of the dominate quadriceps muscle (y) for male and female athletes using their weight (x). A sample of ten male athletes and ten female athletes is listed below.

	Male		Female	
	Weight (x_m)	Quad strength (% of body wt) (y_m)	Weight (x_f)	Quad strength (% of body wt) (y_f)
1	162	108	132	94
2	167	117	135	87
3	191	88	102	96
4	181	109	172	95
5	163	112	127	90
6	147	122	139	86
7	168	51	147	80
8	138	115	134	93
9	167	81	199	75
10	159	76	136	95
Total	1643	979	1423	881

(a) Obtain a ratio estimate of the average quad strength for male and female athletes.

(b) Obtain a combined ratio estimate for the average quad strength of athletes. Assume that $\bar{X}_m = 169.3$ and $\bar{X}_f = 140.2$.

6.18   In Problem 17, the trainers obtained the measures of flexibility on the lower-back muscle sit and reach for each male athlete. They also obtained the number of sit-ups a male athlete did in a minute. A sample of ten athletes from the 104 male college athletes are listed below.

$\bar{X} = 3.79$	x = lower-back muscle sit and reach (cm rotation)	sit-ups (Y)
1	5	41
2	9	56
3	5	51
4	4	54
5	1	46
6	8	56
7	6	42
8	6	40
9	3	36
10	3	32
Total	53	454

(a) Obtain a ratio estimate of the average number of sit-ups per minute for male athletes.

(b) Obtain a 95% confidence interval for the average number of sit-ups per minute for male athletes.

6.19   The Kentucky Educational Reform Act of 1990 (KERA) initiated new school programs. Samples of ten Kentucky school districts' annual accountability indexes for 1992–1993 (X) and 1995–1996 (Y) are listed below. There are 176 school districts in Kentucky. The average index score for Kentucky schools in 1992–1993 is $\bar{X} = 39.0$.

School District	1992–1993 (X)	1995–1996 (Y)
1	43.0	47.8
2	43.5	50.4
3	31.7	35.1
4	37.9	48.1
5	37.8	44.9
6	37.8	45.8
7	30.2	39.4
8	64.5	61.1
9	37.9	45.5
10	38.9	44.5
Total	403.2	462.6

(a) Obtain a ratio estimate of the average accountability index for the 1995–1996 school year.

(b) Obtain a 95% confidence interval for the average accountability index for the 1995–1996 school year.

■ REFERENCES

6.1   Brewer, K. W. R. (1963b). Ratio estimation in finite populations: Some results deducible from the assumption of an underlying stochastic process. *Aust. J. Statist.* **5**, 93–105.

6.2   Durbin, J. (1959). A note on the application of Quenouille's method of bias reduction to the estimation of ratios. *Biometrika,* **46**, 477–480.

6.3   Hartley, H. O. and Ross, A. (1954). Unbiased ratio estimates. *Nature* **174**, 270–271.

6.4   Murthy, M. N. (1957). Ordered and unordered estimators in sampling without replacement. *Sankhyā* **18**, 379–390.

6.5   Nanjamma, N. S., Murthy, M. N., and Sethi, V. K. (1959). Some sampling systems providing unbiased ratio estimators. *Sankhyā* **21**, 299–314.

6.6   Olkin, I. (1958). Multvariate ratio estimation for finite populations. *Biometrika* **45**, 154–165.

6.7   Quenouille, M. H. (1956). Notes on bias in estimation. *Biometrika* **43**, 353–360.

6.8   Rao, P. S. R. S. and Rao, J. N. K. (1971). Small sample results for ratio estimation. *Biometrika* **58**, 625–630.

6.9   Royall, R. M. (1970). On finite population sampling theory under certain linear regression models. *Biometrika* **57**, 377–387.

6.10   Srivenkataramana, T. (1980). A dual to ratio estimator in sample surveys. *Biometrika* **67**, 199–204.

CHAPTER 7

REGRESSION ESTIMATORS

7.1   INTRODUCTION

Like the ratio estimator, the regression estimator is supposed to increase precision by the use of an auxiliary variable x which is highly correlated with y. Here the regression line need not pass through the origin, unlike the case of ratio estimation. The difference between ratio and regression estimators is that a regression estimator is invariant under linear x transformations and goes through the same linear transformation as y. Ratio estimators have the same property but for scale changes only. Unless stated to the contrary, sampling is simple random without replacement. The model is

$$y_i = \alpha + Bx_i + e_i, \qquad i = 1, \ldots, N, \qquad \text{where } \sum_1^N e_i = 0.$$

If b is an estimate of B, then $y_i = \bar{y} + b(x_i - \bar{x})$. Summing the right side on $i = 1, \ldots, N$ and dividing by N, we obtain the estimated regression equation to be

$$\bar{y}_{lr} = \bar{y} + b(\bar{X} - \bar{x}).$$

Then, we take $\hat{Y}_{lr} = N\bar{y}_{lr}$.

N.B. Cochran (1977, pp. 189–203) served as a source for part of this chapter, adapted by permission of John Wiley & Sons, Inc.

7.2   PROPERTIES OF REGRESSION ESTIMATORS

1. They are consistent.
2. They may be biased; however, the ratio of the bias to the standard error is negligible when the sample size is large.
3. A large-sample formula for the variance of the regression estimate is available.

Notice that if $b = 0$, $\bar{y}_{lr} = \bar{y}$, and if $b = \bar{y}/\bar{x}$, then

$$\bar{y}_{lr} = \bar{y} + \bar{y}(\bar{X} - \bar{x})/\bar{x} = \frac{\bar{y}\bar{X}}{\bar{x}} = \hat{\bar{Y}}_R \qquad \text{(the ratio estimator)}.$$

Case when B is Known

Result 7.1.   In simple random sampling, if $B = b_0$ is specified, then the regression estimate of the population mean is unbiased, with variance

$$\text{var}(\bar{y}_{lr}) = \frac{(1-f)}{n} \sum_{i=1}^{N} \left[(y_i - \bar{Y}) - b_0(x_i - \bar{X})\right]^2 / (N-1)$$

$$= \frac{(1-f)}{n}\left(S_y^2 - 2b_0 S_{yx} + b_0^2 S_x^2\right).$$

Proof: $E(\bar{y}_{lr}) = E(\bar{y}) + b_0 E(\bar{x} - \bar{X}) = \bar{Y} + 0 = \bar{Y}.$ ∎

Notice that $\bar{y}_{lr}$ is the sample mean of n quantities $y_i - b_0(x_i - \bar{X})$ whose population mean is $\bar{Y}$. Hence by Result 3.2, var $(\bar{y}_{lr})$ is given by the expression in Result 7.1.

Corollary 7.1.   An unbiased estimate of var $(\bar{y}_{lr})$ is

$$\widehat{\text{var}}(\bar{y}_{lr}) = \frac{(1-f)}{n} \sum_{i=1}^{n} \left[(y_i - \bar{y}) - b_0(x_i - \bar{x})\right]^2 / (n-1)$$

$$= \frac{(1-f)}{n}\left(s_y^2 - 2b_0 s_{yx} + b_0^2 s_x^2\right).$$

Result 7.2.   The value of B that minimizes var $(\bar{y}_{lr})$ is

$$b_0 = S_{yx}/S_x^2 = \sum_{i=1}^{N}(y_i - \bar{Y})(x_i - \bar{X}) / \sum_{i=1}^{N}(x_i - \bar{X})^2$$

which is called the population regression coefficient of y on x. Also

$$\text{min var}(\bar{y}_{lr}) = \frac{(1-f)}{n} S_y^2(1 - \rho^2), \qquad \text{where } \rho = S_{yx}/S_x S_y.$$

Proof: Differentiate $S_y^2 - 2b_0 S_{yx} + b_0^2 S_x^2$ with respect to b_0 and solve for b_0. Substituting the minimizing b_0 into the expression for var $(\bar{y}_{lr})$, we get the desired result.   ∎

Case when B is Unknown

When B is unknown, we estimate it by the least-squares method and set

$$b = \sum_{i=1}^{n}(y_i - \bar{y})(x_i - \bar{x})/\sum_{i=1}^{n}(x_i - \bar{x})^2.$$

Recall that in regression analysis we make the following three assumptions:

1. the relation between y and x is linear,
2. the variance of y for given x is constant, and
3. the population is infinite

In survey analysis, it is reasonable to assume (1) and (2). With the use of b above the linear regression estimate of $\bar{Y}$ is given by

$$\bar{y}_{lr} = \bar{y} + b(\bar{X} - \bar{x}) = \bar{y} - b(\bar{x} - \bar{X}).$$

Define the error e_i by

$$e_i = y_i - \bar{Y} - B(x_i - \bar{X})$$

where B denotes the true value of the regression coefficient.   Then the e_i have the following properties:

1. $\displaystyle\sum_{i=1}^{N} e_i = 0$, and

2. $\displaystyle\sum_{i=1}^{N} e_i(x_i - \bar{X}) = \Sigma(y_i - \bar{Y})(x_i - \bar{X}) - B\sum_{i=1}^{N}(x_i - \bar{X})^2 = 0,$

because of the definition of B. Next

$$b = \sum^{n} y_i(x_i - \bar{x})/\sum(x_i - \bar{x})^2$$
$$= \Sigma\left[\bar{Y} + B(x_i - \bar{X} + e_i\right](x_i - \bar{x})/\Sigma(x_i - \bar{x})^2$$
$$= B + \left[B\Sigma(\bar{x} - \bar{X})(x_i - \bar{x}) + \Sigma e_i(x_i - \bar{x})\right]/\Sigma(x_i - \bar{x})^2$$
$$= B + \Sigma e_i(x_i - \bar{x})/\Sigma(x_i - \bar{x})^2,$$

after writing $x_i - \bar{X} = x_i - \bar{x} + \bar{x} - \bar{X}$.

By Result 3.3, we note that $\sum_1^n e_i(x_i - \bar{x})/(n - 1)$ is an unbiased estimate of $\sum^N e_i(x_i - \bar{X})/(N - 1)$, which by (2) above is zero. Hence $\sum e_i(x_i - \bar{x})/(n - 1)$ is distributed with zero mean. Also, it is known that the standard error of a sample covariance is of order $1/\sqrt{n}$, and that $\sum(x_i - \bar{x})^2/(n-1) = s_x^2$ is of order unity. Hence $(b - B)$, which is the ratio of these quantities, is of order $1/\sqrt{n}$.

In fact, one can easily show that the bias is of $O(n^{-1})$.

$$E(\bar{y}_{lr}) = \bar{Y} - Eb(\bar{x} - \bar{X})$$

$$= \bar{Y} - \text{cov}(b, \bar{x})$$

and since $|\text{cov}(b, \bar{x})| \le \{\text{var}(\bar{x})\ \text{var}(b)\}^{1/2}$

$$\text{cov}(b, \bar{x}) = O(n^{-1}).$$

Sukhatme et al. (1984, p. 239) show that

$$\text{bias}(\bar{y}_{lr}) = \frac{N-n}{N-2} \cdot \frac{B}{n}\left(\frac{\mu_{21}}{\mu_{11}} - \frac{\mu_{30}}{\mu_{20}}\right) + O(n^{-2})$$

where

$$\mu_{rs} = E\left\{(x - \bar{X})^r(y - \bar{Y})^s\right\} = \frac{1}{N}\sum_{i=1}^{N}(x - \bar{X})^r(y_i - \bar{Y})^s, \qquad r, s = 0, 1, \ldots.$$

Williams (1963) provides a procedure for obtaining an unbiased estimate of the bias in $\bar{y}_{lr}$ resulting in an unbiased estimate of $\bar{Y}$. His procedure consists of splitting up the sample into k groups of size n/k (assuming that n is a multiple of k). Let $\bar{y}_i$, $\bar{x}_i$, and b_i, respectively, denote the y and x means, and the least-squares slope estimator based on the ith group of observations. Now $\bar{y}_i$ and $\bar{x}_i$ are conditionally unbiased estimators of $\bar{Y}$ and $\bar{X}$, respectively, given the split of the sample-unit groups. Hence $\widehat{\text{cov}}(b, \bar{x}) = (1 - \frac{n}{N})\frac{1}{k(k-1)}\sum_{i=1}^{k}(\bar{x}_i - \bar{x})(b_i - \bar{b})$ is a conditionally unbiased estimator of $\text{cov}(\bar{x}, b)$, where $\bar{b} = \sum_i^k b_i/k$. Hence $\bar{y}_k^* = \bar{y} + \bar{b}(\bar{X} - \bar{x}) + \widehat{\text{cov}}(b, \bar{x})$ is a conditionally unbiased estimator of $\bar{Y}$. Thus, it is an unbiased estimator of $\bar{Y}$. Williams (1963, Eq. (7)) evaluates an exact expression for $\{\text{var}(\bar{y}_k^*) - \text{var}(\bar{y}_{lr})\}/\text{var}(\bar{y}_{lr})$, and, based on numerical study for $n = 25, 50, 75$ and small values of k, he surmises that the loss of precision in using $\bar{y}_k^*$ is less than 5% when x has a normal distribution. All the above considerations hold in the case of ratio estimators, provided we take the intercept to be zero. For more details see Goodman and Hartley (1958).

Result 7.3.   If b is the least-squares estimate of B and

$$\bar{y}_{lr} = \bar{y} + b(\bar{X} - \bar{x})$$

then for a large simple random sample of size n,

$$\text{var}(\bar{y}_{lr}) \doteq \frac{(1-f)}{n}S_y^2(1 - \rho^2), \qquad \rho = S_{yx}/S_x S_y.$$

Proof: First consider

$$\bar{y}_{lr} - \tilde{y}_{lr} = \bar{y} + b(\bar{X} - \bar{x}) - \bar{y} - B(\bar{X} - \bar{x}) = (b - B)(\bar{X} - \bar{x})$$

where $\tilde{y}_{lr} = \bar{y} + B(\bar{X} - \bar{x})$. Thus, $\bar{y}_{lr} - \tilde{y}_{lr}$ is of the order $1/n$, because both $(b - B)$ and $\bar{x} - \bar{X}$ are of order $n^{-1/2}$. However, the sampling error in $\tilde{y}_{lr}$ is of order $n^{-1/2}$, since it is the error in the sample mean of the variate $(y_i - Bx_i)$. Hence

$$\text{var } \bar{y}_{lr} \doteq \text{var } \tilde{y}_{lr} = \frac{(1 - f)}{n} S_y^2 (1 - \rho^2)$$

(see Result 7.2). Sukhatme et al. (1984, p. 239) show that the correction term in the above approximation is $O(n^{-2})$. ∎

7.3   SAMPLE ESTIMATE OF VARIANCE

Towards an estimate of var $(\bar{y}_{lr})$ we use

$$\widehat{\text{var}} \, (\bar{y}_{lr}) = \frac{(1 - f)}{n(n - 2)} \sum_{i=1}^{n} [(y_i - \bar{y}) - b(x_i - \bar{x})]^2$$

$$= \frac{(1 - f)}{n(n - 2)} \left[\sum (y_i - \bar{y})^2 - b^2 \sum (x_i - \bar{x})^2 \right].$$

A justification for the above estimate is as follows.

From Result 7.3, we have

$$S_e^2 \doteq S_y^2 (1 - \rho^2).$$

Hence

$$\text{var} \, (\bar{y}_{lr}) \doteq \frac{(1 - f)}{n} S_e^2.$$

Also, from Result 3.4, an unbiased estimate of S_e^2 is

$$s_e^2 = \frac{1}{n - 1} \sum_{i=1}^{n} (e_i - \bar{e})^2.$$

Now

$$e_i - \bar{e} = (y_i - \bar{y}) - B(x_i - \bar{x}) = [y_i - \bar{y} - b(x_i - \bar{x}) + (b - B)(x_i - \bar{x})].$$

However, $(b - B)(x_i - \bar{x})$ is of order $n^{-1/2}$ and hence may be neglected relative to the first term, which is of order unity. Hence, for large n, one can use

$$(n - 1)^{-1} \sum_{i=1}^{n} [(y_i - \bar{y}) - b(x_i - \bar{x})]^2$$

as an estimate of S_e^2. Following the classical regression analysis the divisor $(n - 2)$ instead of $(n - 1)$ is suggested.

7.4   COMPARISON OF REGRESSION, RATIO ESTIMATES, AND THE SAMPLE MEAN

Recall that

$$\text{var} (\bar{y}_{lr}) \doteq \frac{(1-f)}{n} S_y^2(1 - \rho^2),$$

$$\text{var} (\bar{y}_R) \doteq \frac{(1-f)}{n} (S_y^2 + R^2 S_x^2 - 2R\rho S_y S_x)$$

and

$$\text{var} (\bar{y}) = \frac{(1-f)}{n} S_y^2.$$

$\bar{y}_{lr}$ is more precise than $\bar{y}$ unless $\rho = 0$. $\bar{y}_{lr}$ is more precise than $\bar{y}_R$ if

$$-\rho^2 S_y^2 \leq R^2 S_x^2 - 2R\rho S_y S_x$$

or

$$(\rho S_y - R S_x)^2 \geq 0 \quad \text{or} \quad (B - R)^2 \geq 0.$$

EXAMPLE 7.1

There are 200 voting precincts in a certain town. The total number of registered voters in that city is 100,000. A simple random sample of six precincts was taken and the following data were obtained after the polls were closed.

Precinct	Number of Registered Voters (x)	Number Voting for a Democratic Party Candidate (y)
1	250	170
2	350	200
3	160	70
4	285	140
5	320	180
6	435	200

Using the ratio method, estimate the total number of voters in that city who are in favor of the Democratic candidate. Also, set up a 95% confidence interval. Computations yield $\bar{X} = 500$, $\bar{x} = 300$, and $\bar{y} = 160$. Thus,

$$\bar{y}_{lr} = \bar{y} + b(\bar{X} - \bar{x}) \equiv 160 + 200b$$

where

$$b = \Sigma y_i (x_i - \bar{x})/\Sigma(x_i - \bar{x})^2$$

$$= 20{,}200/43{,}450 = 0.46.$$

Thus, $\bar{y}_{lr} = 252$. Also,

$$\Sigma(y_i - \bar{y})^2 = 12{,}200.$$

Hence,

$$\widehat{\text{var}}\,(\bar{y}_{lr}) = \frac{(1 - 0.03)}{6(4)}\left[12{,}200 - (0.46)^2(43{,}450)\right]$$

$$= \frac{(0.97)}{24}(12{,}200 - 9194)$$

$$= 121.5\,.$$

Thus,

$$s_{\bar{y}_{lr}} \doteq 11\,.$$

The 95% confidence interval for $\bar{Y}$ is (230,274). By multiplying it by 200 we get the interval for Y.   ◆

7.5   PROPERTIES OF THE REGRESSION ESTIMATOR UNDER A SUPER POPULATION MODEL

Let us assume that the finite population values $y_1, \ldots, y_N$ are randomly selected from an infinite population in which

$$y_i = \alpha + \beta x_i + \epsilon_i, \qquad i = 1, \ldots, N$$

where the ϵ are independent with $E(\epsilon_i|x_i) = 0$ and $E(\epsilon_i^2|x_i) = \sigma_\epsilon^2$. Then

$$\sum(x_i - \bar{x})^2 b = \sum y_i(x_i - \bar{x}) = \sum(x_i - \bar{x})^2\beta + \sum\epsilon_i(x_i - \bar{x})$$

and

$$\bar{y}_{lr} = \bar{y} + b(\bar{X} - \bar{x}) = \alpha + \beta\bar{x} + \bar{\epsilon}_n + b(\bar{X} - \bar{x})$$

$$\bar{Y} = \alpha + \beta\bar{X} + \bar{\epsilon}_N\,.$$

Hence

$$\bar{y}_{lr} - \bar{Y} = (b - \beta)(\bar{X} - \bar{x}) + \bar{\epsilon}_n - \bar{\epsilon}_N$$

$$= \bar{\epsilon}_n - \bar{\epsilon}_N + (\bar{X} - \bar{x})\frac{\sum\epsilon_i(x_i - \bar{x})}{\sum(x_i - \bar{x})^2} \qquad \text{(see p. 145)}\,.$$

Thus $E(\bar{y}_{lr} - \bar{Y}|x_i's) = 0$. That is, $\bar{y}_{lr}$ is model unbiased for $\bar{Y}$ for all n. Also, upon noting that

$$\bar{\epsilon}_n - \bar{\epsilon}_N = \left(\frac{1}{n} - \frac{1}{N}\right)\left(\sum_1^n \epsilon_i\right) - \frac{1}{N}\left(\sum_{n+1}^N \epsilon_i\right)$$

$$\text{var}\,(\bar{y}_{lr}|x_i's) = E\left[(\bar{y}_{lr} - \bar{Y})^2|x_i's\right] = \sigma_\epsilon^2\left[n^{-1} - N^{-1} + \frac{(\bar{X} - \bar{x})^2}{\sum(x_i - \bar{x})^2}\right]\,.$$

Furthermore, one can easily show that the usual least-squares estimator given by

$$s_\epsilon^2 = \sum[(y_i - \bar{y}) - b(x_i - \bar{x})]^2/(n - 2)$$

is model unbiased for σ_ϵ^2 when $n > 2$.

If $E(\epsilon_i^2|x_i) = \sigma_\epsilon^2 v(x_i)(i = 1, \ldots, N)$, where $v(x_i)$ is a known function of x_i, then, using the generalized Gauss-Markov theorem, one can obtain the best linear unbiased estimators of α and β (and consequently the best model unbiased estimator for $\bar{Y}$) by minimizing

$$\sum_{i \in s} (y_i - \alpha - \beta x_i)^2 / v(x_i)$$

with respect to α and β, where s denotes the set of labels (or indices) that are in the sample of size n. The estimators are too complicated to be presented here (see, for instance, Sukhatme et al. (1984, p. 242)). However, when $v(x_i) \equiv 1$, the best (model) unbiased estimator of $\bar{Y}$ reduces to $\bar{y}_{lr} = \bar{y} + b(\bar{X} - \bar{x})$. Then, one can prove the following result pertaining to the optimality of $\bar{y}_{lr}$.

Result 7.4.   Under the super population model with $v(x_i) \equiv 1$, under any sampling scheme, the estimator $\bar{y}_{lr}$ is the best linear unbiased estimator of $\bar{Y}$ with expected mean-square error given by

$$E\{\text{MSE}(\bar{y}_{lr})\} = \frac{\sigma_\epsilon^2}{n}\left\{(1-f) + nE\left[\frac{(\bar{x} - \bar{X})^2}{\sum_{i \in s}(x_i - \bar{x})^2}\right]\right\}.$$

Proof: See Sukhatme et al. (1984, pp. 242–243).   ∎

From $E\{\text{MSE}(\bar{y}_{lr})\}$ we gather that an optimal sampling plan is one which selects the n units such that $(\bar{x} - \bar{X})^2 / \sum_{i \in s}(x_i - \bar{x})^2$ is minimum. Let s^* denote such a sampling scheme. Then we have the following optimality property obtained by Royall (1970).

Result 7.5.   Under the super population model with $v(x_i) = 1$, the sampling plan $(s^*, \bar{y}_{lr})$ is optimal.

An unbiased estimate of $\text{MSE}(\bar{y}_{lr})$ is given by

$$\widehat{\text{MSE}}(\bar{y}_{lr}) = \frac{\hat{\sigma}_\epsilon^2}{n}\left\{(1-f) + \frac{n(\bar{x} - \bar{X})^2}{\sum_{i \in s}(x_i - \bar{x})^2}\right\}$$

where

$$\hat{\sigma}_\epsilon^2 = (n-2)^{-1}\sum_{i \in s}[(y_i - \bar{y})^2 - b(x_i - \bar{x})^2].$$

7.6   REGRESSION ESTIMATES IN STRATIFIED SAMPLING

As in the case of ratio estimates we have two regression estimates, one separate and the other combined. Let $W_h = N_h/N$,

$$\bar{y}_{lrh} = \bar{y}_h + b_h(\bar{X}_h - \bar{x}_h).$$

Then

$$\bar{y}_{lrs} = \sum W_h \bar{y}_{lrh}$$

which is appropriate if the strata have different regression coefficients B_h. On the other hand, if we assume that all the B_h are equal, then

$$\bar{y}_{lrc} = \bar{y}_{st} + b(\bar{X} - \bar{x}_{st})$$

where

$$\bar{y}_{st} = \sum W_h \bar{y}_h, \qquad \bar{x}_{st} = \sum W_h \bar{x}_h, \qquad \bar{X} = \Sigma W_h \bar{X}_h.$$

If the b_h and b are preassigned, then $\bar{y}_{lrs}$ is unbiased for $\bar{Y}$,

$$\text{var}(\bar{y}_{lrs}) = \sum_h W_h^2 \frac{(1 - f_h)}{n_h} (S_{yh}^2 - 2b_h S_{yxh} + b_h^2 S_{xh}^2)$$

and $\text{var}(\bar{y}_{lrs})$ is minimized when $b_h = B_h$ (the true regression coefficient in stratum h) and then

$$\text{min var}(\bar{y}_{lrs}) = \sum_h W_h^2 \frac{(1 - f_h)}{n_h} \left(S_{yh}^2 - \frac{S_{yxh}^2}{S_{xh}^2} \right).$$

Regarding the combined estimator, $\bar{y}_{lrc}$ it is also unbiased for $\bar{Y}$ and

$$\text{var}(\bar{y}_{lrc}) = \sum_h W_h^2 \frac{(1 - f_h)}{n_h} (S_{yh}^2 - 2b S_{yxh} + b^2 S_{xh}^2).$$

The value of b that minimizes the above variance is

$$B_c = \left[\sum W_h^2 \frac{(1 - f_h)}{n_h} S_{yxh} \right] \Big/ \left[\sum_h W_h^2 \frac{(1 - f_h)}{n_h} S_{xh}^2 \right].$$

Notice that B_c is a weighted average of stratum regression coefficients $B_h = S_{yxh}^2/S_{xh}^2$. Towards this let

$$a_h = W_h^2 \frac{(1 - f_h)}{n_h} S_{xh}^2.$$

Then

$$B_c = \sum a_h B_h \Big/ \left(\sum a_h \right).$$

Also one can easily verify that

$$\text{min var}(\bar{y}_{lrs}) = \sum a_h \left(\frac{S_{yh}^2}{S_{xh}^2} - B_h^2 \right)$$

and hence

$$\text{min var}(\bar{y}_{lrc}) = \sum a_h \left(\frac{S_{yh}^2}{S_{xh}^2} - 2B_h B_c + B_c^2 \right).$$

Thus, $\text{min var}(\bar{y}_{lrc}) - \text{min var}(\bar{y}_{lrs}) = \Sigma a_h (B_h - B_c)^2$.

7.7   SAMPLE ESTIMATES

B_h can be estimated by

$$b_h = \sum_i (y_{hi} - \bar{y}_h)(x_{hi} - \bar{x}_h) / \left[\sum_i (x_{hi} - \bar{x}_h)^2 \right].$$

Applying Result 7.3 to each stratum, we obtain (assuming that the n_h are large)

$$\text{var}(\bar{y}_{lrs}) = \sum_h W_h^2 \frac{(1 - f_h)}{n_h} S_{yh}^2 (1 - \rho_h^2).$$

A sample estimate of $S_{yh}^2(1 - \rho_h^2)$ is

$$s_{y,xh} = (n_h - 2)^{-1} \left[\sum_i (y_{hi} - \bar{y}_h)^2 - b_h^2 \sum_i (x_{hi} - \bar{x}_h)^2 \right].$$

Note that the estimate $\bar{y}_{lrs}$ has the same shortcomings as the corresponding ratio estimate, because the ratio of the bias to the standard error may be significantly large.

In the combined estimate, B_c can be estimated by

$$b_c = \sum_h W_h^2 \frac{(1 - f_h)}{n_h(n_h - 1)} \sum_i (y_{hi} - \bar{y}_h)(x_{hi} - \bar{x}_h) / D$$

where

$$D = \sum_h \frac{W_h^2(1 - f_h)}{n_h(n_h - 1)} \sum_i (x_{hi} - \bar{x}_h)^2.$$

If the stratification is proportional, and treating $n_h - 1 \doteq n_h$, we get

$$b_c \doteq \sum_h \sum_i (y_{hi} - \bar{y}_h)(x_{hi} - \bar{x}_h) / \sum_h \sum_i (x_{hi} - \bar{x}_h)^2.$$

Also, since

$$\bar{y}_{lrc} - \bar{Y} = \bar{y}_{st} - \bar{Y} + b_c(\bar{X} - \bar{x}_{st})$$

if the sampling error in b_c is negligible, we have

$$\text{var}(\bar{y}_{lrc}) = \sum_h W_h^2 \frac{(1 - f_h)}{n_h} (S_{yh}^2 - 2B_c S_{yxh} + B_c^2 S_{xh}^2)$$

and

$$\widehat{\text{var}}(\bar{y}_{lrc}) = \sum_h W_h^2 \frac{(1 - f_h)}{n_h(n_h - 1)} \sum_i [(y_{hi} - \bar{y}_h) - b_c(x_{hi} - \bar{x}_h)]^2.$$

EXAMPLE 7.2

Let X_1 denote the weight of a male before he enrolls in a weight watcher's program and Y_1 denote his weight after he completes the program. Similarly, let X_2 denote the weight of a woman before she enrolls in the program and Y_2 her weight after she completes the program. Suppose $N = 250$ is the total number of people enrolled in the program, of which $N_1 = 100$ are males and $N_2 = 150$ are females. We take a simple random sample of $n_1 = 5$ and $n_2 = 5$ from males and females, respectively, and obtain the following data.

Males	Females
$x_{11} = 200, y_{11} = 180$	$x_{21} = 140, y_{21} = 130$
$x_{12} = 170, y_{12} = 155$	$x_{22} = 135, y_{22} = 120$
$x_{13} = 190, y_{13} = 165$	$x_{23} = 150, y_{23} = 130$
$x_{14} = 220, y_{14} = 190$	$x_{24} = 160, y_{24} = 140$
$x_{15} = 250, y_{15} = 220$	$x_{25} = 175, y_{25} = 155$

Assuming that $\bar{X}_1 = 180$, $S_1^2 = 36$, $\bar{X}_2 = 150$, and $S_2^2 = 25$, obtain regression estimates $\bar{y}_{lrh}$ ($h = 1, 2$), assuming that (1) the strata have different regression coefficients and (2) the strata have the same regression coefficient. Also obtain $\widehat{\text{var}}(\bar{y}_{lrs})$ and $\widehat{\text{var}}(\bar{y}_{lrc})$. ◆

Case 1: Different Regression Coefficients

$$W_1 = 0.4 \qquad W_2 = 0.6$$
$$\bar{X}_1 = 180, \ S_1^2 = 36 \qquad \bar{X}_2 = 150, \ S_2^2 = 25$$
$$\bar{x}_1 = 206 \qquad \bar{x}_2 = 152$$
$$\bar{y}_1 = 182 \qquad \bar{y}_2 = 135$$

$$b_1 = \frac{(-2)(-6) + (-27)(-36) + (-17)(-16) + (8)(14) + (38)(44)}{36 + 1296 + 256 + 196 + 1936}$$

$$= \frac{3040}{3720} = 0.817$$

$$\bar{y}_{lr1} = 182 + (0.817)(180 - 206) = 160.76$$

$$b_2 = \frac{(-5)(-12) + (-15)(-17) + (-5)(-2) + (5)(8) + (20)(23)}{144 + 289 + 4 + 64 + 529}$$

$$= \frac{825}{1030} = 0.801$$

$$\bar{y}_{lr2} = 135 + (0.801)(150 - 152) = 133.4$$

$$\bar{y}_{lrs} = .4(160.76) + .6(133.4) = 144.34$$

$$\text{var}(\bar{y}_{lrs}) = \sum_n W_h^2 \frac{(1 - f_n)}{n_h} S_{yh}^2 (1 - \rho_h^2)$$

where an estimate of

$$S_{yh}^2(1 - \rho_h^2) = \frac{1}{n_h - 2}\left[\Sigma(y_{hi} - \bar{y}_h)^2 - b_h^2\Sigma(x_{hi} - \bar{x}_h)^2\right], \qquad h = 1, 2.$$

An estimate of

$$S_{y1}^2(1 - \rho_1^2) = \frac{1}{3}\left[2530 - (.817)^2(3720)\right] = 15.65$$

and an estimate of

$$S_{y2}^2(1 - \rho_2^2) = \frac{1}{3}\left[700 - (.801)^2(1030)\right] = 13.05.$$

Thus,

$$\widehat{\text{var}}(\bar{y}_{lrs}) = (.4)^2\frac{\left(1 - \frac{5}{100}\right)}{5}(15.65) + (.6)^2\frac{\left(1 - \frac{5}{150}\right)}{5}(13.05)$$

$$= 0.4758 + 0.9083$$

$$= 1.384.$$

Case 2: Same Regression Coefficient

$$b_c = \frac{(.4)^2\frac{\left(1 - \frac{5}{100}\right)}{5(4)}(3040) + (.6)^2\frac{\left(1 - \frac{5}{150}\right)}{5(4)}(825)}{(.4)^2\frac{\left(1 - \frac{5}{100}\right)}{5(4)}(3720) + (.6)^2\frac{\left(1 - \frac{5}{150}\right)}{5(4)}(1030)}$$

$$= \frac{23.104 + 14.355}{28.272 + 17.922} = \frac{37.459}{46.194} = 0.8109$$

$$\bar{y}_{lrc} = \bar{y}_{st} + b(\bar{X} - \bar{x}_{st})$$

$$\bar{y}_{st} = (.4)(182) + (.6)(135) = 153.8$$

$$\bar{x}_{st} = (.4)(206) + (.6)(152) = 173.6$$

$$\bar{X} = (.4)(180) + (.6)(150) = 162$$

$$\bar{y}_{lrc} = 153.8 + (.8109)(162 - 173.6) = 144.39.$$

Thus

$$\widehat{\text{var}}(\bar{y}_{lrc}) = (.4)^2\frac{\left(1 - \frac{5}{100}\right)}{5(4)}(45.8461) + (.6)^2\frac{\left(1 - \frac{5}{150}\right)}{5(4)}(39.3494)$$

$$= .3484 + .6847$$

$$= 1.0331.$$

7.8 UNBIASED REGRESSION ESTIMATION

P. Singh and Srivastava (1980) propose a sampling scheme for which the regression estimator is unbiased. Let a population consist of N distinct and identifiable units. Let y_i and x_i be the response value and the value on the auxiliary variable for ith unit $(i = 1, \ldots, N)$. Let

$$\bar{Y} = N^{-1} \sum_1^N y_i, \qquad \bar{X} = N^{-1} \sum_1^N x_i, \qquad x_i' = x_i - \bar{X}, \qquad y_i' = y_i - \bar{Y}.$$

Assume that the auxiliary variable is known for all the population units. The sampling scheme of P. Singh and Srivastava (1980) is as follows.

Step 1: Select two units, for instance, ith and jth units, with their probability of joint selection being proportional to $(X_i - X_j)^2$.

Step 2: Select $(n - 2)$ units from the remaining units of the population by simple random sampling without replacement.

In Step 1 we consider all possible pairs of units and select a pair with the assigned probability. Alternatively, the selection of the first two units may be done as follows.

Step 1a: Select the first unit with probability for the ith unit proportional to $(x_i'^2 + \mu_{20})$, where

$$\mu_{20} = N^{-1} \sum_{i=1}^N x_i'^2.$$

Step 1b: Select the second unit from the remaining $(N - 1)$ units with conditional probability for the jth unit proportional to $(x_j - x_i)^2$, given that the ith unit was selected in the first step. Select $(n - 2)$ units from the remaining units of the population by simple random sampling without replacement. Then the probability of selecting a sample s is

$$p_s = s_x^2 / \left\{ \binom{N}{n} S_x^2 \right\}$$

where

$$\bar{x} = \frac{1}{n} \sum_{r=1}^n x_r, \qquad s_x^2 = \frac{1}{n-1} \sum_1^r (x_i - \bar{x})^2, \qquad S_x^2 = \frac{1}{N-1} \sum_{i=1}^N x_i'^2.$$

The authors show that the usual regression estimator for the above sampling scheme is unbiased. Based on certain empirical study, the authors conclude that the performance of the regression estimate based on the above sampling scheme is highly satisfactory. They also provide another sampling scheme which consists of selecting the first unit with probability for ith unit proportional to $x_i'^2$ and then selecting the $(n - 1)$ units from the remaining $(N - 1)$ units by simple random sampling without replacement. Then the probability of selecting a sample s is

$$p_s = \sum_1^n x_1'^2 / \left\{ \binom{N-1}{n-1} \sum_1^N x_i'^2 \right\}.$$

This scheme also yields an unbiased regression-type estimator, which, however, is not very satisfactory. Their schemes assume that S_x^2 is known where the regression estimate requires only knowledge of $\bar{X}$. No theoretical results on efficiency are known and no decent variance estimate is available.

R. Singh and B. V. Sukhatme (1973) have given several rules for obtaining optimal points of stratification if the data on an auxiliary variable highly correlated with y are available for estimating $\bar{Y}$ via a ratio or regression type of estimators.

■ PROBLEMS

7.1   Do Problem 1 in Chapter 6 using linear regression.

7.2   Do Problem 2 in Chapter 6 using linear regression.

7.3   A smart farmer makes a guess estimate of the weight of apples, X, on each tree in an orchard of $N = 100$ trees. He finds a total weight $X = 5600$ lb. The apples are picked and weighed on a simple random sample of 5 trees, yielding the following results.

Tree Number

	1	2	3	4	5	Total
Actual Weight (Y)	70	78	80	62	55	345
Estimated Weight (X)	65	80	76	65	52	338

Find an estimate of Y using linear regression.

7.4   A certain part of a city has $N = 25{,}000$ houses, and the average assessed value of these houses is 50 (in thousands of dollars). A simple random sample of 6 houses is taken and the following data is obtained.

Property	Assessed Value (in thousands of dollars)	True Value (in thousands of dollars)
1	47.5	52
2	55	60
3	60	58
4	80	84
5	75	90
6	65	72

Using a ratio estimation method, obtain the average value of a house. Assuming that the sample size is large, obtain a 95% confidence interval for the same.

7.5   A travel agent's organization is interested in estimating the effect of per capita income on the amount spent annually for vacation. The trade organization is interested in knowing if low-income groups might purchase travel agents' services if a marketing program were aimed at them.

Per Capita Income	Amount Spent on Travel (annually)
$3,000	$ 20
3,600	40
4,500	55
6,000	150
7,500	3500
8,500	4200
10,000	5000
12,000	5500

Assume that $\bar{X} = 5000$ and N is effectively infinite. Compute $\bar{y}_{lr}$ and an estimate of its standard error.

7.6 For the following data obtain the weighted least-squares estimate of the population regression line. Assume that $\bar{X} = 56$ and that the $\text{var}(\epsilon_i | x)$ is proportional to x^2.

x	y
20	42
30	50
40	55
50	65
60	95
70	120

7.7 One company has 200 sales districts. The total number of client contacts per month is 10,000. A simple random sample of 6 sales districts was taken with the following data.

Sales Value (in thousands of dollars) y	Average # of Client Contacts per Month x
25	17
33	21
82	50
103	57
92	53
160	61

Using the regression method, estimate the total sales of the company.

7.8 There are 500 companies in a city. The total number of employees is 50,000. A simple random sample of 5 companies was taken with the following data.

Expenditure on Web site (in thousands of dollars) y	# of Employees x
10	30
12	50
15	90
25	150
35	310

Using the regression method, estimate the total expenditure on the Web site by the companies in the city.

7.9 Suppose we wish to predict final examination scores in statistics from GRE-Q (quantitative) scores ($n = 20$). Assume $N = 10{,}000$, $\bar{X} = 550$.

x GRE-Q	y Examination
620	65
600	73
590	85
590	80
580	64
560	69
550	78
540	70
530	79
530	70
500	77
480	69
480	64
460	76
440	59
430	44
390	75
380	69
370	54
280	43

$$\bar{x} = 495.00 \qquad \bar{y} = 68.15$$
$$s_x = 91.39 \qquad s_y = 11.245$$

Find an estimate of $\bar{Y}$ using linear regression.

7.10 During an experiment, Dr. Boone examined the effect of varying the water/cement ratio on the strength of concrete that had been aged 28 days. For concrete with a cement content of 200 pounds per cubic yard, he obtained the following data. Let y denote the strength and x the water/cement ratio.

Water/Cement Ratio	Strength (100 ft/pound)
1.21	1.302
1.29	1.231
1.37	1.061
1.46	1.040
1.62	0.803
1.79	0.711

Find an estimate of $\bar{Y}$ using linear regression. Assume $N = 500$, $\bar{X} = 1.5$.

7.11 A member of the school board makes an estimate of the number of children, x, in each of the school districts, $N = 24$ (total number of districts). He estimates X to be 51,500. A random sample of 6 districts results in the following:

District	Actual	Estimated
1	1,099	1,000
2	867	900
3	1,462	1,500
4	2,686	2,900
5	3,185	3,000
6	4,808	4,500
Total	14,107	13,800

Find an estimate of the total number of children and calculate a 95% confidence interval for the total number of children.

7.12 Let X denote the strength of a steel rod before being treated with one of two processes that strengthens the steel. Let Y denote the strength of the rod after the treatment. Let x_1 and y_1 denote the data for treatment A and x_2, y_2 the data for treatment B. Suppose the total number of rods to be treated is $N = 3000$, $N_1 = 1750$ and $N_2 = 1250$. A simple random sample of $n_1 = 5$ and $n_2 = 5$ resulted in the following data.

Treatment A		Treatment B	
$x_{11} = 10$	$y_{11} = 12$	$x_{21} = 13$	$y_{21} = 13.7$
$x_{12} = 10.3$	$y_{12} = 10.5$	$x_{22} = 15.7$	$y_{22} = 17.5$
$x_{13} = 12$	$y_{13} = 12.5$	$x_{23} = 18.1$	$y_{23} = 20$
$x_{14} = 10.5$	$y_{14} = 10.9$	$x_{24} = 14$	$y_{24} = 16$
$x_{15} = 11$	$y_{15} = 12$	$x_{25} = 16.1$	$y_{25} = 18.5$

Assume that $\bar{X}_1 = 10.5$, $S_1^2 = 0.7$ and $\bar{X}_2 = 16$, $S_2^2 = 1.3$. Obtain regression estimates $\bar{y}_{lrh}$ $(h = 1, 2)$, assuming that

(a) the strata have different regression coefficients,

(b) the strata have the same regression coefficient.

Also obtain $\widehat{\text{var}}(\bar{y}_{lrc})$.

7.13 A produce company wishes to estimate the firmness of their cucumbers. Let $N = 1000$, the number of cucumbers. We take a random sample of $n = 5$. Let x denote the number of weeks in storage and y denote the firmness in pounds. Assume $\bar{X} = 16$.

Weeks (x)	Firmness (y)
0	20.1
4	15.9
14	12.5
32	7.9
52	7.2

Find an estimate of Y using linear regression.

7.14 A pharmaceutical company wants to estimate the potency of an antibiotic. One-ounce portions were stored for equal lengths of time at different temperatures and the potency readings were observed. Assume $\bar{X} = 65$, $N = 10,000$.

Temperature (x)	Potency Readings (y)
25	38
30	43
35	29
40	33
50	32
55	26
60	27
70	23
80	19
85	21
90	17
95	14

Find an estimate of Y using linear regression.

7.15 KERA (Kentucky Education Reform Act) made changes to primary school, middle school, and high school programs.[1] Let X_h denote the 1992–1993 accountability indices for each level (4th grade, 8th grade, and 11th–12th grade) and Y_h denote the 1995–1996 accountability indices for each level. There are 1101 schools in the Kentucky accountability system. A sample of five schools per level was taken. Obtain a regression estimate of the 1995–1996 index for each level.

	4th		8th		12th	
	x_1	y_1	x_2	y_2	x_3	y_3
	36.2	48.2	41.4	39.1	39.9	35.2
	43.7	53.7	46.3	45.1	30.9	34.9
	31.6	34.9	44.4	37.5	46.9	51.0
	35.9	49.2	34.2	39.2	28.8	40.4
	41.3	41.7	42.4	45.7	29.1	41.2
N_h	688		212		201	

Assume that $\bar{X}_1 = 38.3$, $\bar{X}_2 = 39.6$, and $\bar{X}_3 = 39.0$.

---

[1] Source for Problems 15 and 16: Kentucky Department of Education (Web address www.kde.state.ky.us).

7.16 KERA (Kentucky Education Reform Act) divided the state into eight regions. Let X_h denote the 1992–1993 accountability indices for each region and Y_h denote 1995–1996 accountability indices for each region. There are 176 school districts in Kentucky ($N = 176$). A sample of n_h school districts is taken from hth region ($h = 1, \ldots, 8$).

	1	2	3	$\bar{X}_h$	N_h
x_1	33.6	34.0	37.8	38.2	25
y_1	37.6	41.6	44.9		
x_2	37.6	35.0	33.9	38.4	28
y_2	42.3	47.2	42.9		
x_3	64.5	34.9	38.2	48.2	4
y_3	61.1	39.8	45.1		
x_4	38.1	40.9	37.9	39.9	27
y_4	46.9	47.8	48.1		
x_5	35.2	37.5	37.9	39.6	23
y_5	53.2	44.4	43.8		
x_6	38.1	30.2	37.9	37.1	31
y_6	40.3	39.4	45.5		
x_7	36.7	38.4	37.5	38.9	23
y_7	45.6	39.9	45.5		
x_8	31.5	37.1	31.1	35.2	15
y_8	38.2	38.7	38.3		

Obtain a regression estimate for the average accountability index for 1995–1996 using (a) separate estimate and (b) combined estimate.

7.17 For the data in Problem 18 in Chapter 6, obtain a regression estimate of the average number of sit-ups per minute for male athletes.

7.18 For the data in Problem 19 in Chapter 6, obtain a regression estimate for the average accountability index for 1995–1996 school year.

■ REFERENCES

7.1 Goodman, L. A. and Hartley, H. O. (1958). The precision of unbiased ratio-type estimators. *J. Amer. Statist. Asso.* **53**, 491–508.

7.2 Royall, R. M. (1970). On finite population sampling theory under certain linear regression models. *Biometrika* **57**, 377–387.

7.3 Singh, P. and Srivastava, A. K. (1980). Sampling schemes providing unbiased regression estimators. *Biometrika* **67**, 205–209.

7.4 Singh, R. and Sukhatme, B. V. (1973). Optimum stratification with ratio and regression methods of estimation. *Ann. Inst. Statist. Math.* **25**, 627–633.

7.5 Sukhatme, P. V., Sukhatme, B. V., Sukhatme, S., and Asok, C. (1984). *Sampling Theory of Surveys with Applications*, (3d ed.) Ames (Iowa): Iowa State University Press.

7.6 Williams, W. H. (1963). The precision of some unbiased regression estimators. *Biometrics* **19**, 352–361.

CHAPTER  8

SYSTEMATIC SAMPLING

Systematic sampling is a sampling scheme which is more convenient than simple random sampling and which ensures that each unit has equal chance of being included in the sample. In systematic sampling, we select every kth unit starting with a unit which corresponds to a number r chosen at random from 1 to k, where k is an integer such that $k = \frac{N}{n}$, the reciprocal of the sampling fraction. The random number r is called the *random start* and k is called the sampling interval. A sample selected by this procedure is called a *systematic sample* with a *random start*. One can easily see that r determines the entire sample. In this procedure, we select with equal probability one of the possible k groups (or samples). Besides the operational convenience, systematic sampling provides estimators that are more efficient than those provided by simple random sampling under certain conditions that are reasonable in practice.

8.1 CIRCULAR SYSTEMATIC SAMPLING

If N/n is not an integer, the actual sample size will be different from that specified, and the resulting sample mean will be a biased estimator for the population mean. We can overcome this by adopting circular systematic sampling devised by Lahiri in 1952 (see Murthy, 1967, p. 139) to the Field Workers of National Sample Survey in India. This goes as follows: Select the random start number from 1 to N and select thereafter kth unit in a cyclical manner till a sample of n units is obtained, where k is an integer nearest to N/n. If r is the random start, then the sample consists of the units corresponding to the numbers

$$\text{and} \qquad \left.\begin{array}{ll} r + jk, & \text{if } r + jk \leq N \\ r + jk - N, & \text{if } r + jk > N \end{array}\right\} \quad j = 0, 1, \ldots, n - 1.$$

This technique ensures that every unit has the same chance of inclusion in the sample.

EXAMPLE 8.1

Let $N = 51$ and $n = 5$, $k = 10$. Let $r = 34$. The sample consists of units numbered 34, 44, 3, 13, 23. ◆

The advantages of the systematic sampling (SY) method are

1. It is easier to draw a sample by this method. It is quick and more efficient.
2. Intuitively, SY seems to be more precise than SRS. Systematic sampling can be viewed as stratified sampling consisting of n strata, each stratum consisting of k units, and we select one unit from each stratum which is located at the same relative position in each stratum. However, in stratified sampling the position in the stratum is determined randomly in each stratum. In other words, the systematic sample is spread more evenly over the population.

Another way of selecting a systematic sample is to take the starting number as $(k + 1)/2$ (or $k/2$) when k is odd (or even). The idea behind this procedure is that the response associated with this centrally located unit is more precise than the one selected at random.

8.2 RELATION TO CLUSTER SAMPLING

Let $N = nk$. Then the k possible systematic samples are as shown in the table below.

	1	2	3	$\cdots$	k
	y_1	y_2	y_3		y_k
	y_{k+1}	y_{k+2}	y_{k+3}		y_{2k}
	$\vdots$	$\vdots$	$\vdots$		$\vdots$
	$y_{(n-1)k+1}$	$y_{(n-1)k+2}$	$y_{(n-1)k+3}$		y_{nk}
Mean	$\bar{y}_1$	$\bar{y}_2$	$\bar{y}_3$	$\cdots$	$\bar{y}_k$

Systematic sampling is equivalent to selecting one of the clusters consisting of n units. We select each of the clusters at random.

8.3 MEAN OF THE SYSTEMATIC SAMPLE

The mean of a systematic sample is unbiased for the population mean, because

$$E(\bar{y}_{sy}) = \frac{1}{k} \sum_{i=1}^{k} \bar{y}_i = \frac{1}{kn} \sum_{i=1}^{k} \sum_{j=1}^{n} y_{ij} = \bar{Y}.$$

8.4   VARIANCE OF THE SYSTEMATIC MEAN

Result 8.1. We have

$$\text{var}\,(\bar{y}_{sy}) = \frac{N-1}{N}\,S^2 - \frac{k(n-1)}{N}\,S^2_{wsy}$$

where

$$S^2_{wsy} = \frac{1}{k(n-1)}\sum_{i=1}^{k}\sum_{j=1}^{n}(y_{ij} - \bar{y}_i)^2$$

is the variance among units that lie within the same systematic sample.

Proof: From the analysis of variance, we have the following identity:

$$(N-1)S^2 = \sum_i\sum_j(y_{ij} - \bar{Y})^2$$

$$= n\sum_i(\bar{y}_i - \bar{Y})^2 + \sum_i\sum_j(y_{ij} - \bar{y}_i)^2\,.$$

However, $\text{var}\,(\bar{y}_{sy}) = \sum_i(\bar{y}_i - \bar{Y})^2/k$. Hence,

$$(N-1)S^2 = nk\ \text{var}\,(\bar{y}_{sy}) + k(n-1)S^2_{wsy}\,. \qquad \blacksquare$$

Corollary 8.1. The mean of the systematic sample is more precise than the mean of SRS if and only if

$$S^2_{wsy} \geq S^2\,.$$

Proof: $\text{var}\,(\bar{y}_{sy}) \leq \text{var}\,(\bar{y})$ if and only if

$$\frac{k(n-1)}{N}\,S^2_{wsy} \geq \frac{N-1}{N}\,S^2 - \left(\frac{N-n}{N}\right)\frac{S^2}{n} = \frac{k(n-1)}{N}\,S^2$$

that is, if and only if $S^2_{wsy} \geq S^2$. $\qquad \blacksquare$

So, the systematic sampling is more precise if the units in the sample are heterogeneous. If they are homogeneous, then they are essentially providing the same information as any one of the units in the systematic sample.

8.5   AN ALTERNATE FORM FOR THE VARIANCE OF $\bar{y}_{SY}$

Result 8.2. We have

$$\text{var}\,(\bar{y}_{sy}) = \frac{S^2}{n}\left(\frac{N-1}{N}\right)[1 + (n-1)\rho_w]$$

where ρ_W is the correlation between pairs of units that are in the same systematic sample. It is given by

$$\rho_W = \frac{E(y_{ij} - \bar{Y})(y_{iu} - \bar{Y})}{E(y_{ij} - \bar{Y})^2}, \qquad j \neq u$$

where the denominator is $\left(\frac{N-1}{N}\right) S^2$ and the numerator is

$$\frac{2}{kn(n-1)} \sum_{i=1}^{k} \sum \sum_{j<u} (y_{ij} - \bar{Y})(y_{iu} - \bar{Y}).$$

That is,

$$\rho_W = \frac{2}{(n-1)(N-1)S^2} \sum_{i=1}^{k} \sum \sum_{j<u} (y_{ij} - \bar{Y})(y_{iu} - \bar{Y}).$$

Proof: We follow Cochran's (1977, p. 209) method of proof. Thus,

$$n^2 k \ \text{var} (\bar{y}_{sy}) = n^2 \sum_{i=1}^{k} (\bar{y}_i - \bar{Y})^2$$

$$= \sum_{i=1}^{k} \left[(y_{i1} - \bar{Y}) + \ldots + (y_{in} - \bar{Y}) \right]^2$$

$$= (N-1)S^2 + 2 \sum_{i} \sum \sum_{j<u} (y_{ij} - \bar{Y})(y_{iu} - \bar{Y})$$

$$= (N-1)S^2 + kn(n-1)\rho_W S^2 \left(\frac{N-1}{N} \right)$$

$$= (N-1)S^2 + (n-1)(N-1)S^2 \rho_W.$$

Hence

$$\text{var} (\bar{y}_{sy}) = \frac{S^2}{n} \left(\frac{N-1}{N} \right) [1 + (n-1)\rho_W]. \qquad \blacksquare$$

Remark 8.1.   Any slight positive correlation within the units of the systematic sample will have a large effect on the $\text{var} (\bar{y}_{sy})$. Thus systematic sampling is beneficial in sampling from populations for which ρ_W is negative.

In the preceding results $\text{var} (\bar{y}_{sy})$ is expressed in terms of S^2, which enables one to compare $\bar{y}_{sy}$ with the mean of SRS. In the following we will express $\text{var} (\bar{y}_{sy})$ in terms of $\text{var} (\bar{y}_{st})$. The strata are composed of the first k units, the second k units, and so on. In our notation, the subscript j in y_{ij} denotes the stratum. Then we have

Result 8.3.   We have

$$\operatorname{var}(\bar{y}_{sy}) = \frac{S_{wst}^2}{n}\left(\frac{N-n}{N}\right)[[1+(n-1)\rho_{wst}]]$$

where

$$S_{wst}^2 = \frac{1}{n(k-1)}\sum_{j=1}^{n}\sum_{i=1}^{k}(y_{ij} - \bar{y}_{.j})^2$$

which is the variance among units that lie in the same stratum and

$$\rho_{wst} = \frac{E(y_{ij} - \bar{y}_{.j})(y_{iu} - \bar{y}_{.u})}{E(y_{ij} - \bar{y}_{.j})^2}$$

$$= \frac{2}{n(n-1)(k-1)}S_{wst}^{-2}\sum_{i=1}^{k}\sum\sum_{j<u}(y_{ij} - \bar{y}_{.j})(y_{iu} - \bar{y}_{.u}).$$

Proof: It is similar to the proof of Result 8.2.   ∎

Corollary 8.2.   A systematic sample has the same precision as the corresponding stratified sample with one unit per stratum provided $\rho_{wst} = 0$.

8.6   ESTIMATION OF SAMPLING VARIANCE

In systematic sampling, it is almost not possible to obtain an unbiased estimate of the variance of either the population mean or population total on the basis of a single sample. This is one of the disadvantages of systematic sampling, since it is unable to provide an estimate of the sampling error. First, let us examine why this is so. Since

$$\operatorname{var}\hat{Y} = E(\hat{Y}^2) - Y^2 = E(\hat{Y}^2) - \left\{\sum_{i=1}^{N}y_i^2 + 2\sum_{i<j}^{N}\sum^{N}y_iy_j\right\}$$

One can estimate unbiasedly estimate $\sum_{i=1}^{N}y_i^2$, but not $\sum^{N}\sum_{i<j}^{N}y_iy_j$, since some of the $\binom{N}{2}$ pairs of units, such as any two neighboring units, have zero chance of being included in any systematic sample when $k \geq 2$. However, it is possible to construct some biased, but useful variance estimators. In the following, we list some of these.

$$\widehat{\operatorname{var}}(\bar{y}_{sy}) = \left(\frac{1}{n} - \frac{1}{N}\right)s_W^2$$

where

$$s_W^2 = (n-1)^{-1}\sum_{j=1}^{n}(y_{ij} - \bar{y}_i)^2$$

is the mean square between units within the systematic sample. Now one can write

$$(n-1)s_W^2 = \sum_{j=1}^{n}(y_{ij} - \bar{Y} + \bar{Y} - \bar{y}_i)^2$$

$$= \sum_{j=1}^{n}(y_{ij} - \bar{Y})^2 - n(\bar{y}_i - \bar{Y})^2.$$

Hence,

$$E s_W^2 = (n-1)^{-1}\left[\frac{1}{k}\sum_{i=1}^{k}\sum_{j=1}^{n}(y_{ij} - \bar{Y})^2 - n \operatorname{var} \bar{y}_{sy}\right]$$

$$= \frac{(N-1)}{N} S^2(1 - \rho_W)$$

after using Result 8.2. Obviously, $\left(\frac{1}{n} - \frac{1}{N}\right)s_W^2$ is not unbiased for $\operatorname{var} \bar{y}_{sy}$ unless $\rho_W = -1/(N-1)$ (then $E s_W^2 = S^2$). Another candidate for the estimate of the variance is

$$\left(\frac{1}{n} - \frac{1}{N}\right)\sum_{j=1}^{n-1}(y_{i,j+1} - y_{ij})^2/2(n-1)$$

which is based on successive differences of the observations in the systematic sample.

If n is large, one can divide up the n observations into m samples of size n/m and obtain the sample means $\bar{y}_{1,n}, \bar{y}_{2,n}, \ldots, \bar{y}_{m,n}$. Then

$$\bar{y}_{sy \cdot m} = m^{-1}\sum_{i=1}^{m}\bar{y}_{i,n}$$

is unbiased for $\bar{Y}$, and an unbiased estimate of the variance of $\bar{y}_{sy \cdot m}$ is

$$\widehat{\operatorname{var}}(\bar{y}_{sy \cdot m}) = \frac{1}{m(m-1)}\sum_{i=1}^{m}(\bar{y}_{i,n} - \bar{y}_{sy \cdot m})^2.$$

When $m = 2$, one subsample can consist of all even members of the sample and the other can consist of all odd members. However, the resulting estimate of the variance is $(\bar{y}_{1,n} - \bar{y}_{2,n})^2/4$, which can have a large bias.

Example 8.2

Susan is interested in finding the average balance in her checking account during the month of April 1997. If her average falls below a certain threshold, then the bank charges her a certain service fee. Susan wants to make sure that the average balance does not fall below the threshold. She takes a systematic sample of dates in the month of April (arranged in the increasing order) and obtains the following data.

Dates Selected	Amount in the Account
2	$3000
8	2500
14	1800
20	1200
26	400

Estimate the average balance for the month of April and obtain a 95% confidence interval for the same.

$$\hat{\bar{Y}}_{sy} = \bar{y}_{sy} = \frac{1}{5}(3000 + 2500 + 1800 + 1200 + 500)$$

$$= 9000/5 = 1800 \, .$$

Since the data is essentially ordered from largest to the smallest, ρ_W will be negative. Consequently, since $E s_W^2 = S_{wsy}^2 > S^2$, we will have

$$\text{var } \bar{y}_{sy} \leq \text{var } (\bar{y}_{ran}) = \frac{S^2}{n}\left(1 - \frac{n}{N}\right) \, .$$

Let s_W^2 be the mean-square error between units. In our example, $N = 30$, $n = 5$, and

$$s_W^2 = \frac{1}{4}\left[(3000 - 1800)^2 + (2500 - 1800)^2 + (1800 - 1800)^2\right.$$

$$+ (1200 - 1800)^2 + (500 - 1800)^2\right]$$

$$= \frac{1}{4}\left[(1200)^2 + (700)^2 + 0 + (600)^2 + (1300)^2\right]$$

$$= 398 \times 10^4/4 = 99.5 \times 10^4 \, .$$

So,

$$\widehat{\text{var }} \bar{y}_{sy} = \frac{99.5 \times 10^4}{5}\left(1 - \frac{1}{6}\right) = 16.5833 \times 10^4 \, .$$

Thus,

$$s_{\bar{y}_{sy}} = 4.07 \times 10^2 \, .$$

Hence, a 95% conservative confidence interval for $\bar{Y}$ is

$$1800 \pm 2(407) = 1800 \pm 814$$

because $\widehat{\text{var }} (\bar{y}_{sy})$ overestimates $\text{var } (\bar{y}_{sy})$. ◆

The precision of the systematic sampling method relative to either stratified or simple random sampling depends on the structure of the population. As n increases, the variance of $\bar{y}_{sy}$ may actually increase, which is contrary to intuition.

8.7   POPULATIONS IN RANDOM ORDER

Systematic sampling is used in populations in which the numbering of the units is random. For instance, we arrange the population according to the surnames of the subjects. Suppose that the response of interest is not related to the surname of the subject. Then there is no trend or stratification in the response variable or no correlation between neighboring values of the response. In this case we expect systematic sampling to be as good as simple random sampling. The following results will throw more light on this aspect.

Result 8.4.   [W. G. Madow and L. H. Madow (1944)]
If we consider all the $N!$ finite populations generated by the $N!$ permutations of any set of numbers $y_1, \ldots, y_N$, then, on the average over these finite populations

$$E\left(\operatorname{var}(\bar{y}_{sy})\right) = \operatorname{var}(\bar{y}).$$

Remark 8.2.   Note that $\operatorname{var}(\bar{y})$ is constant for all permutations of the y_i's. The result points out that if we can conceive the order of the items in a specific finite population as drawn at random from the $N!$ permutations, then systematic sampling is, on the average, equivalent to simple random sampling, since in both the cases the probability of selecting a particular sample of n units is the same, namely $1/\binom{N}{n}$.

The second approach is the assumption of a super population from which the specific finite population is drawn at random.

Let the variables $y_i (i = 1, \ldots, N)$ denote a random sample from a super population such that

$$Ey_i = \mu, \qquad \operatorname{cov}(y_i, y_j) = 0(i \neq j), \qquad \operatorname{var}(y_i) = \sigma_i^2.$$

Then we have the following result of Cochran (1977, Theorem 8.5).

Result 8.5.   With the preceding notation

$$E \operatorname{var}(\bar{y}_{sy}) = E \operatorname{var}(\bar{y}_{\mathrm{ran}}).$$

Proof: Recall that

$$\operatorname{var}(\bar{y}_{\mathrm{ran}}) = \frac{(N-n)}{Nn} \sum_{i=1}^{N} (y_i - \bar{Y})^2 (N-1)^{-1}.$$

Now, writing $y_i - \bar{Y} = y_i - \mu + \mu - \bar{Y}$ and squaring and summing, we have

$$\sum_1^N (y_i - \bar{Y})^2 = \sum_1^N (y_i - \mu)^2 - N(\bar{Y} - \mu)^2$$

$$E N^2 (\bar{Y} - \mu)^2 = E\left[\sum (y_i - \mu)^2 + \sum_{i \neq j}\sum (y_i - \mu)(y_j - \mu)\right]$$

$$= \sum \sigma_i^2 .$$

Then

$$E \ \text{var}\,(\bar{y}_{\text{ran}}) = \frac{N-n}{Nn(N-1)}\left[\sum \sigma_i^2 - N^{-1}\sum \sigma_i^2\right] = \frac{(N-n)}{N^2 n}\sum \sigma_i^2 .$$

Next

$$\text{var}\ \bar{y}_{sy} = k^{-1}\sum_1^k (\bar{y}_u - \bar{Y})^2$$

$$= k^{-1}\left[\sum_1^k (\bar{y}_u - \mu)^2 - k(\bar{Y} - \mu)^2\right]$$

$$= k^{-1}\left[\sum_1^k n^{-2}\left(\sum (y_{uj} - \mu)\right)^2 - k(\bar{Y} - \mu)^2\right]$$

$$E\ \text{var}\ \bar{y}_{sy} = k^{-1}\left[n^{-2}\sum_1^N \sigma_i^2 - kN^{-2}\sum_1^N \sigma_i^2\right]$$

$$= (n^{-1}N^{-1} - N^{-2})\left(\sum \sigma_i^2\right) = \frac{(N-n)}{N^2 n}\left(\sum \sigma_i^2\right). \qquad \blacksquare$$

8.8 POPULATIONS HAVING LINEAR TREND

Let y_i be proportional to i. In particular, we assume that $y_i = i$. Then

$$S^2 = (N-1)^{-1}\left[\sum y_i^2 - N\bar{Y}^2\right] = (N-1)^{-1}\left[\sum i^2 - N\left(\frac{N+1}{2}\right)^2\right]$$

$$= (N-1)^{-1}\left[\frac{N(N+1)(2N+1)}{6} - \frac{N(N+1)^2}{4}\right] = \frac{N(N+1)}{12}.$$

Hence

$$\text{var}\,(\bar{y}_{\text{ran}}) = \left(\frac{N-n}{Nn}\right)S^2 = \frac{n(k-1)}{Nn}\cdot\frac{N(N+1)}{12} = \frac{(k-1)(N+1)}{12}.$$

On the other hand

$$\text{var}\,(\bar{y}_{st}) = \left(\frac{N-n}{Nn}\right) S_W^2 \qquad \text{(see Special Case 3 of Result 5.3 on p. 77)}$$

where

$$S_W^2 = \text{variance within strata} = k(k+1)/12$$

which is obtained by replacing N by k in the expression for S^2. Thus,

$$\text{var}\,(\bar{y}_{st}) = (k^2 - 1)/12n\,.$$

Note that $\bar{y}_2$ exceeds $\bar{y}_1$ by 1, $\bar{y}_3$ exceeds $\bar{y}_2$ by 1, etc. Hence we can, without loss of generality, replace the $\bar{y}_u$ by the integers $1, 2, \ldots, k$ and $\bar{Y}$ by $(k+1)/2$ and obtain

$$\sum_{u=1}^{k}(\bar{y}_u - \bar{Y})^2 = k(k^2 - 1)/12\,.$$

This gives

$$\text{var}\,(\bar{y}_{sy}) = k^{-1}\sum(\bar{y}_u - \bar{Y})^2 = (k^2 - 1)/12\,.$$

Now, from the preceding formulae,

$$\text{var}(\bar{y}_{st}) = (k^2-1)/12n \le \text{var}(\bar{y}_{sy}) = (k^2-1)/12 \le \text{var}(\bar{y}_{\text{ran}}) = (k-1)(N+1)/12.$$

Equality occurs only when $n = 1$. In conclusion, if there is a linear trend, systematic sampling mean is more precise than the mean by simple random sampling; however, it is less precise than the stratified mean.

8.9   FURTHER DEVELOPMENTS IN SYSTEMATIC SAMPLING

A sample of size n can be drawn from two types of populations:

1. The population consists of a finite number N of units with responses y_u attached to uth unit $(u = 1, \ldots, N)$. Earlier we have assumed this type of population.
2. The population consists of a continuum of values on the interval $[0, N]$. A response y_u is made at the point u, $0 \le u \le N$. For this type of infinite population, the sampling interval $k = N/n$ can be any real number. In this case, a random start is chosen with uniform probability on the interval $[0, k]$ and the sample points $r, r + k, \ldots, r + (n-1)k$ are chosen. The sample mean

$$\bar{y}_r = n^{-1}\sum_{j=0}^{n-1} y_{r+jk}$$

has variance

$$k^{-1}\int_0^k (\bar{y}_r - \bar{Y})^2\,dr$$

where

$$\bar{Y} = N^{-1}\int_0^N y_u\,du = \text{the population mean}\,.$$

Centrally Located Systematic Sample

For populations of Type 1, W. G. Madow (1953) proposed a centrally located systematic sampling design which can be described as follows. Instead of selecting a random start from 1 to k, we select the systematic sample with the starting point $r = (k+1)/2$ when k is odd. When k is even, the starting points $r = k/2$ and $r = (k/2)+1$ are each chosen with probability $\frac{1}{2}$. It can be shown that the estimate of the population mean based on this type of design is biased.

Linear Trend with Super Population Model

In some cases, it is reasonable to assume that the finite population of type 1 is itself a random sample from an infinite super population. Then we assume the model

$$y_i = \alpha + \beta i + e_i, \quad i = 1, \ldots,$$

where

$$E(e_i) = 0, \qquad E(e_i^2) = \sigma^2 \quad \text{and} \quad E(e_i e_j) = 0 \qquad \text{for } i \neq j.$$

Then the variance of the sample mean $\bar{y}$ is

$$E \text{ var} (\bar{y}_{sy}) = Ek^{-1} \sum_{i=1}^{k} (\bar{y}_i - \bar{Y})^2$$

$$= \left\{ \beta^2 (k^2 - 1)/12 \right\} + \bar{\sigma}^2$$

where $\bar{\sigma}^2 = \sigma^2 (k-1)/(nk)$. The first term in the expression for $E \text{ var} (\bar{y}_{sy})$ is the variance component due to the linear trend; the second term is due to the random error. Stratified sampling and simple random sampling are two other commonly used designs, and we can compare their efficiencies relative to systematic sampling. Then, Bellhouse (1988, p. 129) gives

$$E \text{ var} (\bar{y}_{ran}) = \left\{ \beta^2 (k-1)(nk+1)/12 \right\} + \bar{\sigma}^2$$

and

$$E \text{ var} (\bar{y}_{st}) = \left\{ \beta^2 (k^2 - 1)/12n \right\} + \bar{\sigma}^2$$

where we assume that a random sample of one unit is taken from each of the n strata comprised of the sets of units $\{1, \ldots, k\}, \{k+1, \ldots, 2k\}, \ldots, \{(n-1)k+1, \ldots, nk\}$. One can easily see that

$$E \text{ var} (\bar{y}_{st}) \leq E \text{ var} (\bar{y}_{sy}) \leq E \text{ var} (\bar{y}_{ran}).$$

Removal of the Linear Trend as a Component of Variance

One concludes that a stratified sampling scheme is the most efficient method of sampling when a linear trend is present. However, there exist several systematic type of sampling designs with $\bar{y}$ as the estimator of $\bar{Y}$ which eliminate the linear trend as a component of variance. Bellhouse and J. N. K. Rao (1975) have found that the centrally located systematic sampling design was the most promising in terms of efficiency. Yates (1948) has suggested an estimator which is obtained by taking the sample mean and then adding weights w and $-w$ to the first and last sample units, respectively. The weight is obtained by setting the estimator equal to the finite population mean under a perfect linear trend. This gives $w = (2r - k - 1)/\{2(n - 1)k\}$, so that the estimator is

$$\bar{y}_r + \frac{2r - k - 1}{2(n - 1)k}\{y_r - y_{r+(n-1)k}\}$$

where r is the starting point. Bellhouse and J. N. K. Rao (1975) studied the efficiency of the above estimator and also obtained an estimator when circular systemating sampling design is adopted. For details see Bellhouse (1988, p. 130).

8.10   OTHER SUPER POPULATION MODELS

Cochran (1946) considered the following autocorrelated scheme in the super population model.

$$E(y_i) = \mu, \qquad E(y_i - \mu)^2 = \sigma^2, \qquad E(y_i - \mu)(y_{i+t} - \mu) = \rho(t)\sigma^2$$

where $\rho(t) \geq \rho(u) \geq 0$ for $t < u$. Then one can compute the expectation of the sampling variance in simple random sampling, stratified random sampling, and systematic sampling. If

$$\rho(i) \geq \rho(i + 1) \geq 0, \qquad i = 1, \dots, N - 1$$

and

$$\delta_i^2 = \rho(i - 1) + \rho(i + 1) - 2\rho(i) \geq 0, \qquad i = 2, 3, \dots, N - 2$$

then systematic sampling is more efficient than either stratified sampling or simple random sampling. Hájek (1959) considers a slightly more general model than that of Cochran and proves that systematic sampling yields minimum variance when the probability of inclusion of the ith unit is proportional to the size X_i of that unit and the estimator is the Horvitz-Thompson estimator. For more details the reader is referred to M. N. Murthy and T. J. Rao (1988, section 9).

A supplementary sample is required in order to obtain an unbiased variance estimator with a single-start systematic sample without making further assumptions on the population model. J. Wu (1984) proposed two procedures for taking supplementary observations, namely (1) a simple random sample or (2) another systematic sample. For each procedure he considers a class of estimators of the population mean (as a weighted mean of the two sample means). A similar weighted class of estimators has been proposed earlier by Zinger (1980). He characterizes the class of nonnegative unbiased estimators of the variance of the estimators of the population mean. He also discusses the choice of the weight as a compromise between efficient estimation of the population mean and nonnegative estimation of its variance.

■ PROBLEMS

8.1   The following constitute values of $y = $ number of employees (in hundreds) in 30 industrial companies in a certain town.

Company	y	Company	y	Company	y
1	1.10	11	0.35	21	4.50
2	0.50	12	0.21	22	3.25
3	2.02	13	1.09	23	1.60
4	0.60	14	4.05	24	1.85
5	0.90	15	3.20	25	0.95
6	0.40	16	1.70	26	0.65
7	0.70	17	2.20	27	0.72
8	1.20	18	1.60	28	0.92
9	0.80	19	1.80	29	2.20
10	0.19	20	2.40	30	1.72

(a) Calculate the efficiency of systematic sampling relative to simple random sampling without replacement in estimating $\bar{Y}$ when the sample size is 3.

(b) Determine the effect of reversing the order of observations in the second set in the table on the relative efficiency.

8.2   The following gives the acreage under cultivation in 15 farms constituting a systematic sample drawn from a county having 300 farms.

Farm	Acreage (y)	Farm	Acreage (y)
1	150	9	115
2	165	10	90
3	275	11	60
4	120	12	140
5	75	13	220
6	80	14	140
7	130	15	85
8	55		

(a) Estimate the total acreage Y under cultivation in the region.

(b) Obtain an estimate of the variance of $\hat{Y}$.

(c) Compare the quantity in (b) with the estimate of the variance of $\hat{Y}$ under the assumption of simple random sampling without replacement.

8.3   The following gives a sample of size 10 from the amount of unpaid balances of $N = 500$ auto loans numbered serially according to the date in which the auto loan was given over a period of 10 years. The company wants to estimate the total amount of unpaid balances.

Auto Loan #	Amount of Unpaid Balance in $1000	Auto Loan #	Amount of Unpaid Balance in $1000
1	3	6	12
2	5	7	10
3	6	8	9
4	10	9	13
5	12	10	8

Treating this as a systematic sample, obtain an estimate of the total amount of unpaid balances. Also, obtain an estimate of its variance.

Hint: Use a biased estimate of the sampling variance.

8.4 A city has listed the home owners according to the real estate taxes they paid on their properties (from the highest to the lowest). If the city is interested in estimating the average real estate taxes a home owner pays, discuss the relative merits of drawing a systematic, stratified, or simple random sampling. Assume that $N = 5000$ and estimate the total real estate taxes the home owners pay in that city on the basis of the following sample (treating it as a systematic sample).

Home Owner	Real Estate Tax in $100	Home Owner	Real Estate Tax in $100
1	10.1	6	7.9
2	9.8	7	7.6
3	9.6	8	7.2
4	8.9	9	6.6
5	8.4	10	5.8

8.5 A men's suiting department store has 3 stores in Lexington, Kentucky, with charge account arranged by the store. Each store has overdue accounts at the front of each store's list. Suppose each store averages about 20 accounts each, with approximately 25% past-due accounts. On a particular day the delinquent accounts are as shown in the following table. The store wants to estimate the proportion of overdue accounts via systematic sampling.

	Store 1	Store 2	Store 3
Account Numbers	1 – 21	22 – 41	42 – 60
Overdue Accounts	3, 7, 18	25, 37, 38, 40	45, 51, 55, 59

(a) List all possible systematic samples of size 5, and compute the variances of the sample proportions.

(b) Compare the quantity in (a) with the corresponding variance if the sample is treated as a simple random sample.

8.6 Mars University has 2000 students living in its dorms. It wishes to improve the quality of food served in the dorms. It wants to estimate the average amount spent by a student (per week) on fast foods such as pizza, hamburgers, etc. It samples every 200th student and obtains the following data.

Student	Amount Spent on Fast Food (in dollars per week)
1	5
2	8
3	3
4	6
5	7
6	8
7	4
8	10
9	6
10	3

Estimate the total amount (per week) spent by students in Mars University on fast food and a bound on its standard error.

■ REFERENCES

8.1   Bellhouse, D. R. (1988). Systematic sampling. *Handbook of Statistics: Sampling* **6** (eds. P. R. Krishnaiah and C. R. Rao). Elsevier Science Publishers B. V., 125–145.

8.2   Bellhouse, D. R. and Rao, J. N. K. (1975). Systematic sampling in the presence of a trend. *Biometrika* **62**, 694–697.

8.3   Cochran, W. G. (1946). Relative accuracy of systematic and random samples for a certain class of populations. *Ann. Math. Statist.* **71**, 164–177.

8.4   Hájek, J. (1959). Optimum strategy and other problems in probability sampling. *Casopis Pro Petsovani Matematiky* **84**, 387–442.

8.5   Koop, J. C. (1963). On splitting a systematic sample for variance estimation. *Ann. Math. Statist.* **42**, 1084–1087.

8.6   Madow, W. G. and Madow, L. H. (1944). On the theory of systematic sampling. *Ann. Math. Statist.* **15**, 1–24.

8.7   Madow, W. G. (1953) . On the theory of systematic sampling III: Comparison of centered and random start systematic sampling. *Ann. Math. Statist.* **24**, 101–106.

8.8   Murthy, M. N. and Rao, T. J. (1988). Systematic sampling with illustrating examples. *Handbook of Statistics: Sampling* **6**, Elsevier Science Publishers B. V., 147–185.

8.9   Murthy, M. N. (1967). *Sampling Theory and Methods.* Statistical Publishing Society, Calcutta, India.

8.10 Wu, Jeff C.F. (1984). Estimation in systematic sampling with supplementary observations. *Sankhyā*, **B46**, part 3, 306–315.

8.11 Yates, F. (1948). Systematic sampling. *Phil. Trans. Roy. Soc.* **A24**, 345–377.

8.12 Zinger, A. (1980). Variance estimation in partial systematic sampling. *J. Amer. Statist. Assoc.* **75**, 205–211.

CHAPTER 9

CLUSTER SAMPLING

9.1 NECESSITY OF CLUSTER SAMPLING

The population units are grouped into a number of clusters. We take a sample of clusters and then take observations on all the units in the selected clusters. Cluster sampling is preferable in terms of cost, because collection of data from adjoining units is cheaper, easier and quicker than observing units chosen at random in the region. For example, it may be cheaper to survey all persons in a selected household rather than the same number of persons chosen at random from a list of all people. Furthermore, operationally it may be more convenient to survey all households in a selected block than to survey a sample of the same number of households chosen randomly from a list of all households in the town. Although it may be economical to carry out cluster sampling, it may be less efficient in terms of precision when compared with a simple random sample consisting of the same number of units. Also, the efficiency of cluster sampling may decrease with increase in cluster size. However, the reduction in cost may offset the decrease in efficiency.

In general, any system of sampling can be construed as cluster sampling, since in all sampling schemes, units are grouped so as to form samples or clusters and one of them is selected with a preassigned probability. Recall that systematic sampling can be taken to be a special case of cluster sampling, since the population is divided into k groups, each group consisting of n units such that $N = nk$, and selecting one group at random.

*Cochran (1977, Chapters 9 and 9A) served as a source for part of this chapter, adapted by permission of John Wiley & Sons, Inc.

9.2   NOTATION

Let N denote the number of clusters in the population, each cluster having M subunits. We select n clusters from these N clusters by simple random sampling without replacement. Let y_{ij} be the value of the characteristic for jth subunit in the ith cluster $j = 1, \ldots, M, i = 1, 2, \ldots, N)$.

$$y_i = \sum_{j=1}^{M} y_{ij} = i\text{th cluster total}$$

$$\bar{y}_i = y_i/M = i\text{th cluster mean per element}$$

$$\bar{Y} = \sum_{i=1}^{N} y_i/N = \text{the mean per cluster}$$

$$\bar{\bar{Y}} = \sum_{i=1}^{N} y_i/NM = \bar{Y}/M = \text{the mean per subunit or element}$$

Then the variance among elements is S^2, where

$$S^2 = \sum_{i=1}^{N} \sum_{j=1}^{M} (y_{ij} - \bar{\bar{Y}})^2/(NM - 1).$$

The mean square within clusters is defined by

$$S_W^2 = \sum_{i=1}^{N} \sum_{j=1}^{M} (y_{ij} - \bar{y}_i)^2/N(M - 1)$$

The mean square between cluster means is given by

$$S_b^2 = \sum_{i=1}^{N} (\bar{y}_i - \bar{\bar{Y}})^2/(N - 1).$$

Also we have the identity

$$\sum_{i}^{N} \sum_{j}^{M} (y_{ij} - \bar{\bar{Y}})^2 = \sum_{i}^{N} \sum_{j}^{M} (y_{ij} - \bar{y}_i)^2 + M \sum_{i=1}^{N} (\bar{y}_i - \bar{\bar{Y}})^2.$$

That is,

$$(NM - 1)S^2 = N(M - 1)S_W^2 + M(N - 1)S_b^2.$$

Define the sample mean of the cluster means by $\bar{\bar{y}}$, where

$$\bar{\bar{y}} = \sum_{i=1}^{n} \bar{y}_i/n.$$

Then we have the following identity

$$\sum_{i=1}^{n}\sum_{j=1}^{M}(y_{ij} - \bar{\bar{y}})^2 = \sum_{i=1}^{n}\sum_{j=1}^{M}(y_{ij} - \bar{y}_i)^2 + M\sum_{i=1}^{n}(\bar{y}_i - \bar{\bar{y}})^2.$$

That is,

$$(nM - 1)s^2 = n(M - 1)s_W^2 + M(n - 1)s_b^2$$

where s^2, s_W^2, and s_b^2 are defined analogous to S^2, S_W^2, and S_b^2 by replacing N by n.

Then we can develop an analysis of variance (Anova) table pertaining to the precision of the data.

9.3 PRECISION OF SURVEY DATA

Let each unit (or cluster) have M subunits. Suppose we have data available for each subunit of a cluster. Then a comparison of the precision of the large and small units can be made. Let us assume that a simple random sample of size n clusters is taken. Then we have the Anova table given in Table 9.1.

TABLE 9.1 Anova for the Sample

Source	d.f.	m.s.
Between clusters	$n - 1$	Ms_b^2
Between subunits within clusters	$n(M - 1)$	s_w^2
Between subunits in the sample	$nM - 1$	$s^2 = \{M(n-1)s_b^2 + n(M-1)s_W^2\}/(nM - 1)$

The estimated variance of a cluster (on a subunit basis) is s_b^2. Also, s^2 can be thought of as an estimate of the variance of a subunit. However, this will be biased, because the sample is not a simple random sample of subunits, since these are sampled in contiguous groups of M units. An unbiased estimate can be obtained from the sample by considering the Anova for the whole population, given in Table 9.2.

TABLE 9.2 Anova for the Population

Source	d.f.	m.s.
Between clusters	$N - 1$	MS_b^2
Between subunits within clusters	$N(M - 1)$	S_W^2
Between subunits in the population	$NM - 1$	$S^2 = \{M(N-1)S_b^2 + N(M-1)S_W^2\}/(NM - 1)$

With simple random sampling s_b^2 is unbiased for S_b^2. It can be shown that s_W^2 is also unbiased for S_W^2. Consequently, $\hat{S}^2$ given by

$$\hat{S}^2 = \{M(N-1)s_b^2 + N(M-1)s_W^2\}/(NM-1)$$

is unbiased for S^2. Also, for large N,

$$\hat{S}^2 \doteq \{Ms_b^2 + (M-1)s_W^2\}/M.$$

If n is large, say ≥ 50, then

$$s^2 \doteq \{Ms_b^2 + (M-1)s_W^2\}/M.$$

So, when N and n are large $s^2 \doteq \hat{S}^2$.

9.4   RELATION BETWEEN VARIANCE AND INTRACLUSTER CORRELATION

Recall that y_{ij} is the observed value of the jth subunit in ith cluster, and y_i is the ith cluster total. We need to distinguish between $\bar{Y} = \sum y_i/N$ =the mean per cluster and the mean per (element) subunit$= \bar{\bar{Y}} = \sum y_i/NM = \bar{Y}/M$.

The variance among elements is

$$S^2 = \sum_i \sum_j (y_{ij} - \bar{\bar{Y}})^2/(NM-1).$$

The intracluster correlation coefficient ρ is defined as

$$\rho = \frac{E(y_{ij} - \bar{\bar{Y}})(y_{ik} - \bar{\bar{Y}})}{E\left\{(y_{ij} - \bar{\bar{Y}})^2\right\}} = \frac{2\sum_i \sum\sum_{j<k}(y_{ij} - \bar{\bar{Y}})(y_{ik} - \bar{\bar{Y}})}{(M-1)(NM-1)S^2}.$$

Notice that the denominator is $(NM-1)S^2/NM$, and the number of terms in the numerator is $NM(M-1)/2$.

Result 9.1.   Suppose a simple random sample of n clusters, each cluster containing M elements, is drawn from the N clusters in the population, then the sample mean per element $\bar{\bar{y}}$ is an unbiased estimate of $\bar{\bar{Y}}$ with variance

$$\text{var}\,(\bar{\bar{y}}) = \frac{(1-f)}{n}\,\frac{NM-1}{M^2(N-1)}S^2[1 + (M-1)\rho]$$

$$\doteq \frac{(1-f)}{nM}S^2[1 + (M-1)\rho], \qquad \text{if } N \text{ is large.}$$

Proof: Recall that y_i denotes the total for the ith cluster and $\bar{y} = \sum_1^n y_i/n$. Then, by Result 3.2, $\bar{y}$ is unbiased for $\bar{Y}$ and has variance

$$\text{var}\,(\bar{y}) = \frac{(1-f)}{n} \cdot \frac{\sum(y_i - \bar{Y})^2}{N-1}.$$

However, $\bar{y} = M\bar{\bar{y}}$ and $\bar{Y} = M\bar{\bar{Y}}$. Thus

$$\operatorname{var}(\bar{\bar{y}}) = \frac{(1-f)}{nM^2} \frac{\sum^N (y_i - \bar{Y})^2}{N-1}$$

and

$$\widehat{\operatorname{var}}(\bar{\bar{y}}) = \frac{(1-f)}{nM^2} \sum_{i=1}^{n} (y_i - \bar{y})^2 (n-1)^{-1}.$$

Now one can write

$$y_i - \bar{Y} = (y_{i1} - \bar{\bar{Y}}) + \cdots + (y_{iM} - \bar{\bar{Y}}).$$

Square on both sides and sum over all N clusters

$$\sum_1^N (y_i - \bar{Y})^2 = \sum_{i=1}^N \sum_{j=1}^M (y_{ij} - \bar{\bar{Y}})^2 + 2 \sum_i \sum_{j<k} \sum (y_{ij} - \bar{\bar{Y}})(y_{ik} - \bar{\bar{Y}})$$

$$= (NM-1)S^2 + (M-1)(NM-1)\rho S^2$$

$$= (NM-1)S^2 [1 + (M-1)\rho] . \qquad\blacksquare$$

Now the desired result follows from the above two calculations. Notice that if a simple random sample of size nM elements is drawn, then

$$\operatorname{var}(\bar{\bar{y}}_{\mathrm{ran}}) = \frac{(1-f)}{nM} S^2 .$$

Thus, if $\rho \geq 0$, then cluster sampling is less precise, and if $\rho \leq 0$, then cluster sampling is more precise. ρ can be expressed in terms of S_b^2 as follows.

Recall that

$$\sum (y_i - \bar{Y})^2 = (N-1)M^2 S_b^2$$

$$= (NM-1)S^2 [1 + (M-1)\rho] .$$

Hence

$$\rho = \frac{(N-1)M^2 S_b^2 - (NM-1)S^2}{(NM-1)(M-1)S^2} \doteq \frac{MS_b^2 - S^2}{(M-1)S^2}$$

when terms of order $1/N$ are neglected. Also, from Table 9.2, we have

$$(NM-1)S^2 = M^{-1} \sum (y_i - \bar{Y})^2 + \sum_i^N \sum_j^M (y_{ij} - \bar{y}_i)^2$$

$$= \frac{(NM-1)}{M} S^2 [1 + (M-1)\rho] + N(M-1)S_w^2 .$$

Hence,

$$S_w^2 = \frac{(NM-1)}{NM} S^2 (1 - \rho) \doteq S^2 (1 - \rho).$$

EXAMPLE 9.1

The Department of Statistics at a certain state university offers several sections of an undergraduate course in statistics for business majors. Assume that the number of sections is $N = 10$ and each section is of the same size, $M = 30$. A random sample of size $n = 2$ sections is selected and a test on college algebra is given to all the students in the selected sections so as to assess the mathematics background of all the students. Assume that the scores range from 0 to 100 and we have the following data:

$$\bar{y}_1 = y_1/30 = 55, \qquad \bar{y}_2 = y_2/30 = 60.$$

Estimate the average score of all students taking the statistics course and obtain a 95% confidence interval for the same.

$$\bar{\bar{y}} = \hat{\bar{Y}} = (55 + 60)/2 = 57.5$$

and

$$\widehat{\text{var}}\,(\bar{\bar{y}}) = \frac{(1 - 0.2)}{2} \frac{\left\{(2.5)^2 + (2.5)^2\right\}}{2 - 1}$$

$$= (0.8)(6.25) = 5.0$$

$$s_{\bar{\bar{y}}} = 2.24.$$

Hence a 95% confidence interval for $\bar{\bar{Y}}$ is

$$\bar{\bar{y}} \pm 2s_{\bar{\bar{y}}}$$

which equals

$$57.5 \pm 4.48.$$ ◆

9.5   ESTIMATION OF M

On the basis of a random sample of subunits one can estimate S^2, which is not affected by M. S_W^2 will be affected by M (in fact it increases with M). In many agricultural surveys S_W^2 seems to be related to M by

$$S_W^2 = AM^g \qquad (g \geq 0)$$

where A and g are constants and typically g is small. If the plot of log S_W against log M is linear, then we have the above relation. Recall that

$$MS_b^2 \doteq MS^2 - (M - 1)S_W^2.$$

If $S_W^2 = AM^g$, by increasing the sample size to MN (i.e., treating the population as a single cluster with MN elements) one can assume the relation $S^2 = A(NM)^g$. Hence,

$$MS_b^2 \doteq AM^g\left[MN^g - (M - 1)\right].$$

9.6 COST ANALYSIS

Let c_1 denote the cost of travel from one subunit to another plus the cost of interview. Also, let the cost of travel from cluster to cluster be proportional to $\sqrt{n}$, where n denotes the number of clusters sampled. Hence the total cost is

$$C = c_1 Mn + c_2 \sqrt{n} \tag{9.1}$$

where c_2 is a given constant. Ignoring the population correction factor, we have

$$V = \text{var}(\bar{\bar{y}}) \doteq S_b^2 / n = \left[S^2 - (M-1)AM^{g-1} \right] / n. \tag{9.2}$$

In order to find the optimal M and, incidentally, n, we will minimize V subject to a fixed C. By solving the quadratic in $\sqrt{n}$ we have

$$\frac{2c_1 M \sqrt{n}}{c_2} = \left(1 + \frac{4Cc_1 M}{c_2^2} \right)^{\frac{1}{2}} - 1. \tag{9.3}$$

Using the Lagrange's approach, we try to minimize

$$C + \lambda V = c_1 Mn + c_2 \sqrt{n} + \lambda V.$$

Setting $\frac{\partial}{\partial n}(C + \lambda V) = 0$ and noting that $\partial V / \partial n = -V/n$, we have

$$c_1 M + \frac{1}{2} c_2 n^{-\frac{1}{2}} = -\frac{\lambda \partial V}{\partial n} = \frac{\lambda V}{n}. \tag{9.4}$$

Also, setting $\frac{\partial}{\partial M}(C + \lambda V) = 0$, we get

$$c_1 n = -\lambda \partial V / \partial M. \tag{9.5}$$

Dividing (9.5) by (9.4), we have

$$-\frac{n}{V}\frac{\partial V}{\partial M} = \frac{c_1 n}{c_1 M + \frac{1}{2}c_2 n^{-\frac{1}{2}}}. \tag{9.6}$$

Substituting $\sqrt{n}$ from (9.3) and simplifying, we obtain

$$\frac{M}{V}\frac{\partial V}{\partial M} = \left(1 + \frac{4Cc_1 M}{c_2^2} \right)^{-\frac{1}{2}} - 1. \tag{9.7}$$

Now substituting the expression for V, we have

$$\frac{AM^{g-1}[gM - (g-1)]}{S^2 - (M-1)AM^{g-1}} = 1 - (1 + 4Cc_1 Mc_2^{-2})^{-\frac{1}{2}} \tag{9.8}$$

which gives the optimum M. Notice that the left side does not involve the cost functions (c_1 and c_2). The right side increases with c_1. So, because of the term $c_1 M$ on right side, M should decrease with c_1. Similarly, M should increase with c_2.

In summary, the optimum M decreases when

1. length of interview increases (c_1 increases)
2. travel becomes cheaper (c_2 decreases)
3. the elements (subunits) become more dense (i.e., c_2 decreases)
4. total amount of money used (C) increases.

EXAMPLE 9.2

Let $c_1 = \$1.0$, $c_2 = \$2.0$, $A = 2$, $g = 1$, and $S^2 = 100$. Then the optimum M given by (9.8) is

$$\frac{2(M-0)}{100-2(M-1)} = 1 - \left\{1 + \frac{4C(1.0)M}{4}\right\}^{-\frac{1}{2}}$$

$$= 1 - \{1 + 1.0CM\}^{-\frac{1}{2}}$$

i.e.,

$$(1 + 1.0CM)^{-\frac{1}{2}} = 1 - \frac{2M}{100 - 2(M-1)}$$

$$= \frac{100 - 2M + 2 - 2M}{100 - 2(M-1)}$$

$$= \frac{102 - 4M}{102 - 2M} = \frac{51 - 2M}{51 - M}$$

$$(1 + 1.0CM)^{\frac{1}{2}} = \frac{51 - M}{51 - 2M}$$

$$(51 - 2M)^2(1 + 1.0CM) = (51 - M)^2$$

$$(51 - 2M)^2 CM = (51 - M)^2 - (51 - 2M)^2$$

$$= M(102 - 3M)$$

$$(51^2 - 204M + 4M^2)C = 102 - 3M$$

$$4CM^2 - (204C - 3)M + 51^2C - 102 = 0$$

$$8CM = (204C - 3) \pm \{(204C - 3)^2$$

$$- 4 \cdot 4C(51^2 C - 102)\}^{\frac{1}{2}}$$

$$\frac{8C}{204}M = \left(C - \frac{3}{204}\right) \pm \left\{\left(C - \frac{3}{204}\right)^2\right.$$

$$\left. - C\left(C - \frac{2}{51}\right)\right\}^{\frac{1}{2}}.$$

If C is large, say > 1, then

$$M \doteq \frac{204}{8} \doteq 26$$

which is independent of C. ◆

9.7 CLUSTER SAMPLING FOR PROPORTIONS

If the response variable takes the value 1 or 0 according as the unit belongs to class C or not, then we are dealing with proportions. Let a_i be the number of subunits in ith cluster that belong to class C. Then, let $p_i = a_i/M$. A simple random sample of n clusters is taken, the average p of the observed p_i is used to estimate the population proportion P. Then we have

$$\text{var}(p) = \frac{N-n}{Nn} \sum_{i=1}^{N} \frac{(p_i - P)^2}{N-1} \doteq \frac{(N-n)}{N^2 n} \sum (p_i - P)^2$$

and

$$s_p^2 = \widehat{\text{var}}(p) \doteq \frac{(N-n)}{Nn(n-1)} \sum_1^n (p_i - p)^2 .$$

Had we taken a simple random sample of size Mn subunits and estimated P, then from the formula for the variance of sample mean from finite populations, we would have

$$\text{var}_{\text{bin}}(p) = \frac{MN - nM}{NM - 1} \cdot \frac{PQ}{nM} \doteq \frac{(N-n)}{N} \frac{PQ}{nM}, \qquad \text{if } N \text{ is large} .$$

Thus the efficiency of the SRS relative to cluster sampling is

$$\frac{\text{var}(p)}{\text{var}_{\text{bin}}(p)} \doteq \frac{M \sum (p_i - P)^2}{NPQ}, \qquad \text{when } N \text{ is large} .$$

It is of interest to determine the sample size required by cluster sampling. We estimate it by the binomial formula and then multiply it by the factor—namely, the efficiency—given by

$$M \sum (p_i - P)^2 / NPQ .$$

If the cluster sizes are unequal, we can modify the above formula.

Example 9.3

Suppose we are interested in estimating the proportion of freshmen in a certain university who own automobiles. Suppose the freshmen dorm consists of 10 floors and 50 rooms on each floor and two students live in each room. We take a random sample of 3 floors and obtain the following data.

Floor #	2	7	9
# of students having automobiles	50	60	45

Obtain an estimate of P, the proportion of freshmen who own automobiles, and a 95% confidence interval for the same.

$$p_1 = 0.5, \qquad p_2 = 0.6, \qquad p_3 = 0.45 .$$

Hence,

$$p = (0.5 + 0.6 + 0.45)/3 = 0.52$$

and

$$
\begin{aligned}
s_p^2 &= \frac{(1 - 0.3)}{3(3 - 1)} \left\{ (0.5 - 0.52)^2 + (0.6 - 0.52)^2 + (0.45 - 0.52)^2 \right\} \\
&= \frac{0.7}{3(2)} (.0004 + .0064 + 0.0049) \\
&= \frac{0.35}{3} (0.0117) = 0.001365
\end{aligned}
$$

$$s_p = 0.037 .$$

So, a 95% confidence interval for P is 0.52 ± 0.074.   ◆

9.8   CASE OF UNEQUAL CLUSTER SIZES

In several applications the sizes of the clusters (for example, number of households in city blocks) are unequal. Let M_i denote the size of the ith cluster unit $(i = 1, \ldots, N)$. We are interested in estimating the population total Y of the y_{ij}. In the following we will provide two methods of estimation, one based on simple random sampling method and the other on the ratio method of estimation.

Estimate Based on Simple Random Sample

Let

$$y_i = \sum_{j=1}^{M_i} y_{ij} = M_i \bar{y}_i$$

denoting the total for ith cluster $(i = 1, \ldots, N)$. Then an unbiased estimate of Y, the population total, is

$$\hat{Y} = \frac{N}{n} \sum_{i=1}^{n} y_i$$

y_i denoting the total for ith cluster $(i = 1, \ldots, N)$, because

$$E(\hat{Y}) = \frac{N}{n} \left(\sum_{j=1}^{N} y_j \right) \frac{n}{N} = Y .$$

Let $\bar{Y} = Y/N$, the population mean per cluster unit. Then from Result 3.2, it follows that

$$\text{var}(\hat{Y}) = \frac{N^2(1-f)}{n} \sum_{i=1}^{N} \frac{(y_i - \bar{Y})^2}{N-1} = \frac{N^2(1-f)}{n(N-1)} \left[\sum_{1}^{N} y_i^2 - (Y^2/N) \right]. \quad (9.9)$$

When the $\bar{y}_i$ change little from unit to unit in each cluster and the M_i vary greatly, then $y_i = M_i \bar{y}_i$ vary greatly, var$(\hat{Y})$ will be large and, consequently, $\hat{Y}$ will be less precise.

Ratio Estimate Based on Size

Let $M_0 = \sum_{i=1}^{N} M_i$ = population size (total number of subunits in the population). If the M_i and M_0 are known, then using $x_i = M_i$ as the auxiliary variable, the ratio estimate of the population total is given by

$$\hat{Y}_R = M_0 \left(\sum_{i=1}^{n} y_i / \sum_{i=1}^{n} M_i \right) = M_0 \times \text{sample mean per element}.$$

Here $R = Y/X = Y/M_0 = \bar{\bar{Y}}$ = the population mean per element.

Assuming that N is large, we can show that (see Result 6.1)

$$\text{var}(\hat{Y}_R) \doteq \frac{N^2(1-f) \sum_{i=1}^{N}(y_i - M_i \bar{\bar{Y}})^2}{n} \frac{}{N-1}$$

$$= \frac{N^2(1-f) \sum_{i=1}^{N} M_i^2 (\bar{y}_i - \bar{\bar{Y}})^2}{n} \frac{}{N-1}. \quad (9.10)$$

Notice that the variance of $(\bar{Y}_R)$ depends on the variability among the means per element and typically will be smaller than var$(\hat{Y})$. However, $\hat{Y}_R$ supposes the knowledge of all M_i and hence M_0, whereas $\hat{Y}$ does not. The reverse is true if we are interested in estimating the population mean per element; the estimate will require the knowledge of the cluster sizes that are included in the simple random sample, because

$$\hat{\bar{\bar{Y}}} = \frac{\hat{Y}}{M_0} = \frac{N}{nM_0} \sum_{i=1}^{n} y_i$$

and

$$\hat{\bar{\bar{Y}}}_R = \frac{\hat{Y}_R}{M_0} = \frac{\sum_{1}^{n} y_i}{\sum_{1}^{n} M_i} = \text{sample mean per element}.$$

EXAMPLE 9.4

Consider the following artificial data consisting of $N = 5$ clusters.

Unit	M_i = size	Cluster Total = y_i	Cluster Mean = $\bar{y}_i$	Cumulative Sum of Clusters $= \sum M_i$	Range Assigned
1	4	20	5	4	1–4
2	2	10	5	6	5–6
3	15	75	5	21	7–21
4	7	49	7	28	22–28
5	12	72	6	40	29–40
Total	40	226			

Suppose we take a random sample of size $n = 2$ clusters, given by 2 and 5. Then

$$\hat{Y} = \frac{5}{2}(10 + 72) = 205$$

$$\hat{Y}_R = 40(10 + 72)/(2 + 12) = 40(82)/14 = 234.3 \,.$$

$$\bar{Y} = \frac{226}{5} = 45.2, \; \bar{\bar{Y}} = \frac{226}{40} = 4.65$$

$$\text{Var}(\hat{Y}) = \frac{25(1 - 0.4)}{2(4)} \left[20^2 + 10^2 + 75^2 + 49^2 + 72^2 - \frac{(226)^2}{5} \right]$$

$$= \frac{7.5}{4}[13710 - 10215.2] = 6552.75$$

$$\sigma_{\hat{Y}} = 80.95$$

$$\text{Var}(\hat{Y}_R) = \frac{7.5}{4} \left[\sum Y_i^2 - 2\bar{\bar{Y}} \sum M_i y_i + \bar{\bar{Y}}^2 \sum M_i^2 \right]$$

$$= \frac{7.5}{4}(13{,}710 - 27{,}481.6 + 13{,}982.055)$$

$$= \frac{7.5}{4}(210.455) = 394.60$$

$$\sigma_{\hat{Y}_R} = 19.86 \qquad \blacklozenge$$

9.9   PROBABILITY SAMPLING PROPORTIONAL TO SIZE

Hansen and Hurwitz (1943) propose selection of clusters with probabilities proportional to their size when the M_i are all known. For example, if we wish to select one cluster out of five in the preceding example, we draw a random number lying between 1 and

40. Suppose that number is 20, which falls in the range assigned to unit 3. So we select unit 3. This method becomes cumbersome, especially when N is large. Lahiri (1951) gives an alternative method which avoids cumulating the M_i. Let $M_{(N)} = \max_i M_i$. Draw a random number between 1 and N; let this be i. Draw another random number m lying between 1 and $M_{(N)}$. If $m \leq M_i$ the ith unit is selected. If not, try another pair of random numbers.

Now consider $n > 1$, and assume that sampling is with replacement. Suppose we want to select a second unit by the cumulative method. Draw a new random number between 1 and 40. Here we allow unit 3 to be chosen again. With this rule, the probabilities of selection remain proportional to the size at each draw.

Case of $n > 1$ (Drawn with Replacement)

Sampling with replacement allows duplicate units in the sample. However, an advantage is that the formulae for the variance of the estimate and the estimate of the variance will be simple. First let us give a general result from which special cases follow.

Result 9.2.   Let the ith cluster unit be selected with probability z_i $(z_i > 0)$, where $\sum_{i=1}^{N} z_i = 1$. Consider an estimate

$$\hat{Y}_{ppz} = \frac{1}{n} \sum_{i=1}^{n} \frac{y_i}{z_i} . \tag{9.11}$$

Then

$$E(\hat{Y}_{ppz}) = Y$$

and

$$\operatorname{var}(\hat{Y}_{ppz}) = \frac{1}{n} \sum_{i=1}^{N} z_i \left(\frac{y_i}{z_i} - Y \right)^2 . \tag{9.12}$$

Proof: Let t_i denote the number of times the ith cluster unit has been drawn in a sample of size n. Notice that t_i can take values $0, 1, \ldots, n$. Since drawing a sample with replacement of size n is equivalent to distributing n balls to N boxes, with the probability of a ball going into ith box being z_i, then the t_i have a multinomial distribution with

$$E(t_i) = nz_i, \quad \operatorname{var}(t_i) = nz_i(1 - z_i) \text{ and } \operatorname{cov}(t_i, t_j) = -nz_iz_j, \quad i \neq j . \tag{9.13}$$

Then we can rewrite $\hat{Y}_{ppz}$ as

$$\hat{Y}_{ppz} = \frac{1}{n} \sum_{i=1}^{N} \frac{y_i}{z_i} t_i$$

where y_i, z_i are fixed and the t_i are random. Thus

$$E(\hat{Y}_{ppz}) = \frac{1}{n} \sum_{i=1}^{N} \frac{y_i}{z_i} n z_i = \sum_{i=1}^{N} y_i = Y,$$

$$\operatorname{var}(\hat{Y}_{ppz}) = n^{-2} \left[\sum_{i=1}^{N} \left(\frac{y_i}{z_i}\right)^2 \operatorname{var} t_i + \sum_{i \ne j}^{N} \sum^{N} \frac{y_i y_j}{z_i z_j} \operatorname{cov}(t_i t_j) \right]$$

$$= n^{-1} \left[\sum_{i=1}^{N} \frac{y_i^2}{z_i} (1 - z_i) - 2 \sum_{i<j}^{N} \sum^{N} y_i y_j \right]$$

$$= n^{-1} \left[\sum_{i=1}^{N} \frac{y_i^2}{z_i} - Y^2 \right]$$

$$= n^{-1} \sum_{i=1}^{N} z_i \left(\frac{y_i}{z_i} - Y\right)^2. \tag{9.14}$$

An alternative form for $\operatorname{var}(\hat{Y}_{ppz})$ can be obtained as follows. Starting with (9.14), we have

$$\operatorname{var}(\hat{Y}_{ppz}) = n^{-1} \left[\sum_{i=1}^{N} \frac{y_i^2}{z_i} \sum_{j \ne i}^{N} z_j - 2 \sum_{i<j} \sum y_i y_j \right]$$

$$= n^{-1} \left[\sum_{i<j} \sum \frac{y_i^2}{z_i} z_j + \sum_{i>j} \sum \frac{y_i^2}{z_i} z_j - 2 \sum_{i<j} \sum y_i y_j \right]$$

$$= n^{-1} \left[\sum_{i<j} \sum \left\{ \frac{y_i^2}{z_i} z_j + \frac{y_j^2}{z_j} z_i - 2 y_i y_j \right\} \right]$$

$$= n^{-1} \sum_{i<j}^{N} \sum^{N} z_i z_j \left(\frac{y_i}{z_i} - \frac{y_j}{z_j}\right)^2. \tag{9.15}$$

∎

Result 9.3. If a random sample of size n is drawn with replacement and the probability is proportional to z_i, then an unbiased estimate of $\operatorname{var}(\hat{Y}_{ppz})$ is given by

$$\widehat{\operatorname{var}}(\hat{Y}_{ppz}) = \sum_{i=1}^{n} \left(\frac{y_i}{z_i} - \hat{Y}_{ppz}\right)^2 / n(n-1). \tag{9.16}$$

Proof: Let $r_i = y_i/z_i$ $(i = 1, \ldots, N)$.   ∎

Let $r_1', \ldots, r_n'$ denote the sampled values. That is, r_j' = value of $r_i = \frac{y_i}{z_i}$ at jth draw with probability z_i.

Let

$$\bar{r}' = \frac{1}{n} \sum_{j=1}^{n} r_j'.$$

Then

$$E(\bar{r}') = E(r_1') = \sum_{i=1}^{N} r_i z_i = Y$$

and

$$\text{var}(\bar{r}') = \frac{1}{n} \sigma_{r_1'}^2.$$

Hence an unbiased estimate of $\text{var}(\bar{r}')$ is

$$\widehat{\text{var}}(\bar{r}') = \frac{1}{n} s_{r'}^2$$

$$= \frac{1}{n} \frac{1}{n-1} \sum_{j=1}^{n} (r_j' - \bar{r}')^2.$$

Another form for the $\widehat{\text{var}}(\hat{Y}_{ppz})$ is

$$\widehat{\text{var}}(\hat{Y}_{ppz}) = \frac{1}{n} \sum_{i<j}^{n} \sum^{n} (r_i' - r_j')^2$$

because, one can write

$$\widehat{\text{var}}(\hat{Y}_{ppz}) = \frac{1}{n} \sum_{i<j}^{N} \sum^{N} (r_i - r_j)^2 a_{ij}$$

where

$$a_{ij} = 1, \qquad \text{if } i\text{th and } j\text{th units are included in the sample}$$

$$= 0, \qquad \text{otherwise}.$$

Hence

$$E\left(\widehat{\text{var}}(\hat{Y}_{ppz})\right) = \frac{1}{n} \sum_{i<j}^{N} \sum^{N} (r_i - r_j)^2 z_i z_j.$$

Special Cases. If $z_i = M_i/M_0$, $M_0 = \sum_{i=1}^{N} M_i$, then

$$\hat{Y}_{ppz} = \hat{Y}_{pps} = \frac{M_0}{n} \sum_{i=1}^{n} \frac{y_i}{M_i} = \frac{M_0}{n} \sum_{i=1}^{n} \bar{y}_i = M_0 \bar{\bar{y}} \qquad (9.17)$$

where $\bar{\bar{y}}$ is the unweighted mean of the unit means. Also, as a special case of (9.14),

$$\text{var}(\hat{Y}_{pps}) = \frac{M_0}{n} \sum_{i=1}^{N} M_i (\bar{y}_i - \bar{\bar{Y}})^2. \qquad (9.18)$$

Also, setting $z_i = M_i/M_0$ in (9.16), it follows that an unbiased estimate of var $(\hat{Y}_{pps})$ is

$$\widehat{\text{var}}(\hat{Y}_{pps}) = M_0^2 \sum_{i=1}^{n} (\bar{y}_i - \bar{\bar{y}})^2/n(n-1) \qquad (9.19)$$

since $\bar{y}_i = y_i/M_i$ and $\hat{Y}_{pps} = M_0 \bar{\bar{y}}$.

Remark 9.1. In some applications the M_i are not known, but a measure of the bigness of the unit is known which is highly correlated with the unit total y_i. For example, the size of a hospital could be in terms of the total number of beds or the average number of occupied beds. Thus, we can consider a measure of size M_i' and the corresponding probability of selection $z_i = M_i'/M_0'$, where $M_0' = \sum_{i=1}^{N} M_i'$.

Remark 9.2. Since one can write var $(\hat{Y}_{ppz})$ as

$$\text{var}(\hat{Y}_{ppz}) = \frac{1}{n} \left(\sum_{1}^{N} y_i^2/z_i - Y^2 \right)$$

note that

$$\text{var}(\hat{Y}_{ppz}) = 0$$

if $z_i = y_i/Y$. Hence one should use as a measure of size, that which is most nearly proportional to the unit totals of the principle items.

9.10 COMPARISON OF THE THREE METHODS

We want to assess the relative accuracies of the three estimates of the population total, namely

1. Simple random sample of clusters: Estimate is $\hat{Y}_u$.
2. Simple random sample of clusters: Ratio to size estimate is $\hat{Y}_R$.
3. Probability proportional to size: Estimate is $\hat{Y}_{pps}$.

Writing $N - 1 \doteq N$ and $E(y_i - \bar{Y})^2 = \frac{1}{N}\sum_1^N (y_i - \bar{Y})^2$ and assuming that the bias in $\hat{Y}_R$ is negligible, we can rewrite (9.9), (9.10), and (9.18) as

$$n \text{ var}(\hat{Y}_u) = (1 - f)E(Ny_i - Y)^2 \qquad (9.20)$$

$$n \text{ var}(\hat{Y}_R) = (1 - f)E\left(\frac{M_i}{\bar{M}}\right)^2 (M_0\bar{y}_i - Y)^2,$$

$$\bar{M} = \sum M_i/N = M_0/N \qquad (9.21)$$

$$n \text{ var}(\hat{Y}_{pps}) = NM_0EM_i(\bar{y}_i - \bar{\bar{Y}})^2 = E\left(\frac{M_i}{\bar{M}}\right)(M_0\bar{y}_i - Y)^2. \qquad (9.22)$$

$\hat{Y}_R$ is superior to $\hat{Y}_{pps}$ if f is substantial. $\hat{Y}_u$ is preferable when y_i is unrelated to M_i. The probability sampling without replacement will be taken up in Chapter 10.

■ PROBLEMS

9.1   A population consists of 3000 elements and is divided into 20 clusters, each containing 150 subunits. A simple random sample of $n = 3$ clusters is drawn. The analysis of variance of the sample data on an element basis is as follows.

Source	df	ms
Between clusters	2	2.5
Within subunits within clusters	447	3.0
Within subunits in the sample	449	3.1

Find unbiased estimates of S^2, S_W^2, and an estimate of S_b^2.

9.2   In planning a sample survey a pilot study was conducted with varying cluster sizes and the estimates of S_W^2 were obtained. The results are summarized in the following table.

Cluster size	s_W^2
15	0.05
20	0.08
25	0.11
30	0.18
35	0.22

On the basis of the above data fit the relation $S_W^2 = AM^g$ $(g > 0)$ and determine A and g.
Hint: Fit a regression line to $\ln S_W^2$ with $\ln M$ as the independent variable.

9.3   The University of Mars is interested in the average amount per week spent on grocers by married graduate students living in a high-rise apartment complex consisting of 15 floors, each floor having 10 apartments. We take a random sample of $n = 3$ floors and obtain the following data.

	Floor 2	Floor 6	Floor 9
	$55	$95	$56
	75	72	68
	65	66	56
	52	76	84
	60	56	69
	72	71	74
	85	65	84
	69	59	79
	57	86	76
	70	64	73
Total	660	710	719

Obtain an estimate of the average amount (per week) spent by a married graduate student on grocers and its standard error.

9.4   Find the optimum value of M (as done in Example 9.2) for the parameter configuration: $c_1 = 1$, $c_2 = 2$, $A = 1$, $g = \frac{1}{2}$, and $S^2 = 100$.

Hint: Assume that c is large and set $x = M^{-1}$, obtain an approximate quartic equation in x which can be solved using Newton's method.

9.5   Suppose we wish to estimate the proportion of Afro-Americans living in a high-rise dormitory consisting of $N = 12$ floors and $M = 50$ rooms on each floor. Suppose we take a random sample of $n = 3$ floors and obtain the following data:

	Floor 2	Floor 6	Floor 9
a_i	4	5	3

Obtain an estimate of P, the proportion of Afro-Americans living in that dorm and a 95% confidence interval for the same.

Hint: Assume that there are two students in each room.

9.6   The University of Kentucky Equal Opportunity Board wishes to estimate the proportion of female professors who have tenured positions in Patterson Office Tower consisting of $N = 15$ floors and $M = 20$ offices per floor. Suppose we take a random sample of $n = 3$ floors and obtain the following data.

	Floor 8	Floor 11	Floor 13
a_i	1	3	5

Obtain an estimate of P, the proportion of female professors who have tenured positions.

9.7   We are interested in a shoe manufacturing company's shoe defective rate on a certain day. There are 24 production lines and each line manufactures 1,000 pairs of shoes in a day. We select 3 lines and gather the following data.

line	2	9	17
# of defective shoes	8	6	7

Obtain an estimate of the defective rate and a 95% confidence interval for the same.

■ REFERENCES

9.1 Cochran, W. G. (1977). *Sampling Techniques*. New York: John Wiley & Sons.

9.2 Hansen, M. H. and Hurwitz, W. N. (1943). On the theory of sampling from finite populations. *Ann. Math. Statist.* **14**, 333–362.

9.3 Lahiri, D. B. (1951). A method for sample selection providing unbiased ratio estimates. *Bull. Intern. Statist. Inst.* **31**, 24–57.

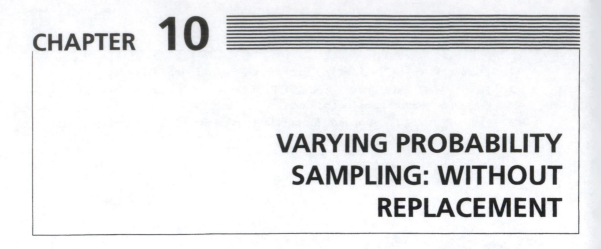

CHAPTER 10

VARYING PROBABILITY SAMPLING: WITHOUT REPLACEMENT

10.1 INTRODUCTION AND PRELIMINARIES

In Chapter 2 we dealt with probability sampling with replacement. Here, we deal with probability sampling without replacement. Let the population consist of elements $U_1, U_2, \ldots, U_N$. A sample of size n is drawn without replacement. Let the probability of selecting the ith element of the population prior to the first draw be $p_{i,1}$ $(i = 1, \ldots, N)$ where

$$p_{i,1} \geq 0, \qquad \sum_{i=1}^{N} p_{i,1} = 1.$$

This constitutes, in a sense, a probability distribution (of selection) for the elements of the population for samples of size one. Since we are sampling without replacement, prior to each succeeding draw we must define a new probability distribution for the remaining elements. These may be based on initial probabilities or can be a completely unrelated set. For the mth draw, let $p_{i,m}$ denote the probability of selecting U_i with

$$p_{i,m} \geq 0, \qquad \sum_i p_{i,m} = 1 \qquad (10.1)$$

where the summation extends only over the $N - m + 1$ remaining elements. The n sets of selection probabilities will be denoted by

$$[p_{i,m}], \qquad m = 1, \ldots, n.$$

Let π_i denote the probability of including U_i in the sample. Then

$$\pi_i = \sum_{m=1}^{n} p_{i,m} \, . \tag{10.2}$$

Now, it is easy to see that

$$\sum_{i=1}^{N} \pi_i = \sum_{m=1}^{n} \sum_{i=1}^{N} p_{i,m} = n \, . \tag{10.3}$$

Also, let

$$\pi_{ij} = P(\text{both } U_i \text{ and } U_j \text{ are included in the sample, } i \neq j) \tag{10.4}$$

$$= \sum_{l \neq k}^{n} \sum^{n} p_{i,l} p_{j,k}, i \neq j \, .$$

Then we have

$$\sum_{\substack{j=1 \\ j \neq i}}^{N} \pi_{ij} = \sum_{l \neq k}^{n} \sum^{n} p_{i,l} \sum_{j \neq i}^{N} p_{j,k}$$

$$= \sum_{l \neq k}^{n} \sum^{n} p_{i,l} = (n-1) \sum_{l=1}^{n} p_{i,l} = (n-1)\pi_i \, . \tag{10.5}$$

Also, consider

$$\sum_{i=1}^{N} \sum_{j>i}^{N} \pi_{ij} = \frac{1}{2} \sum_{i=1}^{N} \sum_{j \neq i}^{N} \pi_{ij} = \frac{1}{2}(n-1) \sum_{1}^{N} \pi_i = \frac{n(n-1)}{2} \, . \tag{10.6}$$

Thus, we have proved the following result.

Result 10.1. In probability sampling without replacement, we have

1. $\displaystyle \sum_{i=1}^{N} \pi_i = \sum_{i=1}^{N} P(U_i \text{ is in the sample}) = n,$

2. $\displaystyle \sum_{\substack{j=1 \\ j \neq i}}^{N} \pi_{ij} = (n-1)\pi_i,$

3. $\displaystyle \sum_{i=1}^{N} \sum_{j>i}^{N} \pi_{ij} = \frac{1}{2}n(n-1).$

Also note that if we define the indicator variables

$$t_i = 1, \qquad \text{if } i \in s$$
$$= 0, \qquad \text{otherwise, for } i = 1, \ldots, n,$$

then

$$E(t_i) = \pi_i.$$

Also

$$\sum_{i=1}^{N} t_i = n.$$

Taking expectation on both sides, we obtain (1) of Result 10.1. Also

$$\left(\sum_{i=1}^{N} t_i\right)^2 = \sum t_i^2 + \sum\sum_{i \neq j} t_i t_j = \sum t_i + \sum\sum_{i \neq j} t_i t_j.$$

Thus

$$\sum\sum_{i \neq j} t_i t_j = n^2 - n.$$

Hence,

$$E\left(\sum\sum_{i \neq j} t_i t_j\right) = \sum_{i \neq j}^{N}\sum^{N} \pi_{ij} = n^2 - n = n(n-1).$$

In general one can show that

$$\sum_{i_1 \neq i_2 \neq \ldots \neq i_r}^{N} \cdots \sum^{N} \pi_{i_1, i_2, \ldots, i_r} = n(n-1)\ldots(n-r+1).$$

Also

$$\sum_{j=1, j \neq i}^{N} \pi_{ij} = \sum_{j \neq i}^{N} E(t_i t_j) = E\left[\sum_{j \neq i}^{N} t_i t_j\right]$$

$$= E\left[t_i \sum_{j \neq i}^{N} t_j\right]$$

$$= E\left[t_i(n - t_i)\right]$$

$$= n\pi_i - \pi_i = (n-1)\pi_i.$$

which provides an alternative proof of 2 in Result 10.1.

There are $\binom{N}{n}$ different samples of size n drawn without replacement from a population of size N, where we assume that at each stage of the draw all remaining undrawn elements have a positive probability of being selected. Since each different sample can be ordered in $n!$ ways, there are

$$S = n! \binom{N}{n}$$

possible samples when order is considered. Let s_n $(s = 1, \ldots, S)$ be the sth such sample of size n. Then, if s_n contains the elements $U_i, U_j, \ldots, U_t$,

$$P(s_n) = p_{i,1}, \; p_{j,2}, \; \ldots, \; p_{t,n} \; . \tag{10.7}$$

For a sample of size n, the probability that U_i is included in the sample is equal to a summation of the probabilities associated with the $n! \binom{N-1}{n-1} = S^{(i)}$ samples that contain U_i. That is,

$$\pi_i = \sum_{s=1}^{S^{(i)}} P(s_n^{(i)}) \tag{10.8}$$

where $s_n^{(i)}$ denotes a sample of size n which includes U_i.

Analogously, the probability that elements U_i and U_j are included in the sample is

$$\pi_{ij} = \sum_{s=1}^{S^{(ij)}} P(s_n^{(ij)}) \tag{10.9}$$

since there are $n! \binom{N-2}{n-2} = S^{(ij)}$ such samples, $s_n^{(ij)}$ denoting a specific one.

10.2   EXPECTED VALUES OF SUMS AND PRODUCT-SUMS

Let y_i denote the response from the unit U_i $(i = 1, \ldots, N)$. Note that not all of the y_i's are necessarily distinct. Then

$$E \left(\sum_{j=1}^{n} y_{i_j} \right) = \sum_{s=1}^{S} p(s_n) \left(\sum_{j=1}^{n} y_{i_j} \right)_{s_n} . \tag{10.10}$$

Factoring the y_i common to the ith element U_i and summing over the population, we have

$$E \left(\sum_{j=1}^{n} y_{i_j} \right) = \sum_{i=1}^{N} y_i \sum_{s=1}^{S^{(i)}} P(s_n^{(i)}) \tag{10.11}$$

$$= \sum_{i=1}^{N} y_i \pi_i .$$

Alternatively,

$$E\left(\sum_{j=1}^{n} y_{i_j}\right) = E\left(\sum_{i=1}^{N} y_i t_i\right) = \sum_{i=1}^{N} y_i E(t_i)$$

$$= \sum_{i=1}^{N} y_i \pi_i .$$

Similarly,

$$E\left(\sum_{j\neq k}^{N} y_{i_j} y_{i_k}\right) = \sum_{s=1}^{S} P(s_n) \left(\sum_{j\neq k} y_{i_j} y_{i_k}\right)_{s_n} \tag{10.12}$$

$$= \sum_{i\neq l}^{N} \sum_{i=1}^{N} y_i y_l \sum_{s}^{S^{(i,l)}} P(s_n^{(i,l)})$$

$$= \sum_{i\neq l}^{N} \sum_{i=1}^{N} y_i y_l \pi_{i,l} .$$

Alternatively,

$$E\left(\sum_{j\neq k}^{N} \sum_{i=1}^{N} y_{i_j} y_{i_k}\right) = E\left(\sum_{j\neq k}^{N} \sum_{i=1}^{N} y_i y_l t_i t_l\right)$$

$$= \sum_{l\neq k}^{N} \sum_{i=1}^{N} y_i y_l \pi_{i,l} .$$

10.3 ESTIMATION OF THE POPULATION TOTAL

Let $Y = \sum_{i=1}^{N} y_i$. Consider the following estimator (linear) of Y,

$$\hat{Y}_1 = \sum_{i=1}^{n} \alpha_i y_i \tag{10.13}$$

where α_i ($i = 1, \ldots, n$) is a constant to be used as a weight for the element selected on the ith draw, and

$$\hat{Y}_2 = \sum_{i=1}^{n} \beta_i y_i \tag{10.14}$$

where β_i is a constant to be used as a weight for the ith *element* whenever it is selected for the sample ($i = 1, \ldots, N$). We may also consider

$$\hat{Y}_3 = \gamma_{s_n} \left(\sum_{i=1}^{n} y_i \right)_{s_n} \qquad (10.15)$$

where γ_{s_n} is a constant to be used as a weight whenever the s_nth sample is selected. It should be pointed out that the α_i are independent of the particular sample that is selected. On the other hand, the β_i and γ_{s_n}, although known constants for a specified sampling procedure, depend on the particular sample selected. We will be interested in determining the best unbiased estimator of Y in the three subclasses of linear estimators.

When we are sampling with equal probabilities of selection for each draw, the α's, β's, and γ's are all equal to N/n for the best linear unbiased estimator of Y for each of the three subclasses. However, it is not justified to claim that

$$\hat{Y} = (N/n) \sum_{i=1}^{n} y_i \qquad (10.16)$$

is the "best" among all possible linear unbiased estimators of Y. Let us find the best unbiased in the subclass characterized by $\hat{Y}_2$. $E(\hat{Y}_2) = Y$ implies that

$$\sum_{i=1}^{N} \pi_i \beta_i y_i = Y = \sum_{1}^{N} y_i$$

or

$$\sum_{i=1}^{N} (\pi_i \beta_i - 1) y_i = 0.$$

If this were to hold for all possible values of the unknown y_i, then $\pi_i \beta_i = 1$ for all i. Hence,

$$\hat{Y} = \sum_{i=1}^{n} \frac{y_i}{\pi_i} \qquad (10.17)$$

is the only unbiased linear estimator in the subclass generated by $\hat{Y}_2$ and this is "best" for that subclass. The above estimator is called the *Horvitz-Thompson (H-T) estimator*. If $\pi_i = ny_i/Y$, then $\hat{Y}$ will have zero variance and the sampling will be optimum.

Although the H-T estimator is not uniformly minimum variance in the class of all unbiased estimators, it is admissible in the class of all unbiased estimators (see Godambe and Joshi (1965)).

EXAMPLE 10.1

Suppose we want to estimate the total number of foreign cars possessed by households in Sadieville, Kentucky. Let

$$N = 10 = \text{total \# of households.}$$

We draw a sample of size 3 without replacement. Let

$$U_1, \ldots, U_{10} \quad \text{be the units and}$$

$$y_1, \ldots, y_{10} \quad \text{be the responses.}$$

Let the π_i be as follows:

$$\pi_i = 0.25 \quad \text{for } i = 1, 3, 5, 6, 8, 9$$

$$= 0.375 \quad \text{for } 2, 4, 7, 10.$$

Suppose you choose U_1, U_4, U_7 in your sample and the responses are $(0, 1, 1)$. Then the Horvitz-Thompson estimator of Y is

$$\hat{Y} = \frac{y_1}{0.25} + \frac{y_4}{0.375} + \frac{y_7}{0.375}$$

$$= 0 + \frac{2}{0.375} = \frac{16}{3} = 5.33.$$

◆

Result 10.2. If $\pi_i > 0 \ (i = 1, \ldots, N)$, then $\hat{Y}_{HT} = \sum_1^n \frac{y_i}{\pi_i}$ is an unbiased estimator of Y, with variance

$$\text{var } \hat{Y}_{HT} = \sum_{i=1}^{N} \frac{(1 - \pi_i)}{\pi_i} y_i^2 + \sum_{i=1}^{N} \sum_{j \neq i}^{N} \frac{(\pi_{ij} - \pi_i \pi_j)}{\pi_i \pi_j} y_i y_j. \tag{10.18}$$

Proof: Recall that

$$t_i = 1, \quad \text{if } U_i \text{ is included in the sample,}$$

$$= 0, \quad \text{otherwise, for } i = 1, \ldots, N.$$

Then

$$E(t_i) = \pi_i, \quad \text{var } t_i = \pi_i (1 - \pi_i)$$

and for $i \neq j$

$$\text{cov}(t_i, t_j) = E(t_i t_j) - E(t_i) E(t_j) = \pi_{ij} - \pi_i \pi_j.$$

Hence, treating the y_i's as fixed and the t_i's as random variables,

$$E(\hat{Y}_{HT}) = E \left(\sum_{i=1}^{N} t_i \frac{y_i}{\pi_i} \right) = \sum_1^N y_i = Y$$

$$\text{var } \hat{Y}_{HT} = \sum_1^N \left(\frac{y_i}{\pi_i} \right)^2 \text{var } t_i + \sum_{i \neq j}^{N} \sum^{N} \frac{y_i y_j}{\pi_i \pi_j} \text{cov}(t_i, t_j)$$

$$= \sum_1^N \left(\frac{1 - \pi_i}{\pi_i} \right) y_i^2 + \sum_{i \neq j}^{N} \sum^{N} \left(\frac{\pi_{ij} - \pi_i \pi_j}{\pi_i \pi_j} \right) y_i y_j.$$

∎

Alternate Expression for $\text{var } \hat{Y}_{HT}$.

From Result 10.1 we have

$$\sum_{\substack{j=1 \\ j \neq i}}^{N} (\pi_{ij} - \pi_i \pi_j) = (n-1)\pi_i - \pi_i(n - \pi_i) = -\pi_i(1 - \pi_i).$$

Using this, we can write

$$\sum_{i=1}^{N}(1 - \pi_i)\pi_i\left(\frac{y_i}{\pi_i}\right)^2 = \sum_{i=1}^{N}\sum_{j \neq i}^{N}(\pi_i\pi_j - \pi_{ij})\left(\frac{y_i}{\pi_i}\right)^2$$

$$= \sum_{i=1}^{N}\sum_{j>i}^{N}(\pi_i\pi_j - \pi_{ij})\left\{\left(\frac{y_i}{\pi_i}\right)^2 + \left(\frac{y_j}{\pi_j}\right)^2\right\}.$$

Hence,

$$\text{var } \hat{Y}_{HT} = \sum_{j>i}^{N}\sum^{N}(\pi_i\pi_j - \pi_{ij})\left\{\left(\frac{y_i}{\pi_i}\right)^2 + \left(\frac{y_j}{\pi_j}\right)^2 - 2\frac{y_i}{\pi_i}\frac{y_i}{\pi_j}\right\}.$$

$$= \sum_{j>i}^{N}\sum^{N}(\pi_i\pi_j - \pi_{ij})\left(\frac{y_i}{\pi_i} - \frac{y_j}{\pi_j}\right)^2. \tag{10.19}$$

Now, using the t method, one can show that an unbiased estimator of the variance of $\hat{Y}_{HT}$ is given by

$$s_{1,\hat{Y}_{HT}}^2 = \sum_{1}^{n}\frac{(1 - \pi_i)}{\pi_i^2}y_i^2 + 2\sum_{j>i}^{n}\sum^{n}\frac{(\pi_i\pi_j - \pi_{ij})}{\pi_i\pi_j\pi_{ij}}y_iy_j. \tag{10.20}$$

Based on the alternative form for the variance of $\hat{Y}_{HT}$, another estimator for $\text{var}(\hat{Y}_{HT})$ is given by

$$s_{2,\hat{Y}_{HT}}^2 = \sum_{j>i}^{n}\sum^{n}\frac{(\pi_i\pi_j - \pi_{ij})}{\pi_{ij}}\left(\frac{y_i}{\pi_i} - \frac{y_j}{\pi_j}\right)^2. \tag{10.21}$$

Remark 10.1.   Since the terms $(\pi_i\pi_j - \pi_{ij})$ often vary widely being sometimes negative, both s_1^2 and s_2^2 tend to be unstable and may assume negative values.

Special Cases.

1. In *simple random sampling*, we have $\pi_i = n/N$ and $\pi_{ij} = n(n-1)/N(N-1)$.
2. In *systematic sampling*, let us assume that $N = kn$, where k is an integer. A systematic sample of size n is obtained by selecting every kth element after choosing a random starting point among the elements numbered 1 through k. The response

associated with U_{ij}, the jth unit in the ith possible sample is denoted by y_{ij}. It readily follows that

$$P(U_{ij}) = 1/k \quad \text{for all } i \text{ and } j$$

$$P(U_{ij}U_{i',j'}) = \begin{cases} 1/k & \text{for } i = i', j \neq j' \\ 0 & \text{for all other pairs of elements,} \end{cases}$$

because the ith sample consists of the elements with subscripts

$$i, \; i + k, \; i + 2k, \; \ldots, \; i + (j-1)k, \; \ldots, \; i + (n-1)k, \quad \text{for } i = 1, \ldots, k.$$

So,

$$\hat{Y} = k \sum_{j=1}^{n} y_{ij} = \frac{N}{n} \sum_{j=1}^{n} y_{ij}.$$

3. Suppose the population is classified into k strata and a random sample is selected from each stratum. Let U_{ij} denote the jth element in the ith stratum, N_i the number of elements in the ith stratum and n_i the size of the random sample drawn from the ith stratum. Then

$$P(U_{ij}) = n_i/N_i \qquad\qquad\qquad \text{for all } j,$$

$$P(U_{ij}U_{i',j'}) = \frac{n_i(n_i - 1)}{N_i(N_i - 1)} \qquad\qquad \text{if } i = i' \text{ and } j \neq j'$$

$$= P(U_{ij})P(U_{i',j'}) = n_i n_{i'}/N_i N_{i'} \qquad \text{for all } j \text{ and } j', i \neq i'.$$

For the above three schemes, the possible estimators $\hat{Y}_1$ and $\hat{Y}_2$ [see (10.13) and (10.14)] are equivalent, because for each of these schemes the probability of including a particular element in the sample is the same either for all elements of the population or for all the elements of the same subpopulation. However, in general, this will not be true.

10.4   APPLICATION OF THE THEORY

The question is how to implement the above theory. Assume that a variable X reasonably correlated with Y is known for each element of the population. The main problems that arise in this regard are:

1. Determine the quantities π_{ij} that will minimize the variance of $\hat{Y}$. (Notice that specifying the π_{ij} determines the π_i, since $\sum_j \pi_{ij} = (n-1)\pi_i$.)

2. Determine the sets $\{p_{i,m}\}$ in order to achieve the π_{ij} thus specified.

3. Assume that the sampler wishes to utilize the information in X for assigning the selection probabilities $\{p_{i,m}\}$. Then we wish to find the conditions required on the relationship between X and Y to obtain gains in efficiency over sampling systems employing the information in X in alternative ways.

These three problems are not independent and a general solution is not available.

Consider first the problem of assigning the π_{ij} as a first approximation to our "optimum" assignment. Suppose we set

$$(n-1)^{-1} \sum_{\substack{j=1 \\ j \neq i}}^{N} \pi_{ij} = \pi_i = nX_i / \sum_{i=1}^{N} X_i . \tag{10.22}$$

If the Y_i are approximately proportional to the X_i, this assignment may be expected to lead to an estimator with small variance. From an examination of the expression for the variance of $\hat{Y}$, it appears that the assignment of the π_{ij} (in terms of the X_i) that leads to minimum variance depends on the joint distribution of X and Y.

In the following, we present some sampling schemes.

Scheme 1 (Horvitz and Thompson (1952)).   A method of defining the set $\{p_{i,m}\}$ that yields an exact solution under certain conditions is as follows.

We wish to select a random sample of size n from N without replacement. Select the first element according to the set $p_{i,1}$ ($i = 1, \ldots, N$), such that $\sum_1^N p_{i,1} = 1$, $p_{i,1} > 0$. At the second and all remaining $(n-1)$ stages of the draw, equal probabilities are assigned to the elements remaining. That is,

$$p_{i,2} = (N-1)^{-1}, \qquad i = 1, \ldots, N-1$$

$$p_{i,3} = (N-2)^{-1}, \qquad i = 1, \ldots, N-2, \text{ etc.}$$

Then,

$$\pi_i = P(U_i \text{ is included in the sample}) \tag{10.23}$$

$$= P(U_i \text{ is chosen on the first draw})$$

$$\quad + P(U_i \text{ is not chosen on the first draw and it is}$$

$$\text{chosen on subsequent draws})$$

$$= p_i + (1 - p_i)\left(\frac{n-1}{N-1}\right), \qquad \text{with } p_i \equiv p_{i1} .$$

Thus,

$$\pi_i = \left(\frac{N-n}{N-1}\right) p_i + \frac{n-1}{N-1} \qquad (i = 1, \ldots, N)$$

$$\pi_{ij} = P(U_i \text{ is chosen on the first draw and } U_j \text{ is}$$

$$\text{chosen on the remaining draws})$$

$$\quad + P(U_j \text{ is chosen on the first draw and } U_i \text{ is}$$

$$\text{chosen on the remaining draws})$$

$$\quad + P(\text{on the first draw neither } U_i \text{ nor } U_j \text{ is chosen,}$$

$$\text{and } U_i \text{ and } U_j \text{ are chosen on subsequent draws}).$$

Thus,

$$
\pi_{ij} = p_i \left(\frac{n-1}{N-1}\right) + p_j \left(\frac{n-1}{N-1}\right) + (1 - p_i - p_j)\left(\frac{n-1}{N-1}\right)\left(\frac{n-2}{N-2}\right) \quad (10.24)
$$

$$
= \left(\frac{n-1}{N-1}\right)\left[\left(\frac{N-n}{N-2}\right)(p_i + p_j) + \frac{n-2}{N-2}\right] \quad (i \neq j, \ i, j = 1, \ldots, n).
$$

Solving for p_i, we have

$$
p_i = \left(\frac{N-1}{N-n}\right)\pi_i - \left(\frac{n-1}{N-n}\right) \quad (i = 1, \ldots, N). \tag{10.25}
$$

So, we should choose p_i subject to two conditions:

1. $p_i \geq 0$,

2. $\displaystyle\sum_{i=1}^{N} p_i = 1$.

Notice that p_i will be negative when $\pi_i < (n-1)/(N-1)$. When p_i, given by (10.25), are positive with $\pi_i = nX_i / \sum_{i=1}^{N} X_i$, the first element would be drawn according to these p_i and equal probabilities would be used for the remaining draws.

Scheme 2 (Horvitz and Thompson (1952)). Let $n = 2$ (which is not unreasonable in stratified sampling with several strata). First, choose $p_{i,1}$ $(i = 1, \ldots, N)$ according to some prior formula. Then, if U_j is selected on the first draw, set

$$
p_{i,2} = p_{i,1}/(1 - p_{j,1}) \qquad \text{for } i \neq j \tag{10.26}
$$

$$
p_{i,2} = 0 \qquad \text{for } i = j.
$$

Now the question is, how to select the $p_{i,1}$? Let us drop the subscript 1 from the $p_{i,1}$. If sampling is done with replacement,

$$
\pi_i = 2p_i(1 - p_i).
$$

If the conditions are such that sampling without replacement is not much different from sampling with replacement, then

$$
\pi_i \doteq 2p_i(1 - p_i)
$$

and p_i will be the approximate solution of

$$
2p_i^2 - 2p_i + 2X_i \left(\sum_{1}^{N} X_i\right)^{-1} = 0
$$

or

$$
p_i^2 - p_i + X_i \left(\sum_{1}^{N} X_i\right)^{-1} = 0 \quad (i = 1, \ldots, N), \tag{10.27}
$$

subject to the conditions $p_i \geq 0$ and $\sum_1^N p_i = 1$. A satisfactory solution is obtained by solving the N quadratic equations and taking the smaller of the two roots. Since the sum of the p_i should be equal to unity, a small adjustment is made by dividing each of the p_i obtained in this manner by their sum. However, this method will break down if any of the desired $\pi_i \geq 1/2$, since the solution to the corresponding quadratic equation will then be imaginary. The above will be reasonable if $N > 10$ and π_i are not dominated entirely by one or two elements.

Whatever the set of selection probabilities adopted with this sampling procedure,

$$\pi_i = p_i + p_i \sum_{\substack{j=1 \\ j \neq i}}^{N} p_j/(1 - p_j) = p_i \left\{ \frac{1 - 2p_i}{1 - p_i} + \sum_{j=1}^{N} \frac{p_j}{1 - p_j} \right\} \qquad (10.28)$$

and

$$\pi_{ij} = p_i p_j \left(\frac{1}{1 - p_i} + \frac{1}{1 - p_j} \right). \qquad (10.29)$$

EXAMPLE 10.2

Suppose we wish to investigate Frankfort, Kentucky, which consists of 10 blocks, the data (artificial) being given in Table 10.1, columns 1–3. We consider drawing a sample of size–2 blocks with probability proportionate to their measure of size (eye-estimated households by driving through the portion of Frankfort). The exact values which the selection schemes are designed to achieve are listed in column (4). The corresponding

TABLE 10.1 Data and Computations: Population of Frankfort, Kentucky

Block	# of households in ith block	eye-estimated # of households	\multicolumn{2}{c}{Scheme 1}		\multicolumn{2}{c}{Scheme 2}	
(1) U_i	(2) Y_i	(3) X_i	(4) $2X_i/\sum_1^N X_i$	(5) p_i^*	(6) π_i	(7) p_i	(8) π_i
1	18	17	0.162	0.055	0.160	0.089 (.078)	0.159 (0.168)
2	10	10*	0.096	0.002	0.113	0.051 (0.044)	0.092 (0.099)
3	20	18	0.171	0.066	0.170	0.094 (0.082)	0.167 (0.176)
4	17	20	0.190	0.088	0.189	0.106 (0.092)	0.083 (0.088)
5	22	21	0.200	0.098	0.198	0.112 (0.098)	0.198 (0.209)
6	25	24	0.228	0.129	0.226	0.131 (0.114)	0.228 (0.241)
7	30	28	0.267	0.172	0.264	0.159 (0.139)	0.273 (0.288)
8	16	16	0.152	0.045	0.151	0.083 (0.072)	0.148 (0.156)
9	35	34	0.324	0.236	0.321	0.203 (0.177)	0.338 (0.357)
10	23	22	0.210	0.109	0.208	0.119 (0.104)	0.209 (0.220)
Totals	216	210	2.000	1.000	2.000	1.147 (1.000)	1.895 (2.000)

Block number 2 with the smallest eye-estimated size is arbitrarily assigned a value of 12 in order to satisfy the condition $2X_i/\sum_1^N X_i > (N - 1)^{-1}$ (otherwise p_i given by (10.25) will be negative).

results of the two proposed schemes are shown in columns (6) and (8); columns (5) and (7) give the selection probabilities for the first draw with scheme 1 and all draws with the second scheme, respectively. When the sample has been drawn according to either of these schemes, the π_{ij} required in (10.18) in order to estimate the variance of $\hat{Y}$ are easily computed from (10.24) and (10.29), respectively. Note that for the standardized p_i in column (7), $\sum_{j=1}^{N} p_j/(1 - p_j) = 1.128$. ◆

Other methods of sample selection have been proposed by Brewer (1963), J. N. K. Rao (1965), Durbin (1967), Murthy (1957), and Samford (1967), which will be discussed below. First we will mention the methods for $n = 2$ for the sake of simplicity and because in nationwide sampling, one uses several small strata with sample size in each stratum being 2.

Brewer's (1963) Method

Let $z_i < \frac{1}{2}$ for all i. Draw U_i as the first element with probability equal to $z_i(1 - z_i)/D(1 - 2z_i)$. Draw U_i as the second element with probability $z_i/(1 - z_j)$ when U_j is the first element drawn and D is chosen so that

$$D = \sum_{i=1}^{N} \frac{z_i(1 - z_i)}{1 - 2z_i} = \frac{1}{2} \sum_{i=1}^{N} \frac{z_i(2 - 2z_i)}{1 - 2z_i} = \frac{1}{2}\left(1 + \sum_{i=1}^{N} \frac{z_i}{1 - 2z_i}\right) \quad (10.30)$$

since $\sum_{i=1}^{N} z_i = \left(\frac{1}{2}\right)\sum_{i=1}^{N} \pi_i = \frac{1}{2} \cdot 2 = 1$. Below we will show that $\pi_i = 2z_i$.

$$\pi_i = P(U_i \text{ is selected on the first draw}) + P(U_i \text{ is selected on the second draw})$$

$$= \frac{z_i(1 - z_i)}{D(1 - 2z_i)} + \sum_{\substack{j=1 \\ j \neq i}}^{N} \frac{z_j(1 - z_j)}{D(1 - 2z_j)} \cdot \frac{z_i}{(1 - z_j)}$$

$$= \frac{z_i}{D}\left[1 + \frac{z_i}{1 - 2z_i} + \sum_{j=1, j \neq i}^{N} \frac{z_j}{1 - 2z_j}\right] = \frac{z_i}{D}\left[1 + \sum_{j=1}^{N} \frac{z_j}{1 - 2z_j}\right] = 2z_i. \quad (10.31)$$

Similarly,

$$\pi_{ij} = \frac{z_i z_j}{D}\left(\frac{1}{1 - 2z_i} + \frac{1}{1 - 2z_j}\right) = \frac{2z_i z_j}{D} \frac{(1 - z_i - z_j)}{(1 - 2z_i)(1 - 2z_j)}. \quad (10.32)$$

Brewer's method uses the $H - T$ estimator, which becomes

$$\hat{Y}_{HT} = \frac{y_i}{\pi_i} + \frac{y_j}{\pi_j} = \frac{1}{2}\left(\frac{y_i}{z_i} + \frac{y_j}{z_j}\right).$$

Consider

$$\pi_i \pi_j - \pi_{ij} = \frac{2z_i z_j}{D(1 - 2z_i)(1 - 2z_j)}\{2D(1 - 2z_i)(1 - 2z_j) - (1 - z_i - z_j)\}$$

where

$$2D(1 - 2z_i)(1 - 2z_j) - (1 - z_i - z_j)$$

$$= \left\{ 1 + \sum_{k=1}^{N} \frac{z_k}{1 - 2z_k} \right\} (1 - 2z_i)(1 - 2z_j) - (1 - z_i - z_j)$$

$$= (1 - 2z_i)(1 - 2z_j) \left\{ \sum_{\substack{k=1 \\ k \neq i,j}}^{N} \frac{z_k}{1 - 2z_k} \right\}$$

$$+ (1 - 2z_i)(1 - 2z_j) + z_i(1 - 2z_j) + z_j(1 - 2z_i) - (1 - z_i - z_j)$$

$$= (1 - 2z_i)(1 - 2z_j) \left(\sum_{\substack{k=1 \\ k \neq i,j}}^{N} \frac{z_k}{1 - 2z_k} \right) > 0.$$

Thus,

$$\pi_i \pi_j - \pi_{ij} > 0 \qquad \text{for all } i \neq j.$$

Thus, the estimate of the variance of the Horvitz-Thompson estimator given by (10.21) is always positive for Brewer's method.   This fact was pointed out by J. N. K. Rao (1965).

Durbin's (1967) Method

Select U_i at the first draw with probability z_i. Then set

$$P(\text{selecting } U_j \text{ at the second draw} \mid U_i \text{ was selected at the first draw})$$

$$= \frac{z_j}{2D} \left\{ \frac{1}{1 - 2z_i} + \frac{1}{1 - 2z_j} \right\}.$$

Note that

$$\sum_{j \neq i}^{N} \frac{z_j}{2D} \left(\frac{1}{1 - 2z_i} + \frac{1}{1 - 2z_j} \right) = \frac{1}{2D} \left(\frac{1 - z_i}{1 - 2z_i} + \sum_{j \neq i}^{N} \frac{z_j}{1 - 2z_j} \right)$$

$$= \frac{1}{2D} \left(1 + \sum_{j=1}^{N} \frac{z_j}{1 - 2z_j} \right) = 1.$$

Proceeding as in Brewer's method, one can show that $\pi_i = 2z_i$. Also

$$P(U_j)P(U_i|U_j) = \frac{z_i z_j}{2D} \left(\frac{1}{1 - 2z_i} + \frac{1}{1 - 2z_j} \right) = P(U_i)P(U_j|U_i) = \pi_{ij}/2$$

so that Durbin's π_{ij} is equal to that of Brewer's given by (10.32).

Samford (1967) has extended Brewer's method to sample sizes n $(n > 2)$ provided $nz_i < 1(i = 1, \ldots, N)$. With his method of sample, the probability that $U_1, U_2, \ldots, U_n$ are included in the sample is proportional to

$$\left(1 - \sum_{i=1}^{n} z_i\right) \prod_{i=1}^{n} z_i / \prod_{i=1}^{n} (1 - nz_i). \tag{10.33}$$

For this method it can be shown that $\pi_i = nz_i$; however, the formula for π_{ij} is complicated. One method suggested by Samford (1967) so as to satisfy (10.33) is as follows.

Samford's Sampling Scheme

This is an extension of Durbin's scheme for $n > 2$. A sample of n different units is to be drawn from a population or stratum in such a way that ith unit has probability nz_i of being drawn into the sample. A mathematical solution of this problem is given by a formula from which the required probability of selection of any possible sample can be calculated. Samford gives three ways in which the required nz_i can be achieved. The most common one in practice would be selecting up to n units *with replacement*, the first drawing being made with probabilities z_i and all subsequent ones with probabilities proportional to $z_i/(1 - nz_i)$, and rejecting completing any sample that does not contain distinct units. The π_{ij}'s are relatively easily calculated, especially for $n = 2$.

Murthy's (1957) Method

This method proposes the selection probabilities for the successive units $U_i, U_j, U_k, \ldots$ to be $z_i, z_j/(1 - z_i), z_k/(1 - z_i - z_j)$, etc. Murthy's estimator follows the earlier work of Des Raj (1956), who produces very clever unbiased estimates based on the specific order in which the n units in the sample were drawn. Murthy (1957) shows that from any estimate one can construct an unordered estimate which is also unbiased and has smaller variance. Murthy's estimator is given by

$$\hat{Y}_M = \sum_{1}^{n} P(s|U_i)y_i/P(s) \tag{10.34}$$

where

$P(s|U_i)$ = the conditional probability of getting the set of units that was drawn,

given that U_i was drawn first,

$P(s)$ = the unconditional probability of getting the set of units that was drawn.

Note that $\sum P(s|U_i) = 1$, where the summation is taken over all samples having U_i as the first unit. Let us show this for $n = 2$ and 3, where we assume that $s = (U_i, U_j)$ and $s = (U_i, U_j, U_k)$, respectively, and the proof for arbitrary n will be obvious. For $n = 2$, $P(s|U_i) = P(U_j|U_i) = z_j/(1 - z_i)$ and $\sum P(s|U_i) = \sum_{\substack{j=1 \\ j \neq i}}^{N} z_j/(1 - z_i) = 1$.

For $n = 3$, with U_j and U_k being the second and third units,

$$\sum P(s|U_i) = \sum_{\substack{j=1 \\ j \neq i}}^{N} \sum_{\substack{k=1 \\ k \neq i,j}}^{N} z_j z_k / (1 - z_i)(1 - z_i - z_j)$$

$$= \sum_{\substack{j=1 \\ j \neq i}}^{N} z_j / (1 - z_i) = 1.$$

Since the coefficient of y_i in the sum $\sum P(s)\hat{Y}_M$ (where the summation is over all possible samples of size n) is unity, we have

$$E\hat{Y}_M = \sum P(s)\hat{Y}_M = \sum_{1}^{N} y_i = Y.$$

Murthy (1957) has obtained var $(\hat{Y}_M)$ and unbiased estimates of it for general n. In the following we will show these computations for $n = 2$.

$$P(s) = \pi_{ij} = z_i P(s|U_i) + z_j P(s|U_j)$$
$$= z_i z_j (2 - z_i - z_j) / (1 - z_i)(1 - z_j).$$

Thus, from (10.34) we have

$$\hat{Y}_M = (2 - z_i - z_j)^{-1} \left\{ (1 - z_j)\frac{y_i}{z_i} + (1 - z_i)\frac{y_j}{z_j} \right\}. \tag{10.35}$$

Then

$$E\hat{Y}_M = \sum_{i<j}^{N} \sum^{N} \left\{ (1 - z_j)\frac{y_i}{z_i} + (1 - z_i)\frac{y_j}{z_j} \right\}$$

$$\cdot (2 - z_i - z_j)^{-1} \frac{z_i z_j (2 - z_i - z_j)}{(1 - z_i)(1 - z_j)}$$

$$= \sum_{i<j} \sum \frac{z_j}{1 - z_i} y_i + \sum_{i<j} \sum y_j \frac{z_i}{1 - z_j}$$

$$= \sum_{i \neq j} \sum y_i \frac{z_j}{1 - z_i} = \sum_{i=1}^{N} y_i = Y.$$

Next,

$$\operatorname{var} \hat{Y}_M = E(\hat{Y}_M)^2 - Y^2$$

$$= \sum_{i<j}^{N}\sum^{N}\left\{(1-z_j)\frac{y_i}{z_i} + (1-z_i)\frac{y_j}{z_j}\right\}^2 \frac{z_i z_j}{(1-z_i)(1-z_j)(2-z_i-z_j)}$$

$$- \left\{\sum_{1}^{N} y_i^2 + 2\sum_{i<j}^{N}\sum^{N} y_i y_j\right\}$$

$$= \sum_{i<j}\sum \frac{(1-z_j)z_j}{(1-z_i)z_i(2-z_i-z_j)} y_i^2$$

$$+ \sum_{i<j}\sum \frac{(1-z_i)z_i}{z_j(1-z_j)(2-z_i-z_j)} y_j^2$$

$$+ 2\sum_{i<j}\sum \left(\frac{1}{2-z_i-z_j} - 1\right) y_i y_j - \sum_{1}^{N} y_i^2$$

$$= \sum_{i<j}\sum \frac{(1-z_i-z_j)z_i z_j}{(2-z_i-z_j)}$$

$$\cdot \left\{\frac{(1-z_j)}{z_i^2(1-z_i)(1-z_i-z_j)} y_i^2\right.$$

$$\left. + \frac{(1-z_i)}{z_j^2(1-z_j)(1-z_i-z_j)} y_j^2 - 2\frac{y_i}{z_i}\frac{y_j}{z_j}\right\} - \sum_{1}^{N} y_i^2$$

$$= \sum_{i\neq j}\sum \frac{(1-z_i-z_j)z_i z_j}{(2-z_i-z_j)}$$

$$\cdot \left\{\frac{1-z_j}{z_i^2(1-z_i)(1-z_i-z_j)} y_i^2 - \frac{y_i y_j}{z_i z_j}\right\} - \sum_{1}^{N} y_i^2 \sum_{j\neq i}^{N} \frac{z_j}{1-z_i}$$

$$= \sum_{j\neq i}^{N}\sum^{N} \frac{(1-z_i-z_j)z_i z_j}{2-z_i-z_j}$$

$$\cdot \left[\left\{\frac{1-z_j}{z_i^2(1-z_i)(1-z_i-z_j)}\right.\right.$$

$$\left.\left. - \frac{2-z_i-z_j}{(1-z_i-z_j)z_i(1-z_i)}\right\} y_i^2 - \frac{y_i y_j}{z_i z_j}\right].$$

Now consider

$$\frac{1 - z_j}{z_i^2(1 - z_i)(1 - z_i - z_j)} - \frac{2 - z_i - z_j}{(1 - z_i - z_j)z_i(1 - z_i)}$$

$$= \frac{(1 - z_j) - z_i(2 - z_i - z_j)}{z_i^2(1 - z_i)(1 - z_i - z_j)}$$

$$= \frac{(1 - z_j) - z_i(1 - z_j) - z_i(1 - z_i)}{z_i^2(1 - z_i)(1 - z_i - z_j)}$$

$$= \frac{(1 - z_i)(1 - z_j) - z_i(1 - z_j)}{z_i^2(1 - z_i)(1 - z_i - z_j)}$$

$$= \frac{(1 - z_i)(1 - z_i - z_j)}{z_i^2(1 - z_i)(1 - z_i - z_j)}$$

$$= z_i^{-2}.$$

Thus,

$$\text{var } \hat{Y}_M = \sum_{i \neq j}^{N}\sum^{N} \frac{(1 - z_i - z_j)z_i z_j}{2 - z_i - z_j} \left\{ \left(\frac{y_i}{z_i}\right)^2 - \frac{y_i y_j}{z_i z_j} \right\}$$

$$= \sum_{i < j}^{N}\sum^{N} \frac{(1 - z_i - z_j)z_i z_j}{2 - z_i - z_j} \left\{ \frac{y_i}{z_i} - \frac{y_j}{z_j} \right\}^{2\dagger}.$$

Since $\sum_{i<j}\sum \pi_{ij} \widehat{\text{var}}(\hat{Y}_M) = \text{var } \hat{Y}_M$, an unbiased estimate of var $\hat{Y}_M$ is given by

$$\widehat{\text{var}}(\hat{Y}_M) = \frac{(1 - z_i)(1 - z_j)(1 - z_i - z_j)}{(2 - z_i - z_j)^2} \left(\frac{y_i}{z_i} - \frac{y_j}{z_j}\right)^2$$

one can easily see that Horvitz-Thompson estimator and Murthy's estimator are quite different. Suppose we compute π_i from Murthy's method of selection and use these π_i in the Horvitz-Thompson's estimator. How do these estimators com-

---

†I thank Professor D. Raghavarao for a useful discussion I had regarding the variance of Murthy's estimator for $n = 2$.

pare? Let us compute this estimator, its variance, and an unbiased estimate for $n = 2$. Here

$$\pi_i = \sum_{j \neq i} P(U_i) P(U_j | U_i) + \sum_{j \neq i} P(U_j) P(U_i | U_j)$$

$$= \sum_{j \neq i}^{N} z_i \frac{z_j}{1 - z_i} + \sum_{j \neq i}^{N} z_j \frac{z_i}{1 - z_j}$$

$$= z_i \left\{ 1 + \sum_{j \neq i}^{N} z_j (1 - z_j)^{-1} \right\} = z_i \left\{ \frac{1 - 2z_i}{1 - z_i} + A \right\}$$

where $A = \sum_{j=1}^{N} z_j (1 - z_j)^{-1}$. We already have computed π_{ij} as

$$\pi_{ij} = z_i z_j (2 - z_i - z_j) / (1 - z_i)(1 - z_j).$$

So,

$$\hat{Y}_{M,HT} = \frac{y_i}{\pi_i} + \frac{y_j}{\pi_j}$$

$$\text{var } \hat{Y}_{M,HT} = \sum_{i<j}^{N} \sum^{N} \frac{z_i z_j}{(1 - z_i)(1 - z_j)}$$

$$\cdot \left[\{1 - 2z_i + A(1 - z_i)\} \{1 - 2z_j + A(1 - z_j)\} \right.$$

$$\left. - (2 - z_i - z_j) \right] \left(\frac{y_i}{\pi_i} - \frac{y_j}{\pi_j} \right)^2$$

after substituting the new values of π_i, π_j and π_{ij} in (10.19). Further, an unbiased estimator of the variance is

$$\widehat{\text{var}} (\hat{Y}_{M,HT}) = (2 - z_i - z_j)^{-1} \left[\{1 - 2z_i + A(1 - z_i)\} \right.$$

$$\cdot \{1 - 2z_j + A(1 - z_j)\} - (2 - z_i - z_j) \right]$$

$$\cdot \left(\frac{y_i}{\pi_i} - \frac{y_j}{\pi_j} \right)^2.$$

It is hard to compare $\text{var} (\hat{Y}_M)$ and $\text{var} (\hat{Y}_{M,HT})$. One may be smaller than the other, depending on the y_i and the choice of z_i.

EXAMPLE 10.3

Let the population consist of four units having the following values. Let the z_i be as given in the table:

Unit	z	y	y/z
1	0.2	1.2	6
2	0.3	1.9	3
3	0.15	1.75	5
4	0.35	3.5	10
Total	1.0	6.35	

Suppose that, using Murthy's method, a sample of size $n = 2$ is drawn and it is (U_1, U_4) (i.e., first U_1 is drawn). Give an estimate of the population total and its standard error. Here $s = (U_1, U_4)$:

$$\hat{Y}_M = \frac{1}{P(s)} \{P(s|U_1)y_1 + P(s|U_4)y_4\}$$

$$P(s|U_1) = P(U_4|U_1) = z_4/(1 - z_1) = 0.35/0.8 = 0.4375$$

$$P(s|U_4) = P(U_1|U_4) = z_1/(1 - z_4) = 0.2/0.65 = 0.3077$$

$$P(s) = z_1 P(s|U_1) + z_4 P(s|U_4)$$

$$= 0.2(0.4375) + 0.35(0.3077) = 0.1952.$$

Then Murthy's estimate of the population total is

$$\hat{Y}_M = \left\{ \frac{0.35}{0.8}(1.2) + \frac{0.2}{0.65}(3.5) \right\} / P(s)$$

$$= (0.525 + 1.077)/0.195 = 8.21$$

which agrees with (10.35), and the estimate of the variance is

$$\widehat{var}(\hat{Y}_M) = \frac{(0.8)(0.65)(1 - 0.2 - 0.35)}{(2 - 0.2 - 0.35)^2}(6 - 10)^2$$

$$= (0.8)(0.65)(0.45)16/1.45 = 2.58. \qquad \blacklozenge$$

10.5   SYSTEMATIC SAMPLING: UNEQUAL PROBABILITIES

Another method related to systematic sampling has been suggested by Madow (1949), which apparently has been used in Indian surveys. Its nice properties are: the sample is easy to draw for any n, it keeps $\pi_i = nz_i$, and it leads to an unbiased estimate of Y, the population total. A disadvantage of the systematic sampling method is the lack of an unbiased estimate of the variance of $\hat{Y}_{sys}$.

A sample of size n is drawn using either the z_i or the measures of size M_i', from which we set $z_i = M_i'/\Sigma M_i' = M_i'/M_0'$. If the M_i' are used, form a column of the cumulative totals T_i of the quantities nM_i'. Using this column, assign a range of size nM_i' to unit i which is contained within the interval $(1, nM_0')$. For selecting a sample of size n, draw a random number r between 1 and M_0' and select the units whose ranges include the numbers $r, r + M_0', \ldots, r + (n - 1)M_0'$. If $nz_i < 1$ (i.e., $nM_i' \leq M_0'$) for all i, any unit has a probability nz_i of being selected, and no unit is selected more than once. If $nz_i > 1$ for one or more units, such units may be selected more than once in the sample, although the average probability of including the ith unit is $\pi_i = nz_i$. Then

$$\hat{Y}_{\text{sys}} = \sum_{i=1}^{n} \frac{y_i}{\pi_i} = \frac{1}{n} \sum_{i=1}^{n} \frac{y_i}{z_i}$$

is an unbiased estimate of Y. Hartley and J. N. K. Rao (1962) study this method when the units are arranged in a random order and, assuming that $nz_i < 1$ for all i, obtain approximate expressions for var $(\hat{Y}_{\text{sys}})$ and its estimate. They are (for large N):

$$\text{var}\,(\hat{Y}_{\text{sys}}) \doteq \sum_{i=1}^{N} \pi_i \left(1 - \frac{(n-1)}{n} \pi_i\right) \left(\frac{y_i}{\pi_i} - \frac{Y}{n}\right)^2 + o(N)$$

$$\widehat{\text{var}}(\hat{Y}_{\text{sys}}) \doteq (n-1)^{-1} \sum_{i<i'}^{n} \sum^{n} \left[1 - (\pi_i + \pi_{i'}) + \frac{1}{n} \sum_{1}^{N} \pi_j^2\right]$$
$$\cdot \left(\frac{y_i}{\pi_i} - \frac{y_{i'}}{\pi_i'}\right)^2 + o(N).$$

Notice that in sampling with replacement, the variance of $\hat{Y}$ is

$$\text{var}\,(\hat{Y}) = \sum_{i=1}^{N} \pi_i \left(\frac{y_i}{\pi_i} - \frac{Y}{n}\right)^2$$

and the characteristic reduction in the variance through the finite population corrections of $\left(1 - \left(\frac{n-1}{n}\right)\pi_i\right)$.

Example 10.4

Consider the following example. Let the number of units be 5. We wish to take a sample of size 2.

Unit	Size M_i'	$T_i = 2\Sigma M_i'$	Assigned range	Unit selected
U_1	4	8	1–8	
U_2	2	12	9–12	
U_3	10	32	13–32	U_3
U_4	3	38	33–38	U_4
U_5	1	40	37–40	
	$M_0' = 20$			

Suppose $r = 15$. Then we select the units whose ranges assigned include the numbers 15, 35 (i.e., units 3 and 4). ◆

J. N. K. Rao, Hartley, and Cochran (1962) present a method of sampling one unit from each of n groups of sizes $N_1, N_2, \ldots, N_n$ into which the population of size N has been decomposed. Sampling within group i is proportional to size of x_i. Let p_j denote the probability of drawing the jth unit in the first draw from the entire population. Then $p_j = x_j / \sum_1^N x_j$. If the jth unit falls in ith group, the true probability that it will be selected is p_j/π_i where

$$\pi_i = \sum_{j \in (\text{group } i)} p_j.$$

The proposed estimator of the population total Y is

$$\hat{Y} = \sum_{i=1}^{n} \frac{y_{k(i)}}{p_i/\pi_{k(i)}}$$

where the suffixes $k(1), \ldots, k(n)$ denote the n units selected one from each of the n groups separately. Let E^* denote the conditional expectation for a given split of the population and $\tilde{E}$ denote the expectation over all possible splits of the population into n groups $N_1, N_2, \ldots, N_n$. Then

$$E^*(\hat{Y}) = \sum_{i=1}^{n} \pi_i \sum_{j=1}^{N_i} \frac{p_j \, y_j}{\pi_i \, p_j} = \sum_{i=1}^{n} Y_i = Y$$

where $Y_i = \sum_{j=1}^{N_i} y_j$. Hence $\hat{Y}$ is unbiased for Y. Also

$$\text{var}(\hat{Y}) = \tilde{E}\left\{ \text{var}(\hat{Y}|N_1, \ldots, N_n) \right\} + \text{var}(E^*(\hat{Y}))$$

$$= \tilde{E}\left\{ \sum_{i=1}^{n} \text{var}\left(\frac{y_{k(i)}}{p_{k(i)}/\pi_i} \Big| N_1, \ldots, N_n \right) \right\} + 0$$

$$= \sum_{i=1}^{n} \tilde{E}\left\{ \text{var}\left(\frac{y_{k(i)}}{p_{k(i)}/\pi_i} \Big| N_1, \ldots, N_n \right) \right\}$$

where

$$\text{var}\left(\frac{y_{k(i)}}{p_{k(i)}/\pi_i} \Big| N_1, \ldots, N_n \right) = \sum_{j=1}^{N_i} \frac{p_j}{\pi_i} \left(\frac{y_j}{p_j/\pi_i} - Y_i \right)^2$$

$$= \sum_{j<k}^{N_i} \sum^{N_i} \frac{p_j \, p_k}{\pi_i^2} \left(\frac{y_j}{p_j/\pi_i} - \frac{y_k}{p_k/\pi_i} \right)^2$$

$$= \sum_{j<k}^{N_i} \sum^{N_i} p_j \, p_k \left(\frac{y_j}{p_j} - \frac{y_k}{p_k} \right)^2.$$

The last but one step follows from an algebraic identity [see (10.19)]. In the last equation we can multiply the summand by $t_j t_k$ and let the upper limits of summation on j and k be N and N, where $t_j = 1$ if j belongs to ith group and zero otherwise ($j = 1, \ldots, N$). Since $N_i(N_i - 1)/N(N - 1) = E(t_j t_k) = $ the probability that a pair of observations in a random split fall into the ith group, we have

$$\tilde{E} \text{ var} \left(\frac{y_{k(i)}}{p_{k(i)}/\pi_i} \Big| N_1, \ldots, N_n \right) = \frac{N_i(N_i - 1)}{N(N - 1)} \sum_{j<k}^{N} \sum^{N} p_j p_k \left(\frac{y_j}{p_j} - \frac{y_k}{p_k} \right)^2$$

$$= \frac{N_i(N_i - 1)}{N(N - 1)} \left[\sum_{j=1}^{N} \frac{y_j^2}{p_j} - Y^2 \right]$$

after squaring and simplifying. Hence

$$\text{var} (\hat{Y}) = \frac{n(\sum_{i=1}^{n} N_i^2 - N)}{N(N - 1)} \left(\sum_{j=1}^{N} \frac{y_j^2}{np_j} - \frac{Y^2}{n} \right).$$

Now, the estimator of Y in sampling with replacement is

$$\hat{Y}' = \sum_{r=1}^{n} \frac{y_r}{np_r}$$

where some of the y_r may be the same and

$$\text{var} (\hat{Y}') = \sum_{i=1}^{N} \frac{y_i^2}{np_i} - \frac{Y^2}{n}.$$

Hence

$$\text{var} (\hat{Y}) = \frac{n(\sum_1^n N_i^2 - N)}{N(N - 1)} \text{ var}(\hat{Y}').$$

Thus var $(\hat{Y})$ is minimized when $N_1 = N_2 = \cdots = N_n = N/n = R$. If R is a positive integer,

$$\min \text{ var} (\hat{Y}) = \left(1 - \frac{n - 1}{N - 1} \right) \text{ var} (\hat{Y}')$$

which shows the reduction in the variance when compared with sampling with replacement. If $N = Rn + k(0 < k < n)$ and R is a positive integer, we choose

$$N_1 = \cdots = N_k = R + 1, \qquad N_{k+1} = N_{k+2} = \cdots = N_n = R$$

and then

$$\text{var} (\hat{Y}) = \left\{ 1 - \frac{n - 1}{N - 1} + \frac{k(n - k)}{N(N - 1)} \right\} \text{ var} (\hat{Y}').$$

Also note that

$$E\left(\frac{y_{k(i)}^2}{p_{k(i)}^2/\pi_{k(i)}}\right) = \tilde{E}E^*\left(\frac{y_{k(i)}^2}{p_{k(i)}^2/\pi_i}\right) = \tilde{E}\left(\sum_{j=1}^{N_i}\frac{y_j^2}{p_j}\right)$$

$$= \tilde{E}\left(\sum_{j=1}^{N}\frac{y_j^2}{p_j}t_j\right) = \frac{N_i}{N}\sum_{j=1}^{N}\frac{y_j^2}{p_j}.$$

Hence,

$$E\left(\sum_{i=1}^{n}\frac{y_{k(i)}^2}{p_{k(i)}^2/\pi_i}\right) = \sum_{j=1}^{N}\frac{y_j^2}{p_j}.$$

Using the fact that

$$\sum_{j=1}^{N}\frac{y_j^2}{p_j} - Y^2 = E\left(\sum_{j=1}^{n}\pi_i\frac{y_{k(i)}^2}{p_{k(i)}^2} - Y^2\right)$$

with

$$Y^2 = (E\hat{Y})^2 = E\left\{\hat{Y}^2 - \widehat{\text{var}}(\hat{Y})\right\}$$

in the expression for var $(\hat{Y})$, we obtain

$$\text{var}(\hat{Y}) = E\left[\widehat{\text{var}}(\hat{Y})\right] = E\left\{\frac{(\sum_1^n N_i^2 - N)}{N(N-1)}\right\}\left\{\sum_{i=1}^{n}\pi_i\frac{y_{k(i)}^2}{p_{k(i)}} - \hat{Y}^2 + \widehat{\text{var}}(\hat{Y})\right\}.$$

Solving for $\widehat{\text{var}}(\hat{Y})$, we have

$$\widehat{\text{var}}(\hat{Y}) = \frac{(\sum N_i^2 - N)}{(N^2 - \sum N_i^2)}\left\{\sum_{i=1}^{n}\pi_i\left(\frac{y_{k(i)}}{p_{k(i)}} - \hat{Y}\right)^2\right\}.$$

When $N_1 = \cdots = N_n = N/n$,

$$\widehat{\text{var}}(\hat{Y}) = (n-1)^{-1}(1-\frac{n}{N})\left\{\sum_{i=1}^{n}\pi_i\left(\frac{y_{k(i)}}{p_{k(i)}} - \hat{Y}\right)^2\right\}.$$

$N_1 = \cdots = N_k = R+1, N_{k+1} = \cdots = N_n = R$ imply that

$$\widehat{\text{var}}(\hat{Y}) = \frac{N^2 + k(n-k) - Nn}{N^2(n-1) - k(n-k)}\left\{\sum_{i=1}^{n}\pi_i\left(\frac{y_{k(i)}}{p_{k(i)}} - \hat{Y}\right)^2\right\}$$

since $\sum N_i^2 - N = R(nR + 2k - n)$ and $N^2 - \sum N_i^2 = N^2 - nR^2 - 2kR - k$.

The estimator of Rao, Cochran, and Hartley (1962) is simple to apply and is applicable for all n. Also it has the desirable property that var $(\hat{Y}) = 0$ when $y_{k(i)}$ is proportional to $p_{k(i)}$. However, $\hat{Y}$ is less precise, because the method of sampling does not keep the probabilities of selection proportional to the size, since $\sum_{j=1}^{N_i} x_j$ ($i = 1, \ldots, n$) are not all equal.

J. N. K. Rao (1988) provides a review of some recent work relevant to mean-square-error (or variance) estimation. He gives a unified approach to deriving MSE of linear estimates of a population total and their nonnegative unbiased estimators. The class of estimators considered by Rao (1988) include the Horvitz-Thompson estimator and Murthy's estimator as particular cases.

EXAMPLE 10.5

Let $n = 2$, $N_1 = 5$, $N_2 = 5$. Farms are grouped as small (< 400 acres) and large (> 400 acres). Let y denote the number of acres on which corn is grown.

Category 1			Category 2		
Acreage	# acres of corn		Acreage	# acres of corn	
x	y	$p_j = x_j/X$	x	y	$p_j = x_j/X$
300	100	0.06	800	250	0.16
200	60	0.04	500	200	0.10
400	120	0.08	600	300	0.12
350	150	0.07	700	290	0.14
250	80	0.05	900	450	0.18
Total 1500	510	0.30	Total 3500	1490	0.70

$X = 1500 + 3500 = 5000$, $Y = 510 + 1490 = 2000$, $\pi_1 = 0.3$, and $\pi_2 = 0.7$. Suppose sampling is done without replacement proportional to size x and we draw a unit from each of the categories. Let $y_{k(1)} = 120$ and $y_{k(2)} = 300$. Then

$$\hat{Y}_{RHC} = \frac{1}{2}\left(\frac{y_{k(1)}}{p_{k(1)}} + \frac{y_{k(2)}}{p_{k(2)}}\right) = \frac{1}{2}\left(\frac{120}{0.08} + \frac{300}{0.12}\right) = \frac{1}{2}(1500 + 2500) = 2000$$

and

$$\widehat{\mathrm{var}}(\hat{Y}_{RHC}) = \left(1 - \frac{2}{10}\right)\left\{0.3\left(\frac{120}{0.08} - 2000\right)^2 + 0.7\left(\frac{300}{0.12} - 2000\right)^2\right\}$$

$$= 0.8\{0.3(2500) + (2500)(0.7)\}$$

$$= (0.8)(2500) = 2000.$$ ◆

10.6   A NEW SYSTEMATIC SAMPLING WITH AN UNBIASED ESTIMATE OF THE VARIANCE

D. Singh and P. Singh (1977) propose a new systematic sampling scheme which provides an unbiased estimator of sampling variance. Their procedure is as follows.

Assume that the population consists of N distinct and identifiable units U_1, $U_2, \ldots, U_N$ and we wish to draw a sample of size n from it. Let u ($\leq n$) and d be two predetermined positive integers. Then

1. select a random number r from 1 to N;
2. starting with r, select u continuous units and thereafter select the remaining $v = n - u$ units with interval d.

The sample space consists of N possible samples, because r can take any value from 1 to N. The sample point corresponding to the random number r is given by

$$s_r = (s'_r, s''_r)$$

where s'_r consists of the unit indices $r + m$ ($m = 0, 1, \ldots, u - 1$) and s''_r consists of the unit indices $r + u - 1 + m'd$ ($m' = 1, \ldots, v$). Since the sampling is circular, unit index $N + r$ stands for unit index r. Since the probability of selecting each sample is $1/N$, the probability measure associated with the selection procedure is

$$P = \{p(s_r)\} : \qquad p(s_r) = \frac{1}{N}, \quad r = 1, 2, \ldots, N.$$

Next, we choose the two parameters u and d such that the following conditions are satisfied:

1. Every sample must contain distinct units only.
2. The probability of including any pair of units in the sample should be positive in order to ensure unbiased variance estimation.

Toward this, Singh and Singh (1977, Theorems 1 and 2) obtain the following result, which is given without proof.

Result 10.3.

1. A sufficient condition for every sample to have all distinct units in it is that $u + vd \geq N$.
2. The probability that any pair of units is included in the systematic sample is positive if $d \leq u$ and $u + vd \geq 1 + (N/2)$.

The sampling procedure described earlier where u and v satisfy the constraints specified in Result 10.3, will be called *new systematic sampling* (nss) procedure.

Let $u = d + t$, where $0 \leq t \leq u - 2$. Then $u + vd \geq 1 + (N/2)$ becomes (after substituting the values of $d = u - t$ and $v = n - u$),

$$u + nu - u^2 - nt + ut - \frac{N}{2} - 1 \geq 0.$$

Now, the left-hand side of the above inequality takes the maximum value when

$$u = (n + t + 1)/2.$$

Substituting this value of u in the above inequality, we obtain

$$\frac{(n + t + 1)^2}{4} \geq nt + \frac{N}{2} + 1$$

which implies that $n \geq t - 1 + \{4t + 2N + 4\}^{\frac{1}{2}}$. The right-hand side of the inequality for n is increasing in t.

Now, setting $t = 0$, we obtain

$$n \geq \{2N + 4\}^{\frac{1}{2}} - 1 \doteq \sqrt{2N}.$$

Although the above imposes a limitation on the sample size, it is possible that one can draw a sample of size as large as $(N - 1)$ by setting $u = n$ and $v = 0$. The limitation that $n \geq \sqrt{2N}$ is not serious when N is large. However, if we wish to select a sample of size n not satisfying the above limitation in more than one phase, the sampling at each phase is by the new systematic sampling. That is, we select the ultimate sample of required size in several stages. In the following we obtain an inequality for the number of phases to be denoted by p.

Let n_i denote the size of the sample satisfying the limitation at the ith phase. That is,

$$n_i \geq (2N)^{\frac{1}{2}} \quad \text{and} \quad n_i \geq (2n_{i-1})^{\frac{1}{2}}, \qquad i \geq 2.$$

Hence,

$$n_i \geq 2^{\frac{1}{2}+\frac{1}{4}+\cdots+\frac{1}{2^{i-1}}} n_0 \geq 2^{\frac{1}{2}+\frac{1}{4}+\cdots+\frac{1}{2^i}} N^{2^{-i}} = 2^{1-2^{-i}} N^{2^{-i}}.$$

Thus the approximate number of phases required (to be denoted by p) to arrive at the sample size n is given by

$$n \geq 2^{1-2^{-p}} N^{2^{-p}}.$$

Hence,

$$\log n \geq (1 - 2^{-p}) \log 2 + 2^{-p} \log N.$$

That is,

$$\log (n/2) \geq 2^{-p} \ln(N/2).$$

Thus,

$$p \geq \{\log \log (N/2) - \log \log (n/2)\} / \log 2.$$

For example, if $n = 25$ and $N = 20,000$, then $p \doteq 2$.

10.7   COMPUTING INCLUSION PROBABILITIES AND ESTIMATION PROCEDURES

Singh and Singh (1977) propose using the Horvitz-Thompson estimator for estimation of the population mean. However, we need the inclusion probabilities of individual as well as pairs of units. Let

$$c_{ti} = P(\text{including } U_i \text{ in the sample at } t\text{th trial})$$

$$t = 1, \ldots, N \quad \text{and} \quad i = 1, \ldots, N$$

where

$$c_{ri} = 1, \qquad \text{if } U_i \in s_r$$
$$= 0, \qquad \text{otherwise.}$$

Hence,

$$\pi_i = P(U_i \text{ is included in the sample})$$

$$= \frac{1}{N} \sum_{i=1}^{N} c_{ti}$$

and

$$\pi_{ij} = P(U_i \text{ and } U_j \text{ are included in the sample})$$

$$= \frac{1}{N} \sum_{t=1}^{N} c_{ti} c_{tj} .$$

Also, for the new systematic sampling procedure,

$$\pi_i = \frac{1}{N}(n \times 1 + (N - n) \times 0) = n/N, \qquad i = 1, \ldots, n .$$

Hence,

$$\hat{Y}_{nss} = \frac{1}{N} \sum_{i=1}^{n} \frac{y_i}{\pi_i} = \frac{1}{n} \sum_{i=1}^{n} y_i = \bar{y}_n .$$

Using the Yates-Grundy (1953) form of the variance of the Horvitz-Thompson estimator, we have

$$\text{var}(\hat{Y}_{nss}) = \frac{1}{N^2} \sum_{j>i}^{N} \sum^{N} \left(1 - \frac{N^2}{n^2} \pi_{ij}\right)(y_i - y_j)^2$$

$$= \frac{N - 1}{N} S^2 - \frac{1}{n^2} \sum_{j>i} \sum \pi_{ij}(y_i - y_j)^2$$

since $\pi_i = \pi_j = n/N$. An unbiased estimator of the variance is

$$\widehat{\text{var}}(\hat{Y}_{nss}) = \frac{1}{N^2} \sum_{j>i}^{n} \sum^{n} \left(\frac{1}{\pi_{ij}} - \frac{N^2}{n^2}\right)(y_i - y_j)^2$$

$$= N^{-2} \sum_{j>i}^{n} \sum^{n} \pi_{ij}^{-1}(y_i - y_j)^2 - n^{-1} \left(\sum_{1}^{n} y_i^2 - n\bar{y}^2\right) .$$

Now $\widehat{\text{var}}(\hat{Y}_{nss})$ is computable, provided π_{ij} is computable. Singh and Singh (1977) obtain explicit expressions for π_{ij} in a series of theorems for the following cases:

1. $N = vd + d + u - 1 = N'$ (say),

2. $N > vd + d + u - 1$,

3. $N < vd + d + u - 1$.

The case 1 is similar to the case $N = nk$ of the usual systematic sampling in the sense that the selection of one more unit results in getting the first unit of the sample repeated. In the following we state the result on inclusion probability for case 1.

Note that for specified u and d there exists one positive integer m satisfying

$$(m - 2)d + 1 \le u \le (m - 1)d + 1 .$$

Further we assume that when $N > vd + u + d - 1$, there is a positive integer k such that $(k - 1)d < N - vd - d - u + 1 \le kd$.

Result 10.4. When $N > vd + d - 1 + u$, the inclusion probabilities for a pair of units (U_i, U_j), $i \ne j$, under the new systematic sampling procedure are:

(i) $N\pi_{ij} = v + 1 - t + \max(0, m - t)$,

$$\text{if } |i - j| = td \text{ or } N - td, \ t = k, k + 1, \ldots, v$$

(ii) $N\pi_{ij} = v - t + \max(0, m - t)$,

$$\text{if } |i - j| = td \text{ or } N - td, \ t = 1, 2, \ldots, (k - 1)$$

(iii) $N\pi_{ij} = u - |i - j|$,   if $|i - j| \le u - i$ ⎤ Excluding the

(iv) $N\pi_{ij} = |i - j| - (N - u)$,   if $|i - j| \ge N - u + 1$ ⎥ case already

(v) $N\pi_{ij} = 1$,   if $u - 1 < |i - j| < md$ ⎥ covered under

(vi) $N\pi_{ij} = 2$,   otherwise.   ⎦ (i) and (ii).

Remark 10.2. If the population is in a random order (i.e., the units are arranged at random) and if we treat the finite population as a simple random sample of size N drawn from a super population, then the variances of $\hat{\bar{Y}}_{\text{nss}}$, $\hat{\bar{Y}}_{\text{sy}}$, and $\bar{Y}_{\text{ran}}$ are all equal.

EXAMPLE 10.6

The following constitute values of $y =$ the number of students from the former U.S.S.R. in 20 universities and colleges in the metropolitan city of Boston.

University/College	y	University/College	y
1	35	11	9
2	20	12	11
3	15	13	14
4	12	14	22
5	18	15	39
6	21	16	26
7	16	17	18
8	20	18	17
9	25	19	12
10	30	20	27

Select a new systematic sample of size $n = 5$ and estimate the average number of students per institution from former U.S.S.R. studying in the city of Boston and estimate its sample variance.

Suppose the selected random number is 15 and let $u = 3$, and $d = 2$. Hence, $v = n - u = 2$. The selected educational institutions are those numbered 15, 16, 17, 19, 1. Then

$$\hat{\bar{Y}} = \bar{y}_n = \frac{1}{5}(39 + 26 + 18 + 12 + 35) = 26$$

and

$$\widehat{\text{var}} \, \bar{y}_n = \frac{1}{400} \sum_{i<j} \sum_{(i,j)\in s} \pi_{ij}^{-1}(y_i - y_j)^2 - n^{-1}\left(\sum y_i^2 - n\bar{y}^2\right)$$

where the π_{ij} will be evaluated using Result 10.4. For the purposes of Result 10.4, it is easy to check that $m = 2$ or 3 and $k = 7$. First,

$$n^{-1}\left(\sum y_i^2 - n\bar{y}^2\right) = \frac{1}{5}\left\{(39 - 26)^2 + (26 - 26)^2 + (18 - 26)^2\right.$$

$$\left. + \ (12 - 26)^2 + (35 - 26)^2\right\}$$

$$= \frac{1}{5}(169 + 0 + 64 + 196 + 81) = 102\,.$$

Next consider

$$\sum_{i<j}\sum \pi_{ij}^{-1}(y_i - y_j)^2 = \pi_{1,15}^{-1}(y_1 - y_{15})^2 + \pi_{1,16}^{-1}(y_1 - y_{16})^2 + \pi_{1,17}^{-1}(y_1 - y_{17})^2$$

$$+ \pi_{1,19}^{-1}(y_1 - y_{19})^2 + \pi_{15,16}^{-1}(y_{15} - y_{16})^2$$

$$+ \pi_{15,17}^{-1}(y_{15} - y_{17})^2 + \pi_{15,19}^{-1}(y_{15} - y_{19})^2$$

$$+ \pi_{16,17}^{-1}(y_{16} - y_{17})^2 + \pi_{16,19}^{-1}(y_{16} - y_{19})^2$$

$$+ \pi_{17,19}^{-1}(y_{17} - y_{19})^2$$

$$= \frac{16}{\pi_{1,15}} + \frac{100}{\pi_{1,16}} + \frac{289}{\pi_{1,17}} + \frac{529}{\pi_{1,19}} + \frac{169}{\pi_{15,16}} + \frac{441}{\pi_{15,17}}$$

$$+ \frac{729}{\pi_{15,19}} + \frac{64}{\pi_{16,17}} + \frac{196}{\pi_{16,19}} + \frac{36}{\pi_{17,19}}.$$

From Result 10.4 (with $m = 2$ or 3 and $k = 7$, here let $m = 3$),

$$\pi_{1,15} = \pi_{1,16} = \pi_{1,17} = \pi_{1,19} = \frac{1}{10}$$

$$\pi_{15,16} = \frac{2}{20}, \qquad \pi_{15,17} = \frac{3}{20}, \qquad \pi_{15,19} = \frac{1}{20}$$

$$\pi_{16,17} = \frac{2}{20}, \qquad \pi_{16,19} = \frac{1}{20}, \qquad \pi_{17,19} = \frac{3}{20}.$$

Hence,

$$\sum_{i<j}\sum \pi_{ij}^{-1}(y_i - y_j)^2$$

$$= 160 + 1000 + 2890 + 5290 + 1690 + 2940 + 14{,}580 + 640 + 3920 + 240$$

$$= 33{,}350.$$

Thus,

$$\widehat{\text{var } \bar{y}_n} = \frac{33350}{400} - 102 = 83.375 - 102 < 0.$$

This is not surprising, because sometimes the estimate of the variance of the Horvitz-Thompson estimator is negative.   ◆

■ PROBLEMS

10.1   Let the population data be as given in the table below.

Unit	z	y	y/z
1	0.1	0.5	5
2	0.2	1.4	7
3	0.3	2.4	8
4	0.4	3.6	9
Total	1.0	7.9	

Objective.   To estimate the population total by selecting two units. Consider two sampling schemes.

(a) The first unit is chosen with varying probability and the second unit is selected with equal probability and without replacement.

(b) Both the units are selected with varying probabilities and without replacement.

Under each sampling scheme, compute the estimate of the population total, its variance and the estimate of the variance.

10.2   Let the population units and their probabilities of selection be as shown in the table below.

Unit	z	y
1	0.2	0.8
2	0.3	0.9
3	0.15	0.75
4	0.25	1.25
5	0.10	0.6
Total	1.0	3.6

Suppose a sample of size $n = 2$ namely (U_2, U_3) is chosen. Give Murthy's estimate of the total and a 95% confidence interval for the same.

10.3   McDonald Corporation wishes to estimate the total annual sales in two adjacent towns. There are 5 McDonald restaurants in each town. Let x denote the receipts (in million of dollars) for the previous year and y^* denote the sales for the first quarter of the current year. We draw one restaurant proportional to size (x) from each town and observe x and y^*. Obtain $\hat{Y}_{RHC}$, the estimate of the total for the current year, and its standard error.

	Town A					Town B			
	x	y^*	$4y^*$	p_j		x	y^*	$4y^*$	p_j
	2.1	0.6	2.4	0.07		1.9	0.5	2.0	0.06
	3.2	0.9	3.6	0.10		4.8	1.3	5.2	0.16
	5.1	1.4	5.6	0.17		2.3	0.7	2.8	0.07
	1.7	0.5	2.0	0.06		1.6	0.5	2.0	0.05
	4.3	1.1	4.4	0.14		3.8	1.1	4.4	0.12
Total	16.4		18.0	0.54	Total	14.4		16.4	0.46

10.4   For the data in Problem 8.1, obtain a new systematic sample of size $n = 5$ with $u = 3$, $d = 2$ and obtain an estimate of the average number of employees in an industrial company in that town. Also, obtain an unbiased estimate of its sampling variance.

■ REFERENCES

10.1   Brewer, K. W. R. (1963a). A model of systematic sampling with unequal probabilities. *Aust. J. Statist.* **5**, 5–13.

10.2   Des Raj (1956). Some estimates in sampling with varying probabilities without replacement. *J. Amer. Statist. Assoc.* **51**, 269–284.

10.3   Durbin, J. (1967). Design of multi-stage surveys for the estimation of sampling errors. *App. Statist.* **16**, 152–164.

10.4   Godambe, V. P. and Joshi, V. M. (1965). Admissibility and Bayes estimation in sampling finite populations, I. *Ann. Math. Statist.* **36**, 1707–1722.

10.5   Hartley, H. O. (1962). Multiple frame surveys. *Proc. Soc. Stat. Sec. Amer. Statist. Assoc.* 203–206.

10.6   Hartley, H. O. and Rao, J. N. K. (1962). Sampling with unequal probabilities and without replacement. *Ann. Math. Statist.* **33**, 350–374.

10.7   Horvitz, D. G. and Thompson, D. J. (1952) A generalization of sampling without replacement from a finite universe. *J. Amer. Statist. Assoc.* **47**, 663–685.

10.8   Madow, W. G. (1949). On the theory of systematic sampling, II. *Ann. Math. Statist.* **20**, 333–354.

10.9   Murthy, M. N. (1957). Ordered and unordered estimators in sampling without replacement. *Sankhyā*, **18**, 379–390.

10.10   Rao, J. N. K. (1965). On two simple schemes of unequal probability sampling without replacement. *J. Ind. Statist. Assoc.* **3**, 173–180.

10.11   Rao, J. N. K. (1988). Variance estimation in sample surveys. *Handbook of Statistics No. 6* (ed., P. R. Krishnaiah and C. R. Rao). Holland: Elsevier Science Publishers B.V., 427–447.

10.12   Rao, J. N. K., Hartley, H. O., and Cochran, W. G. (1962). A simple procedure of unequal probability sampling without replacement. *J. Roy Statist. Soc.* **B24**, 482–491.

10.13   Samford, M. R. (1967). On sampling without replacement with unequal probabilities of selection. *Biometrika* **54**, 499–513.

10.14   Singh, D. and Singh, P. (1977) New systematic sampling. *J. Stat. Planning and Inference* **1**, 163–177.

10.15   Yates, F. and Grundy, P. M. (1953). Selection without replacement from within strata with probability proportional to size. *J. Roy. Statist. Soc.* **B15**, 253–261.

CHAPTER 11

TWO-PHASE AND REPETITIVE SAMPLING

11.1 INTRODUCTION

In the previous chapters we have dealt with how information on an auxiliary variable x can be used to increase the precision of estimates of population mean or total on another variable y. Suppose that no information on x is available, but it can be gathered inexpensively on a large-scale basis; we may be better off collecting such information and then taking y-measurements on a subsample. For example, we wish to take a sample of agricultural holdings with probability proportional to area, and information on area is not available. We take an initial random sample of agricultural holdings and gather information on their areas. Then we take a subsample of holdings with probability proportional to area and collect data on the variable of interest. The initial sample can be used for several purposes: (1) for stratification purposes, or (2) for ratio or regression estimation. Such schemes are called double sampling or two-phase sampling procedures. In the following we will present some applications of this procedure.

11.2 DIFFERENCE ESTIMATION

Recall that the ratio estimator is considered best when the relation between y and x is a straight line passing through the origin. If the relationship is of the form $y - kx = a$ (a

---

N.B. Des Raj (1968, Chapter 7) served as a source for part of this chapter is a constant), it is natural to base the estimator on the differences $y_i - kx_i$. We estimate the difference $\bar{Y} - k\bar{X}$, add this to the estimate of $k\bar{X}$, and thereby obtain an estimate of $\bar{Y}$. Such estimators are called difference estimators. For difference estimators via two-phase sampling, we select an initial sample of size n' without replacement and collect information on x. Then we take a subsample of size $n (n < n')$ without replacement from the initial sample and make y-measurement on it. Let k denote a good guess of the ratio of y to x in the population. Then Des Raj (1968) proposes the following estimate for $\bar{Y}$:

$$\hat{\mu} = \bar{y} - k\bar{x} + k\bar{x}'$$

where $\bar{y}$ and $\bar{x}$ are sample means based on the subsample and $\bar{x}'$ is the mean of x from the first sample. Let

$$E^*(i) = E\{(i)| \text{ the initial sample }\}.$$

Then

$$E(\hat{\mu}) = EE^*(\bar{y} - k\bar{x} + k\bar{x}') = E(\bar{y}') = \bar{Y}.$$

Hence $\hat{\mu}$ is unbiased for $\bar{Y}$. Toward the variance,

$$\text{var}(\hat{\mu}) = E(\text{var}(\hat{\mu}) \mid \text{initial sample}) + \text{var}\left(E^*(\hat{\mu})\right)$$

where

$$\text{var}\left(E^*(\hat{\mu})\right) = \text{var}(\bar{y}') = \left(\frac{1}{n'} - \frac{1}{N}\right) S_y^2$$

$$\text{var}\{(\hat{\mu}) \mid \text{initial sample}\} = \left(\frac{1}{n} - \frac{1}{n'}\right) \sum_1^{n'} \frac{(y_i - kx_i - \bar{y}' + k\bar{x}')^2}{n' - 1}$$

and

$$E \text{ var}\{(\hat{\mu}) \mid \text{initial sample}\} = \left(\frac{1}{n} - \frac{1}{n'}\right) \sum_1^N \frac{(y_i - \bar{Y} - kx_i + k\bar{X})^2}{N - 1}$$

$$= \left(\frac{1}{n} - \frac{1}{n'}\right) (S_y^2 + k^2 S_x^2 - 2k\rho S_x S_y)$$

where N denotes the population size (see Result 3.3 on simple random sampling for the above result). Hence

$$\text{var}(\hat{\mu}) = \left(\frac{1}{n} - \frac{1}{N}\right) S_y^2 - \left(\frac{1}{n} - \frac{1}{n'}\right) kS_x (2\rho S_y - kS_x)$$

$$= S_y^2 \left\{\left(\frac{1}{n} - \frac{1}{N}\right) - \left(\frac{1}{n} - \frac{1}{n'}\right) r (2\rho - r)\right\}$$

where $r = kS_x/S_y.$

If c' and c denote the cost of sampling a unit in the initial and the subsample phases, respectively (where, typically, $c' < c$), the total cost of the two-phase procedure is

$$C = c'n' + cn.$$

If a direct simple random sample is taken for y, then its size n_0 is related by

$$C = n_0 c = n'c' + nc, \quad \text{i.e.,} \quad n_0 = n + (c'n'/c)$$

and the variance of the sample mean based on size n_0 is

$$\left(\frac{1}{n_0} - \frac{1}{N}\right) S_y^2.$$

Thus the double sampling procedure will be more precise (or more efficient) if

$$\frac{1}{n} - \frac{1}{N} - \left(\frac{1}{n} - \frac{1}{n'}\right) r(2\rho - r) < \frac{1}{n_0} - \frac{1}{N}$$

or

$$(2\rho - r)r > \left(\frac{1}{n} - \frac{1}{n_0}\right) \Big/ \left(\frac{1}{n} - \frac{1}{n'}\right)$$

$$= 1 \Big/ \left(1 - \frac{n}{n'}\right)\left(1 + \frac{nc}{n'c'}\right).$$

As a special case, let $k = \rho S_x / S_y = $ the regression coefficient, $n/n' = 1/5$ and $c/c' = 10$.

Then $r = \rho$ and the condition becomes $\rho^2 > 5/12$ or $\rho > 0.645$. Further, for an unbiased estimate of var $(\hat{\mu})$ we have

$$\widehat{\text{var}}(\hat{\mu}) = \left(\frac{1}{n'} - \frac{1}{N}\right) s_y^2 + \left(\frac{1}{n} - \frac{1}{n'}\right) s_d^2$$

where $s_y^2 = (n - 1)^{-1} \sum_1^n (y_i - \bar{y})^2$ and $s_d^2 = (n - 1)^{-1} \sum_1^n [y_i - \bar{y} - k(x_i - \bar{x})]^2$.

Suppose that the second sample is taken independently of the first sample. This, for instance, will be the case if one agency has information only on x and the second agency has information on both x and y. The estimator is still unbiased, because

$$E(\bar{y} - k\bar{x} + k\bar{x}') = \bar{Y} - k(\bar{X} - \bar{X}) = \bar{Y}$$

and

$$\text{var } \hat{\mu} = \text{var}(\bar{y} - k\bar{x}) + \text{var}(k\bar{x}')$$

$$= \left(\frac{1}{n} - \frac{1}{N}\right)(S_y^2 + k^2 S_x^2 - 2k\rho S_x S_y) + k^2 \left(\frac{1}{n'} - \frac{1}{N}\right) S_x^2.$$

Also an unbiased estimator of the variance of $\hat{\mu}$ is

$$\hat{\text{var}}(\hat{\mu}) = \left(\frac{1}{n} - \frac{1}{N}\right) s_d^2 + k^2 \left(\frac{1}{n'} - \frac{1}{N}\right) s_x^2$$

where $s_x^2 = \sum_1^{n'} (x_i - \bar{x}')^2 / (n' - 1)$.

11.3   UNBIASED RATIO ESTIMATION

In order to obtain unbiased ratio estimates of the population total, we employ probability sampling proportional to aggregate size. The initial sample is a simple random sample and the second sample is taken from the first sample with probability proportionate to aggregate x, the variate measured in the first sample. That is, $P(s) = \bar{x}/K\bar{x}'$, where K is chosen such that $\sum_{\text{alls}} P(s) = 1$, and it turns out that $K = \binom{n'}{n}$. Des Raj (1968) proposes the following estimate for the population mean

$$\hat{\bar{Y}} = \frac{\bar{y}}{\bar{x}}\bar{x}'$$

$$E^*\left(\frac{\bar{y}}{\bar{x}}\right) = \frac{\bar{y}'}{\bar{x}'} \quad \text{so that} \quad E\left(\hat{\bar{Y}}\right) = \bar{Y}$$

and he obtains the variance of $\hat{\bar{Y}}$ to be

$$\text{var}\left(\hat{\bar{Y}}\right) = \left[n\binom{n'}{n}\binom{N}{n'}\right]^{-1} \sum_{}^{'''} \bar{x}' \sum_{}^{''} \frac{(\sum_1^n y_i)^2}{\sum_1^n x_i} - \bar{Y}^2$$

where $\sum''$ denotes summation over all possible samples of size n drawn from an initial sample of size n' and $\sum'''$ denotes summation over all possible samples of size n' from the population of size N. Des Raj also gives an approximate estimate for $\text{var}\left(\hat{\bar{Y}}\right)$.

11.4   BIASED RATIO ESTIMATION

Instead of selecting a subsample with probability proportional to aggregate x, suppose we take a simple random *independent* sample and employ the usual ratio estimate

$$\hat{\bar{Y}}_{DR} = \frac{\bar{y}}{\bar{x}}\bar{x}'.$$

Proceeding as in ratio estimation, one can show that

$$E\left(\hat{\bar{Y}}_{DR}\right) = \bar{Y} - E\left[\text{cov}\left(\frac{\bar{y}}{\bar{x}}, \bar{x}|\bar{x}'\right)\right]$$

Also,

$$\text{MSE}\left(\hat{\bar{Y}}_{DR}\right) \doteq \frac{1}{\bar{X}^2}E\left(\bar{y}\bar{x}' - \bar{Y}\bar{x}\right)^2 = \frac{1}{\bar{X}^2}\text{var}\left(\bar{y}\bar{x}' - \bar{Y}\bar{x}\right).$$

Recall that if V and W are independent (writing $VW - EVEW = W^*V^* + (EV)W^* + (EW)V^*$, where $W^* = W - EW$ and $V^* = V - EV$), we have

$$\text{var}\,(VW) = (EW)^2\,\text{var}\,V + (EV)^2\,\text{var}\,W + \text{var}\,V \cdot \text{var}\,W.$$

Applying this result we have

$$\text{var}\,(\bar{y}\bar{x}') = \bar{X}^2\left(\frac{1}{n} - \frac{1}{N}\right)S_y^2 + \bar{Y}^2\left(\frac{1}{n'} - \frac{1}{N}\right)S_x^2 + \left(\frac{1}{n} - \frac{1}{N}\right)\left(\frac{1}{n'} - \frac{1}{N}\right)S_x^2 S_y^2$$

and

$$\text{var}(\bar{Y}\bar{x}) = \bar{Y}^2 \left(\frac{1}{n} - \frac{1}{N}\right) S_x^2,$$

$$\text{cov}(\bar{y}\bar{x}', \bar{x}) = E\{\text{cov}(\bar{y}\bar{x}', \bar{x})|\bar{x}'\} = \bar{X}\left(\frac{1}{n} - \frac{1}{N}\right)\rho S_x S_y.$$

Consequently

$$\text{MSE}\left(\hat{\bar{Y}}_{DR}\right) \doteq \left(\frac{1}{n} - \frac{1}{N}\right)(S_y^2 - 2R\rho S_x S_y + R^2 S_x^2) + \left(\frac{1}{n'} - \frac{1}{N}\right)R^2 S_x^2$$

$$+ \left(\frac{1}{n} - \frac{1}{N}\right)\left(\frac{1}{n'} - \frac{1}{N}\right)\frac{S_y^2 S_x^2}{\bar{X}^2}, \qquad \text{with } R = \bar{Y}/\bar{X}.$$

For all practical purposes, one can neglect the last terms on the right-hand-side expression. Also,

$$s_{\hat{\bar{Y}}_{DR}}^2 = \widehat{\text{MSE}}(\hat{\bar{Y}}_{DR}) \doteq \left(\frac{1}{n} - \frac{1}{N}\right)\sum_1^n \frac{(y_i - \hat{R}x_i)^2}{(n-1)} + \left(\frac{1}{n'} - \frac{1}{N}\right)\hat{R}^2 s_x^2$$

after neglecting the last term.

11.5   REGRESSION ESTIMATION

Let n' be the size of the initial sample and n be the size of the subsample taken out of n'. The estimate of the regression coefficient (to be denoted by b) is computed from the subsample. Then the two-phase regression estimator of $\bar{Y}$ is

$$\hat{\bar{Y}}_{Dlr} = \bar{y} - b(\bar{x} - \bar{x}')$$

where $\bar{y}$ and $\bar{x}$ are based on the subsample and $\bar{x}'$ is based on the initial sample. We will try to obtain the variance of the regression estimator which is valid for large n and n'.

Let $\bar{x}' = \lambda\bar{x} + v\bar{x}''$, where $\lambda = n/n'$, $v = 1 - \lambda$, and $\bar{x}''$ is the mean of the $n'v$ units in the initial sample that are not in the subsample.

Then

$$\hat{\bar{Y}}_{Dlr} = \bar{y} - vb(\bar{x} - \bar{x}'').$$

For sufficiently large n,

$$\hat{\bar{Y}}_{Dlr} \doteq \bar{y} - vB(\bar{x} - \bar{x}''), \qquad B = \rho S_y/S_x.$$

Consequently, we have

$$\operatorname{var}\left(\hat{\bar{Y}}_{Dlr}\right) \doteq \frac{S_y^2}{n'\lambda} + v^2 B^2 \left(\frac{1}{n'\lambda} + \frac{1}{n'v}\right) S_x^2 - \frac{2v B \rho S_x S_y}{n'\lambda}$$

$$= \frac{S_y^2}{n'\lambda} + \frac{(1-\lambda)\rho^2 S_y^2}{n'\lambda} - \frac{2(1-\lambda)\cdot\rho^2 S_y^2}{n'\lambda}$$

$$= \frac{S_y^2}{n'\lambda}\left[(1-\rho^2) + \lambda\rho^2\right] = \frac{S_y^2(1-\rho^2)}{n} + \frac{\rho^2 S_y^2}{n'}$$

$$= \frac{S_y^2}{n}\left[1 - \rho^2(1 - \frac{n}{n'})\right].$$

Based on linear costs, one can explore the condition on ρ^2 for which we are better off with double sampling.

EXAMPLE 11.1

Let $n' = 10$ denote a random sample of people enrolled in a weight-reduction program. We have their initial weights (x's). We take a random sample and obtain their weights (y's). When they leave the program, the following data is obtained. Obtain a two-phase unbiased estimate of $\bar{Y}$ and its standard error.
(*Hint:* Set $k \equiv 1$.) Let $N = 500$.

Sample	x'	y	$d = x - y$
1	120	102	18
2	130		
3	150	136	14
4	205	200	5
5	195		
6	180		
7	155	154	1
8	170		
9	215	206	9
10	145		

Also obtain a regression estimate. Further, assuming that the (x, y) sample is independent of the x'-sample, compute a ratio estimate.
   Computations yield

$$\sum_1^5 y_i = 798, \qquad\qquad \bar{y} = 159.6$$

$$\sum_1^{10} x_i' = 1665, \qquad\qquad \bar{x}' = 166.5$$

$$\bar{d} = 47/5 = 9.4.$$

Hence,

$$\hat{\mu} = -\bar{d} + \bar{x}' = -9.4 + 166.5 = 157.1 .$$

Further,

$$\widehat{\text{var}}(\hat{\mu}) = \left(\frac{1}{10} - \frac{1}{500}\right) s_y^2 + \left(\frac{1}{5} - \frac{1}{10}\right) s_d^2$$

where

$$s_d^2 = \frac{5(627) - (47)^2}{20} = \frac{926}{20} = 46.3$$

$$s_y^2 = \frac{5(135,052) - (798)^2}{20} = \frac{38,456}{20} = 1922.8 .$$

Thus,

$$s_{\hat{\mu}}^2 = \widehat{\text{var}}(\hat{\mu}) = (0.098)(1922.8) + (0.1)(46.3)$$

$$= 193.0644$$

or

$$s_{\hat{\mu}} = 13.89 .$$

Hence a 95% confidence interval for μ is

$$157.1 \pm 2(13.89) .$$

Treating the y sample as our independent sample, we have the following ratio estimate:

$$\bar{y} = 159.6, \qquad\qquad \bar{x} = (120 + 150 + 205 + 155 + 215)/5$$
$$= 845/5 = 169$$

$$\hat{R} = 159.6/169 = 0.944$$

$$\hat{\bar{Y}}_{DR} = \frac{159.6}{169} \times 166.5 = 157.24,$$

$$s_{\hat{\bar{Y}}_{DR}}^2 \doteq \left(\frac{1}{5} - \frac{1}{500}\right) \frac{1}{4} \sum_1^5 (y_i - \hat{R}x_i)^2 + \left(\frac{1}{10} - \frac{1}{500}\right) \hat{R}^2 s_x^2 .$$

After neglecting the last term in the expression for $\text{MSE}(\hat{\bar{Y}}_{DR})$,

$$\frac{1}{4} \sum_1^5 (y_i - \hat{R}x_i)^2 = \frac{1}{4}[(102 - 113.3)^2 + (136 - 141.6)^2 + (200 - 193.5)^2$$

$$+ (154 - 146.3)^2 + (206 - 203)^2]$$

$$= \frac{1}{4}[11.3^2 + 5.6^2 + 6.5^2 + 7.7^2 + 3^2] = 269.59/4 = 67.40,$$

$$s_x^2 = \{5(149,175) - (845)^2\} / 20 = 31,850/20 = 1592.5 .$$

Thus,

$$s^2_{\hat{\bar{Y}}_{DR}} = (0.2 - 0.002)(67.40) + (0.1 - 0.002)(0.944)^2(1592.5)$$

$$= (0.198)(67.40) + (0.098)(1419.13)$$

$$= 13.345 + 139.075$$

$$= 152.42$$

$$s_{\hat{\bar{Y}}_{DR}} = 12.34\,.$$

The 95% confidence interval for $\bar{Y}$ is $157.24 \pm 2(12.34)$.   ◆

Regression Approach

Recall that $\bar{x} = 169$. $x_i - \bar{x}$ are $-49, -19, 36, -14, 46$,

$$\sum (x_i - \bar{x})^2 = 6370\,,$$

$$b = \sum (x_i - \bar{x})y_i / \sum (x_i - \bar{x})^2$$

$$6370b = (-49)(102) + (-19)(136) + 36(200) + (-14)(154) + (46)(206).$$

Thus,

$$b = 6938/6370 = 1.09$$

$$s^2_y = \left\{5(135,052) - (798)^2\right\}/20 = 38,456/20 = 1922.8$$

$$s_y = 43.85.$$

$$s^2_x = 1592.5$$

$$s_x = 39.91.$$

$$r = \hat{\rho} = bs_x/s_y = (1.09)(39.91)/43.85 = 0.99.$$

So,

$$\hat{\bar{Y}}_{Dlr} = 159.6 - (1.09)(169 - 166.5)$$

$$= 159.6 - (1.09)(2.5)$$

$$= 156.9$$

and

$$s^2_{\hat{\bar{Y}}_{Dlr}} = \frac{s^2_y}{5}\left\{1 - r^2(1 - 0.5)\right\}$$

$$= \frac{1922.8}{5}\{1 - 0.49\} = 196.1256,$$

$$s_{\hat{\bar{Y}}_{Dlr}} = 14.00\,,$$

and a 95% confidence interval for $\bar{Y}$ is 156.9 ± 28.

11.6   ESTIMATION BY STRATIFICATION

An initial simple random sample of size n' is taken and the information on the variable x is collected. The sample is stratified into L strata with respect to the x variable. Let n'_h be the number of units falling into the hth strata $(h = 1, \ldots, L)$. From n'_h a simple random subsample of n_h units is taken in order to observe the response variable y.

Then, clearly, n_h constitutes a simple random sample from N_h (which is unknown) in the stratum. Let $\bar{y}_h$ denote the sample mean for y in hth stratum. Then we take the estimator of the population mean to be

$$\hat{\bar{Y}}_{D,st} = \sum_{h=1}^{L} a_h \bar{y}_h$$

where $a_h = n'_h/n'(h = 1, \ldots, L)$. Notice that $n'_h(h = 1, \ldots, L)$ are multinomial $(n', W_1, \ldots, W_L)$ where $W_h = N_h/N$ (where N denotes the size of the population).

In particular, $E(a_h) = W_h$ and $\text{var}(a_h) = bW_h(1-W_h)$, where $b = \frac{N}{N-1}\left(\frac{1}{n'} - \frac{1}{N}\right)$ and $\text{cov}(a_h, a_k) = -bW_hW_k(h \neq k)$. Also note that $E(\bar{y}_h) = \bar{Y}_h$ and $\text{var}(\bar{y}_h) = \left(\frac{1}{n_h} - \frac{1}{N_h}\right)S_h^2$.

$$E\left(\hat{\bar{Y}}_{D,st}\right) = EE\left(\sum a_h \bar{y}_h | a_h\right) = \sum \bar{Y}_h E(a_h) = \sum W_h \bar{Y}_h = \bar{Y}.$$

Furthermore

$$\text{var}\left(\hat{\bar{Y}}_{D,st}\right) = E\left\{\text{var}\left(\hat{\bar{Y}}_{D,st} | a_1, \ldots, a_L\right)\right\} + \text{var}\left(E\hat{\bar{Y}}_{D,st} | a_1, \ldots, a_L\right)$$

$$= T_1 + T_2 \quad \text{(say)}$$

where

$$T_1 = E\sum a_h^2 \text{ var}(\bar{y}_h)$$

$$= \sum \text{var}(\bar{y}_h)\left[bW_h(1 - W_h) + W_h^2\right]$$

and

$$T_2 = \text{var}\left(\sum a_h \bar{Y}_h\right) = b\sum \bar{Y}_h^2 W_h(1 - W_h) - b\sum\sum_{h\neq k} \bar{Y}_h \bar{Y}_k W_h W_k$$

$$= b\sum W_h \bar{Y}_h^2 - b\left(\sum W_h \bar{Y}_h\right)^2$$

$$= b\sum W_h(\bar{Y}_h - \bar{Y})^2.$$

Thus

$$\text{var}\left(\hat{\bar{Y}}_{D,st}\right) = \sum \left(\frac{1}{n_h} - \frac{1}{N_h}\right) W_h^2 S_h^2$$

$$+ b \sum W_h(1 - W_h) \left(\frac{1}{n_h} - \frac{1}{N_h}\right) S_h^2$$

$$+ b \sum W_h(\bar{Y}_h - \bar{Y})^2.$$

Note that the second and third terms can be construed to be the price (in terms of precision) we have to pay in not having information on x for the entire population, because the first term constitutes the variance obtained from a stratified random sample. Also, when N is large, $b \doteq 1/n'$. If $n_h/n \doteq W_h$,

$$\text{var}\left(\hat{\bar{Y}}_{D,st}\right) \doteq \frac{1}{n} \sum W_h S_h^2 + \frac{1}{n'} \sum W_h \left(\bar{Y}_h - \bar{Y}\right)^2.$$

Des Raj (1968, p. 243, Exercise 57) (see Problem 11.3 on page 243) provides an unbiased estimator of the variance of $\sum a_h \bar{y}_h$ when n_h/N_h and $1/N$ are negligible. Further, if the n_h are small when compared with n', an unbiased estimate of the variance of $\sum a_h \bar{y}_h$ becomes

$$\sum_{h=1}^{L} a_h^2 s_h^2/n_h.$$

For the cost functions considered in Section 11.2, the variance of the estimator based on the simple random sample of size n_0 is approximately

$$\frac{1}{n_0} \sum W_h S_h^2 + \frac{1}{n_0} \sum W_h \left(\bar{Y}_h - \bar{Y}\right)^2.$$

Hence, the between strata contribution to the variance would be much smaller with the two-phase sampling procedure.

EXAMPLE 11.2

Let $n' = 20$, the size of a random sample of farms taken in a certain county, and their acreages are noted. They are then classified as small (≤ 200 acres), medium ($200 < x \leq 400$), and large (> 400) farms. Simple random samples of sizes 3, 2, and 2 farms are taken from categories 1, 2, and 3, respectively, and the response variable $y = \#$ of acres on which corn is grown. The following data is obtained. Assume $N = 1000$. Estimate $\bar{Y}$ and obtain a 95% confidence interval for the same.

	Small	Medium	Large
	$y_{11} = 120$	$y_{12} = 250$	$y_{13} = 400$
	$y_{21} = 80$	$y_{22} = 150$	$y_{23} = 520$
	$y_{31} = 160$		
n'_h	10	5	5
n_h	3	2	2
$a_h = n'_h/n'$	0.5	0.25	0.25
$\bar{y}_h$	120	200	460
s_h^2	1600	5000	7200

$$\hat{\bar{Y}}_{D,st} = \sum_{h=1}^{3} a_h \bar{y}_h = \frac{1}{2}(120) + \frac{1}{4}(200) + \frac{1}{4}(460)$$

$$= 225$$

$$s^2_{\bar{Y}_{D,st}} = \sum_{h=1}^{3} a_h^2 s_h^2/n_h = \frac{1600}{2^2(3)} + \frac{5000}{4^2(2)} + \frac{7200}{4^2(2)}$$

$$= 133.33 + 156.25 + 225 = 514.58$$

$$s_{\bar{Y}_{D,st}} = 22.68.$$

A 95% confidence interval for $\bar{Y} = 225 \pm 2(22.68)$.   ◆

11.7   REPETITIVE SURVEYS

So far we have been discussing one-time surveys with different sampling designs. However, many surveys are repetitive in nature. Many medical surveys are follow-up studies over a period of time. Most governmental surveys are conducted repeatedly at fixed intervals. Repetitive surveys are similar to double sampling procedures. Question is how to utilize the information from the first sample in the second sample. Current estimates can be enriched by the previous information. Des Raj (1968, p. 153) illustrates how the first sample could be used to obtain estimates from the second sample.

For example, let a simple random sample of size n x-measurements be taken. A random subsample of size $m = n\lambda$ is retained for use on a second occasion. Let y-measurements be taken on them (actually x and y are the same variates, but we denote them by x and y in order to distinguish from which sample they arose). Also, on the second occasion, an independent random sample of size $u = n - m = nv(v = 1 - \lambda)$ is selected (unmatched with the first sample) and y-measurements are taken on the u units. Let us ignore the finite population corrections and assume that x and y have the same variance S^2. The population mean at the time of the first sample will be denoted by μ_1 and that at the time of the second sample be denoted by μ_2. For estimating μ_2

we can have the following two independent estimates:

$$\hat{\mu}_{2,u} = \frac{1}{u} \sum_1^u y_i$$

is based on the unmatched part, and the other is the difference estimator

$$\hat{\mu}_{2,m} = \left(\frac{1}{m} \sum_1^m y_i - \frac{1}{m} \sum_1^m x_i \right) + \frac{1}{n} \sum_1^n x_i .$$

Thus

$$E(\hat{\mu}_{2,m}) = EE(\hat{\mu}_{2,m}|x_i's) = E\left(\frac{1}{n} \sum y_i - \frac{1}{n} \sum x_i + \frac{1}{n} \sum x_i \right)$$

$$= E\left(\frac{1}{n} \sum_1^n y_i \right) = \mu_2 .$$

That is, $\hat{\mu}_{2,m}$ is unbiased for μ_2. Also,

$$\text{var}(\hat{\mu}_{2,u}) = \frac{S^2}{u} = \frac{S^2}{nv} = 1/W_{2,u} \quad \text{(say)} .$$

Further,

$$E(\hat{\mu}_{2,m}|x_1, \ldots, x_n) = \frac{1}{n} \sum_1^n y_i$$

$$\text{var}\left(E(\hat{\mu}_{2,m}|x_1, \ldots, x_n) \right) = \frac{S^2}{n} .$$

Also

$$\text{var}(\hat{\mu}_{2,m}|x_1, \ldots, x_n) = \left(\frac{1}{m} - \frac{1}{n} \right) \cdot \frac{1}{n-1} \sum_1^n \left[y_i - x_i - \frac{1}{n} \sum (y_i - x_i) \right]^2$$

and

$$E\{ \text{var}(\hat{\mu}_{2,m}|x_1, \ldots, x_n) \} = \left(\frac{1}{m} - \frac{1}{n} \right) \frac{1}{N-1} \sum_1^N [y_i - \mu_2 - (x_i - \mu_1)]^2$$

$$= \left(\frac{1}{m} - \frac{1}{n} \right)(S^2 + S^2 - 2\rho S^2) = \frac{2(1-\lambda)S^2(1-\rho)}{n\lambda} .$$

Hence

$$\text{var}(\hat{\mu}_{2,m}) = \frac{S^2}{n\lambda} \{ \lambda + (1-\lambda)(2 - 2\rho) \}$$

$$= \frac{S^2}{n\lambda} \{ 1 + (1-\lambda)(1 - 2\rho) \} = 1/W_{2,m} \quad \text{(say)}$$

To obtain a best unbiased estimate of μ_2, we can weigh $\hat{\mu}_{2,u}$ and $\hat{\mu}_{2,m}$ by the reciprocals of their variances and obtain

$$\hat{\mu}_2 = (W_{2,u}\hat{\mu}_{2,u} + W_{2,m}\hat{\mu}_{2,m})/(W_{2,u} + W_{2,m})$$

and

$$\text{var}\,(\hat{\mu}_2) = (W_{2,u} + W_{2,m})^{-1}$$

$$= \frac{S^2}{n}[1 + (1 - 2\rho)v]\left[1 + (1 - 2\rho)v^2\right]^{-1}.$$

Now, one can obtain the optimal value of v by solving the equation

$$\frac{\partial}{\partial v}\,\text{var}\,(\hat{\mu}_2) = 0, \qquad \text{namely} \qquad (1 - 2\rho)v^2 + 2v - 1 = 0.$$

The admissible solution is $v = \frac{\sqrt{2(1-\rho)}-1}{1-2\rho} = \{1+\sqrt{2(1-\rho)}\}^{-1}$ and hence $\lambda = 1-v = \frac{\sqrt{2(1-\rho)}}{1+\sqrt{2(1-\rho)}}$. With this choice of v, $1 + (1 - 2\rho)v = \{2(1 - \rho)\}^{\frac{1}{2}}$ and $1 + (1 - 2\rho)v^2 = 2\sqrt{2(1 - \rho)}\{\sqrt{2(1 - \rho)} - 1\}/(1 - 2\rho)$. Hence

$$\text{min var}\,(\hat{\mu}_2) = \frac{S^2}{n}\left(\frac{1}{2} + \sqrt{\frac{1 - \rho}{2}}\right) < \frac{S^2}{n} \qquad \text{if } \rho > \frac{1}{2}$$

where $\frac{S^2}{n}$ would be the variance of $\frac{1}{n}\sum_1^n y_i$ (which ignores the first sample; i.e., an independent sample of size n is taken on the second occasion). Thus for making current estimates (using the difference estimator) it is best to replace a portion of the first sample with a new independent sample. Further, the relative reduction in precision is

$$1 - \left(\frac{1}{2} + \sqrt{\frac{1 - \rho}{2}}\right) = \frac{1}{2}\left(1 - \sqrt{2(1 - \rho)}\right)$$

which is presented in Table 11.1 for selected values of ρ.

TABLE 11.1   The Proportion of the First Sample to Be Retained

ρ	$s = \sqrt{2(1 - \rho)}$	$\lambda = s/(1 + s)$	Relative reduction in precision $= (1 - s)/2$
0.5	1	0.5	0
0.6	0.8944	0.47	0.05
0.7	0.7746	0.44	0.11
0.8	0.6324	0.39	0.18
0.9	0.4472	0.31	0.28
0.95	0.3162	0.24	0.34
1.0	0	0	0.50

EXAMPLE 11.3

Unemployment rate[1] in the following counties in the state of Kentucky is measured in three years and is given as follows.

Name of County	Unemployment Rate		
	1994	1995	1996
Fayette	3.4	2.3	2.1
Jefferson	4.6	4.2	4.3
Jessamine	3.1	2.8	1.9
Montgomery	7.9	8.0	4.3
Woodford	3.2	1.9	1.8
Nelson	6.3	6.3	6.6
Shelby	3.2	3.2	2.2
Pike	7.6	8.2	9.5
Logan	4.7	4.7	3.7

Take the first five counties' data for 1995 as the first sample. Assume that $\rho = 0.8$ and use Fayette County as the portion of the first sample to be retained for use in 1996. Use the last four counties' data for 1996 as the second sample. Find the best unbiased estimate of the unemployment rate in Kentucky in 1996.

Here

$$\lambda = 0.2, \qquad m = 1, \quad \text{and} \quad u = 4$$

$$\hat{\mu}_{2,u} = \frac{1}{4}(6.6 + 2.2 + 9.5 + 3.7) = 5.5$$

$$\hat{\mu}_{2,m} = 2.1 - 2.3 + \frac{1}{5}(2.3 + 4.2 + 2.8 + 8.0 + 1.9)$$

$$= -0.2 + 3.84 = 3.64$$

$$W_{2,u} = 4/s^2 \qquad \text{and} \qquad W_{2m} = \frac{1}{(1 - 0.48)}s^{-2} = \frac{1}{(0.52s^2)}.$$

Then the best unbiased estimate of μ_2 is

$$\hat{\mu}_2 = \{4(5.5) + (3.64/0.52)\} / \{4 + (0.52)^{-1}\} = 4.896. \qquad \blacklozenge$$

■ PROBLEMS

11.1   We wish to estimate the number of inpatients in a large metropolitan city on a certain day. Let $N = 30$, the number of hospitals. We take a random sample of size $n' = 10$ hospitals and observe the number of beds x' in each of the selected hospitals. Then we

---

[1] *Source:* 1994 data from *Kentucky Deskbook of Economic Statistics*, 1996. For 1995 and 1996 data, see Kentucky Labor Force Estimates.

take a random sample of size $n = 5$ out of the above sample and observe y, the number of inpatients in each of the five selected hospitals. The following data is gathered. Obtain a two-phase unbiased estimate of $\bar{Y}$ and a 95% confidence interval for $\bar{Y}$ (use two-phase and regression approaches).

Sample	x	y	$d = x - y$
1	250		
2	300	160	140
3	400		
4	275	170	105
5	450	300	150
6	500		
7	550		
8	475	385	90
9	280		
10	575	395	180

11.2 A book on the history of Kentucky has just been published. We are interested to know how many copies of the book have been sold in Lexington, Kentucky, during the first week of the issue of this book. The total number of outlets is $N = 40$. They are classified in terms of square footage as small (≤ 400 sq ft), medium (between 400 and 1000 sq ft) and large (> 1000 sq ft). A random sample of $n' = 15$ outlets is taken and their sizes noted. A simple random sample of size 2 outlets is taken from each category, and the response variable y = number of books on the history of Kentucky sold during the first week. The following data is yielded.

	Small	Medium	Large
	$y_{11} = 25$	$y_{21} = 40$	$y_{31} = 75$
	$y_{12} = 35$	$y_{22} = 55$	$y_{32} = 85$
n'_h	6	5	4
n_h	2	2	2
$a_h = n'_h/n'$	6/15	5/15	4/15

Find an estimate of $\bar{Y}$ and a 95% confidence interval for the same.

11.3 [Des Raj, 1968, Problem 57]   An unbiased estimator of the variance of $\sum a_h \bar{y}_h$ is given by

$$\frac{n'}{n' - 1} \sum_h \left[\left(a_h^2 - \frac{a_h}{n'} \left(\frac{N - n'}{N - 1} \right) \right) \frac{s_h^2}{n_h} + \frac{N - n'}{n'(N - 1)} a_h (\bar{y}_h - \sum a_h \bar{y}_h)^2 \right]$$

provided n_h/N_h and $1/N$ are negligible. Show further that the estimator of variance reduces to $\sum a_h s_h^2/n_h$ if the n_h are small when compared with n'.

11.4   A firm with 25 factories wants to check the condition of numerical control machines. The total number of numerical control machines is $N = 1000$. A random sample of $n' = 10$ factories was taken, and the number of numerical control machines x' in each of the factories was obtained. Then we take a random sample of size $n = 5$ out of the above sample and obtain y, the number of machines found with signs of deterioration. The following data is gathered. Obtain a two-phase unbiased estimate of $\bar{Y}$ and a 95% confidence interval for $\bar{Y}$. Use two-phase, and regression approaches.

Sample	x	y	$d = x - y$
1	50		
2	55		
3	51	10	41
4	40		
5	35	6	29
6	52		
7	40	7	33
8	60		
9	28	3	25
10	25	2	23

11.5   We are interested in the investment in information technology by restaurants in a certain town. There are $N = 80$ restaurants in the town. They are classified as small (monthly sales less than or equal to $30,000), medium (monthly sales between $30,000 and $100,000), and large (monthly sales greater than $100,000). We took a simple random sample of $n' = 15$ restaurants and their sizes were noted. A simple random sample of size 2 restaurants is taken from each category and the response variable y = amount of dollars invested in information technology in 1996 is noted. The following data is yielded.

	Small	Medium	Large
	$y_{11} = 5,000$	$y_{21} = 10,000$	$y_{31} = 20,000$
	$y_{12} = 6,000$	$y_{22} = 8,000$	$y_{32} = 15,000$
$n'_h = 6$		5	4
$n_h = 2$		2	2
$a_h = n'_h/n'$	6/15	5/15	4/15

Find an estimate of $\bar{Y}$ and a 95% confidence interval for the same.

11.6   The state of Kentucky wants to determine the average daily attendance of its schools. There are 176 (N) school districts in Kentucky. We take a random sample of $n' = 10$ school districts and record the number of students in each district (x'). A random sample of five school districts is taken (n) from the above sample and the daily attendance is obtained. Obtain a two-phase unbiased estimate of $\bar{Y}$ and a 95% confidence interval for $\bar{Y}$. Use two-phase and regression approaches.

School District	Enrollment (x')	Average (Jan. '97) Daily Attendance (y)	$d = x - 7$
1 Clinton	1522	1429	93
2 Carter	5256		
3 Graves	4290		
4 Harlan	5686	5242	444
5 Harlan Ind.	945	835	110
6 Knox	4932	4136	796
7 Laurel	8825	7630	1195
8 Mason	2824		
9 Mayfield Ind.	1405		
10 Dayton Ind.	1367		

11.7 Unemployment rate[2] in the following states in the United States is measured in three years and is given as follows.

Name of State	Unemployment Rate 1994	1995	1996
Kentucky	5.4	6.6	6.3
Minnesota	4.0	4.6	4.3
California	8.6	8.2	7.4
Texas	6.4	6.5	5.9
New York	6.9	6.9	6.9
Wisconsin	4.7	3.7	3.5
Washington	6.4	6.4	6.5
Mississippi	6.6	6.1	6.1
Massachusetts	6.0	5.4	4.3

Take the first five states' data for 1995 as the first sample. Assume that $\rho = 0.8$ and use the state of New York as the portion of the first sample to be retained for use in 1996. Use the last four states' data for 1996 as the second sample. Find the best unbiased estimate of the unemployment rate in United States in 1996.

■ REFERENCES

11.1 Des Raj (1968). *Sampling Theory*. New York: McGraw Hill Book Company.

---

[2] Source: *Bureau of Labor Statistics*. Website address—
http://stats.bls.gov/news.release.stgune.t01.htm

CHAPTER **12**

TWO-STAGE SAMPLING

12.1 INTRODUCTION

In cluster sampling we choose a random sample of size n clusters and do 100% subsampling in each selected cluster. However, it may be more efficient to increase the number of clusters to be selected and to draw random samples of size m_i from the ith selected cluster ($i = 1, \ldots$). Here the clusters constitute the primary-stage (or first-stage) units (psu's or fsu's) and the subunits selected from each cluster constitute the second-stage units (ssu's). This is called two-stage sampling, which is usually used in large surveys such as a Gallup poll involving the sampling of housing units. In general we can have multistage sampling. For example, towns could be the primary units, the farms in each town be the secondary units and the plots in each farm be the third stage units. Also it should be noted that an r-stage design becomes a stratified $(r - 1)$-stage design when all the fsu's are included in the sample. Furthermore, multistage sampling may be the only feasible procedure in some practical situations where a reasonable sampling frame of ultimate or last observational units is not available and the cost of obtaining such a frame is very high.

N.B. Murthy (1967, pp. 323–338) served as a source for this chapter.

12.2   NOTATION

Let N denote the number of groups or clusters and ith cluster contain M_i units ($i = 1, \ldots, N$). Let y_{ij} denote the value of the response for the jth ssu in the ith cluster. Then the population total Y is given by

$$Y = \sum_{i=1}^{N} Y_i = \sum_{i=1}^{N} \sum_{j=1}^{M_i} y_{ij} \tag{12.1}$$

where Y_i denotes the total for ith cluster. n denotes the sample of fsu's selected according to any probability sampling scheme and from the ith fsu, m_i ssu's are selected.

12.3   ESTIMATION OF POPULATION TOTALS

If the total values of the selected fsu's were known, it would be possible to obtain an estimator of Y with the aid of the probability scheme adopted at the first stage as in cluster sampling. However, in two-stage sampling the totals of the selected fsu's are not known and they ought to be estimated on the basis of the selected ssu's using the probability scheme implemented in selecting them. Thus

$$\hat{Y}_i = \sum_{j=1}^{m_i} a_{ij} y_{ij} \tag{12.2}$$

where a_{ij} is the inflation factor at the second-stage selection, and hence the estimate of the population total is

$$\hat{Y} = \sum_{i=1}^{n} b_i \hat{Y}_i = \sum_{i=1}^{n} b_i \sum_{j=1}^{m_i} a_{ij} y_{ij} . \tag{12.3}$$

For instance, if the sampling is simple random without replacement at both the stages, we have

$$b_i = \frac{N}{n} \quad \text{and} \quad a_{ij} = \frac{M_i}{m_i} .$$

Then $\hat{Y} = \frac{N}{n} \sum_{i=1}^{n} M_i \bar{y}_i$, where $\bar{y}_i = \frac{1}{m_i} \sum_{j=1}^{m_i} y_{ij}$. Analogously, if the fsu's are selected with probabilities $\{p_i\}(i = 1, \ldots, N)$ with replacement and the m_i ssu's are selected with probabilities $\{p_{ij}\}$ with replacement, then

$$b_i = \frac{1}{n p_i} \quad \text{and} \quad a_{ij} = \frac{1}{m_i p_{ij}} .$$

In deriving the expected values and variances of the estimates, one has to consider the selection procedures at all the stages. Let E_i denote the expectation with respect to random variables associated with ith-stage sampling units $(i = 1, 2, \ldots)$. Thus

$$E(\hat{Y}) = E_1 E_2(\hat{Y})$$

and

$$\mathrm{var}\,(\hat{Y}) = E_1(\mathrm{var}_2\, \hat{Y}) + \mathrm{var}_1\left(E_2(\hat{Y})\right) \tag{12.4}$$

where $\mathrm{var}_i\,(\cdot)$ denotes variance of $(\cdot)$ with respect to the ith stage sampling units $(i = 1, 2)$.

Next let us consider some sampling designs.

12.4   TWO-STAGE SCHEME WITH SIMPLE RANDOM SAMPLING

Suppose we take a simple random sample of n fsu's and then select a simple random sample of m_i ssu's from the ith fsu $(i = 1, \ldots, n)$. An estimate of Y is

$$\hat{Y} = \frac{N}{n} \sum_{i=1}^{n} \frac{M_i}{m_i} \sum_{j=1}^{m_i} y_{ij} \tag{12.5}$$

where $P(i = k) = 1/N$ and $P(j = l|i) = 1/M_i$, $1 \le k \le N$ and $1 \le l \le M_i$.

Then

$$E(\hat{Y}) = E_1 E_2(\hat{Y}) = E_1\left(\frac{N}{n} \sum_{i=1}^{n} y_i\right) = Y$$

where y_i denotes the total over all ssu's in the ith sample fsu. That is, $\hat{Y}$ is unbiased for Y.

Case 1:   Suppose we do simple random sampling without replacement at both the stages. Then

$$\mathrm{var}\,(\hat{Y}) = \mathrm{var}_1\,(E_2\hat{Y}) + E_1\,(\mathrm{var}_2\,\hat{Y})$$

$$= \mathrm{var}_1\left(\frac{N}{n} \sum_{i=1}^{n} y_i\right) + E_1\left\{\frac{N^2}{n^2} \sum_{i=1}^{n} M_i^2(1 - f_i)\frac{\sigma_{wi}'^2}{m_i}\right\}$$

$$= N^2 M'^2(1 - f)\frac{\sigma_b'^2}{n} + \frac{N}{n} \sum_{i=1}^{N} M_i^2(1 - f_i)\frac{\sigma_{wi}'^2}{m_i} \tag{12.6}$$

where $f = n/N$, $f_i = m_i/M_i$, $M' = \sum_{i=1}^{N} M_i/N$,

$$\sigma_b'^2 = (N-1)^{-1} \sum_{i=1}^{N} \left(\frac{M_i}{M'} \bar{Y}_i - \bar{Y} \right)^2, \qquad \sigma_{wi}'^2 = (M_i - 1)^{-1} \sum_{j=1}^{M_i} (y_{ij} - \bar{Y}_i)^2 \quad (12.7)$$

and $\bar{Y}_i$ denotes the mean of ith fsu in the population and $\bar{Y} = Y/NM'$. An unbiased estimator of var $(\hat{Y})$ can be obtained, provided unbiased estimators for $\sigma_{wi}'^2$ and $\sigma_b'^2$ are available. An unbiased estimator of $\sigma_{wi}'^2$ is given by

$$s_{wi}^2 = \frac{1}{m_i - 1} \sum_{j=1}^{m_i} (y_{ij} - \bar{y}_i)^2. \qquad (12.8)$$

Since

$$\sigma_b'^2 = \frac{1}{(N-1)M'^2} \left(\sum_{i=1}^{N} M_i^2 \bar{Y}_i^2 - \frac{Y^2}{N} \right)$$

where $NM'\bar{Y} = Y$, let us try to obtain unbiased estimators of $\sum_{i=1}^{N} M_i^2 \bar{Y}_i^2$ and Y^2. Since $\bar{Y}_i^2 = E_2(\bar{y}_i^2) - \text{var}_2(\bar{y}_i)$, an unbiased estimator of $\bar{Y}_i^2$ is

$$\bar{y}_i^2 - \widehat{\text{var}}_2(\bar{y}_i) = \bar{y}_i^2 - (1 - f_i)\frac{s_{wi}^2}{m_i}.$$

Similarly, an unbiased estimator of Y^2 is $\hat{Y}^2 - \widehat{\text{var}}(\hat{Y})$. Thus, since $\frac{N}{n} \sum_{i=1}^{n} M_i^2 \{\bar{y}_i^2 - \widehat{\text{var}}(\bar{y}_i)\}$ is unbiased for $\sum_{k=1}^{N} M_k^2 \bar{Y}_k^2$, we have

$$\widehat{\text{var}}(\hat{Y}) = \frac{N^3(1-f)}{n^2(N-1)} \left[\sum_{i=1}^{n} M_i^2 \left\{ \bar{y}_i^2 - (1 - f_i)\frac{s_{wi}^2}{m_i} \right\} \right]$$

$$- \frac{N(1-f)}{n(N-1)} \left\{ \hat{Y}^2 - \widehat{\text{var}}(\hat{Y}) \right\}$$

$$+ \left(\frac{N}{n} \right)^2 \sum_{i=1}^{n} M_i^2 (1 - f_i)\frac{s_{wi}^2}{m_i}.$$

Hence,

$$\left\{ 1 - \frac{(N-n)}{n(N-1)} \right\} \widehat{\text{var}}(\hat{Y}) = \frac{N^3(1-f)}{n^2(N-1)} \left[\sum M_i^2 \bar{y}_i^2 - \frac{n}{N^2} \hat{Y}^2 \right]$$

$$+ \frac{N^2(n-1)}{n^2(N-1)} \sum_{i=1}^{n} M_i^2 (1 - f_i)\frac{s_{wi}^2}{m_i}.$$

Thus,

$$\frac{N(n-1)}{n(N-1)} \widehat{\text{var}}(\hat{Y}) = \text{RHS}.$$

So,

$$\widehat{\text{var}}(\hat{Y}) = \frac{N^2(1-f)}{n(n-1)} \left[\sum_{i=1}^{n} M_i^2 \bar{y}_i^2 - \frac{n}{N^2} \hat{Y}^2 \right]$$

$$+ \frac{N}{n} \sum_{i=1}^{n} M_i^2 (1-f_i) \frac{s_{w_i}^2}{m_i}. \tag{12.9}$$

Also,

$$(n-1)^{-1} \left[\sum_{i=1}^{n} M_i^2 \bar{y}_i^2 - \frac{n}{N^2} \hat{Y}^2 \right] = (n-1)^{-1} \left[\sum_{i=1}^{n} \hat{Y}_i^2 - n(M'\hat{\bar{Y}})^2 \right],$$

$$\text{since } \hat{Y} = N M' \hat{\bar{Y}}$$

$$= (n-1)^{-1} \sum_{i=1}^{n} (\hat{Y}_i - M'\hat{\bar{Y}})^2,$$

$$\text{since } \sum_{1}^{n} \hat{Y}_i = n M' \hat{\bar{Y}}$$

$$= s_b^2.$$

The latter notation for s_b^2 is used by several authors.

EXAMPLE 12.1

Mars University has 10 locations where personal computers (PCs) are available. The Vice President for Academic Computing wants to estimate the average number of hours the PCs were down for repairs in the past month. Since the locations are widely scattered, the VP decides to take a random sample of locations (clusters) and at each location take a simple random sample of PCs. The following data is obtained with $n = 3$ and $m_i = 0.2M_i$. Assume that $\sum_{i=1}^{10} M_i = 250$ (or $M' = 25$).

Downtime for PCs

Location	M_i	m_i	Downtime	$\bar{y}_i$	s_i^2
1	30	6	3, 4, 2, 4, 5, 6	4	2.0
2	25	5	4, 5, 2, 6, 3	4	2.5
3	20	4	5, 6, 4, 5	5	0.67

Using the above data, estimate the average downtime per machine and obtain a 95% confidence for the same.

estimate of the total downtime $=$

$$\hat{Y} = \frac{10}{3}[30(4) + 25(4) + 20(5)]$$

$$= \frac{10}{3}(320) = 3200/3 \text{ hours}$$

$\hat{\bar{Y}} =$ estimate of the average downtime per machine

$$= \frac{3200}{3(250)} = 4.267 \text{ hours}$$

$$\widehat{\text{var}}\,(\hat{Y}) = \frac{10^2(0.7)}{3 \times 2}\left[30^2(4)^2 + 25^2(4)^2 + 20^2(5^2) - \left(\frac{3200}{3}\right)^2 \cdot \frac{3}{100}\right]$$

$$+ \frac{10(0.8)}{3}\left[30^2\frac{(2.0)}{6} + 25^2\frac{(2.5)}{5} + 20^2\frac{(0.67)}{4}\right]$$

$$= 11.667[34,400 - 34,133.33] + (2.667)(300 + 312.5 + 67)$$

$$= (11.667)(266.67) + (2.667)(679.5)$$

$$= 4923.4654$$

$$s_{\hat{Y}} = 70.17 .$$

Hence,

$$s_{\hat{\bar{Y}}} = s_{\hat{Y}}/250 = 0.28, \qquad 95\% \text{ CI} = 4.267 \pm 0.561 . \qquad \blacklozenge$$

Case 2: With replacement at the first stage and without replacement at the second stage. Please note that if a first-stage unit repeats itself, we draw a fresh simple random sample of specified size without replacement from that unit.

Then the unbiased estimator of Y given by (12.5) remains the same and its sampling variance is given by

$$\text{var}\,(\hat{Y}) = N^2 M'^2 \frac{\sigma_b^2}{n} + \frac{N}{n}\sum_{i=1}^{N} M_i^2(1 - f_i)\frac{\sigma_{w_i}'^2}{m_i} \qquad (12.10)$$

where $\sigma_b^2 = (N - 1)\sigma_b'^2/N$.

Also, since the n unbiased estimates of Y obtained from the n sample fsu's given by

$$t_i = N M_i \bar{y}_i , \qquad i = 1, \ldots, n \qquad (12.11)$$

are mutually independent and have the same sampling variance, an unbiased estimate of the variance of $\hat{Y} = n^{-1} \sum_{i=1}^{n} t_i$ is given by

$$\widehat{\text{var}}(\hat{Y}) = \frac{1}{n(n-1)} \sum_{i=1}^{n} (NM_i \bar{y}_i - \hat{Y})^2 = N^2 \frac{M'^2 s_b^2}{n} \tag{12.12}$$

where

$$s_b^2 = \frac{1}{n-1} \sum_{i=1}^{n} \left(\frac{M_i}{M'} \bar{y}_i - \hat{\bar{Y}} \right)^2, \qquad \hat{\bar{Y}} = \hat{Y}/NM'. \tag{12.13}$$

Case 3:   Sampling with replacement at both the stages.

Here also the estimator $\hat{Y}$ given by (12.5) is unbiased and its variance is given by

$$\text{var}(\hat{Y}) = N^2 M'^2 \left(\frac{\sigma_b^2}{n} + \frac{\sigma_w^2}{nm} \right)$$

where $m_i = m$, $\sigma_w^2 = \frac{1}{N} \sum_{i=1}^{N} \frac{M_i}{M'} \sigma_{wi}^2$, $\sigma_{wi}^2 = \frac{M_i-1}{M_i} \sigma_{wi}'^2$, and $f_i = \frac{m}{M_i}$.

Since the fsu's are selected with replacement, an unbiased estimator of the variance of $\hat{Y}$ is given by (12.12).

Remark 12.1.   If we are interested in estimating the population mean $\bar{Y} = Y/NM'$, an unbiased estimator of $\bar{Y}$ can be obtained by dividing $\hat{Y}$ by NM', provided the value of M' is known ahead of time. The variance of $\hat{\bar{Y}}$ and its unbiased estimate are obtained by dividing the var $(\hat{Y})$ and $\widehat{\text{var}}(\hat{Y})$ by $N^2 M'^2$. If M' is unknown, it can be estimated by the mean number of ssu's in the n sample fsu's. Then the estimator of $\bar{Y}$ is

$$\hat{\bar{Y}} = \frac{N}{n} \sum_{i=1}^{n} \frac{M_i}{m_i} \sum_{j=1}^{m_i} y_{ij} \Big/ \frac{N}{n} \sum_{i=1}^{n} M_i \tag{12.14}$$

which is a ratio of two unbiased estimators. In general, the estimator of $\bar{Y}$ given by (12.14) will be biased.

12.5   COMPARISON WITH SINGLE-STAGE AND CLUSTER SAMPLING

The two-stage sampling reduces to cluster sampling if $m_i = M_i (i = 1, \ldots, n)$ and hence the sampling variances of estimators for cluster sampling can be obtained by setting $f_i \equiv 1$ in the variances of the estimators in the two-stage sampling. In order to evaluate the efficiency of two-stage procedure relative to single-stage and cluster sampling for a specified total sample size in terms of number of ultimate units, let us consider the simple case of $M_i \equiv M$ and $m_i \equiv m$. Then

$$\hat{\bar{Y}} = \frac{1}{mn} \sum_{i=1}^{n} \sum_{j=1}^{m} y_{ij} \tag{12.15}$$

and its variance with simple random sampling with replacement at the first stage and without replacement at the second stage takes the form of

$$\text{var}\,(\hat{\bar{Y}}) = \frac{\sigma_b^2}{n} + \frac{M-m}{M-1}\frac{\sigma_w^2}{nm}. \tag{12.16}$$

Recall from Chapter 9 on cluster sampling that σ_b^2 and σ_w^2 can be expressed in terms of the population variance σ^2 and the intraclass correlation coefficient ρ, namely

$$\sigma_b^2 = \frac{\sigma^2}{M}\{1 + (M-1)\rho\} \quad \text{and} \quad \sigma_w^2 = \frac{M-1}{M}\sigma^2(1-\rho). \tag{12.17}$$

We obtain (after some elementary simplification)

$$\text{var}\,(\hat{\bar{Y}}_t) = \frac{\sigma^2}{mn}\{1 + (m-1)\rho\} \tag{12.18}$$

where the subscript t denotes two-stage sampling.

If the specified total number of units is mn, the variances of the estimators of $\bar{Y}$ in cluster sampling and single-stage sampling are given by

$$\text{var}\,(\hat{\bar{Y}}_c) = \frac{\sigma^2}{mn}\{1 + (M-1)\rho\}$$

and

$$\text{var}\,(\hat{\bar{Y}}_r) = \frac{\sigma^2}{mn} \tag{12.19}$$

where the subscripts c and r, respectively, denote cluster sampling and simple random sampling. Clearly one can see that

$$\text{var}\,(\hat{\bar{Y}}_r) \leq \text{var}\,(\hat{\bar{Y}}_t) \leq \text{var}\,(\hat{\bar{Y}}_c) \tag{12.20}$$

provided $\rho \geq 0$, which is possible in practice when nearby units are grouped to form the clusters or fsu's. Hence, the two-stage sampling scheme is more efficient than the cluster sampling and less efficient than the single-stage sampling.

On the other hand, if sampling is simple random sampling with replacement at both the stages, then

$$\text{var}\,(\hat{\bar{Y}}_t) = \frac{\sigma_b^2}{n} + \frac{\sigma_w^2}{mn}$$

$$= \frac{\sigma^2}{mn}\left[\frac{m}{M} + \frac{M-1}{M}\{1 + (m-1)\rho\}\right]. \tag{12.21}$$

Now we see that $\text{var}\,(\hat{\bar{Y}}_t) \geq \text{var}\,(\hat{\bar{Y}}_r)$ since $\rho \geq -1/(M-1)$.

One can consider other sampling schemes such as probability sampling proportional to the size of an auxiliary variable and with replacement. For example, in studying the cost-of-living survey of industrial workers, the factories may be treated as fsu's and selected with probability proportional to size (with replacement), where size is the number of workers. However, such considerations are beyond the scope of this book.

In general when $m_i \equiv m$, var $(\hat{Y})$ is of the form

$$\frac{1}{n}\left(A_1 + \frac{A_2}{m}\right) + A_3 \tag{12.22}$$

where A_1, A_2, and A_3 are functions of the population parameters and are free of the sample sizes m and n. Furthermore, $A_3 = 0$ if sampling is done with replacement at the first stage. From (12.22) we infer that n plays a more important role than that of m in determining the precision of the estimate.

Optimal Choice of m and n

In two-stage sampling the total cost c could be written as

$$c = c_0 + nc_1 + nmc_2 \tag{12.23}$$

where c_0 denotes the overhead cost, c_1 is the cost per single first-stage unit, and c_2 is the cost per single second-stage unit.

Suppose that the total cost is fixed at c'. Then the optimum values of n and m that would minimize the variance of $\hat{Y}$ can be obtained as follows. From (12.23) the value of n for given m is

$$n \doteq (c' - c_0)/(c_1 + mc_2).$$

For this value of n, var $(\hat{Y})$ becomes

$$\begin{aligned}
\text{var}(\hat{Y}) &= \left(\frac{c_1 + c_2 m}{c' - c}\right)\left(A_1 + \frac{A_2}{m}\right) + A_3 \\
&= \frac{c_1 A_1}{c' - c_0}\left\{\left(m\frac{c_2}{c_1} + \frac{1}{m}\frac{A_2}{A_1}\right) + 1 + \frac{c_2 A_2}{c_1 A_1}\right\} + A_3. \tag{12.24}
\end{aligned}$$

Hence it suffices to minimize with respect to m the quantity

$$\frac{mc_2}{c_1} + \frac{A_2}{mA_1}.$$

The solution is $m_0 = (A_2 c_1 / A_1 c_2)^{\frac{1}{2}}$, and the corresponding value of n is

$$n_0 = \frac{(c' - c_0)(A_1/c_1)^{\frac{1}{2}}}{(A_1 c_1)^{\frac{1}{2}} + (A_2 c_2)^{\frac{1}{2}}}.$$

Substituting m_0 in (12.24), we obtain the minimum variance to be

$$\text{var}(\hat{Y}) = (c' - c_0)^{-1}\left\{(A_1 c_1)^{\frac{1}{2}} + (A_2 c_2)^{\frac{1}{2}}\right\}^2 + A_3. \tag{12.25}$$

We illustrate the above by the following example.

EXAMPLE 12.2

Let $c_1 = 200$, $c_2 = 5$, $A_1 = 200$, $A_2 = 125$, $A_3 = 0$, $c' - c_0 = 2250$. Then $m_0 = 5$ and $n_0 = 10$. Hence

$$\text{var}\,(\hat{Y}) = \frac{1}{2250}\,\{225\}^2 = 22.5\,.$$

Next we will find the optimal m_0 and n_0 that would minimize the cost for a specified variance, namely $\text{var}\,(\hat{Y}) = V_0$. Then for any m, the value of n is

$$n = \frac{A_1 + A_2 m^{-1}}{V_0 - A_3}$$

and

$$c - c_0 = (V_0 - A_3)^{-1}(A_1 + A_2 m^{-1})(c_1 + mc_2)$$

$$= A_1 c_1 (V_0 - A_3)^{-1}\left\{\left(\frac{mc_2}{c_1} + \frac{A_2}{mA_1}\right) + \left(1 + \frac{A_2 c_2}{A_1 c_1}\right)\right\}\,. \quad (12.26)$$

Thus it suffices to minimize $\frac{mc_2}{c_1} + \frac{A_2}{mA_1}$.

Then the optimal value of $m = m_0$ is the same as before, and the optimal value of n is

$$n_0 = (V_0 - A_3)^{-1}\left\{(A_1 c_1)^{\frac{1}{2}} + (A_2 c_2)^{\frac{1}{2}}\right\}\left(\frac{A_1}{c_1}\right)^{\frac{1}{2}}\,.$$

Substituting the value of m_0 in (12.26), we obtain

$$c - c_0 = (V_0 - A_3)^{-1}\left\{(A_1 c_1)^{\frac{1}{2}} + (A_2 c_2)^{\frac{1}{2}}\right\}^2\,. \quad (12.27)$$

$\blacklozenge$

EXAMPLE 12.3

As in Example 12.2 take $c_1 = 200$, $c_2 = 5$, $A_1 = 200$, $A_2 = 125$, $V_0 - A_3 = 22.5$. Then $m_0 = 5$, $n_0 = 10$, and $c - c_0 = \frac{225^2}{22.5} = 2250$.

$\blacklozenge$

12.6 PROBABILITY SAMPLING FOR A TWO-STAGE DESIGN

Let the universe consists of N primary sampling units with the ith such unit containing M_i secondary units. Let y_{ij} be the value of some characteristic Y of the jth subsampling unit of the ith primary sampling unit. We wish to estimate the population total

$$T = \sum_{i=1}^{N}\sum_{j=1}^{M_i} y_{ij}$$

from a sample of n primary units, where m_i subsampling units are drawn from the ith primary unit if it is included in the sample. The primary units are drawn without replacement using arbitrary probabilities of selection for each draw. Suppose an overall sampling rate t is specified in advance and the m_i are defined by

$$m_i = \frac{t M_i}{\pi_i} \quad (i = 1, \dots, n)$$

where π_i now denotes the prior probability that the ith primary unit will be included in a sample of n such units. The subsampling units are drawn without replacement with equal probabilities of selection for those remaining prior to each draw (that is, subsampling is by simple random sampling).

One difficulty that arises is that the m_i may not be integers. We can choose the closest integral value for m_i. We shall ignore the bias introduced by this. Also, the values of M_i need not be known in advance of the primary unit selection stage of the draw. Since every subsampling unit will have the same chance of being included in the sample, an unbiased estimate of T is

$$\hat{T} = \frac{1}{t} \sum_{i=1}^{n} \sum_{j=1}^{m_i} y_{ij}$$

$$E\hat{T} = \frac{1}{t} E \sum_{i=1}^{n} \left(E \sum_{j=1}^{m_i} y_{ij} \,|\, i\text{th primary unit is selected.} \right)$$

$$= \frac{1}{t} E \sum_{i=1}^{n} \frac{m_i}{M_i} \left(\sum_{j=1}^{M_i} y_{ij} \right)$$

$$= E \sum_{i=1}^{n} \frac{T_i}{\pi_i} = T, \qquad \text{where } T_i = \sum_{j=1}^{M_i} y_{ij}.$$

If $\pi_i > 0$ for all i,

$$\text{var}\,(\hat{T}) = \sum_{i=1}^{N} T_i^2 \left(\frac{1 - \pi_i}{\pi_i} \right) + \sum_{i \neq j}^{N} \sum^{N} T_i T_j \frac{\pi_{ij} - \pi_i \pi_j}{\pi_i \pi_j} + \sum_{i=1}^{N} \frac{M_i (M_i - m_i)}{m_i \pi_i} \sigma_i^2$$

where

$$T_i = \sum_{j=1}^{M_i} y_{ij} = M_i \mu_i$$

and

$$\sigma_i^2 = \sum_{j=1}^{M_i} (y_{ij} - \mu_i)^2 / (M_i - 1).$$

The first two terms in the expression for the variance of $\hat{T}$ make up the usual between primary unit component of variance, the last term being the within component.

Since an unbiased estimate of the within component is given by

$$\frac{1}{t} \sum_{i=1}^{n} \frac{M_i - m_i}{\pi_i} s_i^2, \qquad \text{with} \qquad s_i^2 = \sum_{j=1}^{m_i} \frac{(y_{ij} - \bar{y}_i)^2}{m_i - 1}$$

and

$$\bar{y}_i = \frac{1}{m_i} \sum_{j=1}^{m_i} y_{ij}$$

we have an unbiased estimate of var $(\hat{T})$ given by

$$s_{\hat{T}}^2 = -\hat{T}^2 + \sum_{i=1}^{n} \frac{\hat{T}_i^2}{\pi_i} + \sum_{i \neq j}^{n} \sum_{j}^{n} \frac{\hat{T}_i \hat{T}_j}{\pi_i \pi_j} + \frac{1}{t} \sum_{i=1}^{n} (M_i - m_i) s_i^2$$

where

$$\hat{T}_i = M_i \bar{y}_i = \frac{M_i}{m_i} \sum_{j=1}^{m_i} y_{ij}.$$

The following general result of Des Raj (1966) will be useful in evaluating the variances and their unbiased estimates. First let us specify the design. Let n psu's be selected from N without replacement with unequal probabilities. First assume that the sample psu's are completely enumerated (single-stage sampling). (That is, $y_i = Y_i$.) In order to estimate the population total consider the general estimator

$$\sum_{i=1}^{N} a_{is} y_i$$

where a_{is} $(i = 1, \ldots, N)$ are real numbers predetermined for every sample s, with the restriction that $a_{is} = 0$ whenever the sample does not include the ith psu $(i = 1, \ldots, N)$. The above estimator is unbiased implies that

$$E(a_{is}) = 1 \qquad \text{for every } i$$

and

$$\text{var}\,(\Sigma a_{is} y_i) = \sum_{i}^{N} y_i^2 \, \text{var}\,(a_{is}) + \sum_{i}^{N} \sum_{j \neq i}^{N} y_i y_j \, \text{cov}\,(a_{is}, a_{js}).$$

Let

$$f(y) = \Sigma\, b_{is} y_i^2 + \sum_{i}^{n} \sum_{j \neq i}^{n} d_{ijs} y_i y_j \tag{12.28}$$

be an unbiased estimator of var $(\Sigma a_{is} y_i)$, where, like a_{is}, the real numbers b_{is}, d_{ijs} are predetermined for every sample s. Hence,

$$E(b_{is}) = \text{var}\,(a_{is}). \tag{12.29}$$

Now, consider the multistage case in which the psu's are subsampled independently in a specified manner. For given i, let t_i (based on sampling at the second and subsequent stages) be an unbiased estimator of Y_i. Also, let

$$\text{var}\,(t_i|i) \;=\; \sigma_i^2$$

and $\hat{\sigma}_i^2$ be an estimator such that $E(\hat{\sigma}_i^2|i) = \sigma_i^2$.

Let an unbiased estimator of the population total be given by

$$\hat{Y} = \sum_{i=1}^{N} a_{is} t_i \tag{12.30}$$

where

$$\text{var}\,(\hat{Y}) \;=\; V(\Sigma a_{is} y_i) + \sum_i E(a_{is}^2)\sigma_i^2 \,.$$

Then we have the following result.

Result 12.1. [Des Raj, 1966, p. 392] With the preceding notation we have

$$E\left[f(t) + \Sigma a_{is}\hat{\sigma}_i^2\right] \;=\; \text{var}\,(\hat{Y}) \tag{12.31}$$

where

$$f(t) \;=\; \Sigma b_{is} t_i^2 + \sum_{\substack{j\neq i}}^{n} \sum^{n} d_{ijs} t_i t_j \,.$$

Proof:

$$Ef(t) \;=\; E\left[\Sigma b_{is}\{\,\text{var}\,(t_i|i) + y_i^2\} + \sum_{\substack{j\neq i}}^{n}\sum^{n} d_{ijs} y_i y_j\right]$$

$$=\; Ef(y) + \Sigma\,\text{var}\,(a_{is})\sigma_i^2$$

$$=\; Ef(y) + \Sigma\left\{E(a_{is}^2) - \{E(a_{is})\}^2\right\}\sigma_i^2$$

$$=\; \text{var}\,(\hat{Y}) - \Sigma\sigma_i^2 \,.$$

Now, the result follows upon noting that $\Sigma a_{is}\hat{\sigma}_i^2$ is an unbiased estimator of $\Sigma\sigma_i^2$. ∎

Thus the rule for estimating the variance in multistage sampling can be summarized in the following steps:

1. Obtain an unbiased estimator of the variance in single-stage sampling.
2. Obtain a copy of it by replacing y_i by its unbiased estimate t_i $(i = 1, 2, \ldots)$.
3. Copy the estimator of the stratum total in single-stage sampling by substituting $\hat{\sigma}_i^2$ for y_i.
4. The sum of the two copies will be an unbiased estimator of the variance in the multistage case.

Remark 12.2. The expressions for the var $(\hat{Y})$ and $\widehat{\text{var}}\,(\hat{Y})$ in the two-stage case can be gotten as special cases of the general result of Des Raj (1966). See also the remark of Des Raj (1966, p. 395).

■ PROBLEMS

12.1 A certain city has 80 blocks. We select a sample of 10 blocks using simple random sampling without replacement. From each block 5 households were drawn randomly without replacement. The number of VCR's in each household were recorded. The data is as follows

Sample block	No. of households	# of VCR's in sample households				
		1	2	3	4	5
1	100	1	2	1	1	0
2	150	0	1	1	1	2
3	80	1	0	0	1	1
4	100	2	2	2	1	1
5	120	1	2	1	2	1
6	150	1	1	1	1	1
7	75	0	0	0	0	1
8	100	1	1	1	1	2
9	80	2	1	2	1	1
10	125	1	2	2	1	2

Obtain an unbiased estimate of the total number of VCR's in the city and an unbiased estimate of its variance.

12.2 A two-stage sampling design was planned in order to estimate the average household weekly expenditure Y on groceries in a certain town. Use blocks as the first-stage units and households as the second-stage units. Assume sampling will be done randomly with replacement at each stage. To help in planning the survey, a pilot survey was conducted which yielded (i) $\hat{\bar{Y}} = \$100$, (ii) estimate of between-blocks variation $\sigma_b^2 = 75$, (iii) estimate of between-households variation within blocks $\sigma_w^2 = 36$, (iv) cost of travel per block, $c_1 = \$10$, and (v) cost of surveying each household, $c_2 = \$1$. Assume the overhead cost $c_0 = \$1000$. Determine the optimum number of blocks and number of households in each sampled block to be sampled when the total cost is fixed at \$5000. Also compute the minimum variance of the estimate attained.

12.3 For the problem in Example 12.1, suppose we have the following data.

Location	M_i	m_i	p_i = Proportion of PCs requiring repair
1	30	6	0.37
2	25	5	0.20
3	20	4	0.25

Estimate the proportion of PCs requiring repair at the Mars University.

12.4   A hamburger chain has restaurants in 40 cities. A company official wishes to estimate the proportion of restaurants that do not meet a certain specified cleanliness criterion. He or she resorts to a two-stage sampling. A simple random sample of 5 cities is drawn and the following data is obtained.

City	Number of restaurants of the chain in city	Number of restaurants sampled	Number not meeting the criterion
1	20	4	1
2	30	6	2
3	40	8	2
4	25	5	1
5	15	3	0

Estimate the proportion of restaurants of the chain that do not meet the cleanliness criterion.

12.5   Mars University wants to estimate the total number of calls placed by its employees during one day. The university consists of $N = 100$ departments, and the ith department has M_i employees $(i = 1, \ldots, N)$. A simple random sample of $n = 5$ departments is taken, a random sample of 20% of the employees is taken, and the following data is obtained.

Dept. number	Number of employees	Number of employees Sampled	Number of calls Made
1	20	4	4, 5, 6, 3
2	30	6	2, 4, 7, 5, 3, 6
3	15	3	6, 7, 6
4	25	5	3, 6, 4, 5, 2
5	35	7	5, 6, 4, 7, 3, 2, 1

Assuming that at Mars University the total number of employees is 1500, estimate the average number of phone calls an employee makes and set up a 95% confidence interval for the same.

12.6   A marketing agency wants to estimate the weekly sales of boxes of a certain brand of detergent soap in a certain region of the United States which has $N = 25$ cities. The agency takes a simple random sample of $n = 5$ cities and takes a simple random sample of supermarkets in the chosen city. The following data is obtained.

City	Number of supermarkets	Number of supermarkets sampled	$\bar{y}_i$	s_i^2
1	40	8	50	15
2	35	7	42	9
3	45	9	55	14
4	25	5	35	10
5	30	6	45	12

Assume that the total number of supermarkets in that region is 750, estimate the total number of boxes of the detergent that were sold during that week in that region, and obtain a 95% confidence interval for the same.

12.7   The mayor of Heavenhill wants to estimate the proportion of property owners in a section of the city who are in favor of a proposed zoning change. The section is dividied into 10 residential areas, each containing homogeneous residents. Four of the residential ones are chosen at random and about 25% of the residents in each area are selected at random and their responses are noted. The results are as follows:

Area	Number of property owners	Number of property owners sampled	Number in favor of zoning change
1	40	10	2
2	60	15	2
3	52	13	3
4	36	9	1

Assuming that the total number of property owners in that section of the city is 400, estimate the true proportion of property owners that are in favor of the zoning change and obtain a 95% confidence interval for the same.

12.8   The city of Marine wants to estimate the number of senior citizens (65 years or older) that reside in a huge federally subsidized housing complex. The complex has 10 buildings and each building has 50 units. In order to expedite matters, the city resorts to a two-stage sampling scheme.   First it draws a random sample of three buildings, draws a random sample of 10 units from each building, and counts the number of senior citizens residing in each unit. The following data is obtained.

Building number	$\bar{y}_i$ = Average number of senior citizens per unit	s_i^2 = sample variance
1	1.3	0.16
2	0.9	0.25
3	1.1	0.36

Estimate the total number of senior citizens residing in that complex and obtain a 95% confidence interval for the same.

12.9   We are interested in estimating the number of computers in a certain company that have access to the Web. The company has 10 factories. We select a sample of 3 factories using simple random sampling without replacement. From each factory, 4 departments are selected randomly without replacement. The number of computers with access to the Web is recorded.

Sample factory	# of departments	# of computers with access to the web			
		1	2	3	4
1	7	3	4	5	2
2	8	4	4	4	3
3	6	2	3	3	3

Obtain an unbiased estimate of the total number of computers in the company that have access to the web and an unbiased estimate of its variance.

12.10   The strength of pillars in a coal mine is measured to determine the load each pillar can carry—that is, how heavy the coal in the pillar is. A coal mine has 10 panels (entries) and approximately 1000 pillars per panel. Since a sample from one pillar can cost $500, we take a random sample of panels (clusters) and take a random sample of pillars at each selected panel. Five samples are taken from two panels and their strengths determined to hundreds of pounds per squared inch. The following data is obtained.

Panel	4	7
	28	21
	32	47
	41	35
	22	26
	14	22
$\bar{y}_i$	27.4	30.2
M_i	985	1025
m_i	5	5
s_i^2	103.8	118.7

Obtain an estimate of the average strength of the pillars at the mine. Also obtain an unbiased estimate of its variance.

■ REFERENCES

12.1   Des Raj (1966). Some remarks on a simple procedure for sampling without replacement. *J. Amer. Statist. Assoc.* **61**, 391–397.

12.2   Murthy, M. N. (1967). *Sampling Theory and Methods.* Calcutta, India: Statistical Publishing Society.

CHAPTER 13

NONSAMPLING ERRORS

13.1 INTRODUCTION

Aside from sampling errors (which can be attributed to the stochastic nature of the responses), there are several ways in which other errors may occur.

1. **Errors of reporting.** The income a man reports to the tax authorities may differ from what he told his girl friend. A child's age reported by his mother to a bus driver may be different from what she tells other parents. Few people know their exact weight, height or the number of cigarettes they smoke per day. Thus, it's almost impossible to gather correct information.

2. **Nonresponse errors.** Respondents will throw away the questionnaires and do not respond to reminders. Sometimes those who respond may belong to one class and nonrespondents to another class, thus leading to biased samples.

3. **Errors in sample selection.** The bananas exhibited in the window may be different from those inside the store. The selected sample may be biased by the survey or when random sampling is not strictly observed.

13.2   EFFECT OF NONRESPONSE ON SAMPLE MEAN AND PROPORTION

Let us now consider the effects of nonresponse on the sample estimate. Let N_1 denote the number responding to a certain questionnaire (denote it by stratum I). Let $W_1 = N_1/N$, $W_2 = N_2/N$, where $N = N_1 + N_2$. That is, W_2 denotes the proportion of nonresponse in the population. If we draw a random sample of size n from stratum I and $\bar{y}_1$ denotes the sample estimate, then the bias in the sample mean due to "nonavailability" is

$$E(\bar{y}_1) - \bar{Y} = \bar{Y}_1 - \bar{Y} = \bar{Y}_1 - (W_1\bar{Y}_1 + W_2\bar{Y}_2) \qquad (13.1)$$
$$= W_2(\bar{Y}_1 - \bar{Y}_2).$$

Since stratum II is unobservable, the size of the bias is unknown, except when we make a guess on $\bar{Y}_2$. However, if the data is continuous, the usual confidence bounds on $\bar{Y}_2$ with high confidence are usually so wide as to be meaningless. However, when one is sampling for proportions, there is some hope because P_2 (the proportion in the nonresponse part of the population) is bounded by unity when we are setting confidence limits on P. Suppose that n is the size of the random sample and n_1 of out n respond. If n_1 is sufficiently large, a 95% confidence interval for P_1 is

$$p_1 \pm 2\sqrt{p_1(1 - p_1)/n_1}$$

when the finite population correction is ignored where p_1 is the sample proportion. A conservative confidence interval can be obtained by setting $P_2 = 0$ when finding $\hat{P}_L$ and $P_2 = 1$ when finding $\hat{P}_U$. Thus, 95% confidence limits for P are

$$\hat{P}_L = W_1\left(p_1 - 2\sqrt{p_1(1 - p_1)/n_1}\right) + 0 \cdot W_2 \qquad (13.2)$$

$$\hat{P}_U = W_1\left(p_1 + 2\sqrt{p_1(1 - p_1)/n_1}\right) + 1 \cdot W_2. \qquad (13.3)$$

If W_2 is unknown, Cochran (1977, p. 362) proposes the following procedure for obtaining conservative confidence limits for p. In calculating $\hat{P}_L$, assume that all sample nonrespondents would have given a negative response (i.e., set $W_1 = 1$ and $P_2 = 0$). For computing $\hat{P}_U$ assume that all sample nonrespondents would have given a positive response (i.e., set $W_1 = 1$ and $P_2 = 1$). Note that since $W_1 = 1$, we set $n_1 = n$.

EXAMPLE 13.1 _____

Let $n = 500$, $n_1 = 400$, and $p_1 = 15\%$, so that 75 members in the sample respond positively and the nonresponse rate is 20%. Then (in percentages)

$$\hat{P}_L = 15 - 2\sqrt{15(85)/500} = 15 - 3.2 = 11.8\%$$
$$\hat{P}_U = 35 + 2\sqrt{35(65)/500} = 35 + 4.3 = 39.3\%.$$

If the number of nonresponses is zero and if the true proportion has to lie within a specified amount d of the sample proportion with confidence $1 - \alpha$, i.e.,

$$P\left(|p - P| \leq d\right) \geq 1 - \alpha \tag{13.4}$$

then

$$n = z_\alpha^2 P(1 - P)/d^2 \leq z_\alpha^2/4d^2 \tag{13.5}$$

where z_α is the standard normal deviate such that the area to the right of z_α is $\alpha/2$.   ◆

When specialized for proportions, the bias due to nonavailability from (13.1) becomes

$$b = W_2(P_1 - P_2)$$

and we can easily see that

$$m(W_2, P_1) = -W_2(1 - P_1) \leq b \leq W_2 P_1 = M(W_2, P_1) \tag{13.6}$$

and the range of b is $W_2(P_1 + 1 - P_1) = W_2$ which is independent of P_1. Also,

$$\max |m(W_2, P_1)| = |m(W_2, 0)| = W_2$$
$$\max M(W_2, P_1) = M(W_2, 1) = W_2$$

whereas $|m| < M$ implies that $P_1 > \frac{1}{2}$ and hence

$$\min\left(|m|, M\right) = \left| m\left(W_2, \frac{1}{2}\right) \right| = M\left(W_2, \frac{1}{2}\right) = \frac{W_2}{2}.$$

Hence, if we want to assure that $|b|$ is small, it is most advantageous to use a question in the survey for which P_1 is close to $\frac{1}{2}$. Also, (13.6) can be improved if, via some prior information, we can narrow down the range for P_2 from $0 \leq P_2 \leq 1$. Next, we will present the result of Birnbaum and Sirken (1950) pertaining to the sample size required to meet the specifications in (13.4) when nonresponses are present.

13.3   REQUIRED SAMPLE SIZE WHEN NONRESPONSE IS PRESENT

If we draw a random sample of size n, it can be partitioned as follows:

	yes	no	total
available	n_{11}	n_{10}	$n_{1.}$
not available	n_{01}	n_{00}	$n_{0.}$
			n

As an estimate of P_1, we use

$$U = n_{11}/n_{1.} \tag{13.7}$$

$$E(U) = EE\left(\frac{n_{11}}{n_{1.}}|n_{1.}\right) = E\left(\frac{1}{n_{1.}}n_{1.}P_1\right) = P_1.$$

$$\sigma^2_{(U)} = \text{var } U = E(U^2) - P_1^2$$

and

$$E(U^2) = E\left[\left(\frac{n_{11}}{n_{1.}}\right)^2\right] = EE\left(\frac{n_{11}^2}{n_{1.}^2}|n_{1.}\right)$$

$$= E\left(\frac{n_{1.}P_1(1 - P_1) + n_{1.}^2 P_1^2}{n_{1.}^2}\right)$$

$$= P_1(1 - P_1)E\left(\frac{1}{n_{1.}}\right) + P_1^2.$$

Thus,

$$\sigma^2_{(U)} = P_1(1 - P_1)E(n_{1.}^{-1}). \tag{13.8}$$

Without loss of generality, we can assume that $n_{1.}$ is positive. (Otherwise the survey will be disregarded.) Thus, $n_{1.}$ is a positive Bernoulli variable with zero-value excluded. Now, using Stephan's (1945) results, we assert that if $W_2 = 1 - W_1$ is so small that

$$K = nW_1W_2^n/(1 - W_2^n)$$

is negligible, then

$$E(n_{1.}^{-1}) = 1/(n + 1)W_1. \tag{13.9}$$

Thus, if K is sufficiently small,

$$\sigma^2_{(U)} = P_1(1 - P_1)/(n + 1)W_1. \tag{13.10}$$

An intuitive interpretation of the expression in (13.10) is as follows: $\sigma^2_{(U)}$ is equal to the variance of the proportion of those answering "yes" in a random sample of size $(n + 1)W_1$ taken from the subpopulation of those who are available.

Now we will give a result of Birnbaum and Sirken (1950).

Result 13.1. With the preceding notation, when some responses are not available, the value of n that assures the given "precision" δ with confidence $1 - \alpha$ is approximately

$$n \doteq \frac{z_\alpha^2}{4\delta(\delta - W_2)W_1} - 1. \tag{13.11}$$

Proof: The error due to using U as an estimate of P (true proportion in the population who say "yes") is

$$H = U - P = U - P_1 + P_1 - P = S + b$$

where $S = U - EU$ is the sampling error and b is the bias. We wish to determine n so that

$$P(|H| \le \delta) \ge 1 - \alpha$$

for specified δ and α. We have

$$P_n(P_1, b) = P(|H| \le \delta) = P(-b - \delta \le S \le -b + \delta)$$

$$= \frac{1}{\sqrt{2\pi}} \int_{-(b+\delta)/\sigma_S}^{(-b+\delta)/\sigma_S} e^{-t^2/2}\, dt \tag{13.12}$$

where σ_S^2 is given by (13.10). From (13.6) we know that $|b| \le W_2$. Since the bias component of H alone may be as large as W_2, the precision δ must be greater than W_2. ∎

Suppose that $P_1 > 0.5$. Notice that $P_n(P_1, b)$ is symmetric in b. That is,

$$P_n(P_1, -b) = \Phi\left(\frac{\delta + b}{\sigma_S}\right) - \Phi\left(\frac{-\delta + b}{\sigma_S}\right) = P_n(P_1, b)$$

and

$$\frac{\partial P_n}{\partial b} = \frac{1}{\sigma_S}\left\{ \phi\left(\frac{\delta + b}{\sigma_S}\right) - \phi\left(\frac{\delta - b}{\sigma_S}\right)\right\} \begin{smallmatrix} < \\ = \\ > \end{smallmatrix}\, 0 \quad \text{according as} \quad b \begin{smallmatrix} > \\ = \\ < \end{smallmatrix}\, 0.$$

That is, P_n is increasing in b for $b < 0$ and decreasing in b for $b > 0$. Now, using (13.6), we have

$$\min_b P_n = \min\{P_n(P_1, -W_2(1 - P_1)), P_n(P_1, W_2 P_1)\}. \tag{13.13}$$

If $P_1 > 0.5$, $W_2(1 - P_1) < P_1 W_2$ or $-W_2(1 - P_1) > -W_2 P_1$,

$$\min_b P_n \ge P_n(P_1, -W_2 P_1) = P_n(P_1, W_2 P_1)$$

$$= \Phi\left(\frac{\delta - W_2 P_1}{\sigma_S}\right) - \Phi\left(\frac{-\delta - W_2 P_1}{\sigma_S}\right)$$

$$\ge \Phi\left(\frac{\delta - W_2 P_1}{\sigma_S}\right) - \Phi\left(\frac{-\delta + W_2 P_1}{\sigma_S}\right)$$

$$= 2\Phi\left(\frac{\delta - W_2 P_1}{\sigma_S}\right) - 1. \tag{13.14}$$

Now, minimizing the right-side expression in (13.14) is equivalent to minimizing $(\delta - W_2 P_1)/\sigma_S$, since Φ is an increasing function. Now, when $0.5 \leq P_1 \leq 1$, set $x = P_1 - 0.5$ and minimize

$$\frac{\{\delta - W_2(0.5 + x)\} \{(n + 1)W_1\}^{1/2}}{\left(\frac{1}{4} - x^2\right)^{1/2}} \tag{13.15}$$

with respect to x, and find that it is minimized at

$$x = W_2/2(2\delta - W_2)$$

or

$$P_1 = \delta/(2\delta - W_2). \tag{13.16}$$

With this P_1,

$$\frac{\delta - W_2 P_1}{\sigma_S} = 2\{\delta(\delta - W_2)(n + 1)W_1\}^{1/2}. \tag{13.17}$$

Thus, using this in (13.14), we have

$$\min_b P_n \geq 2\Phi\left(2\{\delta(n + 1)(\delta - W_2)W_1\}^{1/2}\right) - 1 \tag{13.18}$$

for $\frac{1}{2} \leq P_1 \leq 1$.

Similar result holds for $0 \leq P_1 \leq \frac{1}{2}$. Thus,

$$P(|H| \leq \delta) \geq 2\Phi\left(2\{\delta(n + 1)(\delta - W_2)W_1\}^{1/2}\right) - 1.$$

Since

$$\lim_{n \to \infty} (\text{RHS in (13.18)}) = 1$$

it is always possible to find for given δ and W_2 a value of n such that

$$2\Phi\left(2\{\delta(n + 1)(\delta - W_2)W_1\}^{1/2}\right) - 1 \geq 1 - \alpha = 2\Phi(z_\alpha) - 1.$$

Solving for n, we get (13.11). This completes the proof of the assertion.

Let us denote n satisfying (13.11) by $n(\delta, \alpha, W_2)$. If $W_2 = 0$, n given by (13.11) coincides with (13.5). In Table 13.1 we provide values of n for selected values of W_2 and δ for $\alpha = .05$.

TABLE 13.1   Giving the Values of n
Satisfying (13.11)

		\multicolumn{3}{c}{δ}		
		0.2	0.1	0.05
	0	24	96	384
W_2	0.05	38	201	∞
	0.10	53	∞	∞

13.4 CONDITIONAL INFERENCE WHEN NONRESPONSE EXISTS

Recall that n_1 denotes the number of responses in a simple random sample of size n and W_1 the proportion in the response stratum. In this case, conditioning on the observed value of n_1 can be questionable, since the distribution of n_1 depends on the unknown W_1 which is involved in the parameter of interest, namely the population mean $\bar{Y} = W_1\bar{Y}_1 + W_2\bar{Y}_2(W_2 = 1 - W_1)$. Also the sample mean $\bar{y}_1$ of respondents is unconditionally biased, since $E(\bar{y}_1) = \bar{Y}_1 \neq \bar{Y}$. Thus, it is necessary to assume a model for response mechanism even in the unconditional set up, unless a subsample of nonrespondents is also sampled. Oh and Scheuren (1983) propose a simple model in which the probability of response if contacted is the same for all units, say p^*. That is, data is missing at random. Then the distribution of n_1 depends only on p^* and hence we can condition on n_1, if p^* is assumed known (or at least partially known or is unrelated to $\bar{Y}$). Oh and Scheuren (1983) have shown that conditionally given n_1, the sample $s(n_1)$ of respondents behaves like a simple random sample of size n_1 from the population as a whole. Hence $\bar{y}_1$ is conditionally unbiased, and an unbiased estimate of its conditional variance is

$$\widehat{\text{var}}(\hat{y}_1) = (n_1^{-1} - N^{-1})s_{n_1,y}^2$$

where

$$(n_1 - 1)s_{n_1,y}^2 = \sum_{i \in s(n_1)} (y_i - \bar{y}_1)^2.$$

Also, the confidence interval $\bar{y}_1 \pm z_{\alpha/2}\{\widehat{\text{var}}(\hat{y}_1)\}^{\frac{1}{2}}$ is conditionally correct (approximately for large n_1). We can also define the Horvitz-Thompson estimator (assuming that p^* is known) as

$$\hat{y}_{HT} = \frac{n_1}{E(n_1)}\bar{y}_1 = \sum_{i \in s(n_1)} \frac{y_i}{np^*}$$

which is conditionally biased; however, it becomes unbiased when averaged over the distribution of n_1. J. N. K. Rao (1988, p. 25) mentions a ratio estimator which is often justifiably used on the basis of efficiency for general designs.

13.5 CALL-BACKS

In order to avoid a large number of nonresponses in the sample, it is customary to call back the nonrespondents (especially those who are not home) a fixed number of times. Consider the following table which gives the percentages of response and the associated percentage of households with children under 2 years of age by the number of calls. The data from Hilgard and Payne (1944) and cited by P. S. R. S. Rao (1983) are from a survey of 3265 urban households through personal interviews.

	Number of the Call				
	1	2	> 2	Nonresponse	Total
Percentage of response	63.5	22.2	14.3	0	10.0
Percentage of households with small children among those responded	17.2	9.5	6.2	0	13.9

This table shows that adult members of households with young children are more likely to be at home when the interviewer calls. This implies that if the interviewer stopped after the first call, the responses would over-represent the households having small children. Thus, if the target population were all households, then there would be a biasing effect on the estimates for variables correlated with small children. In practice, call-backs should be stopped after a few attempts. The obvious reason is "cost." Since this is a major concern for most surveys, we need a model that would determine the total cost of field operations of the sample survey.

In the following we will assess the total expected cost derived by Birnbaum and Sirken (1950). Toward this we need the further following notation. If a subject is not available for an interview in all k calls, he is considered "not available." Let

$p_1^{(j)}$ = probability of a subject being nonavailable in the first, second, ..., $(j-1)$st call and being available on the jth call ($j = 1, \ldots, k$);

$p_0^{(k)} = 1 - \sum_{j=1}^{k} p_1^{(j)}$ = probability of subject being not available within k calls;

$n_{1.}^{(j)}$ = number of those subjects in the sample of size n available exactly at the jth call;

β_j = total cost due to a subject available exactly at the jth call including the cost of the interview ($j = 1, \ldots, k$);

γ_k = total cost due to a subject nonavailable up to and including the kth call;

C = total cost of field operations of the sample survey.

Then

$$C = \sum_{j=1}^{k} n_{1.}^{(j)} \beta_j + \gamma_k \left(n - \sum_{j=1}^{k} n_{1.}^{(j)} \right) \tag{13.19}$$

$$= \sum_{j=1}^{k} (\beta_j - \gamma_k) n_{1.}^{(j)} + n\gamma_k .$$

Since $E(n_{1.}^{(j)}) = np_1^{(j)}$, the expected cost of a sample survey consisting of sample size n and k call-backs is

$$E(C) = n \left[\sum_{j=1}^{k} (\beta_j - \gamma_k)p_1^{(j)} + \gamma_k \right]. \qquad (13.20)$$

Now, since the distribution of $(n_{1.}^{(1)}, \ldots, n_{1.}^{(k)})$ is multinomial, with

$$\text{var}(n_{1.}^{(j)}) = np_1^{(j)}(1 - p_1^{(j)})$$

$$\text{cov}(n_{1.}^{(i)}, n_{1.}^{(j)}) = -np_1^{(i)}p_1^{(j)}, \qquad i \neq j = 1, \ldots, k$$

we have

$$\text{var}(C) = n \sum_{j=1}^{k} (\beta_j - \gamma_k)^2 p_1^{(j)}(1 - p_1^{(j)})$$

$$- n \sum_{j \neq i}^{k} \sum^{k} (\beta_i - \gamma_k)(\beta_j - \gamma_k)p_1^{(i)}p_1^{(j)}$$

$$= n \left[\sum_{j=1}^{k} (\beta_j - \gamma_k)^2 p_1^{(j)} - \left\{ \sum_{j=1}^{k} (\beta_j - \gamma_k)p_1^{(j)} \right\}^2 \right]$$

$$= n \left[\sum_{j=1}^{k} (\beta_j - \gamma_k)^2 p_1^{(j)} - \left(\frac{E(C)}{n} - \gamma_k \right)^2 \right]. \qquad (13.21)$$

For given precision δ and confidence $1 - \alpha$, we can now determine k and n such that

$$P(|H| \leq \delta) \geq 1 - \alpha$$

and

$$E(C) \text{ is as small as possible}.$$

Setting $n(\delta, \alpha, W_2)$ given by (13.11) equal to $n(\delta, \alpha, p_0^{(k)})$ and substituting this in (13.20), we obtain

$$E_k(C) = n(\delta, \alpha, p_0^{(k)}) \left[\sum_{j=1}^{k} (\beta_j - \gamma_k)p_1^{(j)} + \gamma_k \right] \qquad (13.22)$$

which, for given δ and α, depends only on k. Now we wish to minimize $E_k(C)$ with respect to k and find the value of $k = \tilde{k}$ which minimizes (13.22). Birnbaum and Sirken (1950) suggest the following trial-and-error procedure.

First, determine the smallest integral value k' of k such that

$$\sum_{j=1}^{k'} p_1^{(j)} \geq 1 - \delta$$

and compute $E_{k'}(C)$ from (13.22). Then compute $E_k(C)$ for all values of $k > k'$ for which the constants $p_1^{(j)}$, β_j ($j = 1, 2, \ldots, k$), and γ_k are empirically known, and choose for $\tilde{k}$ the value of k minimizing $E_k(C)$. Once $\tilde{k}$ is obtained, $n(\delta, \alpha, p_0^{(k)})$ is determined from (13.11). For $k = \tilde{k}$, the variance of C is obtained from (13.21).

EXAMPLE 13.2

Consider the following empirical values.

j	$p_1^{(j)}$	β_j
1	0.63	$1.00
2	0.25	$1.40
3	0.10	$1.80

and $\gamma_3 = \$1.05$. Use $\alpha = .05$ and $\delta = .10$. Then

$$p_0^{(3)} = 1 - (0.63 + 0.25 + 0.1) = 0.02$$

$$n(0.10, 0.05, 0.02) = \frac{(1.96)^2}{4(0.1)(0.98)(0.10 - 0.02)} - 1$$

$$= \frac{3.8416}{0.03136} - 1 = 122.$$

Expected cost is

$$E_3(C) = 122\,[-0.05(0.63) + 0.35(0.25) + 0.75(0.10) + 1.05]$$

$$= 122(-0.0315 + 0.0875 + 0.075 + 1.05) = 122(1.181) = \$144.08$$

$$\sigma^2(C) = 122\,\big[(-0.05)^2(0.63) + (0.35)^2(0.25) + (0.75)^2(0.10) - (1.181 - 1.05)^2\big]$$

$$= 122(0.001575 + 0.030625 + 0.05625 - 0.017161)$$

$$= 122(0.071289) = 8.697258$$

$$\sigma(C) = \$2.949.\qquad\qquad\blacklozenge$$

The nonrespondents can be classified as not-at-home, refuse-to-answer (temporarily or permanently). Deming (1953) provides a flexible mathematical model for incorporating the consequences of various call-back policies (see also Cochran, 1977, pp. 367–368). The population is classified into r classes according to the probability that the respondent will be found at home.

Let

$$W_{ij} = \text{probability that a respondent in } j\text{th class will be reached on or before the } i\text{th call;}$$

$$p_j = \text{proportion of the population falling in the } j\text{th class;}$$

$$\mu_j = \text{mean response for the } j\text{th class;}$$

$$\sigma_j^2 = \text{variance of the response for the } j\text{th class.}$$

Let us further assume that $W_{ij} > 0$ for $j = 1, \ldots, r$. If $\bar{y}_{ij}$ denotes the sample mean for those in class j who were reached on or before the ith call, it is assumed that $E(\bar{y}_{ij}) = \mu_j$. The true population mean for the response is

$$\bar{\mu} = \sum_j p_j \mu_j . \tag{13.23}$$

The subjects in the sample who have been reached after i calls are classified as follows: in the first class and interviewed, ..., in the rth class and interviewed and the $(r+1)^{\text{th}}$ class consists of all those not yet interviewed after r calls.

   If n_0 is the initial size of the sample, the numbers falling in the $r+1$ classes have a multinomial distribution with parameters n_0, $W_{i1}p_1$, ..., $W_{ir}p_r$, $(1 - \sum_{j=1}^{r} W_{ij}p_j)$. If n_i denotes the number of interviews in i calls, then

$$E(n_i) = n_0 \sum_{j=1}^{r} W_{ij} p_j . \tag{13.24}$$

For fixed n_i, $n_{ij} = $ the number of interviews in the jth class ($j = 1, \ldots, r$) have a multinomial distribution with probabilities $W_{ij}p_j / \sum_{j=1}^{r} W_{ij}p_j$. So,

$$E(n_{ij}|n_i) = \frac{n_i W_{ij} p_j}{\Sigma W_{ij} p_j} = n_i \tilde{p}_{ij} \text{ (say)} . \tag{13.25}$$

Hence, if $\bar{y}_i$ is the sample mean computed after i calls,

$$E(\bar{y}_i|n_i) = E\left(\frac{\Sigma n_{ij} \bar{y}_{ij}}{n_i} \Big| n_i \right) = \frac{\Sigma n_i W_{ij} p_j \mu_j}{n_i \Sigma W_{ij} p_j} \tag{13.26}$$

$$= \frac{\Sigma W_{ij} p_j \mu_j}{\Sigma W_{ij} p_j} = \bar{\mu}_i .$$

Since the right-hand side is free of n_i, the unconditional expectation of $\bar{y}_i$ is also $\bar{\mu}_i$. The bias in the estimate $\bar{y}_i$ is $\bar{\mu}_i - \bar{\mu}$. Similarly,

$$\text{var}(\bar{y}_i|n_i) = \text{var}\left(\frac{\Sigma n_{ij} \bar{y}_{ij}}{n_i} \Big| n_i \right) .$$

Let

$$\tilde{E}(\cdot) = E\{(\cdot)|n_i\} .$$

Then

$$\text{var}\,(\bar{y}_i\,|\,n_i) = n_i^{-2}\tilde{E}\left\{\sum_{j=1}^{r}n_{ij}(\bar{y}_{ij} - \bar{\mu}_i)\right\}^2$$

$$= n_i^{-2}\tilde{E}\left[\Sigma n_{ij}^2(\bar{y}_{ij} - \bar{\mu}_i)^2 + \sum\sum_{j\neq k}n_{ij}n_{ik}(\bar{y}_{ij} - \bar{\mu}_i)(\bar{y}_{ik} - \bar{\mu}_i)\right]$$

$$= n_i^{-2}\tilde{E}\left[\Sigma n_{ij}^2\left\{\frac{\sigma_j^2}{n_{ij}} + (\mu_j - \bar{\mu}_i)^2\right\} + \sum\sum_{j\neq k}n_{ij}n_{ik}(\mu_j - \bar{\mu}_i)(\mu_k - \bar{\mu}_i)\right]$$

$$= n_i^{-1}\Sigma \tilde{p}_{ij}\sigma_j^2 + n_i^{-2}\tilde{E}\left[\sum_{j=1}^{r}n_{ij}(\mu_j - \bar{\mu}_i)\right]^2 , \qquad (13.27)$$

since $\tilde{E}(n_{ij}) = n_i\tilde{p}_{ij}$.
  Next consider

$$\tilde{E}\left[\sum_{j=1}^{r}n_{ij}(\mu_j - \bar{\mu}_i)\right]^2 = \tilde{E}\left[\sum_{j=1}^{r}(n_{ij} - n_i\tilde{p}_{ij})(\mu_j - \bar{\mu}_i)\right]^2$$

since

$$\Sigma \tilde{p}_{ij}(\mu_j - \bar{\mu}_i) = 0 \qquad \text{(by the definition of } \bar{\mu}_i\text{)}.$$

Thus,

$$\tilde{E}\left[\sum_{j=1}^{r}n_{ij}(\mu_j - \bar{\mu}_i)\right]^2 = \tilde{E}\left[\sum_{j=1}^{r}(n_{ij} - n_i\tilde{p}_{ij})^2(\mu_j - \bar{\mu}_i)^2 + \sum\sum_{j\neq k}\right.$$

$$\left. (n_{ij} - n_i\tilde{p}_{ij})(n_{ik} - n_i\tilde{p}_{ik})(\mu_j - \bar{\mu}_i)(\mu_k - \bar{\mu}_i)\right]$$

$$= \Sigma n_i\tilde{p}_{ij}(1 - \tilde{p}_{ij})(\mu_j - \bar{\mu}_i)^2$$

$$- \sum\sum_{j\neq k}n_i\tilde{p}_{ij}\tilde{p}_{ik}(\mu_j - \bar{\mu}_i)(\mu_k - \bar{\mu}_i)$$

$$= n_i\,\Sigma \tilde{p}_{ij}(\mu_j - \bar{\mu}_i)^2 - \left[\sum_{j=1}^{r}\tilde{p}_{ij}(\mu_j - \bar{\mu}_i)\right]^2$$

$$= n_i\,\Sigma \tilde{p}_{ij}(\mu_j - \bar{\mu}_i)^2 . \qquad (13.28)$$

Using (13.28) in (13.27), we have

$$\operatorname{var}(\bar{y}_i \,|\, n_i) = n_i^{-1} \left[\sum_{j=1}^{r} \tilde{p}_{ij} \left\{ \sigma_j^2 + (\mu_j - \bar{\mu}_i)^2 \right\} \right]$$

$$= \frac{\sum_{j=1}^{r} W_{ij} p_j \left\{ \sigma_j^2 + (\mu_j - \bar{\mu}_i)^2 \right\}}{n_i \, \Sigma \, W_{ij} p_j}.$$

Now, since

$$E\left(\frac{1}{n_i}\right) = E\left(\frac{1}{n_i - n_0 \, \Sigma \, W_{ij} p_j + n_0 \, \Sigma \, W_{ij} p_j}\right)$$

$$= (n_0 \, \Sigma \, W_{ij} p_j)^{-1} E\left\{ 1 + \frac{n_i - n_0 \, \Sigma \, W_{ij} p_j}{n_0 \, \Sigma \, W_{ij} p_j} \right\}^{-1}$$

$$\doteq (n_0 \, \Sigma \, W_{ij} p_j)^{-1} + O(n_0^{-2}),$$

we have

$$\operatorname{var}(\bar{y}_i) = \frac{\sum_{j=1}^{r} W_{ij} p_j \left\{ \sigma_j^2 + (\mu_j - \bar{\mu}_i)^2 \right\}}{n_0 (\Sigma \, W_{ij} p_j)^2} + O(n_0^{-2}). \qquad (13.29)$$

Finally, toward the mean-square error (MSE) of $\bar{Y}_i$, we have

$$\operatorname{MSE}(\bar{Y}_i) = \operatorname{var}(\bar{y}_i) + (\bar{\mu}_i - \bar{\mu})^2.$$

Let c_k denote the cost per completed interview of the kth call ($k = 1, \ldots, i$). The expected number of responses in the kth call is $\Sigma(W_{kj} - W_{k-1,j})p_j$. Then the expected total cost of making i calls is $n_0 C(i)$, where

$$C(i) = c_1 \, \Sigma \, W_{1j} p_j + c_2 \, \Sigma (W_{2j} - W_{1j}) p_j + \cdots = \sum_{j=1}^{r} p_j \sum_{k=1}^{i} (c_k - c_{k+j}) W_{k,j}$$

$$(13.30)$$

with $c_{i+1} = 0$.

EXAMPLE 13.3

Let a population consist of three classes. Let $p_1 = 0.40$, $p_2 = 0.50$, and $p_3 = 0.10$. At the first call, let

$$W_{11} = 0.55, \qquad W_{12} = 0.40, \qquad W_{13} = 0.05.$$

At the second and subsequent calls, the conditional probabilities that a subject responds, given that he was missed previously, are 0.8, 0.5, 0.3. Also, let $\mu_1 = 60$, $\mu_2 = 50$, $\mu_3 = 45$ (as %).

	Class		
	1	2	3
p_j	0.40	0.50	0.10
W_{ij}	$0.55 + (0.45)\left[1 - (0.2)^{i-1}\right]$	$0.40 + (0.6)\left[1 - (0.5)^{i-1}\right]$	$0.05 + (0.95)\left[1 - (0.7)^{i-1}\right]$
μ_j (as %)	60	50	45
$p_j W_{ij}$	$0.22 + (0.18)\left[1 - (0.2)^{i-1}\right]$	$0.2 + (0.30)\left[1 - (0.5)^{i-1}\right]$	$0.005 + (0.095)\left[1 - (0.7)^{i-1}\right]$
$\mu_j p_j W_{ij}$	$13.2 + (10.8)\left[1 - (0.2)^{i-1}\right]$	$10 + (15.0)\left[1 - (0.5)^{i-1}\right]$	$0.225 + (4.275)\left[1 - (0.7)^{i-1}\right]$

$$\bar{\mu} = \Sigma \, p_j \mu_j = 60(0.40) + 50(0.50) + 45(0.10)$$

$$= 53.5.$$

Computations yield the following results:

Number of calls required (i)	Expected number of responses	Bias $= \mu_i - \bar{\mu}$
1	$0.425n_0$	1.618
2	$0.7475n_0$	−8.234
3	$0.87125n_0$	0.588

◆

13.6   A PROBABILISTIC MODEL FOR NONRESPONSE

Response rates in industrialized countries have considerably decreased. The apparent reasons are twofold. (1) People are spending less time at home, and (2) the general public has more doubts today about the usefulness of sample surveys. In order to reduce refusal rates, most survey organizations spend considerable resources on informing the general public about the importance of survey results and the confidentiality of survey data. It is futile to attempt to model the efficiency of such activities. The most effective means of reducing the nonresponse rate is to make several attempts to obtain responses from the nonrespondents. However, call-backs are also a strain on the survey budget. Hence, it is worthwhile to explore reasonable rules for allocating resources between the initial sample and the call-backs. Thomsen and Tesfu (1988) propose a probabilistic model for nonresponse from which one can easily obtain estimable variance, an estimable nonresponse bias after each call-back. Hence, it is possible to study the relation between mean-square error and the number of call-backs. Thus one can determine the number of call-backs that are reasonable.

The Model

The possible outcomes when an interviewer makes an attempt to interview a selected unit are

1. We get a response.
2. No response is obtained and the interviewer decides to call back.
3. No response is obtained and the interviewer classifies the unit as nonresponse (refusal).

Let p_1 denote the probability that outcome (1) occurs at the first call and p_0 denote the probability that outcome (3) occurs at the first call. Also let Δp_1 be the probability of outcome (1) in the second and subsequent calls.

It is reasonable to assume that p_0 remains constant from call to call. We also expect Δ to exceed unity, because the interviewer may use ingenious methods such as finding from neighbors or parents when the people will be available or making appointments, etc.

Let T denote the number of call-backs after which the interviewer obtains a response. Then

$$P(T = t) = \begin{cases} p_1, & \text{if } t = 1 \\ (1 - p_1 - p_0)(1 - \Delta p_1 - p_0)^{t-2}\Delta p_1, & \text{if } t \geq 2. \end{cases}$$

The model can be generalized by allowing p_1 to vary among units. One can assume that p_1 has a prior beta distribution or that p_1 is constant within certain subclasses in the population but varies between them. Let us assume the latter.

An Application of the Model

Thomsen and Tesfu (1988) illustrate their model by means of a Norwegian fertility survey. The aim of the survey is to estimate the mean number of live births in the population. Nonresponses can result in a serious bias because response rate is a function of the household size. Hence we wish to determine the effect of call-backs on the bias and the mean-square error. We poststratify women in the sample into seven strata. Poststratum i consists of those women with i live births ($i = 0, 1, \ldots, 6$). Note that the last stratum includes women with 6 or more live births. We assume that p_i and Δ are constant within each poststratum, but vary from stratum to stratum.

Let n denote the sample size and $N_0, N_1, \ldots, N_6$ denote the number of women falling into the poststrata (in the population). Then the expected number of responses at the jth call in stratum i is $N_i P(T_i = j)$, where

$$P(T_i = j) = \begin{cases} p_{1,i}, & \text{if } j = 1 \\ (1 - p_{1i} - p_0)(1 - \Delta_i p_{1i} - p_0)^{j-2}\Delta_i p_{1i}, & \text{if } j \geq 2. \end{cases}$$

Let z_{ij} be the observed number of responses in stratum i at the jth call. The following equations will give simple estimates of N_i, p_{1i} and Δ_i, p_o:

$$N_i p_{1i} = z_{i1}$$

$$N_i(1 - p_{1i} - p_0)\Delta_i p_{1i} = z_{i2}$$

$$N_i(1 - p_{1i} - p_0)(1 - \Delta_i p_{1i} - p_0)\Delta_i p_{1i} = z_{i3}, \qquad \text{for } i = 0, 1, \ldots, 6.$$

The relevant data is presented in Table 13.2.

TABLE 13.2[1] Number of Responses at Each Call
and Certain Estimates

Number of responses at each call

Poststratum	Call		
	1	2	3
0	311	387	199
1	258	248	134
2	487	410	158
3	261	199	88
4	107	79	30
5	37	15	9
6	12	7	3
Total	1483	1345	610

Estimates of N_i, Δ_i, p_{1i}, and p_0

Stratum	$\hat{N}_i$	$\hat{\Delta}_i$	$\hat{p}_{1i}$	
0	1380	1.840	0.226	
1	1049	1.470	0.245	
2	1433	1.490	0.347	
3	771	1.356	0.339	$\hat{p}_0 = 0.099$
4	287	1.398	0.373	
5	96	0.783	0.383	
6	30	1.717	0.400	

In order to estimate the bias and the variance of the respondent mean, let y_i denote the number of live births for the ith selected woman and let

$$a_i = \begin{cases} 1, & \text{if the } i\text{th selected woman is a respondent} \\ 0, & \text{otherwise.} \end{cases}$$

The respondent sample mean can be written as

$$\bar{y}_s = \sum_{i=1}^{n} y_i a_i / \sum_{1}^{n} a_i .$$

Now, let

$$q_j = P(\text{a woman in the sample belongs to poststratum } j|$$

the woman is a respondent), $\quad j = 0, 1, \ldots, 6.$

Hence, we have after the first call

$$q_j = N_j p_{1j} / \sum_{j=0}^{6} N_j p_{1j}$$

---
[1] Reproduced with permission from Elsevier Science Publishers.

and after $k(k \geq 2)$ calls,

$$q_j = \frac{N_j p_{1j} + \sum_{i=2}^{k} N_j (1 - p_{1j} - p_0)(1 - \Delta_j p_{1j} - p_0)^{i-2} \Delta_j p_{1j}}{\sum_{j=0}^{6} \{ N_j p_{1j} + \sum_{i=2}^{k} N_j (1 - p_{1j} - p_0)(1 - \Delta_j p_{1j} - p_0)^{i-2} \Delta_j p_{1j} \}}$$

$j = 0, 1, \ldots, 6.$

$$E(\bar{y}_s) = E E(\bar{y}_s | a_1, \ldots, a_n) = E(y_1) = \sum_{j=1}^{5} j q_j + 6.5 q_6$$

and

$$\text{var}(\bar{y}_s) = E\{\text{var}(\bar{y}_s | a_1, \ldots, a_n)\} + \text{var}\{E(\bar{y}_s | a_1, \ldots, a_n\}$$

$$= E\left\{ \frac{\sum_{i=1}^{n} a_i^2 \text{var}(y_i)}{\{(\sum_1^n a_i)\}^2} \right\} \doteq \frac{\text{var } y_1}{E(\sum_1^n a_i)}$$

$$= \left[\sum_{j=0}^{5} j^2 q_j + (6.5)^2 q_6 - E^2(y_1) \right] / E\left(\sum_1^n a_i\right)$$

where the average number of live births per woman in poststratum 6 is assumed to be 6.5.

Using estimates $\hat{N}_j$, $\hat{p}_{1j}$, $\hat{\Delta}_j$, and $\hat{p}_o$, one can obtain estimates for the q_j, namely $\hat{q}_j$, and hence estimates of $E(\bar{y}_s)$ and $\text{var}(\bar{y}_s)$. From official records, the mean in the total selected sample $\bar{y}$ will be known, so that

$$\text{bias}(\bar{y}_s) = E(\bar{y}_s) - E(\bar{y})$$

can be found.

The authors provide the bias and the mean-square error for a specified number of calls and these are presented in Table 13.3.

TABLE 13.3[2] Estimated Bias and Mean-Square Error by Number of Calls

	Number of calls									
	1	2	3	4	5	6	7	8	9	10
Bias	0.34	0.21	0.17	0.14	0.13	0.13	0.12	0.12	0.12	0.12
MSE	0.116	0.044	0.028	0.021	0.018	0.017	0.016	0.015	0.015	0.015

One surmises that the bias and the MSE are both substantially reduced after 3 to 4 calls and the usefulness of making further call-backs is small.

---

[2] Reproduced with permission from Elsevier Science Publishers.

13.7   RANDOMIZED RESPONSES TO SENSITIVE QUESTIONS

In certain situations, when we are eliciting answers to sensitive questions such as having AIDS or having extramarital affairs, the answers either are evasive or are not given. In this situation, we may resort to randomized responses. For example, if π_A is the true population of people having the characteristic A, Warner (1965) has shown that it is possible to estimate π_A without the respondent revealing his or her personal status regarding this question.

The randomizing device (for example, throwing a die, selecting a ball out of a box containing predetermined white and red balls) selects one of two statements, each resulting in a "yes" or "no" response to be presented to the subject. The interviewer does not know which question the subject has answered. However, the interviewer knows the probabilities P and $1 - P$ with which the two statements are presented. The main idea is the respondent is sure that he/she is not revealing his/her personal status with regards to the sensitive issue.

Let the two statements be

"I have the characteristic A" (presented with probability P).
"I do not have the characteristic A" (presented with probability $1 - P$).

In a random sample of size n, suppose that m are positive responses. Then,

$$\hat{\phi} = m/n$$

where

$$\phi = P\pi_A + (1 - P)(1 - \pi_A) = (2P - 1)\pi_A + 1 - P.$$

When P is known,

$$\hat{\pi}_{AW} = \frac{\hat{\phi} - (1 - P)}{2P - 1} \qquad (P \neq \frac{1}{2} \text{ and "}W\text{" denotes Warner (1965))}.$$

One can easily see that $\hat{\pi}_A$ is the maximum-likelihood estimate (MLE) of π_A and that $E(\hat{\pi}_A) = \pi_A$, since $\hat{\phi}$ is the MLE of ϕ and $E\hat{\phi} = \phi$,

$$\text{var}(\hat{\pi}_{AW}) = \frac{\phi(1 - \phi)}{n(2P - 1)^2}.$$

Since

$$1 - \phi = (2P - 1)(1 - \pi_A) + (1 - P)$$

we have

$$\phi(1 - \phi) = (2P - 1)^2 \pi_A(1 - \pi_A) + P(1 - P).$$

Then we can write

$$\text{var}(\hat{\pi}_{AW}) = \frac{\pi_A(1 - \pi_A)}{n} + \frac{P(1 - P)}{n(2P - 1)^2}. \tag{13.31}$$

The first term in $\text{var}(\hat{\pi}_{AW})$ would have been the variance if all the subjects answered truthfully to the direct question whether they have characteristic A. The second term could be very large, depending on the value of P.

EXAMPLE 13.4

A school district wishes to estimate the proportion of middle-school students that use drugs. The interviewer selects a sample of $n = 500$ students from a population of 2500. Each student is asked to pick a card from a deck of cards in which 85% of the cards read "I use drugs" and the remaining 15% read "I do not use drugs." Let us compute an approximate 95% confidence interval for the proportion of middle-school students who use drugs. Let the number of yeses be 90. Then we have

$$\phi = 90/500 = 0.18$$

$$\hat{\pi}_{AW} = \{0.18 - (1 - 0.85)\} / (2(0.85) - 1) = 0.03/0.7 = 0.04$$

$$\widehat{\text{var}}(\hat{\pi}_{AW}) = 0.04(1 - 0.04)/500 + 0.85(1 - 0.85)/\{500(2(0.85) - 1)^2\}$$

$$= 0.000768 + 0.0005204$$

$$= 0.000597,$$

$$95\%\,\text{CI} = 0.04 \pm 2(0.0244) = 0.04 \pm 0.05.$$

◆

Alternative Method

Horwitz, Shah, and Simmons (1967) suggested that the subject's cooperation will improve if the second statement is unrelated to the first question. For instance, the second statement can be "I was born in California." Then the probability of a "yes" is

$$\phi = P\pi_A + (1 - P)\pi_U$$

where π_U is the proportion in the sampled population who were born in California. If π_U is known, the MLE of π_A is

$$\hat{\pi}_{AU} = \frac{\hat{\phi} - (1 - P)\pi_U}{P}$$

with variance

$$\text{var}(\hat{\pi}_{AU}) = \frac{\phi(1 - \phi)}{nP^2}.$$

We can set up the following experiment so that π_U is known. Let a box contain red, white, and blue balls with known proportions P_1, P_2, P_3, respectively. If one draws a red ball, he should answer the sensitive question. If he draws a white or a blue ball, he should answer the second statement: "The color of this ball is white." Thus,

$$\pi_U = P_2/(P_2 + P_3).$$

Case When π_U Is Unknown

We can have two random samples of sizes n_1 and n_2 with proportions P_1, P_2 $(P_1 \neq P_2)$ for the sensitive question. Denoting by ϕ_1, ϕ_2 the proportions of positive responses in the populations defined by the choices P_1 and P_2, we have

$$\phi_1 = P_1\pi_A + (1 - P_1)\pi_U$$
$$\phi_2 = P_2\pi_A + (1 - P_2)\pi_U .$$

Eliminating π_U, we get

$$\pi_A = \frac{(1 - P_2)\phi_1 - (1 - P_1)\phi_2}{P_1 - P_2} .$$

Then an unbiased estimate of π_A is

$$\hat{\pi}_{AU} = \frac{\hat{\phi}_1(1 - P_2) - (1 - P_1)\hat{\phi}_2}{P_1 - P_2}$$

having the variance

$$\operatorname{var}(\hat{\pi}_{AU}) = (P_1 - P_2)^{-2}\left[\frac{(1 - P_2)^2\phi_1(1 - \phi_1)}{n_1} + \frac{(1 - P_1)^2\phi_2(1 - \phi_2)}{n_2}\right] .$$

In order to set up a $(1 - \alpha)$ confidence interval for π_{AU}, in $\operatorname{var}(\hat{\pi}_{AU})$ one can replace $\phi_1(1-\phi_1)$ and $\phi_2(1-\phi_2)$ by $1/4$ their maximum values or by $\hat{\phi}_1(1-\hat{\phi}_1)$ and $\hat{\phi}_2(1-\hat{\phi}_2)$, respectively. One can minimize the above variance with respect to n_1 and n_2 subject to $n_1 + n_2 = n$. Then we choose n_1 and n_2 such that

$$\frac{n_1}{n_2} = \frac{(1 - P_2)}{(1 - P_1)}\left\{\frac{\phi_1(1 - \phi_1)}{\phi_2(1 - \phi_2)}\right\}^{1/2}$$

and with this choice of n_1 and n_2,

$$\min \operatorname{var}(\hat{\pi}_{AU})$$

$$= \frac{1}{n(P_2 - P_1)^2}\left[(1 - P_2)\{\phi_1(1 - \phi_1)\}^{1/2} + (1 - P_1)\{\phi_2(1 - \phi_2)\}^{1/2}\right]^2 .$$

Extension to Estimation of Population Mean

A subgroup of size n_i subjects get to answer the sensitive question with probability P_i and to answer the nonsensitive question with probability $(1 - P_i)(i = 1, 2)$. The response variable Z_i for a subject is distributed as a mixture of two distributions with mixing probabilities P_i, $(1 - P_i)$.

If the two distributions have means μ_A and μ_U, and variances σ_A^2 and σ_U^2, then

$$Z_i = \begin{cases} X & \text{with probability } P_i \\ Y & \text{with probability } (1 - P_i). \end{cases}$$

Hence,

$$E(Z_i) = P_i\mu_A + (1 - P_i)\mu_U ,$$

$$\begin{aligned} \text{var}(Z_i) &= E\{Z_i - P_i\mu_A - (1 - P_i)\mu_U\}^2 \\ &= P_i E\{X - P_i\mu_A - (1 - P_i)\mu_U\}^2 \\ &\quad + (1 - P_i)E\{Y - P_i\mu_A - (1 - P_i)\mu_U\}^2 \\ &= P_i\{\sigma_A^2 + (1 - P_i)^2(\mu_A - \mu_U)^2\} + (1 - P_i)\{\sigma_U^2 + P_i^2(\mu_A - \mu_U)^2\} \\ &= P_i\sigma_A^2 + (1 - P_i)\sigma_U^2 + P_i(1 - P_i)(\mu_A - \mu_U)^2 . \end{aligned}$$

An unbiased estimate of μ_A is

$$\hat{\mu}_{AU} = \frac{(1 - P_2)\bar{z}_1 - (1 - P_1)\bar{z}_2}{P_1 - P_2} .$$

Again we can minimize the variance of $\hat{\mu}_{AU}$ with respect to n_1 and n_2 subject to the constraint $n_1 + n_2 = n$. Also, for the estimate of the variance of $\hat{\mu}_{AU}$ we have

$$\widehat{\text{var}}(\hat{\mu}_{AU}) = (P_1 - P_2)^{-2}\left\{(1 - P_2)^2\bar{z}_1(1 - \bar{z}_1)n_1^{-1} + (1 - P_1)^2\bar{z}_2(1 - \bar{z}_2)n_2^{-1}\right\} .$$

EXAMPLE 13.5

Let $n_1 = 20$, $n_2 = 30$, $P_1 = 0.85$, $P_2 = 0.75$, $\hat{\sigma}_1 = 0.08$, and $\hat{\phi}_2 = 0.05$. Then

$$\hat{\mu}_{AU} = \{0.08(0.25) - 0.05(0.15)\}/0.10$$

$$= 0.0125/0.10 = 0.125 .$$

An upper bound for var $(\hat{\mu}_{AU})$ is

$$\text{var}(\hat{\mu}_{AU}) \leq \frac{(0.10)^{-2}}{4}\left\{\frac{(0.25)^2}{20} + \frac{(0.15)^2}{30}\right\}$$

$$= \frac{1}{0.04}\{0.003125 + 0.00075\} = 0.096875 .$$

Thus, a 95% confidence interval for μ_{AU} is

$$0.125 \pm (1.96)(0.311)$$

i.e.,

$$0.125 \pm 0.610 .$$

Next,

$$\widehat{\operatorname{var}}\,(\hat{\mu}_{AU}) = (0.10)^{-2}\left\{\frac{(0.25)^2(0.08)(0.92)}{20} + \frac{(0.15)^2(0.05)(0.95)}{30}\right\}$$

$$= (0.10)^{-2}\{0.00023 + 0.0000356\} = 0.02656.$$

Thus, a 95% confidence interval for μ_{AU} is

$$0.125 \pm (1.96)(0.1629)$$

i.e.,

$$0.125 \pm 0.319.$$

◆

13.8   MEASUREMENT ERRORS*

Measurement errors do occur in practice and much attention has been paid to their study. Let y_i denote the true value of the response by the ith unit denoted by U_i. Let a simple random sample of n units be drawn from the N units and also let x_{ij} = the value reported by jth enumerator on U_i, $i = 1, \ldots, h$ and $j = 1, \ldots, m$.

The simple model considered in the literature is

$$x_{ij} = y_i + \alpha_j + e_{ij} \tag{13.32}$$

where

α_j = the bias of the jth enumerator in repeated observations on all units

e_{ij} = the error when the jth enumerator reports on the ith unit

where $E(e_{ij}|i, j) = 0$, $E(e_{ij}^2) = S_e^2$ and the errors are uncorrelated.

We assume that the number of replications $n_{ij} = 1$ or 0. Let

$$n_{i.} = \sum_{j=1}^{m} n_{ij} = \text{number of observations on } U_i$$

$$n_{.j} = \sum_{i=1}^{h} n_{ij} = \text{the number of observations made by the } j\text{th enumerator}$$

$$\bar{x}_{.j} = \frac{1}{n_{.j}}\sum_{i=1}^{h} n_{ij}y_{ij} = \text{the mean of all the } n_{.j} \text{ observations made by the } j\text{th enumerator}$$

$$\bar{x}_{..} = \frac{1}{n}\sum_{i}\sum_{j} n_{ij}y_{ij} = \text{the mean of all the } n \text{ observations made on the } h \text{ units in the sample}$$

---

* Sukhatme et al. (1984, pp. 450–454) served as a source for the material of this section.

Then

$$\bar{x}_{.j} = \frac{1}{n_{.j}} \sum_{i=1}^{h} (n_{ij}y_i + n_{ij}\alpha_j + n_{ij}e_{ij})$$

$$= \frac{1}{n_{.j}} \sum_{i=1}^{h} y_i n_{ij} + \alpha_j + \frac{1}{n_{.j}} \sum_{i=1}^{h} n_{ij}e_{ij} \tag{13.33}$$

Similarly

$$\bar{x}_{..} = \frac{1}{n} \sum_{i=1}^{h} y_i n_{i.} + \frac{1}{n} \sum_{j=1}^{m} \alpha_j n_{.j} + \frac{1}{n} \sum_i \sum_j e_{ij} n_{ij} . \tag{13.34}$$

Suppose we make the following assumptions

1. The m enumerators constitute a simple random sample out of the population of M enumerators.
2. The h units in the sample are randomly allocated to the different enumerators.
3. $n_{.j} = n/m = \bar{n}$ (say).
4. $n_{i.} = n/h = p$.

Then equations (13.33) and (13.34) become

$$\bar{x}_{.j} = \frac{1}{\bar{n}} \sum_{1}^{h} n_{ij}y_i + \alpha_j + \frac{1}{\bar{n}} \sum_i n_{ij}e_{ij} . \tag{13.35}$$

$$\bar{x}_{..} = \frac{1}{h} \sum_{i=1}^{h} y_i + \frac{1}{m} \sum_{j=1}^{m} \alpha_j + \frac{1}{n} \sum_i \sum_j n_{ij}e_{ij} . \tag{13.36}$$

Also

$$E(\bar{x}_{.j}) = \frac{1}{N} \sum_{i=1}^{N} y_i + \frac{1}{M} \sum_{1}^{M} \alpha_j = \mu + \bar{\alpha} \tag{13.37}$$

and

$$E(\bar{x}_{..}) = \mu + \bar{\alpha} . \tag{13.38}$$

One can obtain

$$\text{var}(\bar{x}_{.j}) = \left(\frac{1}{\bar{n}} - \frac{1}{N}\right) S_y^2 + \left(1 - \frac{1}{M}\right) S_\alpha^2 + \frac{S_e^2}{\bar{n}}$$

$$\doteq \frac{1}{\bar{n}} \left(S_y^2 + S_e^2\right) + S_\alpha^2 \qquad \text{if } M \text{ and } N \text{ are large} \tag{13.39}$$

and

$$\text{var}\,(\bar{x}_{..}) = \left(\frac{1}{h} - \frac{1}{N}\right) S_y^2 + \left(\frac{1}{m} - \frac{1}{M}\right) S_\alpha^2 + \frac{S_e^2}{n}$$

$$\doteq \frac{S_y^2}{h} + \frac{S_\alpha^2}{m} + \frac{S_e^2}{n} \tag{13.40}$$

where

$$S_y^2 = \frac{1}{N-1} \sum_{i=1}^{N} (y_i - \mu)^2, \qquad S_\alpha^2 = \frac{1}{M-1} \sum_{j=1}^{M} (\alpha_j - \bar{\alpha})^2. \tag{13.41}$$

Note that, although the α usually vary from enumerator to enumerator, $\bar{\alpha}$ is not negligible.

Since the variance of a single observation drawn from an infinite population when M is large is

$$S_x^2 = S_y^2 + S_\alpha^2 + S_e^2 \tag{13.42}$$

one can write

$$\text{var}\,(\bar{x}_{..}) = \frac{S_x^2}{h} + S_\alpha^2 \left(\frac{1}{m} - \frac{1}{h}\right) + S_e^2 \left(\frac{1}{n} - \frac{1}{h}\right). \tag{13.43}$$

Formula (13.43) points out that the sampling variance of the estimator is not entirely due to random variation in the selection of the sample units, but is inflated by the variability in the biases of the enumerators. Consequently, the formulae given in the previous chapters underestimate the actual sampling variance of the estimators. Also note that

$$\text{var}\,(\bar{x}_{..}) = \frac{S_x^2}{h} \qquad \text{if } m = h = n \text{ or if } \alpha_j \text{ is constant for all } j \text{ and } n = h.$$

One can also estimate S_e^2 and S_α^2 (namely the components of variance) from the sample. For details, the reader is referred to Sukhatme et al. (1984, Section 11.5).

■ PROBLEMS

13.1   Suppose we interested in knowing the prevalence of the use of marijuana in a certain town. Let $n = 600$ be the total number of people contacted and $n_1 = 500$ be the number who responded. If the number of people responding positively (i.e., say yes) is 60, obtain a 95% confidence interval for P, the true proportion of people who have used in the past or are currently using marijuana.

13.2   Consider the following empirical values:

j	p_j	β_j
1	0.50	$1.05
2	0.30	$1.50
3	0.15	$1.75

and $\gamma_3 = \$1.00$. Then $p_0^{(3)} = (1 - 0.50 - 0.30 - 0.15) = 0.05$. Using $\alpha = .05$ and $\delta = 0.10$, compute

$$n(0.10, 0.05, 0.05), \qquad E_3(C), \qquad \text{and} \qquad \text{var}(C).$$

(For relevant formulae, see Section 13.5.)

13.3 A school district wishes to estimate the proportion of middle school students that are experiencing disharmony between their parents. The interviewer selects a sample of $n = 200$ students from a population of 2500. Each student is asked to select a card from a deck of cards in which 25% of the cards read "I am experiencing disharmony between my parents" and the remaining 75% read "I am not experiencing disharmony between my parents." Each student answers yes or no to the question on the selected card. Suppose the total number of yeses is 96. Obtain a 95% confidence interval for the proportion of middle-school students experiencing disharmony between their parents.

13.4 Suppose that the student newspaper at Jupiter College is interested in estimating the number of students that are homosexual. The total number of students is 10,000. A random sample of 100 students is taken and each student is asked to toss a biased coin with $P(H) = 0.8$ (the result of which the interviewer is not supposed to know). If the coin shows up heads, the student is asked to answer yes or no to the question, (a): "I am a homosexual." If the coin results in a tail, the student is asked to answer yes or no to question (b): "I am heterosexual." Suppose that 45 students give "yes" for their response. Obtain a 95% confidence interval for the number of students that are homosexual.

13.5 The student newspaper at Mars University wants to assess the proportion of students that cheat on their examinations. A random sample of 200 students out of the total number of students, namely 10,000, is taken. Each student is asked to answer yes or no to the question (a): "Sometimes I cheat on my examinations," if the biased coin with $P(H) = 0.6$ he/she tosses results in a head. If the toss results in a tail, the student is asked to answer yes or no to the question (b): "I never cheat on my examinations." Suppose that 90 students give "yes" for their responses. Obtain a 95% confidence interval for the proportion of students that cheat on their examinations.

13.6 The local newspaper in a town called Mint Julep is interested in estimating the proportion of people who have cheated on their spouses. They take a random sample of size 100 adults (the town consists of 12,000 people). Each chosen adult is asked to toss a biased coin with $P(H) = 0.6$ and to answer yes or no to the question (a): "I cheated on my spouse," if the toss results in a head. If the toss results in a tail, he/she will answer the question (b): "I did not cheat on my spouse." Suppose that 42 adults in the sample give "yes" for their responses. Obtain a 95% confidence interval for the population of adults who cheat on their spouses.

13.7 Suppose the number of students attending Jupiter University is 10,000, of which 50% are males. The student newspaper is interested in estimating the number of people who use drugs. Suppose it draws a random sample of size $n_1 = 100$ male students. Each selected male student is asked to pick a card from a deck of cards in which 85% of the cards read "I use drugs" and the remaining 15% read "I am from California." Also, it draws a random sample of size $n_2 = 100$ female students. Each selected female student is asked to pick a card from a deck of cards in which 75% of the cards read "I use drugs" and the remaining 25% read "I am from California." Suppose 8 male students and 5 female students answer yes. Obtain a 95% confidence interval for the proportion of students at Jupiter University that use drugs.

13.8   Suppose the number of students attending Mars University is 10,000, of which 50% are males. The student newspaper is interested in estimating the proportion of students who cheat on their examinations. Suppose it draws a random sample of size $n_1 = 100$ male students and each selected student is asked to pick a card from a deck of cards in which 85% of the cards read "I cheat on examinations" and the remaining 15% read "I come from the state of New York." The newspaper also draws an independent random sample of size $n_2 = 100$ female students. Each selected female student is asked to pick a card from a deck of cards in which 75% of the cards read "I cheat on examinations" and the remaining 25% read "I come from the state of New York." Suppose that 12 male students and 8 female students answer yes. Set up a 95% confidence interval for the proportion of students at Mars University that cheat on examinations.

■ REFERENCES

13.1   Birnbaum, Z. W. and Sirken, M. G. (1950). Bias due to nonavailability in sampling surveys. *J. Amer. Statist. Assoc.* **45**, 98–111.

13.2   Cochran, W. (1977). *Sampling Techniques,* 3rd ed., New York: John Wiley & Sons.

13.3   Deming, W. E. (1953). On a probability mechanism to attain an economic balance between the resultant error of non-response and the bias of non-response. *J. Amer. Statist. Assoc.* **48**, 743–772.

13.4   Hilgard, E. R. and Payne, S. L. (1944). Those not at home: Riddle for polsters. *Public Opinion Quarterly* **8**, 254–261.

13.5   Horwitz, D. G., Shah, B. V., and Simmons, W. R. (1967). The unrelated randomized response model. *Proc. Soc. Statist. Section, Amer. Statist. Assoc.* 663–685.

13.6   Oh, H. L. and Scheuren, F. J. (1983). Weighting adjustment for unit nonresponse. In *Incomplete Data in Sample Surveys*, Vol 2, (ed. I. Olkin and D.B. Rubin). New York: Academic Press, 143–184.

13.7   Rao, J. N. K. (1988). Variance estimation in sample surveys. *Handbook of Statistics*, No. 6 (ed. P. K. Krishnaiah and C. R. Rao). New York: North Holland, 427–447.

13.8   Rao, P. S. R. S. (1983). Callbacks, followups and repeated telephone calls. in: *Incomplete Data in Sample Surveys*, Vol. 2 (ed. I. Olkin and D.B. Rubin,), New York: Academic Press, 33–44.

13.9   Stephan, F. F. (1945). The expected value and variance of the reciprocal and other negative powers of a positive Bernoullian variate. *Ann. Math. Statist.* **16**, 50–62.

13.10 Sukhatme, P. V., Sukhatme, B. V., Sukhatme, S., and Asok, C. (1984). *Sampling Theory of Surveys with Applications* (3rd ed.). Ames: Iowa State Univ. Press.

13.11 Thomsen, I. and Tesfu, D. (1988). On the use of models in sampling from finite populations. *Handbook of Statistics: Sampling,* Vol. 6 (ed. P. K. Kristiraiah and C. R. Rao). New York: North Holland, 369–397.

13.12 Warner, S. L. (1965). Randomized response: a survey technique for eliminating evasive answer bias. *J. Amer. Statist. Assoc.* **60**, 63–69.

CHAPTER 14

BAYESIAN APPROACH FOR INFERENCE IN FINITE POPULATIONS

14.1 INTRODUCTION

After Godambe (1955) showed the nonexistence of minimum-variance unbiased estimators for the total of a finite population for which the labels of the units in the population are a variable, there has been renewed interest and research in the application of various inferential approaches like Bayes, empirical Bayes, the super population approach, pseudolikelihood and fiducial idea to the finite-population problem. These approaches can be viewed as incorporating prior information into inference. Ericson (1969) introduced a subjectivist Bayes approach to problems of inference and sample design for finite populations. He points out that Bayesian models are straightforward and they provide simple ways of handling problems of nonresponse, response error, and response bias. Ericson (1988) summarizes some of these results, which form the basis of this chapter.

14.2 NOTATION AND THE MODEL

We assume that the finite population consists of N distinguishable units labeled by the integers $1, 2, \ldots, N$. Let $\eta = \{1, 2, \ldots, N\}$ denote the label set and $\mathbf{Y} = (Y_1, Y_2, \ldots, Y_N)$ where Y_i is the unknown value (it could be vector valued) of some characteristic associated with the ith population unit. We are interested in making inferences about $\mathbf{Y}$ or some function g of $\mathbf{Y}$. Our main interest would be to estimate

$T = g(Y) = \sum_{i=1}^{N} Y_i$ or $\bar{y} = T/N$. We also assume that there is a known vector $\mathbf{X}_i = (X_{i1}, \ldots, X_{ip})'$ of concomitant variables available for each $i \in \eta$. Let $\mathbf{X}$ denote the $N \times p$ matrix of these variables.

Note that the label $i \in \eta$ is a convenient coding of some true label which may contain some information about Y_i. For instance, the label could be a person's name, the serial number of an automobile, the names of the streets defining a city block, etc. The following model is flexible so as to distinguish the information about Y_i carried by $i \in \eta$ and by $\mathbf{X}_i$.

Let (s, y_s) denote a sample where $s = (i_1, \ldots, i_n) \subseteq \eta$ is the set of distinct unit labels comprising the sample and $y_s = (y_{i_1}, \ldots, y_{i_n})$, where y_{i_j} is the response or characteristic observed on sample unit i_j. Then $y_{i_j} = Y_{i_j}$ if no nonresponse and no response bias or error exists. If one or more of the latter exists, one can assume that $y_{i_j} = Y_{i_j} +$ some unknown bias + error. Such extended models have been considered by Ericson (1983b), Little (1982), and Rubin (1976). However, for our discussion in this chapter we assume the simpler model $y_{i_j} = Y_{i_j}$, for $i_j \in s$.

A sample design is defined by S, the set of all subsets of η, together with $p_{\mathbf{x}}(s)$, a discrete probability measure on S. That is, $p_{\mathbf{x}}(s) \geq 0$ and $\sum_{s \in S} p_{\mathbf{x}}(s) = 1$. Also for any s in S let $n(s)$ be the sample size, the number of elements in s. Notice that we have excluded sample designs with replacement. In doing so, we do not incur any loss of generality, because for any design (s, y_s) is a minimal sufficient statistic. Further, note that the sample design may depend on the values of $\mathbf{X} = (\mathbf{X}_1, \ldots, \mathbf{X}_N)$.

For any sample (s, y_s) define the matrix operator $\mathbf{S}(\mathbf{Y}) = (Y_{i_1}, \ldots, Y_{i_n})$ and its complement $\bar{\mathbf{S}}(\mathbf{Y}) = (Y_{j_1}, \ldots, Y_{j_{N-n}})$ for $j_k \in \eta - s$. For the sake of definiteness assume that $i_1 < \cdots < i_n$ and $j_1 < \cdots < j_{N-n}$. Then the likelihood function of $\mathbf{Y}$ is

$$l(\mathbf{Y}|s, y_s) = \begin{cases} kp_{\mathbf{x}}(s) & \text{for } \{\mathbf{Y}|\mathbf{S}(\mathbf{Y})\} = y_s \\ 0 & \text{otherwise} \end{cases} \tag{14.1}$$

where $k > 0$ is some constant. For any prior distribution of $\mathbf{Y}$ denoted by $p(\mathbf{Y}|\mathbf{X})$ (the prior may depend on the known $\mathbf{X}$), the posterior of $\mathbf{Y}$ is given by

$$p(\mathbf{Y}|s, y_s) = \begin{cases} \frac{p(\mathbf{Y}|\mathbf{X}) p_{\mathbf{x}}(s)}{p_{s(\mathbf{Y})}(y_s|\mathbf{X})} & \text{for } \{\mathbf{Y}|S(\mathbf{Y})\} = y_s \\ 0 & \text{otherwise} \end{cases} \tag{14.2}$$

where $p_{s(\mathbf{Y})}(y_s|\mathbf{X})$ is the marginal prior on $S(\mathbf{Y})$.

Note that the likelihood function given in (14.1) is not very different from the most uninformative likelihood function (namely the one that is constant for all $\mathbf{Y}$), since it does not depend on the design by which (s, y_s) was observed. This has led some to conclude that the sample design is irrelevant from a Bayesian point of view and that randomization plays no role. Another consequence of the posterior in (14.2) is that some research workers adopted the modeling of a super population approach in which $\mathbf{Y}$ constitutes a random sample of N units drawn from some super population having density function $f(Y_i|\theta)$, where θ is either known or has a prior density with known parameters (see, for instance, Kolehmarnen (1981)). The concept of a super population is a partial specification of a prior distribution.

In spite of the uninformative nature of the likelihood, by specification of reasonable priors, $p(\mathbf{Y}|\mathbf{X})$, one often obtains useful inferences (posterior distributions) on various functions $g(\mathbf{Y})$, and when the priors are suitably diffuse, the resulting Bayes estimators or their limits coincide with those obtained by the classical sampling distribution viewpoint. Also one can establish the Bayes optimality of the traditional sampling designs such as stratified and two-stage sampling.

14.3   SOME BASIC RESULTS

It seems to be a formidable task to assign an N-dimensional prior distribution. This is made easy by the application of notions of exchangeability, partitioning of η, modeling prior knowledge of the relation between $\mathbf{Y}$ and $\mathbf{X}$, use of randomization, etc. The reasonable approach is the use of linear Bayes estimators which rely only on the specification of low moments of the prior distributions, and the subsequent results are based on this approach. Linear Bayes estimators have been discovered and rediscovered by several researchers. The following basic result plays a crucial role, which says that if one approximates the posterior mean by a 'best' linear function of the observed data, then that estimator is equivalent to the one resulting from a multivariate normal distribution.

Result 14.1.   [Ericson, 1983a]   Let $\mathbf{X}_1 (n_1 \times 1)$, and $\mathbf{X}_2 (n_2 \times 1)$ be any jointly distributed random vectors having means μ_1 and μ_2 and covariance matrix

$$\Sigma = \begin{bmatrix} \Sigma_{11} & \Sigma_{12} \\ \Sigma_{21} & \Sigma_{22} \end{bmatrix}. \tag{14.3}$$

If

$$E(\mathbf{X}_1|\mathbf{X}_2) = \mathbf{P}\mathbf{X}_2 + \gamma \tag{14.4}$$

for some $\mathbf{P}(n_1 \times n_2)$ and $\gamma(n_1 \times 1)$ not depending on $\mathbf{X}_2$, or if $\mathbf{P}$ and γ are chosen to minimize

$$E_{\mathbf{X}_2} \| E(\mathbf{X}_1|\mathbf{X}_2) - \mathbf{P}\mathbf{X}_2 - \gamma \|^2 \tag{14.5}$$

then

$$\mathbf{P}\mathbf{X}_2 + \gamma = \Sigma_{12}\Sigma_{22}^{-1}\mathbf{X}_2 + (\mu_1 - \Sigma_{12}\Sigma_{22}^{-1}\mu_2). \tag{14.6}$$

Also

$$E_{\mathbf{X}_2} \operatorname{var}(\mathbf{X}_1|\mathbf{X}_2) - (\Sigma_{11} - \Sigma_{12}\Sigma_{22}^{-1}\Sigma_{21}) \le 0 \tag{14.7}$$

(i.e., the matrix on the left side of (14.7) is negative semidefinite) and equality holds in (14.7) if (14.4) is valid.

Notice that (14.4) holds if $\mathbf{X}_1$ and $\mathbf{X}_2$ have a multivariate normal distribution. If (14.4) fails to be satisfied, the best linear approximation to $E(\mathbf{X}_1|\mathbf{X}_2)$ and the upper bound for $E_{\mathbf{X}_2} \operatorname{var}(\mathbf{X}_1|\mathbf{X}_2)$ given by (14.5) and (14.7) are still valid, respectively.

The above result is used in the sequel to characterize the posterior mean of $\mathbf{Y}, T$, and $\bar{Y}$ in several cases and the prior expectation of the posterior covariance matrix of $\mathbf{Y}$. The latter is useful in determining optimal sample designs.

A special case of Result 14.1 is the following corollary due to Ericson (1975).

Corollary 14.1. Let $\xi (= \mathbf{X}_1)$ and $\mathbf{X}(= \mathbf{X}_2)$ be any $n + 1$ jointly distributed random variables such that $E(\xi) = m$, $\text{var}\,\xi = v(\xi) < \infty$, $\mathbf{V}(\mathbf{X})$ the variance-covariance matrix of $\mathbf{X}$ is positive definite, and $E(X_i|\xi) = \xi$ for $i = 1, 2, \ldots, n$, where $\mathbf{X} = (X_1, \ldots, X_n)$. If either

$$E(\xi|\mathbf{X}) = \mathbf{Xa} + b, \qquad \mathbf{a} = (a_1, \ldots, a_n)' \tag{14.8}$$

or $\mathbf{a}$ and b are chosen to minimize

$$E_\mathbf{X}[E(\xi|\mathbf{X}) - \mathbf{Xa} - b]^2 \tag{14.9}$$

then

$$\mathbf{Xa} + b = \frac{E(\xi|\mathbf{X})EV(\hat{\xi}|\xi) + \hat{\xi}v(\xi)}{v(\xi) + EV(\hat{\xi}|\xi)} \tag{14.10}$$

where

$$\hat{\xi} = \hat{\xi}(\mathbf{X}) = \mathbf{1}[\mathbf{V}(\mathbf{X})]^{-1}\mathbf{X}'/\mathbf{1}[\mathbf{V}(\mathbf{X})]^{-1}\mathbf{1}'$$

$(\mathbf{1} = (1, 1, \ldots, 1))$ is the usual weighted least-squares estimator of ξ with respect to either the variance-covariance matrix $\mathbf{V}(\mathbf{X})$ or $E_\xi V(\mathbf{X}|\xi)$, and $\mathbf{V}(\hat{\xi}|\xi)$ stands for var $\hat{\xi}$ for given ξ. Further

$$E_\mathbf{X}V(\xi|\mathbf{X}) \leq v(\xi)\left[1 - v(\xi)\mathbf{1}(\mathbf{V}(\mathbf{X}))^{-1}\mathbf{1}'\right] = v(\xi)\left[\frac{EV(\hat{\xi}|\xi)}{v(\xi) + EV(\hat{\xi}|\xi)}\right] \tag{14.11}$$

with equality in (14.11) if (14.8) holds.

Thus, the Bayes estimator of ξ is a weighted average of a classical estimator and the prior mean, with weights proportional to natural measures of the precision of each. For optimal designs, one naturally minimizes the right-side quantity in (14.11). Applications of Corollary 3.1 will be provided.

14.4   SIMPLE RANDOM SAMPLING

One of the simplest designs is simple random sampling without replacement of size n. Since every subset n of the N population elements has the same probability of constituting the sample, the design consists of the pair $(S, p_x(s))$, where

$$p_x(s) = \begin{cases} 1/\binom{N}{n} & \text{if } n(s) = n \\ 0 & \text{otherwise.} \end{cases} \tag{14.12}$$

The essence of this design is that the N population units are indistinguishable in the sense that for inferential purposes a subset of n units is as good as any other subset of n units. Here there is no information about $\mathbf{Y}$ contained in the unit labels. Then the sample is selected using randomization so as to avoid any biases and to provide "objectivistic" sampling distributions for various statistics. This property can be interpreted (by the subjectivists) as though the variate values were exchangeable in the sense of de Finetti (1937).

The relation between the inference about the finite population mean μ via the simple random sampling approach and the inference made by a subjectivist Bayesian via an exchangeable prior on **Y** is very close. Let us assume that there are no concomitant variables **X** and the Y_i's are scalars.

The variables $Y_1, Y_2, \ldots, Y_N$ are said to be exchangeable whenever the distribution of any subset of $r(1 \le r \le N)$ of the Y_i's is the same as that of any other subset of r of the Y_i's. Suppose we impose a prior distribution on **Y** under which the Y_i's are exchangeable with mean $E(Y_i) = m$, var $Y_i = V(Y_i) = v$, and covariance, cov $(Y_i, Y_j) = c$ for all i and $j \ne i$. Let μ be the mean of Y_i in the finite population and let $\sigma^2 = \sum_{i=1}^{N}(Y_i - \mu)^2/N$ be the finite population variance. Further, let $\bar{y}$ be the mean based on a sample of size n drawn from the population of size N. Then we have the following result.

Result 14.2. If the variables $Y_1, Y_2, \ldots, Y_N$ are exchangeable with means, variances and covariances as defined above, then

  i. $E(\mu) = E(\bar{y}) = m$,

  ii. $V(N\mu) = N$ var $Y_1 + N(N-1)$ cov (Y_1, Y_2), Thus $V(\mu) = [v + (N-1)c]/N$.

  iii. Similarly one can show that

$$V(n\bar{y}) = n[v + (n-1)c]$$

  iv. $\quad E(N\sigma^2) = N$ var $Y - NE(\mu - m)^2$

$$= Nv - \frac{1}{N}E\left(\sum_{1}^{N}(Y_i - m)\right)^2$$

$$= Nv - \frac{1}{N}[Nv + N(N-1)c] = (N-1)(v-c).$$

  v. $E(\bar{y}|\mu, \sigma^2) = \mu$, and

  vi. $V(\bar{y}|\mu, \sigma^2) = \dfrac{(N-n)\sigma^2}{(N-1)n}$

and the latter two results are well known for the simple random sample design.

Note that the properties (i)–(iv) are those of the prior distribution only; no sampling design has been specified. Further, it may be shown that under an exchangeable prior on Y, given the N population variate values, namely the Y_i's but not the units with which they are associated, the probability that any pre-specified subset of size n of the population elements will assume the values given by any collection of n of the N population values is equal to $1/\binom{N}{n}$, which is the same as the objective probability that the subset was selected by simple random sampling.

Bayes Linear Estimator

Let us assume that we have an exchangeable prior on $\mathbf{Y}$ of the kind described above and we select a sample s, consisting of $Y_i = y_i$ for $i \in s$. Now apply Corollary 14.1 by taking $\mu = \xi$ and $(s, y_s) = x$, a realization of $\mathbf{X}$. One could also apply Result 14.1 directly to Y, partitioned into $\mathbf{S}(\mathbf{Y})$ and $\bar{\mathbf{S}}(\mathbf{Y})$ corresponding to the sampled and unsampled Y_i's. In either case the posterior mean of μ or the Bayes linear estimator of μ, denoted by $\tilde{\mu}$ and given by (14.10) is

$$\tilde{\mu} = \frac{\bar{y}V(\mu) + mEV(\bar{y}|\mu, \sigma^2)}{V(\mu) + EV(\bar{y}|\mu, \sigma^2)} \tag{14.13}$$

where

$$EV(\bar{y}|\mu, \sigma^2) = \frac{(N-n)E(\sigma^2)}{n(N-1)} . \tag{14.14}$$

Also from (14.11) we have

$$E_{(s,y_s)}V\left(\mu|(s, y_s)\right) \leq V(\mu) \cdot \frac{EV(\bar{y}|\mu, \sigma^2)}{V(\mu) + EV(\bar{y}|\mu, \sigma^2)} . \tag{14.15}$$

Note that if $V(\mu)$ becomes large whereas $E(\sigma^2)$ remains fixed, then $\tilde{\mu}$ tends to $\bar{y}$ and the precision on the right-hand side of (14.15) will tend to $EV(\bar{y}|\mu, \sigma^2)$.

Remark 14.1.   Although randomization and random sampling are not required formally by the Bayesian approach with an exchangeable prior, Ericson (1988, p. 220) makes a case for randomization which, costing a little to the subjectivist, may buy him much in terms of the utility of his sample to others having diverse views of inference.

EXAMPLE 14.1

Let $N = 1000$, $n = 50$, $m = 10$, $v = 100$, and $c = 5$. Then

$$V(\mu) = \{100 + 5(995)\}/1000 = 5.095$$

and $$EV(\bar{y}|\mu, \sigma^2) = \frac{950}{999 \times 50} \cdot \frac{999}{1000}(100 - 5) = \frac{361}{200} = 1.805$$

Thus the Bayes linear estimator is

$$\tilde{\mu} = 0.738\bar{y} + 0.262m = 2.62 + 0.738\bar{y} . \qquad \blacklozenge$$

14.5   HYPERGEOMETRIC-BINOMIAL MODEL

In this section we consider a special model called the hypergeometric-binomial model and obtain an explicit expression for the Bayes estimator.

Let N be the size of the population and M denote the size of the subpopulation having a certain characteristic. Let

$$Y_i = 1, \quad \text{if } i\text{th unit has the characteristic}$$

$$= 0, \quad \text{otherwise } (i = 1, \ldots, N).$$

Let n denote the size of the simple random sample. Then

$$P(\mathbf{Y} = \mathbf{y}|M) = \binom{M}{x}\binom{N-M}{n-x} \Big/ \binom{n}{x}\binom{N}{n} \quad \text{if } x = \sum_1^n y_i$$

$$= 0, \qquad\qquad\qquad\qquad\qquad \text{otherwise.}$$

Also, if $X = Y_1 + \cdots + Y_n$, then

$$f(x|M) = P(X = x|M) = \binom{n}{x} P(\mathbf{Y} = \mathbf{y}|M).$$

Suppose that M is an unobservable integer-valued random variable, the distribution of which is determined by the quality of the process. We further assume that the prior distribution of M is given by

$$g(m) = \binom{N}{m} p^m (1-p)^{N-m}, \qquad m = 0, 1, \ldots, N$$

where the hyper parameter p can be interpreted as the probability that any subject in the population will have the characteristic independently of all the other subjects in the population. We assume that p is small, say $p < \frac{1}{2}$. Then

$$f(x) = \sum_{m=0}^{N} f(x|m)g(m)$$

$$= \sum_{m=0}^{N} \frac{\binom{m}{x}\binom{N-m}{n-x}}{\binom{N}{n}} \binom{N}{m} p^m (1-p)^{N-m}$$

$$= \sum \binom{n}{x}\binom{N-n}{m-x} p^m (1-p)^{N-m}$$

$$= \binom{n}{x} p^x (1-p)^{n-x}$$

$$\times \sum \binom{N-n}{m-x} p^{m-x} (1-p)^{N-n-(m-x)}.$$

Thus,

$$f(x) = \binom{n}{x} p^x (1-p)^{n-x}, \qquad x = 0, 1, \ldots, n.$$

Lemma 14.1.   Let $Z = M - X$. Then the posterior probability of Z for given X is

$$P(Z = z|X = x) = \binom{N - n}{z} p^z (1 - p)^{N-n-z}, \qquad z = 0, 1, \ldots, N - n.$$

Proof:

$$
\begin{aligned}
P(Z = z|X = x) &= P(Z = z, X = x)/P(X = x) \\
&= P(Z = z)P(X = x|Z = z)/P(X = x) \\
&= P(M = z + x)P(X = x|M = z + x)/P(X = x) \\
&= \frac{\binom{N}{z+x} p^{z+x}(1 - p)^{N-(z+x)} \binom{z+x}{x} \binom{N-z-x}{n-x} / \binom{N}{n}}{\binom{n}{x} p^x (1 - p)^{n-x}} \\
&= \binom{N - n}{z} p^z (1 - p)^{N-n-z}.
\end{aligned}
$$

Hence,

$$
\begin{aligned}
P(M = m|X = x) &= P(Z = m - x|X = x) \\
&= \binom{N - n}{m - x} p^{m-x}(1 - p)^{N-n-(m-x)}, \\
& \qquad m = x, \ldots, N - n + x. \qquad \blacksquare
\end{aligned}
$$

Lemma 14.2.   We have, for the hypergeometric binomial model,

1. $v = \operatorname{var} Y = p(1 - p)$, $\operatorname{var} M = Np(1 - p)$,
2. $c = \operatorname{cov}(Y_i, Y_j) = -p^2/N$,
3. $NV(\mu) = v + (N - 1)c = p - 2p^2 + p^2/N$,
4. $EV(\bar{y}|\mu, \sigma^2) = \frac{(N-n)}{Nn}(v - c) = \frac{(N-n)}{Nn}\{p(1 - p) + p^2/N\}$, and
5. $V(\mu) + EV(\bar{y}|\mu, \sigma^2) = \frac{p(1-p)}{n} - \frac{(n-1)}{Nn}p^2$.

Proof: From Lemma 14.1, we have

$$E(M|X) = (N - n)p + X$$

and hence

$$EM = Np.$$

Further,

$$v = \operatorname{var} Y = E\{\operatorname{var}(Y|M)\} + \operatorname{var}\{E(Y|M)\}$$

$$= E\left[\frac{M}{N}\left(1 - \frac{M}{N}\right)\right] + \operatorname{var}\left(\frac{M}{N}\right)$$

$$= E\left(\frac{M}{N}\right) - E\left(\frac{M^2}{N^2}\right) + E\left(\frac{M^2}{N^2}\right) - \left\{E\left(\frac{M}{N}\right)\right\}^2$$

$$= p - p^2$$

$$\operatorname{var} M = E\{\operatorname{var}(M|X)\} + \operatorname{var}(EM|X)$$

$$= E\{(N-n)p(1-p)\} + \operatorname{var}\{(N-n)p + X\}$$

$$= (N-n)p(1-p) + np(1-p)$$

$$= Np(1-p).$$

Next,

$$c = \operatorname{cov}(Y_1, Y_2) = E(\operatorname{cov}(Y_i, Y_2)|M) + \operatorname{cov}(E(Y_1|M), E(Y_2|M))$$

$$= EE\{Y_1 Y_2|M\} - E\{E(Y_1|M) \cdot E(Y_2|M)\} + \operatorname{var}(M/N)$$

$$= E\left\{\frac{M}{N}\frac{(M-1)}{N}\right\} - E\left[\left(\frac{M}{N}\right)^2\right]$$

$$= -\frac{1}{N^2}E(M) + \frac{1}{N^2}Np(1-p) = -p^2/N$$

and (3)–(5) follow from their definitions. ∎

Consequently, the Bayes linear estimator of μ is

$$\tilde{\mu} = \frac{V(\mu)\bar{y} + pEV(\bar{y}|\mu, \sigma^2)}{\frac{p(1-p)}{n} - \frac{(n-1)}{Nn}p^2}$$

where the weights $V(\mu)$ and $EV(\bar{y}|\mu, \sigma^2)$ are given by Lemma 14.2,

$$\tilde{\mu} = \frac{\left(\frac{p-2p^2}{N} + \frac{p^2}{N^2}\right)\bar{y} + p \cdot \frac{(N-n)}{Nn}\left\{p(1-p) + \frac{p^2}{N}\right\}}{\frac{p(1-p)}{n} - \frac{(n-1)}{Nn}p^2}$$

$$= \frac{n\left(1 - 2p + \frac{p}{N}\right)\bar{y} + (N-n)\left(1 - p + \frac{p}{N}\right)p}{N(1-p) - (n-1)p}.$$

14.6   STRATIFIED SAMPLING

The prior information about Y_i contained in the label i and/or in the concomitant variable X_i, may be used to partition η in such a way that within each element of the partition, the Y_i's are approximately exchangeable a priori. Such partitioning may be by geographic region, sex and race, farm size, etc. This is analogous to the traditional stratification of the population so as to achieve within-stratum homogeneity.

Let $\eta_k, k = 1, 2, \ldots, K$ be the k strata (a partition of η). Let N_k be the number of units in η_k, Y_{ik} be the value of the variable for the ith unit in kth stratum and $\mathbf{Y}_k = (Y_{1k}, \ldots, Y_{N_k,k})$. Further, let μ_k and σ_k^2 be the mean and variance of the Y_{ik}'s in the kth stratum. That is,

$$\mu_k = N_k^{-1} \sum_{i=1}^{N_k} Y_{ik} \quad \text{and} \quad \sigma_k^2 = \sum_{i=1}^{N_k} (Y_{ik} - \mu_k)^2 / N_k \qquad (14.16)$$

and let

$$\mu = \sum_{k=1}^{K} N_k \mu_k / N = \text{the overall population mean}. \qquad (14.17)$$

Now assume that within the kth stratum the Y_{ik}'s have an exchangeable prior with mean m_k, variance v_k, and covariance $c_k (k = 1, \ldots, K)$. Also assume that the prior distributions are such that the observations in different strata are uncorrelated. That is, $\text{cov}(Y_{ik}, Y_{hj}) = 0$ for $k \neq j$. A sample s of n observations is obtained with n_k being the sample size in the kth stratum ($0 \leq n_k \leq N_k$), and for $(i, k) \in s$ one observes $Y_{ik} = y_{ik}$. Denote this sample by (s, y_s) and let $\bar{y}_k$ be the sample mean from the kth stratum.

Bayes Linear Estimator

By a routine generalization of the results for the simple random sampling design, one can show that the Bayes linear estimator of μ is

$$\tilde{\mu} = \sum_{k=1}^{K} \frac{N_k}{N} \left\{ \frac{\bar{y}_k V(\mu_k) + m_k EV(\bar{y}_k | \mu_k, \sigma_k^2)}{V(\mu_k) + EV(\bar{y}_k | \mu_k, \sigma_k^2)} \right\} = \sum_{k=1}^{K} \left(\frac{N_k}{N} \right) \tilde{\mu}_k \qquad (14.18)$$

where $\tilde{\mu}_k$ is (14.13) with subscript k added on.

Further

$$E_{(s,y_s)} V(\mu | (s, y_s)) \leq \sum_{k=1}^{K} \left(\frac{N_k}{N} \right)^2 V(\mu_k) \cdot \frac{EV(\bar{y}_k | \mu_k, \sigma_k^2)}{V(\mu_k) + EV(\bar{y}_k | \mu_k, \sigma_k^2)} \qquad (14.19)$$

where $V(\mu_k)$ and $EV(\bar{y}_k | \mu_k, \sigma_k^2)$ are given by Result 14.2 (ii) and (14.14), respectively, with subscript k added on. Here also, if the prior on the μ_k's is vague in the sense that $V(\mu_k)$ becomes large and $E(\sigma_k^2)$ is fixed, then

$$\tilde{\mu} \approx \sum_{k=1}^{K} \left(\frac{N_k}{N} \right) \bar{y}_k \qquad (14.20)$$

and

$$E_{(s,y_s)} V(\mu|(s, y_s)) \; \dot{\le} \; \sum_{k=1}^{K} \left(\frac{N_k}{N} \right)^2 \left\{ \frac{(N_k - n_k)E(\sigma_k^2)}{(N_k - 1)n_k} \right\} \tag{14.21}$$

which coincide with the expressions obtained by the classical sampling theory.

EXAMPLE 14.2

Consider the following numerical example. Suppose that we are interested in estimating the proportion of female students at Mars University using stratified sampling by class (freshmen, sophomore, junior, senior). The sizes of these strata N_k, sizes of the samples n_k drawn from the strata, prior proportions p_k of female students in the strata, and estimated proportions $\bar{y}_k$ are shown in the table:

Stratum	1	2	3	4
N_k	6500	6000	4000	3500
n_k	650	600	400	350
p_k	0.5	0.5	0.5	0.5
$\bar{y}_k$	0.58	0.51	0.45	0.48

Then the Bayes estimates of the proportions of female students in each stratum (using the formula $\hat{p}_k = \bar{y}_k + \alpha_k(p_k - \bar{y}_k)$[1] with $\alpha_k = (1 - n_k/N_k)$) are

Stratum	1	2	3	4
$\hat{p}_k$	0.508	0.501	0.49	0.498

Note that the Bayes estimates are very close to the prior proportion, since the ratios $n_k/N_k = 0.1$ are relatively small. Therefore, the Bayes estimate $\hat{p}$ of the overall population proportion is

$$\hat{p} = \sum_{k=1}^{4} \left(\frac{N_k}{N} \right) \hat{p}_k$$

$$= \left(\frac{6500}{20,000} \right)(0.508) + \left(\frac{6000}{20,000} \right)(0.501)$$

$$+ \left(\frac{4000}{20,000} \right)(0.495) + \left(\frac{3500}{20,000} \right)(0.498)$$

$$= 0.1651 + 0.1503 + 0.099 + 0.08715 = 0.50155 \,. \qquad \blacklozenge$$

---

[1] The Bayes linear estimator in each stratum assumes this form when $\bar{y}_k = \sum_1^{n_k} y_{ik}/n_k$, where the y_{ik} are i.i.d. Bernoulli (p_k) variables.

14.7 TWO-STAGE SAMPLING

Bayesian analogies can be obtained for cluster sampling and two (or higher) stage sampling schemes. Let us consider the special case of equal primary sampling unit sizes. The unequal size case can be handled in an analogous manner. Let Y_{ik} denote the value associated with the ith unit in the kth primary sampling unit (psu). In the traditional two stage sampling design, we take a random sample of psu's and then a random sample of units within each of the selected psu's. Let there be K psu's and M subunits within each psu and let $N = MK$. Note that cluster sampling is a special case of two-stage sampling in the sense that a complete census of each selected psu is taken and the psu's are called clusters.

Let μ_k and σ_k^2 be the unknown mean and variance within the kth psu. Also, let $\mu = \sum_{k=1}^{K} \mu_k / K$ be the overall population mean and let

$$\sigma^2 = \sum_{k=1}^{K} \sum_{i=1}^{M} (Y_{ik} - \mu)^2 / N. \tag{14.22}$$

Recall that

$$\mu_k = \frac{1}{M} \sum_{i=1}^{M} Y_{ik} \quad \text{and} \quad \sigma_k^2 = \frac{1}{M} \sum_{i=1}^{M} (Y_{ik} - \mu_k)^2. \tag{14.23}$$

Then we can write σ^2 as

$$\sigma^2 = \sigma_b^2 + \sigma_w^2 \tag{14.24}$$

where

$$\sigma_b^2 = \sum_{k=1}^{K} (\mu_k - \mu)^2 / K \quad \text{and} \quad \sigma_w^2 = \sum_{k=1}^{K} \sigma_k^2 / K. \tag{14.25}$$

Bayesian interpretation of classical sampling theory has been obtained by Ericson (1975) and related work by Bellhouse et al. (1977) and Sundberg (1983). The assumed class of prior distributions satisfy:

A1: conditional on μ_k and σ_k^2, the Y_{ik}'s are exchangeable for $i = 1, \ldots, M$ and also for $k \neq h$, Y_{ik}, and Y_{jh} are independent for all i and j.

A2: For $k = 1, \ldots K$, the ordered pairs (μ_k, σ_k^2) are exchangeable bivariate random vectors such that

$$E(\mu_k) = m, \quad V(\mu_k) = v, \quad \text{cov}(\mu_k, \mu_k') = c, \quad E(\sigma_k^2) = \phi \tag{14.26}$$

where $|c| < v/(K-1)$. The condition on c ensures the positive definiteness of the variance-covariance matrix of the psu means.

Then we have the following straightforward results of Ericson (1988).

Result 14.3. Let $\bar{y}_k$ be the mean of any subset of n_k units drawn from the kth psu. If a prior distribution on $\mathbf{Y}$ satisfies condition A1 above, then

$$E(Y_{ik}|\mu_k, \sigma_k^2) = E(\bar{y}_k|\mu_k, \sigma_k^2) = \mu_k \tag{14.27}$$

$$V(Y_{ik}|\mu_k, \sigma_k^2) = \sigma_k^2 \tag{14.28}$$

$$\text{cov}\,(Y_{ik}, Y_{jk}|\mu_k, \sigma_k^2) = -\sigma_k^2/(M-1) \tag{14.29}$$

and

$$V(\bar{y}_k|\mu_k, \sigma_k^2) = \frac{(M-n_k)\sigma_k^2}{(M-1)n_k} \tag{14.30}$$

where $V(\cdot)$ denotes the variance of $(\cdot)$.

Result 14.4. If the prior distribution on $\mathbf{Y}$ satisfies assumptions A1 and A2, then

$$E(\mu) = E(\bar{y}_k) = E(Y_{ik}) = m,$$

$$V(\mu) = \{v + (K-1)c\}/K \tag{14.31}$$

$$E(\sigma_w^2) = \phi, \quad E(\sigma_b^2) = (K-1)(v-c)/K \tag{14.32}$$

$$V(Y_{ik}) = \phi + v,$$

$$\text{cov}\,(Y_{ik}, Y_{jk}) = v - \phi(M-1)^{-1} \quad \text{for } j \neq i \tag{14.33}$$

$$\text{cov}\,(Y_{ik}, Y_{jh}) = \text{cov}\,(\bar{y}_k, \bar{y}_h) = c, \quad k \neq h \tag{14.34}$$

$$V(\bar{y}_k) = v + \frac{(M-n_k)\phi}{(M-1)n_k}, \quad E(\mu_k|\mu) = E(\bar{y}_k|\mu) = \mu \tag{14.35}$$

$$E_\mu V(\bar{y}_k|\mu) = E(\sigma_b^2) + \frac{(M-n_k)E(\sigma_w^2)}{(M-1)n_k} \tag{14.36}$$

and

$$E_\mu \,\text{cov}\,(\bar{y}_k, \bar{y}_h|\mu) = -E(\sigma_b^2)/(K-1). \tag{14.37}$$

Proof: (14.31) and (14.32) are trivial. To obtain (14.33) consider

$$E(Y_{ik} - m)^2 = E(Y_{ik} - \mu_k)^2 + E(\mu_k - m)^2$$

$$= E(\sigma_k^2) + v = \phi + v \tag{14.38}$$

$$\text{cov}\,(Y_{ik}, Y_{jk}) = E(Y_{ik} - m)(Y_{jk} - m)$$

$$= E(Y_{ik} - \mu_k)(Y_{jk} - \mu_k) + E(\mu_k - m)^2 \tag{14.39}$$

$$= -E(\sigma_k^2)/(M-1) + v$$

$$= -\phi(M-1)^{-1} + v.$$

Toward (14.34) consider, for $k \neq h$,

$$
\begin{aligned}
\text{cov}\,(Y_{ik}, Y_{jh}) &= E(Y_{ik} - m)(Y_{jh} - m) \\
&= E(Y_{ik} - \mu_k)Y_{jh} - \mu_h) + \text{cov}\,(\mu_k, \mu_h) = 0 + c\,.
\end{aligned}
$$

Similarly

$$
\begin{aligned}
\text{cov}\,(\bar{y}_k, \bar{y}_h) &= E(\bar{y}_k - m)(\bar{y}_h - m) \\
&= E(\bar{y}_k - \mu_k)(\bar{y}_h - \mu_h) + \text{cov}(\mu_k, \mu_h) = 0 + c\,.
\end{aligned}
$$

To get (14.35), consider

$$
\begin{aligned}
V(\bar{y}_k) &= E(\bar{y}_k - m)^2 \\
&= E(\bar{y}_k - \mu_k + \mu_k - m)^2 \\
&= E(\bar{y}_k - \mu_k)^2 + V(\mu_k) \\
&= EV(\bar{y}_k)|\mu_k, \sigma_k^2) + v \\
&= \frac{(M - n_k)}{(M - 1)n_k} E(\sigma_k^2) + v \\
&= \frac{(M - n_k)\phi}{(M - 1)n_k} + v
\end{aligned}
$$

and

$$
E(Y_k|\mu) = EE(Y_k|\mu_k)|\mu) = E(\mu_k|\mu) = \sum_{j=1}^{K} \mu_j \cdot \frac{1}{K} = \mu\,,
$$

since the μ_k are exchangeable. Toward (14.36) consider

$$
\begin{aligned}
V(\bar{y}_k|\mu) &= E(\bar{y}_k - \mu)^2|\mu) = E(\bar{y}_k - \mu_k)^2|\mu) + V(\mu_k|\mu) \\
&= \frac{(M - n_k)E(\sigma_k^2|\mu)}{(M - 1)n_k} + E\{(\mu_k - \mu)^2|\mu\}\,.
\end{aligned}
$$

However,

$$
E(\sigma_k^2|\mu) = \frac{1}{K}\sum_{j=1}^{K}\sigma_j^2 = \sigma_w^2
$$

and

$$
E\{(\mu_k - \mu)^2|\mu\} = \frac{1}{K}\sum_{j=1}^{K}(\mu_j - \mu)^2 = \sigma_b^2\,.
$$

Using these, we obtain (14.36). Finally consider

$$
\begin{aligned}
\mathrm{cov}\,(\bar{y}_k, \bar{y}_h | \mu) &= E\{(\bar{y}_k - \mu)(\bar{y}_h - \mu) | \mu\} \\
&= E\{(\bar{y}_k - \mu_k)(\bar{y}_h - \mu_k) | \mu\} + E\{(\mu_k - \mu)(\mu_h - \mu) | \mu\} \\
&= 0 + \frac{1}{K(K-1)} \sum_{i \neq j} \sum (\mu_i - \mu)(\mu_j - \mu) \\
&= -\frac{1}{K(K-1)} \sum_{j=1}^{K} (\mu_j - \mu)^2 = -\frac{1}{(K-1)} \sigma_b^2 .
\end{aligned}
$$

Now (14.37) is obtained by taking expectation on both sides of the preceding equation. ∎

Bayes Linear Estimator

Suppose we select a sample of r psu's $(1 \leq r \leq K)$ and then select n_k observations from kth sampled psu $(1 \leq n_k \leq M)$. Applying Corollary 14.1 to the joint distribution of μ and the $\bar{Y}_k$'s, Erickson (1988, p. 205) obtains the posterior mean of μ of the best linear approximation to be

$$
\tilde{\mu} = \frac{m EV(\hat{\mu}|\mu) + \hat{\mu} V(\mu)}{V(\mu) + EV(\hat{\mu}|\mu)} \tag{14.40}
$$

where $\hat{\mu}$ is the BLUE (best linear unbiased estimator) or WLSE (weighted least-squares estimator) of μ, given here by

$$
\hat{\mu} = \sum_{i=1}^{r} v_i \bar{Y}_i \Big/ \sum_{i=1}^{r} v_i \tag{14.41}
$$

$$
v_i = \left[\frac{K E(\sigma_b^2)}{K-1} + \frac{(M - n_i) E(\sigma_w^2)}{(M-1)n_i} \right]^{-1} \tag{14.42}
$$

$$
EV(\hat{\mu}|\mu) = \frac{E(\sigma_b^2)}{(K-1)} \left[\frac{K \sum_{i=1}^{r} v_i^2 - (\sum_{i=1}^{r} v_i)^2}{(\sum_{i=1}^{r} v_i)^2} \right]
$$

$$
+ \sum_{i=1}^{r} v_i^2 \left[\frac{(M - n_i) E(\sigma_w^2)}{(M-1)n_i (\sum_{i=1}^{r} v_i)^2} \right] . \tag{14.43}
$$

Also, it follows from (14.11) that

$$
EV(\mu|(s, Y_s)) \leq V(\mu) \left[1 - \frac{V(\mu) \sum_{i=1}^{r} v_i}{1 + c \sum_{i=1}^{r} v_i} \right] . \tag{14.44}
$$

Here also, if the prior information about μ becomes weak, the posterior mean of μ approaches $\hat{\mu}$, the BLUE of μ.

EXAMPLE 14.3 _____

Let $K = 5, r = 2, M = 100, n_1 = n_2 = 20, E\sigma_w^2 = 10, v = 50$, and $c = 5$. Then

$$E(\sigma_b^2) = \frac{4}{5}(50 - 5) = 36 \text{ [see (14.32)]}$$

$$V(\mu) = \{50 + 4(5)\}/5 = 14$$

$$v_1 = v_2 = \left[\frac{5(36)}{4} + \frac{(100 - 20)10}{49(20)}\right] = (45.40)^{-1} = 0.022,$$

$$\hat{\mu} = \frac{1}{2}(\bar{Y}_1 + \bar{Y}_2)$$

$$EV(\hat{\mu}|\mu) = \frac{36}{4}\left[\frac{5(2)(0.022)^2 - (0.044)^2}{(0.044)^2}\right]$$

$$+ 2 \cdot (0.022)^2\left[\frac{80(10)}{99(20)(0.044)^2}\right]$$

$$= 13.7.$$

Thus

$$\tilde{\mu} = \frac{m(13.7) + \hat{\mu}(14)}{13.7 + 14} = 0.505m + 0.495\hat{\mu}.$$

Similarly, Ericson (1988) considers Bayes ratio and regression estimators which are somewhat complicated (mathematically) and hence are not presented here. ◆

Next we consider response error and bias.

14.8 RESPONSE ERROR AND BIAS

As mentioned earlier the Bayesian approach naturally incorporates nonsampling biases and errors. Here we concentrate on response biases and errors. Ericson's (1988) method is a generalization of Schlaifer's (1959) approach. The prior information on bias and errors would be based on the sampler's previous experience. We consider the model in which all the observations are tainted.

Model. Let us observe for each $i \in s$,

$$X_i = Y_i + \beta + \epsilon_i \qquad (14.45)$$

where β is some unknown constant or average response bias and the ϵ_i are unobservable response errors. Let $(s, \mathbf{x}_s)$ be the observed sample, where $\mathbf{x}_s = (x_{i_1}, \ldots, x_{i_n})$ for $i_j \epsilon s$. We assume that there exists some prior information regarding β and the ϵ_i's which is incorporated into a joint prior distribution of $(\mathbf{Y}, \beta, \epsilon)$, where $\epsilon = (\epsilon_1, \ldots, \epsilon_N)'$ given by

$$f(\mathbf{Y}, \beta, \epsilon) = f(\beta, \epsilon|\mathbf{Y})f(\mathbf{Y}). \qquad (14.46)$$

Under the model (45) suppose that we have a symmetric prior on $\mathbf{Y}$ with

$$E(Y_i) = m, \qquad V(Y_i) = v, \qquad \text{and} \qquad \text{cov}(Y_i, Y_j) = c$$

$$i = 1, \ldots, N, \qquad i \neq j. \tag{14.47}$$

Also assume that the joint prior on (β, ϵ) conditional on $\mathbf{Y}$ has moments given by

$$E(\beta|\mathbf{Y}) = \bar{\beta}, \, V(\beta|\mathbf{Y}) = v_\beta, \, E(\epsilon_i|\mathbf{Y}) = 0,$$

$V(\epsilon_i|\mathbf{Y}) = v_\epsilon$ and the ϵ_i's are uncorrelated and $\text{cov}(\epsilon_i, \beta|\mathbf{Y}) = 0$, for all $i = 1, \ldots, N$.

Now let us observe $(s, \mathbf{x}_s)$ based on a sample s of n units. Let $\mathbf{Y}_s$ be the unknown vector of Y_i's for $i \in s$ and let $\mathbf{Y}_r((N - n) \times 1)$ be the unknown vector defined for the unsampled units. Using the assumptions made on the model given by (14.45), one can readily obtain

$$E(X_i) = m + \bar{\beta}, \qquad i = 1, \ldots, n,$$

$$E(Y_j) = m, \qquad j = 1, \ldots, N \tag{14.48}$$

$$\text{var } X_i = v + v_\beta + v_\epsilon, \qquad i = 1, \ldots, n \tag{14.49}$$

$$\text{cov}(X_i, X_j) = c + v_\beta, \qquad i \neq j = 1, \ldots, n$$

$$\text{cov}(X_i, Y_i) = v, \qquad i = 1, \ldots, n \tag{14.50}$$

and

$$\text{cov}(X_i, Y_j) = c, \quad i \neq j, \quad i = 1, \ldots, n, \quad j = 1, \ldots, N. \tag{14.51}$$

When $(\mathbf{Y}_r', \mathbf{Y}_s', \mathbf{X}_s')'$ have the mean vector and the covariance matrix given by (14.48)–(14.50), Ericson (1988) applies Result 14.1 by taking $\mathbf{X}_1 = (\mathbf{Y}_r', \mathbf{Y}_s')'$ and $\mathbf{X}_2 = \mathbf{X}_s$. After letting $\mu = \sum_{i=1}^N Y_i/N$, Ericson (1988) gives the posterior mean of μ to be (at least approximately)

$$E(\mu|s, \mathbf{x}_s)) = \frac{\text{var}(\mu)(\bar{X}_s - \bar{\beta}) + E_\mu \text{var}(\bar{X}_s|\mu)m}{\text{var } \bar{Y} + v_\beta + (v_\epsilon/n)} \tag{14.52}$$

where

$$\text{var}(\mu) = \{v + (N - 1)c\}/N,$$

$$\text{var}(\bar{Y}) = \{v + (n - 1)c\}/n \tag{14.53}$$

$$E_\mu\{\text{var}(\bar{X}_s|\mu)\} = \frac{(N - n)(v - c)}{Nn} + \frac{v_\epsilon}{n} + v_\beta \tag{14.54}$$

$$\bar{X}_s = \frac{1}{n}\sum_{i \in s} X_i \qquad \text{and} \qquad \bar{Y}_s = \frac{1}{n}\sum_{i \in s} Y_i \tag{14.55}$$

Also,

$$E_{\mathbf{x}_s}\{\text{var}(\mu|(s, x_s))\} \leq \frac{(\text{var } \mu) E_\mu\{\text{var}(\bar{X}_s|\mu)\}}{\text{var } \bar{Y}_s + (v_\epsilon/n) + v_\beta}. \tag{14.56}$$

Notice that the posterior mean of μ is the weighted average of the prior mean of μ and a simple "unbiased" estimator of μ with weights inversely proportional to the prior variance of μ and the prior expectation of the sampling variance of the estimator. Also note that the Bayes estimator of μ remains a linear combination of m and $\bar{X}_s - \bar{\beta}$, even if one does a complete census of the population. Also the upper bound to $E_{x_s}\{\text{var}(\mu|(s, \mathbf{x}_s))\}$ is never less than

$$\text{var}(\mu) \cdot \frac{v_\beta + (v_\epsilon/N)}{\text{var}(\mu) + v_\beta + (v_\epsilon/N)}. \tag{14.57}$$

Further note that in (14.53) $v - c = E(\sigma^2)$, where $\sigma^2 = \sum_{i=1}^{N}(X_i - \mu)^2/(N-1)$, the finite population variance.

Ericson (1988, Section 8.3) shows how to combine results from tainted observations with those from untainted observations. These results will not be presented here.

EXAMPLE 14.4

Let $N = 1000$, $n = 50$, $v = 16$, $c = 2$, $\bar{\beta} = 2$, $v_\beta = 3$, and $v_\epsilon = 25$. Then

$$\text{var } \mu = \frac{16 + (999)2}{1000} = 2.014$$

$$\text{var } \bar{Y} = \frac{16 + (49)2}{50} = 2.28$$

$$E_\mu \text{ var}(\bar{X}_s|\mu) = \frac{(1000 - 50)(16 - 2)}{(1000)(50)} + \frac{25}{50} + 3$$

$$= 0.266 + 0.5 + 3 = 3.766.$$

Thus the posterior mean of μ is given by

$$E(\mu|s, x_s) = \frac{2.014(\bar{X}_s - 2) + 3.766m}{2.28 + 3 + 0.5}$$

$$= \{2.014(\bar{X}_s - 2) + 3.766m\}/5.78$$

$$= 0.348\bar{X}_s + 0.652m - 0.697. \qquad \blacklozenge$$

■ PROBLEMS

14.1 We draw a simple random sample of $n = 100$ from a finite population of size $N = 5000$. If $m = 20$, $v = 100$, and $c = 10$, find the Bayes linear estimator of μ.

14.2 A simple random sample of $n = 15$ households was drawn from a city consisting of $N = 15{,}000$ households. If $\bar{y} = 4.0$, $m = 3$, $v = 25$, and $c = 2$, find the Bayes estimator of μ, the average number of people per household in that city.

14.3 In a small town of population $N = 100$, a random sample of size $n = 10$ was drawn and found that one of them has AIDS. Find the Bayes estimator of the total number of people (M) in the town who are suffering from AIDS. Assume that the prior distribution of M is binomial $(n, 0.1)$.

Hint: Use Lemma 14.2.

14.4 In a random sample of size $n = 25$, a certain diagnostic machine gave false alarms in one case. Find the Bayes estimator of the true proportion of cases in which the machine will give a false alarm. Assume that N is large, and the prior distribution of p is uniform $(0,1)$.

Hint: Use Lemma 14.2.

14.5 In two-stage sampling from a population, let $K = 10$, $r = 2$, $M = 50$, $n_1 = n_2 = 10$, $E\sigma_w^2 = 10$, $v = 25$, and $c = 2$. Find the Bayes linear estimator of μ as a linear combination of m and $\hat{\mu}$.

14.6 In two-stage sampling from a population, let $K = 20$, $r = 5$, $M = 40$, $n_1 = n_2 = 10$, $E\sigma_w^2 = 10$, $v = 50$, and $c = 2$. Obtain the Bayes linear estimator of μ.

14.7 Suppose that we are interested in estimating the proportion of students at Mars University who are currently using or have used drugs in the past. Suppose the sampling is done with stratifying the students by sex (i.e., males and females). Assume that the number M_k in kth stratum that is exposed to the drugs has a prior binomial distribution with parameters N_k and p_k $(k = 1, 2)$. The sizes of the strata, sizes of the samples n_k, the p_k and the sample proportions are shown in the table.

	Males	Females
N_k	5000	6000
n_k	500	600
p_k	0.1	0.05
$\hat{p}_k$	0.15	0.07

Find the Bayes linear estimator of the overall proportion of students that is exposed to drugs at Mars University.

14.8 A television station in a certain town is interested in estimating the proportion of the population of that town that watched a certain program aired on TV the night before. The station people take a random sample of males, females and children. Assume that the number M_k in the kth stratum is binomial (N_k, p_k) $(k = 1, 2, 3)$ and the data are as follows.

	Males	Females	Children
N_k	6500	7000	8000
n_k	130	140	160
p_k	0.4	0.5	0.2
$\hat{p}_k$	0.5	0.6	0.3

Find the Bayes linear estimator of proportion of people in that town that watched the program.

■ **REFERENCES**

14.1   Bellhouse, D. R., Thompson, M. E., and Godambe, V. P. (1977). Two-stage sampling with exchangeable prior distribution. *Biometrika* **64**, 97–103.

14.2   deFinetti, B. (1937). La Prevision, ses lois logiques, ses sources subjectives. Annales de L'Institut Henri Poincaré **7**, 1–68. Appearing in English translation with new notes in *Studies in Subjective Probability* (ed. H. E. Kyburg and H. E. Smokler) New York: John Wiley & Sons, 1964.

14.3   Ericson, W. (1969). Subjective Bayesian models in sampling finite populations: stratification. *New Developments in Survey Sampling* (ed. N. L. Johnson and H. Smith),New York: John Wiley & Sons, 326–357.

14.4   Ericson, W. (1975). *A Bayesian Approach to Two-Stage Sampling*. Tech. Report AFFDL-TR–75–145. *Air Force Dynamic Laboratory*. Wright Patterson AFB, Ohio, 1–25.

14.5   Ericson, W. (1983a). *A Bayesian Approach to Regression Estimation in Finite Populations*. Tech. Report No. 120, Department of Statistics, Univ. of Michigan, 1–21.

14.6   Ericson, W. (1983b). *Response Bias and Error in Sampling Finite Populations*. Tech. Report No. 122. Dept. of Statistics, Univ. of Michigan.

14.7   Ericson, W. A. (1988). Bayesian Inference in Finite Populations. *Handbook of Statistics* (Chapter 9) (ed. P. R. Krishnaiah and C. R. Rao).New York: Elsevier Science Publishers. B.V. 213–246.

14.8   Godambe, V. P. (1955). A unified theory of sampling from finite populations. *J. Roy. Statist. Soc.* **B17**, 269–278.

14.9   Kolehmarnen, O. (1981). Bayesian models in estimating the total of a finite population. Towards a general theory. *Scand. J. Statist.* **8**, 27–32.

14.10   Little, R. J. A. (1982). Models for nonresponse in sample surveys. *J. Amer. Statist. Assoc.* **77**, 237–250.

14.11   Rubin, D. B. (1976). Inference and missing data. *Biometrika* **63**, 581–590.

14.12   Schlaifer, R. (1959). *Probability and Statistics for Business Decisions*. New York: McGraw Hill.

14.13   Sundberg, R. (1983). The prediction approach and randomized population type models for finite population inference for two-stage samples. *Scand. J. Statist.* **10**, 223–238.

Then the estimator

$$\tilde{\theta} = \frac{1}{g} \sum_{i=1}^{g} \tilde{\theta}_i = g\hat{\theta} - \frac{(g-1)}{g} \sum_{i=1}^{g} \hat{\theta}_{-i} \tag{15.2}$$

has bias of order n^{-2}.

Tukey (1958) suggested that the g-values given by (15.1) can approximately be treated as independent and identically distributed variables in several situations. Then the statistic

$$\sqrt{g}(\tilde{\theta} - \theta)/s_{\tilde{\theta}} \tag{15.3}$$

where

$$(g-1)s_{\tilde{\theta}}^2 = \sum_{i=1}^{g} (\tilde{\theta}_i - \tilde{\theta})^2$$

should have approximate t distribution with $(g-1)$ degrees of freedom. This statistic could be used to obtain a confidence interval for θ. Tukey (1958) called the estimator $\tilde{\theta}$ the jackknifed one with the hope that it would be a rough-and-ready statistical tool.

Miller (1974) surveyed the results on the jackknife, and this paper served as a basis for the following. Since much of the subsequent research in this area has been advanced on the assumption that $g = n$ and $h = 1$, subsequently, we assume the same and the results can easily be generalized for arbitrary h.

Quenouille (1956) also proposed a jackknifed estimator which eliminates the $O(n^{-2})$ term from the bias. The second-order jackknife estimator of θ is

$$\tilde{\theta}^{(2)} = \frac{n^2 \tilde{\theta} - (n-1)^2 \sum_{j=1}^{n} \tilde{\theta}_{-j}/n}{n^2 - (n-1)^2} \tag{15.4}$$

where $\tilde{\theta}_{-j}$ is the estimator obtained by applying (15.2) to the sample of size $n-1$ with the jth observation removed. When expressed in terms of the original estimator $\hat{\theta}$, the second-order jackknife takes the form of

$$\tilde{\theta}^{(2)} = (2n-1)^{-1} \left[n^3 \hat{\theta} - (2n^2 - 2n + 1)(n-1) \left(\frac{1}{n} \sum \hat{\theta}_{-i} \right) \right.$$

$$\left. + (n-1)^2 (n-2) \left\{ \frac{2}{n(n-1)} \sum_{i<j} \hat{\theta}_{-ij} \right\} \right] \tag{15.5}$$

where $\hat{\theta}_{-ij}$ denotes the original estimator applied to the sample of size $n-2$ with the ith and jth observations removed. Then

$$E(\tilde{\theta}^{(2)}) = \theta + O(n^{-3}). \tag{15.6}$$

CHAPTER 15

THE JACKKNIFE METHOD

15.1 INTRODUCTION

The jackknife method was originally designed by Quenouille (1949, 1956) for reducing the bias of an estimator. An attractive feature of the jackknife method is that it can be applied in complicated situations where parametric modeling or theoretical treatment is impossible.

15.2 THE GENERAL METHOD

Quenouille (1949) gave a technique for reducing the bias of a serial correlation estimator, which is based on splitting the sample into two equal parts. In his 1956 paper he generalized the idea as follows. Split the sample into g equal groups of size h each. That is, $n = gh$. Let $X_1, \ldots, X_n$ be a random sample. Let $\hat{\theta}$ denote an estimator of the unknown parameter θ based on the sample of size n. Let $\hat{\theta}_{-i}$ be the estimate of θ based on the sample of size $(g-1)h$, where the ith group of size h has been deleted. Let

$$\tilde{\theta}_i = g\hat{\theta} - (g-1)\hat{\theta}_{-i} \qquad (i = 1, \ldots, g). \tag{15.1}$$

Schucany, Gray, and Owen (1971) suggest modifying the weights in order to achieve complete unbiasedness when the bias has only first and second terms in $1/n$ (i.e., $E(\hat{\theta}) = \theta + \frac{a_1}{n} + \frac{a_2}{n^2}$). Their estimator is

$$\tilde{\theta}^{(2)*} = \frac{1}{2}\left[n^2\hat{\theta} - 2(n-1)^2 \left(\frac{1}{n}\sum \theta_{-i} \right) \right.$$

$$\left. + (n-2)^2 \left\{ \frac{2}{n(n-1)} \sum_{i<j} \hat{\theta}_{-ij} \right\} \right] \tag{15.7}$$

They also obtain a generalized jackknife estimate as follows. Let $\hat{\theta}_1$ and $\hat{\theta}_2$ be two estimators of θ based on all parts of the data such that

$$E(\hat{\theta}_1) = \theta + f_1(n)b(\theta) \quad \text{and} \quad E\hat{\theta}_2 = \theta + f_2(n)b(\theta).$$

Then the estimator

$$\hat{\theta}^* = \{f_2(n)\hat{\theta}_1 - f_1(n)\hat{\theta}_2\}/\{f_2(n) - f_1(n)\} \tag{15.8}$$

is unbiased for θ.

EXAMPLE 15.1

The first-order jackknife given by (15.2) fits into the form (15.8) with $\hat{\theta}_1 = \hat{\theta}$, $\hat{\theta}_2 = \sum \hat{\theta}_{-i}/n$

$$f_1(n) = 1/n \quad \text{and} \quad f_2(n) = 1/(n-1).$$

One can easily generalize (15.8) for eliminating k separate terms in the bias, each of which factorizes into distinct functions of n and θ. In order to achieve this we need $k+1$ estimators whose expectations have the special form (see equation (2.6) in Miller (1974)). ◆

Gray et al. (1972) point out an interesting connection between the jackknife technique and the e_1 transformation which is used in numerical analysis to hasten the speed of convergence of a series. For a slowly converging series of numbers

$$S_n = \sum_{i=1}^{n} a_i \tag{15.9}$$

the transformation

$$e_1(S_n) = \frac{S_n - \rho(n)S_{n-1}}{1 - \rho(n)} \tag{15.10}$$

where $\rho(n) = a_n/a_{n-1} \neq 1$, will increase the rate of convergence to the limit S_∞. The analogy here is

$$S_n \sim E(\hat{\theta}), \quad S_{n-1} \sim E\left(\Sigma \hat{\theta}_{-i}/n \right),$$

$$S_\infty = \theta, \quad \rho(n) \sim (n-1)/n.$$

Notice that the jackknife estimate can be viewed as a linear extrapolate to $0 = 1/\infty$ from $\hat{\theta}$ at $1/n$ and $\Sigma \hat{\theta}_{-i}/n$ at $1/(n-1)$.

There are other methods for bias reduction. However, no systematic study exists for comparing the asymptotic effectiveness of jackknife in bias reduction with other procedures.

Certain Examples

Example (i)

Let θ denote the population mean and $\hat{\theta} = \bar{x} = \sum_1^n x_i/n$. When $h = 1$, $g = n$, we have

$$\hat{\theta}_{-i} = (n\hat{\theta} - x_i)/(n-1).$$

Let

$$\hat{\theta}_{(\cdot)} = \frac{1}{n}\sum_{i=1}^n \hat{\theta}_{-i}.$$

Then

$$\hat{\theta}_{(\cdot)} = \hat{\theta}, \qquad \hat{\theta}_{-i} - \hat{\theta}_{(\cdot)} = (\bar{x} - x_i)/(n-1)$$

and hence

$$\widehat{\text{var}} = \frac{(n-1)}{n}\sum_{i=1}^n (\hat{\theta}_{-i} - \hat{\theta}_{(\cdot)})^2 = \sum(x_i - \bar{x})^2/n(n-1)$$

the usual nonparametric estimate for the variance of an average $\bar{X}$. ◆

Example (ii)   [Efron, 1982, p. 14]

Let

$$\hat{\theta} = \sum_{i=1}^n (x_i - \bar{x})^2/(n-1)$$

and let

$$\mu_k = E\{(X - EX)^k\} \qquad \text{and} \qquad \hat{\mu}_k = n^{-1}\sum_{i=1}^n (x_i - \bar{x})^k.$$

By the definition of $\hat{\theta}$, we have

$$(n-2)\hat{\theta}_{-i} = \sum_{\substack{j=1 \\ j\neq i}}^n (x_j - \bar{x}_{-i})^2 \qquad \text{where } (n-1)\bar{x}_{-i} = \sum_{\substack{j=1 \\ j\neq i}}^n x_j$$

$$= (n\bar{x} - x_i).$$

Thus

$$(n-2)\hat{\theta}_{-i} = \sum_{\substack{j=1 \\ j\neq 1}}^{n}\left\{x_j - \frac{(n\bar{x} - x_i)}{n-1}\right\}^2$$

$$= \sum_{\substack{j=1 \\ j\neq i}}^{n}\left\{x_j - \bar{x} - \frac{(\bar{x} - x_i)}{n-1}\right\}^2$$

$$= \sum_{j=1}^{n}\left\{x_j - \bar{x} - \frac{(x_i - \bar{x})}{n-1}\right\}^2 - \left(\frac{n}{n-1}\right)^2(x_i - \bar{x})^2$$

$$= (n-1)\hat{\theta} + \frac{n}{(n-1)^2}(x_i - \bar{x})^2 - \frac{n^2}{(n-1)^2}(x_i - \bar{x})^2$$

$$= (n-1)\hat{\theta} - \frac{n}{n-1}(x_i - \bar{x})^2.$$

Consequently

$$(n-2)\hat{\theta}_{(\cdot)} = (n-2)n^{-1}\sum \hat{\theta}_{-i} = (n-1)\hat{\theta} - \hat{\theta} = (n-2)\hat{\theta}$$

and

$$(n-2)(\hat{\theta}_{-i} - \hat{\theta}_{(\cdot)}) = \hat{\theta} - \frac{n}{n-1}(x_i - \bar{x})^2.$$

Hence

$$(n-2)^2\sum(\hat{\theta}_{-i} - \hat{\theta}_{(\cdot)})^2 = \sum_1^n\left\{\frac{n}{n-1}(x_i - \bar{x})^2 - \hat{\theta}\right\}^2$$

$$= \left(\frac{n}{n-1}\right)^2\sum(x_i - \bar{x})^4 - n\hat{\theta}^2$$

$$= \left(\frac{n}{n-1}\right)^2 n\hat{\mu}_4 - n\left(\frac{n}{n-1}\right)^2\hat{\mu}_2^2.$$

Thus

$$\widehat{\text{var}} = \frac{n-1}{n}\sum(\hat{\theta}_{-i} - \hat{\theta}_{(\cdot)})^2$$

$$= (n-2)^{-2}\cdot\frac{n^2}{n-1}(\hat{\mu}_4 - \hat{\mu}_2^2).$$

We also have the following lemma.

Lemma 15.1. $\text{var }\hat{\theta} = n^{-1}\left[\mu_4 - \frac{n-3}{n-1}\mu_2^2\right].$

Proof: Let $y_i = x_i - \xi$ where $\xi = EX$ and also let $E\hat{\theta} = \sigma^2$. Then we can write

$$(n-1)\hat{\theta} = \sum_1^n (y_i - \bar{y})^2$$

$$= \frac{n-1}{n} \sum y_i^2 - \frac{1}{n} \sum\sum_{j\neq k} y_j y_k .$$

Hence

$$(n-1)(\hat{\theta} - \sigma^2) = \frac{n-1}{n} \sum (y_i^2 - \sigma^2) - \frac{1}{n} \sum\sum_{j\neq k} y_j y_k .$$

Thus

$$(n-1)^2 \operatorname{var} \hat{\theta} = (n-1)^2 E\{(\hat{\theta} - \sigma^2)^2\}$$

$$= E\left\{ \frac{n-1}{n} \sum (y_i^2 - \sigma^2) - \frac{1}{n} \sum\sum_{j\neq k} y_j y_k \right\}^2$$

$$= n^{-2} E\left[(n-1)^2 \left\{ \sum (y_i^2 - \sigma^2)^2 + \sum\sum_{i\neq k} (y_i^2 - \sigma^2)(y_j^2 - \sigma^2) \right\} \right.$$

$$\left. + \left(\sum\sum_{j\neq k} y_j y_k \right)^2 - 2(n-1) \sum_i \sum\sum_{j\neq k} (y_i^2 - \sigma^2) y_j y_k \right]$$

$$= n^{-2} \left[(n-1)^2 n E(y^2 - \sigma^2)^2 + 4E \left(\sum\sum_{j<k} y_i y_k \right)^2 \right]$$

$$= n^{-2} \left[n(n-1)^2 E(y^4 - \sigma^4) + 4\frac{n(n-1)}{2} \sigma^4 \right]$$

$$\operatorname{var} \hat{\theta} = n^{-1} \left[\mu_4 - \left(\frac{n-3}{n-1} \right) \mu_2^2 \right].$$

Hence $\widehat{\operatorname{var}}$ compares very well with $\operatorname{var} \hat{\theta}$.   ◆

Example (iii)   [The sample median]
Let $X_{(1)} \leq X_{(2)} \leq \cdots \leq X_{(n)}$ be the ordered sample of size n drawn from a population having F and f for its distribution and density functions, respectively, having θ for its median, while $n = 2m$ and m is a positive integer. Then the sample median is given by

$$\hat{\theta} = (X_{(m)} + X_{(m+1)})/2 .$$

Then

$$\hat{\theta}_{-i} = X_{(m+1)} \qquad \text{for } i \leq m$$

$$= X_{(m)} \qquad \text{for } i > m$$

$$\hat{\theta}_{(\cdot)} = \hat{\theta}$$

and

$$\sum_{i=1}^{n}(\hat{\theta}_{-i} - \hat{\theta}_{(\cdot)})^2 = \frac{n}{4}(X_{(m+1)} - X_{(m)})^2$$

$$\widehat{\text{Var}} = \frac{n-1}{n}\sum_{i=1}^{n}(\hat{\theta}_{-i} - \hat{\theta}_{(\cdot)})^2$$

$$= \frac{n-1}{4}(X_{(m+1)} - X_{(m)})^2 .$$

From the asymptotic results of Pyke (1965) we have

$$n\,\widehat{\text{var}} \xrightarrow{\text{law}} \frac{1}{4f^2(\theta)}\left(\frac{\chi_2^2}{2}\right)^2 \qquad \text{as } n \to \infty$$

where $[\chi_2^2/2]^2$ is a random variable with mean 2 and variance 20, whereas it is well known that (see, for instance, Kendall and Stuart (1958))

$$n \text{ var } \hat{\theta} \to 1/4f^2(\theta) .$$

Thus, $\widehat{\text{var}}$ is not even a consistent estimator of var $\hat{\theta}$. ◆

Example (iv)   [Ratio estimation]
Let Y and Z be random variables having means μ_Y, μ_Z, variances μ_{YY}, μ_{ZZ}, and covariance μ_{YZ}. We wish to estimate $\theta = \log(\mu_Y/\mu_Z)$. Then, the ratio estimate is given by $\hat{\theta} = \log(\bar{y}/\bar{z})$, where $\bar{y}$ and $\bar{z}$ are sample means based on the sample $((Y_i, Z_i), i = 1, \ldots, n)$. Recall that the delta method is based on Taylor's expansion of $\hat{\theta}$ around θ given by

$$\hat{\theta} = \theta + (\bar{z} - \mu_Z)/\mu_Z - (\bar{y} - \mu_Y)/\mu_Y .$$

Then

$$\text{var } \hat{\theta} \doteq n^{-1}[\mu_{YY}/\mu_Y^2 + \mu_{ZZ}/\mu_Z^2 - 2\mu_{YZ}/\mu_Y\mu_Z]$$

and the estimate of var $\hat{\theta}$ is obtained by replacing the population moments by the sample moments. Efron (1982, Table 3.2) compares the jackknife, the bootstrap and the delta method via 100 Monte Carlo trials of size $n = 10$ with (a) $Y \sim$ uniform $(0,1)$, $Z \sim$ standard exponential, Y is independent of Z and (b) $Y \sim$ uniform $(0,1)$, $2Z \sim$ (standard exponential)^2, Y is independent of Z. He surmises that the jackknife estimate of var $\hat{\theta}$ is almost unbiased. ◆

Example (v)

Let $\hat{\theta} = g(\overline{x})$, where g is some smooth function. Then

$$\hat{\theta}_{-i} = g\left(\frac{n\overline{x} - x_i}{n-1}\right) \doteq (g(\overline{x}) + \left(\frac{\overline{x} - x_i}{n-1}\right) g'(\overline{x}).$$

Hence

$$\hat{\theta}_{(\cdot)} \doteq g(\overline{x}) = \hat{\theta}.$$

Thus

$$\widehat{\mathrm{var}}\,\hat{\theta} = \frac{n-1}{n}[g'(\overline{x})]^2 \cdot (n-1)^{-2} \sum (x_i - \overline{x})^2$$

$$= [g'(\overline{x})]^2 \frac{\hat{\sigma}^2}{n}$$

where

$$\hat{\sigma}^2 = \sum (x_i - \overline{x})^2/(n-1).$$

Next the variance of $\hat{\theta} = g(\overline{x})$ is obtained by the delta method. We expand $g(\overline{x}) \doteq g(\mu) - (\overline{x} - \mu)g'(\mu)$, where $\mu = E(X)$. Hence

$$\mathrm{var}\,\hat{\theta} \doteq [g'(\mu)]^2 \, \mathrm{var}\,(\overline{X}).$$

Thus an estimate of $\mathrm{var}\,\hat{\theta}$ is obtained by replacing μ by $\overline{x}$ and σ^2 by $\hat{\sigma}^2$. Thus the delta method gives the same estimate of variance as the jackknife. ◆

Note that all the above examples are discussed in Efron (1982, Chapter 3).

15.3   MAIN APPLICATIONS

Jackknife estimates could usefully be employed in ratio and regression estimation. For a sample $(X_i, Y_i), i = 1, \ldots, n$, of paired random variables with $E(X_i) = \mu$ and $E(Y_i) = \eta$, the problem is to estimate $\theta = \eta/\mu$. In sample surveys, the auxiliary population mean μ is assumed to be known. Then $\hat{\eta} = \hat{\theta}\mu$, where $\hat{\theta}$ is the ratio estimate based on the bivariate sample of size n. Typically the ratio estimate of η will be more precise than the usual estimator $\overline{Y}$.

Durbin (1959) considered ratio estimation of β via the jackknife in the model

$$Y_i = \alpha + \beta X_i + e_i \tag{15.11}$$

where the e_i are independent and identically distributed either as normal or gamma. He studied the jackknife estimator of β of the form (2) with $g = 2$. He established that, neglecting terms of order n^{-4}, the jackknife estimator has both smaller bias and smaller variance than $\overline{Y}/\overline{X}$ when the e_i have a normal distribution. If the errors have a gamma distribution with coefficient of variation less than 1/4, the jackknife reduces the bias more, increases the variance slightly, and thereby reduces the mean-square error, when compared with $\overline{Y}/\overline{X}$. J. N. K. Rao (1965) and, J. N. K. Rao and Webster (1966) established that the optimal choice of g is n for the normal as well as the gamma auxiliary distribution. It should be noted that there are other alternative estimators besides the jackknife estimator.   The jackknife estimator is not always the best; however, it is not far behind the best estimator. Brillinger (1966) provides another application of the jackknife procedure in various types of sample surveys.

15.4   INTERVAL ESTIMATION

It has been shown that Tukey's conjecture pertaining to the distribution of the studentized version of the jackknife estimator is valid. That is, the statistic (15.3) has an approximate t distribution or a normal distribution for large g. The proofs consist of a power series expansion of $\tilde{\theta}$ in terms of the random variables $Y_1, \ldots, Y_n$, showing that the linear term in the expansion gives the correct behavior and the other terms are negligible for large g. Let $\theta = f(\mu)$, where $\mu = E(Y_i)$. Then Miller (1964) showed that for $\hat{\theta} = f(\overline{Y})$ the limiting distribution of the estimate of θ obtained from (15.3) with $g = n$ is standard normal provided that var $Y_i = \sigma^2 < \infty$ and f has bounded second derivative in the neighborhood of μ.

Miller (1974, Section 4.2) discusses the infinitesimal jackknife introduced by Jaeckel which serves as a bridge between the jackknife and the theory of robust estimation of the location of a symmetric distribution (see Huber (1972) for robust estimation).

15.5   TRANSFORMATIONS

People who advocate jackknife estimates suggest that variance stabilizing transformation on the estimator be performed before jackknifing it. Examples are jackknifing $\log s^2$ and $\tanh^{-1} r$ instead of s^2 and r where r denotes the sample correlation coefficient.   Sometimes transformation is a must in order to prevent distortion of the results. For instance, consider inference on σ^2. Without the log transformation, the pseudovalues $ns^2 - (n-1)s_{-i}^2$ can be negative. The jackknife method is blind to the negativity of the pseudovalues. With the log transformation, a negative pseudovalue corresponds to a small variance.

Miller (1974) applied the arc tan transformation to the correlation coefficients obtained from data on two methods of measuring blood flow. A standard method (DYE) is to inject dye into the pulmonary artery and sample the blood flow from the aorta. A computer integrates the experimentally determined curves of dye concentration to obtain a blood-flow measurement. The electromagnetic flow probe method (EFP) is a recent procedure. In it a cuff placed around the aorta creates an electrical field to measure the blood flow. The DYE method has more variability and the EFP has serious calibration problems. In order to assess the level of agreement between these two methods, simultaneous measurements were made on nine dogs. The data is:

DYE	1.15	1.70	1.42	1.38	2.80	4.70	4.80	1.41	3.90
EFP	1.38	1.72	1.59	1.47	1.66	3.45	3.87	1.31	3.75

The jackknife estimates of the correlation coefficient on the original and transformed values are presented in Table 15.1.[1]

---

[1] The data and Table 15.1 are reproduced here with the permission of Oxford University Press.

TABLE 15.1   Correlation Coefficients and Pseudo-values for Control Blood Flow Data with and without Transformation

i	r_{-i}	$\tilde{r}_i$	$\tanh^{-1} r_{-i}$	$\widetilde{\tanh}^{-1} r_{-i}$
0	0.944	–	1.780	–
1	0.941	0.978	1.743	2.076
2	0.943	0.956	1.768	1.876
3	0.943	0.956	1.768	1.876
4	0.941	0.977	1.745	2.060
5	0.977	0.690	2.218	−1.724
6	0.940	0.986	1.735	2.140
7	0.921	1.139	1.593	3.276
8	0.940	0.986	1.735	2.140
9	0.958	0.837	1.925	0.620

The untransformed jackknife estimate is $\tilde{r} = 0.945$ and its standard error is 0.041. The jackknife has increased the estimated value of ρ slightly, probably in the wrong direction. Because of the size of the standard error, the confidence interval for ρ will have its upper bound exceeding unity. The transformed values give $\widetilde{\tanh}^{-1} r = 1.593$, which is equivalent to an estimate of ρ of 0.921. The standard error of $\widetilde{\tanh}^{-1} r = 0.471$ yields a 95% confidence for ρ to be $(0.469, 0.991)$. The negative pseudovalue, -1.724, makes the interval so broad.

15.6   THE BIAS IN THE JACKKNIFE ESTIMATE OF THE VARIANCE

Efron and Stein (1981) investigate the jackknife estimate of variance for a statistic $S(X_1, \ldots, X_n)$ which is a symmetric function of i.i.d. random variables X_i. They show that the jackknife variance estimate tends always to be biased upward. This will be discussed in the following.

The Quenouille-Tukey jackknife provides very useful estimates of bias and variance that are of nonparametric nature. If $X_1, X_2, \ldots, X_n$ are i.i.d. random variables, let $S(X_1, \ldots, X_n)$ be a statistic designed to estimate a certain parameter of interest. We assume that S is symmetric in the arguments, that is, it is invariant with respect to all permutations of the arguments. Let

$$S_{(i)} = S(X_1, X_2, \ldots, X_{i-1}, X_{i+1}, \ldots, X_n) \tag{15.12}$$

the value of S computed when X_i is deleted from the sample. Then the jackknife estimate of var $S(X_1, \ldots, X_n)$ is

$$\widehat{\text{var}}S(X_1, \ldots, X_n) = \frac{n-1}{n} \sum_{i=1}^{n} \left[S_{(i)} - \overline{S} \right]^2 \tag{15.13}$$

where

$$\overline{S} = \frac{1}{n} \sum_{i=1}^{n} S_{(i)} \tag{15.14}$$

The estimate given by (15.13) is typically the variance estimate for the jackknife version of S given by $nS - (n-1)\overline{S}$. However, we can think of it either as the variance estimate of S itself or $S_{(i)}$. Note that $\widehat{\text{var}}\, S(X_1, \ldots, X_n)$ is defined entirely with respect to samples of size $n - 1$ rather than n. It would be helpful to view $\widehat{\text{var}}\, S(X_1, \ldots, X_n)$ as estimating the true variance, namely, $\text{var}\, S(X_1, \ldots, X_n)$, in two distinct steps: (i) a direct estimate of $\text{var}\, S(X_1, \ldots, X_{n-1})$, the variance for sample of size $n - 1$, and (ii) an adjustment to go from sample size $n - 1$ to sample size n. The direct estimate is

$$\widetilde{\text{var}}\, S(X_1, \ldots, X_{n-1}) = \sum_{i=1}^{n} [S_{(i)} - \overline{S}]^2 \tag{15.15}$$

and the sample size modification is

$$\widehat{\text{var}}\, S(X_1, \ldots, X_n) = \frac{n-1}{n} \widetilde{\text{var}}\, S(X_1, \ldots, X_{n-1}). \tag{15.16}$$

Note that (15.15) and (15.16) give (15.13).

Let
$$\mu = ES \quad \text{(the grand mean)} \tag{15.17}$$

$$A_i(x_i) = E\{S|X_i = x_i\} - \mu \quad (i\text{th main effect}) \tag{15.18}$$

$$B_{i,j}(x_i, x_j) = E\{S|X_i = x_i, X_j = x_j\} - E(S|X_i = x_i)$$
$$- E\{S|X_j = x_j\} + \mu \tag{15.19}$$

$$((i, j)\text{th second-order interaction), etc.}$$

Then Efron and Stein (1981) give the following decomposition of S.

Lemma 15.2.   [Decomposition lemma]   The random variable $S(X_1, \ldots, X_n)$ can be expressed as

$$S(X_1, \ldots, X_n) = \mu + \sum_i A_i(X_i) + \sum\sum_{i<j} B_{i,j}(X_i, X_j)$$

$$+ \sum\sum\sum_{i<j<k} C_{i,j,k}(X_i, X_j, X_k) + \cdots$$

$$+ H(X_1, X_2, \ldots, X_n) \tag{15.20}$$

where all $2^n - 1$ random variables on the right side of (15.20) have mean 0 and are mutually uncorrelated with each other.

Proof: The coefficient of μ on the right side of (15.20) is

$$1 - \binom{n}{1} + \binom{n}{2} - \binom{n}{3} + \cdots = (1 - 1)^n = 0.$$

Similarly the coefficient of $E\{S|X_i\}$ is $(1-1)^{n-1} = 0$ and the coefficient of $E\{S|X_i, X_j\}$ is $(1-1)^{n-2} = 0$, etc. $H(X_1, \ldots, X_n)$ has as its first term $S(X_1, \ldots, X_n)$, which is the only term that does not cancel. This establishes the decomposition (15.20). Also note that

$$EA_i(X_i) = E\{E(S|X_i) - \mu\} = 0. \tag{15.21}$$

Similarly

$$E\{B_{ij}(X_i, X_j)|X_i\} = E\{C_{ijk}(X_i, X_j, X_k)|X_i, X_j\} = \cdots$$

$$= E\{H(X_1, \ldots, X_n)|X_1, \ldots X_{n-1}\} = 0. \tag{15.22}$$

Hence all the random variables on the right have mean zero and correlation zero.   ∎

Remark 15.1. The above decomposition is a generalization of Hajek's (1968) projection of S into the space of linear statistics. The expansion (15.20) is unique in the sense that once the properties (15.21)–(15.22) hold, the terms μ, A_i, B_{ij}, C_{ijk}, $\ldots$ must be given by (15.17)–(15.19).

Letting

$$\alpha_i = \alpha(X_i) = nA_i(X_i), \qquad \beta_{ij} = \beta(X_i, X_j) = n^2 B_{ij}(X_i, X_j)$$

$$\gamma_{ijk} = \gamma(X_i, X_j, X_k) = n^3 C_{ijk}(X_i, X_j, X_k), \qquad \cdots$$

we can write (15.20) as

$$S(X_1, X_2, \ldots, X_n) = \mu + \frac{1}{n}\sum \alpha_i + \frac{1}{n^2}\sum\sum_{i<j}\beta_{ij} + \frac{1}{n^3}\sum\sum\sum_{i<j<k}\gamma_{ijk}$$

$$+ \cdots + n^{-n}\eta_{1,2,\ldots,n}. \tag{15.23}$$

EXAMPLE 15.2

Let $S(X_1, X_2, \ldots, X_n) = n^{-1}\sum_{i=1}^{n}(X_i - \overline{X})^2$, where $\overline{X} = \sum_1^n X_i/n$, where the X's have mean ξ and variance σ^2. Then writing

$$S = n^{-1}\sum_{i=1}^{n}(X_i - \xi)^2 - n^{-2}\left\{\sum(X_i - \xi)\right\}^2$$

$$= n^{-1}\left\{(1 - n^{-1})\sum(X_i - \xi)^2 - 2n^{-1}\sum\sum_{i<j}(X_i - \xi)(X_j - \xi)\right\}$$

we obtain

$$\mu = \frac{n-1}{n}\sigma^2, \qquad \alpha_i(X_i) = \left(\frac{n-1}{n}\right)\{(X_i - \xi)^2 - \sigma^2\}$$

and

$$\beta_{ij}(X_i, X_j) = -2(X_i - \xi)(X_j - \xi)$$

and all higher-order terms are equal to zero.

If $\sigma_\alpha^2 = \operatorname{var}\alpha_i(X_i)$, $\sigma_\beta^2 = \operatorname{var}\beta(X_i, X_j)$, $\sigma_\gamma^2 = \operatorname{var}\gamma(X_i, X_j, X_k)$ etc., we have

$$\operatorname{var} S(X_1, \ldots, X_n) = \frac{\sigma_\alpha^2}{n} + \binom{n-1}{1}\frac{\sigma_\beta^2}{2n^3} + \binom{n-1}{2}\frac{\sigma_\gamma^2}{3n^5} + \cdots + \frac{\sigma_\eta^2}{n^{2n}} \quad (15.24)$$

Then we state the main result of Efron and Stein (1981).   ◆

Theorem 15.1.

$$E\{\widetilde{\operatorname{var}}\, S(X_1, X_2, \ldots, X_{n-1})\} - \operatorname{var} S(X_1, X_2, \ldots, X_{n-1})\}$$

$$= \frac{1}{2}\binom{n-1}{1}\frac{\sigma_\beta^2}{(n-1)^3} + \frac{2}{3}\binom{n-2}{2}\frac{\sigma_\gamma^2}{(n-1)^5} + \cdots \quad (15.25)$$

there being $(n-2)$ terms on the right side of (15.25).

Corollary 15.1. $E\{\widetilde{\operatorname{var}}\, S(X_1, X_2, \ldots, X_{n-1})\} \geq \operatorname{var} S(X_1, X_2, \ldots, X_{n-1}).$

Proof: See Efron and Stein (1981, p. 589).   ∎

EXAMPLE 15.3

Let $S(X_1, \ldots, X_n) = n^{-1}\sum_1^n (X_i - \overline{X})^2$, where $EX_i = \xi$ and $\operatorname{var} X_i = \sigma^2$. Then

$$E\{\widetilde{\operatorname{var}}\, S(X_1, \ldots X_{n-1})\} - \operatorname{Var} S(X_1, X_2, \ldots, X_{n-1})$$

$$= \frac{1}{2}\binom{n-2}{1}\frac{\sigma_\beta^2}{(n-1)^3}$$

where

$$\beta_{ij} = \beta(X_i, X_j) = -2(X_i - \xi)(X_j - \xi)$$

$$\sigma_\beta^2 = 4\operatorname{var}\{(X_i - \xi)(X_j - \xi)\}$$

$$= 4 \cdot E\{(X_i - \xi)^2(X_i - \xi)^2\} = 4\sigma^4.$$

◆

■ PROBLEMS

15.1   Let a random sample of size 5 guinea pigs be taken and their weights be (1, 2, 3, 4, 5). Find the first-order and second-order Quenouille estimators of the average weight of the guinea pigs.
Hint: See Equations (15.2) and (15.5) and let $g = 5$ and $h = 1$.

15.2   For the data in Problem 15.1, suppose we want to estimate the population variance. Find the first-order Quenouille estimator of the population variance, using $g = 5$ and $h = 1$.

15.3   Compute an estimate of the variance of the estimate obtained in Problem 15.2. (See Example (ii).)

15.4   Let a random sample of 6 guinea pigs be taken and their weights be (1, 2, 3, 4, 5, 6). Proceed as in Example (iii) and evaluate the asymptotic estimated variance of the sample median and compare it with the well-known variance of the sample median.
Hint: See Example (iii).

15.5   A random sample of 5 pairs of mutual funds is obtained and yielded the following data for the percentage of returns for the year 1996.

Load (X)	18.2	9.5	12.0	21.1	10.2
Noload (Y)	10.9	11.7	20.2	15.6	12.9

Find the first-order Quenouille estimate of the ratio of the average percentage of returns for the year 1996. Also, compare the jackknife and delta method variance estimates.
Hint: Let $\theta = \log(\mu_X/\mu_Y)$. See Example (iv).

15.6   For the data in Problem 15.1, suppose we are interested in estimating the square of the population mean. Compare the jackknife and delta method variance estimates.
Hint: See Example (v).

■ REFERENCES

15.1   Brillinger, D. R. (1966). The application of the jackknife to the analysis of sample surveys, *Commentary* **8**, 74–80.

15.2   Durbin, J. (1959). A note on the application of Quenouille's method of bias reduction to the estimation of ratios, *Biometrika* **46**, 477–480.

15.3   Efron, B. (1982). *The Jackknife, the Bootstrap and Other Resampling Plans*. Society for Industrial and Applied Mathematics #38, Philadelphia, PA.

15.4   Efron, B. and Stein, C. (1981). The jackknife estimate of variance, *Ann. Statist.* **9**, 586–596.

15.5   Gray, H. L., Watkins, T. A., and Adams, J. E. (1972). On the jackknife statistic, its extensions, and its relations to e_n-transformations, *Ann. Math. Statist.* **43**, 1–30.

15.6   Hajek, J. (1960). Asymptotic normality of simple linear rank statistics under alternatives, *Ann. Math. Statist.* **39**, 325–346.

15.7   Huber, P. (1972). Robust statistics: A review, *Ann. Math. Statist.* **43**, 1041–1067.

15.8   Kendall, M. and Stuart, A. (1958). *The Advanced Theory of Statistics*. London: Griffin.

15.9   Miller, R. G. (1964). A trustworthy jackknife, *Ann. Math. Statist.* **35**, 1594–1605.

15.10   Miller, R. G. (1974). The jackknife - a review, *Biometrika* **61**, 1–15.

15.11   Pyke, R. (1965). Spacings, *J. Roy. Statist. Soc.* **B27**, 395–449.

15.12   Quenouille, M. H. (1949). Approximate tests of correlation in time series, *J. Roy. Statist. Soc.* **B11**, 68–84.

15.13   Quenouille, M. H. (1956). Notes on bias in estimation, *Biometrika* **52**, 647–649.

15.14   Rao, J. N. K. (1965). A note on the estimation of ratios by Quenouille's method, *Biometrika* **52**, 647–649.

15.15   Rao, J. N. K. and Webster, J. (1966). On two methods of bias reduction in the estimation of ratios, *Biometrika* **53**, 571–577.

15.16   Schucany, W. R., Gray, H. L., and Owen, D. B. (1971). On bias reduction in estimation, *J. Amer. Statist. Assoc.* **66**, 524–533.

15.17   Tukey, J. W. (1958). Bias and confidence in not-quite large samples (abstract), *Ann. Math. Statist.* **29**, 614.

CHAPTER 16

THE BOOTSTRAP METHOD

16.1   INTRODUCTION

The attraction of the jackknife and the bootstrap methods is that they can be applied to complicated situations where parametric modeling and/or theoretical treatment is impossible. Efron[1] (1979) pioneered the bootstrap method and then expanded on several situations (e.g., the estimation of the population median) where the bootstrap is superior to the jackknife. (See also Efron and Tibshirani, 1993.)

16.2   THE BOOTSTRAP METHOD

Let $X_1, X_2, \ldots, X_n$ be a random sample from a population having $F(x)$ and $f(x)$ for its distribution and density functions, respectively. Let θ be a parameter of interest and $\hat{\theta}(X_1, \ldots, X_n)$ be an estimate of θ which is symmetric in $X_1, \ldots, X_n$. We write the standard deviation of $\hat{\theta}$ as

$$\sigma_{\hat{\theta}} = \sigma(F, n, \hat{\theta}) = \sigma(F). \tag{16.1}$$

The last notation is to make it clear that the standard deviation is a function of the unknown distribution function F. The bootstrap estimate of the standard deviation is

---

[1] Efron (1982) served as a source for this chapter.

obtained by replacing the unknown F by $\hat{F}$, the maximum-likelihood estimate of F. That is,

$$\hat{\sigma}_{\hat{\theta}} = \sigma(\hat{F}). \tag{16.2}$$

EXAMPLE 16.1

The sample mean $\bar{x}$ estimates the population mean μ. The standard deviation of $\bar{x}$ is $(\mu_2/n)^{\frac{1}{2}}$, where

$$\mu_2 = E(X - \mu)^2, \qquad \mu = EX.$$

Hence,

$$\hat{\sigma}_{\bar{X}} = (\hat{\mu}_2/n)^{\frac{1}{2}} \qquad \text{where} \hat{\mu}_2 = n^{-1} \sum_{i=1}^{n} (x_i - \bar{x})^2$$

where $x_1, \ldots, x_n$ and $\bar{x}$ denote the observed values of $X_1, \ldots, X_n$ and $\bar{X}$, respectively.

Since $\hat{\mu}_2$ is biased downward (i.e., $E\hat{\mu}_2 < \mu_2$), we can rescale $\hat{\mu}_2$ by multiplying with a factor $n/(n-1)$, and hence we have

$$\widehat{SD} = \hat{\sigma}_{\bar{X}} = \left\{ (n-1)^{-1} \sum_{1}^{n} (x_i - \bar{x})^2 \right\}^{\frac{1}{2}}. \tag{16.3}$$

Usually $\sigma(F)$ does not have an explicit form. In order to compute $\widehat{SD}$, we proceed with the following Monte Carlo algorithm.

1. Let $\hat{F}$ be the MLE of F (i.e., it assigns probability mass $1/n$ at each observation x_i.

2. Draw a bootstrap sample from $\hat{F}$, namely $X_1^*, \ldots, X_n^*$ distributed identically as $\hat{F}$, and calculate $\hat{\theta}^* = \hat{\theta}(X_1^*, \ldots, X_n^*)$.

3. Repeat step 2 B times (where B is large) and obtain the bootstrap replications $\hat{\theta}_1^*, \ldots, \hat{\theta}_B^*$ and compute

$$\widehat{SD} = \left\{ \sum_{j=1}^{B} (\hat{\theta}_j^* - \bar{\hat{\theta}}^*)^2 / (B-1) \right\}^{\frac{1}{2}} \tag{16.4}$$

where

$$\bar{\hat{\theta}}^* = \sum_{j=1}^{B} \hat{\theta}_j^* / B.$$

If we let $B \to \infty$, then $\widehat{SD}$ in (16.4) equals SD given by (16.1). In practice, we want B to be finite because of computational costs. Based on some numerical computations, Efron (1982, p. 28) infers that $B = 100$ is as good as $B = 200, 512,$ or 1000.   ◆

EXAMPLE 16.2

Let the random sample consist of 5 guinea pigs whose weights are 1, 2, 3, 4, and 5 pounds:

$$\bar{x} = (1 + 2 + 3 + 4 + 5)/5 = 3$$

$$s^2 = \frac{1}{4} \sum_1^5 (x_i - 3)^2 = \frac{10}{4} = 2.5$$

$$\text{standard error of } \bar{X} = \frac{s}{\sqrt{n}} = (2.5/5)^{\frac{1}{2}} = 0.707 .$$

Now let us draw $B = 10$ bootstrap samples.   Using the random-number tables, we obtain the samples to be

$$(1, 2, 2, 3, 5), \quad (3, 4, 5, 5, 2), \quad (1, 3, 4, 1, 2), \quad (5, 3, 1, 4, 2), \quad (5, 4, 4, 2, 5)$$
$$(3, 3, 4, 1, 5), \quad (4, 1, 2, 2, 5), \quad (4, 4, 2, 4, 2), \quad (2, 5, 3, 2, 4), \quad (5, 4, 1, 5, 5)$$

yielding

$$\hat{\theta}_1^* = 2.6, \quad \hat{\theta}_2^* = 3.8, \quad \hat{\theta}_3^* = 2.2, \quad \hat{\theta}_4^* = 3, \quad \hat{\theta}_5^* = 4,$$
$$\hat{\theta}_6^* = 3.2, \quad \hat{\theta}_7^* = 2.8, \quad \hat{\theta}_8^* = 3.2, \quad \hat{\theta}_9^* = 3.2, \quad \hat{\theta}_{10}^* = 4,$$
$$\bar{\hat{\theta}}^* = 3.2,$$

and

$$\sum_1^{10} (\hat{\theta}_j^* - \bar{\hat{\theta}}^*)^2 = 105.6 - 10(3.2)^2 = 3.2 .$$

Thus,

$$\widehat{SD} = (3.2/9)^{1/2} = 0.596 .$$

Notice that $\widehat{SD}$ is not close to the standard error of $\bar{X}$ because B is very small.   ◆

16.3   BOOTSTRAP METHODS FOR GENERAL PROBLEMS

Let $\mathbf{X} = (X_1, \ldots, X_n)$ and $R(\mathbf{X}, F)$ a function of $\mathbf{X}$ which is of interest to us. Suppose we wish to estimate some characteristic of the distribution of R, say $E_F R$ or $P_F(R < a)$ for specified a. We proceed along the lines of the bootstrap algorithm, except that in step 2 we compute

$$R^* = R(\mathbf{X}^*, \hat{F})$$

instead of $\hat{\theta}$, and at step 3 we compute the characteristic of R that we are interested in. For example, if we are interested in estimating $E_F R$, we compute

$$E_* R^* = B^{-1} \sum_{j=1}^B R_j^* .$$

On the other hand, if we are interested in $P_F(R < a)$, we compute

$$P_*(R^* < a) = \{ \#(R_j^* < a) \} / B .$$

16.4   THE BOOTSTRAP ESTIMATE OF BIAS

If we wish to estimate the bias of a functional estimate $\hat{\theta}(\hat{F})$ of $\theta(F)$, namely $\theta(\hat{F}) - \theta(F)$, then we take $R(\mathbf{X}, F) = \theta(\hat{F}) = \theta(\hat{F}^*) - \theta(\hat{F}) = \hat{\theta}^* - \hat{\theta}$ where $\hat{\theta}^* = \theta(\hat{F}^*)$, $\hat{F}^*$ being the empirical distribution based on the bootstrap sample $\mathbf{X}^*$. That is, $\hat{F}^*$ assigns probability mass M_i^*/n on x_i where M_i^* is the number of times x_i appears in the bootstrap sample.

The bootstrap estimate of bias is

$$\widehat{\text{Bias}} = E_* R^* = \frac{1}{B} \sum_{j=1}^{B} \hat{\theta}_j^* - \hat{\theta} = \bar{\hat{\theta}}^* - \hat{\theta}. \tag{16.5}$$

In Example 16.2, $\bar{\hat{\theta}}^* = 3.2$ whereas $\hat{\theta} = 3$, and hence

$$\widehat{\text{Bias}} = 3.2 - 3.0 = 0.2.$$

Remark 16.1. The estimate $\hat{\theta}$ need not be the same functional as θ. For example, $\theta(F) = E_F X$ and $\hat{\theta} = $ sample median. If we write the bias as

$$\widehat{\text{Bias}} = E_F \hat{\theta} - \theta(F) = \beta(F, n, \hat{\theta}, \theta) = \beta(F)$$

a function of the unknown F when once the sample size n, and the form $\hat{\theta}(\cdot, \ldots, \cdot)$ and $\theta(\cdot)$ are fixed, then the bootstrap estimate of the bias is

$$\widehat{\text{Bias}} = \beta(\hat{F}).$$

Efron (1982, Theorem 6.1) has proved that if $\hat{\theta} = \theta(\hat{F})$ is a quadratic functional, then

$$\widehat{\text{Bias}}_{\text{Boot}} = \frac{n-1}{n} \widehat{\text{Bias}}_{\text{Jack}}.$$

16.5   CASE OF FINITE SAMPLE SPACE

The bootstrap method is much more transparent when the sample space is finite. In particular, let X take values $1, 2, \ldots, L$ only. Then the distribution F can be written in terms of $\mathbf{f} = (f_1, \ldots, f_L)$, where

$$f_i = P_F(X = i) \quad \text{and} \quad \hat{\mathbf{f}} = (\hat{f}_1, \ldots, \hat{f}_L)$$

where $\hat{f}_i = \#(x_j = i)/n$. Here the general random variable $R(\mathbf{X}, F)$ takes the form of

$$R(\mathbf{X}, F) = Q(\hat{\mathbf{f}}, \mathbf{f}) \tag{16.6}$$

where Q is some function of $\hat{f}$ and f, provided $R(\mathbf{X}, F)$ is invariant under all permutations of the X_i. Note that $n\hat{\mathbf{f}}$ has a multinomial distribution with n for the number of trials and $\mathbf{f}$ for the true probability vector. In brief,

$$\hat{\mathbf{f}} \mid \mathbf{f} \sim \frac{1}{n} \text{Mult}_L(n, \mathbf{f}). \tag{16.7}$$

The bootstrap distribution of $X_1^*, \ldots, X_n^*$ which are distributed i.i.d. on $\hat{F}$ can be evaluated in terms of $\hat{f}^* = (\hat{f}_1^*, \ldots, \hat{f}_L^*)$, where $\hat{f}_i = \#(X_j^* = l)/n$. Thus,

$$\hat{\mathbf{f}}^* \mid \mathbf{f} \sim \frac{1}{n} \operatorname{Mult}_L(n, \hat{\mathbf{f}}). \tag{16.8}$$

As Efron puts it, "The bootstrap method estimates the unobservable distribution of $Q(\hat{\mathbf{f}}, \mathbf{f})$ under (16.7) by the observable distribution of $Q^* = Q(\hat{\mathbf{f}}^*, \hat{\mathbf{f}})$ under (16.8)." As a special case, consider the following example.

EXAMPLE 16.3

Let $X \overset{d}{=}$ Bernoulli with $P(X = 0) = f_1$ and $P(X = 1) = f_2$. Let $\theta(\mathbf{f}) = f_2$ and $R(\mathbf{X}, F) = Q(\hat{\mathbf{f}}, \mathbf{f}) = \hat{f}_2 - f_2$, the deviation of the observed from the true frequency for the second category. Then the bootstrap distribution of

$$Q^* = \hat{f}_2^* - \hat{f}_2$$

is

$$\frac{1}{n} B(n, \hat{f}_2) - \hat{f}_2$$

where $B(n, \hat{f}_2)$ is a binomial random variable with n trials and $\hat{f}_2$ for the probability of a success. The first two moments of the bootstrap distribution of Q^* are

$$E_* Q^* = 0 \quad \text{and} \quad \operatorname{var}_* Q^* = \hat{f}_1 \hat{f}_2 / n.$$

As $n \to \infty$, both $\hat{\mathbf{f}} - \mathbf{f}$ under (16.7) and $\hat{\mathbf{f}}^* - \hat{\mathbf{f}}$ under (16.8) approach the same L-dimensional normal distribution $(\mathbf{0}, \Sigma/n)$, where $\Sigma_f = f_i(1 - f_i)$ for the diagonal elements and $-f_i f_j$ for the off-diagonal elements.

Efron asserts that for a well-behaved function Q, the bootstrap distribution of Q^* is asymptotically the same as the true distribution of Q. This justifies estimation of $E_F R$ by $E_* R^*$, when n is sufficiently large.

When the sample space is not finite, it has been shown in the statistical literature that for certain choices of Q, the asymptotic distribution of R converges to the true distribution of R (the convergence rate faster than the rate of convergence in the usual central limit theorem). For references, see Efron (1982, p. 35). ◆

EXAMPLE 16.4

[Binomial case] Let the random sample of size 10 from the Bernoulli population yield

$$(X_0, \ldots, X_9) = (0, 1, 1, 0, 0, 0, 1, 0, 1, 0)$$

(i.e., $X_1 = X_2 = X_6 = X_8 = 1$, and $X_0 = X_3 = \cdots = X_9 = 0$). Then the subscripts associated with the X's of the 10 bootstrap sample sizes are:

$$(1, 7, 4, 5, 9, 6, 8, 6, 3, 3), \quad (8, 5, 6, 4, 6, 1, 3, 7, 9, 3)$$
$$(7, 1, 5, 7, 9, 9, 4, 1, 3, 6), \quad (6, 4, 2, 6, 5, 6, 5, 1, 9, 7)$$
$$(8, 6, 1, 3, 5, 7, 9, 4, 7, 3), \quad (1, 9, 3, 5, 7, 1, 4, 6, 8, 7)$$
$$(3, 7, 2, 9, 3, 5, 8, 8, 1, 1), \quad (9, 1, 5, 6, 1, 5, 4, 7, 5, 4)$$
$$(6, 6, 9, 1, 3, 5, 4, 8, 1, 5), \quad (8, 8, 9, 7, 9, 6, 1, 2, 1, 1)$$

We want to estimate $\hat{f}_2 - f_2$, where $\hat{f}_2 = 4/10 = 0.4$. The bootstrap sample of $\hat{f}_2$ is $(\hat{f}_{2,1}^*, \ldots, \hat{f}_{2,10}^*)$ given by

$$(0.4, 0.4, 0.2, 0.5, 0.3, 0.4, 0.3, 0.3, 0.5, 0.7)$$

yielding $\bar{\hat{f}}_2^* = \frac{1}{10}(0.4 + \cdots + 0.7) = 0.40$. Thus, the bootstrap estimate of the bias $\hat{f}_2 - f_2$ is

$$\bar{\hat{f}}_2^* - \hat{f}_2 = 0.40 - 0.40 = 0.00.$$

We do not expect this zero-bias phenomenon all the time.   ◆

16.6 REGRESSION PROBLEMS

Up till now, we have been discussing one-sample problems in which the random variables X_i have the same distribution F. Bootstrapping methods can readily be applied to more complex structures. In the following, we will discuss applicability of bootstrap methods to regression problems.

Consider the model

$$Y_i = g_i(\beta) + \epsilon_i, \qquad i = 1, \ldots, n. \tag{16.9}$$

Let y_i denote the observed value of $Y_i (i = 1, \ldots, n)$. We assume that the functions $g_i(\cdot)$ are of known form, depending on some specified vector of constants (or covariates) c_i, while β is a $p \times 1$ vector of unknown parameters. The errors ϵ_i are i.i.d. as F, where either $E_F \epsilon_i = 0$ or the ϵ_i have median zero. Having observed $\mathbf{Y} = (Y_1, \ldots, Y_n)'$ as $\mathbf{y} = (y_1, \ldots, y_n)'$, we wish to estimate the parameter vector β by some criterion such as minimizing the distance $D(\mathbf{y}, \eta)$ between $\mathbf{y}$ and the vector of predictors

$$\eta(\beta) = (g_1(\beta), \ldots, g_n(\beta))'.$$

That is,

$$\hat{\beta} : \min_{\beta} \; D(\mathbf{y}, \eta(\beta)). \tag{16.10}$$

The usual choice of D is $D(\mathbf{y}, \eta) = \sum_{i=1}^{n}(y_i - \eta_i)^2$, $\eta_i = g_i(\beta)$. We further assume that the model is too complicated to be handled by the standard analysis. For example, $g_i(\beta) = \exp(c_i\beta)$, F is of unknown form, and $D(\mathbf{y}, \eta) = \sum_{1}^{n}|y_i - \eta_i|$. Then the bootstrap algorithm described in Section 16.2 can be modified as follows:

1. Construct $\hat{F}$ which assigns probability mass $1/n$ at each observed residual,

$$\hat{\epsilon}_i = y_i - g_i(\hat{\beta}). \tag{16.11}$$

2. Draw a bootstrap sample $\epsilon_1^*, \ldots, \epsilon_n^*$ and hence the bootstrap sample denoted by

$$Y_i^* = g_i(\hat{\beta}) + \epsilon_i^*, \qquad i = 1, \ldots, n \tag{16.12}$$

where the ϵ_i^* are i.i.d. as $\hat{F}$ and calculate

$$\hat{\beta}^* : \quad \min_\beta \; D\left(\mathbf{Y}^*, \eta(\beta)\right). \tag{16.13}$$

3. Repeat step 2 independently B times, obtaining bootstrap replications, $\hat{\beta}_1^*, \ldots, \hat{\beta}_B^*$.

Suppose we are interested in estimating the covariance matrix of the $\hat{\beta}$'s. Then the bootstrap estimate of the covariance matrix is

$$\widehat{\text{Cov}} = \frac{1}{B-1} \sum_{j=1}^{n} (\hat{\beta}_j^* - \bar{\hat{\beta}}^*)(\hat{\beta}_j^* - \bar{\hat{\beta}}^*)'. \tag{16.14}$$

Special Case: Linear Regression. In this case, $g_i(\beta) = \mathbf{c}_i\beta$, where $\mathbf{c}_i$ is a $1 \times p$ vector of unknown covariates. We also take $D(\mathbf{y}, \eta) = \Sigma(y_i - \eta_i)^2$. Let $\mathbf{C}$ be the $n \times p$ matrix with $\mathbf{c}_i$ for the ith row and $\mathbf{G} = \mathbf{C}'\mathbf{C}$. For simplicity, we assume that the first element in each row vector $\mathbf{c}_i$ is unity and $\mathbf{G}$ is of full rank p. In this case we can obtain an explicit expression for the estimate of the covariance.

Note that $\hat{F}$ has mean 0 and variance $\hat{\sigma}^2 = \sum_{i=1}^{n} \hat{\epsilon}_i^2/n$ and

$$Y_i^* = \mathbf{c}_i\hat{\beta} + \epsilon_i^* \tag{16.15}$$

is the standard linear model written with a different notation. The standard linear model theory yields

$$\hat{\beta}^* = \mathbf{G}^{-1}\mathbf{C}'Y^* \qquad \text{and} \qquad \widehat{\text{cov}} = \hat{\sigma}^2\mathbf{G}^{-1}. \tag{16.16}$$

That is, the bootstrap estimate of the standard estimate of covariance differs from the standard estimate of covariance in the sense that it uses $\hat{\sigma}^2 = \sum_1^n \hat{\epsilon}_i^2/n$ instead of $\Sigma\hat{\epsilon}_i^2/(n - p)$ in order to estimate σ^2. Notice that it also differs from the jackknife estimate (see (3.13) of Efron, 1982).

Remark 16.2. Efron (1982, p. 36) remarks that $\hat{\sigma}^*$ might give a small value and consequently the bootstrap estimate of the covariance will be small, thereby giving a foolishly optimistic assessment of $\text{cov}(\hat{\beta})$. In the polynomial regression model, this situation can be averted by using an unbiased estimate of σ^2. However, in the general case, the picture is not clear.

Bootstrapping Pairs versus Bootstrapping Residuals

We have two choices for bootstrapping a regression model. The method suggested in this section is bootstrapping the residuals. That is, the bootstrap sample will be

$$\mathbf{x}^* = \left\{ (\mathbf{c}_1, \mathbf{c}_1\hat{\beta} + \hat{\epsilon}_{i_1}), \ \ldots, \ (\mathbf{c}_n, \mathbf{c}_n\hat{\beta} + \hat{\epsilon}_{i_n}) \right\} \tag{16.17}$$

where $(i_1, \ldots, i_n)$ is a random sample of integers 1 through n with replacement. Bootstrapping the pairs will yield a sample

$$\mathbf{x}^* = \left\{ (\mathbf{c}_{i_1}, y_{i_1}), \ \ldots, \ (\mathbf{c}_{i_n}, y_{i_n}) \right\}. \tag{16.18}$$

Now the question is, which bootstrap method is better? The answer depends on the validity of the regression model (16.9), which implies that the error between y_i and its mean $\mu_i = \mathbf{c}_i\beta$ is free of $\mathbf{c}_i$, it has the same distribution "F" irrespective of the value of $\mathbf{c}_i$. This is a strong assumption which may fail to hold even if $\mu_i = \mathbf{c}_i\beta$.

EXAMPLE 16.5

Let Y denote the monthly income (in thousands of dollars) and c denote the age of a person (in years). Let the regression model be

$$Y_i = \beta c_i + \epsilon_i, \qquad i = 1, \ldots,$$

where $E\epsilon_i = 0$, $\operatorname{var}\epsilon_i = \sigma^2$. Consider the following data:

$$(20, 0.8), (25, 1.1), (30, 1.2), (35, 1.3), (40, 1.5).$$

We are interested in finding our estimate of the variance of $\hat{\beta}$. The least-squares estimate of β is

$$\hat{\beta} = \sum_{i=1}^{5} c_i y_i / \sum_{1}^{5} c_i^2 = \frac{185}{4750} = 0.039$$

$$\hat{y}_i = \hat{\beta} c_i$$

$$\hat{\epsilon}_i = y_i - \hat{y}_i = y_i - \hat{\beta} c_i$$

$$\hat{\epsilon}_1 = 0.8 - 0.78 = 0.02, \qquad \hat{\epsilon}_2 = 1.1 - 0.975 = 0.125,$$

$$\hat{\epsilon}_3 = 1.2 - 1.17 = 0.03,$$

$$\hat{\epsilon}_4 = 1.3 - 1.365 = -0.065 \qquad \text{and} \qquad \hat{\epsilon}_5 = 1.5 - 1.56 = -0.06$$

$$\operatorname{var}\hat{\beta} = \frac{\hat{\sigma}^2}{\Sigma c_i^2} \qquad \text{where } \hat{\sigma}^2 = \frac{\sum_1^5 \hat{\epsilon}_i^2}{5-1} = \frac{0.02475}{4} = 0.0062.$$

Let us compute the bootstrap estimate of $\widehat{var}$. Let us draw $B = 10$ bootstrap samples. Let us use the random numbers generated in Example 16.2:

$$(1, 2, 2, 3, 5), (3, 4, 5, 5, 2), \text{etc.}$$

Let us bootstrap the residuals. Then the bootstrap samples are given by:

(20, 0.8),	(25, 1.1),	(30, 1.295),	(35, 1.395),	(40, 1.56),
(20, 0.81),	(25, 0.91),	(30, 1.11),	(35, 1.305),	(40, 1.685),
(20, 0.8),	(25, 1.005),	(30, 1.105),	(35, 1.385),	(40, 1.685),
(20, 0.72),	(25, 0.978),	(30, 1.19),	(35, 1.365),	(40, 1.685),
(20, 0.72),	(25, 0.91),	(30, 1.105),	(35, 1.49),	(40, 1.56),
(20, 0.81),	(25, 1.005),	(30, 1.105),	(35, 1.385),	(40, 1.56),
(20, 0.715),	(25, 0.995),	(30, 1.295),	(35, 1.49),	(40, 1.56),
(20, 0.715),	(25, 0.91),	(30, 1.295),	(35, 1.365),	(40, 1.685),
(20, 0.905),	(25, 0.915),	(30, 1.17),	(35, 1.49),	(40, 1.495),
(20, 0.72),	(25, 0.911),	(30, 1.19),	(35, 1.305),	(40, 1.56)

Then the bootstrap sample of $\hat{\beta}^*$ is

$$0.0408, \quad 0.390, \quad 0.0400, \quad 0.0399, \quad 0.0389,$$
$$0.0390, \quad 0.0405, \quad 0.0409, \quad 0.0396, \quad 0.0381,$$

yielding $\bar{\hat{\beta}}^* = 0.03967$ and

$$\sum_1^{10} (\hat{\beta}_j^* - \bar{\hat{\beta}}^*)^2/9 = (0.01574469 - 0.01573709)/9$$

$$= 0.0000076/9 = 0.00000084$$

which is the bootstrap estimate of $\text{var} \, \hat{\beta}$. Notice that this is much smaller than the true value. ◆

16.7   BOOTSTRAP CONFIDENCE INTERVALS

If we wish to set up a 95% confidence interval for a parameter θ, then we can roughly set it to be

$$\hat{\theta} \pm 2\widehat{SD}.$$

On the other hand, if we want to be more precise, after generating the bootstrap values, $\hat{\theta}_1, \ldots, \hat{\theta}_B$, we can set the $(1 - \alpha)$ confidence interval to be

$$(\hat{\theta}_{k_1}^*, \hat{\theta}_{k_2}^*)$$

where

$$k_1 = [n\alpha/2] \quad \text{and} \quad k_2 = [n(1 - \alpha/2)].$$

EXAMPLE **16.6**

For the problem in Example 16.5, an 80% bootstrap confidence interval for β is (0.0381, 0.0408). ◆

16.8   APPLICATION OF BOOTSTRAP METHODS IN FINANCE AND MANAGEMENT CASES

The bootstrap method is essentially a computer-intensive nonparametric statistical method which empirically measures the variability of any statistic without relying on traditional normality assumptions (see Diaconis and Efron, 1983). Hence, bootstrap methods have been very attractive to research workers in Finance and Management Science. For example, bootstrap methods have been used

1. to study the time-series behavior of exchange rates and the empirical distribution of exchange rates (see Levich and Thomas, 1993, or Kho, 1996);

2. to examine the ability of dividend yields for predicting the long-term returns by stocks (see Goetzmann and Jorion, 1993);

3. to calculate the capability indices of production processes (see Franklin and Wasserman, 1992); and

4. to determine the reorder point in inventory management (see Wang and S. S. Rao, 1992).

■ PROBLEMS

16.1   Let the random sample consist of 6 guinea pigs whose weights are (1, 2, 3, 4, 5, 6). Find the bootstrap estimate of the SD based on 10 bootstrap samples.

16.2   Let X_i be distributed as Bernoulli with $P(X = 0) = f_1$ and $P(X = 1) = f_2$. On the basis of 10 bootstrap samples, obtain the bootstrap estimate of $\hat{f}_2 - f_2$ where we have the sample (1, 0, 0, 1, 0).

16.3   For the data in Example 16.5, let the regression model be

$$Y_i = e^{-c_i \beta} + \epsilon_i \quad (i = 1, 2, \ldots).$$

Use the least-squares method and compute the bootstrap estimate of the variance of $\hat{\beta}$.

16.4   We are interested in comparing the yields of loaded and nonloaded mutual funds. We randomly select a sample of 5 from each type of mutual fund. The following is the returns for the year 1996.

Loaded 18.2	9.5	12.0	21.1	10.2
Nonloaded 10.9	11.7	20.2	15.6	12.9

Find the bootstrap estimate of the SD for each fund based on 10 bootstrap samples.

16.5   The following data have been collected from the experiment of life span of a certain type of electric lamp (in hours):

$$2000, 1800, 1900, 1950, 2050, 2000 .$$

Find an 80% confidence interval for the mean based on 10 bootstrap samples.

■ REFERENCES

16.1   Diaconis, P. and Efron, B. (1983). Computer-intensive methods in statistics. *Scientific American*, May 1983, 116–130.

16.2   Efron, B. (1981). The jackknife estimate of variance. *Ann. Statist.* **9**, 586–596.

16.3   Efron, B. (1982). *The Jackknife, The Bootstrap and Other Resampling Plans*, SIAM Publication No. 38, Philadelphia, PA.

16.4   Efron, B., and Tibshirani, R. (1993), *An Introduction to the Bootstrap*. New York: Chapman and Hall.

16.5   Efron, B. (1979), Bootstrap methods: Another look at the jackknife. *Ann. Statist.* **7**, 1–26.

16.6   Franklin, L. A. and Wasserman, G. S. (1992), Bootstrap lower confidence limits for capability indices. *Journal of Quality Technology* **24**:4, 196–210.

16.7   Goetzmann, W. N. and Jorion, P. (1993), Testing the predictive power of dividend yields. *Journal of Finances* **48**:2, 663–679.

16.8   Kish, L. and Frankel, M. R. (1974). Inference from complex surveys. *Jour. Roy. Stat. Soc.* **B36**, 1–37.

16.9   Kho, B. (1996). Time-varying risk premia, volatility, and technical trading rule profits: Evidence from foreign currency future markets. *Journal of Financial Economics* **41**:2, 249–290.

16.10   Levich, R. M. and Thomas, L. R. III (1993), The significance of technical trading-rule profits in the foreign exchange market: A bootstrap approach. *Journal of International Money and Finance* **12**:5, 451–474.

16.11   Wang, M. and Rao, S. S. (1992), Estimating reorder points and other management science applications by bootstrap procedure. *European Journal of Operational Research* **56**:3, 332–342.

CHAPTER 17

SMALL-AREA ESTIMATION

17.1 INTRODUCTION

The term *small* or *local area* is commonly used to denote a small geographical region such as a country, a municipality, or a census division. Regression methods for improving local-area estimates was first used by Hansen, Hurwitz, and Madow (1953, pp. 483–486). It has been popularized by Erickson (1974). Other methods that are used are empirical Bayes (EB), hierarchical Bayes (HB), and empirical best linear unbiased prediction (EBLUP). In this regard, quite useful are the review papers by J. N. K. Rao (1986), Chaudhuri (1992), and Ghosh and J. N. K. Rao (1984).[1] Some of the applications of small-area estimation methods are given below:

1. Federal State Cooperative Program (FSCP) is interested in obtaining reliable and consistent series of county population estimates. The FSCP helps the Census Bureau's postcensual estimate program.

2. Fay and Herriot (1979) wanted to estimate the per capita income (PCI) for several small places. These estimates could be used (by the Treasury Department with the help of the U.S. Census Bureau) in allocating funds to the local governments within the different states, under the General Revenue Sharing Program. For instance, the Census Bureau obtained the current estimates of PCI (per capita

---

[1] Ghosh and Rao (1994) served as a source for the material of this chapter.

335

income) by multiplying the 1970 census estimates of PCI in 1969 (based on a 20% sample) by ratios of an administrative estimate of PCI in the current year and an analogously derived estimate for 1969. Fay and Herriot (1979) suggest better estimates based on the EB method and show that they have smaller average errors than either the census sample estimates or the county averages. The Fay-Herriot (1969) method was adopted by the Census Bureau in 1974.

3. This deals with the issue of adjustment by the population undercount in the 1980 census. The population counts in 3000 counties and 39,000 civil divisions were used by the Congress in allocating 100 billion dollars a year during the early 1980s to the different state and local governments. An undercount is the difference between omissions and erroneous inclusions in the census and hence it is positive. Erickson and Kadane (1985) and Erickson, Kadane, and Tukey (1980) suggest weighted averages of sample estimates and systematic regression estimates of the 1980 census undercount, similar to those of Fay and Herriot (1979) for PCI. These authors also suggest using regression methods for areas where no sample data are available. Although several people applaud these regression methods, others like Freedman and Navidi (1986, 1992) criticized them for not validating their model and for not explicitly mentioning the assumptions made.

4. This concerns the estimation of areas under corn and soy beans for each of 12 counties in the North-Central Iowa using farm interview data together with LANDSAT satellite data (see Battese, Harter, and Fuller, 1988).

17.2 DEMOGRAPHIC METHODS

Demographers have been using a variety of methods for estimating (locally) the population and other characteristics of interest during the postcensual years. Purcell and Kish (1980) call these methods symptomatic accounting techniques (SAT). These techniques utilize current data from administrative registers together with related data from the latest census. The diverse registration data include "symptomatic" variables such as the number of births and deaths, of existing new housing units, and of school enrollments.

In the following we briefly describe the Vital Rates (VR) method, Census Component Method II (CM-II), the Administrative Records (AR) method, and the Housing Unit (HU) method.

VR Method

In a given year t, let b_t (d_t) the annual number of births (deaths) be known for a certain local area. The crude birth (death) rates r_{1t} (r_{2t}) for that local area are estimated by

$$r_{1t} = r_{10}(R_{1t}/R_{10})\ \{r_{2t} = r_{20}(R_{2t}/R_{20})\} \tag{17.1}$$

where r_{10} (r_{20}) denote the crude birth (death) rate for the local area in the latest census year $(t = 0)$ while R_{1t} (R_{2t}) and R_{10} (R_{20}), respectively, denote the crude birth (death) rates in the current and census years for a larger area that includes the local area. Then the population for the local area at year t is estimated as

$$P_t = \frac{1}{2}\left(\frac{b_t}{r_{1t}} + \frac{d_t}{r_{2t}}\right). \tag{17.2}$$

Note that the efficiency of the VR method depends on the assumption that

$$r_{1t}/r_{10} \approx R_{1t}/R_{10} \quad \text{and} \quad r_{2t}/r_{20} \approx R_{2t}/R_{20} \, .$$

The composite method is an extension of the VR method which sums independently computed age-sex-race specific estimates based on births, deaths, and school enrollments.

EXAMPLE 17.1

For a certain small county in the state of Kentucky, the total number of births in 1995 was 400 and the total number of deaths was 350. The birth and death rates (according to the 1990 census) were 2% and 1.8%, respectively, for both the county and the state, and the same for the state of Kentucky for 1995 were 2.1% and 1.9%, respectively. Using the VR method, estimate the population of that county in 1995.

$$r_{1t} = 0.02 \left(\frac{2.1}{2} \right) = 0.021$$

$$r_{2t} = 0.018 \left(\frac{1.9}{1.8} \right) = 0.019 \, .$$

The population of that county in 1995 is

$$P_t = \frac{1}{2} \left(\frac{400}{r_{1t}} + \frac{350}{r_{2t}} \right) = \frac{1}{2} (19{,}047.619 + 18{,}421.053)$$

$$\doteq 18{,}735. \qquad \blacklozenge$$

CM-II Method. Unlike the previous methods, this takes into account the net migration. If m_t denotes the net migration into the local area during the period since the last census, then an estimate of P_t is

$$P_t = P_0 + b_t - d_t + m_t \tag{17.3}$$

where P_0 denotes the population of the local area in the census year $t = 0$. The m_t is further divided into military and civilian migration. The former is readily available from administrative records, while the CM-II estimates the civilian migration from school enrollments. However, the AR method estimates the net migration from records of individuals as opposed to collective units such as schools.

HU Method. Let H_t denote the number of occupied housing units at time t, PPH_t denote the average number of persons per housing unit at time t, and GQ_t be the number of persons in group quarters at time t. Then P_t is given by

$$P_t = (H_t)(PPH_t) + GQ_t \, . \tag{17.4}$$

Note that all the quantities on the right side of (17.4) need to be estimated. Smith and Lewis (1980) propose various methods of estimating these quantities.

17.3   MULTIPLE REGRESSION METHODS

Most of the methods mentioned above become special cases of multiple linear regression. Regression-symptomatic procedures employ multiple regression with symptomatic variables as independent variables in order to estimate the local-area populations. Two such procedures that are in use are the ratio-correlation method and the difference-correlation methods. In the following we will describe the ratio-correlation methods.

Ratio-Correlation Method

Let $0, 1$, and $t \ (> 1)$ denote the consecutive census years and the current year, respectively. Also, $P_{i\alpha}$ and $S_{ij\alpha}$ denote the population and the value of the jth asymptomatic variable for the ith local area $(i = 1, \ldots, m)$ in the year $\alpha \ (= 0, 1, t)$. Further, let $p_{i\alpha} = P_{i\alpha}/\sum_i P_{i\alpha}$ and $s_{ij\alpha} = S_{ij\alpha}/\sum_i S_{ij\alpha}$ denote the corresponding proportions, and

$$R'_i = p_{i1}/p_{i0}, \qquad R_i = p_{it}/p_{i1}, \qquad r'_{ij} = s_{ij1}/s_{ij0}, \qquad r_{ij} = s_{ijt}/s_{ij1}. \quad (17.5)$$

Using the data $(R'_i, r'_{i1}, \ldots, r'_{ip}; i = 1, \ldots, m)$ and via multiple regression, we first fit

$$R'_i = \hat{\beta}'_0 + \hat{\beta}'_1 r'_{i1} + \cdots + \hat{\beta}'_p r'_{ip} \quad (17.6)$$

where the $\hat{\beta}'$'s denote the estimated regression coefficients which relate the ratio of the population proportions between the two census years to the corresponding changes r'_{ij} in the proportions for the symptomatic variables. In a similar fashion, the changes in the post-censual period, namely R_i, are predicted by

$$\tilde{R}_i = \hat{\beta}'_0 + \hat{\beta}'_1 r_{i1} + \cdots + \hat{\beta}'_p r_{ip} \quad (17.7)$$

using r_{ij}, the known changes in the symptomatic proportions in the postcensual period and the estimated regression coefficients $\hat{\beta}'_j \ (j = 0, 1, \ldots, p)$. Finally, the current population counts P_{it}, are estimated by

$$\tilde{P}_{it} = \tilde{R}_i p_{i1}\left(\sum_i P_{it}\right) \quad (17.8)$$

where the total current count, namely $\sum_i P_{it}$, is obtained from other sources.

Difference-Correlation Method

In the difference-correlation method, differences between the populations at the two pairs of time points, $(0, 1)$ and $(1, t)$, are used instead of their ratios. Notice that the above regression-symptomatic procedure uses the regression coefficients $\hat{\beta}'_j$ in the last intercensal period. However, applicable changes in the statistical relationship can lead to errors in the current postcensal estimates. The sample-regression method of Erickson (1974) overcomes this defect by using sample estimates of the R_i to compute the current regression equation. Suppose sample estimates of the R_i are available for k of the m local areas, say $\hat{R}_1, \ldots, \hat{R}_k$. Then we fit the regression equation

$$\hat{R}_i = \hat{\beta}_0 + \hat{\beta}_1 r_{i1} + \cdots + \hat{\beta}_p r_{ip} \tag{17.9}$$

to the data $(\hat{R}_i, r_{i1}, \ldots, r_{ip})$ from the k sampled areas instead of (17.7) and then obtain the sample regression estimates $\hat{R}_{i(\text{reg})}$ for all the areas using the known symptomatic ratios r_{ij} $(i = 1, \ldots, m)$:

$$\hat{R}_{i(\text{reg})} = \hat{\beta}_0 + \hat{\beta}_1 r_{i1} + \cdots + \hat{\beta}_p r_{ip}. \tag{17.10}$$

Using 1970 census data and sample data from the current population survey (CPS), Erickson (1974) showed that the reduction of mean error is small when compared with the ratio-correlation method. The success of the sample regression method depends on the size and the quality of the samples and the nature of the symptomatic variables.

EXAMPLE 17.2

In the State of Kentucky (known as the Commonwealth of Kentucky) there are $m = 120$ counties. Let the periods 1980, 1990 and 1997 be denoted by 0, 1 and t, respectively. Let $p = 1$ (i.e., we use only one symptomatic variable). Suppose we take a sample of $k = 10$ counties and, using Ericson's (1974) method, we fit a linear regression to the data

$$(\hat{R}_i, r_{i1}), \quad i = 1, \ldots, k$$

and obtain

$$\hat{R}_i = 0.05 + 1.05 r_{i1}, \quad i = 1, \ldots, 120.$$

Assume that

$$\sum_{i=1}^{m} P_{it} = 3.1 \times 10^6.$$

Using $r_{11} = 1.01$ and $p_{11} = 0.073$, estimate the population of Fayette County in 1997. Let it be denoted by P_{1t}. Then

$$P_{1t} = \hat{R}_1 p_{11} \left(\sum_{i=1}^{m} P_{it} \right)$$

$$= \{0.05 + 1.05(1.01)\}(0.073)(3.1 \times 10^6)$$

$$= 1.1105(0.073)(3.1 \times 10^6)$$

$$= 251,306. \qquad \blacklozenge$$

17.4   SYNTHETIC ESTIMATORS

Suppose an unbiased estimate is available for a large area from a sample survey. When the estimate is used to derive estimates for subareas (with the assumption that the subareas have the same characteristics as the large area), such estimates are called *synthetic* estimates. The National Center for Health Statistics was the first to use synthetic estimation in order to obtain state estimates of long- and short-term physical disabilities from the National Health Interview Survey data. In the following we will describe this method of estimation.

Suppose the population is partitioned into large domains r and that reliable direct estimators $\hat{Y}'_{\cdot r}$ of the totals $Y_{\cdot r}$ are available from the survey data. Suppose the small areas i cut across the g large domains so that $Y_{\cdot r} = \sum_i Y_{ir}$, where Y_{ir} is the total for cell (i, r). Also, assume that auxiliary information in the form of totals X_{ir} is also available. Then a synthetic estimator of small area total $Y_i = \sum_r Y_{ir}$ is given by

$$\hat{Y}_i^s = \sum_r (X_{ir}/X_{\cdot r})\hat{Y}'_{\cdot r} \tag{17.11}$$

where $X_{\cdot r} = \sum_i X_{ir}$. Note that the estimator in (17.11) has the consistency property, namely,

$$\sum_i \hat{Y}_i^s = \sum_r \hat{Y}'_{\cdot r} = \hat{Y}'$$

the direct estimator of the population total.

The direct estimator $\hat{Y}'_{\cdot r}$ used in (17.11) is usually a ratio estimator of the form

$$\hat{Y}'_{\cdot r} = \left[\left(\sum_{l \in s_{\cdot r}} w_l y_l \right) / \left(\sum_{l \in s_{\cdot r}} w_l x_l \right) \right] X_{\cdot r}$$

$$= (\hat{Y}_{\cdot r}/\hat{X}_{\cdot r}) X_{\cdot r} \tag{17.12}$$

where $s_{\cdot r}$ is the sample in the large domain r and w_l is the sampling weight given to the lth element. For this choice, the synthetic estimator (17.11) assumes the form of

$$\hat{Y}_i^s = \sum_r (\hat{Y}_{\cdot r}/\hat{X}_{\cdot r}) X_{ir} .$$

If $E\hat{Y}'_{\cdot r} = Y_i$, then the design bias of $\hat{Y}_i^s$ is

$$E(\hat{Y}_i^s) - Y_i \doteq \sum_r \{Y_{\cdot r}/X_{\cdot r} - Y_{ir}/X_{ir}\} X_{ir}$$

which is not zero unless $Y_{ir}/X_{ir} = Y_{\cdot r}/X_{\cdot r}$ for all r. When $X_{ir} = N_{ir}$, the population count, the latter condition is equivalent to

$$\frac{1}{N_{ir}} Y_{ir} = \bar{Y}_{ir} = \frac{1}{N_{\cdot r}} Y_{\cdot r} = \bar{Y}_{\cdot r} \qquad \text{for all } r$$

which implies that the small-area mean in each domain r is equal to the overall domain mean. However, such an assumption is quite strong and will invariably not be valid. Thus, the synthetic estimators for some of the areas can be highly design biased. Toward the mean-squared error of $\hat{Y}_i^s$ we have

$$
\begin{aligned}
\text{MSE } \hat{Y}_i^s &= E(\hat{Y}_i^s - Y_i)^2 \\
&= E(\hat{Y}_i^s - \hat{Y}_i + \hat{Y}_i - Y_i)^2 \\
&= E(\hat{Y}_i^s - \hat{Y}_i)^2 + E(\hat{Y}_i - Y_i)^2 + 2E(\hat{Y}_i - Y_i)(\hat{Y}_i^s - \hat{Y}_i) \\
&= E(\hat{Y}_i^s - \hat{Y}_i)^2 - E(\hat{Y}_i - Y_i)^2 + 2 \text{ cov}(\hat{Y}_i^s, \hat{Y}_i)
\end{aligned}
$$

after writing $\hat{Y}_i^s - \hat{Y}_i$ in the third term as $\hat{Y}_i^s - Y_i + Y_i - \hat{Y}_i$, where we assume that the bias in $\hat{Y}_i^s$ is negligible. If $\text{cov}(\hat{Y}_i, \hat{Y}_i^s) \doteq 0$, where $\hat{Y}_i$ is a direct, unbiased estimator of Y_i, an approximate unbiased estimator of MSE of $\hat{Y}_i^s$ is

$$
\text{MSE}(\hat{Y}_i^s) = (\hat{Y}_i^s - \hat{Y}_i)^2 - v(\hat{Y}_i) \tag{17.13}
$$

where $v(\hat{Y}_i)$ is a design-unbiased estimator of the variance of $\hat{Y}_i$. Also, since the estimators in (17.13) are highly unstable, it is customary to average these estimators over i in order to obtain a stable estimator of MSE (see Gonzalez, 1993). Further, the assumption that the $\text{cov}(\hat{Y}_i, \hat{Y}_i^s) \doteq 0$ may be reasonable in practice, since $\hat{Y}_i^s$ is much less variable than $\hat{Y}_i$.

17.5 COMPOSITE ESTIMATORS

In order to balance the possible bias of a synthetic estimator with the instability of a direct estimator, it is customary to consider a weighted average of the two estimators, namely

$$
\hat{Y}_i^c = w_i \hat{Y}_{1i} + (1 - w_i)\hat{Y}_{2i} \tag{17.14}
$$

where $\hat{Y}_{1i}$ is a direct estimator, $\hat{Y}_{2i}$ is an indirect estimator, and w_i is a suitably chosen weight $(0 \le w_i \le 1)$. For instance, one can set $\hat{Y}_{1i} = \hat{Y}_i$ (an unbiased estimator) and $\hat{Y}_{2i} = \hat{Y}_i^s$. With the above choice for $\hat{Y}_{1i}$ and $\hat{Y}_{2i}$, we find the optimal weights, namely $w_i(\text{opt})$, which will minimize MSE of $\hat{Y}_i^c$ with respect to w_i, subject to

$$
\text{cov}(\hat{Y}_i, \hat{Y}_i^s) = 0
$$

where

$$
\text{MSE}(\hat{Y}_i^c) = w_i^2 V(\hat{Y}_i) + (1 - w_i)^2 \text{MSE } \hat{Y}_i^s .
$$

Setting the derivative with respect to w_i equal to zero, we obtain

$$w_i(\text{opt}) = \text{MSE}(\hat{Y}_i^s) / \left\{ \text{MSE}(\hat{Y}_i^s) + V(\hat{Y}_i) \right\}. \qquad (17.15)$$

Thus,

$$\hat{w}_i(\text{opt}) = \widehat{\text{MSE}}(\hat{Y}_i^s) / (\hat{Y}_i^s - \hat{Y}_i)^2. \qquad (17.16)$$

However, these weights can be very unstable. To overcome this, Purcell and Kish (1979) use a common weight w and then minimize the average MSE, namely $m^{-1} \sum_{i=1}^{m}$ $\text{MSE}(\hat{Y}_i^c)$ with respect to w. Elementary computations yield

$$\hat{w}(\text{opt}) = 1 - \sum_i v(\hat{Y}_i) / \sum_i (\hat{Y}_i^s - \hat{Y}_i)^2. \qquad (17.17)$$

If the variances of the $\hat{Y}_i$ are approximately equal, then (17.17) becomes

$$\hat{w}(\text{opt}) = 1 - m\bar{v} / \sum_i (\hat{Y}_i^s - \hat{Y}_i)^2 \qquad (17.18)$$

where $\bar{v} = \frac{1}{m} \sum v(\hat{Y}_i)$.

Simple weights w_i that depend only on the domain counts of the domain totals of a covariate X have been proposed in the literature. For example, Drew, M. P. Singh, and Choudary (1982) propose

$$w_i(D) = \begin{cases} 1, & \text{if } \hat{N}_i \geq \delta N_i \\ \hat{N}_i / (\delta N_i), & \text{otherwise} \end{cases} \qquad (17.19)$$

where $\hat{N}_i$ is the direct, unbiased estimator of the known domain population size N_i and δ is arbitrarily chosen so as to control the contribution of the synthetic estimator. $\delta = 2/3$ is currently used by the Canadian Labor Force Survey. Särndal and Hidiroglow (1989) propose

$$w_i(S) = \begin{cases} 1, & \text{if } \hat{N}_i \geq N_i \\ (\hat{N}_i | N_i)^{h-1}, & \text{otherwise} \end{cases} \qquad (17.20)$$

where h is arbitrarily chosen. They recommend $h = 2$ as a general-purpose value. Note that the weights in (17.19) and (17.20) coincide when $\delta = 1$ and $h = 2$.

To get more insight into the weights (17.17) and (17.20), consider the special case of simple random sampling of n elements from a population of N elements. Here $\hat{N}_i = N(n_i/n)$ where n_i is the sample size (which is random) in ith domain. If $\delta = 1$ in (17.19), then $w_i(D) = w_i(S) = 1$ if n_i is at least as large as $E(n_i) = n(N_i/N)$. Thus, the estimators which depend on the sample sizes cannot be strengthened by the related domains, even when $E(n_i)$ is not large enough to make the direct estimators $\hat{Y}_i$ reliable. However, when $\hat{N}_i < N_i$ and $h = 2$, $w_i(D)$ equals $w_i(S)$ and decreases as n_i decreases. Consequently, more weight is given to the synthetic component as n_i decreases. Thus, the weights behave well, unlike in the case of $\hat{N}_i \geq N_i$. One disadvantage of the simple-minded weights $w_i(D)$ or $w_i(S)$ is that they do not take into account the size of the between-area variation relative to the within-area variation for the characteristic of interest.

EXAMPLE **17.3**

Let Y_{ij} denote the wages and salaries of jth firm in the ith census division and X_{ij} the corresponding gross income (in millions of dollars) in a certain country. Let $\bar{Y}_i$ and $\bar{X}_i$ denote the true small area means ($i = 1, \ldots, 4$). Let a random sample of size $n = 10$ business firms out of $N = 100$ be drawn and the sample values be denoted by (y_{ij}, x_{ij}), $j = 1, \ldots, n_i$ and $i = 1, \ldots, 4$. The following artificial data is obtained:

Simple random sample of $n = 10$

Area	N_i	$\bar{X}_i$	$\bar{Y}_i$		Area	n_i	x_{ij}	$\bar{x}_i$	y_{ij}	$\bar{y}_i$
1	15	55	12		1	2	30	35	6	9
2	30	45	8				40		12	
3	45	92	22		2	3	35	31	2	5
4	10	125	25				28		3	
							30		10	
					3	3	100	95	40	25
							110		25	
							75		10	
					4	2	150	135	23	20
							120		17	

Then we obtain the following estimator:

1. **Ratio-synthetic (RS) estimator.**   Let $\bar{x} = 71.8$, $\bar{y} = 14.8$ be the overall sample means. Then,

$$\bar{Y}_{i,\text{RS}} = (\bar{y}/\bar{x})\bar{X}_i = \frac{14.8}{71.8}\bar{X}_i = 0.206\bar{X}_i \qquad (i = 1, \ldots, 4).$$

Thus, $\hat{\bar{Y}}_{i,\text{RS}}$ ($i = 1, \ldots, 4$) are, respectively, 11.34, 9.28, 18.96, 25.7.

2. **Sample-size dependent (SD) estimator.**

$$\hat{\bar{Y}}_{i,\text{SD}} = \begin{cases} \hat{\bar{Y}}_{i,lr} = \begin{cases} \bar{y}_i + (\bar{y}/\bar{x})(\bar{X}_i - \bar{x}_i), & \text{if } w_i \geq W_i \\ \frac{w_i}{W_i}(\hat{\bar{Y}}_{i,lr}) + \left(1 - \frac{w_i}{W_i}\right)\hat{\bar{Y}}_{i,\text{RS}}, & \text{if } w_i < W_i \end{cases} \end{cases}$$

where $\hat{\bar{Y}}_{i,lr}$ is a "survey regression" estimator, $(\bar{y}_i, \bar{x}_i)$ are the sample means for ith area, $w_i = n_i/n$, and $W_i = N_i/N$.

This estimator corresponds to the weight (17.19) with $\delta = 1$ or the weight (17.20) with $h = 2$.

The survey regression estimators of the area means are given by

$$\hat{\bar{Y}}_{i,lr} = \bar{y}_i + (\bar{y}/\bar{x})(\bar{X}_i - \bar{x}_i), \qquad i = 1, \ldots, 4.$$

Computations yield

$$\bar{y}/\bar{x} = 14.8/71.8 = 0.206$$

$$\hat{\bar{Y}}_{1,lr} = 9 + 0.206(55 - 35) = 13.12$$

$$\hat{\bar{Y}}_{2,lr} = 5 + 0.206(45 - 31) = 7.89$$

$$\hat{\bar{Y}}_{3,lr} = 25 + 0.206(92 - 95) = 24.38$$

and

$$\hat{\bar{Y}}_{4,lr} = 20 + 0.206(125 - 135) = 17.94.$$

Since $w_i \geq W_i$ for $i = 1, 2,$ and 4,

$$\hat{\bar{Y}}_{1,SD} = 13.12$$

$$\hat{\bar{Y}}_{2,SD} = 7.89$$

$$\hat{\bar{Y}}_{4,SD} = 17.94$$

and since $w_3 < W_3$,

$$\hat{\bar{Y}}_{3,SD} = \frac{0.3}{0.45}(24.38) + \left(1 - \frac{0.3}{0.45}\right)(18.96)$$

$$= 22.57.$$

Except for $\hat{\bar{Y}}_{4,SD}$, the other sample-size dependent estimators are reasonable. ◆

Ghosh and J. N. K. Rao (1994) also discuss the empirical Bayes and hierarchical Bayes estimators, which will not be presented here.

■ PROBLEMS

17.1 For Gerard County in the Commonwealth of Kentucky the total number of births in 1995 was 300 and the total number of deaths was 280. The birth and death rates (according to the 1990 census) were 2% and 1.9%, respectively for both the county and the state, and the same for the Commonwealth of Kentucky for 1995 were 2.1% and 1.9%, respectively. Using the VR method, estimate the population of Gerard County in 1995.

17.2 With the data as in Example 17.2, assuming that for Jefferson County $p_{21} = 0.26$ and $r_{21} = 1.01$, estimate the population of Jefferson County for 1997.

17.3   Let Y_{ij} denote the wages and salaries of the jth firm in the ith census division of a certain country and X_{ij} the corresponding gross business income (in millions of dollars) in that country. Let $\bar{Y}_i$ and $\bar{X}_i$ denote the true small-area means ($i = 1, \ldots, 8$). Let a random sample of size $n = 20$ business firms out of $N = 120$ be drawn and the sample values be denoted by (y_{ij}, x_{ij}), $j = 1, \ldots, n_i$, and $i = 1, \ldots, 8$. The following (artificial) data is obtained.

Small-area sizes, N_i, and means $(\bar{Y}_i, \bar{X}_i)$ for a synthetic population ($N = 120$).

Area	N_i	$\bar{X}_i$	$\bar{Y}_i$
1	10	106	21
2	5	47	6
3	16	90	18
4	12	105	17
5	32	94	14
6	20	89	15
7	10	165	24
8	15	91	12

Data from a simple random sample drawn from the synthetic population ($n = 20$, $N = 120$).

Area	n_i	x_{ij}	y_{ij}	Area	n_i	x_{ij}	y_{ij}
1	3	34	6	5	4	75	12
		58	15			60	10
		77	19			55	9
2	2	25	4			40	7
		35	7	6	3	76	12
3	3	70	12			65	10
		50	8			42	9
		45	7	7	1	150	21
4	2	90	18	8	2	85	10
		75	15			72	9

Compute the ratio-synthetic (RS) estimators and the sample-size dependent (SD) estimators for the eight areas.

■ REFERENCES

17.1   Battese, G. E., Harter, R. M., and Fuller, W. A. (1988). An error component model for prediction of county crop areas using survey and satellite data. *J. Amer. Statist. Assoc.* **83**, 28–36.

17.2   Chaudhuri, A. (1992). Small domain statistics: A review. Tech. Rep. ASC/92/2, Indian Statistical Institute, Calcutta.

17.3   Drew, D., Singh, M. P., and Choudary, G. H. (1982). Evaluation of small area estimation techniques for the Canadian Labour Force Survey. *Survey Methodology* **8**, 17–47.

17.4   Erickson, E. P. (1974). A regression method for estimating populations of local areas. *J. Amer. Statist. Assoc.* **69**, 867–875.

17.5   Erickson, E. P. and Kadane, J. B. (1985). Estimating the population in a census year (with discussion). *J. Amer. Statist. Assoc.* **80**, 98–131.

17.6   Erickson, E. P., Kadane, J. B., and Tukey, J. W. (1989). Adjusting the 1981 census of population and housing. *J. Amer. Statist. Assoc.* **84**, 927–944.

17.7   Fay, R. E. and Herriot, R. A. (1979). Estimates of income for small places: An application of James-Stein procedures to census data. *J. Amer. Statist. Assoc.* **74**, 269–277.

17.8   Freedman, D. A. and Navidi, W. C. (1986). Regression models for adjusting the 1980 census (with discussion). *Statist. Sci.* **1**, 1–39.

17.9   Freedman, D. A. and Navidi, W. C. (1992). Should we have adjusted the U.S. census of 1980? (with discussion). *Survey Methodology* **18**, 3–74.

17.10   Ghosh, M. and Rao, J. N. K. (1994). Small area estimation: An appraisal. *Statistical Science* **9**, No. 1, 55–91.

17.11   Gonzalez, M. E. (1973). Use and evaluation of synthetic estimators. In *Proceedings of the Social Statistics Section*, 33–36, American Statistical Association, Washington, D.C.

17.12   Hansen, M., Hurwitz, W. N., and Madow, W. G. (1953). *Sample Survey Methods and Theory*, Vol. 1. New York: Wiley & Sons.

17.13   Purcell, N. J. and Kish, L. (1979). Estimation for small domain. *Biometrics* **35**, 365–384.

17.14   Rao, J. N. K. (1986). Synthetic estimators. SPREE and best model based predictors. In *Proceedings of the Conference on Survey Research Methods in Agriculture*, 1–16, U.S. Dept. Agriculture, Washington, D.C.

17.15   Särndal, C. E. and Hidiroglow, M. A. (1989). Small domain estimation: A conditional analysis. *J. Amer. Statist. Assoc.* **84**, 266–275.

17.16   Smith, S. K. and Lewis, B. B. (1980). Some new techniques for applying the housing unit method of local population estimation. *Demography* **17**, 323–340.

CHAPTER 18

IMPUTATIONS IN SURVEYS

18.1   INTRODUCTION

In surveys a response may be incomplete, or in two-phase sampling, certain items may be unavailable. Under these circumstances, it is convenient to impute values for the missing items.

In a survey, the respondents may answer only some of the questions, resulting in what is called *partial nonresponse*. Call-back approach may not yield 100% response because it may be impossible, impractical, or too expensive to reach the respondents again. Imputation is the estimation of individual items missing from the survey response. Sande (1982) gives a personal guide to the possibilities for imputation and the problems associated with them. In the following we will summarize his ideas.

Typically, in a survey the items are interrelated and imputing items in this situation will be somewhat different from those where only a single variable is imputed. In the case of a complex situation, pragmatism will be an overriding factor in dealing with partial nonresponse. Partial nonresponse can arise (i) due to the unavailability of data for a certain survey unit, or (ii) due to the inconsistency of a certain component item—for example, someone's height is 10 feet. Now the question is how to deal with partial nonresponse. Here are some of the possibilities.

1. Ignore all the records with missing values. This may result in loss of an appreciable part of the data. The "missings" are seldom random, and the procedures that are adopted will lead to biased estimates.

2. Publish the unknown values as a category. This is better than possibility 1 but ignores the partial information that may be available in the other variables. Most often the users of the data make adjustments for the "unknowns" without looking at the microdata and without the knowledge of the collection process.

3. Adjust (or reweight) each estimate, ignoring the missing values. This is a variation of possibility 1, which may lead to inconsistent estimates in the sense that edits or constraints on the data may be violated.

4. Fill in the missing values by plausible (i.e., realistic) and consistent estimates. This is called *imputing the missing values*.

Remark 18.1.   Please note that estimation of individual values in a data set is known as the "missing observation" problem in ANOVA (analysis of variance) and the "incomplete data" problem in multivariate analysis.

18.2   GENERAL RULES FOR IMPUTING

Any method of imputing must conform to certain edits. Typically we would like to transform the data so that normality-based procedures can be applied. However, such transformations usually result in transformation of the edits that make them more difficult to deal with. Also, the imputer does not usually have much time to modify the data after they have been collected. "Imputation does not solve any specific estimation problem more satisfactorily than classical estimation techniques for incomplete data, and it may do a lot worse" (Sande, 1982, p. 147).

Typically we will be estimating a large number of parameters, and the mathematical problem, assuming the model is correct, is formidable. If we estimate these parameters in groups, there is no guarantee that the overall set of estimates would be consistent in the sense that there might exist a complete data set that would yield the same set of estimates.

By imputing a consistent (in the sense that the edits are not violated) value for each missing item, one can easily estimate the population parameters of interest such as means, proportions, ratios, etc. However, the precision of the estimates is not assured. The use of imputed data makes the estimates less reliable. The imputer is faced with ethical problems if the microdata is made available to others. He should identify the missing items that are imputed. If one wants to explore relationships between variables, the use of imputed values could be misleading.

In summary, the general criteria to be met by the procedure adopted by the imputer are:

1. It will impute values that are consistent.

2. It will reduce the nonresponse bias and preserve the relationships between items as far as possible.

3. It will be suitable for any pattern of missing items.

4. It can be set up ahead of time.

5. Its effect on the bias and precision of the estimate can be evaluated.

18.3   METHODS OF IMPUTATION

Imputation techniques can be simple or sophisticated. If one can guess ahead of time what fields are most likely to cause problems, it would be wise to include in the survey questionnaire one or more correlated variables or get data on these correlated variables from auxiliary sources. Some of the techniques of imputing are:

1. Use of *ad hoc* values.
2. **Poststratification** and use of the poststratum marginal mean or another typical value.
3. **Model the relationships** among the variables.

    If some of the (numerical) response variables $Y = (Y_1, \ldots, Y_k)$ are missing and there are no suitable predictor variables X, one can model the joint distribution of Y using the complete responses in Y and then, for each missing response in $Y = (Y_1, \ldots, Y_k)$, predict the marginal expectation of the missing Y_i, given the Y's that are present. That is, for ith observation,

$$\hat{Y}_{i,\text{missing}} = E(Y_{i,\text{missing}}|Y_{\text{present}} = Y)$$

where we partition Y into Y_{missing} and Y_{present}. However, the assumption of normality for the distribution of Y was used by research workers, which may not be a plausible assumption, and also the edit structure is not taken into account.

However, simple ratio or regression techniques are often used. For instance, at Statistics Canada, 160 items were collected (from administrative documents) for a small sample of businesses and five major items were collected from other sources for the entire population. Suppose we wish to impute the 160 items for the nonsampled businesses. After stratification by size and industry, a ratio type of imputation is given by

$$\hat{x}_i = \left(\sum_p x_i \Big/ \sum_p Y_i \right) Y_i$$

where x is related to major item Y and the ith record requires imputation, p denotes the sample of complete records with all 160 items present. Because of the structure of the data, the edits are satisfied, but the imputations do not reflect the real structure of the data that have a lot of zero values. That is, the imputed records are not realistic and the marginal distributions are distorted. However, the ratio estimates are acceptable to Statistics Canada and permit variance estimation.

4. **Use of historic data** such as last month's or last year's response from the same unit. This is used in monthly surveys when the same units are surveyed in consecutive months.
5. **Use of proxy data** from another source, like another file, perhaps from medical or tax records. If an exact match is not available (because identifiers have been removed for reasons of confidentiality), one may be satisfied with a statistical match or classification variables such as age, sex, and place of birth. For example, one may use last year's sample survey as a source of data for statistical matching and imputation for this year's survey. Statistical matching is closely related to hot-deck and nearest-neighbor techniques.

6. **Hot-deck procedures.** There is not agreement on the precise definition of a hot-deck procedure. Usually it stands for an imputation procedure that employs such records from the current survey to supply missing values and involves a random or pseudo-random choice. There seem to be two main versions of a hot-deck procedure that are currently used mainly in categorical data.

   (a) The sequential hot deck used by U.S. Census and

   (b) The random-choice procedure used by the Canadian Census and Labor Force Survey. For a description of these procedures, see Sande (1982, p. 149).

   Hot-deck methods lead to estimators with (in simple cases) variances larger than the variance of the usual expansion estimates of means and totals (see, e.g., Ernest, 1980). However, there may be a reduction in the bias. Sande (1982) points out that hot-deck methods should produce imputed data sets that appear more realistic and do a better job of showing the distributional properties.

7. **Nearest-neighbor procedures** use current survey data as a source of individual data records with similar characteristics to supply values for missing items. Unlike hot-deck procedures, these procedures are suitable when one is matching with numeric data. Nearest-neighbor procedures can be converted into hot-deck procedures by choosing the "donor" record at random from m nearest neighbors instead of taking the nearest satisfactory record. Both types of procedures can be viewed as forms of nonparametric regression, that is, regression without an explicit model.

8. **Use of hybrid methods.** No single imputational procedure is satisfactory. Some *ad hoc* imputations are typically combined with more sophisticated methods. Sometimes a two-stage procedure is used. Another procedure is the use of a regression model followed by the addition of a residual value chosen by hot-deck or some other random process. Then

$$Y_{\mathrm{imp}} = \hat{Y} + \hat{\epsilon}$$

where $\hat{Y}$ is the predicted value obtained from the fitted model which is based on the complete observations, and $\hat{\epsilon}$ is the estimated residual that may be obtained by hot deck from the actual residuals of the fitted values or randomly generated by using the estimated distribution of residuals.

Devices for Expediting the Imputation Procedure

1. Formulation of the edit procedures so as to reduce the number of possible missing configurations.

2. Transformation of the data. It is more natural to impute proportions than absolute numbers.

3. Dividing the record into segments and imputing one segment at a time. Each pass is conditional on the preceding ones being complete.

18.4   EVALUATION OF IMPUTATION PROCEDURES

Imputation affects the quality of estimates.   Hence, it is desirable to determine, even approximately, the magnitude of the effect of imputation, the most relevant concern being the effect on bias and variance of the estimates (mean, ratio, etc.).   Theoretical treatment of imputation procedures is quite difficult. The easiest case is the use of poststratum mean under simple random sampling, where the variance conditional on the poststratum is easy to evaluate and the unconditional variance is somewhat more difficult. A considerable amount of theoretical work has been done, although most of it in the univariate case under simple random sampling where the edit constraints are ignored.

There also has been a fair amount of empirical work comparing various imputation procedures. When theory fails, one can always resort to a simulation study.   Rubin (1978) advocates the generation of several sets of imputed values under different models or sets of assumptions. This enables one to obtain estimates of the imputation error so that the effects of different models can be studied. This method is applicable only to imputation techniques that employ some random component such as hot-deck or Bayesian procedures.   This approach has been found to be useful and informative.

In conclusion, quite often almost unlimited and unpredictable demands are made on some data sets. Anyone faced with the problem of an imputation procedure will have to choose some compromise between what is technically effective and what is operationally expedient. Sande (1982) believes that the real problem of imputation is the interaction with editing. However, the problem of studying the properties of imputation procedures under realistic conditions is a very difficult one.

EXAMPLE **18.1**

A fast-food restaurant corporation wishes to estimate the average annual sales at its various restaurants. A random sample of $n = 9$ restaurants from the corporation's 1000 restaurants is drawn. Let x be the receipts (in millions of dollars) for the previous year and let y be the receipts for the current year. Assume $\bar{X} = 2.43$ million. Two restaurants did not report their current year receipts at the time of the study. Using an ignorable hot-deck model (see Remark 18.3 on page 353 for the definition) with $m = 2$, obtain a ratio estimate of the average sales at these fast-food restaurants for the corporation and also set up a 95% confidence interval for the same.

Resaurant	x	y
1	2.1	2.5
2	3.2	3.6
3	5.1	5.4
4	1.7	?
5	4.3	4.4
6	1.9	2.1
7	4.8	?
8	3.3	2.6
9	1.6	1.8

If the complete data set were available, the ratio estimator $\bar{X}\bar{y}/\bar{x}$ would be used as a point estimate and the associated 95% interval estimate would be

$$\frac{\bar{X}\bar{y}}{\bar{x}} \pm \frac{1.96}{n^{\frac{1}{2}}} (SD)$$

where

$$SD^2 = \sum_{i=1}^{n} (y_i - x_i \bar{y}/\bar{x})^2/(n-1).$$

However, y responses for units 4 and 7 are missing. For the first nonrespondent unit 4, the closest matching units are 9 and 6. For the nonrespondent unit 7, the closest matching units are units 3 and 5. For the ignorable hot-deck model, the missing values for y are obtained by drawing at random from the two closest matches. So, under this model, the multiple $m = 2$ imputations are as follows:

	Repetition 1	Repetition 2
Unit 4	1.8	2.1
Unit 7	4.4	5.4

Then the completed data sets are

	Set 1			Set 2	
	x	y		x	y
1	2.1	2.5	1	2.1	2.5
2	3.2	3.6	2	3.2	3.6
3	5.1	5.4	3	5.1	5.4
4	1.7	1.8	4	1.7	2.1
5	4.3	4.4	5	4.3	4.4
6	1.9	2.1	6	1.9	2.1
7	4.8	4.4	7	4.8	5.4
8	3.3	2.6	8	3.3	2.6
9	1.6	1.8	9	1.6	1.8
Total	28	28.6	Total	28	29.9
Means	3.111	3.178	Means	3.11	3.32

Estimate of $\bar{Y}$ when $\bar{X} = 2.43$ is 2.482   Estimate of $\bar{Y}$ is 2.595
Variance $= SD^2 = 0.1471$ Variance $= SD^2 = 0.1452$

The pooled estimate of $\bar{Y} = (2.482 + 2.595)/2 = 2.5385$.

The associated estimated average within variance $= (0.1471 + 0.1452)/2 = 0.14615$.

The estimated between variance $= \left[(2.482 - 2.5385)^2 + (2.595 - 2.5385)^2\right]$
$= 0.006384$.

The variances are combined as follows.

$$\text{estimated total variance} = (\text{estimated average within variance}) +$$

$$(1 + m^{-1})(\text{estimated between variance})$$

$$= 0.14615 + \frac{3}{2}(0.006384)$$

$$= 0.15573 .$$

95% confidence interval for $\bar{Y}$ is

$$2.5385 \pm \frac{1.96}{3}(0.15573)^{\frac{1}{2}} = 2.5385 \pm 0.2578 .$$

Thus, the 95% confidence interval for $\bar{Y}$ is $(2.2807, 2.7963)$.   ◆

Remark 18.2.   Note that the factor $(1+m^{-1})$ is an adjustment for using a finite number of imputations (see Rubin, 1987, p. 21). Also, we can obtain sharper confidence intervals by using the appropriate quantities of the t distribution with degrees of freedom computed as a simple function of the variance components. In our case, it is $8+1 = 9$.

Remark 18.3.   Rubin (1987, p. 22) proposes a modification to the hot-deck model given by: "a nonrespondent will tend to have a value of y, p% higher (or lower) than the matching respondent's value of y where p can be as small as 5% or as large as 20%." One can generate analogous computed data sets for this model and obtain the corresponding confidence intervals. Rubin (1987) calls such a model a *nonignorable hot-deck model*. If a modification is not used, then it is called an *ignorable hot-deck model*.

18.5   SECONDARY DATA ANALYSIS WITH MISSING OBSERVATIONS

Quite often a data set having missing observations is completed by using imputed values. The question is how to improve the secondary data analysis by examining the interrelation between different imputation methods and the methods of secondary data analysis when there are both observed and imputed values. Assume throughout that the missing data cannot be regarded as missing at random (MAR). Wang, Sedransk, and Jinn (1992) study such interplay in a simple linear regression model set-up when the main objectives of the secondary data analysis are confidence intervals for the regression coefficients. They also investigate the performance of confidence intervals based on multiple imputations. In the following we will present some of their results.

Let us assume that a reasonable knowledge is available about the missing data process. Let Y denote the variable of interest. Let $z_i = 1$ if the ith unit selected in the sample is a respondent and $z_i = 0$ otherwise. Then the desirable procedure is the one based on the likelihood, namely, $f(z_1, \ldots, z_n; y_1 \ldots, y_r | \theta)$, where $y_1, \ldots, y_r$ are the observed values of Y corresponding to the respondents (i.e., $z_1 = \cdots = z_r = 1$ and $z_{r+1} = \cdots = z_n = 0$) and θ denotes the parameters for the data and response processes. However, the feasibility of likelihood-based inference is limited. Alternative strategies available to the secondary data analyst are:

1. Use only the observed values.
2. Treat the completed data (containing both observed and imputed values) as if they were all observed (i.e., "uncritical" estimation).
3. Proceed as in item 2 for estimation of location parameters, but use improved estimators of variance.
4. Base inferences on multiple imputed data sets.

Most people opt for 1 or 2. Use of 3 or 4 requires the knowledge of the specific technique employed for imputing. Strategy 4 holds greatest promise when the missing values cannot be regarded as MAR.

18.6   A PROCEDURE FOR ASSESSING THE QUALITY OF INFERENCES

In order to study the interplay of different imputation techniques, Wang, Sedransk, and Jinn (1992) choose a simple, but yet prototypical, analytical goal of influence about the parameters of a simple linear regression. That is, they assume

$$Y_i = \beta_0 + \beta_1 X_i + \epsilon_i, \quad i = 1, \ldots, n \quad (18.1)$$

where the ϵ_i are independent with $\epsilon_i \sim$ normal$(0, \sigma^2)$. The value of the auxiliary variable X is assumed to be known for each unit and the probability of a response on Y is $g(R|Y, X)$. The authors propose the following model for the probability of response:

$$g(R|y, x) = \alpha_1 \{1 - \alpha_2 \exp(-\alpha_3 y)\} . \quad (18.2)$$

They note that this model fits (using PROC NLIN in SAS) well the data from some business detail file. To simplify analysis, the authors propose the special case of (18.2), namely,

$$g(R|y, x) = 1 - \exp(-\alpha y) \quad (18.3)$$

because the general conclusions based on (18.3) will hold for (18.2) as well.

Assume that in a random sample of size n, there are r responses on Y and n responses on X $(r < n)$. The completed data set is denoted by

$$\{(y_i, x_i): \quad i = 1, \ldots, r; \quad (y_i^*, x_i), \quad i = r + 1, \ldots, n\} \quad (18.4)$$

where y_i^* is the imputed value.

Then we have

$$\hat{\beta}_{1c} = \sum_{i=1}^{n} y_i^+ (x_i - \bar{x}_n) / \sum_{i=1}^{n} (x_i - \bar{x}_n)^2 \quad (18.5)$$

$$\hat{\beta}_{0c} = n^{-1} \sum_{i=1}^{n} y_i^+ - \hat{\beta}_{1c} \bar{x}_n \quad (18.6)$$

and

$$\hat{\sigma}_n^2 = \sum_{i=1}^{n} (y_i^+ - \hat{y}_i^+)^2 / (n - 2) \quad (18.7)$$

where

$$\bar{x}_n = n^{-1} \sum_1^n x_i$$

$$y_i^+ = y_i \qquad \text{for } i = 1, \ldots, r$$
$$ = y_i^* \qquad \text{for } i = r+1, \ldots, n$$

and

$$\hat{y}_i^+ = \hat{\beta}_{0c} + \hat{\beta}_{1c} x_i \, .$$

Assuming that n is sufficiently large, the confidence intervals for β_0 and β_1 (based on singly imputed values) are given by

$$\hat{\beta}_{kc} \pm z_{\gamma/2} \left\{ \widehat{\text{var}} \, \hat{\beta}_{kc} \right\}^{\frac{1}{2}}, \qquad k = 0, 1 \tag{18.8}$$

where $\widehat{\text{var}}\,(\hat{\beta}_{kc})$ is the usual estimate of the variance of $\hat{\beta}_{kc}$ evaluated using the completed data set in (18.4) and $z_{\gamma/2}$ is such that $\Phi(z_{\gamma/2}) = 1 - \gamma/2$.

Expressions analogous to (18.5), (18.6), (18.7), and (18.8) can be obtained if the estimates are based only on observed values of y by changing n to r and denote the resultant estimates by $\hat{\beta}_{1r}$, $\hat{\beta}_{0r}$, and $\hat{\sigma}_r^2$. This alternative method will be called N. Consider the following general-purpose imputation methods that are currently in use.

1. **Mean imputation overall [MO].**   Each missing value is replaced by a constant, which is the overall mean of the respondents' values of Y. That is, $y_i^* = \bar{y}_r$, $i = r+1, \ldots, n$.

2. **Random imputation overall [R].**   Given a sample of size n with $n - r$ missing values, a random sample of size $n - r$ is taken with replacement from the r observed values. The selected respondents are called "donors" and their values are randomly assigned to the nonrespondents.

3. **Simple regression imputation [RG].**   Using the respondents' data, β_0 and β_1 are estimated and then for the nonrespondents

$$y_i^* = \hat{\beta}_{0r} + \hat{\beta}_{1r} x_i, \qquad i = r+1, \ldots, n \, .$$

4. **Random regression imputation [RRN].**   The $n-r$ residuals are drawn randomly from the normal $(0, \hat{\sigma}_r^2)$ population and are added to the y_i^* specified in item 3.

5. **Random regression imputation [RRS].**   A random sample of size $n - r$ is taken with replacement from the r observed residuals,

$$\{y_i - \hat{\beta}_{0r} - \hat{\beta}_{1r} x_i : i = 1, 2, \ldots, r\}$$

and these are added to the y_i^* given in item 3.

6. **Random imputation within adjustment cells [RC].**   Method R is applied within the adjustment cells, where an adjustment cell consists of all units having values of X within a specified interval.

EXAMPLE 18.2

A certain part of a city has $N = 25,000$ houses and the average assessed value of these houses is $X = 50$ (in thousands of dollars). A simple random sample of 6 houses is taken and the following data is obtained.

Property	Assessed Value	True Value
1	47.5	52
2	55	60
3	60	58
4	80	84
5	75	?
6	65	72

Suppose the true value for unit #5 is missing. Here $n = 6$, $r = 5$. We illustrate the various methods of imputation.

1. MO: $y_5^* = 326/5 = 65.2$.
2. R: We draw a number randomly (from $1, \ldots, 6$). Suppose it happens to be 3. Then $y_5^* = 58$.

2.′ Nearest-neighbor approach yields $y_5^* = 84$ (since $x = 80$ is closest to 75).

3. RD: Linear regression is fitted to the 5 complete observed pairs, and the least-squares regression line is given by

$$y = 3.08 + 1.01x.$$

So,

$$y_5^* = 3.08 + 1.01(75) = 78.83.$$

4. RRN: $\hat{\sigma}^2 = 15.2465$. A randomly drawn normal deviate (corresponding to a random number 0.75) is 0.6745. Hence,

$$y_5^* = 78.83 + 0.6745(15.2465)^{\frac{1}{2}} = 81.46.$$

5. RRS: The residuals are 0.94, 1.36, −5.68, 0.11, 3.26. Suppose we select 1.36 randomly out of these and, hence,

$$y_5^* = 78.83 + 1.36 = 80.19.$$

6. RC: Method 2′ comes close to method 6.   ◆

18.7   BAYESIAN METHOD

Bayesian method provides the basis for satisfactory secondary data analysis when the missing data cannot be regarded as MAR and we do have knowledge of the nonresponse process. The imputations (single or multiple) are obtained from the unconditional distribution of the values of Y corresponding to the nonresponding units given the sample data. One of the components of this unconditional distribution is the posterior distribution, f_2 of $\beta = (\beta_0, \beta_1)'$. We assume that σ^2 is known and assume a noninformative prior distribution for β. Then f_2 is proportional to the likelihood of β given the data. Thus, the imputations $y_{r+1}, \ldots, y_n$ are taken from the density

$$f(y_{r+1}, \ldots, y_n | y_1, \ldots, y_r; x_1, \ldots, x_n; z_1, \ldots, z_n; \sigma^2)$$

$$= \int \cdots \int f_1(y_{r+1}, \ldots, y_n | \beta, \sigma^2, x_1, \ldots, x_n; z_1, \ldots, z_n)$$

$$\times \ f_2(\beta | y_1, \ldots, y_r; x_1, \ldots, x_n; z_1, \ldots, z_n; \sigma^2) d\beta \qquad (18.9)$$

where $z_1 = \cdots = z_r = 1$ and $z_{r+1} = \cdots = z_n = 0$ are the indicator functions for the respondents and the nonrespondents, respectively. Rubin (1987) has shown that the following procedure provides confidence intervals with (approximately) correct coverage probabilities: The distribution f_2 in (18.9) can be shown to be proportional to

$$K \left\{ \exp\left[-\alpha \left\{ \sum_{i=r+1}^{n} (\beta_0 + \beta_1 x_i) \right\} - (2\sigma^2)^{-1} \left\{ \sum_{i=1}^{r} (y_i - \beta_0 - \beta_1 x_i)^2 \right\} \right] \right\}$$

where

$$K = \prod_{i=r+1}^{n} \Phi\left\{ (\beta_0 + \beta_1 x_i)\sigma^{-1} - \alpha\sigma \right\} \Phi\left((\beta_0 + \beta_1 x_i)\sigma^{-1} \right)$$

and Φ denotes the distribution function of a standard normal variable. For the examples considered by Wang et al. (1992), $(\beta_0 + \beta_1 x_i)/\sigma$ is sufficiently large so that one can set $K \doteq 1$. Hence, f_2 can be reasonably approximated by the bivariate normal distribution. Thus,

$$f_2(\beta | y_1, \ldots, y_r; x_1, \ldots, x_n; z_1, \ldots, z_n; \sigma^2)$$

is normal with mean η and Σ for the var-cov matrix, where

$$X_r' = \begin{pmatrix} 1, \ldots, 1 \\ x_1, \ldots, x_r \end{pmatrix}, \qquad X_r^{*'} = \begin{pmatrix} 1, \ldots, 1 \\ x_{r+1}, \ldots, x_n \end{pmatrix}$$

$$Y_r' = (y_1, \ldots, y_r), \qquad \hat{\beta}_r = (X_r'X_r)^{-1}X_r'Y_r$$

$$A = (X_r'X_r)/\sigma^2, \qquad \Sigma = A^{-1}$$

$$c = 2\alpha 1'X_r^* \text{ with } 1 \text{ as a column vector of } (n-r) \text{ ones and}$$

$$\eta' = -(c - 2\hat{\beta}_r'A)A^{-1}/2.$$

In order to obtain a sample from (18.9) we follow the following procedure.

1. Select $\beta = \beta^*$ from f_2 in (18.9).

2. Given β^*, choose $\hat{y}_j$ from the conditional distribution of y_j for given x_j, β^*, and σ^2, namely the normal distribution with mean $\beta_0^* + \beta_1^* x_j$ and variance σ^2.

3. Select a random number u_j from the uniform $(0, 1)$ distribution.

4. If $u_j \leq \exp(-\alpha \hat{y}_j)$, then $y_j = \hat{y}_j$. Otherwise, repeat steps 2–4 until an acceptable value of y_j is obtained. Repeat the steps 2–4 independently for $j = r+1, \ldots, n$. Using $\hat{y}_{r+1}, \ldots, \hat{y}_n$ and the observed data values $y_1, \ldots, y_r$, calculate $\hat{\beta}_{0c}$, $\hat{\beta}_{1c}$, and the estimated covariance matrix using $(y_1, \ldots, y_r, \hat{y}_{r+1}, \ldots, \hat{y}_n)$. The entire procedure consisting of steps 1–4 is repeated m times. Then the $(1 - \gamma)\, 100\%$ confidence interval for β_0 or β_1 is

$$\bar{Q}_m \pm t_\nu(\gamma/2) T_m^{\frac{1}{2}} \tag{18.10}$$

where $\bar{Q}_m$ and $\bar{U}_m$ are, respectively, the averages over the m replications of the estimates of β and the estimated variance-covariance matrices each evaluated using a completed data set,

$$T_m = \bar{U}_m + (1 + m^{-1}) B_m ,$$

B_m is the variance among replicates, namely,

$$B_m = \sum_{l=1}^{m} (Q_l - \bar{Q}_m)^2 / (m - 1) ,$$

and $t_\nu(\gamma/2)$ is the $100\,\{1 - (\gamma/2)\}$ percentage point of the t distribution with ν degrees of freedom, where

$$\nu = (m - 1)(1 + r_m^{-1})^2$$

and

$$r_m = (1 + m^{-1}) B_m / \bar{U}_m$$

(see also Rubin, 1987, Section 3.3).

Remark 18.4.   If the response function is something other than (18.3), one may proceed as in steps 1–4 (after replacing $\exp(-\alpha \hat{y}_j)$ with $1 - g(R|\hat{y}_j, x_j)$) and take the additional steps that led to (18.1). However, it should be noted that the posterior density of β, namely f_2, may not have a simple form. If it does not, one may sample from f_2 using the rejection sampling method applied by Zeger and Karim (1991, Section 5.1).

Special Case. Suppose β_0 is known and only β_1 is unknown. Then the conditional distribution of β_1 for given $y_1, \ldots, y_r; x_1, \ldots, x_n; z_1, \ldots, z_n; \sigma^2$ is normal, the mean and variance of which will be computed below.

$$\hat{\beta}_{1r} = \sum_1^r x_i y_i / \sum_1^r x_i^2$$

$$A = \sum_1^r x_i^2 / \sigma^2$$

$$\Sigma = A^{-1} = \sigma^2 / \sum_1^r x_i^2$$

$$c = 2\alpha \sum_{j=r+1}^n x_j$$

$$\eta = \sigma^2 \alpha \frac{\sum_{j=r+1}^n x_j}{\sum_1^r x_i^2} + \frac{\sum_1^r x_i y_j}{\sum_1^r x_i^2} = \left(\sum_1^r x_i^2 \right)^{-1} \left\{ \sigma^2 \alpha \sum_{r+1}^n x_j + \sum_1^r x_i y_i \right\}.$$

We illustrate the earlier procedure by means of the following example with $m = 2$.

EXAMPLE 18.3

Consider the rearranged data of Example 18.1.

Property	Assessed Value	True Value
1	47.5	52
2	55	60
3	60	58
4	80	84
5	65	72
6	75	?

Here $n = 6$ and $r = 5$. Assume that $\beta_0 = 3$ and $\sigma^2 = 16$ and $\alpha = 0.02$.

$$\hat{\beta}_{1r} = 20{,}650/19{,}506.25 = 1.059 \approx 1.06$$

$$\eta = (19{,}506.25)^{-1} \{16(0.02)(75) + 20{,}658\}$$

$$= 20{,}682/19{,}506.25 = 1.0603$$

and

$$\Sigma = 16/19{,}506.25 = 0.00082$$

$$\sqrt{\Sigma} = 0.0286 \approx 0.03.$$

First we draw 5 random number given by

$$0.87, 0.72, 0.89, 0.79, 0.92$$

and the corresponding normal deviates are

$$1.13, 0.58, 1.23, 0.80, 1.41.$$

Thus, the random sample from normal $(\beta_0 + \hat{\beta}_{1r}x_6, \sigma^2)$ is

$$\hat{y}_j : 87.02, 84.82, 87.42, 85.7, 88.14.$$

Then $e^{-\alpha \hat{y}_j} = e^{-0.02\hat{y}_j} : 0.18, 0.18, 0.17, 0.18, 0.17$. We draw a random sample of size 5 from uniform $(0, 1)$ distribution and obtain

$$u_j : 0.19, 0.23, 0.15, 0.93, 0.10.$$

Since $u_j \leq \exp(-\alpha y_j)$ for $j = 3$ and 5, we set $y_j = \hat{y}_j$ $(j = 3, 5)$ and reject the rest of the y_j's.

Now using $(y_1, \ldots, y_5, y_6)$, we compute $\hat{\beta}_1$ based on two completed data sets:

$$\sum_1^6 x_i^2 = 19,506.25 + (75)^2 = 25,131.25.$$

Therefore,

$$\hat{\beta}_{1,1} = \{20,658 + 75(87.42)\} / 25,131.25 = 1.083,$$

$$\hat{\beta}_{1,2} = \{20,658 + 75(88.14)\} / 25,131.25 = 1.085,$$

$$\hat{Q}_m = (\hat{\beta}_{1,1} + \hat{\beta}_{1,2})/2 = 1.084$$

$$\bar{U}_1 = \Sigma_1 = \sigma^2/\Sigma_{i=1}^6 x_i^2 = 16/25,131.25 = 0.0006367$$

since Σ_1 is the same for both the completed data sets,

$$B_m = (1.083 - 1.084)^2 + (1.085 - 1.084)^2$$
$$= 0.000002$$

and

$$T_m = 0.0006367 + \frac{3}{2}(0.000002) = 0.0006387$$

$$T_m^{\frac{1}{2}} = 0.0253.$$

Suppose we wish to set up a 95% confidence interval for β_1.

$$r_m = \frac{3}{2}(0.000002)/0.0006367 = 0.0047118$$

$$\nu = \left\{1 + (0.0047118)^{-1}\right\}^2 = (213.23)^2 \doteq 45,468.$$

Hence,

$$t_\nu(0.025) = z_{0.025} = 1.96.$$

Hence, a 95% confidence interval for β_1 is

$$1.084 \pm (1.96)(0.0253) = 1.084 \pm 0.05. \qquad \blacklozenge$$

18.8   COMPARISON OF THE VARIOUS IMPUTATION METHODS

Wang et al. (1992) carried out extensive simulation studies for various values of β_0, β_1, σ^2, α, and $X_1, \ldots, X_n$. They take $\beta_1 = 3$, $\beta_1 = 5$, $\sigma^2 = 1$, and $n = 25$ and use 1000 simulated values. Recall that the expected response rate given $X_1, \ldots, X_n$ is (after using (18.3))

$$E\left((r/n)|X_1, \ldots, X_n; \alpha\right) = n^{-1} \sum_{i=1}^{n} \int \left\{1 - e^{-\alpha y}\right\} h(y|x_i)\, dy$$

where $h(y|x)$ is the density function defined by (18.1). The authors use trial-and-error computational methods to select α so that $E\left((r/n)|x_1, \ldots, x_n; \alpha\right)$ has a specified value. For the examples considered by them, the expected response rates estimated from the 1000 simulations are 0.45, 0.65, and 0.76, corresponding to $\alpha = 0.01, 0.02$, and 0.03. They tabulate the estimated bias$(\hat{\theta})$ and bias$(\hat{\theta})/sd(\hat{\theta})$ for $\hat{\theta} = \hat{\beta}_{0c}, \hat{\beta}_{1c}$, and $\hat{\sigma}_c^2$ (using both observed and imputed values) corresponding to methods N, MO, R, RG, and RRN. The results for RRS are similar to those of RRN. The estimated standard error of the estimate of $B_1 = \text{bias}(\hat{\theta})$ is $B_1/B_2(1000)^{\frac{1}{2}}$, where $B_2 = \text{bias}(\hat{\theta})/sd(\hat{\theta})$. The authors draw the following conclusions:

MO and R are unsatisfactory and N, RG and RRN provide significant improvement over MO and R. The bias$(\hat{\theta})$, the bias$(\hat{\theta})/sd(\hat{\theta})$ are satisfactory for N and RRN, and the biases for N and RRN change little as α ranges from 0.01 to 0.03. For MO, R, and RG, the absolute values of the biases tend to decrease as α increases.

Further, the authors study the estimated properties of two-sided confidence intervals for β_0 and β_1 of the form (18.8) or the analogous form based only on the observed values of y. In particular, they estimate the probability P_{kL} (P_{kU}) that the lower (upper) bound of the confidence interval for β_k exceeds (is less than) β_k ($k = 0, 1$). Clearly, (see their Tables 4 and 5) MO and R are totally unacceptable (because the P_{0L} and P_{1U} are close to one and the P_{0U} and P_{1L} are close to zero. Also, neither RG nor RRN is satisfactory (although preferable to MO and R) because the P_{kL} and P_{kU} ($k = 0, 1$) are close to 30%. When using only the observed y's, N is the best alternative, even though the (estimated) actual confidence coefficients differ from the nominal levels by 3% to 4%.

The authors also consider two other response functions besides (18.3), namely

$$P(R|y) = \exp(-\alpha y)$$

$$P(R|y) = c_0 + c_1 y + c_2 y^2$$

where the values of α and the c_i are chosen so as to have expected response rates of about 0.65 (corresponding to $\alpha = 0.02$) and the c_i to generate a symmetric U-shaped response function. The empirical results differ somewhat from those presented in their Tables 3, 4 and 5, but the rank order of preference among the various methods is remarkably consistent with that based on the response function given by (18.3). Thus, N is the best choice for the set of examples considered by the authors. One may improve the performance of N by replacing $z_{\gamma/2}$ in (18.8) by $t_{r-2,\gamma/2}$ (the corresponding percentage point on the t distribution which depends on r).

They also compare confidence intervals (18.8) (based on observed y's only) and (18.10) and note that the estimated confidence coefficient of (18.10) is larger than the nominal confidence coefficient, whereas the reverse is true for (18.8).

In summary, for any response function, a data set completed with a single set of general-purpose imputations is unlikely to be reliable. Inferences about β_0 and β_1 using only the observed values may be satisfactory, whereas inferences about other parameters such as the overall mean may not be satisfactory. If the data are MAR or nearly so, there is no reason to include in the analysis any imputed values, provided suitable software is available for carrying out the designed analysis with missing data. Otherwise, one can resort to multiple imputation methods and the methods described in Lee, Rancourt, and Särndal (1991) and J. N. K. Rao and Shao (1992). We should also emphasize that "easy" methods of analysis are not likely to be satisfactory.

18.9   MULTIPLE IMPUTATION FOR INTERVAL ESTIMATION

Although we touched upon the Bayesian method in Section 18.7, here we deal with the multiple imputation method for interval estimation in some detail. We assume that we have a random sample with nonresponse that can be ignored. If we impute a value for each missing datum under some model for nonresponse, we have a completed data set and we can carry out the usual methods of analyzing the data. However, single imputation has the major drawback in the sense that the missing values are treated as if they were known, thereby resulting in unreliable inferences, because the variability from not knowing the missing values is ignored. However, multiple imputation, which was proposed by Rubin (1978), not only has the advantages of single imputation but also avoids its drawbacks by replacing each missing datum with two or more values representing a distribution of likely values. Using multiple imputations, one can make two or more complete-data analysis. Hence, one can combine the several complete-data inferences in a simple way that reflects both within-imputation variability and between-imputation variability.

One can understand the theoretical justification for multiple imputation from a Bayesian point of view. Our main objective is to draw an inference about a population quantity from a survey where missing data is present and we assume that the posterior distribution of the missing data (i.e., their conditional distribution given the observed data) is available. Then the posterior distribution of the population quantity is obtained by averaging its complete-data posterior distribution (namely, the conditional distribution given both the observed and the missing data) over the posterior distribution of the missing data.

In order to express it mathematically, let Y_1 denote the set of observed values, Y_2 the set of missing values, and Q be the population quantity of interest. Then the posterior density of Q can be expressed as

$$h(Q|Y_1) = \int g(Q|Y_1, Y_2) f(Y_2|Y_1) \, dY_2 \qquad (18.11)$$

where $f(\cdot)$ denotes the posterior density of the missing values and $g(\cdot)$ is the complete-data posterior density of Q.

Now we can interpret the multiple imputations as simulated draws from the posterior distribution of the missing data. Thus, multiple imputation is a simulation device which enables the investigator to approximate the actual posterior distribution of Q.

18.10   NORMAL-BASED ANALYSIS OF A MULTIPLE IMPUTED DATA SET

Let Q be a scalar (not a vector-valued) quantity to be estimated. If there were no nonresponse, let $\hat{Q}$ be an estimate of Q having an estimated variance U and assume that $\hat{Q} - Q$ is normally distributed with mean 0 and variance U. Now suppose that due to nonresponse, only n_1 of the data values are observed—that is, $Y_1 = (Y_1, \ldots, Y_{n_1})$ and Y_2 is the vector of $n_0 = n - n_1$ missing values ($n_0 > 0$). With m imputations of Y_2, created under a single nonresponse model, there are m completed data sets yielding m values of $\hat{Q}$ and U, say

$$(\hat{Q}_{*l}, U_{*l}), \qquad l = 1, \ldots, m .$$

Then,

$$Q - \hat{Q}_{*.} \sim \text{normal}(0, T_*) \qquad (18.12)$$

where

$$\hat{Q}_{*.} = \sum_{l=1}^{m} \hat{Q}_{*l}/m \qquad (18.13)$$

$$T_* = \hat{W} + ((m + 1)/m) \, \hat{B} \qquad (18.14)$$

$$\hat{W} = \sum_{l=1}^{m} U_{*l}/m \, (\text{average within-imputation variance of } (\hat{Q}_{*.} - Q)$$

and

$$\hat{B} = \sum_{l=1}^{m} (\hat{Q}_{*l} - \hat{Q}_{*.})^2/(m - 1)$$

which is the between-imputation variance of $\hat{Q}_{*.} - Q$. The factor $(m+1)/m$ multiplies $\hat{B}$ as an improvement for modest m because it reflects the extra variability of $\hat{Q}_{*.}$ based on a finite rather than an infinite number of imputations. Interval inferences for Q based on (18.12) are given by

$$I(Y_1) = \hat{Q}_{*.} \pm kT_*^{\frac{1}{2}}, \qquad k = z_{\alpha/2} \tag{18.15}$$

where, for example, $\alpha = .05$ yields $k = 1.96$ and $\alpha = 0.10$ yields $k = 1.645$.

When m is small, one can base the confidence on t distribution and obtain

$$I(Y_1) = \hat{Q}_{*.} \pm t_{\nu,\alpha/2} T_*^{\frac{1}{2}} \tag{18.16}$$

where

$$\nu = \left[1 + \frac{m}{m+1} \frac{\hat{W}}{\hat{B}} \right]^2 (m - 1). \tag{18.17}$$

Also, ν is large, and hence, (18.16) is close to (18.15) when $\hat{W}$ is large relative to $\hat{B}$ (i.e., when the response rate is high). However, ν is close to $m - 1$, the degrees of freedom associated with $\hat{B}$ when $\hat{B}$ is large relative to $\hat{W}$. Rubin (1986) provides a Bayesian justification for the factor $m/(m+1)$ in (18.17). An explanation of the factor $m/(m+1)$ in (18.17) is as follows:

Let $\hat{Q}_\infty$ be the estimate (18.13) based on an infinite degrees of freedom. Then the variance of $\hat{Q}_\infty$ is estimated by $\hat{W} + \hat{B}$. Also, based on m imputations,

$$\text{var}(\hat{Q}_{*.}) = E\left[\text{var}(\hat{Q}_{*.}|Y_1) \right] + \text{var}\left[E(\hat{Q}_{*.}|Y_1) \right]$$

$$= E(B_\infty)/m + \text{var}(\hat{Q}_\infty),$$

where B_∞ denotes the conditional variance of $\hat{Q}_{*l}$ given Y_1 and $\hat{B}$ its unbiased estimate. Thus, the estimated variance of $\hat{Q}_{*.}$ based on m imputations is $(\hat{W} + \hat{B}) + \hat{B}/m$. For a justification of (18.17), see Rubin and Schenker (1986, p. 368).

Rubin and Schenker (1986) study the performance of several multiple imputation methods designed for discrete data, namely,

1. **Single random (SR) imputation.** This SR method draws n_0 components of Y_2 with replacement from the n_1 values in Y_1. This is also known as *hot-deck* method. The variability is underestimated (thereby leading to narrow confidence intervals) because the SR method draws the components of Y_2 with replacement from Y_1 rather than first drawing θ from its posterior distribution and then drawing Y_2 from its conditional posterior distribution, given the drawn value of θ.

2. **Bayesian bootstrap (BB) imputation [Rubin (1981)].**   Let the population random variable be discrete, taking on one of the values $d_1, \ldots, d_K$ with probabilities $\theta_1, \ldots, \theta_K$, respectively. If the improper prior (namely, Dirichlet prior) with density proportional to $\prod_{i=1}^{K} \theta_i^{-1}$ is imposed on the vector $\theta = (\theta_1, \ldots, \theta_K)$, then the posterior distribution of θ is the Dirichlet distribution with density proportional to $\prod_{i=1}^{K} \theta_i^{q_i - 1}$ and K-dimensional mean vector $\hat{\theta} = (\hat{\theta}_1, \ldots, \hat{\theta}_K)$ where $\hat{\theta}_i = q_i/n_1$ and q_i =number of times d_i appears in Y_1. Components of θ corresponding to values of d_i not appearing in Y_1 will be zero with probability one. The BB method first draws a value θ^* of θ from this posterior distribution. Then the components of Y_2 are independently drawn from among $d_1, \ldots, d_K$ using the probabilities in θ^*.

3. **Approximate Bayesian bootstrap (ABB) imputation.**   A simple approximation to the BB method that is more direct from the computation point of view is as follows. First, draw the components of an n_1-dimensional vector X with replacement from Y_1. Then draw the n_0 components of Y_2 with replacement from X. The only difference between ABB and BB method is that instead of drawing θ from the Dirichlet posterior distribution as in the BB method, the ABB method draws θ from a scaled multinomial distribution. The distributions used for θ in the BB and ABB methods have the same mean vectors and the same correlations; however, the variances for the ABB method are $(n_1 + 1)/n_1$ times the variances for the BB method (see Rubin, 1981).

Toward imputation methods for continuous data, the authors propose the following:

4. **Fully normal (FN) imputation.**   Let the data be a random sample from a normal (μ, σ^2) distribution where $\theta = (\mu, \sigma^2)$. If the prior distribution of θ has density proportional to σ^{-2}, then the posterior distribution of σ^2 is $(n_1 - 1)s_1^2/\chi_{n_1 - 1}^2$, and the conditional posterior distribution of μ given σ^2 is normal $(\bar{y}_1, \sigma^2/n_1)$. The FN method first draws a value (μ^*, σ^{*2}) of (μ, σ^2) from the posterior distribution of (μ, σ^2): σ^{*2} is drawn from $(n_1 - 1)s_1^2/\chi_{n_1 - 1}^2$ and then μ^* is drawn from normal $(\bar{y}_1, \sigma^{*2}/n_1)$. The n_0 components of Y_2 are then drawn as a random sample from normal (μ^*, σ^{*2}) population.

5. **Imputation adjusted for uncertainty in the mean and variance (MV).**   If the assumption of normality is not valid, it is desirable to let the observed data Y_1 influence the shape of the distribution of imputed values for Y_2. Then the MV method is as follows. First μ^* and σ^{*2} are drawn as in the FN method. Next the components of an n_0-dimensional vector $X = (X_1, \ldots, X_{n_0})$ are drawn with replacement from Y_1. Then, under repeated draws from Y_1, $Z_i = (X_i - \bar{y}_1)\left[(n_1 - 1)s_1^2/n_1\right]^{-\frac{1}{2}}$ has expected value zero and variance 1 $(i = 1, 2, \ldots)$. The n_0 components of Y_2 are set equal to $\mu^* + \sigma^* Z_i, i = 1, \ldots, n_0$. Note that if the values in Y_1 are left-skewed, then the MV method will lead to left-skewed imputations for Y_2. On the other hand, the FN method will lead to symmetric imputations for Y_2 irrespective of the distribution of values in Y_1.

18.11   CONFIDENCE INTERVAL FOR POPULATION MEAN FOLLOWING MULTIPLE IMPUTATION

We let $Q = \mu =$ the population mean. If there are no missing values, $(\bar{y} - \mu)$ is approximately normally distributed with mean 0 and sample variance s^2/n, where $\bar{y}$ and s^2 are the sample mean and variance based on n observations. Then the quantities introduced in Section 18.10 take the following special forms:

$$\hat{Q} = \bar{y}, \qquad U = s^2/n, \qquad \hat{Q}_{*l} = \bar{y}_{*l} \qquad \text{and} \qquad U_{*l} = s^2_{*l}/n$$

the latter two quantities denoting the values of $\bar{y}$ and s^2/n in the lth data set completed by multiple imputation, $l = 1, \ldots, m$. Then by (18.13) and (18.14), μ is estimated by

$$\bar{y}_{*.} = \sum_{l=1}^{m} \bar{y}_{*l}/m \tag{18.18}$$

and the variance of $\bar{y}_{*.} - \mu$ is estimated by

$$T_* = \sum_{l=1}^{m} s^2_{*l}/(mn) + \frac{(m+1)}{m} \sum_{l=1}^{m} (\bar{y}_{*l} - \bar{y}_{*.})^2/(m-1). \tag{18.19}$$

Hence, by (18.15), the confidence interval for μ is given by

$$I(Y_1) = \bar{y}_{*.} \pm k T_*^{\frac{1}{2}} \tag{18.20}$$

where k is $z_{\alpha/2}$ or $t_{\nu,\alpha/2}$, and ν is given by (18.17).

Asymptotic Expressions for the Coverage Probabilities

Let $r = n_1/n$ and $1 - \alpha$ be the nominal coverage probability. The authors give (as n becomes large):
For SR method,

$$\left.\begin{array}{c}\text{coverage}\\\text{probability}\end{array}\right\} = P\left\{|Z| \le t_{\nu_1,\alpha/2}\left[\frac{mr}{r - r^2 + m}\right.\right.$$

$$\left.\left. + \frac{(m+1)r(1-r)}{(r - r^2 + m)(m-1)}\chi^2_{m-1}\right]^{\frac{1}{2}}\right\} \tag{18.21}$$

and for all other methods,

$$\left.\begin{array}{c}\text{coverage}\\\text{probability}\end{array}\right\} = P\left\{|Z| \le t_{\nu_2,\alpha/2}\left[\frac{mr}{1 - r + m}\right.\right.$$

$$\left.\left. + \frac{(m+1)(1-r)}{(1 - r + m)(m-1)}\chi^2_{m-1}\right]^{\frac{1}{2}}\right\} \tag{18.22}$$

where Z is a standard normal variable,

$$\nu_1 = \nu_2 = \infty \text{ for normal-based analysis}$$

and for the t-based analysis

$$\nu_1 = (m - 1)\left[1 + \frac{m}{m+1} \cdot \frac{(m-1)}{(1-r)\chi^2_{m-1}} \right]^2 \tag{18.23}$$

and

$$\nu_2 = (m - 1)\left[1 + \frac{m}{m+1} \cdot \frac{r(m-1)}{(1-r)\chi^2_{m-1}} \right]^2. \tag{18.24}$$

When $m = 1$, the t-based analysis is not defined and $\chi^2_{m-1} \equiv 0$. For rigorous proof of (18.21)–(18.24) the reader is referred to Schenker (1985). However, the authors provide the following heuristic justification for the same.

The coverage probability associated with the multiple imputed interval

$$= P(\bar{y}_{*.} - kT_*^{\frac{1}{2}} \le \mu \le \bar{y}_{*.} + kT_*^{\frac{1}{2}}) = P\left[\left| \sqrt{n}\frac{(\bar{y}_{*.} - \mu)}{s_1} \right| \le k(nT_*/s_1^2)^{\frac{1}{2}} \right].$$

The preceding probability statement involves the random variables,

$$\sqrt{n}(\bar{y}_{*.} - \bar{y}_1)/s_1, \quad n\hat{W}/s_1^2 \quad \text{and} \quad n\hat{B}/s_1^2.$$

Note that

$$\bar{y}_{*l} - \bar{y}_{*.} = \bar{y}_{*l} - \bar{y}_1 + \bar{y}_1 - \bar{y}_{*.} = (1 - r)\{(\bar{y}_{0l} - \bar{y}_1) - (\bar{y}_{0.} - \bar{y}_1)\}$$

where $\bar{y}_{0.} = \sum_1^m \bar{y}_{0l}/m$ and $\bar{y}_{0l}$ is the lth average of the $(n - n_1)$ imputed values. It is easy to see that for $l = 1, \ldots, m$,

$$\sqrt{n}(\bar{y}_{*l} - \bar{y}_1)/s_1|(Y_1, r)$$

converge to i.i.d. normals with mean zero and variance that depends only on r because of the central limit theorem. Hence,

$$\sqrt{n}(\bar{y}_{*.} - \bar{y}_1)/s_1|(Y_1, r) \quad \text{and} \quad n\hat{B}/s_1^2|(Y_1, r)$$

are asymptotically independent with normal and scaled χ^2_{m-1} distributions, respectively. Also, note that conditioning on (Y_1, r) can be replaced by conditioning on $(\bar{y}_1, s_1^2, r)$. Further, $\sqrt{n}(\bar{y}_{*.} - \mu)/s_1|r$ is normal $(0, r^{-1})$.

The limiting scaled χ^2_{m-1} distribution of $n\hat{B}/s_1^2|(Y_1, r)$ does not depend on Y_1. So, $n\hat{B}/s_1^2$ has the same scaled χ^2_{m-1} distribution, independent of $\sqrt{n}(\bar{y}_{*.} - \mu)/s_1$, asymptotically, for given r. The factors involving r and m in (18.21)–(18.24) reflect asymptotic variances obtained by letting n tend to infinity in Appendix A (see pp. 372–373 of Rubin and Schenker (1986)) in which the authors derive the coverage probabilities for normal data with $m = \infty$ and finite n for various methods.

Remark 18.5. It should be noted that the imputation methods are invariant under location shifts and scale changes. In other words, if the data are transformed as $Y_i \rightarrow aY_i + b$, the imputed values are also transformed in the same fashion. Hence, the coverage probability results for $\mu = 0$ and $\sigma = 1$ will apply for all μ and σ. Also, based on some simulation study, the authors claim that as n tends to ∞, with $r = n_1/n$, m, μ, σ, and F (the underlying distribution of the observations) fixed, "the coverage probability resulting from a particular imputation method is the same for essentially all F."

Certain General Conclusions

The authors tabulate the percentages in expressions (18.21) and (18.22) for nominal levels of coverage, namely 90% and 95% when $m = 1$ and $m = \infty$. However, when $m = 1$, only the normal-based analysis is possible, because the between-imputation component of variance cannot be estimated. Also, when $m = \infty$, the t-based analysis is identical to the normal-based analysis, since $\nu_1 = \nu_2 = \infty$. The authors draw the following conclusions.

1. Substantial gains are possible with multiple imputation rather than with single imputation, and these gains diminish with the increase in the rate of response.

2. Multiple imputation methods that adjust for uncertainty due to parameter estimation are superior to SR imputation; however, the effect becomes modest as the response rate increases.

3. Large-sample coverages for values of m between 2 and ∞ are not presented by the authors because these can be obtained by simple linear interpolation in $1/(m-1)$ between the coverages for $m = 2$ and $m = \infty$. For example, the coverages for $m = 3$ are nearly halfway between the coverages for $m = 2$ and $m = \infty$.

4. The FN and MV methods are superior to all of the other methods. The performance of the SR method is the worst. This shows that it is better to adjust for uncertainty in the parameters when imputing, especially when r is small.

It is impossible to carry out $m = \infty$ imputations in practice. Only $2 \leq m \leq 10$ imputations are routinely possible. The authors carry out an extensive Monte Carlo study of the coverage for normal data with six factors, A–F, and 900 replications, where

A = method of analysis: normal-based, t-based;

B = nominal level of the confidence interval: 90%, 95%;

C = method of imputation: SR, BB, ABB, FN, MV;

D = number of imputations per missing value (m): 1, 2, 3, 5, 10;

E = sample size (n): 20, 50, 100;

F = response rate (r) = 0.4, 0.5, 0.6, 0.7, 0.8, 0.9.

The authors also carry out a simulation study of the coverage probability for certain non-normal data generated from the Laplace (i.e., double exponential) and log normal distributions (i.e., $\log Y$ is distributed normal $(0, 1)$) with 2500 replications. Based on the simulation studies, the authors recommend the MV method with the t-based analysis, especially when n_1 is small. For the MV method with $m = 2$, the coverage is within 3% of the nominal level when $r \geq 0.60$ (within 2% when $r \geq 0.7$) for exactly normal data with small n or essentially any data with large n. When $m \equiv 3$, the coverages are within 2% of the nominal level when $r \geq 0.4$ for normal data with small n or essentially any data with large n.

EXAMPLE 18.4

This is to illustrate the FN imputation method described in Section 18.10. Assume that σ is known. If the prior distribution of $\theta = \mu$ has a density proportional to σ^{-2}, then the posterior distribution of μ is normal $(\bar{y}_1, \sigma^2/n_1)$.

Consider the following scores in the final examination of a certain graduate course in statistics at the University of Kentucky in Fall 1997:

Student #	1	2	3	4	5	6	7	8	9	10	11
Score out of 100	88	86	87	80	83	60	90	88	96	82	?

The score for one student is missing. Assume that $\sigma^2 = 100$. Here $n_1 = 10$, $n_0 = 1$. Suppose 0.61 is a random number drawn from uniform $(0, 1)$ distribution. Then the corresponding normal deviate is 0.28. So, $\theta^* = \mu^* = (0.28)10/\sqrt{10} + 84 = 0.88 + 84 = 84.9$. Then let us draw a random sample of size $m = 3$ from normal $(\mu^*, 10^2)$. Again we draw 3 random numbers lying between 0 and 1 and obtain the corresponding normal deviates and from them the imputed values for y_{11}. The computations are

$$
\begin{array}{cccl}
& 0.40, & 0.01, & 0.34 \\[4pt]
& -0.25, & -2.33, & -0.41 \\[4pt]
\hat{y}_{11} & 82.4, & 61.6, & 80.8, \quad \text{Ex:} \quad 82.4 = -0.25(10) + 84.9 \\[4pt]
\bar{y}_{*l} & 83.8, & 82.0, & 83.7, \quad \text{Ex:} \quad \bar{y}_{*1} = (840 + 82.4)/11 = 83.85 \\[8pt]
s^2_{*l} & 82.43, & 127.82, & 83.13, \quad \text{Ex:} \quad s^2_{*1} = \dfrac{11(78171.76) - (922.4)^2}{110}.
\end{array}
$$

Hence,

$$\bar{y}_{*.} = 83.17$$

$$T_* = \frac{1}{33}(82.43 + 127.82 + 83.13) + \frac{4}{6}\left\{(83.8)^2 + (82.0)^2 + (83.7)^2 - 3(83.17)^2\right\}$$

$$= 8.89 + \frac{4}{6}(0.38) = 9.14$$

$$\nu = 2\left[1 + \frac{3}{4}(8.89)\left(\frac{0.38}{2}\right)^{-1}\right]^2 = 2[1 + 35.09]^2 = 2605.28.$$

A 95% confidence interval for μ is

$$83.17 \pm (1.96)(9.14)^{\frac{1}{2}}$$

i.e.,

$$83.17 \pm 5.93$$

and the true value was 78.   ◆

EXAMPLE 18.5

For the data in Example 18.4, let us proceed with the MV method. As before, we have $\sigma^2 = 100$ and $\mu^* = 84.9$.

Now let the random sample of size $m = 3$ with replacement from Y_1 (the non-missing data) be

$$90, \ 83, \ 86.$$

Since $\sum_1^{10} y_i = 840$ and $\sum_1^{10} y_i^2 = 71{,}382$, we compute $\bar{y}_1 = 84$ and $(n_1 - 1)s_1^2 = 822$ and

$$\left\{ \frac{(n_1 - 1)s_1^2}{n_1} \right\}^{\frac{1}{2}} = 9.07.$$

Hence,

$$z_i : \ 0.66, \ -0.11, \ 0.22, \qquad \text{Ex:} \ \ z_1 = (90 - 84)/9.07 = 0.66.$$

and

$$\hat{y}_{11} = \mu^* + \sigma z_i : \ \ 91.5, \ 83.8, \ 87.1$$

$$\bar{y}_{*l} : \ \ 84.68, \ 83.98, \ 84.28$$

$$s_{*l}^2 : \ \ 87.31, \ 82.20, \ 83.07.$$

Thus,

$$\bar{y}_{*.} = (84.68 + 83.98 + 84.28)/3 = 84.31$$

$$T_* = \frac{1}{33}(87.31 + 82.20 + 83.07)$$

$$+ \frac{4}{6}\left\{(84.68)^2 + (83.98)^2 + (84.28)^2 - 3(84.31)^2\right\}$$

$$= 7.65 + \frac{4}{6}(21{,}326.46) - 21{,}324.528)$$

$$= 7.65 + \frac{4}{6}(1.933) = 8.94$$

$$T_*^{\frac{1}{2}} = 2.99$$

$$\nu = 2\left[1 + \frac{3}{4}(7.65)\left(\frac{1.933}{3}\right)^{-1}\right] = 2(1 + 5.94)^2 = 96.23.$$

Hence, a 95% confidence interval for μ is

$$84.31 \pm (1.96)(2.99)$$

$$84.31 \pm 5.86 .$$

Note that the MV method leads to a shorter confidence interval than the FN method.   ◆

■ PROBLEMS

18.1   With the data in Example 18.1, using a nonignorable hot-deck model with $m = 2$, and assuming that a nonrespondent has a 10% higher sales than the matching respondent (nonrespondent bias), obtain a ratio estimate of the average sales at these fast-food restaurants for the corporation. Also, set up a 95% confidence interval for the same.

18.2   Suppose we wish to estimate the grade-point average of graduating seniors at Mars University. Let $N = 1000$, the number of graduate seniors. We take a sample of $n = 9$ students. Let x denote their SAT scores and y denote the grade-point average at the University. Assume $\bar{X} = 600$. There were two students whose final GPAs were not available.

Student #	x	y
1	550	2.8
2	630	3.1
3	570	2.9
4	650	?
5	700	3.5
6	520	3.0
7	720	3.6
8	660	3.5
9	575	?

Using a nonignorable hot-deck model with $m = 2$, assuming that a nonrespondent has a 5% lower GPA than the matching respondent (nonrespondent bias), obtain a ratio estimate of the average grade-point average of a graduate senior at the University of Mars, and also set up a 95% confidence interval for the same.

18.3   For the data in Example 18.1, using an ignorable hot-deck model with $m = 2$, obtain a ratio estimate of the average sales at these fast-food restaurants for the corporation and also set up a 95% confidence interval for the same.

18.4   The following data gives the heights (x) and weights (y) of a random sample of size 6. Height for one subject is missing. Estimate it by the various methods discussed in Section 18.6. Assume that $\bar{X} = 68$ inches.

x (in inches)	60	70	65	61	62	72
y (in pounds)	115	185	160	?	140	190

18.5   For the data given in Problem 18.4, using an ignorable hot-deck model with $m = 2$, obtain a ratio estimate of the average weight of men and also set up a 95% confidence interval for the same.

18.6 The following data is obtained for a random sample of size 6 students who have completed the MBA program at Mars University. The data includes each student's GPA.

x (GMAT score)	470	570	458	480	530	550
y (MBA GPA)	2.3	3.5	3.3	3.2	3.7	?

Using an ignorable hot-deck model with $m = 2$, obtain a ratio estimate of the average MBA GPA of the MBA graduates at Mars University. Also, obtain a 95% confidence interval for the same. Use $\bar{X} = 495$.

18.7 Consider the following artificial data. Using the procedure of Section 18.7 and assuming that $\beta_0 = -1$, obtain a 95% confidence interval for β_1 with $m = 2$ imputations.

x	1	2	3	4	5	6
y	3	2	8	8	11	?

18.8 For the data in Problem 18.6, using the procedure of Section 18.7 and assuming that $\beta_0 = 2.7$, obtain a 95% confidence interval for β_1 with $m = 2$ imputations.

18.9 The maximum daily rainfall in a certain city in the United States for the years 1961–1970 is as follows:

$$1.25, \ 3.30, \ 1.86, \ 1.51, \ 3.00, \ 3.48, \ 2.12, \ 4.68, \ 2.28, \ 2.12.$$

Assume that the data is normal (μ, σ^2) with $\sigma^2 = 1.0$. Pretend that the last observation, namely y_{11}, is missing. Following the procedure given in Section 18.10, impute $m = 3$ values for the missing datum and obtain a 95% confidence interval for μ.

18.10 For the data in Problem 18.9, do the same thing using the MV method, since the data may not be normally distributed.

18.11 The following data gives the amount of money (in dollars) a random sample of $n = 11$ of shoppers spent at a grocery store:

$$2.50, \ 10.36, \ 16.42, \ 20.72, \ 33.46, \ 21.18, \ 19.25, \ 8.24, \ 11.68, \ 43.80, \ 36.42.$$

Assume that the data is normal (μ, σ^2), where $\sigma^2 = 49$. Pretend that the last observation, namely y_{11}, is missing. Following the procedure given in Section 18.10, impute $m = 3$ values for the missing datum and obtain a 95% confidence interval for μ.

18.12 For the data in Problem 18.11, do the same thing using the MV method.

■ REFERENCES

18.1 Ernest, L. F. (1980). Variance of the estimated mean for several imputation procedures. *Proceedings of the Section on Survey Research Methods, American Statistical Association*, 716–720.

18.2 Kalton, G. and Kasprzyk, D. (1986). The treatment of missing survey data. *Survey Methodology*, Statistics Canada **12**, 1–16.

18.3 Lee, H., Rancourt, E., and Särndal, C. (1991). Experiments with variance estimation from survey data with imputed values. *Proceedings of the Survey Research Methods Section, Amer. Statist. Assoc.* 690–695.

18.4   Platek, R. and Gray, G. B. (1978). Nonresponse and imputation. *Survey Methodology,* Statistics Canada **4**, 144–177.

18.5   Rao, J. N. K. and Shao, J. (1992). Jackknife variance estimation with survey data under hot-deck imputation. *Biometrika* **79**, No. 4, 811–822.

18.6   Rubin, D. B. (1976). Inference and missing data. *Biometrika* **63**, 581–592.

18.7   Rubin, D. B. (1978). Multiple imputations in sample surveys—A phenomenological Bayesian approach to nonresponse. *Proceedings of the Section on Survey Research Methods, American Statistical Association* 20–28.

18.8   Rubin, D. B. (1979). Illustrating the use of multiple imputations to handle nonresponse in sample surveys. *Proc. International Statistical Institute,* Manila, 517–532.

18.9   Rubin, D. B. (1981). The Bayesian bootstrap. *The Annals of Statistics* **9**, 130–134.

18.10 Rubin, D. B. (1986). *Multiple Imputation for Nonresponse in Surveys.* New York: John Wiley.

18.11 Rubin, D. B. and Schenker, N. (1986). Multiple imputation for interval estimation from simple random samples with ignorable nonresponse. *Journal of the American Statistical Association* **81**, 316–374.

18.12 Sande, I. G. (1982). Imputation in surveys: coping with reality. *The American Statistician* **36**, 145–152.

18.13 Schenker, N. (1985). *Multiple Imputation for Internal Estimation from Surveys with Ignorable Nonresponse.* Ph.D. dissertation, University of Chicago, Department of Statistics.

18.14 Wang, R., Sedransk, J., and Jinn, J. H. (1992). Secondary data analysis when there are missing observations. *Journal of American Statistical Association* **87**, 952–961.

18.15 Zeger, S. and Karim, M. (1991). Generalized linear models with random effects: Gibbs sampling approach. *Journal of the American Statistical Association* **86**, 79–86.

Chapter 1

2. **(b)** $\mathbf{W} = \begin{pmatrix} -1.33 \\ 2.83 \\ 0.5 \end{pmatrix}$ **(c)** $\mathbf{W} = \begin{pmatrix} 0.5 \\ 0 \\ 0.5 \end{pmatrix}$

4. Let $T = \Sigma w_i X_i$. Then T is MVU if $w_i = \frac{1}{n}$ $(i = 1, \ldots, n)$, i.e., $T^* = \bar{X}$ is MVU. Next, suppose T is MVU. Let $Z = X_i - X_j$. Then $\operatorname{cov}(T, X_i - X_j) = 0$. This implies that $w_i = w_j$ $(i \neq j)$ for all i. Then $\sum_1^n w_i = 1$, implies that $w_i = \frac{1}{n}$.

Chapter 2

4. $\pi_i = z_i + z_i \sum_{j=1}^4 \frac{z_j}{1-z_j}$

i	π_i
1	0.235
2	0.441
3	0.608
4	0.716

$$\operatorname{cov}(a_i, a_j) = E(a_i a_j) - \pi_i \pi_j$$

$$E(a_i a_j) = P(a_i = 1, a_j = 1)$$

$$= P(U_{i_1} = U_i \text{ and } U_{i_2} = U_j)$$

$$+ P(U_{i_1} = U_j \text{ and } U_{i_2} = U_i)$$

$$= z_i \left(\frac{z_j}{1 - z_i} \right) + z_j \left(\frac{z_i}{1 - z_j} \right)$$

375

i	var a_i
1	0.180
2	0.247
3	0.238
4	0.203

$\mathrm{cov}(a_1, a_2) = -0.0564$

$\mathrm{cov}(a_1, a_3) = -0.0667$

$\mathrm{cov}(a_1, a_4) = -0.0571$

$\mathrm{cov}(a_2, a_3) = -0.1074$

$\mathrm{cov}(a_2, a_4) = -0.0824$

$\mathrm{cov}(a_3, a_4) = -0.0639$

$$\mathrm{var}\ \hat{\bar{Y}}_{HT} = \frac{1}{4^2}\left[\sum \frac{y_i^2}{\pi_i^2}\ \mathrm{var}\ a_i + 2\sum\sum_{i<j} \frac{y_i y_j}{\pi_i \pi_j}\ \mathrm{cov}(a_i, a_j)\right]$$

$$= \frac{1}{16}[9.538 + 2(-4.358)]$$

$$= 0.0514$$

For DesRaj's estimate, let $r_i = \frac{y_i}{Nz_i} - \bar{Y}$. Since $\bar{Y} = 1.75$,

$$r_1 = -0.5$$

$$r_2 = -0.25$$

$$r_3 = 0$$

$$r_4 = 0.25$$

$$\mathrm{var}(\hat{\bar{Y}}_D) = \left\{\frac{1}{2} - \frac{1}{4}(0.3)\right\}(0.0625) - \frac{1}{4}(0.015)$$

$$= \underline{0.0228}.$$

Chapter 3

1. var $\bar{y} = 5/12$.
3. $(44012.9, 71987.1)$
5. $\hat{Y}_1 = 220$, $\hat{Y}_2 = 244.4$, var $\hat{Y}_1 = 3638.57$, var $\hat{Y}_2 = 2050.53$
7. $\hat{R} = 329/21 = 15.6$, i.e., the confidence interval is $15.6 \pm 2.2622(0.696)$
15. $0.04 \pm 2.0634(0.04)$, i.e., $(0, 0.123)$
18. $0.732 \pm 1.96(0.0172)$

Chapter 4

1. $\hat{n}_0 = \frac{z^2 q}{r^2 p} = 270$. Since $\hat{n}_0/N = 0.27$, we use finite population correction and obtain

$$n = \frac{\hat{n}_0}{\left(1 + \frac{\hat{n}_0 - 1}{N}\right)} = 213.13 \simeq 214.$$

3. $P[(p - P) \leq 0.1P] = 0.95$

$$n = \frac{(1.96)^2(0.2)(0.8)}{(0.01)(0.2)^2} = 384 \times 400 = \underline{1536.64}\,.$$

Let $d = (0.1)(0.2) = 0.02$,

$$n = \frac{NPQz^2}{(N - 1)d^2 + PQz^2} = 1506.9 \approx 1507\,.$$

4. $N = 77{,}853$, $m = 10$, $P = 0.1$,

$$E(n) = \frac{m(N + 1)}{M + 1}$$

$$\hat{M} = NP = 77{,}853(0.1) \simeq 7785.3$$

$$E(n) \doteq 10(77{,}853 + 1)/\{7785.3 + 1\} = 99.99 \simeq 100\,.$$

6. $P\,(|p - P| \leq 0.3P) = 0.95$,

$$\frac{n_0(0.3)^2 P^2}{P(1 - P)} = 1.96^2$$

$$n_0 = 384$$

and

$$n = \frac{n_0}{1 - \frac{1}{N} + \frac{n_0}{N}} \doteq 142\,.$$

Alternatively one can use $n = NPQz^2/\{(N - 1)d^2 + PQz^2\}$ with $d = (0.3)(0.1) = 0.03$.

9. $A = $ expected profit $= 100N - N^2\frac{PQ}{n} - cn$,

$$\frac{\partial A}{\partial n} = 0 \Rightarrow$$

$$n = N\sqrt{\frac{PQ}{c}}$$

$$n = N\sqrt{\frac{PQ}{c}} = 222\,.$$

Chapter 5

1.
$P_{w,\text{edu}} = 0.578$, $s_p = 0.0175$, 95% CI is 0.577 ± 0.035,
$P_{w,\text{rel}} = 0.608$, $s_p = 0.0176$, 95% CI is 0.6077 ± 0.0345,
$P_{w,\text{pol}} = 0.575$, $s_p = 0.0181$, 95% CI is 0.576 ± 0.0355.

2. $s_{p,\text{edu}} = 0.0173$, $\bar{y}_{w,\text{edu}} = 0.6174$,
$s_{p,\text{rel}} = 0.0176$, $\bar{y}_{w,\text{rel}} = 0.6343$.

4. $n_i \equiv 61$.

$$(\bar{y}_{st} - \bar{Y})/s(\bar{y}_{st}) \overset{d}{=} N(0, 1)$$

$$\bar{y}_{st} = \frac{1}{8}(31.7) = 3.9625$$

$$\text{var}(\bar{y}_{st}) = \frac{1}{(64)(61)} \cdot \sum_{n=1}^{8} s_n^2 = (3904)^{-1}(4.7505)$$

$$= 0.00122$$

$$s_{\bar{y}_{st}} = 0.0349$$

$$95\% \text{ CI is } 3.9625 \pm 1.96(0.0349) = 3.96256 \pm 0.06836 \text{ i.e., } (3.894, 4.031).$$

$$df \doteq 494.$$

6. $n_1 = 96, n_2 = 3, n_3 = 1$.

7. If $W_1 = W_2 = W_3 = W_4 = \frac{1}{4}$,

$$\bar{y}_{st} = 5891.1$$

$$s_{\bar{y}_{st}} = 1385.448.$$

14. (a) $p = 0.06$, 95% CI is 0.06 ± 0.0468, i.e., $(0.0132, 0.1068)$

(b) $p_{st} = 0.0542, s_{\bar{y}_{st}} = 0.0161$, CI is $(0.0226, 0.0858)$

(c) st is more precise

17. Stratum 1: $(0.8, 0.9)$

Stratum 2: $(0.9, 1.0)$

Stratum 3: $(1.0, 1.10)$

Chapter 6

1. Recall that

$$\hat{Y}_{RS} = \sum_{k=1}^{2} \frac{y_k}{x_k} \cdot X_k$$

and

$$\text{MSE}(\hat{Y}_{RS}) = \frac{1}{100} \sum_{i=1}^{100} (\hat{Y}_{RS,i} - Y)^2$$

$$= \frac{1}{100} \left[\sum (\hat{Y}_{RS,i}^2 - 2Y \sum_{1}^{100} \hat{Y}_{rs,i} \right] + Y^2$$

$$= 66.47754$$

where

$$\sum_{i=1}^{100} \hat{Y}_{RS,i} = 8628.109 \text{ and } \sum_{i=1}^{100} \hat{Y}_{RS,i}^2 = 751,038.8.$$

Given that $N_h = 5, n_h = 2, h = 1, 2$,

$$\hat{Y}_{RC} = \frac{\sum_{1}^{2} y_h}{\sum_{1}^{2} x_h} X$$

$$\text{MSE}(\hat{Y}_{RC}) = \frac{1}{100} \left(\sum_{i=1}^{100} \hat{Y}_{RC,i}^2 - 2Y \sum \hat{Y}_{RC,i} \right) + Y^2 = 62.5625$$

since

$$\sum_{i=1}^{100} \hat{Y}_{RC,i} = 8660.804 \text{ and } \sum_{i=1}^{100} \hat{Y}_{RC,i}^2 = 756,336.1.$$

Hence,

$$MSE(\hat{Y}_{RS}) - MSE(\hat{Y}_{RC}) = 66.48 - 62.56 = 3.92.$$

To see if the difference in the MSE's is due to bias or variance, we can calculate $var(\hat{Y}_{RS})$ and $var(\hat{Y}_{RC})$. Now,

$$var(\hat{Y}_{RS}) = E[\hat{Y}_{RS} - 86.28109]^2 = 65.96$$

and

$$var(\hat{Y}_{RC}) = E[\hat{Y}_{RC} - 86.60804]^2 = 62.4$$

Thus,

$$var(\hat{Y}_{RS}) - var(\hat{Y}_{RC}) = 3.55.$$

Hence,

$$(Bias\hat{Y}_{RC})^2 - (Bias\hat{Y}_{RS})^2 = 3.92 - 3.55 = 0.37.$$

Thus, the difference in the MSE's is largely due to the variance of the estimates, and not due to the bias.

Remark. See the enclosed program for evaluating all possible samples and the relevant quantities.

3. $\hat{R} = 176/161 = 1.1$ and

$$\widehat{var}(\hat{R}) = \frac{\left(1 - \frac{10}{2000}\right)}{10(16.1)^2} \left[64.2667 + 1.1^2(61.6556) - 2(1.1)55.7556\right]$$

$$= 0.006687.$$

Thus, $s_{\hat{R}} = 0.08177$. Hence, a 95% CI for R is

$$1.1 \pm 2.2622(0.08177) \text{ i.e., } (0.908, 1.278).$$

5. $N_1 Sd_1/\sqrt{c_1} = 100(10)/\sqrt{5} = 447.2136,$
   $N_2 Sd_2/\sqrt{c_2} = 150(12)/\sqrt{6} = 734.8469,$ and
   $N_3 Sd_3/\sqrt{c_3} = 120(15)/\sqrt{4} = 900.$
   Thus,

$$\sum_{i=1}^{3} N_i Sd_i/\sqrt{c_i} = 2082.0605.$$

Hence, our optimum allocation of $n = 25$ to the 3 strata is:

$$n_1 = 25(447.2136/2082.0605) = 5.37 \doteq 5$$

$$n_2 = 25(734.8469/2082.0605) = 8.82 \doteq 9$$

$$n_3 = 25(900/2082.0605) = 10.81 \doteq 11.$$

6. Let $\hat{R}_i$ be the ratio estimate with the ith pair (x_i, y_i) deleted. Then we obtain

$$\begin{array}{llll}
\hat{R}_1 = 310/690, & \hat{R}_2 = 315/695, & \hat{R}_3 = 308/680, & \hat{R}_4 = 300/670, \\
\hat{R}_5 = 290/660, & \hat{R}_6 = 295/665, & \hat{R}_7 = 305/678, & \hat{R}_8 = 298/665, \\
\hat{R}_9 = 288/655, & \hat{R}_{10} = 285/660, & \hat{R}_{11} = 306/682. &
\end{array}$$

Also,

$$\hat{R} = 310/740 = 0.4189.$$

Hence,

$$\hat{R}_- = \frac{1}{11}\sum_{j=1}^{n}\hat{R}_j \doteq \frac{1}{n}(4.9044) \doteq 0.4459.$$

Thus, the jackknife estimate of R is

$$R_Q = 11\hat{R} - 10\hat{R}_- = 11(0.4189) - 4.459 = 0.4469.$$

8. $\hat{R} = 550/730 = 0.7534.$

$$\widehat{\text{var}}(\hat{R}) = \left\{62.5 + (0.7534)^2580 - 2(0.7534)(137.5)\right\}/5(146)^2$$

$$= 0.0017315 \text{ (see p. 118 for the formula)}.$$

So,

$$s_{\hat{R}} = 0.0416.$$

13. Using a ratio estimate for $\hat{Y}$, we have

$$\hat{\bar{Y}}_R = \hat{R}\bar{X} = \frac{.381}{30.2}(3) = 37.8477$$

$$\widehat{\text{var}}(\hat{\bar{Y}}_R) = \frac{\left(1 - \frac{10}{10^5}\right)}{(10)9}(185.9258)$$

$$= 2.06564.$$

Thus,

$$s(\hat{\bar{Y}}_R) = 1.4272.$$

Hence, a 95% CI for $\bar{Y}$ is

$$37.8477 \pm 2.2622(1.4372) \text{ i.e., } (34.596, 41.099).$$

```
*        Chapter 6, Problem 1
*        This program computes the MSE and VAR for=20
*        Yhatratioseparate and Yhatratiocombined
*        (i.e. the ratio population estimates)
*
 program ratio=20
*
*        VARIABLE DECLARATION
*        i & j give the srs for stratum 1
*        k & l give the srs for stratum 2
*        X1=3Dtotal x for stratum 1
*        X2=3Dtotal x for stratum 2
*        Y1=3Dtotal y for stratum 1
*        Y2=3Dtotal y for stratum 2
*        xs1=3Dtotal x for stratum 1's srs
*        xs2=3Dtotal x for stratum 2's srs
*        ys1=3Dtotal y for stratum 1's srs
*        ys2=3Dtotal y for stratum 2's srs
*        estrs=3Dseparate ratio estimate (section 6.9)=20
*        estrc=3Dcombined ratio estimate (section 6.9)
```

```
*=09
 integer i,j,k,l
 real strat1(5,2), strat2(5,2)=09
 real X, Y, X1, X2, Y1, Y2
 real xs1, xs2, ys1, ys2
 real estrs estrc
 real trs1, trs2, trc1, trc2
 real means, meanc
*=09
*     LET'S FILL THEM UP
*
 strat1(1,1)=3D2
 strat1(1,2)=3D1
 strat1(2,1)=3D4
 strat1(2,2)=3D3
 strat1(3,1)=3D8
 strat1(3,2)=3D7
 strat1(4,1)=3D10
 strat1(4,2)=3D8
 strat1(5,1)=3D14
 strat1(5,2)=3D10
*
 strat2(1,1)=3D8
 strat2(1,2)=3D1
 strat2(2,1)=3D16
 strat2(2,2)=3D13
 strat2(3,1)=3D20
 strat2(3,2)=3D12
 strat2(4,1)=3D25
 strat2(4,2)=3D15
 strat2(5,1)=3D30
 strat2(5,2)=3D17
*=09
 X1=3D38
 X2=3D99
 X=3DX1+X2
 Y1=3D29
 Y2=3D58
 Y=3DY1+Y2
 xs1=3D0
 xs2=3D0
 xs1=3D0
 ys2=3D0
 estrc=3D0
 estrs=3D0
 trs1=3D0
 trs2=3D0
 trc1=3D0
 trc2=3D0
*
*     LET'S PICK THE SAMPLES & FIND THE TOTALS
*     NECESSARY TO CALCULATE THE MSE and VAR
```

```
*
 do i=3D2,5
  do j=3D1,i-1
   do k=3D2,5
    do l=3D1,k-1
             xs1=3Dstrat1(i,1)+strat1(j,1)
     xs2=3Dstrat2(k,1)+strat2(l,1)
     ys1=3Dstrat1(i,2)+strat1(j,2)
     ys2=3Dstrat2(k,2)+strat2(l,2)
     estrs=3Dys1*X1/xs1+ys2*X2/xs2
     trs1=3Dtrs1+estrs
     trs2=3Dtrs2+estrs*estrs
     estrc=3D(ys1+ys2)*X/(xs1+xs2)
     trc1=3Dtrc1+estrc
     trc2=3Dtrc2+estrc*estrc
             enddo=20
   enddo
  enddo
 enddo
*
*     MSE computation
*
 means=3Dtrs1/100
 meanc=3Dtrc1/100
*
 print *,'The MSE for separate is', (trs2-2*Y*trs1)/100+Y*Y
 print *,'Note:  Total sum for separate estimates is',trs1
 print *,'       and total sum for squared sep. est. is',trs2
 print *,'The variance for separate is',trs2/100-means*means
 print *
 print *,'The MSE for combined is', (trc2-2*Y*trc1)/100+Y*Y
 print *,'Note:  Total sum for combined estimates is',trc1
 print *,'       and total sum for squared comb. est. is',trc2
 print *,'The variance for combined is',trc2/100-meanc*meanc
*
 end
```

Chapter 7

3. Y =actual weight,
X =estimated weight,
$N = 100, n = 5, \bar{X} = 67.6, \bar{Y} = 69,$

$$\bar{Y}_{lr} = \bar{Y} + b(\bar{X} - \bar{x})$$

$$b = 438/481.2 = 0.91$$

$$\hat{Y} = N\hat{\bar{Y}}_{lr}$$

$$= 100(69) + 100(0.91)(\bar{X} - \bar{x})$$

$$= 100(69) + 91(56 - 67.6)$$

$$= 100(69) - 11.6 \times 91 = \underline{5844.14}.$$

5. $\bar{x} = 6887.5, \bar{y} = 2308.125, \bar{X} = 5000,$

$$b = 0.732$$

$$\bar{Y}_{lr} = 926.475$$

$$\widehat{var}(\bar{Y}_{lr}) = \frac{1}{8(6)}\left[42{,}547{,}996.9 - (0.732)^2(712.8750)\right], \quad 1 - \rho \doteq 1,$$

$$= 91{,}513.3258$$

$$s(\bar{Y}_{lr}) = 302.51.$$

6. Given $\bar{X} = 56$, we wish to minimize

$$\sum \left(\frac{y_i - \alpha - \beta x_i}{x_i}\right)^2.$$

Differentiating with respect to α and β, respectively, we obtain

$$\sum \left(\frac{y_i}{x_i^2} - \frac{\alpha}{x_i^2} - \frac{\beta}{x_i}\right) = 0,$$

$$\sum \left(\frac{y_i}{x_i} - \frac{\alpha}{x_i} - \beta\right) = 0.$$

That is,

$$0.27181 - 0.005118\alpha - 0.15929\beta = 0$$

and

$$9.73929 - 0.15929\alpha - 6\beta = 0,$$

yielding

$$\alpha = 14.9, \quad \beta = 1.228.$$

Verify that this leads to a minimum. Thus

$$\hat{\bar{Y}} = 14.9 + 1.228\bar{X}$$

$$= 14.9 + 1.228(56) = 83.668.$$

9. $\bar{x} = 495, \bar{y} = 18.15, b = 0.0748,$

$$\bar{y}_{lr} = 68.15 + 0.0748(550 - 495) = 72.26.$$

11. $\bar{X}_1 = 10.5$, $s_1^2 = 0.7$, $\bar{X}_2 = 16$, $s_2^2 = 1.3$,

$$b_1 = 1.596/2.452 = 0.6509$$

$$b_2 = 18.634/15.588 = 1.1954$$

$$\bar{y}_{lr_1} = 11.411$$

$$\bar{y}_{lr_2} = 17.881$$

$$\bar{y}_{lr_s} = 14.107$$

$$\text{var}(\bar{y}_{lr_s}) = 0.0522$$

$$b_c = \frac{3.76366}{3.52221} = 1.067,$$

$$\bar{y}_{lr_c} = 14.0107$$

$$\widehat{\text{var}}(\bar{y}_{lr_c}) = 0.0487.$$

13. $\bar{y}_{lr} = 25.018$, $b = -0.3351$.

15. $\bar{y}_{lr_s} = 42.478$, $\bar{y}_{lr_c} = 42.359$.

Chapter 8

1.
$$S^2 = \frac{1}{29} \sum_1^{30} (y_i - \bar{Y})^2 = 1.2218$$

$$S_{wsy}^2 = 1.58331 \text{ (a)}$$

$$= 1.36941 \text{ (b)}$$

$$\text{var}(\bar{y}_{\text{ran}}) = \frac{1-f}{n} \cdot S^2 = \frac{(1 - \frac{3}{30})}{3}(1.2218) = 0.36654.$$

(a) $\text{var}(\bar{Y}_{sy}) = \frac{N-1}{N} S^2 - \frac{k(n-1)}{N} S_{wsy}^2 = 0.12553$. Then,

$$\frac{\text{var}(\bar{y}_{sy})}{\text{var}(\bar{y}_{\text{ran}})} = \frac{0.12553}{0.36654} = 0.34.$$

SRS is 34% as effective as systematic sampling.

(b) $\text{var}(\bar{y}_{sy}) = 0.26813$, $\dfrac{\text{var}(\bar{y}_{sy})}{\text{var}(\bar{y}_{\text{ran}})} = 0.73$.

3.
$$\bar{y}_{sy} = 8.8$$

$$s_w^2 = \frac{97.6}{9} = 10.84$$

$$\widehat{\text{var}}(\bar{y}_{sy}) = \left(\frac{1}{10} - \frac{1}{500}\right) \frac{97.6}{9} = 1.06275$$

$$\widehat{\text{var}}(\hat{Y}_{sy}) = (500)^2 \, \text{var}(\bar{y}_{sy}) = 265,689.$$

5.
$$\text{var}(\hat{p}_{sy}) = \frac{1}{12}[3(0.055) + 5(0.036)] = 0.02903$$

$$\text{var}(\hat{p}_{\text{ran}}) = \frac{(1-f)PQN}{n(N-1)} = 0.03496 > \text{var}(\hat{p}_{sy}).$$

6.
$$\hat{Y}_{sy} = N\bar{y}_{sy} = 2000(6) = 12{,}000$$

$$\widehat{\text{var}}(\bar{y}_{sy}) = \left(\frac{1}{10} - \frac{1}{2000}\right)\frac{48}{4} = 0.5306$$

$$\widehat{\text{var}}(\hat{Y}_{sy}) = 2{,}122{,}666.6$$

$$s(\hat{\bar{Y}}) = 1456.94$$

Chapter 9

1. $s_b^2 = 2.5/150 = 0.0167,\ S_w^2 = 3.0.$ Also, an unbiased estimate of S^2 is
$$\hat{S}^2 = \left[M(N-1)s_b^2 + N(M-1)s_w^2\right]/(NM-1)$$
$$= [150(20-1)(0.0167) + 20(150-1)(3.0)]/\{20(150)-1\}$$
$$= 2.9978.$$

2. If $S_w^2 = AM_i^g$, $\log S_w^2 = \alpha + \beta\log M_i$. Using the calculator, $\hat{\alpha} = -7.8652,\ \hat{\beta} = 1.7865,$
$$A = e^{\hat{\alpha}} = 3.84 \times 10^{-4}, \qquad g = 1.7865.$$

3.

Floor	Averages
2	$\bar{y}_1 = \dfrac{660}{10} = 66$
6	$\bar{y}_2 = \dfrac{710}{10} = 71$
9	$\bar{y}_9 = \dfrac{719}{10} = 71.9$

An estimate of the average amount spent by a married graduate student is
$$\hat{\bar{Y}} = \bar{\bar{y}} = (66 + 71 + 71.9)/3 = 208\cdot9/3 = 69.63.$$

Using the formula on p. 181),
$$\widehat{\text{var}}(\bar{y}) = \frac{(1-\frac{3}{15})}{3}\cdot\frac{1}{2}\cdot(20.2067) = 2.6942$$

$$s_{\bar{y}} = 1.64.$$

4. If $M = y^2$, the equation becomes
$$\frac{y^2 + 1}{2(100y - y^2 + 1)} = 1 - (1 + cy^2)^{-\frac{1}{2}}$$

or
$$\frac{1}{1 + cy^2} = \left(\frac{200y - 3y^2 + 1}{200y - 2y^2 + 2}\right)^2.$$

That is,

$$P(y) = 9cy^b - 1200cy^5 + (39994c + 5)y^4 + (-400 + 400c)y^3 + (2 + c)y^2 - 400y - 3 = 0.$$

Maple gives

c	y	$M = y^2$
250	66.693	4448
500	66.687	4448
1000	66.682	4447

If c is large, we can solve for y from

$$P^*(y) = 9y^4 - 1200y^3 + 39{,}994y^2 + 400y + 1 = 0.$$

Root of the equation is 66.672 yielding $M = 4446$.

5.

Floor	Proportion of Afro-American
2	$p_1 = \dfrac{4}{100} = 0.04$
6	$p_6 = \dfrac{5}{100} = 0.05$
9	$p_9 = \dfrac{3}{10} = 0.03$

Estimate of the true proportion $= p = (0.04 + 0.05 + 0.03)/3 = 0.04$,

$$s_p^2 = \frac{\left(1 - \frac{3}{12}\right)}{3(2)}(0.0002) = 0.000025$$

$$s_p = 0.005.$$

95% confidence interval for the true proportion is

$$0.04 \pm (4.3027)(0.0005), \text{ i.e., } (0.0185, \ 0.0615).$$

Chapter 10

1. Scheme I:
$\pi_1 = 0.4, \pi_2 = 0.467, \pi_3 = 0.533, \pi_4 = 0.6,$
$\pi_{12} = 0.1, \pi_{13} = 0.133, \pi_{14} = 0.167, \pi_{23} = 0.167, \pi_{24} = 0.2, \pi_{34} = 0.233.$

$$\text{var } \hat{Y}_{HT} = 3.8801.$$

If units U_1 and U_4 are selected in your sample, then

$$\hat{Y}_{HT} = 7.25 \text{ and } \widehat{\text{var}}\hat{Y}_{HT} = 9.8826.$$

Scheme II: $\sum_{i=1}^{4} \dfrac{z_j}{1 - z_j} = 1.4564,$

$\pi_1 = 0.2345, \pi_2 = 0.4413, \pi_3 = 0.6083, \pi_4 = 0.7159,$
$\pi_{12} = 0.0472, \pi_{13} = 0.0762, \pi_{14} = 0.1111, \pi_{23} = 0.1607, \pi_{24} = 0.2334, \pi_{34} = 0.3714.$

$$\text{var } \hat{Y}_{HT} = 1.1796.$$

If, for instance, units U_1 and U_4 are selected in your sample, then

$$\hat{Y}_{HT} = 7.1608 \text{ and } \widehat{\text{var}}\hat{Y}_{HT} = 4.2871.$$

2. $n = 2$ and (U_2, U_3) is your sample. Then $p(s|U_2) = 0.2143$, $p(s|U_3) = 0.3529$, and $p(s) = 0.1172$. Hence,

$$\hat{Y}_M = 3.9040,$$

$$\widehat{\text{var}}\hat{Y}_M = 0.5448,$$

$$s_{\hat{Y}_M} = 0.7381.$$

95% confidence interval for Y_M is $3.9040 \pm 2(0.7381)$.

Chapter 11

1. $\bar{y} = 282$, $\bar{x}' = 405.5$, $\bar{d} = 133$, $s_d = 35.986$.
   Two Phase:

$$\hat{\mu} = -133 + 405.5 = 272.5$$

$$\text{var}\,\hat{\mu} = 981.6,$$

$$s_{\hat{\mu}} = 31.33.$$

95% confidence interval for μ is $272.5 \pm 2(31.33)$.
   Regression Approach:

$$\bar{x} = 415,$$

$$b = 0.8632,$$

$$\hat{\rho} = 0.9601,$$

$$\bar{x}'' = 396,$$

$$s_y = 113.0597,$$

$$s_x = 125.7478,$$

$$\hat{\bar{Y}}_{D,lr} = 273.799,$$

$$s(\hat{\bar{Y}}_{D,lr}) = 37.12.$$

95% confidence interval for $\bar{Y}$ is $273.799 \pm 2(37.22)$.

2. $N = 40$, $n' = 15$, $\hat{\bar{Y}}_{D,st} = 49.1667$, $s(\hat{\bar{Y}}_{D,st}) = 3.468$.
   95% confidence interval for $\bar{Y}$ is $49.1667 \pm 2(3.468)$.

4. $N = 1000$, $n = 5$, $n' = 10$.

$$\bar{x}' = 43.6,$$

$$\bar{y} = 5.6,$$

$$\bar{d} = 30.2$$

$$\hat{\mu} = 13.4$$

$$s_{\hat{\mu}} = 2.48.$$

95% confidence interval for $\mu = \bar{Y}$ is $13.4 \pm 2(2.48)$.

Regression Approach:

$$\bar{x} = 35.8,$$

$$b = 0.3083,$$

$$s_x = 10.33,$$

$$\hat{\rho} = 0.99,$$

$$\hat{\bar{Y}}_{D,lr} = 8.005,$$

$$s(\hat{\bar{Y}}_{D,lr}) = 1.023.$$

95% confidence interval for $\bar{Y}$ is $8.005 \pm 2(1.023)$.

5. $N = 80, n' = 15, n = 2.$

$$\bar{Y}_{D,st} = 9266.67,$$

$$s(\bar{Y}_{D,st}) = 8.456 \times 10^2.$$

95% confidence interval for $\bar{Y}$ is 9266.67 ± 1692.

6. $N = 176, n' = 10, n = 5,$ set $k = 1.$

$$\bar{x}\prime = 3705.2,$$

$$\bar{y} = 3854.4,$$

$$s_y^2 = 7,814,807.3$$

$$\bar{d} = 527.6,$$

$$s_d^2 = 221,929.3$$

$$\hat{\mu} = 3178.1,$$

$$s_{\hat{\mu}} = 871.36.$$

95% confidence interval for $\bar{Y}$ is $3178.1 \pm 2(871.36)$.

Regression Approach:

$$b = 0.864,$$

$$s_x = 3230.16,$$

$$s_y = 2795.5,$$

$$\hat{\rho} = 0.998,$$

$$\hat{\bar{Y}}_{D,lr} = 3270.1,$$

$$s(\hat{\bar{Y}}_{D,lr}) = 885.78.$$

95% confidence interval for $\bar{Y}$ is $3270.1 \pm 2(885.78)$.

7. $\rho = 0.8, n = 5, m = 1, \lambda = 0.2, u = 4, v = 0.8,$

$$\hat{\mu}_{2,u} = 5.1,$$

$$\hat{\mu}_{2,m} = 6.56,$$

$$W_{2,u} = 4/S^2,$$

$$W_{2,m} = 4/0.52S^2.$$

Hence,

$$\hat{\mu}_2 = \frac{4(0.51) + (4/0.52)(6.56)}{4 + (4/0.52)} = 6.602.$$

Chapter 12

1. $N = 80, n = 10, f = 1/8, M_1 = \cdots = M_{10} = 5,$

$$\hat{Y} = \Sigma M_i \bar{y}_i = 8(1223) = 9784,$$

$$\widehat{\text{var}}(\hat{Y}) = 1,841,141.33, \quad s_{\hat{y}} = 1356.89.$$

2. Approach I:

$$\text{var}(\hat{\bar{Y}}_t) = \frac{75}{n} + \frac{36}{mn}$$

$$5000 = 1000 + 10n + 1 \cdot nm \Rightarrow mn = 4000 - 10n$$

Hence,

$$\text{var}(\hat{\bar{Y}}_t) = \frac{75}{n} + \frac{36}{4000 - 10n}.$$

Value of n that minimizes $\text{var}(\hat{\bar{Y}}_t)$ is $n_0 = 328.1 \doteq 329$. Hence,

$$m_0 = 2.19 \doteq 3.$$

$$\min \text{ var}(\hat{\bar{Y}}_t) = 0.2787 \text{ (with } n_0 = 328.1 \text{ and } m_0 = 2.19\text{)}.$$

Approach II: Let $(\Sigma M_i)^2 = A_0$. Then

$$\text{var}(\hat{Y}) = (\Sigma M_i)^2 \text{ var}(\hat{\bar{Y}}_t) = \frac{1}{n}\left(75A_0 + \frac{36A_0}{m}\right).$$

Let $A_1 = 75A_0, A_2 = 36A_0, A_3 = 0, C_0 = 1000, C' = 5000, C_1 = 10, C_2 = 1.$

$$m_0 = \left(\frac{A_2 C_1}{A_1 C_2}\right)^{1/2} = 2.19 \doteq 3$$

$$n_0 = \frac{(C' - C_0)(A_1/C_1)^{1/2}}{(A_1 C_1)^{1/2} + (A_2 C_2)^{1/2}} = 328.11 \doteq 329$$

$$\text{var}(\hat{Y}) = (C' - C_0)^{-1}\left\{(A_1 C_1)^{1/2} + (A_2 C_2)^{1/2}\right\} + A_3$$

$$\min \text{ var}(\hat{\bar{Y}}) = \frac{1}{A_0}\text{ var }\hat{Y} = \frac{1}{4000}(\sqrt{750} + \sqrt{36})^2 = 0.2787.$$

5. $N = 100$, $n = 5$, $f = 0.05$, $f_i = m_i/M_i = 0.20$, $\sum_1^N M_i = 1500$.

$$\hat{Y} = \frac{N}{n} \Sigma M_i \bar{y}_i \doteq 11{,}200,$$

$$\hat{\bar{Y}} = \text{Estimate of the average \# of phone calls an employee makes}$$

$$= \frac{\hat{Y}}{\sum_1^N M_i} = \frac{11{,}200}{1500} = 7.4667$$

$$\widehat{\text{var}}(\hat{Y}) = 475(64950 - 62720) + 16(1845 \cdot 8333)$$

$$= 1088783.33,$$

$$s_{\hat{Y}} = 1043.45$$

$$s_{\hat{\bar{Y}}} = 1043.45/1500 = 0.6956.$$

95% confidence interval for $\bar{Y}$ is $7.4667 \pm 2(0.6956)$.

6. $N = 25$, $n = 5$, $\sum_1^N M_i = 750$, $f = 0.2$.

$$\hat{Y} = 40{,}850,$$

$$\widehat{\text{var}}(\hat{Y}) = 25(14{,}874{,}650 - 13{,}349{,}780) + 4(10{,}775)$$

$$= 38{,}164{,}850,$$

$$s_{\hat{Y}} = 6177.77.$$

95% confidence interval for Y is $40{,}850 \pm 2(6177.77)$.

8. $N = 10$, $n = 3$, $M_i = M = 50$, $f = 0.3$, $m_i = m = 10$, $f_i = 0.2$.

$$\hat{Y} = 550,$$

$$\widehat{\text{var}}(\hat{Y}) = 11.6667(9275 - 9075) + \frac{2000}{3}(0.77)$$

$$= 2846.6667,$$

$$s_{\hat{Y}} = 53.35.$$

Hence, 95% confidence interval for Y is $550 \pm 2(53.35)$.

9. $N = 10$, $n = 3$, $f = 0.3$, $m_i = m = 4$,

$$\hat{Y} = 236.666,$$

$$\widehat{\text{var}}(\hat{Y}) = 11.6667(1772.5 - 1680.3333) + 3.3333(11.5)$$

$$= 1113.61,$$

$$s_{\hat{Y}} = 33.37.$$

Chapter 13

1. $\hat{P}_L = 0.0755$.
   $\hat{P}_U = 0.3021$.
2. (a) $n = 202$. (b) $E_3(C) = \$260.075$, $\text{var } C = 315.75$.
3. $0.54 \pm 2(0.071)$
4. $0.4167 \pm 2(0.0829)$
5. $0.25 \pm 2(0.1759)$
6. $0.10 \pm 2(0.2468)$
7. $0.125 \pm 2(0.7529)$
8. $0.18 \pm 2(0.0909)$

Chapter 14

1. $\tilde{\mu} = \{10.018\bar{y} + 0.882(10)\}/10.9 = 0.919\bar{y} + 0.809$
2. $\tilde{\mu} = \dfrac{4(2.0015) + 3(1.5318)}{2.0015 + 1.5318} = 3.57$
3. $\tilde{\mu} = 8.91/81 = 0.11$. Hence, $\hat{M} = N\tilde{\mu} = 100(0.11) = 11$.
5. $v_1 = v_2 = 0.042$, $EV(\hat{\mu}|\mu) = 9.608$, $V(\mu) = 4.3$. Thus,

$$\tilde{\mu} = \frac{m(9.608) + \hat{\mu}(4.3)}{9.608 + 4.3} = 0.691m + 0.309\hat{\mu}.$$

6. $E(\sigma_w^2) = 45.6$, $v_1 = v_2 = 0.0205$. $EV(\hat{\mu}|\mu) = 21.9846$, $V(\mu) = 4.4$. So,

$$\hat{\mu} = 0.833m + 0.167\hat{\mu}.$$

7. $\tilde{p}_1 = 0.104$, $\tilde{p}_2 = 0.0519$.

$$\tilde{p} = \frac{5000}{11000}(0.104) + \frac{6000}{11000}(0.0519) = 0.076.$$

8. $\tilde{p}_1 = 0.4$, $\tilde{p}_2 = 0.5$ and $\tilde{p}_3 = 0.2$. Thus,

$$\tilde{p} = \{6500(0.4) + 7000(0.5) + 8000(0.2)\}/21{,}500 = 0.358.$$

Chapter 15

1. $\hat{\theta} = 3, \hat{\theta}_{-1} = 3.5, \hat{\theta}_{-2} = 3.25, \hat{\theta}_{-3} = 3, \hat{\theta}_{-4} = 2.75, \hat{\theta}_{-5} = 2.5$.

$$\tilde{\theta}_i = i \quad (i = 1, \ldots, 5), \quad \tilde{\theta} = 3.$$

Second order estimator: $\tilde{\theta}_{-1} = 3.5, \tilde{\theta}_{-2} = 3.25, \tilde{\theta}_{-3} = 3, \tilde{\theta}_{-4} = 2.75, \tilde{\theta}_{-5} = 2.5$. Hence,

$$\tilde{\theta}^{(2)} = 3.$$

2. $S = 2.5, S_{-1} = 1.667, S_{-2} = 2.917, S_{-3} = 3.333, S_{-4} = 2.917, S_{-5} = 1.667$,

$$\tilde{S} = 2.4992.$$

3. $\hat{\theta}_{-1} = 1.667, \hat{\theta}_{-2} = 2.917, \hat{\theta}_{-3} = 3.333, \hat{\theta}_{-4} = 2.917, \hat{\theta}_{-5} = 1.667$,

$$\tilde{\theta}_{(\cdot)} = \frac{1}{n}\sum_1^n \hat{\theta}_{-i} = 2.5002,$$

$$\widehat{\text{var}}(\hat{\theta}) = \frac{(n-1)^2}{n} \cdot \frac{1}{n-1}\Sigma(\hat{\theta}_{-i} - \hat{\theta}_{(\cdot)})^2 = \frac{16}{5} \times 0.6074 = 1.944.$$

Alternate way: $\bar{x} = 3$, $\hat{\mu}_4 = \frac{1}{n}\sum_1^n (x_i - \bar{x})^4 = 6.8$.

$$\hat{\mu}_2 = \frac{1}{n}\Sigma(x_i - \bar{x})^2 = 2,$$

$$\widehat{\text{var}}(\hat{\theta}) = \frac{1}{(5.2)^2} \cdot \frac{25}{4}(6.8 - 4) = 1.944.$$

6. $g(\bar{x}) = \bar{x}^2$, $\bar{x} = 3$, $\hat{\sigma}^2 = 2.5$. So, $\hat{\theta} = \bar{x}^2 = 9$.

$$\hat{\theta}_{-i} \doteq g(\bar{x}) + \frac{(\bar{x} - x_i)}{n-1}g'(\bar{x}) = \bar{x}^2 + \frac{(\bar{x} - x_i)}{n-1}2\bar{x},$$

$\hat{\theta}_{-1} = 12, \hat{\theta}_{-2} = 10.5, \hat{\theta}_{-3} = 9, \hat{\theta}_{-4} = 7.5, \hat{\theta}_{-5} = 6$. Thus,

$$\tilde{\theta}_{(\cdot)} = 9.$$

$$\widehat{\text{var}}(\hat{\theta}) = \frac{n-1}{n}\Sigma(\hat{\theta}_{-i} - \hat{\theta}_{(\cdot)})^2 = 18.$$

If we use the delta method,

$$\widehat{\text{var}}(\hat{\theta}) = \left[g'(\bar{x})\right]^2 \text{var}(\bar{x}) = \left[g'(\bar{x})\right]^2 \frac{\hat{\sigma}^2}{n}$$

$$= (2\bar{x})^2 \frac{(2.5)^2}{5} = 18.$$

Chapter 16

1. $\bar{x} = 3.5$, $s^2 = 3.5$, $\sigma_{\bar{x}} = (3.5/6)^{1/2} = 0.7638$. Suppose the bootstrap samples are given by

   (1,4,1,1,1,1), (5,3,6,2,1,1), (1,6,4,1,6,4), (6,6,1,1,4,1), (4,2,2,3,6,4), (6,5,3,2,5,5), (5,5,3,3,3,5), (1,2,2,5,3,4), (2,2,4,1,3,4), (3,6,2,2,5,2).

   Then

   $$\begin{array}{lllll} \hat{\theta}_1^* = 1.5, & \hat{\theta}_2^* = 3, & \hat{\theta}_3^* = 3.667, & \hat{\theta}_4^* = 3.167, & \hat{\theta}_5^* = 3.5, \\ \hat{\theta}_6^* = 4.333, & \hat{\theta}_7^* = 4, & \hat{\theta}_8^* = 2.833, & \hat{\theta}_9^* = 2.667, & \hat{\theta}_{10}^* = 3.333, \end{array}$$

   and

   $$\bar{\hat{\theta}}^* = 3.2$$

   $$\widehat{SD} = \left\{\frac{1}{9}\sum_1^{10}(\hat{\theta}_i^* - \bar{\hat{\theta}}^*)^2\right\}^{1/2} \doteq 0.7888.$$

   Bootstrap confidence interval for θ. It is given by

   $$\hat{\theta} \pm 1.96(\widehat{SD})$$

   or

   $$(\hat{\theta}_{(k_1)}^*, \hat{\theta}_{(k_2)}^*)$$

   where $(\hat{\theta}_{(1)}^* < \cdots < \hat{\theta}_{(10)}^*)$ are the ordered $\hat{\theta}_i^*$ and $k_1 = n\alpha/2$ and $k_2 = n(1-\alpha/2)$. Hence an 80% confidence interval for θ is (1.5, 4) since $k_1 = 1$, and $k_2 = 9$.

2. X is distributed as Bernoulli with $P(X = 0) = f_1$ and $P(X = 1) = f_2$. Given the sample is $(X_1, \ldots, X_5) = (1, 0, 0, 1, 0)$, on the basis of 10 bootstrap samples we wish to estimate $\hat{f}_2 - f_2$. Suppose the superscripts associated with the X's of the 10 bootstrap samples are given by

   (2,1,5,2,3), (1,3,3,2,3), (5,5,5,5,3), (5,5,3,4,1), (4,2,3,5,3), (4,2,4,2,4), (4,5,1,3,2), (5,4,2,3,5), (2,3,2,3,4), (3,3,4,3,3).

$$\hat{f}_{2,1}^* = 0.2, \quad \hat{f}_{2,2}^* = 0.2, \quad \hat{f}_{2,3}^* = 0, \quad \hat{f}_{2,4}^* = 0.4, \quad \hat{f}_{2,5}^* = 0.2,$$
$$\hat{f}_{2,6}^* = 0.6, \quad \hat{f}_{2,7}^* = 0.4, \quad \hat{f}_{2,8}^* = 0.2, \quad \hat{f}_{2,9}^* = 0.2, \quad \hat{f}_{2,10}^* = 0.2 .$$

Then

$$\bar{\hat{f}}_2^* = \frac{1}{10}(0.2 \times 6 + 0.4 \times 2 + 0.6) = 0.26 .$$

Also,

$$\hat{f}_2 = 0.4 .$$

Thus,

$$\bar{\hat{f}}_2^* - \hat{f}_2 = 0.26 - 0.4 = -0.14 .$$

3. Model is

$$Y_i = \exp(-c_i \beta) + \epsilon_i \quad (i = 1, 2, \ldots) .$$

Let $h(\beta) = \Sigma \epsilon_i^2 = \Sigma (Y_i - \exp(-c_i \beta))^2$. $\frac{\partial h}{\partial \beta} = 0$ implies

$$g(\beta) = \Sigma c_i y_i \exp(-c_i \beta) - \Sigma c_i \exp(-2c_i \beta) = 0 .$$

This is a nonlinear equation in β. Hence, we solve it by iterative method such as the Newton's method. To find an approximate solution, we take the first two terms in the expansion of the exponential function and obtain

$$\Sigma c_i y_i (1 - c_i \beta) \doteq \Sigma c_i (1 - 2c_i \beta)$$

yielding

$$\beta_0 = (\Sigma c_i - \Sigma c_i y_i)/(2\Sigma c_i^2 - \Sigma c_i^2 y_i) = -0.010234 .$$

Now, following the Newton's method, we obtain

$$g(\beta) = g(\beta_0) + (\beta - \beta_0)g'(\beta_0) = 0$$

yielding

$$\beta_1 = \beta_0 - \{g(\beta_0)/g'(\beta_0)\} .$$

After ten iterations, we obtain

$$\hat{\beta} = -0.0067744 .$$

Letting $\hat{y}_i = \exp(-c_i \hat{\beta})$ and $\hat{\epsilon}_i = y_i - \hat{y}_i$, $i = 1, \ldots$, we obtain

$$\hat{\epsilon}_1 = -0.3451, \quad \hat{\epsilon}_2 = -0.0845, \quad \hat{\epsilon}_3 = -0.0254,$$
$$\hat{\epsilon}_4 = 0.0324, \quad \hat{\epsilon}_5 = 0.1888 .$$

Using the delta method, we obtain

$$dy = -c \exp(-c\beta)d\beta .$$

Hence,

$$\text{var } y \doteq c^2 \exp(-2c\beta)(\text{var } \beta) .$$

Hence,

$$\widehat{\text{var}}\hat{\beta} = (\widehat{\text{var}} \, y) \cdot \frac{1}{n} \sum_1^5 c_i^{-2} \exp(2c_i \hat{\beta}) = 3.809747 \times 10^{-5}$$

where

$$\widehat{\text{var}} \, y = \Sigma \hat{\epsilon}_i^2/(n-1) = 0.0406 .$$

In order to compute the bootstrap estimate of $\text{var}(\hat{\beta})$, we draw $B = 10$ bootstrap samples. Using random numbers the generated subscripts of the X's in the bootstrap samples are

(1,2,2,3,5), (3,4,5,5,2), (1,3,4,1,2), (5,3,1,4,2), (5,4,4,2,5), (3,3,4,1,5), (4,1,2,2,5), (4,4,2,4,2), (2,5,3,2,4), (5,4,1,5,5).

Let us bootstrap the residuals and then the bootstrap samples are given by

$$(c_i, y_i = \exp(-\hat{\beta}c_i) + \hat{\epsilon}_{j_i}, \quad i = 1, \ldots, 5)$$

where $(j_1, \ldots, j_5)$ is bootstrap sample of size 5 subscripts obtained from $(1,2,3,4,5)$. For example, the first bootstrap sample is

$$(20, 0.80), (25, 1.099), (30, 1.141), (35, 1.242), (40, 1.500).$$

Using the enclosed program in *S-plus*, we obtain the bootstrap sample of $\hat{\beta}$ as

$$\hat{\beta}_1 = -0.0061103, \quad \hat{\beta}_2 = -0.0082364, \quad \hat{\beta}_3 = -0.0032450,$$
$$\hat{\beta}_4 = -0.0051161, \quad \hat{\beta}_5 = -0.0084160, \quad \hat{\beta}_6 = -0.0060150,$$
$$\hat{\beta}_7 = -0.0058794, \quad \hat{\beta}_8 = -0.0061554, \quad \hat{\beta}_9 = -0.0068663,$$
$$\hat{\beta}_{10} = -0.0081755.$$

From this sample we compute

$$\widehat{\mathrm{var}}(\hat{\beta}^*) = 2.551918 \times 10^{-6}$$

which is much smaller than the estimate of the variance of $\hat{\beta}$ obtained via the delta method.

4. (1) Loaded. Let $(x_1, \ldots, x_5) = (18.2, 9.5, 12.0, 21.1, 10.2)$, $\bar{x} = 14.2$, $S^2 = 26.635$, $\sigma_{\bar{x}} = (S^2/n)^{1/2} = 2.308$. Let the bootstrap samples obtained using random number table be (we give the subscripts of the x's):

$$(1,2,2,3,5), (3,4,5,5,2), (1,3,4,1,2), (5,3,1,4,2), (5,4,4,2,5), (3,3,4,1,5), (4,1,2,2,5), (4,4,2,4,2), (2,5,3,2,4),$$
$$(5,4,1,5,5).$$

$$\hat{\theta}_1^* = 11.88, \quad \hat{\theta}_2^* = 12.6, \quad \hat{\theta}_3^* = 15.8, \quad \hat{\theta}_4^* = 14.2, \quad \hat{\theta}_5^* = 14.42,$$
$$\hat{\theta}_6^* = 14.7, \quad \hat{\theta}_7^* = 13.7, \quad \hat{\theta}_8^* = 16.46, \quad \hat{\theta}_9^* = 12.46, \quad \hat{\theta}_{10}^* = 13.98.$$

Thus, $\bar{\hat{\theta}}^* = 14.02$, $\widehat{SD} = 1.4495 < 2.308 = \sigma_{\bar{x}}$.

(2) Unloaded. $(y_1, \ldots, y_5) = (10.9, 11.7, 20.2, 15.6, 12.9)$. $\bar{y} = 14.26$, $S^2 = 14.193$, $\sigma_{\bar{x}} = (14.193/3)^{1/2} = 1.6848$. Let the bootstrap samples obtained using random number table be (we give the subscripts of the y's):

$$(1,2,2,3,5), (3,4,5,5,2), (1,3,4,1,2), (5,3,1,4,2), (5,4,4,2,5), (3,3,4,1,5), (4,1,2,2,5), (4,4,2,4,2), (2,5,3,2,4),$$
$$(5,4,1,5,5).$$

$$\hat{\theta}_1^* = 13.48, \quad \hat{\theta}_2^* = 14.66, \quad \hat{\theta}_3^* = 13.86, \quad \hat{\theta}_4^* = 14.26, \quad \hat{\theta}_5^* = 13.74,$$
$$\hat{\theta}_6^* = 15.96, \quad \hat{\theta}_7^* = 12.56, \quad \hat{\theta}_8^* = 14.04, \quad \hat{\theta}_9^* = 14.42, \quad \hat{\theta}_{10}^* = 13.04.$$

Thus, $\bar{\hat{\theta}}^* = 14.002$, $\widehat{SD} = 0.9354 < 1.6848 = \sigma_{\bar{x}}$.

5. The sample is

$$(x_1, x_2, x_3, x_4, x_5, x_6) = (2000, 1800, 1900, 1950, 2050, 2000).$$

Subscripts of the 10 bootstrap samples are:

$$(1,4,1,5,6,6), (5,3,1,2,1,6), (1,6,4,6,1,4), (1,1,6,6,4,1), (4,2,2,3,6,4), (1,5,3,2,5,5), (5,5,3,3,3,5), (1,2,2,6,3,4),$$
$$(2,2,4,1,3,4), (3,1,2,2,5,2).$$

$$\hat{\theta}_1^* = 2000, \quad \hat{\theta}_2^* = 1958.33, \quad \hat{\theta}_3^* = 1983.33, \quad \hat{\theta}_4^* = 1991.67, \quad \hat{\theta}_5^* = 1900,$$
$$\hat{\theta}_6^* = 1975, \quad \hat{\theta}_7^* = 1975, \quad \hat{\theta}_8^* = 1908.33, \quad \hat{\theta}_9^* = 1900, \quad \hat{\theta}_{10}^* = 1891.67.$$

$$k_1 = n\alpha/2 = 10(0.2)/2 = 1$$

$$k_2 = n(1 - \alpha/2) = 10(0.9) = 9.$$

Order statistics of the $\hat{\theta}_i^*$ are

$$(\hat{\theta}_{10}^* < \hat{\theta}_5^* < \hat{\theta}_9^* < \hat{\theta}_8^* < \hat{\theta}_2^* < \hat{\theta}_6^* < \hat{\theta}_7^* < \hat{\theta}_3^* < \hat{\theta}_3^* < \hat{\theta}_1^*).$$

Hence, an 80% confidence interval for the mean is

$$(\hat{\theta}_1^*, \hat{\theta}_9^*) = (1891.67, 1991.67).$$

Chapter 16, Problem 3

```
new <- function(C, Y){
    # This is Splus program for problem 3, Chapter 16.
    # C <- c(20,25,30,35,40)
    # Y <- c(0.8,1.1,1.2,1.3,1.5)
    sum1 <- 0
    sum2 <- 0
    for (i in 1:5){
        sum1 <- sum1 + C[i] - C[i]*Y[i]
        sum2 <- sum2 + 2*(C[i]^2) - Y[i]*(C[i]^2)
    }
    betai <- sum1/sum2
    print('initial value of beta is:')
    print(betai)
    for (i in 1:10){
        sum3 <- 0
        sum4 <- 0
        for (j in 1:5){
            sum3 <- sum3 + C[j]*Y[j]*exp(-betai*C[j]) -
                    C[j]*exp(-2*betai*C[j])
            sum4 <- sum4 - C[j]^2*Y[j]*exp(-betai*C[j]) +
                    2*C[j]^2*exp(-2*betai*C[j])
        }
        betai <- betai - sum3/sum4
        print('betai is :')
        print(betai)
        print('sum3 is; ')
        print(sum3)
    }
    sum5 <- 0
    sum6 <- 0
    for(i in 1:5){
        yhati <- exp(-betai*C[i])
        errori <- Y[i] - yhati
        sum5 <- sum5 + errori^2
        sum6 <- sum6 + (1/C[i]^2)*exp(2*betai*C[i])
        print('errori is:')
        print(errori)
    }
    varyhat <- sum5/4
    print('varyhat is; ')
    print(varyhat)
    varbetahat <- (varyhat*sum6)/5
    print('varbetahat is: ')
    varbetahat
}
```

Chapter 17

1. $r_{1t} = 0.02\left(\frac{2.1}{2}\right) = 0.021$, $r_{2t} = 0.019\left(\frac{1.9}{1.9}\right) = 0.019$. The population of the county in 1995 was

$$P_t = \frac{1}{2}\left(\frac{300}{0.021} + \frac{280}{0.019}\right) = \frac{1}{2}(29022.5) = 14511.$$

2. Suppose that

$$\hat{R}_i = 0.05 + 1.05r_{i1}, \quad i = 1, \ldots, 120,$$

$$m = 120,$$

$$\sum_{i=1}^{m} P_{it} = 3.1 \times 10^6.$$

Since $P_{21} = 0.26$, $r_{21} = 1.01$, $\hat{R}_2 = 0.05 + 1.05(1.01) = 1.1105$,

$$P_{2t} = 1.1105 \times 0.26 \times 3.1 \times 10^6 = 895{,}063.$$

3. $N = 120$, $n = 20$.

$$\sum_{i=1}^{8} \sum_{j=1}^{n_i} y_{ij} = 220, \qquad\qquad \bar{y} = 220/20 = 11,$$

$$\sum_{i=1}^{8} \sum_{j=1}^{n_i} x_{ij} = 1279, \qquad\qquad \bar{x} = 1279/20 = 63.95,$$

$$\hat{\bar{Y}}_i^{RS} = \frac{\bar{y}}{\bar{x}} \bar{X}_i = \frac{11}{63.95} \bar{X}_i = 0.172 \bar{X}_i.$$

i	1	2	3	4	5	6	7	8
$\bar{X}_i$	106	47	90	105	94	89	165	91
$\bar{Y}_i^{RS}$	18.23	8.08	15.48	18.06	16.17	15.31	28.38	15.65
w_i	0.15	0.1	0.15	0.1	0.2	0.15	0.05	0.1
W_i	1/12	1/24	2/15	1/10	4/15	1/6	1/12	1/8

For $i = 1, 2, 3, 4$, $w_i \geq W_i$. Hence,

$$\hat{\bar{Y}}_1^{SD} = \frac{40}{3} + 0.172\left(106 - \frac{165}{3}\right) = 21.88$$

$$\hat{\bar{Y}}_2^{SD} = \frac{11}{2} + 0.172(47 - 30) = 8.42$$

$$\hat{\bar{Y}}_3^{SD} = 9 + 0.172\left(90 - \frac{165}{3}\right) = 15.02$$

$$\hat{\bar{Y}}_4^{SD} = \frac{33}{2} + 0.172\left(105 - \frac{165}{2}\right) = 20.37.$$

For $i = 5, 6, 7, 8$, $w_i < W_i$. Hence,

$$\hat{Y}_5^{REG} = 9.5 + 0.172(94 - 57.5) = 15.78$$

$$\hat{Y}_5^{SD} = \frac{0.2}{4/15} \times 15.78 + \left(1 - \frac{0.2}{4/15}\right) 16.168 = 15.877$$

$$\hat{Y}_6^{REG} = \frac{31}{3} + 0.172(89 - 61) = 15.149$$

$$\hat{Y}_6^{SD} = \frac{0.15}{1/6}(15.49) + \left(1 - \frac{0.15}{1/6}\right) \times 15.308 = 15.165$$

$$\hat{Y}_7^{REG} = 21 + 0.172(165 - 150) = 23.58$$

$$\hat{Y}_7^{SD} = \frac{0.05}{1/12}(23.58) + \left(1 - \frac{0.05}{1/2}\right)(28.38) = 25.5$$

$$\hat{Y}_8^{REG} = 9.5 + 0.172(91 - 78.5) = 11.65$$

and

$$\hat{Y}_8^{SD} = \frac{0.1}{1/8}(11.65) + \left(1 - \frac{0.1}{1/8}\right)(15.652) = 12.45.$$

Chapter 18

4. $\bar{X} = 68$ inches, $n = 6, r = 5$.

1. Mean imputation overall $(MO) = y_4^* = 790/5 = 158$.
2. Random imputation overall $(R) = y_4^* = 115$ (if the random number drawn is 1).
3. Simple regression

$$\hat{\beta}_{1c} = 5.99, \quad \hat{\beta}_{0c} = -236.142.$$

Hence the regression line is

$$y = -236.142 + 5.99x.$$

When $x = 61$, $y_4^* = 129.248$.

Random regression imputation (RRN). If $y_i = -236.142 + 5.99x_i$, $(i = 1, 2, \ldots)$,

$$\hat{y}_1 = 123.258, \quad \hat{y}_2 = 183.158, \quad \hat{y}_3 = 153.208,$$
$$\hat{y}_5 = 135.238, \quad \hat{y}_6 = 195.138,$$

$$\hat{\sigma}^2 = \sum_{i=1}^{n}(y_i - \hat{y}_i)^2/(n-2) \text{ (based only on observed } y_i)$$

$$= 55.598.$$

Suppose the random number in (0.1) to be 0.73. Then the corresponding standard normal deviate is 0.61. Hence,

$$y_4^* = 129.248 + 0.61(55.598)^{1/2} = 133.78.$$

Random regression imputation (RRS). We find the residuals are

$$-8.258, \quad 1.842, \quad 6.792, \quad 4.762, \quad -5.138.$$

If 4.762 is randomly selected out of these residuals, then

$$y_4^* = 129.248 + 4.762 = 134.01.$$

7. Assume that $\beta_0 = -1$, $\sigma^2 = 4$ and $\alpha = 0.02$. We are also given that $n = 6$, $r = 5$ and $m = 2$.

    i. $\hat{\beta}_{1r} = 118/55 = 2.146$

    ii. $\eta = \frac{1}{55} \{4(0.02)6 + 118\} = 2.1542$

    iii. $\Sigma = A^{-1} = 4/55 = 0.0727$, $\sqrt{\Sigma} = 0.27$.

    iv. Next, we draw five random numbers given by

$$0.77, \quad 0.93, \quad 0.69, \quad 0.61, \quad 0.75.$$

Then the corresponding normal deviates are

$$0.74, \quad 1.47, \quad 0.5, \quad 0.26, \quad 0.68.$$

    v. Now,

$$\beta_0 + \hat{\beta}_{1r} x_6 = -1 + 2.1455 \times 6 = 11.873.$$

Thus the random sample of size 5 from normal $(\beta_0 + \hat{\beta}_{1r} x_6, \sigma^2)$ is

$$\hat{y}_j : \quad 13.353, \quad 14.813, \quad 12.873, \quad 12.393, \quad 13.233.$$

    vi. Next,

$$e^{-0.02 \hat{y}_j} : \quad 0.77, \quad 0.74, \quad 0.77, \quad 0.78, \quad 0.77.$$

    vii. Now we draw a random sample of size 5 from uniform (0,1):

$$0.96, \quad 0.35, \quad 0.23, \quad 0.96, \quad 0.94.$$

    viii. Since $u_j \leq \exp(-\alpha y_j)$ for $j = 2, 3$, we set $y_j = \hat{y}_j$ (for $j = 2, 3$) and reject the rest of the y_j's. Now, using $(y_1, \ldots, y_5, y_6)$ we compute $\hat{\beta}$ based on two completed data sets:

$$\sum_1^6 x_i^2 = 91,$$

$$\hat{\beta}_{1,1} = \left\{ \sum_1^r x_i y_i + x_6(14.813) \right\} / 91$$

$$= 206.878/91 = 2.2734.$$

Similarly,

$$\hat{\beta}_{1,2} = 2.1455$$

$$\hat{Q}_m = (\hat{\beta}_{1,1} + \hat{\beta}_{1,2})/2 = 2.2095$$

$$\Sigma_1 = \bar{U}_1 = \sigma^2 / \sum_1^6 x_i^2 = 4/91 = 0.004.$$

Here, Σ_1 is the same for both the selected data sets. We have

$$B_m = \sum_{l=1}^{m}(Q_l - \bar{Q}_m)^2/(m-1)$$

$$= (2.2734 - 2.2095)^2 + (2.1455 - 2.2095)^2$$

$$= 0.008179.$$

ix. Now,

$$T_m = \bar{U}_m + (1 + m^{-1})B_m$$

$$= 0.044 + (3/2)(0.008179) = 0.05627$$

$$T_m^{1/2} = 0.2372.$$

x. 95% confidence interval for β_1. We need

$$r_m = (1 + m^{-1})B_m/\bar{U}_m = 0.2788$$

$$v = (m-1)(1 + r_m^{-1})^2 = 21.0387$$

$$t_v(0.025) \doteq 1.96.$$

Hence, a 95% confidence interval for β_1 is

$$2.2095 \pm 1.96(0.2372) \quad \text{i.e., } (1.7446, 2.6744).$$

9. $\sigma^2 = 1, n = 10, n_0 = 1, m = 3, \bar{y} = 25.6/10 = 2.56.$
We will use the FN method and find the missing observation y_{11}.

i. Suppose 0.92 is a random number drawn from the uniform (0,1) distribution. Then the corresponding normal deviate is 1.41. Hence,

$$\theta^* = \mu^* = z\sigma/\sqrt{n_1} + \bar{y} = \frac{1.41}{\sqrt{10}} + 2.56 = 3.01.$$

ii. $z\sigma + \mu^* = z(1) + 3.01.$ Then we obtain

$$\bar{y}_{*l} : 2.59, 2.60, 2.60$$

$$s_{*l}^2 : 0.9938018, 1.0001655, 1.0001655$$

$$\bar{y}_{*.} = (2.59 + 2.60 + 2.60)/3 \doteq 2.60.$$

$$T^* = \hat{W} + \frac{4}{3}B^*$$

$$T^* = \frac{2.9941328}{33} + \frac{4}{6}(20.2281 - 20.2280)$$

$$= 0.0907313 + \frac{4}{3}(0.00005)$$

$$= 0.0907973$$

$$T^{*1/2} = 0.3013.$$

Further,

$$v = 2\left[1 + \frac{3}{4}\left(\frac{0.0907313}{0.0001}\right)\right]^2 \doteq 928,842.93.$$

Here, a 95% confidence interval for μ is

$$2.60 \pm 1.96(0.3013)$$

$$2.60 \pm 0.59\,,$$

or

$$(2.01, 3.19)\,.$$

10. Using the data in Problem 18.9, we use the MV method to find the confidence interval for μ. (In this case, the data may not be normally distributed.) We are given that $\sigma^2 = 1$, $\mu^* = 3.01$.

   i. Let the random sample of size $m = 3$ with replacement from y_i (the non-missing data) be

$$y_2 = 3.30, \quad y_6 = 3.48 \text{ and } y_9 = 2.28\,.$$

   ii. Since

$$\sum_1^{10} y_i = 25.6 \text{ and } \sum y_i^2 = 75.3922,$$

   we compute

$$\bar{y}_1 = 25.6/10 = 2.56 \text{ and } s_1^2 = 1.0951$$

   and

$$(n_1 - 1)s_1^2 = 9.8559\,.$$

   Hence,

$$z_i = (y_i - \bar{y}_1)/\left\{ \frac{(n_1 - 1)s_1^2}{n_1} \right\}^{1/2}, \quad i = 2, 6 \text{ and } 9\,.$$

$$z_i = 0.7454, \quad 0.9267, \quad -0.2820$$

   and

$$\hat{y}_{11} = \mu^* + \sigma z_i : 3.7554, \quad 3.9367, \quad 2.728$$

$$\bar{y}_{*l} : 2.6687, \quad 2.6852, \quad 2.5753$$

$$s_{*l}^2 : 1.1155, \quad 1.1579, \quad 0.9882\,.$$

   Hence,

$$\bar{y}_{*.} = (2.6687 + 2.6852 + 2.5753)/3 = 2.6431$$

$$T_* = (1.1155 + 1.1579 + 0.9882)(33)^{-1} + \frac{4}{3}\left(\frac{0.006496}{2} \right)$$

$$= 0.1031$$

$$T_*^{1/2} = 0.3212$$

$$\nu = 2\left[1 + \frac{3}{4} \frac{(0.09884)}{0.003248} \right]^2 = 1135.0969\,.$$

   Thus, 95% confidence interval for μ is

$$2.643 \pm (1.96)(0.321)$$

or

$$(2.014, 3.273)\,.$$

LIST OF CUMULATIVE REFERENCES

1. Aoyama, H. (1954). A study of the stratified random sampling. *Ann. Inst. Statist. Math.* **6**, 1–36.

2. Avadhani, M. S. and Sukhatme, B. V. (1965). Controlled simple random sampling. *J. Ind. Soc. Agri. Statist.* **17**, 34–42.

3. Avadhani, M. S. and Sukhatme, B. V. (1967). Controlled sampling with varying probabilities with and without replacement. *Aust. J. Statist.* **9**, 8–15.

4. Avadhani, M. S. and Sukhatme, B. V. (1973). Controlled sampling with equal probabilities and without replacement. *Internat. Statist. Rev.* **41**, 175–182.

5. Basu, D. (1958). On sampling with and without replacement. *Sankhyā* **20**, 287–294.

6. Basu, D. (1971). An essay on the logical foundations of survey sampling, I. *In Foundations of Statistical Inference* (ed. V. P. Godambe and D. S. Sprott). Toronto: Holt, Rinehart, and Winston, pp. 203–242.

7. Battese, G. E., Harter, R. M., and Fuller, W. A. (1988). An error component model for prediction of county crop areas using survey and satellite data. *J. Amer. Statist. Assoc.* **83**, 28–36.

8. Bellhouse, D. R. (1988). Systematic sampling. *Handbook of Statistics: Sampling*, Vol. 6 (ed. P. R. Krishnaiah and C. R. Rao). Elsevier Science Publishers B. V., 125–145.

9. Bellhouse, D. R. (1988). A brief history of random sampling methods. Chapter 1 of *Handbook of Statistics #6* (ed. P. R. Krishnaiah and C. R. Rao). New York: North Holland, pp. 1–4.

10. Bellhouse, D. R. and Rao, J. N. K. (1975). Systematic sampling in the presence of a trend. *Biometrika* **62**, 694–697.

11. Bellhouse, D. R., Thompson, M. E. and Godambe, V. P. (1977). Two-stage sampling with exchangeable prior distribution. *Biometrika* **64**, 97–103.

12. Birnbaum, Z. W. and Sirken, M. G. (1950). Bias due to nonavailability in sampling surveys. *J. Amer. Statist. Assoc.* **45**, 98–111.

13. Bowley, A. L. (1926). Measurement of the precision attained in sampling. *Bull. Interm. Statist. Inst.* **22**, Supplement to Liv. 1 6–62.

14. Brewer, K. W. R. (1963a). A model of systematic sampling with unequal probabilities. *Aust. J. Statist.* **5**, 5–13.

15. Brewer, K. W. R. (1963b). Ratio estimation in finite populations: some results deducible from the assumption of an underlying stochastic process. *Aust. J. Statist.* **5**, 93–105.

16. Brillinger, D. R. (1966). The application of the jackknife to the analysis of sample surveys. *Commentary* **8**, 74–80.

17. Bryant, E. C., Hartley, H. O., and Jessen, R. J. (1960). Design and estimation in two-way stratification. *J. Amer. Statist. Assoc.* **55**, 105–124.

18. Burstein, H. (1975). Finite population correction for binomial confidence limits. *J. Amer. Statist. Assoc.* **70**, 67–69.

19. Chakrabarti, M. C. (1963). On the use of incidence matrices of designs in sampling from finite populations. *J. Indian Statist Assoc.* **1**, 78–85.

20. Cassel, C. M, Särndal, C. E., and Wretman, J. H. (1977). *Foundations of Inference in Survey Sampling.* New York: John Wiley & Sons, p. 44.

21. Chaudhuri, A. (1992). Small domain statistics: A review. Tech. Rep. ASC/92/2, Indian Statistical Institute, Calcutta.

22. Cochran, W. G. (1946). Relative accuracy of systematic and random samples for a certain class of populations. *Ann. Math. Statist.* **71**, 164–177.

23. Cochran, W. G. (1961). Comparison of methods for determining strata boundaries. *Bull. Internat. Statist. Inst.* **38** (Part II), 345–358.

24. Cochran, W. G. (1977). *Sampling Techniques,* 3d ed. New York: John Wiley & Sons.

25. Cochran, W. G. (1978). Laplace's ratio estimator in *Contributions to Survey Sampling and Applied Statistics* (ed. H. A. David). New York: Academic Press.

26. Chung, J. H. and DeLury, D. B. (1950). *Confidence Limits for the Hypergeometric Distribution.* Toronto: University of Toronto Press.

27. Clopper, C. J. and Pearson, E. S. (1934). The use of confidence or fiducial limits illustrated in the case of the binomial. *Biometrika* **26**, 404–413.

28. Cornfield, J. (1944). On samples from finite populations. *J. Amer. Statist. Assoc.* **39**, 236–239.

29. Cox, D. R. (1952). Estimation by double sampling. *Biometrika* **39**, 217–227.

30. Dalenius, T. (1950). The problem of optimum stratification. *Skand. Aktuartidskr* **33**, 203–213.

31. Dalenius, T. (1957). *Sampling in Sweden.* Stockholm: Almquist and Wiksell.

32. Dalenius, T. and Gurney, M. (1951). The problem of optimum stratification II. *Skand. Aktuartidskr.* **34**, 133–148.

33. Dalenius, T. and Hodges, J. L. (1957). The choice of stratification points. *Skand. Aktuartidskr.* **3–4**, 198–203.

34. Dalenius, T. and Hodges, J. L. (1959). Minimum variance stratification. *J. Amer. Statist. Assoc.* **54**, 88–101, correction *JASA* **58**, (1963), p. 1161.

35. Das, A. C. (1951). On two phase sampling and sampling with varying probabilities without replacement. *Bull. Internat. Statist. Inst.* **33**, 105–112.

36. deFinetti, B. (1937). La Prevision, ses lois logiques, ses sources subjectives. Annales de L'Institut Henri Poincaré **7** 1–68. Appearing in English translation with new notes in *Studies in Subjective Probability* (ed. H. E. Kyburg and H. E. Smokler) New York: John Wiley & Sons, 1964.

37. Deming, W. E. (1953). On a probability mechanism to attain an economic balance between the resultant error of non-response and the bias of non-response. *J. Amer. Statist. Assoc.* **48**, 743–772.

38. Deming, W. E. (1960). *Sampling Design in Business Research.* New York: John Wiley & Sons.

39. DesRaj (1956). Some estimates in sampling with varying probabilities without replacement. *J. Amer. Statist. Assoc.* **51**, 269–284.

40. DesRaj (1966). Some remarks on a simple procedure for sampling without replacement. *J. Amer. Statist. Assoc.* **61**, 391–397.

41. DesRaj (1968). *Sampling Theory.* New York: McGraw-Hill Book Company.

42. DesRaj, and Khamis, S. H. (1958). Some remarks on sampling with replacement. *Ann. Math. Statist.* **29**, 550–557.

43. Diaconis, P. and Efron, B. (1983). Computer-intensive methods in statistics. *Scientific American*, May 1983, 116–130.

44. Drew, D., Singh, M. P., and Choudary, G. H. (1982). Evaluation of small area estimation techniques for the Canadian Labour Force Survey. *Survey Methodology* **8**, 17–47.

45. Durbin, J. (1959). A note on the application of Quenouille's method of bias reduction to the estimation of ratios. *Biometrika* **46**, 477–480.

46. Durbin, J. (1967). Design of multi-stage surveys for the estimation of sampling errors. *App. Statist.* **16**, 152–164.

47. Efron, B. (1979), Bootstrap methods: Another look at the jackknife. *Ann. Statist.* **7**, 1–26.

48. Efron, B. (1981). The jackknife estimate of variance. *Ann. Statist.* **9**, 586–596.

49. Efron, B. (1982). *The Jackknife, the Bootstrap and Other Resampling Plans.* Society for Industrial and Applied Mathematics #38, Philadelphia, PA.

50. Efron, B. and Stein, C. (1981). The jackknife estimate of variance, *Ann. Statist.* **9**, 586–596.

51. Efron, B., and Tibshirani, R. (1993). *An Introduction to the Bootstrap.* New York: Chapman and Hall.

52. Ekman, G. (1959). An approximation useful in univariate stratification. *Ann. Math. Statist.* **30**, 219–229.

53. Erdös, P. and Rényi, A. (1959). On the central limit theorem for samples from a finite population. *Pub. Math. Inst. Hungarian Acad. Sci.* **4**, 49–57.

54. Erickson, E. P. (1974). A regression method for estimating populations of local areas. *J. Amer. Statist. Assoc.* **69**, 867–875.

55. Erickson, E. P. and Kadane, J. B. (1985). Estimating the population in a census year (with discussion). *J. Amer. Statist. Assoc.* **80**, 98–131.

56. Erickson, E. P., Kadane, J. B., and Tukey, J. W. (1989). Adjusting the 1981 census of population and housing. *J. Amer. Statist. Assoc.* **84**, 927–944.

57. Ericson, W. (1969). Subjective Bayesian models in sampling finite populations: stratification. *New Developments in Survey Sampling* (ed. N. L. Johnson and H. Smith). New York: John Wiley & Sons, 326–357.

58. Ericson, W. (1975). *A Bayesian Approach to Two-Stage Sampling.* Tech. Report AFFDL-TR–75–145. *Air Force Dynamic Laboratory.* Wright Patterson AFB, Ohio, 1–25.

59. Ericson, W. (1983a). *A Bayesian Approach to Regression Estimation in Finite Populations.* Tech. Report No. 120, Department of Statistics, Univ. of Michigan, 1–21.

60. Ericson, W. (1983b). *Response Bias and Error in Sampling Finite Populations.* Tech. Report No. 122. Department of Statistics, Univ. of Michigan.

61. Ericson, W. A. (1988). Bayesian Inference in Finite Populations. *Handbook of Statistics* (Chapter 9) (ed. P. R. Krishnaiah and C. R. Rao). Elsevier Science Publishers. B.V., 213–246.

62. Ernest, L. F. (1980). Variance of the estimated mean for several imputation procedures. *Proceedings of the Section on Survey Research Methods, American Statistical Association*, 716–720.

63. Fay, R. E. and Herriot, R. A. (1979). Estimates of income for small places: An application of James-Stein procedures to census data. *J. Amer. Statist. Assoc.* **74**, 269–277.

64. Feller, W. (1968). *An Introduction to Probability Theory and its Applications.* Vol. 1 (Third Edition), New York: John Wiley & Sons.

65. Franklin, L. A. and Wasserman, G. S. (1992). Bootstrap lower confidence limits for capability indices. *Journal of Quality Technology* **24**:4, 196–210.

66. Freedman, D. A. and Navidi, W. C. (1986). Regression models for adjusting the 1980 census (with discussion). *Statist. Sci.* **1**, 1–39.

67. Freedman, D. A. and Navidi, W. C. (1992). Should we have adjusted the U.S. census of 1980? (with discussion). *Survey Methodology* **18**, 3–74.

68. Ghosh, M. and Rao, J. N. K. (1994). Small area estimation: An appraisal. *Statistical Science* **9**, No. 1, 55–91.

69. Godambe, V. P. (1955). A unified theory of sampling from finite populations. *J. Roy. Statist. Soc.* **B17**, 269–278.

70. Godambe, V. P. and Joshi, V. M. (1965). Admissibility and Bayes estimation in sampling finite populations, I. *Ann. Math. Statist.* **36**, 1707–1722.

71. Goetzmann, W. N. and Jorion, P. (1993). Testing the predictive power of dividend yields. *Journal of Finances* **48**:2, 663–679.

72. Gonzalez, M. E. (1973). Use and evaluation of synthetic estimators. In *Proceedings of the Social Statistics Section*, 33–36, American Statistical Association, Washington, D.C.

73. Goodman, L. A. and Hartley, H. O. (1958). The precision of unbiased ratio-type estimators. *J. Amer. Statist. Asso.* **53**, 491–508.

74. Goodman, R. and Kish, L. (1950). Controlled selection—a technique in probability sampling. *J. Amer. Statist. Assoc.* **45**, 350–372.

75. Gray, H. L., Watkins, T. A., and Adams, J. E. (1972). On the jackknife statistic, its extensions, and its relations to e_n-transformations. *Ann. Math. Statist.* **43**, 1–30.

76. Hájek, J. (1959). Optimum strategy and other problems in probability sampling. *Casopis Pro Petsovani Matematiky* **84**, 387–442.

77. Hájek, J. (1960). Limiting distribution in simple random sampling from a finite population. *Pub. Math. Inst. Hungarian Acad. Sci.* **5**, 361–374.

78. Hájek, J. (1968). Asymptotic normality of simple linear rank statistics under alternatives, *Ann. Math. Statist.*, **39**, 325–346.

79. Haldane, J. B. S. (1945). On a method of estimating frequencies. *Biometrika* **33**, 222–225.

80. Hansen, M. H., Dalenius, T., and Tepping, B. J. (1985). The development of sample surveys of finite populations, in *A Celebration of Statistics* (ed. A. C. Atkinson and S. E. Fienberg). New York: Springer-Verlag, pp. 327–354.

81. Hansen, M. H. and Hurwitz, W. N. (1943). On the theory of sampling from finite populations. *Ann. Math. Statist.* **14**, 333–362.

82. Hansen, M., Hurwitz, W. N., and Madow, W. G. (1953). *Sample Survey Methods and Theory*, Vol. 1. New York: John Wiley & Sons.

83. Hansen, M.H., Madow, W. G. and Tepping, B. J. (1983). An evaluation of model-dependent and probability-sampling inferences in sample surveys. *J. Amer. Statist. Assoc.* **78**, 776–793. Comments and rejoinder, 794–807.

84. Hartley, H. O. (1962). Multiple frame surveys. *Proc. Soc. Stat. Sec. Amer. Statist. Assoc.* 203–206.

85. Hartley, H. O. and Rao, J. N. K. (1962). Sampling with unequal probabilities and without replacement. *Ann. Math. Statist.* **33**, 350–374.

86. Hartley, H. O. and Ross, A. (1954). Unbiased ratio estimates. *Nature* **174**, 270–271.

87. Hess, I., Sethi, V. K., and Balakrishnan, T. R. (1966). Stratification: A practical investigation. *J. Amer. Statist. Assoc.* **61**, 74–90.

88. Hilgard, E. R. and Payne, S. L. (1944). Those not at home: Riddle for polsters. *Public Opinion Quarterly* **8**, 254–261.

89. Holt, D. and Smith, T. M. F. (1979). Post-stratifcation *J. Roy. Statist. Soc.* **A142**, 33–46.

90. Horvitz, D. G. and Thompson, D. J. (1952). A generalization of sampling without replacement from a finite universe. *J. Amer. Statist. Assoc.* **47**, 663–685.

91. Horvitz, D. G., Shah, B. V., and Simmons, W. R. (1967). The unrelated randomized response model. *Proc. Soc. Statist. Section, Amer. Statist. Assoc.*, 663–685.

92. Huber, P. (1972). Robust statistics: A review. *Ann. Math. Statist.* **43**, 1041–1067.

93. Kalton, G. and Kasprzyk, D. (1986). The treatment of missing survey data. *Survey Methodology*, Statistics Canada **12**, 1–16.

94. Kendall, M. and Stuart, A. (1958). *The Advanced Theory of Statistics*. London: Griffin.

95. Kho, B. (1996). Time-varying risk premia, volatility, and technical trading rule profits: Evidence from foreign currency future markets. *Journal of Financial Economics* **41**:2, 249–290.

96. Kish, L. and Frankel, M. R. (1974). Inference from complex surveys. *Jour. Roy. Stat. Soc.* **B36**, 1–37.

97. Kolehmarnen, O. (1981). Bayesian models in estimating the total of a finite population. Towards a general theory. *Scand. J. Statist.* **8**, 27–32.

98. Koop, J. C. (1963). On the axioms of sample formation and their bearing on the construction of linear estimators in sampling theory for finite universes. *Metrika* **17**, 81–114, 165–204.

99. Koop, J. C. (1963). On splitting a systematic sample for variance estimation. *Ann. Math. Statist.* **42**, 1084–1087.

100. Korwar, R. M. and Serfling, R. J. (1970). On averaging over distinct units in sampling with replacement. *Ann. Math. Statist.* **41**, 2132–2134.

101. Lahiri, D. B. (1951). A method for sample selection providing unbiased ratio estimates. *Bull. Intern. Statist. Inst.* **31**, 24–57.

102. Lanke, J. (1975). *Some Contributions to the Theory of Survey Sampling*. Lund: A B Svenska Siffror, pp. 41–42.

103. Lee, H., Rancourt, E., and Särndal, C. (1991). Experiments with variance estimation from survey data with imputed values. *Proceedings of the Survey Research Methods Section, Amer. Statist. Assoc.*, 690–695.

104. Levich, R. M. and Thomas, L. R. III (1993). The significance of technical trading-rule profits in the foreign exchange market: A bootstrap approach. *Journal of International Money and Finance* **12**:5, 451–474.

105. Little, R. J. A. (1982). Models for nonresponse in sample surveys *J. Amer. Statist. Assoc.* **77**, 237–250.

106. Madow, W. G. (1949). On the theory of systematic sampling, II. *Ann. Math. Statist.* **20**, 333–354.

107. Madow, W. G. (1953). On the theory of systematic sampling, III: comparison of centered and random start systematic sampling. *Ann. Math. Statist.* **24**, 101–106.

108. Madow, W. G. and Madow, L. H. (1944). On the theory of systematic sampling. *Ann. Math. Statist.* **15**, 1–24.

109. Mahalanobis, P. C. (1946). Recent experiments in statistical sampling in the Indian Statistical Institute. *J. Roy. Statist. Soc.* **A109**, 325–378, reprinted in *Sankhyā* **20** (1958), 1–68.

110. Mahalanobis, P. C. (1952). Some aspects of the design of sample surveys. *Sankhyā* **12**, 1–7.

111. Miller, R. G. (1964). A trustworthy jackknife. *Ann. Math. Statist.* **35**, 1594–1605.

112. Miller, R. G. (1974). The jackknife—a review. *Biometrika* **61**, 1–15.

113. Mosteller, F. (1978). Nonsampling errors, in W. M. H. Kruskal and J. M. Tanur (eds.), *The International Encyclopedia of Statistics*. New York: Free Press, 208–229.

114. Murthy, M. N. (1957). Ordered and unordered estimators in sampling without replacement. *Sankhyā* **18**, 379–390.

115. Murthy, M. N. (1962). Variance and confidence interval estimation. *Sankhyā* **24**(B), 1–12.

116. Murthy, M. N. (1967). *Sampling Theory and Methods*. Statistical Publishing Society, Calcutta, India.

117. Murthy, M. N. and Rao, T. J. (1988). Systematic sampling with illustrating examples. *Handbook of Statistics: Sampling*, Vol. 6. Elsevier Science Publishers B. V., 147–185.

118. Nanjamma,N. S., Murthy, M. N., and Sethi, V. K. (1959). Some sampling systems providing unbiased ratio estimators. *Sankhyā* **21**, 299–314.

119. Neter, J. and Waksburg, J. (1964). A study of response errors in expenditure data from households interviews. *J. Amer. Statist. Assoc.* **59**, 18–55.

120. Neyman, J. (1934). On the two different aspects of the representative method: The method of stratified sampling and the method of purposive selection. *J. Roy. Statist. Soc.* **97**, 558–606.

121. Neyman, J. (1938). Contributions to the theory of sampling human populations. *J. Amer. Statist. Assoc.* **33**, 101–116.

122. Oh, H. L. and Scheuren, F. J. (1983). Weighting adjustment for unit nonresponse. In *Incomplete Data in Sample Surveys*, Vol. 2 (ed. I. Olkin and D. B. Rubin). New York: Academic Press, 143–184.

123. Olkin, I. (1958). Multvariate ratio estimation for finite populations. *Biometrika* **45**, 154–165.

124. Panel on Incomplete Data, Committee on National Statistics (1983). *Incomplete Data in Sample Surveys*. Vol 1: *Report and Case Studies* (Madow, Nisselson, Olkin, eds.) Vol 2: *Theory and Bibliographies* (Madow, Olkin, Rubin, eds.) Vol 3: *Proceedings of the Symposium* (Madow and Olkin, eds.) New York: Academic Press.

125. Pathak, P. K. (1961). On the evaluation of moments of distinct units in the sample. *Sankhyā* **A23**, 415–420.

126. Pathak, P. K. (1962). On simple random sampling with replacement. *Sankhyā*, **A24**, 287–302.

127. Platek, R. and Gray, G. B. (1978). Nonresponse and imputation. *Survey Methodology*, Statistics Canada **4**, 144–177.

128. Purcell, N. J. and Kish, L. (1979). Estimation for small domain. *Biometrics* **35**, 365–384.

129. Pyke, R. (1965). Spacings. *J. Roy. Statist. Soc.* **B27**, 395–449.

130. Quenouille, M. H. (1949). Approximate tests of correlation in time series. *J. Roy. Statist. Soc.* **B11**, 68–84.

131. Quenouille, M.H. (1956). Notes on bias in estimation. *Biometrika* **52**, 647–649.

132. Rao, J. N. K. (1965). A note on the estimation of ratios by Quenouille's method. *Biometrika* **52**, 647–649.

133. Rao, J. N. K. (1965). On two simple schemes of unequal probability sampling without replacement. *J. Ind. Statist. Assoc.* **3**, 173–180.

134. Rao, J. N. K. (1966). Alternative estimators in pps sampling for multiple characteristics. *Sankhyā* **A23**, 47–60.

135. Rao, J. N. K. (1968). Some small sample results in ratio and regression estimation. *Jour. Ind. Stat. Assoc.* **6**, 160–168.

136. Rao, J. N. K. (1975). On the foundations of survey sampling. In *A Survey of Statistical Design and Linear Models*, ed. J. N. Srivastava. New York: American Elsevier Publishing Co., 489–505.

137. Rao, J. N. K. (1985). Conditional inference in survey sampling. *Survey Methodology*, **II**, No. 1, 15–31.

138. Rao, J. N. K. (1986). Synthetic estimators: SPREE and best model based predictors. In *Proceedings of the Conference on Survey Research Methods in Agriculture*, 1–16, U.S. Department of Agriculture, Washington, D.C.

139. Rao, J. N. K. (1988). Variance estimation in sample surveys. *Handbook of Statistics No. 6* (ed. P. R. Krishnaiah and C. R. Rao). Holland: Elsevier Science Publishers B.V., 427–447.

140. Rao, J. N. K., Hartley, H. O. and Cochran, W. G. (1962). A simple procedure of unequal probability sampling without replacement. *J. Roy Statist. Soc.* **B24**, 482–491.

141. Rao, J. N. K. and Shao, J. (1992). Jackknife variance estimation with survey data under hot deck imputation. *Biometrika* **79**, No. 4, 811–822.

142. Rao, J. N. K. and Webster, J. (1966). On two methods of bias reduction in the estimation of ratios, *Biometrika* **53**, 571–577.

143. Rao, P. S. R. S. (1983). Callbacks, followups and repeated telephone calls. In *Incomplete Data in Sample Surveys*, Vol. 2 (ed. I. Olkin and D. B. Rubin). New York: Academic Press, 33–44.

144. Rao, P. S. R. S. and Rao, J. N. K. (1971). Small sample results for ratio estimation. *Biometrika* **58**, 625–630.

145. Rosen, B. (1964). Limit theorems for sampling from finite populations. *Ark. Mat.* **28**, 383–424.

146. Roy Choudhury, D. K. (1956). Integration of several pps. surveys. *Science and Culture* **22**, 119–120.

147. Royall, R. M. (1970). On finite population sampling theory under certain linear regression models. *Biometrika* **57**, 377–387.

148. Rubin, D. B. (1976). Inference and missing data. *Biometrika* **63**, 581–592.

149. Rubin, D. B. (1978). Multiple imputations in sample surveys—A phenomenological Bayesian approach to nonresponse. *Proceedings of the Section on Survey Research Methods, American Statistical Association*, 20–28.

150. Rubin, D. B. (1979). Illustrating the use of multiple imputations to handle nonresponse in sample surveys. *Proc. International Statistical Institute*, Manila, 517–532.

151. Rubin, D. B. (1981). The Bayesian bootstrap. *The Annals of Statistics* **9**, 130–134.

152. Rubin, D. B. (1987). *Multiple Imputation for Nonresponse in Surveys*. New York: John Wiley & Sons.

153. Rubin, D. B. and Schenker, N. (1986). Multiple imputation for interval estimation from simple random samples with ignorable nonresponse. *J. Amer. Statist. Assoc.* **81**, 366–374.

154. Samford, M. R. (1967). On sampling without replacement with unequal probabilities of selection. *Biometrika* **54**, 499–513.

155. Sande, I. G. (1982). Imputation in surveys: coping with reality. *The American Statistician* **36**, 145–152.

156. Särndal, C. E. and Hidiroglow, M. A. (1989). Small domain estimation: A conditional analysis. *J. Amer. Statist. Assoc.* **84**, 266–275.

157. Satterthwaite, F. E. (1946). An approximate distribution of estimates of variance components. *Biometrics* **2**, 110–114.

158. Schenker, N. (1985). *Multiple Imputation for Internal Estimation from Surveys with Ignorable Nonresponse*. Ph.D. dissertation, University of Chicago, Department of Statistics.

159. Schlaifer, R. (1959). *Probability and Statistics for Business Decisions*. New York: McGraw-Hill.

160. Schucany, W. R., Gray, H. L., and Owen, W. E. (1971). On bias reduction in estimation, *J. Amer. Statist. Assoc.* **66**, 524–533.

161. Serfling, R. J. (1968). Approximately optimal stratification. *J. Amer. Statist. Assoc.* **63**, 1298–1309.

162. Seth, G. R. and Rao, J. N. K. (1964). On the comparison between simple random sampling with and without replacement. *Sankhyā,* **A26**, 85–86.

163. Sethi, V. K. (1963). A note on optimum stratification of populations for estimating the population means. *Aust. J. Statist.* **5**, 20–33.

164. Singh, D. and Singh, P. (1977). New systematic sampling. *J. Stat. Planning and Inference* **1**, 163–177.

165. Singh, P. and Srivastava, A. K. (1980). Sampling schemes providing unbiased regression estimators. *Biometrika* **67**, 205–209.

166. Singh, R. and Sukhatme, B. V. (1973). Optimum stratification with ratio and regression methods of estimation. *Ann. Inst. Statist. Math.* **25**, 627–633.

167. Smith, S. K. and Lewis, B. B. (1980). Some new techniques for applying the housing unit method of local population estimation. *Demography* **17**, 323–340.

168. Smith, T. M. F. (1976). The foundations of survey sampling: A review. *J. Roy. Statist. Soc.* **A139**, 183–204.

169. Stephan, F. F. (1945). The expected value and variance of the reciprocal and other negative powers of a positive Bernoulli variate. *Ann. Math. Statist.* **16**, 50–62.

170. Srivenkataramana, T. (1980). A dual to ratio estimator in sample surveys. *Biometrika* **67**, 199–204.

171. Sukhatme, P. V., Sukhatme, B. V., Sukhatme, S., and Ashok, C. (1984). *Sampling Theory of Surveys with Applications*, 3rd ed. Ames, Iowa: Iowa State University Press.

172. Sundberg, R. (1983). The prediction approach and randomized population type models for finite population inference for two-stage samples. *Scand. J. Statist.* **10**, 223–238.

173. Taga, Y. (1953). On optimum balancing between sample size and number of strata in subsampling. *Ann. Inst. Statist. Math.* (Tokyo) **4**, 95–102.

174. Taga, Y. (1967). On optimum stratification for the objective variable based on concomitant variables using prior information. *Ann. Inst. Statist. Math.* (Tokyo) **19**, 101–129.

175. Thomsen, I. and Tesfu, D. (1988). On the use of models in sampling from finite populations. *Handbook of Statistics: Sampling*, Vol. 6 (ed. P. K. Kristiraiah and C. R. Rao). New York: North Holland, 369–397.

176. Tschuprow, A. A. (1923). On the mathematical expectation of the moments of frequency distributions in the case of correlated observations. *Metron* **2**, 461–493, 646–680.

177. Tukey, J. W. (1950). Some sampling simplified. *J. Amer. Statist. Assoc.* **45**, 501–519.

178. Tukey, J. W. (1958). Bias and confidence in not-quite large samples (abstract). *Ann. Math. Statist.* **29**, 614.

179. Wang, M. and Rao, S. S. (1992). Estimating reorder points and other management science applications by bootstrap procedure. *European Journal of Operational Research* **56**:3, 332–342.

180. Wang, R., Sedransk, J., and Jinn, J. H. (1992). Secondary data analysis when there are missing observations. *Journal of American Statistical Association* **87**, 952–961.

181. Warner, S. L. (1965). Randomized response: a survey technique for eliminating evasive answer bias. *J. Amer. Statist. Assoc.* **60**, 63–69.

182. Wilks, S. S. (1962). *Mathematical Statistics.* New York: John Wilely & Sons, p. 369.

183. Williams, W. H. (1963). The precision of some unbiased regression estimators. *Biometrics* **19**, 352–361.

184. Wu, Jeff C. F. (1984). Estimation in systematic sampling with supplementary observations. *Sankhyā* **B46**, part 3, 306–315.

185. Yates, F. (1948). Systematic sampling *Phil. Trans. Roy. Soc.* **A24**, 345–377.

186. Yates, F. and Grundy, P. M. (1953). Selection without replacement from within strata with probability proportional to size. *J. Roy. Statist. Soc.* **B15**, 253–261.

187. Zeger, S. and Karim, M. (1991). Generalized linear models with random effects: Gibbs sampling approach. *Journal of the American Statistical Association* **86**, 79–86.

188. Zinger, A. (1980). Variance estimation in partial systematic sampling. *J. Amer. Statist. Assoc.* **75**, 205–211.

AUTHOR INDEX

SUBJECT INDEX

A

a nonrespondent, 353
absolute error, 68
access to the Internet, 113
Administrative Records method, 336
admissibility, 46
admissible, 46, 201
AIDS, 61, 108–109, 307
almost unbiased, 315
alternative estimators, 317
analysis of variance, 164, 179
analytical surveys, 3
ancillary statistic, 91
ANOVA, 179, 348
approximate Bayesian bootstrap (ABB) imputation., 365
AR, 336
AR method, 337
arc tan transformation, 317
assumption of normality, 365
asymptotic distribution, 328
asymptotic expressions, 366
asymptotic normality, 38
asymptotic properties, 3
asymptotic results, 315
asymptotic variances, 367
asymptotically independent, 367

auxiliary distribution, 316–317
auxiliary information, 42, 340
auxiliary population mean, 316
auxiliary sources, 349
auxiliary variable, 14, 116, 143, 155, 156, 187, 253, 354
auxiliary variables, 131

B

balanced incomplete block designs, 51
Bayes, 289
Bayes estimator, 306
Bayes estimators, 291
Bayes linear, 297
Bayes linear estimate, 307
Bayes linear estimator, 294, 297, 298, 303, 306–307
Bayes optimality, 291
Bayes ratio and regression estimators, 304, 306
Bayesian analogies, 300
Bayesian approach, 289, 294, 304
Bayesian bootstrap (BB) imputation, 365
Bayesian estimators, 42
Bayesian interpretation, 300
Bayesian method, 356, 362
Bayesian models, 289

Bayesian procedures, 351
Bernoulli density function, 56
Bernoulli numbers, 45
Bernoulli population, 328
best linear unbiased estimator, 121–122
best unbiased estimator, 40
best unbiased estimators, 40
between-area variation, 342
between-imputation variability, 362
between-imputation variance, 364
bias, 131
bias of a functional estimate, 327
bias of a ratio estimate, 123
bias reduction, 312
biased downward, 325
biased estimators, 5
biased ratio estimation, 232
biased upward, 318
biases, 119
(BIB), 51
binomial, 35
binomial case, 328
binomial distribution, 54, 56
binomial random variable, 328
bivariate normal distribution, 357
bivariate random vectors, 300